# Encyclopedia of Comic Books and Graphic Novels

# ENCYCLOPEDIA OF COMIC BOOKS AND GRAPHIC NOVELS

## VOLUME 2: M–Z

### M. KEITH BOOKER, EDITOR

**GREENWOOD**

AN IMPRINT OF ABC-CLIO, LLC
Santa Barbara, California • Denver, Colorado • Oxford, England

**Library of Congress Cataloging-in-Publication Data**

Encyclopedia of comic books and graphic novels / M. Keith Booker, editor.
     p. cm.
    Includes bibliographical references and index.
    ISBN 978-0-313-35746-6 (set) — ISBN 978-0-313-35747-3 (set : ebook) — ISBN 978-0-313-35748-0 (vol. 1 : alk. paper ) — ISBN 978-0-313-35749-7 (vol. 1 : ebook) — ISBN 978-0-313-35750-3 (vol. 2 : alk. paper) — ISBN 978-0-313-35751-0 (vol. 2 : ebook)
  1. Comic books, strips, etc.—Dictionaries.   I.  Booker, M. Keith.
  PN6707.E49   2010
   741.403—dc22     2010002233

ISBN: 978-0-313-35746-6
EISBN: 978-0-313-35747-3

14  13  12  11  10    1  2  3  4  5

This book is also available on the World Wide Web as an eBook.
Visit www.abc-clio.com for details.

Greenwood
An Imprint of ABC-CLIO, LLC

ABC-CLIO, LLC
130 Cremona Drive, P.O. Box 1911
Santa Barbara, California 93116-1911

This book is printed on acid-free paper ∞

Manufactured in the United States of America

For Benjamin Booker, Skylor Booker, and Adam Booker

# Contents

# Alphabetical List of Entries

# Topical List of Entries

## Individual Comic Book and Graphic Novel Titles or Characters

*Action Comics*
*Adventure Comics*
*Alice in Sunderland*
*All-American Comics*
*All Star Comics*
*Alpha Flight*
*Amazing Fantasy*
*American Born Chinese*
*American Flagg*
*American Splendor*
Ant-Man
Aquaman
Archie
Arkham Asylum
*Astro City*
*Authority, The*
*Avengers*
*Barefoot Gen*
Batman
*Batman & Dracula*
*Binky Brown Meets the Holy Virgin Mary*

*Birth of a Nation*
*Black Condor, The*
*Blackhawk*
*Black Hole*
Black Panther
Black Widow
*Blankets*
Blue Beetle, The
*Blueberry*
*Bone*
*Buddha*
*Cages*
Captain America
Captain Marvel
Casper the Friendly Ghost
*Castle Waiting*
Catwoman
*Cerebus the Aardvark*
*City of Glass*
*Civil War*
*Classics Illustrated*
Conan the Barbarian
*Concrete*
*Contract with God, A*

## Individual Writers and Artists

## Themes and Genres

Adaptations from Other Media
Cold War
Crime Comics
Educational Comics
Espionage
European Comics
Fantasy
Feminism
Folklore in Comics
Funny Animal Comics
Gay and Lesbian Themes
History in Comics
Horror Comics
Jungle Comics
Manga
Memoir/Slice-of-Life
    Themes
Mutants
Nazis
Politics and Politicians
Post-Apocalyptic Narratives
Race and Ethnicity
Religion
Romance Comics
Satire
Science Fiction
Superheroes

Underground and Adult Comics
Vampires and Zombies
War Comics
Westerns (Comics)
Youth Culture in Comics

## Comics Publishers

Charlton Comics
Dark Horse Comics
DC Comics
EC Comics
Fantagraphics
Image Comics
Kitchen Sink Press
Marvel Comics
Milestone Comics
Quality Comics
Warren Publishing

## Miscellaneous

Ages of Comics
Comics Code
Comics Scholarship
Eisner Awards
Harvey Awards
Merchandising and Licensing
Retcon
Wertham, Fredric

**MADMAN.** The Madman of Snap City is the star of multiple series by comics auteur **Mike Allred**, including *Madman*, *Madman Adventures*, *Madman Comics*, and *Madman Atomic Comics*. Combining Allred's interest in metaphysical speculation, pop-culture kitsch, and **superhero** action, these titles have established Allred's reputation as a talented and increasingly ambitious craftsman and storyteller.

Allred's narrative began in the 1992 *Madman* miniseries published by Tundra. When readers first meet the title character, he is a disfigured, childlike amnesiac prone to sudden fits of horrifying violence and introspective ruminations on the nature of existence—a dual nature that finds expression in the yo-yos, slingshots, and other children's toys that he has converted into weapons. Though his precognitive and psychic powers offer him insights into the souls of others, Madman is a mystery to himself. Beneath his mask, he is Frank Einstein—a character Allred had previously spotlighted in *Grafik Muzik* (1990) and *Creatures of the Id* (1990)—the victim of a car crash brought back to life by the brilliant but unbalanced Dr. Boiffard. One of Frank's few ties to his forgotten past life is his costume: His only memory is of reading comics starring his childhood hero, Mr. Excitement, and he finds it soothing to wear his idol's distinctive exclamatory lightning bolt design. Aided by his faithful girlfriend Joe, and Boiffard's partner, Dr. Flem, Frank begins to make a new life and piece together the remains of his old one. His peaceful existence, though, is often shattered by the minions of the evil Monstadt, a former ally of Boiffard's obsessed with the secret of eternal life.

This first series was a critical success and drew particular attention for Allred's clean-lined and dynamic visual style, a style influenced by **Alex Toth**, Jack Cole, and Bruno Premiani, and informed by Allred's affection for pop culture ephemera of all sorts. Allred continued to chronicle the exploits of Frank and his friends in a second three-issue Tundra series, *Madman Adventures*. This series, which cast its protagonist adrift in time and had him meet a centuries-old alien in South America, saw Allred moving away from his emphasis on Madman's occasional fits of rage and focusing more on the combination of graceful action, whimsical comedy, and metaphysical speculation now commonly associated with Allred's work. The next series, *Madman Comics*, ran for 20 issues at **Dark Horse** and includes Allred's most sustained exploration of the retro-futuristic Snap City and its inhabitants—including mutant street beatniks, runaway robots, demonic detectives, and men with vomit for skin. This series also developed Allred's exploration of the nature of identity when the open-hearted and heroic Frank discovered that in his previous life he had been a deadly assassin named Zane Townsend.

After featuring Madman as an ensemble character in the spin-off title *The Atomics*, Allred launched a fourth series for the character through his own imprint, AAA Pop. *Madman Atomic Comics* ran for 17 issues. Although he did not abandon the light-hearted adventure characteristic of previous incarnations, Allred began to place a greater emphasis on religious and philosophical questions and on formal experimentation—including an issue in which each panel was drawn in the style of a different artist from comics history and an issue in which the action was superimposed upon a continuous background. Though Allred ended the series in 2009, he has indicated that Madman and his supporting cast will play a significant role in future projects.

*Brannon Costello*

**MANGA.** Manga (*man*, frivolous, *ga*, drawings) is a term that refers to the collective comics traditions of Japan. Although manga is similar in many ways to American and **European comics**—and the similarities have increased as manga has increased in global popularity—it is distinctive in its content, creative style, and published format. Like much of Japanese pop culture, manga represents a synthesis of traditional, indigenous art styles with Western influences, resulting in a uniquely Japanese end product.

## History

One of the traditional forms that influenced manga were the *Ukiyo-e*, woodblock prints of daily life, landscapes, and legendary episodes. Other influences include the *Emakimono*, a traditional narrative art painted on scrolls. From the Meiji Period (1868–1912) until World War II, Japan became culturally and economically accessible to the West. Early Japanese cartoonists were inspired by published cartoons in American and French humor magazines and newspapers. Magazines were created explicitly to imitate these influential Western magazines, which provided a popular forum for creators to share their work with an increasingly affluent and educated public. A few popular and enduring characters were created in this period, including Ryuichi Yokoyama's *Fuku-chan* (1938) and Suiho Tagawa's *Norakuro* (1931).

Before World War II, manga barely resembled the popular mass medium it would eventually become, and was published in newspapers, humor magazines, and books. The outbreak of war limited the resources available to publishers, and after the war widespread economic turmoil and the political upheaval of the occupation changed much about the business and the art of manga. Manga remained popular through these troubled times, largely through appealing to the reliable children's market. Manga magazines for children would continue, and eventually proliferate, while new methods of delivering entertainment to children and young adults would appear.

Arguably the most influential publication format for manga at the time was the *akabon*, or "red book," referring to the use of red ink as a half-tone color for interior black-and-white line art. Akabon titles were cheaply published on inexpensive paper, at roughly the size of

Manga action. Photofest

contemporary manga volumes, or *tankobon*. Akabon titles introduced work from new, highly original and influential creators such as **Osamu Tezuka** and Tetsuya Chiba. Other important artists, such as Yoshihiro Tatsumi and Sanpei Shirato, presented their work in *kamishibai*, or paper theaters. A kamishibai artist would travel with his display, a series of images drawn on paper or cardboard, and narrate a story while selling cheap candies or trinkets to the accumulated children. Meanwhile, as a cheap alternative to the cost of buying books, rental libraries or *kashibonya* sprang up, offering manga volumes to readers at rates such as 10 yen for two days.

By the 1950s and 1960s, the manga publishing business shifted into its current paradigm: new work would be serialized in magazines, released quarterly, monthly, or even weekly. These magazines, including those issued weekly, would extend to the hundreds of pages and would be sold at affordable prices. Serialized manga stories would be compiled into *tankobon* volumes, containing roughly 150–200 pages. Such *tankobon* would become the permanent print edition of a given manga storyline. The original magazines containing the same content would become superfluous: the American predilection for collectability in comic books largely does not translate to Japanese manga magazines and volumes. After 1970 and through today, manga became stratified into a variety of well-defined genres designed to appeal to commercial audiences.

## Genre

Manga is marketed in several basic genres, which are determined by the intended audience of a given work. Within each genre are several formulas, which can target very specific reader interests, although a work might contain elements of multiple formulas or genres. An example of this is the recent series *Hikaru no Go* (1998) by Yumi Hotta and Takeshi Obata. This series focuses on the subject of competitive hobbies and pursuits, specifically the traditional Japanese board game, *Go*. Manga about such personal pursuits are very popular—there are series about most popular sports and hobbies, all featuring the same basic plot elements, such as the impetuous, youthful beginner, the seemingly invincible opponents, the obsession with minute details and perfectionism, and so forth. This formula is part of a genre called *shonen* manga, which is manga geared toward a young, male readership, primarily focused on readers under the age of 18 years old. The popular American manga magazine *Shonen Jump* focuses on such titles, as does the Japanese *Shonen Jump* franchise and many other magazines in Japan. Tezuka dominated early *shonen* manga: his early trilogy *Lost World* (1948), *Metropolis* (1949), and *Next World* (1951), along with his later series *Astro Boy* (1952), set the tone for *shonen* manga and had innumerable imitators throughout the 1950s and 1960s. Later *shonen* creators influenced by Tezuka include Shotaro Ishinomori, who created *Cyborg 009* (1964) and Mitsutero Yokoyama, creator of *Tetsujin 28-Go* (1956, an animated version of this manga series was released in the United States as *Gigantor*). *Shonen* is arguably the dominant genre of manga both in Japan and worldwide, and includes such series as *Dragon Ball* (1984) by Akira Toriyama, *Rurouni Kenshin* (1994) by Nobuhiro Watsuki, and *Naruto* (1999) by Masashi Kishimoto.

*Shojo* is another major genre of manga in Japan, focusing on stories for young girls, though as in the case of shonen manga, the stories have appeal to a diversity of readers. *Shojo* manga does include **romance** themed stories, although the diversity of stories available to female readers is a distinct characteristic of manga. Tezuka is again recognized for creating one of the first *shojo* series, *Ribon no Kishi* (1954, translated as *Princess Knight*). Tezuka's *shojo* series introduced an important trope in *shojo* manga: sexual ambiguity and androgynous characters. In the 1970s, *shojo* had a wave of popularity, coming from series such as Riyoko Ikeda's *The Rose of Versailles* (1972), a historical drama centered around the French Revolutionary period; and *Swan* (1976) by Kyoko Ariyoshi, which follows the struggles of a young ballerina. By the 1970s, female creators were becoming more heavily involved in the creation of *shojo* manga, and current *shojo* manga titles are almost exclusively created by women. One noteworthy formula in *shojo* manga, called *magic girl*, features main characters that are almost the equivalent of Japanese superheroes. Magic girl characters dress up in elaborate costumes and fight evil foes, yet with **fantasy** elements instead of a focus on crime, common to **superhero** comics.

Magic girl titles include *Sailor Moon* (1992) by Naoko Takeuchi and *Cardcaptor Sakura* (1996) by CLAMP. Other popular *shojo* manga titles include *Fruits Basket* (1999) by Natsuki Takaya and *Kare Kano* (1996) by Masami Tsuda. Many Japanese magazines publish *shojo* manga, including long-running titles such as *Nakayoshi* and *Margaret*; in the United States, the magazine *Shojo Beat* also serializes *shojo* manga.

*Kodomo* manga is manga aimed at children but not toward a specific gender orientation. Although some kodomo manga resemble *shojo* or *shonen* manga, *kodomo* stories tend to avoid the masculine action of *shonen* manga or the youthful romance of *shojo* manga, and to focus instead on whimsical stories and cute characters. One of the most influential *kodomo* series is *Doraemon* (1969), created by the creative duo Fujio-Fujiko. This series follows the adventures of a robotic time-traveling cat and a young boy named Nobita. Other *kodomo* manga include popular, cute franchise characters such as *Pokemon* (1996).

*Seinen* and *josei* manga refer to manga created for adult male and female readers, respectively. *Seinen* manga has been particularly popular in the West. Popular *seinen* titles include *Akira* (1982) by Katsuhiro Otomo, *Ghost in the Shell* (1989), and *Appleseed* (1985) by Masamune Shirow, and *Gantz* (2000) by Hiroya Oku. *Seinen* manga largely avoids the popular art and storytelling styles prevalent in *shonen* and *shojo* manga, and features stories with adult themes, as well as, in some cases, increased violence and nudity. Relatively less popular, *josei* manga often adopts the style found in *shojo* manga, with a focus on more mature storylines and sexuality. Only a few *josei* manga have been translated for American audiences: among the few are *XXXHolic* (2003) and *Chobits* (2001) by CLAMP, *Nodame Cantabile* (2001) by Tomoko Ninomiya, and *Nana* (2000) by Ai Yazawa.

Alternative comics are frequently, though not universally, referred to in Japan as *gekiga*. This term, which translates as "dramatic pictures," was coined by Yoshihiro Tatsumi as a preferred term for the style of comics he began publishing in 1957. While *seinen* and *josei* manga are in many ways adult-oriented versions of *shonen* and *shojo* manga, *gekiga* is not targeted toward readers of a specific age or gender. Influential magazines that featured alternative and experimental manga were *Garo* and *COM*, the latter published by Tezuka. *Gekiga* and other alternative manga have been rare in the United States; although in recent years with the boom in manga publishing more *gekiga* have begun to appear in the United States. From 1997 until 2002, manga publisher Viz issued the magazine *Pulp*, which largely focused on *gekiga* and alternative manga. Regular *Pulp* columnist and former *Garo* editor Chikao Shiratori assembled the book *Secret Comics Japan*, published by Viz in 2000. *Secret Comics Japan* highlighted artists such as Junko Mizuno, who draws unusual childlike characters with a cute, though frequently sexual style; and Usamaru Furuya, who illustrates four-panel strips that often explore social, religious or philosophical ideas as well as creating humor. Among other important efforts to bring *gekiga* to the United States are recent series by Tezuka, including **Buddha** (1972) and *Phoenix* (1967); Yoshihiro Tatsumi's work has gained significant attention in the West due in large part to the advocacy of the American

Typical manga drawing style. Photofest

indie comics artist Adrian Tomine, and several titles by Tatsumi have been translated and published in English.

The diversity of stories available in Japanese manga, accessible from very young to very old readers, and including children's humor, **fantasy**, **science fiction**, **Westerns**, romance, action stories, comedy, **horror**, and even pornography have led comics fans and creators in the United States to question the narrow focus of American comics on superhero stories.

## Artistic Style

The most commonly perceived artistic conventions in manga, particularly for Western readers, are the peculiar conventions manga utilizes for character design. Often characters will have disproportionately large eyes combined with small, delicately drawn noses and mouths. Characters may often be indistinguishable save for costuming and elaborate, and at times outlandishly colored, hairstyles. In some types of manga there is a preference for illustrating both male and female characters with thin, feminine qualities.

This style largely originates with Tezuka, who was distinctly influenced in his artistic style by Walt Disney cartoons that were being shown in Japan during the post-war occupation. Tezuka's conventions in character design were a major influence on his fellow artists for many years, particularly his use of childlike proportions, large eyes, and thick arms and legs. By the 1970s, other artists had expanded the parameters of manga style—some artists, including Tezuka, continued to use the familiar style, inked in a heavy line, while some artists would use a completely realistic style, thickly inked with pen and brush. The style that became popular with *shojo* comics featured the now-stereotypical style with androgynous characters, large eyes and unique hairstyles, and in the 1970s this style became popular as the preferred mainstream style of manga. The basic conventions of this style are predominant in all but the more experimental and adult-oriented manga, and Japanese artists have built around this cartooning style a unique vocabulary of manga cartooning.

Artists may have different preferences for drawing in this mainstream style, depending on their alignment within the genre system. For example, a *shonen* artist may draw an image with a clear, heavy line without much artistic embellishment. A seinen artist may draw this style with heavy penwork and thoroughly rendered textures, or alter the mainstream style slightly towards more adult proportions. *Shojo* artists, on the other hand, might draw the mainstream style with a very light, nimble line and a heavy use of filled grey-tones instead of hand-rendered textures.

Other differences between Japanese manga and Western comic book styles abound, some of which are superficial, others which demonstrate the differences between how Japanese and non-Japanese readers perceive comics. Minor differences include the symbolic elements in manga, such as the use of a large, single sweat drop to symbolize worry or frustration, nosebleeds to symbolize lust, or shading of the eyes to symbolize embarrassment. More intriguingly, in America the preference for illustrating motion is to clearly illustrate a fixed scene with the moving element, such as a person, illustrated as moving within the scene. In Japan, illustrators show motion in a scene by having the moving element, such as a person, fixed within the center of the panel, surrounded by a background of motion lines.

As in Western comics, manga uses rendered sound effects—words drawn within the visual space of the story—to demonstrate sounds. In the United States, the use of sound effects in comics primarily derives from the physical, action-oriented stories in superhero comics. Outside of superhero comics there has been a reluctance to use sound effects, except perhaps in a more subdued way. In manga, however, sound effects are almost universally embraced regardless of the content of the story or its' targeted audience. While Western comics often use sound effects to clearly denote loud sounds, such as explosions or crashes, manga often utilizes sound effects to indicate subtle actions, such as a character grabbing an item or making an expression. In some situations in manga there is a sound effect used to indicate silence itself.

One surprising fact to new manga readers in the United States is that the pages of manga volumes are published in the reverse order of an English-language book. This is not unique specifically to manga, but is a reflection of how virtually all books and magazines published in Japanese are formatted.

Manga utilizes a publishing format that is much smaller than comics in the United States. In the United States, original comic art is most often drawn on heavy paper, such as bristol board or illustration board, in 11-by-14 inch sheets. Manga art is typically drawn on sheets that are 8.7-by-11.3 inches, known as the international paper format A4. The finished art is reduced in size only slightly for full-size magazine printing, but is reduced much further for reproduction in book-format volumes roughly 5-by-7 inches in size. The format can vary based upon a number of factors, such as the choice of the artist or the preferences of the publisher, and books are often published in larger or smaller formats.

A given manga title typically bears the name of a single creator, or at times a creative team whose members are largely responsible for the creation of the story and artwork. Manga creators are referred to as *manga-ka*, and are also referred to by the respectful title *sensei*, much like doctors, teachers, or politicians. As is the case in American comics, *manga-ka* are responsible to an editor, who represents the financial interests of the publisher as well as coordinating the production aspects of the finished manga. In the United States, the control an editor has over the creative aspects of the work that is produced depends on a variety of factors, such as the importance of the project, the perceived value of a creator or creative team, or the editorial policies of the publisher. In Japan, however, an editor generally holds a great deal of creative power, regardless of the *manga-ka* involved.

During the plotting stage of a manga work, the *manga-ka* will typically draft out the work in a notebook or on a series of folded sheets of paper referred to as a *name* (pronounced "nah-meh"). The *manga-ka* will then submit the *name* to their editor, who may approve some parts or request revisions in others. After the final storyline is agreed upon, the *manga-ka* coordinates the illustration of the story with their own personal art staff, which is often a group of several people, each in charge of specialized tasks in the creative process. The *manga-ka* or an assistant will lay out the page, rendering the panel boundaries, and the *manga-ka* reserves the primary task of rendering the characters on the page. It may be the assistants' jobs to render background elements, background figures, add tones and lettering, and fill in black or color areas of the page. This division of labor allows for the relatively speedy production time that manga is known for, and all the while the editor is in charge of verifying that the *manga-ka* is producing the required number of pages to meet deadlines. Also, working as an assistant for an established *manga-ka* allows for new artists to earn their way into establishing their own careers as *manga-ka*.

Of course, not all manga creators utilize such a system. Experimental and alternative manga artists are rarely even paid for their work, much less are given a staff to assist in the creative process. Despite this, these *manga-ka* are not only given a forum for public exposure, but they are given almost total creative control over their own work, which is atypical in mainstream manga.

Outside of the mainstream, yet still influential, are the manga fanzines referred to as *dojinshi*. *Dojinshi* are produced and published by independent creative teams outside of the corporate system, often by artists who aspire to work in that system. *Dojinshi* are difficult to characterize, since they are produced independently of the commercial manga editorial system. *Dojinshi* are often printed in thin, black-and-white magazine-style pamphlets, and may contain stories using established manga characters in unlicensed fan stories that may focus on character relationships and other fan-oriented expectations.

*Dojinshi*, along with mainstream and other manga, are often sold in the context of large trade shows, analogous to the American comic conventions. The largest one is Comic Market, otherwise known as Comiket, held twice a year in Tokyo. Comiket is the largest public comic convention in the world, although it consists entirely of a sales floor for publishers and creators to sell their work. Much like comic conventions in America, Comiket and similar Japanese manga conventions allow fans to socialize and explore different and difficult to obtain manga.

## Manga in English

Manga was first brought to the United States by the artist Henry Yoshitaka Kiyama, whose *Four Immigrants Manga* was privately published in 1931 and featured comic stories about his experience as a Japanese immigrant in San Francisco, California, between 1904 and 1924. Kiyama's work had relatively little impact outside of the San Francisco Japanese immigrant community, and was quickly forgotten, but has been rediscovered recently due to the book's translation by noted manga scholar Frederik Schodt.

After World War II, manga made its American debut with work by Keiji Nakazawa, a survivor of the atomic bomb that fell on Hiroshima in 1945. Nakazawa documented his experiences in *I Saw It* and the fictionalized series *Barefoot Gen.* The translation and publication were coordinated by an all-volunteer group known as Project Gen, and the result was published by small press imprints such as Educomics and Last Gasp starting in 1982.

In the 1980s, following the popularity of imported "anime" (essentially animated versions of manga) series such as *Astro Boy*, *Speed Racer*, and *Battle of the Planets*, American comic book fans and artists showed great interest in Japanese manga and anime. The artist **Frank Miller**, who would later be known for **Batman: The Dark Knight Returns** and the **Sin City** series, wrote and illustrated the miniseries **Ronin**, published by **DC Comics** in 1983. In the series, Miller tells the story of a reborn samurai warrior who fights a time-traveling demon in a decadent futuristic city. The artwork is clearly inspired by Japanese artists such as Goseki Kojima, the artist of the legendary samurai manga **Lone Wolf and Cub.**

At the same time, established independent publishers such as Eclipse Comics and First Comics began to publish manga titles such as *Lone Wolf and Cub* by Kazuo Koike and Kojima, *Appleseed* by Masamune Shirow, and other titles. Another new manga publisher in the early 1980s was Viz Comics. Viz's original publication lineup included *Nausicaä of the Valley of the Wind* by Hayao Miyazaki and *Crying Freeman* by Kazuo Koike and Ryoichi Ikegami. **Marvel Comics's** imprint Epic also published manga, including excerpts in their flagship magazine *Epic Illustrated*, and ongoing series such as *Akira* by Katsuhiro Otomo.

At the end of the 1980s, manga was a modestly successful, if obscure publishing niche. As Eclipse and First folded by the early 1990s, the new publisher **Dark Horse Comics** gained attention by publishing manga along with their licensed and original titles in both the comic book periodical format and the graphic novel paperback format, such as *Ghost in the Shell* by Masamune Shirow, *Blade of the Immortal* by Hiroaki Samura, and eventually reprints of *Akira* and *Lone Wolf and Cub*.

Anime releases in the mid-to-late 1990s, such as *Dragon Ball Z* and *Pokemon*, helped to raise the profile of manga to the level of a major publishing force. One new publishing upstart, Mixx Publications, began publishing *shojo* titles that were then rare in the United States, such as *Sailor Moon*. Mixx, which was later renamed Tokyopop, revolutionized how manga was published in America. While other publishers were printing manga in the format of comic books before compiling them into digest format paperback collections, Tokyopop bypassed the comic book format entirely, publishing titles in a significantly cheaper paperback format designed to mimic the original Japanese editions. Tokyopop promoted their manga titles to major bookstore chains, particularly the Borders and Waldenbooks chain, rather than direct-market comic book stores. Eventually, all of the major American manga publishers would adopt a similar business model, selling hundreds of titles in high volume at all of the major bookstore chains as well as many of the major media retail outlets and online. By the mid 2000s, some manga titles were appearing on bestseller lists, attracting the notice of some of the largest book publishers. Viz became a publishing subsidiary of the Japanese publishing conglomerates Shogakukan and Shueisha, and Tokyopop negotiated a business partnership with HarperCollins. DC Comics founded a manga publishing imprint, CMX. Random House began publishing manga under a new branch of its science fiction and fantasy imprint Del Rey, in partnership with the Japanese publisher Kodansha. Finally, Hachette Book Group founded Yen Press to publish original titles as well as licensed content from Japan.

Manga's explosive popularity in America has additionally led some American and European artists and writers to explore the style. As discussed previously, comic artists such as Miller have been incorporating manga drawing techniques since the 1980s, often in comics that otherwise offered little resemblance to manga. After 2000, however, Western artists began to create artwork that revealed a sincere devotion to manga beyond simple emulation. This type of manga became known collectively as OEL—Original English Language—manga. Significant creators include Bryan Lee O'Malley, creator of *Scott Pilgrim* (2004); Chynna Clugston, creator of *Blue Monday* (2000), Becky Cloonan, creator of *East Coast Rising* (2006) and artist for *Demo* (2004), written by Brian Wood; and Kazu Kibuishi, creator of *Daisy Kutter* (2006) and *Amulet* (2008), as well as the editor for *Flight*, an anthology that includes manga-inspired comics. Manga has also inspired a number of popular webcomics, such as *MegaTokyo* and *AppleGeeks*, as well as video games, animation, and other media.

In addition to its influence on the American comics industry, manga is also leading a trend in what some are referring to as *world comics*, a style of comics that embraces international themes and styles. By embracing manga style, creators from Europe, Asia, and the Americas are able to craft work that crosses borders and interests.

**Selected Bibliography:** Gravett, Paul. *Manga: Sixty Years of Japanese Comics.* New York: Harper Design, 2004; Kinsella, Sharon. *Adult Manga: Culture and Power in*

*Contemporary Japanese Society*. London: Routledge Curzon, 2000; Schodt, Frederik. *Manga! Manga! The World of Japanese Comics*. Tokyo: Kodansha, 1983.

*Robert O'Nale*

**MANHUNTER.** Manhunter is the name given to a group of vigilante crime-fighting heroes appearing in **DC Comics** since the 1940s (not to be confused with the DC superhero J'onn J'onzz, known as the Martian Manhunter). There have been four significant versions of the character. The first two Manhunters appeared during the 1940s. **Quality Comics** introduced its Manhunter, Donald Richards, created by Tex Blaisdell and Alex Kotzky, in *Police Comics* #8, March 1942. Paul Kirk, National (DC) Comics' Manhunter, first appeared in 1940 as a non-costumed private detective in *Adventure Comics* #58. In 1942, **Joe Simon** and **Jack Kirby** revised the character, giving him the familiar blue-and-red costume and the "Manhunter" name in issue #73. The two characters share little else but the name. DC purchased the Quality Comics characters in the late 1950s, and the two characters only retroactively interacted in the 1980s *All-Star Squadron* and other DC Comic titles.

Dan Richards, with his canine companion Thor (later revealed to be a Manhunter android in the 1988 *Millennium* crossover), became a mystery man to hunt down the killer for whose deeds his brother was framed. Afterwards, the Richards Manhunter's adventures involved crime fighting otherwise ordinary thugs and criminals. The character is killed by Mark Shaw in the 2004 *Manhunter* series.

Paul Kirk, a big game hunter and private detective, becomes Manhunter after the death of his close friend and city police commissioner. His **Golden Age** adventures are of relatively little note, though he is historically important, if only because he was a creation of Simon and Kirby. Archie Goodwin and **Walt Simonson** revised the character in the 1970s as a backup story for *Detective Comics* (beginning with #437 and ending in #443).

Placed in suspended animation by a secret organization, Kirk re-emerges to work as the organization's assassin, trained in the martial arts and embedded with a healing factor. On discovering their goal of global domination, Kirk turns on his benefactors and dies by the end of the story arc. This version is seen as a product of its time and represents seminal work on new characters to transition superhero comics away from their **Silver Age** innocence. (A clone of Paul Kirk appears as Manhunter in **Kurt Busiek**'s *Power Company* series.)

The 1988 DC crossover *Millennium* launched the next incarnation of the Manhunter character, in a series written by John Ostrander that ran for 24 issues into 1990. Attorney Mark Shaw turns on the Manhunter cult that recruited him. The Shaw Manhunter works as bounty hunter and his antagonist is Dumas, a shape-shifting mercenary. The series reveal is that Shaw is Dumas and that his split personalities are a result of government experimentation (a plot line that would be finally resolved in the third 2000-era series). Another *Manhunter* series, written by Steven Grant, was launched in 1994 after the *Zero Hour* crossover and lasted 12 issues.

The third *Manhunter* series, created by writer Marc Andreyko, ran from October 2004 to January 2009. This popular series features Kate Spencer as a prosecuting attorney who, fed up with the acquittal of various supervillains, pieces together various superhuman devices to take on the Manhunter persona. The series would find Spencer taking on established villains and interacting with DC heroes while struggling to be a single parent. Even with fan support to save the series, it was canceled with issue #38 in January 2009. The Spencer Manhunter also appears in *Birds of Prey* and later becomes the District Attorney of Gotham City in the 2009 **Batman:** *Streets of Gotham* series.

*D. R. Hammontree*

**MAN OF STEEL, THE.** A six-issue miniseries published by **DC Comics** in 1986 that retells the origin story of **Superman**, *The Man of Steel* was written and penciled by **John Byrne**. The first issue is set initially on Krypton, a coldly scientific world where even skin-to-skin contact has been prohibited between Kryptonians. There, Jor-El and Lara remove their infant son from his gestation chamber to send him rocketing towards Earth, escaping the destruction of his native planet. Through a flashback of scenes from Superman's childhood we learn how Jonathan and Martha Kent found the infant sent from Krypton and raised him as their own, and how gradually, throughout puberty, Superman developed his amazing powers. The issue ends with Superman publicly saving a crashing experimental space-plane, which prompts him to create a costumed persona with which to operate as a **superhero**.

The remaining issues are highly episodic and are used to establish various aspects and characters from the Superman mythos. While Lois Lane does appear as a reporter covering the test flight of the experimental plane in the first issue, the remaining supporting cast from the *Daily Planet*—Perry White and Jimmy Olsen—is introduced in the second issue along with Lex Luthor (though he is little more than a shadowy figure inside a limousine). The third installment shows the first meeting between Superman and another costumed hero, **Batman**, who enlists his help in tracking down a Gotham City jewel thief. The fourth and fifth issues focus on Superman's rivalry with Lex Luthor, he at first trying to place Superman on retainer in issue four, then cloning him in issue #5 after realizing Superman cannot be bought. Luthor inadvertently unleashes the clone (a pale white copy of Superman without his high regard for justice or life—Byrne's updated version of Bizarro) and later in the same issue Superman is forced to stop the rampage of his alter ego. To end the series Byrne has Superman return to Smallville and explore his origins, both as an immigrant to Earth and as a Kryptonian through confronting a holographic projection of his father from his spacecraft.

Byrne's miniseries was the most extensive **retcon** of Superman up to its publication. Previous stories had changed details involved in Superman's origin—1948's "The Origin of Superman!" changed the design of Kryptonian clothing, placing emblems reminiscent of superhero costumes on the inhabitants, and 1961's "The Story of Superman's Life" added the expanded cast of characters, such as Krypto and Supergirl's Father, Zor-El, which had appeared under Mort Weisinger's run as editor; however, Byrne's miniseries was the first large-scale reboot for the character. The previous year had seen the publication of **Crisis on Infinite Earths**, a 12-issue maxi-series that was produced to simplify the continuity of DC's universe of characters, eliminating several canonical stories and synthesizing others in an effort to make the fictional histories of DC's universe coherent. Byrne, coming from successful runs on **X-Men** and **Fantastic Four**, was DC President Jeanette Khan's pick to revitalize the Superman franchise, and his revisions reflect many of the current trends in comics at the time.

Byrne's most important revision was to diminish the long-standing opposition between Clark Kent and Superman. Under Byrne's authorship, Superman no longer felt so distant from humanity since his powers had only gradually developed and his Clark Kent persona, no longer used simply to cover-up his abilities, was more integrated into his identity. Clark Kent becomes an assertive, likeable fellow in *The Man of Steel*, which means that finally, after nearly 50 years of publication, Lois Lane can believably find him attractive. This innovation allows for a depth of interpersonal relationships not possible with the earlier Superman who merely used Clark Kent as a disguise, and for a Lois whose only male peer at the *Daily Planet* had been a cowardly weakling. Lois no longer assumes that Superman has a secret identity, either, giving more honesty to the interactions between Clark, Lois, and Superman. The Kents likewise become a viable source for interpersonal relationships since Superboy was eliminated from continuity, and Byrne keeps them alive to help Clark transition into his new role of Superman. Even Lana Lang receives new depth as, instead of a bitter rival to Lois for Superman's affections, she becomes a heartbroken childhood friend who is the only outsider to know Superman's secret identity. Superman's power-levels were also toned down to increase the drama of his encounters with supervillains, who no longer had to rely solely on Kryptonite to have a fighting chance against the Man of Steel.

Other elements of the mythos that Byrne eliminated were Supergirl, the bottle city of Kandor, and the numerous Kryptonian artifacts and escaped zoo creatures that were prone to run amok on Earth. Byrne returned Superman to his unique status as the sole survivor of Krypton. Acting on an idea from collaborator **Marv Wolfman**, Byrne also transforms Lex Luthor from a mad-scientist into possibly the only thing that seemed more sinister to an audience in the 1980s: a wall-street fat-cat with a billion-dollar payroll and a heart of stone.

*The Man of Steel* title was also used in a regularly published series from 1991 to 2003, and Byrne's conception of Superman remained canon for almost two decades until **Superman: Birthright** was published (2003–4), once again reworking Superman's origins. His work, though, especially the Lex Luthor renovation, has remained influential in the mythos, with a major impact not only on subsequent comics (paving the way for Superman and Lois's eventual marriage in 1996) but on treatment of the Superman character on television in Bruce Timm's *Superman: The Animated Series* as well as the series from the mid-1990s, *Lois and Clark*, and the new millennium's

*Smallville*, all of which focus on interpersonal relationships and feature corporate Luthors.

*Jackson Jennings*

**MARVEL BOY.** "Marvel Boy" is a name used for a variety of characters in comic books published by Marvel and its precursors. The first Marvel Boy, a **superhero** with the power of Hercules, created by **Joe Simon** and **Jack Kirby**, had only two appearances: one in *Daring Mystery Comics* in 1940, and another (in a version that could be interpreted as an entirely different character) in *USA Comics* in 1943. "I don't recall that one," Simon later said about the character.

The second Marvel Boy, created by **Stan Lee** and Russ Heath, made his debut in *Marvel Boy* #1 in 1950. Bob Grayson is a teenager raised on the planet Uranus, where his father flew in a space ship. He is given a set of powerful accessories by the local aliens and returns to Earth as a costumed hero. The character stopped appearing regularly in 1951, but had a handful of further appearances over the next 55 years. In 2006, writer Jeff Parker re-introduced Grayson in the *Agents of Atlas* miniseries, revising his history in the process. Parker established that Marvel Boy was a member of the group now known as the Agents of Atlas in the 1950s, but then returned to Uranus, where he remained until the present. Now simply called "Bob" by his friends, the character became one of the protagonists of Parker's new monthly *Agents of Atlas* series.

In 1977, another Marvel character using the name Marvel Boy debuted in **Captain America** #217. This time, it is young Wendell Vaughn who comes in possession of powerful Uranian artifacts and uses them as a superhero. The character does not keep the Marvel Boy moniker for long, however, and is now better known as Quasar. In *The Thing* #32, published in 1985, a telekinetic youth named Vance Astrovik begins calling himself Marvel Boy. He continues using the name while appearing in *New Warriors* at first, but changes it in 1993. Better known as Justice, he now appears in **Avengers: The Initiative**. Meanwhile, he passed on the Marvel Boy name to a minor character named David Banks in the limited series *Justice: Four Balance* (1994).

In 2000, writer **Grant Morrison** and artist J. G. Jones created the miniseries *Marvel Boy*. Its protagonist is Noh-Varr, a young member of a humanoid alien race from a parallel universe. Noh-Varr is on his way home from a diplomatic mission when his ship is shot down by Marvel Universe super-villain Dr. Midas. The only survivor of the crash, Noh-Varr is imprisoned by Midas, but quickly escapes due to his superior, nano-active physiology, which, among many other superhuman features, is capable of self-repair fueled by the ingestion of matter—such as waste. Following his escape, Noh-Varr declares war on humanity. He carves block-sized expletives into Manhattan and fights opponents such as Hexus the Living Corporation, a parasitic alien life form; a group of very expensive super-soldiers called the United Nations Bannermen; and Oubliette, Dr. Midas's daughter, who is forced to wear a mask by her father at all times and believes herself to be horribly scarred. Eventually, Noh-Varr and Oubliette, who discovers she was lied to, team up to defeat Midas. In the final issue, Noh-Varr is imprisoned, but announces his intention to turn the prison into the capital of his new empire. A follow-up series by Morrison was promised, but never materialized. Nonetheless, Noh-Varr, now also known as **Captain Marvel**, was re-introduced in 2007 and currently appears in *Dark Avengers*.

**Selected Bibliography:** Daniels, Les. *Marvel: Five Fabulous Decades of the World's Greatest Comics*. New York: Harry N. Abrams, 1991.

*Marc-Oliver Frisch*

**MARVEL COMICS.** One of the two (along with **DC**) publishing houses that have dominated the American comic book industry since the early 1960s, Marvel has produced comics in a wide variety of styles and genres, but it is primarily known for its **superhero** comics. The company's most recognizable characters include **Spider-Man**, the **Incredible Hulk**, and the **X-Men**.

Martin Goodman founded the company as **Timely** Publications in 1939. The Sub-Mariner and the Human Torch were early hits, but Timely had difficulty building on their success until the introduction of **Captain America** in early 1941. The patriotic hero, created by **Joe Simon** and **Jack Kirby**, was an immediate smash. Another important figure at Marvel, **Stan Lee**, came to the company in 1940. Lee's talents lay in writing and editing. When Simon and Kirby left at the end of 1942, Lee became the major editor and writer at the company for the next 30 years.

The fortunes of the company, now operating as Atlas Comics, were buoyed by the general popularity of comics during and immediately after World War II. Though the company continued to rely on its popular **superheroes**, it also diversified into other types of comics, especially as the popularity of superheroes declined after the war. As **crime**, **romance**, and **Westerns** became popular, the company followed industry trends and added these genres to its lineup. By 1950, they were producing more than 80 monthly titles in a wide variety of genres, though many titles were short-lived. In the 1940s and 1950s, the company derived its success primarily by copying what was successful at other publishers rather than by innovation.

The industry decline in the mid-1950s hit the company hard. Although Atlas published some crime and **horror** comics, its lineup was diverse enough that the **Comics Code** had little direct impact. Though almost all publishers suffered from the bad publicity surrounding comics, the situation at Atlas was exacerbated by distribution problems. After the collapse of distributor American News in 1957, the company found itself with no distributor for its 75 monthly titles. It survived only because Goodman struck a deal with DC, under which DC distributed eight Marvel books a month (16 bimonthly titles) through its Independent News distributorship. The 16 titles were filled with completed stories from inventory.

Late in 1958, Atlas began to publish newly commissioned material again. Kirby and other artists returned, and the company produced a number of largely forgettable comics. In 1960, when Goodman learned of the success of DC's **Justice League of**

**America**, he directed Lee to create a superhero team. Lee and Kirby developed an entirely new superhero team, the **Fantastic Four**, who debuted in *Fantastic Four* 1 (November 1961), by which time the company was publishing under the Marvel Comics brand name. Lee and Kirby adopted a new approach to the genre, making their stories more character driven and their protagonists less idealized. Their general approach, and the Fantastic Four in particular, proved successful. Marvel followed up by introducing more new superheroes over the next several years, sometimes in new eponymous titles like *The Incredible Hulk* (May 1961), *The X-Men* (September 1963), and *Daredevil: The Man Without Fear* (April 1964), but more often in its remaining mystery and **science fiction** comics. For example, Marvel introduced Spider-Man (by Lee and artist **Steve Ditko**) in *Amazing Fantasy* 15 (1962), and **Thor** first appeared in *Journey Into Mystery* 83 (1962). These titles not only served as tryout books for Marvel, but also allowed the company to remain within the limits imposed on them by the distribution agreement with DC. This issue forced Marvel to cancel the relatively popular *The Incredible Hulk* title in 1963 (after six issues) to make room for a Spider-Man comic. The limitations of the agreement continued to be a problem for Marvel until 1968, when it signed a national newsstand deal with Curtis Circulation Company.

The Marvel characters are known for their complex (for superhero comics) emotional and psychological traits and for being less than perfect. They are often ambivalent about their roles as superheroes, and conflict among them is common. This approach attracted the juvenile audience that was, at that time, the majority of the comic book audience; but Marvel comics were also very popular on college campuses, and enjoyed an aura of hipness throughout the 1960s.

In the early 1960s, Marvel also introduced an innovation in production, the "Marvel Method." Because Lee wrote nearly all of Marvel's titles, he started working with a method that allowed him to create comics more quickly by relying on the storytelling skills of his artists. Lee would provide a brief plot outline to the artist, who would then be responsible for turning this plot into pictures. Lee would then provide the dialogue. This method worked well because he had talented artists like Kirby and Ditko working with him.

Marvel passed DC as the largest publisher in 1968, when it was finally able to publish more titles because of its new distribution arrangement with Curtis, but sales were down throughout the industry. Sales of superhero comics were flat, and other traditional genres were disappearing. In the 1970s, Marvel developed a new profitable genre with its **fantasy** titles like *Conan the Barbarian*. Marvel was instrumental in getting the Comics Code revised in 1971. Lee had published an anti-drug story in *Spider-Man* 96–98 (May-July 1971) without the approval of the code (which forbade the very mention of drug use), and the code was relaxed somewhat after that. Marvel also made a move toward socially conscious stories, introducing African American heroes like **Luke Cage** and The **Black Panther**, while having their other characters deal with problems like alcoholism and poverty.

Marvel was wholly owned by Goodman until 1969, when he sold the company to Cadence Industries. The 1970s were a tumultuous period for Marvel; the company had some spectacular failures like the attempts to publish feminist comics (*The Cat*) and to co-opt the underground movement with the short-lived magazine *Comix Book*. At the same time, the company began focusing on the comic book fans that would be the bulk of the future audience for the medium. A new version of the X-Men debuted in 1975, and became a mainstay of Marvel's superhero lineup. Jim Shooter became editor-in-chief in 1977; during his decade-long tenure, Marvel aggressively courted the profitable direct market.

In the 1970s and 1980s, Marvel was also developing its characters into Hollywood properties. Under Cadence's control, the company built a substantial presence in television animation, creating cartoons featuring both its own and licensed characters. In 1985, Cadence sold Marvel (by then the "Marvel Entertainment Group") for $46 Million to New World Pictures, a television and film production company interested in exploiting Marvel's characters.

New World got little chance to exploit those ideas, as financial trouble forced them to sell Marvel to financier Ronald Perelman in 1989. Under Perelman's control, Marvel diversified and expanded its business by leveraging its position in the comic book industry to borrow money and acquire new subsidiaries. As the comic book industry faltered after 1993, the company had difficulty servicing its debt. In December 1996, the Marvel Entertainment Group filed for bankruptcy to reorganize its debt. The bankruptcy was resolved in 1998 when the company was re-merged with Toy Biz (which had been spun off in 1994). In 2005, after the success of the *Spider-Man* and *X-Men* film franchises, the subsidiary Marvel Studios began to produce films based on Marvel characters, instead of licensing the characters to other companies. By 2009, Marvel was still a major part of the comic book industry, but the company itself has become more of a media company, with comics still playing an important role. At the end of August 2009, the Walt Disney Company announced that it planned to purchase full ownership of Marvel for $4 billion in cash and stock, an acquisition that would place Marvel in a position analogous to DC, which is owned by the Time-Warner media conglomerate.

*Mark C. Rogers*

**MARVELS.** A 1994 limited comic book series written by **Kurt Busiek** and illustrated by **Alex Ross**, *Marvels* is notable for its synergy of artwork and storyline. It is also notable for its retelling of the history of the **Marvel** universe from the perspective of the unassuming bystanders always on the front lines: the ordinary citizens of New York. A sequel series, *Marvels: Eye of the Camera*, by Busiek and illustrator Jay Anacleto, would follow 15 years later, in 2009.

In traditional superhero comics, stories are told around the interplay of heroes and villains: **Batman** fights the Joker, the **Fantastic Four** tangle with Dr. Doom, and so on. Much like the extras in a movie, the citizens of New York, Gotham, or the like are relegated to the background; their lives are unimportant simply because they do not have super powers or are integral to the plotline. Not so with *Marvels*. It is the average person who becomes the hero of the story.

Busiek weaves a tale that puts Phil Sheldon—a photographer and budding writer for a local newspaper—at the heart of the story, chasing the exploits of various superheroes living in New York. Through his eyes and photographs we see the origins of some of the most infamous heroes and villains in the Marvel universe. The ordinary and fantastic live side-by-side in New York.

The prologue to *Marvels* opens with a narrative from a Frankenstein-inspired creation: a man made of fire. Fueled by scientific discovery, but shunned by a conservative society, scientist Phineas Thomas Horton realizes the world is not ready for his creation, thus he secures him away from public harm. However, in 1939 the man of fire is freed by accident, once again able to roam the streets in hopes of being able to control his "gift." Thus begins *Marvels* as a new interpretation to the origin of the first (android) Human Torch, the forerunner of the better-known (but very different) character from the Fantastic Four.

With gloriously romantic overtones and emblematic visual aspects of different decades in the 20th century, Busiek introduces such characters as Prince Namor, Angel, **Captain America**, and a newly minted reporter named J. Jonah Jamieson. Through Sheldon's perspective readers find out why he calls the superheroes marvels "Marvels I called them—and that's what they were. Next to that—what were we?" The supremacy of the human race becomes secondary to those whose powers are greater than average people.

Chronologically, the first chapter provides a beginning to the Marvel universe. Ross's artwork brings to life not only the grandeur of the superheroes themselves, but also a glimpse into life during each era covered by the series. Ross's award-winning style fleshes out the people and events in his iconic vivid style to provide the reader an authentic experience.

The second chapter, "Monsters Among Us," reflects the care-free attitude of America during the 1950s and 1960s. Fascination with superheroes still lingers, but at times it gives way to the more mundane and practical aspects of their triumphs: who pays to clean up the mess left in the wake of their battles? Likewise, a fear of those that are different—**mutants**—begins to grow among the masses. Secularism arrives and people feel threatened by those not really all that different from themselves.

Thematically, the second chapter is more about tolerance and understanding than super heroes battling one another. Introducing characters like the **X-Men** and **Iron Man**, the storyline gives *Marvels*'s characters humanistic qualities, like fear and loathing. Riots and xenophobia occur, and readers see an apparent metaphor for the **Cold War** mentality.

The third chapter, "Judgment Day," is grandeur on a global scale: Galactus versus the **Silver Surfer** and the Fantastic Four. It is the traditional scenario most superhero comic books utilize at some point: the battle for the very existence of the planet; but Busiek infuses the characters with the moralistic compass of humans, taking readers into the "what if" aspects of this battle. Religious and apocalyptic overtones abound as this chapter starts to have Phil and company question what it means to be fallible, until they are saved by the Fantastic Four and return to their normal existence, questioning the need for the marvels at all. Frustrated, Sheldon shouts to a crowd: "Are you so busy digging for garbage you can't even admit to yourselves that you're grateful?"

Finally, the "The Day She Died" echoes the end of Sheldon's career and the beginning of life as an author of Marvels, an homage to the heroes that he spent a lifetime reporting on and defending. He recounts their treatment by the citizens of the planet they have spent a lifetime defending. Central to the chapter are **Spider-Man** and his arch enemies, Doctor Octopus and the Green Goblin. It is here that readers see the impact of death on Phil Sheldon, when Gwen Stacy perishes at the hand of the Goblin. This becomes a question of faith for Sheldon—faith in the marvels that he so vehemently supported and wrote about through the years. In the end, Sheldon realizes that even superheroes are only human.

It is worth noting that *Marvels* is not without a sense of humor. For instance, while referencing a quote about King Arthur, characters that look like John and Jackie Kennedy are in the same elevator with Phil Sheldon. Liza Minnelli and Bea Arthur are seen at a black-tie gala, and Howard Hughes is notably present in the book. The seriousness of the text gives in to these small specks of humor, strategically placed throughout the four chapters. In addition to the text itself, the graphic novel includes some behind-the-scenes commentary on how the artwork was created, source material, and editorials by **Stan Lee** and **Scott McCloud**.

All in all, *Marvels* does more than retell the origins of the Marvel universe and its key figures; its goal is to re-envision and add character and humanity to its long and rich history. Phil Sheldon is the ordinary everyman, but in the end, readers find him anything but ordinary—he is the epitome of what it takes to be a real superhero.

*Alec R. Hosterman*

## MARVEL SUPER HEROES SECRET WARS.

*Secret Wars* is one of the first crossover comic book series to blend both the heroes and the villains of the **Marvel** universe in a story that helped re-position the comics giant. It is considered one of the seminal limited edition crossovers that led to other comic book publishers doing the same, like **DC's** *Crisis on Infinite Earths*. Yet its genesis was never about developing a great storyline and series for the Marvel universe; instead, the series was conceived as a marketing ploy to sell their upcoming action figures line. Ironically, the action figures didn't make a dent in their niche, but *Marvel Super Heroes Secret Wars* became the best selling comic book series of all time for Marvel.

Published between 1984 and 1985, the 12-part series was conceived of and written by Jim Shooter, penciled by Mike Zeck and Bob Layton, and edited by Tom DeFalco. The series opens with members of the **X-Men** (Storm, Colossus, Cyclops, Magneto, Nightcrawler, Rogue, Wolverine, Professor X, and Lockhead the Dragon); the **Avengers** (**Captain America**, **Captain Marvel**, Hawkeye, **Iron Man**, She-Hulk, **Thor**, and the Wasp);

and the **Fantastic Four** (Human Torch, Thing, and Mister Fantastic); as well as the **Hulk**, **Spider-Man**, and Spider-Woman, transported to "Battleworld," a planet deep in the recesses of the galaxy. There, a voice declaring itself to be the Beyonder, states, "I am from beyond! Slay your enemies and all that you desire shall be yours! Nothing you dream of is impossible for me to accomplish!" Thus begins the secret wars.

In similar fashion, the enemies of the super heroes are also brought to the planet, but are placed in a different fortress, and are given the same ultimatum as the heroes. The villains include the Absorbing Man, Doctor Doom, Doctor Octopus, Enchantress, Kang the Conqueror, Klaw, Lizard, Molecule Man, Titania, Ultron, Volcana, and the Wrecking Crew (Piledriver, Wrecker, Thunderball, and Bulldozer). A "neutral," third party, Galactus, is also brought to the netherworld. Not intimidated by the Beyonder's declaration, Doctor Doom and Galactus both fly off into space to confront the Beyonder, only to be turned away, thrown back into the fray like one would swat a fly at a family picnic. Having both the heroes and the villains see this defeat, and knowing Galactus was presumably the most powerful individual in the universe, the combatants decide to play the war games. But with this defeat, Galactus decides his destiny is not with the villains, much to the dismay of Doctor Doom, and leaves to create his own camp.

After the initial battle in the first issue, the X-Men feel it is in their best interest to break away from the rest of the group and create their own camp as well. As **mutants**, they feel they are unlike the other heroes and disdain the authoritative leadership of Captain America. This causes some animosity among the heroes, fueled by the dissonance of being transported to an unknown world, and in-fighting occurs.

As the series continues, good battles evil in a contest of champions. In book 4, Molecule Man drops an entire mountain on the heroes, who are saved by the strength of the Hulk, holding up the mass. In book eight, the heroes take the offense and go after the villains. These battles become the framework for *Secret Wars*, but on its own would not make this a significant piece in Marvel's history. Rather, it is in the subplots and character development that the series makes its mark, creating a depth of humanity and realness for readers.

Doctor Doom drives one of these significant subplots. It is his quest for ultimate power that drives him to conclude that he should battle the Beyonder one-on-one, setting his sights on stealing his power for his own use. Siphoning off a part of Galactus's power, Doom mounts an attack against the Beyonder and inevitably steals the source of his power. With the help of the heroes, the Beyonder regains his power and decides to end the games, albeit ever-so-humbled by mere humans.

*Secret Wars* is a multilayered, complex series that does more than provide a prototypical good superhero versus bad supervillain storyline. It is one of the first to bring together a multitude of company-wide titles into one series, and one (as noted previously) that inspired several other imitators at other comic book publishers. It is in this collaboration that we see the humanity and the every day struggle of learning to deal with egos, both with the humans and the villains.

Another significant aspect of the series is that of an all-powerful being in control of one's fate. The character of the Beyonder is akin to that of an omnipotent being—a god-like individual who has the power to create and to destroy, merely on a whim. This sets up themes of life, death, and what constitutes real power. For instance, in one issue the Wasp dies in battle but then in another she is brought back to life.

In addition, several important changes and additions were made to the Marvel universe. Professor X was able to walk on the Battleworld, and thus joined his X-Men in battle. The villainesses Titania and Volcana were created by Doctor Doom. Julia Carpenter was introduced as the second Spider-Woman. Most famously, Spider-Man gets a new black costume (later revealed to really be an alien symbiote) in book eight. Finally, the Thing decides to stay behind to find himself, a journey self-discovery (thereby leading to She-Hulk becoming the fourth member of the Fantastic Four). When the heroes and villains are transported back to Earth, the events on the Battle-world become part of each book's own lore.

In the end, *Secret Wars* was a financial success; and in 1985, Marvel released *Secret Wars II*, a nine-part series where the Beyonder comes to Earth to battle the superheroes. Likewise, *Secret Wars* spawned such series as the *Infinity Gauntlet*, the *Infinity War*, the *Infinity Crusade*, and **Civil War**, but none are as impactful and successful as the original.

*Alec R. Hosterman*

**MATT, JOE** (1963–). Best known for his unflinchingly revealing and unflattering autobiographical series *Peepshow*, first published in 1992, Joe Matt is an American artist and writer who is well known for writing about things many people would rather keep private. His works generally take his own life as primary subject material, ranging from his suburban childhood and Catholic upbringing to his notorious and well-documented obsession with pornography and allegedly somewhat lax work ethic.

Born in Philadelphia in 1963, Matt began drawing comics in 1987 toward the end of his time studying at the Philadelphia College of Art, though his interest in collecting comics as a child later developed into an extensive accumulation of vintage *Gasoline Alley* strips. Matt's tightly-packed panel style, in which he often directly addresses the reader, developed during this time frame, though his panels gradually became more open and easier to read. (One early self-referential piece pokes fun at how many tiny panels he could pack into a single page.) These strips, spanning 1987 to 1991 (initially published in 1992 as *Peepshow: The Cartoon Diary of Joe Matt* by **Kitchen Sink Press** and republished five years later by Drawn & Quarterly), tend to be single-page stand-alone pieces rather than smaller parts telling an ongoing sequential story.

Matt moved to Canada in 1988 and became part of the "Toronto Three" consisting of himself, **Chester Brown** (*I Never Liked You*), and **Seth** (*Palookaville*), both accomplished comics creators. All published by Drawn & Quarterly, these three creators often reference one another in their works, including illustrated forewords to collections and in-jokes about convention hyjinx. Some of these appear in Matt's work; *Peepshow*, first published in 1992, shifts in narrative style to tell these longer stories.

*The Poor Bastard* (1997) collects issues (#1 through #6) in relaying the story of Matt's move to Canada and his relationship and subsequent messy breakup with his girlfriend Trish; this collection is suffused with all the things that make Joe Matt's work so cringingly autobiographical. His "Jam Sketchbook" appeared in 1998, collecting a series of collaborative illustrated works with other notable comics creators including Julie Doucet, Adrian Tomine, and **Will Eisner**. *Fair Weather* (2002) details an event in Matt's childhood (issues #7 through #10) and *Spent*, published five years later, focuses most specifically on Matt's fascination with pornography.

Nominated for four **Harvey Awards** for his work on *Peepshow*, including Best New Talent in 1990, Matt has also worked as a colorist for a number of mass-market superhero comics including **Batman/Grendel—Limited Series** (which earned him a 1989 Harvey nomination). In 2004, there was discussion of translating *The Poor Bastard* into an animated series for HBO to be produced by Matt and David X. Cohen; these plans never came to fruition and the series never appeared. Matt currently lives and works in Los Angeles, where he is working on a book-length work about living in L.A.

*Anne Thalheimer*

## MAUS: A SURVIVOR'S TALE.

**MAUS: A SURVIVOR'S TALE.** Art **Spiegelman**'s two-volume account (1986, 1991) of his parents' experiences in Poland during World War II and his own struggles to come to terms with the identity of a second-generation Holocaust survivor won him a special Pulitzer Prize in 1992. Among the book's many visual innovations are its dense black-and-white line drawings, its mixing of images from multiple time periods within the same panel, and its allegorical representations of human beings as animals: **Nazis** as cats, Poles as pigs, Americans as dogs, the French as frogs, and Jews as mice. The covers to both volumes feature expressionless mice, dressed in human clothing, cowering beneath a swastika surmounted by a stylized cat's face. This symbolic choice represents not only the predator-prey relationships existing among ethnic groups during World War II, but also the anonymity that history imposes upon even its most devastated victims.

In 1972, Spiegelman drew the first "Maus" strip, a three-page exploration of the stories that his father Vladek told him about the Holocaust (collected in *Breakdowns*, 1977 and 2008). Its animal characters and references to Nazi brutality and extremist survival measures are familiar to readers of *Maus*. However, the first strip evidences a more conventionally cartoonish style and traditional representation of father-son roles. Here, a relatively young, healthy Vladek narrates his memories to 10-year-old Artie, tucking him into bed at the end of the strip with the admonition, "It's time to go to sleep, Mickey," rather than the heartbreaking admission, "I'm tired from talking, Richieu [Vladek's first son, who died during the war], and it's enough stories for now . . ." that closes the second volume of *Maus*. In this later rendering, an adult Artie stands listening to these words while looking down at the elderly Vladek, already falling asleep in his bed. The work continued to evolve between 1980 and 1986 during its serialization in Spiegelman and wife Françoise Mouly's underground magazine *RAW*. The shifts in perspective and style that occur between the initial strip and the final volumes reflect the present-day conflicts between father and son. This relationship becomes as central to the work as its considerations of wartime social and political conditions.

*Maus* is narrated in three layers: the story of Vladek's and his wife Anja's travails during the Holocaust, Vladek's efforts to explain various incidents to Artie, and Artie's attempts to represent his father's story accurately while grappling with their often discordant relationship. This complex structure helps to illuminate the book's subtitle, *A Survivor's Tale*, which likely refers to the impact of the Holocaust on both Vladek's and Artie's lives. Such ambiguity of meaning is also present in the two volumes' individual titles, *My Father Bleeds History* and *And Here My Troubles Began*, which suggest not only the torment that Vladek must undergo as he recounts the war for his son but also Artie's fight to come to terms with his own guilt. He remains painfully aware that he did not experience the Holocaust, much less die as his parents' first child did, yet he seeks to capture it for his own creative work.

Many of the representational choices that Spiegelman made in *Maus* reflect the violence and deprivations of war. The story's panels are often densely packed with details, as in a panel near the beginning of *Maus I*, where Vladek gets onto his exercise bike to begin narrating the story. His bike represents a way for him to maintain cardiac health, yet the repeated images of his furious pedaling on a stationary machine suggest that he is not progressing into the future. His concentration-camp number is clearly visible on his left forearm, while Artie sits surrounded by books and college pennants from his own past. Spiegelman notes that he learned this economy of design from his father's insistence upon using every inch of available space, a hard-earned lesson from the war. He also illustrates the ways in which history persists into the present day by juxtaposing images of past and present within the same panel, as when Vladek tells Artie about four Jews hanged for dealing goods on the black market. Their dangling feet and anguished faces persist through three additional panels, and their memory brings tears to the contemporary storyline as well. Spiegelman also uses some more conventional comic-book tropes to highlight these themes, including textual sound effects, panels shaped like a Star of David or crossed by enormous swastikas to underline the hunted Jews' sense of vulnerability, and panels whose contents spill into the gutters, suggesting the impossibility of containing such difficult truths.

One of *Maus*'s most important subjects is the father-son relationship. Spiegelman's exploration of generational differences allows him to tell Vladek's story while rejecting many of the narrative conventions central to other accounts of the Holocaust. Readers learn at the beginning of the first volume that Artie has come to visit in order to record Vladek's story for a book he is writing. This apparent reconciliation is hardly a smooth one, however, as Vladek repeatedly tells Artie not to include information that is, however, present in the book. Artie does not allow his father the space to process the events he has witnessed, but chooses instead to judge his actions. Volume I closes, for instance, with Artie calling Vladek a murderer for choosing to burn Anja's diaries.

Artie also refuses to portray his father as a heroic, selfless survivor of disaster; rather, he fights with him over his miserly ways and commiserates with his second wife, Mala, over Vladek's poor treatment.

*Maus's* groundbreaking qualities exist in both its approach to Holocaust history and its role in bringing increased critical attention and literary respectability to the graphic novel. Spiegelman has noted that he chose his drawing style and animal characters in reference to the anti-Semitic cartoons included in Nazi magazine *Der Stürmer*, which portrayed Jews as rats, as well as period films that contrast portraits of the Nazis as perfectly proportioned human beings with Jews living in crowded, dirty ghettos. He also cites his childhood viewing of Mickey Mouse, Tom and Jerry, and Krazy Kat as inspiration for his characters, though the stark drawings also recall newsreel footage of survivors staring through the barbed-wire fences of concentration camps. The book acknowledges its own artistic lineage in several ways: it includes "Prisoner on the Hell Planet," a 1972 comic whose human characters attempt to deal with the aftermath of Anja's suicide; it confronts the guilt produced by the first volume's commercial success; and it acknowledges its author's individual limitations. Spiegelman's use of sources from popular culture, politics, and personal life makes *Maus* not only an essential intervention in Holocaust studies but also a testament to the powerful historical work of graphic narratives.

**Selected Bibliography:** Chute, Hillary. "'The Shadow of a Past Time': History and Graphic Representation in *Maus*." *Twentieth Century Literature* 52(2) (Summer 2006): 199–230; Geis, Deborah R., ed. *Considering* Maus: *Approaches to Art Spiegelman's "Survivor's Tale" of the Holocaust*. Tuscaloosa: University of Alabama Press, 2003.

*Jennifer D. Ryan*

**MCCLOUD, SCOTT** (1960–). Born Scott McLeod in Boston, Massachusetts, comic book writer, artist, and theorist McCloud is best known for his attempts to understand the comics art form and reshape the comic book industry. In 1982, McCloud received his BFA in illustration from Syracuse University and took a job in the production department at **DC Comics**. While at DC he began working on his own original comic, *Zot!* Eclipse Comics published the first issue of *Zot!* in 1983 and the series ran for 36 issues. *Zot!* won the **Jack Kirby** Award for Best New Series in 1985 and McCloud received the Russ Manning Award for Most Promising Newcomer.

McCloud wrote the first draft of the Creator's Bill of Rights for a 1988 summit of independent comics creators. The document articulated rights—such as full ownership of creations, return of original artwork, and equitable sharing of profits from creative work—that had not generally been granted to creators by the mainstream comic book publishers.

McCloud's fame within and far beyond the comic book industry began in 1993 with the publication of *Understanding Comics*, a nonfiction graphic novel that presented his theories about the inner workings of the comics art form. It is an ambitious work that, in addition to providing a definition, history and vocabulary for understanding comics, attempts to explain visual communication, symbol use and the artistic process. *Understanding Comics* almost immediately became the most important work in the comics studies field and continues to profoundly influence the work of comics creators and scholars. The book won the industry's two leading awards, the **Eisner Award** and the **Harvey Award**, and was widely and favorably reviewed in the mainstream media.

In 2000 McCloud followed-up with *Reinventing Comics*, his manifesto, in comics format, about how the comics industry needs to evolve. He was already well-known in the online comics community as a pioneer and promoter of web-comics, but his enthusiastic portrayal of a digital future for comics in *Reinventing Comics* made McCloud a guru in the web-comics community. McCloud's trilogy of theory in comics form was completed in 2006 with the publication of *Making Comics*, a how-to book for aspiring comic book creators.

The concepts in these works have captured the imaginations of diverse audiences beyond the comics industry and garnered McCloud invitations to speak at Harvard University, Microsoft, The Smithsonian, Pixar, and many other venues. He has been a consultant on projects at a number of institutions, including The National Cancer Institute, The Defense Advanced Research Projects Agency, and The Xerox Palo Alto Research Center. In 2008 he created a 38-page comic to introduce Google's "Chrome" browser.

Even after he began to establish himself as a theorist, McCloud continued to create comics. In 1997 and 1998 he scripted issues #2 through #13 of DC's *Superman Adventures*. Also in 1998, McCloud's first attempt at computer-generated artwork, *The New Adventures of Abraham Lincoln*, received lukewarm, or worse, response from fans and critics. McCloud accepted a couple of more assignments from DC, including script and layouts in 2004 for the three part prestige series *Superman: Strength*, but after the 1998 launch of his ScottMcCloud.com Web site most of his comics output has been in the form of web-comics, including *Zot! Online* beginning in 2000. As of this writing, McCloud is at work on a new graphic novel with the working title *The Sculptor*.

*Randy Duncan*

**MCFARLANE, TODD** (1961–). Originally from Calgary, Alberta, Canada, McFarlane made his artistic debut in American comics in *Coyote* #11 in 1985 for **Marvel Comics**. Soon after, he also began working for **DC Comics** on the series *Infinite Inc.* His continued success led him to add work from both *Batman: Year Two* and *Incredible Hulk* to his portfolio. His significant rise to the top came when he began drawing *The Amazing Spider-Man* in 1988. Here, McFarlane would craft the famous nemesis, Venom, and with his growing popularity, would be given the opportunity to both write and draw his own *Spider-Man* series in August, 1990. The debut issue sold over 2.5 million copies; the best-selling issues at the time and still one of the best-selling issues of all time.

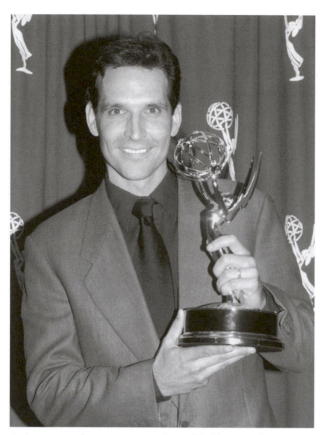

Animator and executive producer Todd McFarlane poses with Emmy award he won August 28, 1999 at the Prime-time Creative Arts Emmy Awards in Pasadena for Outstanding Animated Program for *Todd McFarlane's Spawn* on HBO. © Rose Prouser/Reuters/Corbis

McFarlane took a hiatus from Marvel in August, 1991. By early 1992, he left Marvel altogether to form **Image Comics** with Erik Larsen, **Jim Lee**, Rob Liefeld, Whilce Portacio, Marc Silvestri, and Jim Valentino. Under the new organization, the artists kept the rights to their intellectual properties. As both writer and artist, McFarlane launched *Spawn* as his first project launched through Todd McFarlane Productions, his production studio under Image Comics. *Spawn* #1 sold approximately 1.7 million copies, the highest single-issue sale for an independent publisher to date. After the first seven issues, McFarlane brought on additional writer talent while he continued on as artist. In 1994, McFarlane oversaw the **Spawn**/Batman crossover with DC Comics; which was part of the fanfare to drive comic speculation and sales that dominated the 1990s.

McFarlane sought the maximum potential for his intellectual properties. His creation of McFarlane Toys in 1994 provided him a range of merchandizing opportunity for his properties including toys, clothing, and other goods featuring Spawn. This company also picked up other properties to sell merchandise for including *Akira*, *Alien*, KISS, Metal Gear Solid, and *X-Files*. By the end of the 1990s, McFarlane Toys has become a powerhouse within the toy industry. While continuing his work with Image Comics, in 1996, McFarlane also opened McFarlane Entertainment, the film and animation studio which would work with New Line Cinema for the feature film adaptation of *Spawn* (1997) and with HBO for the animated series *Todd McFarlane's Spawn* (1997–99). *Spawn* was also turned into a Japanese **manga** series, *Shadows of Spawn* (1998–99).

McFarlane's legacy comes not just from his establishment of Image Comics and a new business model for the creators of comics; he also stood ahead of the curve in terms of marketing his intellectual properties in numerous venues, leading the way for major players such as Marvel and DC Comics.

**Selected Bibliography:** Khoury, George et al. *Image Comics: The Road to Independence.* TwoMorrows Publishing, 2007; Vaughan, Kenton, Dir. *Todd McFarlane—The Devil You Know.* DVD. New York: New Video Group, 2002.

*Lance Eaton*

**McKEAN, DAVID (DAVE)** (1962–). Dave McKean has been a professional illustrator, sculptor, comic book artist and writer, videographer, filmmaker, and musician. After graduating from Berkshire College of Art & Design in 1986, he traveled to New York seeking work. Failing to find work in mainstream comics, McKean illustrated **Neil Gaiman**'s *Violent Cases* in 1987, beginning an ongoing collaboration. After work on *Hellblazer* and *Black Orchid* (again with Gaiman), McKean began creating covers for Gaiman's seminal series *Sandman.* Often manipulated photographs or collages and incorporating digital art in the latter half of the 75-issue run, these covers had a number of distinctive characteristics. The title character was almost never on the cover. The title itself did not always appear bannered atop the cover. Objects from nature (leaves, insects, fish) were often collaged into cover images. Despite these irregular aspects, or possibly because of them, the covers were a popular aspect of *Sandman*.

In 1989, McKean illustrated **Grant Morrison's Batman** story, *Arkham Asylum.* Expanding on the ideas **Frank Miller** alluded to in *The Dark Knight Returns, Arkham Asylum* was an exploration of the nature of madness, using the Batman/Joker relationship as a vehicle to examine concepts of sanity. By creating visual analogues specific to each inmate's madness, McKean reinforced Morrison's taut script.

McKean's work draws to mind the chaotic and aggressive style of Ralph Steadman, though the comic artist most often mentioned as similar to McKean is **Bill Sienkeweicz.** This comparison plays out strongly in McKean's 496-page opus *Cages.* Completed between 1980 and 1996, the 10-issue series was collected in a single volume by **Kitchen Sink Press** in 1998 and republished by NBM in 1992. McKean's fluid lines and gracefully distorted figures evoke comparison to European comic masters, notably Lorenzo Mattoti.

As of this writing, McKean has illustrated Tarot decks, over 100 CD covers, over 50 book covers, and 20 children's books, 4 of which were written by Gaiman. He has illustrated or contributed to over 30 different graphic novels. Of these, Gaiman wrote four, exclusive of *The Sandman* series. Two others were based on specific rock albums: *Rolling Stones Voodoo Lounge* (art and script by McKean) and *Alice Cooper: The Last Temptation.* McKean collaborated with Cooper on the CD cover and booklet.

McKean's interest in music extends beyond the visual. A jazz/blues pianist and singer, he occasionally performs publicly at conventions. McKean owns his own record label, *Feral Records*, with saxophonist Iain Ballamay. As a videographer and filmmaker, he has collaborated with Buckethead and Bill Bruford. A DVD compilation of his short films, *Keanoshow*, was released in 2008. He contributed design ideas to two of the Harry Potter films. McKean directed the feature film *Mirrormask*, scripted by Gaiman.

Dave McKean, contemplating his direction of the 2005 film *MirrorMask*. Columbia Pictures/Photofest

McKean has worked as a graphic designer for corporate clients including Sony. He won the Alph-Art, Pantera and **Harvey Awards** for *Cages*, best film awards from four European film festivals for *Mirrormask*, and an **Eisner Award** Best Publication Design.

***See also:*** Sandman, The

**Selected Bibliography:** McKean, Dave. *Dust Covers: The Collected Sandman Covers*. New York: DC Comics, 1997, http://www.dave mckean.com.

*Diana Green*

# MEMOIR/SLICE-OF-LIFE THEMES.

The term memoir or slice of life describes a form of story that many see as a recent innovation in graphic fiction, concentrating on the realistic details of everyday life rather than the spectacular and fantastic worlds that are often associated with comics. These works offer experimental, novelistic aspects of the medium, explore long and often harsh realities of life and human nature, and inhabit profound, shocking, and disturbing corners of the human experience. Paul Gravett calls them stories that "turn the personal and specific into something universal and inclusive" (20). In reality, slice of life comics existed at the medium's inception.

One of the first comics, *The Yellow Kid*, could be seen as the first slice of life cartoon. *The Yellow Kid* was a doppelganger for the public mentality, silly, violent, quickly entertained, and easily patronized; the kid was a stand-in for New York's teeming immigrant, semi-literate, worker population, the new America of century's end. R. F. Outcault's character first appeared in 1894 in a few cartoons before he became the star of *Hogan's Alley* in Joseph Pulitzer's Sunday edition of his newspaper, *The New York World*. The University of Virginia American Studies Web site lauds Outcault as "present(ing) a turn-of-the-century theater of the city." Speaking in a strange sort of criminal argot of the poor, the Kid caused a sensation. His shirt itself constituted the word balloon for the comic strip and often his messages straddled social commentary and naked advertisement. Holding a record player he said, "listen te de woids of wisdom wot de phonograff will give yer." His pidgin English expressions, his long draping body sweater/nightshirt, and his Charlie Brown bald hair style (used by the poor to combat lice) made him the darling of the lower classes, giving them a champion and commentator.

Winsor McKay's strip *Little Nemo in Slumberland* (1905–14), while purporting to be a pure fantasy of a child's evening nocturnes, explored the psyche of childhood desires. Nemo would indulge in a fantasy world of eating, playing, and ice skating. McKay's later *Dream of a Rarebit Fiend* (1904–13), explored the fantasies of adults (city life, stock market, subways, etc.) in a similar fashion. When the comic book began to achieve popularity in the 1930s, real societal issues and personal autobiography quietly crept into the publications. Paul Gravett described comics' popularity as "a secret retreat from parents and siblings, a private way of facing fears and fantasies, (and ) a trove of big important tales to read over and over" (20). **Joe Shuster** and **Jerry Siegel** were two immigrant kids with dreams of merging into the great melting pot of American society and gave their character **Superman** their same hopes and ambitions. Superman was an immigrant who had lost everything, including his native homeland, his family, and his identity to come to the United States. It was hard for readers to tell where Superman's fiction ended and their truth began. Superhero creators did not neglect real world problems. **Jack Kirby** and **Joe Simon** evoked their own experiences in World War II in their **Captain America**, *Guardian*, and *Fighting American* superhero strips. Even before his later graphic novels, **Will Eisner**'s long running **Spirit** comic strip dealt with inner city squalor, tenements, and society's refuse. Often *The Spirit* was only a supporting character to more complex urban tragedies. Eisner portrayed life's losers with sensitivity and emotional complexity. The post-war Noir period signaled a decline in **superheroes** and a new interest in **romance, war,** and **horror**. Returning veterans, as well as comics, had to face the complexities and anxieties of post-war life at home. **EC** Comics used suggestive metaphors and featured stories of **zombies**, cannibalism, and vampirism arguing that the post-war society was filled with predatory forces. Rampant consumerism, unemployment, and higher prices were fears and worries of the postwar recession. Even optimistic space adventures like **DC**'s *Mystery in Space*, reflected new fears about exploration and unconquered worlds.

By the 1960s, the counter-culture was producing **underground and adult comics** that ridiculed conventional society, and was experimenting with autobiographical motifs. **Robert Crumb** used the vehicle of the comic format to discuss the drug culture, but also a cynical and insightful attitude towards his own life. However, it was Justin Green's **Binky Brown Meets the Holy Virgin Mary** that boldly moved into pure autobiography in 1972. Green exposed his complicated guilt about religion and the obsessive compulsive disorder that governed his life. He would dream of women's underwear and nuns without their habits. He conflated his sexual desires and neuroses with his upbringing in a religious school. He agonized about his lusts and felt that his natural human urges were horrific sins. He fantasized about his punishment before the nuns. Others, such as like **Art Spiegelman** and Crumb were emboldened to go further and make their own life stories the center of the their comic world.

Though much of Crumb's early output was episodic in **Zap**, *Hup*, **Weirdo**, and other venues, his tales regarding the women in his life were eventually anthologized in the full-length collection, **My Troubles with Women**. In this album Crumb explored his own obsessions with women, starting with his pre-fame days where he idealized women as an unattainable goal and wrote strips like "Footsy," subtitled, "the true story of how I became a teen-age sex pervert." He admits, "but, I've been lucky—oh so lucky! A few of these wondrous beings have allowed me to have my way with them." This declaration is followed by a typical Crumb image of Crumb glomming on to the leg of an Amazon woman of gigantic proportions. Crumb's images go beyond realism to grotesque caricatures featuring his exaggerated eyes, hideous glasses, an anemic body and a lecherous expression. He writes, "my whole trouble with women is that I'm too much into 'em." Yet Crumb's narrative progresses beyond lecherous infatuation with the female form. Crumb becomes famous and has his fill of women and his fetishes. He writes about one conquest, saying, "she's cute but we're just two sweaty animals going at it, like cows or pigs." Readers are continually reminded of Crumb's low self-esteem, his humor, and his honesty about himself; but Crumb has a wider vision, maturing and growing beyond his mere lusts. He marries Arline, his soul mate of sorts, and becomes a father. Still, his puzzling relationship with women continues. He has a mid-life crisis and writes and draws ironically about his failure to work. He reemerges with "Arline and Bob," a strip about domestic life and the manner in which his young daughter Sophie dominates his life in the same manner women dominated his life before. Only now, Crumb, instead of being dominated by his urges, is dominated by his daughter's urges, whims, needs, and phobias. In the strip, he describes his bouts of depression, sitting in bed, and moping about his life. He then shows his wife Arline the finished midlife strip, and she threatens to cry if he does not draw her in a more flattering manner. Even when happily married and a family man, Crumb still has female troubles.

As the **Comics Code** began to lose its censoring force in the 1970s, more adult comic experiments began to arise. Eisner produced the dark but deeply moving **A Contract with God** stories in 1978. Eisner's novelistic depiction of 1930s Jewish tenement life in the Bronx at 55 Dropsie Avenue featured edgy portrayals of people left in a rundown apartment dwelling. Eisner never calls these tales directly autobiographical, but they clearly are derived from his life experiences. There is a cast of losers and wannabes including a pedophile superintendent; a greedy little Lolita child who steals the super's money and kills his dog; a gigolo addict; a broken-down opera diva; a secretary who vacations in the country and dreams of a wealthy husband; and Willie, a young man who loses his virginity to a worldly older woman.

Other comics took a more intellectual view of nonfiction material. **Scott McCloud** chose to talk about the comics medium and explain how the combination of words and pictures was a unique art form. In his seminal, *Understanding Comics* (1993), he explained how comics were a part of his own life and how the comics form has altered how we see the world. McCloud, posing in the comic as narrator and pivotal spokesman for the medium, suggests that the comic medium is a pivotal piece of society's mythic structure. He sees comics as all-American art form, and like a documentary filmmaker he takes readers behind the scenes, explaining everything from panel structure, to point of view, to styles of comics. Autobiography, comics history, and technique have strangely merged in McCloud's life. Having published several comics explaining the medium, the way he has drawn himself (literally) into the medium has made his life a part of the form he describes.

More often than not, autobiographical comics tell common tales of individual lives, and while earlier autobiographical works of Robert Crumb, Justin Green, and **Harvey Pekar** broke taboos about sex and perversion, later memoirs dealt with simpler slice of life issues portrayed in compelling images and poetic writing. Craig Thompson's graphic novel *Blankets* (2003) explores a young man's coming of age in a deeply religious community. In the lengthy narrative, the protagonist begins to question the assumptions of his religious foundation. He falls in love and experiences his first romance, breaking from his religious and family beliefs and tentatively charting a new course for his life. He explores the difficult territory of self-discovery and experiencing a larger world than his origins. Not only is the subject matter adult in the most novelistic way, but Thompson's work treads a fine line between traditions and innovation. Thompson draws in a regular traditional comic style, with wide-eyed characters and gangly cartoon bodies. However, these characters are not caricatures or superheroes, but normal people with small flaws and mild expressions. Thompson's pacing emulates real life and events unfold slowly. His parents enforce a strict church doctrine in his family household, but the adolescent Thompson slowly grows to see a larger world by visits to church camp. There, theoretically, the attendees are to become more devout, but many of the kids go just to escape the watchful eyes of their controlling parents. In one scene, the other students make fun of Thompson for reading his Bible, and he even prays to God to forgive his peers for ridiculing him. More touching is his burgeoning relationship with the kind and good-hearted Raina, a girl he meets at the church camp. Their closeness and growing understanding awaken his passion and normal degree of teenage lust, but Thompson is deeply conflicted about his feelings. Is this temptation or real love? If Raina is a Christian too, than why would she want to have a physical relationship instead of abstinence? Thompson wrestles with his sexual identity and his pangs of first love in an often amusing, confusing, and heartbreaking way that all people who were adolescents remember and ponder in later life.

Some comics blur the lines between fairytale and reality. J. M. DeMatteis and Jon J. Muth's epic fairy tale *Moonshadow* (1985–87) tells the story of a young enchanted boy coming of age among a host of quirky acquaintances. Along the way he sees his mother die, experiences other losses, and grows to maturity. Tinged with elements of philosophy and folk wisdom the story has resonances in our everyday world. When Moonshadow's mother is murdered, he goes to see a slimy funeral director. "Unkshuss talked: I listened. He proposed: I agreed. He billed: I paid." DeMatteis's fantasy world of strange journeys and odd friends is much like Crumb's real world of hollow dreams and faint ambitions, tinged with the stuff of reality. Danny Fingerroth argues that

DeMatteis expresses "a disarming conviction of man's potential and the beauty to be found in life" (94).

Marjane Satrapi's *Persepolis* (2003–5) tells the story of her childhood and growth in modern Iran in the time after the Shah and during the blooming power of Islamic fundamentalists. She is shaken by fearful childhood experiences that are described with simplicity but with dark and rich resonances. At one point she is accosted by a league of women fundamentalists who want to report her to the local police for not wearing the traditional women's veil. She cries and lies her way out of prosecution, but it is a frightening, embarrassing experience that terrifies her. She has an uncle who is accused of crimes against the Islamic revolution, and he is to be put to death. He has a choice of one visitor and he requests young Marjane be that one guest. It is an awesome responsibility for a little girl, but she is brave and hugs her uncle. He calls her "the star of his life" and the little girl he wished he had. After his death, the papers write "Marxist spy punished." However, Satrapi's story is not mournful or self-pitying. Bad things happen to people she loves. A neighbor next door is bombed and her playmate is killed, buried in the rubble. She is given a chance to escape at the end of the autobiography's first volume, but she cannot leave her family for fear she will never see them again. It is a simple and moving account of a little girl who wants nothing more than to be left at peace, to play Madonna records, and to be free of war and internal spies.

Not all graphic experiments in nonfiction are such personal tomes. Some like Larry Gonick's *A Cartoon History of the Universe* (1990) seeks to tell a massive story, literally the history of the universe from the Big Bang to the present in a quirky and irreverent way. Gonick is neither a defender or denier of any religious or philosophical view, but he plants them all in the story of man's rise. People, dinosaurs, and mammals are shown full of energy and individualism. His story of King Saul and David is typically funny. Saul's daughter, Michal wishes to marry David and Saul sets an impossible condition. "She's yours—If you bring me 100 foreskins of the Philistines!" David's reply, "No problem." Gene Kannenberg writes that it is an "irreverent, but informative and alternative way of delivering a history lesson packed with quirky facts" (74). Gonick places the dinosaurs and man's precursors on an equal footing, and he has fun with the writers of the Bible and the Greeks, who are by turns inspired and mired in their beliefs and philosophies. In any event the rise of civilization is chronicled with humor and a wise eye towards man's many foibles. While not strictly a memoir, it is one man's quirky view of our cultural history.

Bryan Talbot's *Alice in Sunderland* (2007) is an encyclopedic journey into the world of *Alice in Wonderland*, the life of Lewis Carroll, and the town of Sunderland, England, as well as a macrocosmic view of the world and history. Talbot makes remarkable connections between the bizarre, the coincidental, the cosmic, and the minor. The parallels in the life of writer, Charles Lutwidge Dodgson (Carroll), his trip down the rabbit hole with Alice, and the larger vision of the world of Carroll and the economic, political, and social events since his era are intertwined. It would be easy to write Talbot off as a strange eccentric with a gift for seeing conspiracies and connections that others cannot envision, but Talbot has a larger agenda. He is seeking to make a visual codex to the work of Carroll and tie that motif and text to the events of the next hundred years and illustrate the inextricable links between seemingly unrelated events. Danny Fingeroth explains, "He immerses you in history, not just that of Alice and Carroll, but also of England, America, religion, entertainment (including comics), war, disease, birth, death and everything inbetween" (67).

Nick Bertozzi's *The Salon* (2007) is a more limited cultural experiment in history and art but no less exciting than Talbot's gambit. Bertozzi writes about the period of early 20th-century modern art with Picasso, Satie, Braque, Gertrude Stein, Edward Muybridge, and other vibrant personalities existing in turn of the century Paris. He places this remarkable, complex time in the frame of a murder mystery; a mysterious lady in blue paint is killing off avant-garde artists, and Georges Braque, his lusty friend Picasso, the Steins and Gertrude's paramour Alice B. Toklas have to find the cause and murderer or risk the same end themselves.

Spiegelman's **Maus** (1986) was a creative experiment that made autobiographical comics not only respectable, but profound. Spiegelman tells the desperate story of his father, Vladek, a concentration camp survivor, but in an unconventional way. Rather than simply another holocaust memoir, he wanted to illustrate the story using the ho-locaust images to explore ideas about humanity and inhumanity. In his tale, the Jewish people are allegorically portrayed as Mice, the Polish as Pigs, and the **Nazi** oppressors are viewed as cats. This dark metaphorical structure not only produces a view of racism, it uses the comedy structure of Disney cartoons to pointedly undercut and increase the drama. Comedic cats and mice are rarely equated with worldwide tragic events, but here, we are forced to confront the most horrific acts of man's depravity against man in the friendly and winsome guise of a cat-and-mouse cartoon. Reading *Maus* is disturbing for many, because while enjoying the tale, the reader feels guilt for obtaining pleasure from so much human suffering. To complicate matters further, Spiegelman's tale has a modern connection, since his father was a living character at the time and the adult Spiegelman struggles to understand his damaged parent within the comic. As a son, he cannot understand his father's incredible anguish as a survivor, and he conse-quently cannot comfort this parent who grew up under such extraordinary conditions. As is often the case, Spiegelman finds that those closest to a victim of tragedy can be the least understanding; the event is too close, too prescient, and too demanding for relatives to engage it. Spiegelman's novel shows the private face of suffering.

**Daniel Clowes**'s experiments in the graphic novel format provide a humorous and often surreal lens to critique society. In his popular **Eightball** anthology series (1989–) from **Fantagraphics** books, Clowes was able to lampoon contemporary social conditions. Various stories have been revived in separate graphic novels. In *David Boring* (2000) he addresses the protagonist's sexual obsession with a perfect woman, being stranded on a desert island, and the apocalypse. *Like A Velvet Glove Cast in Iron* (2005) is Clowes's *Finnegans Wake*, a disturbed, modern Ulyssean/Kafkaesque journey where protagonist Clay Loudermilk seeks his lost wife, meets bizarre surreal characters, and undergoes unsettling metamorphoses. In *Art School Confidential*, Clowes ridicules the pretentious world of art students and the pomposity of art education with wry observations such as, "the only thing of less value than one of your paintings will be your BFA diploma." Rocco Versaci argues that Clowes's "real intent is to explore the psychologies of the town's oddball citizens" (17).

Clowes is most widely known for **Ghost World**, a series of short comic tales from *Eightball* translated into a successful 2001 film, which follows the seemingly aimless wandering (and wondering) of two urban, nomadic, post-high school teen girls who are looking for a meaningful role in life. M. Keith Booker describes Clowes's work as an exploration of "the alienation and ennui of postmodern youth," (87) and *Ghost World*'s teen protagonists are the embodiment of that condition. Enid Coleslaw is the outspoken, angry, punk misanthrope and her friend, Becky Dishwaller is the naïve puzzled cooler partner in their rambling, semiotic approach to the modern city. While Enid critiques boys, jobs, schools, and society, she is also lost and unhappy, stuck in the quagmire between adolescence and true adult life. Yet Clowes carefully removes the outer layers of polite camaraderie and analytically dissects contemporary intimacy between two girl friends that are nearly a singular consciousness. When Enid thinks she is accepted to school at Swarthmore it portends a monumental breakup for partners who have shared their most secret thoughts. When Rebecca complains that Enid does not want her along, Enid retorts, "it has EVERYTHING to do with you, you remember every little detail I wish I could forget"(74). Clowes strikes at the horrible burden of intimacy in a fragmentary society that values aloofness and alienation over any sense of community. *Ghost World*'s visual language underscores the banality and lack of reality of life in postindustrial America, making the girls' estrangement and confusion more plausible.

In *It's a Bird* (2004) writer Steven Seagle and artist Teddy Kristiansen take the figure of **Superman** and work it into a personal memoir of a character dealing with life realities. Seagle's protagonist, Steve, is a comic-book author offered the chance to write the *Superman* strip, which causes him to ponder the problems of omnipotence. His opening line is "what I think about most is the big red 'S'." Danish artist Teddy Kristiansen's work is extremely chilling, showing the influence of Fritz Lang's expressionistic *Metropolis*. Seagle's script plays off of that dark, almost monochromatic world, juxtaposing Kristiansen's dull coloring with the notion of a fantastic world of comic culture. Though Kristiansen's style is abstract, these people are not grotesques, just sympathetic flawed humans worthy of compassion. Seagle's Steve ponders Superman's might while dealing with disturbing family traumas. His father has gone missing, and he is haunted by the fact that he has a genetic propensity for Huntington's Disease, an incurable and fatal genetic condition. Instead of jumping at the opportunity of a lifetime, Steve balks at the idea becoming reticent and prickly. He thinks he cannot write Superman stories and lacks empathy with the character. He proclaims, "there's no access point to the character for me." Steve has watched his mother die, he fears marrying a long time paramour for fear of making more children with the fatal disease, and he fears for his missing father;

he feels anything but super. Seagle sees the massive gulf between puny human experience and the overwhelming cosmic-ness of an omnipotent character like Superman. *It's a Bird* brings the Superman myth to everyone, suggesting that the **man of steel** could make anyone feel inadequate.

It was fitting that one of the greatest innovators of comics, Will Eisner, ended his career on another inventive experimental work. In the late 1970s, inspired by underground comics telling personal tales, Eisner embarked on a series of autobiographical comic projects that illustrated his worldview. Even in *The Spirit*, Eisner purposefully sidelined his protagonist on occasion to focus on a totally inconsequential supporting character. In essence, Eisner was inserting alterative short stories into the superhero medium back in the 1940s; but in the aftermath of 9/11, surrounded by the rage of conspiracy stories and fears of foreign terrorism that haunted the United States, Eisner turned to an absurd and vile primal conspiracy theory that had haunted him his whole life, *The Protocols of the Elders of Zion*. This sham document, an obvious forgery created by anti-liberal repressive factions in the Tsarist government of Nicholas II, was intended as a conspiracy theory linking Jewish groups to a plot of world domination as a pretext/rationale for punishing Jews through a series of *pogroms*. Eisner wanted to uncover this conspiracy about conspiracies, and he used the formula he had honed so well in the 1940s, the character-driven mystery suspense tale that he had perfected in *The Spirit* to such superb effect, to explore the bizarre twists and turns in this fable. Here he begins with the tale of Maurice Joly, the French scribe who in 1864 created "The Dialogue in Hell Between Machiavelli and Montesquieu." The work was a critique of Napoleon III and was intended to tarnish his rule and regime. It was used in the creation of the text of *The Protocols*. In 1921 *The London Times* did an expose revealing the absurdity of the document and dismantling its claims, yet it still persisted. In the story, Eisner is embodied by journalist Philip Graves, who seeks to know how the lies of the Protocols persisted so long and have continued to have such a negative effect. He asks a bookseller how such a weapon of mass deception could survive when "that document is shown to be a fake?" The bookseller calmly responds, "no matter people will buy it anyway . . . because they need to justify the conduct they may later be ashamed of."

Using the dependable mystery format, Eisner links the *Protocols* to the larger issue of peoples' fear of social change. Eisner grapples with the kind of conservatism that leads people to believe outrageous stories that support the status quo. Holocaust deniers, 9/11 deniers, and Iraq conspiracy buffs are all part of this unlikely crop of scenarios promoted as truth. Eisner also returns the graphic novel to its origins in didactic instructional materials explaining history and social behavior. Eisner's last work was a fitting end and summation of the graphic novel's progress, invoking novelistic, nonfiction, didactic, and graphic elements in one package.

Paul Gravett said that comics are important because "they are often the first pieces of fiction that a young boy or girl chooses for themselves"(20). Gravett thinks they help us build interior worlds. Rocco Versaci suggests that "we are drawn to others' lives out of the desire to connect with and learn from their stories" (76). What the memoir/slice of life comic has achieved is to make graphic novels the full partner of other contemporary forms of literature and communication, both liberating the form from ghettoes of superheroes, adolescent fantasy, and crude illustrative styles and linking graphic storytelling to film, other media, and life itself.

**Selected Bibliography:** Booker, M. Keith *"May Contain Graphic Material": Comic Books, Graphic Novels, and Film.* Westport, CT: Praeger, 2007; Fingeroth, Danny. *The Rough Guide to Graphic Novels.* London: Rough Guides, 2008; Gravett, Paul. *Graphic Novels, Stories to Change Your Life.* New York: Collins Design, 2005; Kannenberg, Gene. Jr. *500 Essential Graphic Novels.* New York: Collins Design, 2008; Versaci, Rocco. *This Book Contains Graphic Language: Comics as Literature.* New York: Continuum, 2007; Wood, Mary. "The Yellow Kid on the Paper Stage." *Xroads* (March 9, 2009). http://xroads. virginia.edu/~ma04/wood/ykid/intro.htm.

*Stuart Lenig*

**MERCHANDISING AND LICENSING.** Merchandising and licensing are twin industry practices that involve utilizing characters and stories created in one medium for the marketing of ancillary products. Licensing refers to the practice of selling or renting the rights to characters for use in other media (television, film, advertising), while merchandising is the sale and creation of products, such as toys, lunchboxes, or video-games, based on those characters. Licensing and merchandising have always been an important part of the American and Japanese comic book industries. However, as large media interests acquired publishers, and the number of media outlets expanded from the 1970s to the 1990s, licensing and merchandising became much more important in the American comic book industry.

Generally, two types of licensing have played roles in the comic book industry. In the first type, properties from other media (largely television and film) are licensed to comic book publishers who then produce comics based on the characters. This has been significant in the American industry since the 1950s. After the adoption of the Comics Code in 1954, Dell became the largest American publisher largely because it held the license to publish comics based on the Disney characters. Dell and its successor company, Gold Key, published many licensed titles through the 1960s, including comics based on such oddities as *The Beverly Hillbillies* television series and Disney's film version of *Swiss Family Robinson*. In this type of licensing, the comic books, produced as extra commodities to profit from the popularity of characters, are the merchandising.

The second type of licensing generally reverses this process. Comic book publishers license their characters to other companies. This process also has a long history in the industry. For example, **DC**'s iconic superhero **Batman** made his comic book debut in 1939; by 1943, the character was appearing in *The Batman*, a 15-episode movie serial. *Batman and Robin*, another serial, followed in 1949. From 1966 to 1968, the campy live-action *Batman* television series was a prime-time hit; it was also successful in syndication through the 1970s and 1980s and spawned a feature film in 1966. In the 1970s, the character was featured as part of the *Superfriends* cartoon series. In 1989, Warner Brothers, by then the owner of DC Comics, released a darker, massively successful *Batman* film that was followed by three sequels over the next decade. The franchise was rebooted in 2005 with *Batman Begins*.

Each of these media appearances increased the visibility of the character, and expanded his appeal beyond comic books. Batman has become part of the larger American (and to a lesser extent international) culture; many people who have never read comic books can identify the character. This allows DC to license the character's image for a wide range of purposes, from common toys and juvenile clothing to more elaborate art and advertising uses. Successful licensing programs have generally increased the ability of comic book publishers to sell merchandise based on their characters.

In the United States, DC has long been the king of licensing and merchandising among comic book publishers. The company owns **Superman**, Batman and Robin, and **Wonder Woman**, the most widely known characters in the **superhero** genre. DC has relentlessly exploited their name recognition by using the characters in television and feature films. DC has long been part of larger media interests. It was purchased in 1968 by Kinney National Services, which purchased Warner Brothers film studio in 1969 and formed Warner Communications in 1971. Due to subsequent consolidation in mass media industries, DC later became part of Time-Warner, one of the largest international media conglomerates. Even though DC has generally trailed **Marvel Comics** as the largest publisher of comic books since the late 1960s, the company's media connections have ensured that its licensing efforts have been more lucrative.

Licensing and merchandising has also been an important source of revenue for Marvel. In 1969, Marvel's founder Martin Goodman sold the company to Cadence Industries, a conglomerate that used Marvel's characters to market some of their own products, such as children's vitamins. Under Cadence's control, Marvel also developed a substantial presence in television animation. In 1985, Cadence sold Marvel to New World Pictures for $46 million. Three years later, financial trouble forced New World to sell the company to financier Ronald Perelman. Perelman used Marvel's position in the comic book industry to buy companies that enhanced Marvel's ability to sell licensed products. Before it went into bankruptcy in 1996, Marvel had purchased trading card manufacturers, juvenile publishing interests, and part of Toy Biz, a toy company. Marvel financed some of the Toy Biz purchase by granting the company an exclusive, perpetual, worldwide license to make toys based on the Marvel characters.

Despite the fact that Marvel's value to both New World and Perelman clearly lay in licensable characters, the company has historically not been as successful as DC in developing their licenses. As late as 1985, Marvel derived only about eight percent of its revenue from licensing; In the same year, well before the wave of Batman products brought forth by the 1989 film, DC derived over 60 percent of its income from licensing. The success of the *Spider-Man* and *X-Men* film franchises at the beginning of the 21st century brought considerable new licensing income to Marvel, and in 2005 Marvel Studios began producing its own films, rather then licensing characters or doing co-productions.

From the 1960s through the 1980s, DC and Marvel were the industry leaders in licensing, just as they were in comic book publishing. Other companies also licensed their characters, but they were less successful, partially because their characters were less valuable. By the late 1980s merchandising and licensing were the driving force behind the American comic book industry. In 1989, the Batman license alone contributed some $390 million to Time-Warner's bottom line. This was more money than was generated by the gross sales of the entire comic book industry.

In addition to the licensing success of the *Batman* film, two other developments in the 1980s brought new attention to the role of licensing in the industry. The first was the success of **Dark Horse Comics**, which began as a small independent publisher that published both creator-owned and company-owned titles. The success of some of these early titles gave the company enough capital to buy licenses from Hollywood films, initially *Aliens*, then *Predator* and *Terminator*. Dark Horse employed these licenses in all sorts of titles and combinations. Dark Horse's new connections in Hollywood also allowed the company to work licensing the other way; several Dark Horse comics, notably *The Mask* and *Timecop*, became feature films. By creating close connections with Hollywood, Dark Horse carved out a profitable niche doing both types of licensing. By the 1990s, much of the company's revenue came from publishing licensed *Star Wars* comics.

The second big development in comic book licensing and merchandising in the 1980s was the *Teenage Mutant Ninja Turtles*. Created by Peter Laird and Kevin Eastman in 1984 as a black and white independent comic, the turtles became a licensing goldmine. During the late 1980s and early 1990s, over $2 billion worth of turtle-related merchandise was sold. The runaway success of the turtles meant that the comic book industry began to be seen as a cheap way to develop profitable licenses.

Many of the comic book publishers that started up after 1990 were explicitly more interested in license creation than in publishing comic books. Video game publisher Acclaim video games purchased Valiant Comics in 1994 for $65 million and developed videogames such *Turok: Dinosaur Hunter*, based on their comics' properties. Between 1990 and 1996, comic book publishers were founded by a number of media companies. The clearest attempt at developing licenses was Tekno Comics, which hired celebrities and fan favorite comics creators to develop concepts for comics such as *Leonard Nimoy's Primortals*. Tekno lost money and got out of comic book publishing in 1997, but not before developing some minor licensing agreements. Like Tekno, most of the other companies were short-lived in comics publishing.

While the possibility of a big licensing hit like the *Teenage Mutant Ninja Turtles* was slim, most comic book publishers actively pursued opportunities to sell their characters outside the medium in the 1990s, particularly for toys, feature films, and animated television. **Todd McFarlane**, one of the founders of **Image Comics**, licensed his popular **Spawn** character for a feature film and an adult animated series. McFarlane also developed his own toy company, which he used to market Spawn and other action figures to both the traditional toy audience and adult collectors.

Merchandising and licensing revenue have often been at the center of disputes about creator's rights. **Jerry Siegel** and **Joe Shuster**'s many lawsuits with DC for the ownership of Superman, for example, were spurred by their recognition of the value of the character's licensing rights. While creators may have been reasonably (by industry standards, at least) compensated for the creation of comic books, they have often received no share of the far greater profits derived from the licensing and merchandising of characters they have created.

*Mark C. Rogers*

**MIGNOLA, MIKE** (1960–). Though his reputation rests largely on his role as the creator of the *Hellboy* series, Mike Mignola is a prominent artist and writer whose work has spanned several titles and characters. He is noted for his distinctive style, which **Alan Moore** once described as "German expressionism meets **Jack Kirby**."

Growing up in the Bay Area of California, Mignola developed an early passion for monster movies and horror novels, and concluded at an early age that he wanted to grow up to be a comic book artist. His initial entry into the comics industry was through a self-published fanzine called *The Comic Reader*. A graduate of the California College of Arts and Crafts, Mignola transitioned from fan to professional when he began providing covers and illustrations soon after his move to New York in 1982. A year later, Mignola got his first series work as the penciler for **Marvel**'s *Rocket Raccoon*. Following its success as a cult title, Mignola provided illustrations, covers and inks with his trademark style for *Alpha Flight*, *The Incredible Hulk*, and other **Marvel superhero** titles.

In 1988, Mignola left Marvel to work for their competitor **DC Comics**, which had begun to publish comics with the kind of sophisticated subject matter that appealed to Mignola, such as Alan Moore's *Watchmen* and *The Dark Knight Returns* by **Frank Miller**. His first contributions at DC were as artist on a *Phantom Stranger* miniseries and on *The World of Krypton*. During his tenure at DC, he was recognized as an accomplished artist, with a distinctly dark and shadowy style, which is evident on the covers for the **Batman:** *A Death in the Family* series. He also lent his Kirby-esque art for *Gotham by Gaslight*, an alternative reality Batman series set in 19th-century Gotham that featured Jack the Ripper.

In 1992, **Dark Horse Comics** signed on for a comic book adaptation of Francis Ford Coppola's film, *Bram Stoker's Dracula* and Mignola was hired to provide the inside illustrations. Later, Mignola, along with Miller, Art Adams, and **John Byrne**, went to Dark Horse and pitched a new imprint that featured characters—not merely the retelling of established stories. This finally led to Mignola's signature character, Hellboy. An orphaned demon who fights to save the world from evil, Hellboy formally debuted in 1994 in *The Seed of Destruction*, scripted by Byrne. Eventually Mignola took over writing duties as more Hellboy series were published.

While Hellboy can certainly be considered the most significant creation of Mignola's career, he has also been active in other endeavors. In 2001, he joined the production team for Walt Disney's *Atlantis: The Lost Empire*. The experience helped him when he became the concept artist for Guillermo del Toro's *Blade II*. During this time Mignola and del Toro forged plans to produce a live-action *Hellboy* movie. The project came to fruition when it opened in 2004 to both financial and fan approval—enough to warrant a sequel. Mignola went on to adapt a comic book one-shot for television, *The Amazing Screw-On Head*, about a mechanical head called to the rescue by President Lincoln.

In addition to enjoying worldwide popularity, Mignola has won eight **Eisner Awards** for his writing and illustrating work on *Hellboy*. While he continues to occasionally write and illustrate *Hellboy* issues, he has handed over the reins of the growing franchise to artists, including Ryan Sook and Derek Thompson.

**Selected Bibliography:** Brayshaw, Christopher. "Between Two Worlds: The Mike Mignola Interview." *Comics Journal* (August 1996): 65.

*Richard L. Graham*

## MILESTONE COMICS.

In 1993, the comics business in the United States was booming, and many new approaches were tested on the seemingly ever-growing audience. One of the most distinctive of these was Milestone Comics, a group of comic books published as an imprint of **DC Comics**, but set in a separate universe.

Behind the start of Milestone Comics stood Milestone Media, a group created in 1992 by the African American artists and writers Dwayne McDuffie, Denys Cowan, Derek T. Dingle and Michael Davis. McDuffie was the chief writer/editor and Cowan did all the initial character and other design tasks. Their reason for launching this initiative was in response to the way minority characters had been treated in American mainstream comics, either being included as token characters or simply not being included at all.

The origin story of the Milestone universe was a massive gang conflict, called "The Big Bang," which ended with the police using an experimental tear gas, killing many of the gang members and mutating the rest, giving them various super powers. This was the origin of the majority of the super-powered characters in the Milestone universe, often called the Dakotaverse after the fictional Midwestern city of Dakota in which most of the stories take place.

The first year of Milestone Comics saw the publication of four titles: *Blood Syndicate* by Ivan Velez, Jr. and Chriscross, *Hardware* by McDuffie and Cowan, *Icon* by McDuffie and MD Bright, and *Static* by Robert Washington III and John Paul Leon. The titles were, in effect, clever African American variations on mainstream **superhero** team comics, **Iron Man**, **Superman**, and **Spider-Man**, respectively. *Icon* included a distinctive female superhero, Rocket, as well as a hilarious parody of Marvel's **Luke Cage**, named Buck Wild. The response was good, both from readers and critics, and the following year another three titles were added: *Kobalt* by John

Rozum and Arvell Jones, *Shadow Cabinet* by Washington and Leon, and *Xombi* by John Rozum and Cowan.

When the whole comics industry went into a slump, Milestone similarly suffered. In 1995, they had to cancel some of their lowest selling titles, a trend that continued in 1996 despite the cross-over *Worlds Collide*, which included several major DC comic books, and a number of separate miniseries. Milestone finally shut down their whole comic book line in 1997, ending many of the books in mid-story.

In the aftermath of the closing of all the titles, Milestone Media kept going, mostly as a licensing company, and has had some success, such as the re-launching of the title *Static* in conjunction with the animated TV series *Static Shock*, which ran for 52 episodes between the years 2000 and 2004. A *Static* trade paperback was released in 2009.

In 2008, Milestone announced that the characters from Milestone Comics would be integrated into the DC universe, and this was initiated in 2009, beginning with the introduction of the Shadow Cabinet in the title ***Justice League of America***, which at the time was written by McDuffie, and adding Static to the roster of ***Teen Titans***.

**Selected Bibliography:** Brown, Jeffrey A. *Black Superheroes, Milestone Comics, and Their Fans.* Jackson: University Press of Mississippi, 2001.

*Fredrik Strömberg*

**MILLAR, MARK** (1969–). Born in Scotland, UK, Mark Millar is a comics writer whose significant works include ***The Authority***, *Ultimates*, and *Wanted*. He has won multiple Eagle Awards amongst others. His work is characterized by religious themes, a polemical style and a postmodernist mix of superheroics and **satire**.

Millar's first comics work was for Trident Comics on *Saviour* (1989–90). During the next decade he worked on titles including *Crisis* (#31, 1989), *Judge Dredd Megazine* ("Red Razors" series 1991–95) *Sonic the Comic*, and *2000 AD* (including Thargs Future Shocks, Robo-Hunter, Tales from Beyond Science and Maniac 5, 1989–93). His work for *2000 AD* also involved the notorious collaboration with **Grant Morrison** on *Big Dave* (1993).

His work for **DC Comics** began to appear in 1994 with ***Swamp Thing*** (issues #140–71; issues #140–43 were co-written with Morrison) to great critical acclaim, although the title did not gain enough sales to avoid subsequent cancellation. He also published the miniseries *Skrull Kill Krew* with Morrison for **Marvel** in 1995. He subsequently continued working for DC on titles such as ***JLA***, ***The Flash***, and ***Superman*** Adventures.

In 2000 he took over *The Authority* for DC Wildstorm, but creative differences and delays led him to quit in 2001, although DC would subsequently publish his ***Elseworlds*** style one-shot ***Superman: Red Son*** (2003). His *Ultimate X-Men* was released from 2001 to 2003 for *Ultimate Marvel* and he also published *The Ultimates* (a new version of Marvel's ***The Avengers***) under this imprint from 2002 to 2007. To date, he has continued to work on titles for Marvel including *Marvel Knights **Spider-man***

(2004), *Ultimate **Fantastic Four*** (2004, 2005–6), ***Civil War*** (2006) a Marvel summer crossover that garnered exceptional sales, and *1985* (2008). His current work for Marvel includes *Wolverine* and *Fantastic Four*.

Millarworld, his creator-owned line, was launched in 2004, and is published by multiple, competing companies including Avatar, Top Cow, **Image Comics**, and **Dark Horse**. Titles published to date include *Wanted, Chosen, The Unfunnies, Kick-Ass* and *War Heroes*. *Chosen* is expected to continue publication under Image Comics as part of Millar's proposed trilogy *American Jesus*. A film version of *Wanted* was released in 2008, and *Kick-Ass* is currently being filmed by Matthew Vaughn, although Millar has said he has no interest in moving into the film industry.

*Julia Round*

**MILLER, FRANK** (1957– ). Born in Maryland, Frank Miller is a comics writer/artist and film director whose significant publications include ***Daredevil, Ronin, Batman: The Dark Knight Returns, Sin City***, and ***300***. He has won multiple **Eisner Awards**, Kirby Awards, and **Harvey Awards**. His work is characterized by realism and brutal themes, although he has come under attack for his patriotic politics, and has been accused of misogyny, exploitative violence, and homophobia.

Miller's first publication was *The Twilight Zone* #84 for Gold Key Comics in September 1978. He followed this with penciling jobs for both **DC** and **Marvel** comics. These included *Weird War Tales* #64 and #68 and *Unknown Soldier* #219 for DC Comics, and *Warlord of Mars* #18, *Spectacular Spiderman* #27–28, and multiple *Marvel Spotlight* and *Team-Up* titles for Marvel comics. He became best known for his work on the series *Daredevil*, which he began illustrating with #158 in 1979. His realistic and evocative depictions of New York brought new attention to the title, which moved from bi-monthly to monthly publication. Miller took over as writer and penciler with #168 in 1981, which also featured the first appearance of his popular character creation, Elektra.

Miller continued to write various *Daredevil* issues for Marvel in the 1980s and also published various works for DC, including the futuristic samurai six-part series *Ronin* (1983) and the four-part miniseries *Batman: The Dark Knight Returns* (1986), to great critical acclaim. *The Dark Knight Returns* was felt by many fans to be a reclamation of the character's original dark roots and was key in developing the trend for grim and gritty **superhero** comics at this time. Miller also published the origin story *Batman: Year One* (*Batman* #404–7) for DC in 1987.

In the late 1980s, Miller left DC due to a dispute over the proposed comics ratings system and distributed his work via Epic Comics (*Elektra Lives Again*) and **Dark Horse** (including *Hard Boiled, Give me Liberty*). His first completely solo work, the film noir-inflected series *Sin City*, was published by Dark Horse in 1991. Later in this decade Miller became one of the founding members of Dark Horse's Legend imprint, which would release the majority of *Sin City*. During this time Miller also published various *Daredevil* and *Elektra* comics with Marvel (including *Elektra: Assassin* (1986)

Author and Executive Producer Frank Miller on the set of the 2007 film *300*, directed by Zack Snyder. Warner Bros./Photofest

and *Daredevil: Man Without Fear* (1993) and contributed work to Image Comics (**Spawn**). In 1998 his graphic novel *300* was released by Dark Horse. In 2001 Miller released the three-part series *The Dark Knight Strikes Again* with DC, for whom he is also currently writing *All Star Batman and Robin* (2005–).

Miller's work has also been featured in cinema, where it often closely replicates the visual style and pacing of his comics. He co-wrote the movies *Robocop 2* (1990) and *Robocop 3* (1993), and also co-directed (with Robert Rodriguez) the *Sin City* movie (2005), with a sequel in production at the time of this writing. His solo directorial debut, an adaptation of **Will Eisner's The Spirit** (co-scripted by Eisner and Miller), was released in 2009. Movie versions of *Daredevil* (2003) and *300* (2007) have also been released based on Miller's stories.

*Julia Round*

**MOEBIUS.** *See* **Giraud, Jean**

**MOONEY, JIM** (1919–2008). James Noel ("Jim") Mooney was born into a privileged New York family. He left high school before graduating in order to attend art class, and while there he got his first job illustrating a Henry Kutner story in *Weird Tales*. An extremely prolific artist whose career lasted from the 1940s into the 21st century, he was the signature artist of Supergirl in **Action Comics** from 1959 to 1968.

Other notable characters drawn by Mooney include **Batman**, **Spider-Man**, Tommy Tomorrow, The Legion of Super-Heroes, Man-Thing, Ms. Marvel and Omega the Unknown.

After losing their fortune, Mooney's family moved to Hollywood, California, where Mooney grew up. Seeing the success of comic books, Mooney hitchhiked back to New York where he drew The Moth for *Mystery Men Comics* in the early 1940. For a few short weeks Mooney then worked at the Eisner & Iger shop, but did not feel that his skills were sufficiently professional when compared to the studio's artists. During World War II, Mooney worked with **Stan Lee** at **Timely Comics** drawing **funny animal comics**. In 1946, Mooney applied for, and got, the job as the Batman artist (replacing Dick Sprang) on the basis of his Moth work (**DC Comics** had once sued him over its likeness to Batman). He especially enjoyed drawing the Bill Finger scripts. He would be with DC for the next 22 years.

During most of his tenure as the Supergirl artist (where he created Streaky the Super-cat), Mooney lived in Los Angeles and had a studio on Hollywood Boulevard. There he was able to do other artistic work and spend time with friends and fans. Mooney left DC Comics in the late 1960s and returned to **Marvel**, where he started inking **John Romita Sr.**'s illustrations for *Amazing Spider-Man* and ultimately would take it over before moving on to pencil and ink other Marvel series.

Relocating to Florida in the mid 1970s, Mooney focused on interior art pages rather than covers, as the location made it impossible to have the necessary editorial meetings. Although he worked in numerous genres and with many major characters, it was the quirky, non-mainstream comics and stories that Mooney enjoyed doing the most since they gave him an opportunity for greater artistic freedom. Man-Thing and Omega the Unknown were highest upon this list. Some five decades after Mooney became a professional artist he finally felt he came into his own in terms of his skill, considering *A Trip to Necropolis* (1989), and *Lakota: The Thunder Makers* (2007), both with writer Mark Ellis, to be his best works. The nickname "Gentleman Jim" (given Mooney by Stan Lee) was an appropriate moniker. Mooney was the consummate professional, extremely amiable and dependable, never late with his work, and able to tell a good story with clean, natural lines. He represents all the legendary comic book artists from the earliest days that saw what they did not as an art form, but as a job that was about entertaining the readers.

*Jeff McLaughlin*

**MOORE, ALAN** (1953–). Celebrated English comic book writer, best known for *Watchmen*, one of the **adult comics** of the 1980s (along with **Frank Miller's *The Dark Knight Returns*** and **Art Spiegelman's *Maus***), which contributed to the rise of the graphic novel format. Moore came to the attention of U.S. publisher **DC Comics** with his work for **Marvel** UK, writing *Captain Britain*, and his work for **science fiction** weekly *2000 AD*, to which he contributed a number of twilight zone-style short stories, as well as the very popular *The Ballad of Halo Jones*. However, it was in the short-lived rival to *2000 AD*, *Warrior*, that Moore had the most freedom, creating *V for Vendetta* and *Marvelman* (known as *Miracleman* in the United States). These dark, highly political stories highlighted the bleakness of Britain under the rule of Prime Minister Thatcher, with a brooding sense of dissatisfaction and a clear distrust of authority that indicated Moore's anarchist leanings. When recruited by DC Comics in the early 1980s, Moore was given the ailing *Swamp Thing* title. Here, his fascination with the arcane and the political was evident in his reinvention of Swamp Thing as gothic **horror** meets ecological parable. In these stories Moore introduced John Constantine, later to get his own title, *Hellblazer*, a vehicle for Moore's interest in the occult. These comics became the backbone of DC's Vertigo line of comics for mature readers. Moore became renowned for his elaborate scripts and his ability to deconstruct generic clichés. *Watchmen* is the prime example. Intended as the last word on the **superhero** genre, Moore's complex and intricate story, with a literary handling of narrative, pacing and time, is perfectly matched by **Dave Gibbons**'s artwork, and actually rekindled interest in superheroes. Having become something of a celebrity in comics, Moore's success prompted the British invasion of U.S. comics, and he has been a huge influence on fellow British writers **Grant Morrison**, **Neil Gaiman**, **Warren Ellis**, and **Mark Millar**. DC bought *V for Vendetta*, which had been unfinished at the time of *Warrior's* demise, and Moore completed the story. This was, like *Watchmen*, hugely popular and critically acclaimed, as were his **Superman** stories, the last in the original Superman continuity before it was revised by **John Byrne**. His **Batman** story, *The Killing Joke*, with artwork by British artist Brian Bolland, was even more celebrated. Building on this success Moore moved towards independent publishing, partly a desire to move away from superheroes but also because he felt ill-used by DC concerning the royalties from *Watchmen*. Moore turned his back on the mainstream to work on projects such as *A Small Killing*, with Oscar Zarate, *Big Numbers*, with **Bill Sienkiewicz**, *From Hell*, with **Eddie Campbell**, and *Lost Girls*, with Melinda Gebbie. The last two started in the short-lived *Taboo* magazine, published by Moore's own company, Mad Love. When these independent ventures failed, Moore returned to mainstream comics, despite his feeling that most publishers took advantage of creators. His decision to return was partly based on the fact that **Image Comics**, the new independent publisher, published only creator-owned comics. For Image, he wrote *1963*, a six-issue parody of Marvel comics, before working on **Jim Lee**'s *WildC.A.T.s* and Rob Liefeld's *Supreme*. Moore made the best of this, eventually producing his own ABC line of comics as part of Wildstorm, Jim Lee's company, which was itself part of Image. Highlights were **Promethea** and **The League of Extraordinary Gentlemen**. In the meantime, *From Hell* and *Lost Girls* were completed and Moore published his first novel, *Voice of the Fire*. Several of Moore's comics have been made into Hollywood films, none particularly successfully, although *Watchmen* was a commercial success, and attempted to remain true to its source. Frustrated by such **adaptations** Moore has insisted that his name be removed from the credits of film adaptations of his work. Perhaps more than any other single writer, Moore has shown that comics are a medium with enormous literary potential, while also using his writing to celebrate what makes comics powerful and unique—their ability to twist time and space together.

*Chris Murray*

**MORE FUN COMICS.** Originally titled *New Fun, More Fun Comics* was the first series published by National Allied Publications, Inc., the first of several companies that would eventually merge into **DC Comics**. Its first issue, cover dated February 1935, is often considered the first American comic of all-new material, although Dell's newspaper-ish 1929 series *The Funnies* arguably has a similar claim. National Allied publisher Major Malcolm Wheeler-Nicholson was inspired by The Funnies and British weeklies, adopting the former's tabloid size along with stiffer covers.

The book shrunk slightly and changed its title to *More Fun* with issue #7. With issue #9 it joined National Allied's other title, *New Comics*, in the now-standard size and the word "Comics" was added to the cover (and in the indicia about a year later). Both titles would be bought at auction by *Detective Comics*, Inc. after Wheeler-Nicholson was forced into bankruptcy. He had already lost his share of the purchasing company, originally a partnership between him and his printer. Afterwards, Nicholson was left only with a percentage ownership in his original title.

Notable early features include the debut of **Superman** creators **Jerry Siegel** and **Joe Shuster** on two series in issue #6. "Henri Duval" was short-lived, but "Dr. Occult" lasted 27 issues and is the oldest character still appearing in the DC universe. His run included one storyline with the character in a caped costume as a trial run for the still unpublished Superman. "Sandra of the Secret Service" was an unusual action feature with a female lead. "Wing Brady," the **Western** "Jack Woods," and "The Magic Crystal of History" were other long-running pre-**superhero** features. Another Siegel and Shuster feature, "Calling All Cars" (later "Radio Squad") ran for 80 issues, by far the longest of the early features. All stories in this period began at no more than one page in length, slowly growing as comic books diverged from newspaper strips. After DC purchased the title, most existing features were cancelled or moved to *Adventure Comics* and replaced by a new round of adventure and detective strips.

Superheroes, by then well-established in DC's other anthologies, entered *More Fun* in early 1940 with the Spectre and then Dr. Fate dominating the covers. By late 1941, Johnny Quick, **Green Arrow**, and **Aquaman** had been added, and during the early war years only one non-superhero feature remained. However, in 1943 the comedy feature "Dover and Clover" (twin detectives) replaced "Radio Squad." Dr. Fate and the Spectre exited soon after, but Superboy, one of the last major superheroes, debuted in issue #101.

With issue #108, *More Fun* became the first of DC's anthologies to switch away from superheroes, moving to an all-humor format. The superheroes moved to *Adventure Comics*, with the comedic hero Genius Jones coming to *More Fun* in return. The humorous adventure series "Jiminy and the Magic Book" was the last cover feature to be added, but the new direction was ultimately unsuccessful. In keeping with its tradition of firsts, *More Fun Comics* became the first of DC's eight main anthologies to be canceled with issue #127, cover dated November 1947.

*Henry Andrews*

**MORRISON, GRANT** (1960–). Born and raised in Glasgow, Scotland, Morrison started his professional career in the late 1970s and early 1980s working for **DC** Thomson in Dundee, publishers of *The Beano* and *The Dandy*, while also working for independent comics such as *Near Myths*. At DC Thomson, Morrison wrote and drew issues of the **science fiction** comic *Starblazer*, before turning exclusively to writing. In the mid-1980s he started work for **Marvel** UK, writing short Doctor Who stories, and for the short-lived but very influential *Warrior*, which also featured work by **Alan Moore**. At Marvel UK, which mainly published licensed material, he wrote the Zoids script in *Spider-Man and Zoids*, turning a story about warring robot dinosaurs into an apocalyptic story about obsession and fate. This was far more than the story deserved, and was an indication that Morrison was ready to tackle a much more demanding project. The opportunity came when Morrison began work for *2000 AD*, creating their first **superhero**, Zenith, in 1987. This was an intelligent deconstruction of superhero comics, at a time when Moore's **Watchmen** had made such things extremely marketable, but this was not a cheap copy of *Watchmen*; rather it was about the occult, the apocalypse, and transformation, referencing the poetry of William Blake, and drawing on spiritualist Aleister Crowley, popular fashion and music, and a host of other eclectic sources. It was also about the influence of American comics on British comics, and was carried off with irony and precision, aided by stylish artwork by Steve Yeowell. Following the success of *Watchmen*, **DC Comics** started head-hunting new British talent, and Morrison was the obvious target. Morrison would eventually contribute to the new Vertigo line of adult comics produced by DC; however, his early work with DC saw him revamping second-rate superhero comics such as *Animal Man* and *Doom Patrol*, following a pattern established by Moore with **Swamp Thing**. In *Animal Man* the story became a platform for Morrison's animal rights views, and ultimately twisted in on itself in a postmodern deconstruction of the comics form itself. Likewise, *Doom Patrol* became a surreal rumination on madness, disability and art that quickly caught the attention of readers, and soon it came under the Vertigo banner.

Never content to simply knock out genre fare, Morrison continued to make a name for himself with his strange vision of **Batman**'s world in the graphic novel *Arkham Asylum*, with artwork by **Dave McKean**. At this time he was still producing work for the British market, including the controversial stories *St. Swithin's Day* and *The New Adventures of Hitler*, as well as a reworking of Dan Dare, simply called *Dare*. Morrison's most mature and personal work emerged in the mid-1990s, and included *Flex Mentallo* (1996), and arguably his most important project, *The Invisibles* (1994–2000). He also wrote the enormously popular **Justice League of America** series *JLA* (1996). Morrison continued to balance personal work with mainstream success, with *The Filth* (2002) and *We3* (2004) on one hand, and **Marvel Boy** for

Marvel and *The Flash* for DC, and has helmed several radical re-workings of major titles, notably *New X-Men*. His run on *All-Star Superman*, with artwork by Frank Quitely, produced some of the best Superman stories since the 1960s, and in his "Batman R.I.P." storyline, Bruce Wayne disappeared and later appeared to be dead. Beyond comics Morrison has become involved in writing scripts and treatments for films and computer games. He has written two plays and several short stories, many of which are collected in the anthology *Lovely Biscuits* (1999).

*Chris Murray*

**MOTTER, DEAN** (1953–). Dean Motter is an American designer, art director, and comic-book writer and illustrator. His first published work as a writer of comics was *The Sacred and the Profane*, printed in the **science fiction** anthology magazine *Star Reach* in 1977–78; he later revived this series in *EPIC Illustrated* (1983–84) in collaboration with artist Ken Steacy. Motter is most often associated with the character Mister X and the two noir-inflected *Terminal City* miniseries he wrote for the Vertigo imprint of **DC Comics**. Motter's Web site draws attention to his design work in comics, as Creative Services Art Director at DC Comics in the 1990s, and work outside comics on album covers and other commercial projects.

Motter was the first writer on the stories featuring Mister X, published by Vortex Comics beginning in 1984. He has scripted the adventures of the character for more than 20 years, including most recently another revival of the character for **Dark Horse Comics** (*Mister X: Condemned*). Motter also wrote the series *Terminal City* for DC/ Vertigo, drawn by Michael Lark, and wrote and drew the series *The Prisoner*, a comic-book follow-up tom the popular British TV show, also for DC. His *Batman: Nine Lives* (also illustrated by Lark and published by DC in their **Elseworlds** series) won the 2003 **Eisner Award** for publication design. Motter served as art director for DC in the 1990s, and has at different times headed up a design agency.

*Mister X* was a comic that followed the adventures of the titular architect as he tried to save Radiant City, an urban landscape that was driving its residents insane. X propounded the theory of "psychetecture, the theory that the very shape and size of a room could alter a person's mood or neuroses" (Motter, 77). X felt responsible because his designs for Radiant City should have fostered a utopia, but because corners were cut, the effect was instead to create a dystopia. The visual look of Mister X, bald head and round sunglasses and wearing a sharp lapelled black trench coat, made the character immediately recognizable, and early appearances were drawn by some outstanding talents, including the **Hernandez Brothers**, Ty Templeton, and Paul Rivoche. Later collaborator **Seth** developed a bold new style working on the book that built an artistic bridge to his work on *Palookaville* and elsewhere.

Motter's interest in the urban landscape recurs in much of his work, a significant element in his two *Terminal City* miniseries for DC/Vertigo as well as in his short-lived *Electropolis* book for **Image Comics**. In nearly all of his work, concerns of plot are sublimated to design; as the urban background increasingly dominates the frame, foregrounded plots sometimes get lost in noir twists that never quite untwist enough to provide satisfying narrative resolutions. That said, Motter's work remains consistently interesting because of his focus on architectural design and forced perspectives, a signature style that is recognizably his as much as it is possible to trace its forbears.

**Selected Bibliography:** Arndt, Richard. "The Star-Reach Bibliography." *Enjolra's World—Comic Book Annotations and Bibliographies* (May 2006). Enjolrasworld.com, http://www.enjolrasworld.com/Richard%20Arndt/Star-Reach.htm; "Dean Motter" (January 11, 2009). LAMBIEK.NET, http://lambiek.net/artists/m/motter_dean. htm; "Dean Motter Bibliography." (2006). deanmotter.com, http://deanmotter.com/ biblio1.htm; "Dean Motter Biography." (2006). deanmotter.com, http://deanmotter. com/pubbio.htm; Motter, Dean. *Mister X: The Definitive Collection Volume One.* New York: iBooks, 2004.

*Matthew Dube*

**MUTANTS.** The term "mutants" has been widely used in reference to mutated humans within genre fiction, particularly **science fiction** from the 1950s onward. It had sparse application in comics despite the growth of **horror** and science fiction comics in the 1950s. However, **Stan Lee**'s usage of the term in *X-Men* #1 (1963) to apply to humans whose superhuman powers naturally develop at puberty, has become one of the mostly widely used and recognized tropes within comics. While other publishers have used the term over the years, its current meaning within comics is predominately associated with **Marvel Comics,** and in particular their line of X-Men titles. Lee explained that his reasoning for creating mutants was to avoid repeatedly having to spend time on creating complex and new origin stories.

Though there is some speculation about previous uses of the term mutant prior to Lee, he first used and defined it in *X-Men* #1. In the first issue, the concept of mutants being the next step in human evolution is not directly explained, but the story's villain, Magneto, proclaims, "The first phase of my plan shall be to show my power . . . to make homo sapiens bow to homo superior!" This indicates a separate, higher species of humans with the nomenclature of "superior." Additionally, Professor X explains to the new student, Jean Grey, "Jean, there are many mutants walking the earth . . . and more are born each year." The observations of X and Magneto combined to serve as the foundation for explaining mutants as the next evolutionary step for humankind. Often, this evolution is identified in an "X-gene" that manifests at puberty in the form of a mutant power. However, in that first issue, before the word "gene" became well-known, Professor X simply explained to Grey, "You, Miss Grey, like the other four students at this most exclusive school, are a mutant! You possess an extra power . . . one which ordinary humans do not!! That is why I call my students . . . X-Men for Ex-tra power!" However, given that Professor X's parents worked on the nuclear bomb, there is some indication that this somehow became a catalyst for his mutant manifestation; or at least his parents symbolically represent the influence and relevance of the Atomic Age in mutant narratives.

Initially, Marvel gave mutants singular or a limited range of superpowers; essentially matching one superpower to each mutant. However, as Marvel expanded its universe and its cast of mutants, either current mutants' powers expanded or new characters were introduced with several mutant powers. For example, Jean "Marvel Girl/Phoenix" Grey was initially a mere telepath, but over the years she developed her telepathy further and became a vessel for the Phoenix Force. Some characters manifested multiple mutations, as in the case of Kurt "Nightcrawler" Wagner, who was blue, had three digits per appendage and had a tail, while also being able to teleport. Other mutants, particularly second generation mutants (mutants born of mutants or other characters with superpowers), often had several superpowers. Nathan "Cable" Summers and Franklin Richards are the best examples of these. Additionally, Marvel has hinted that first generation mutants have the potential to go through a second mutation, including Henry "Beast" McCoy, and Emma "White Queen" Frost. While mutant powers can vary significantly, the powers that reappear time and again in popular, strong, or influential mutants include: telepathy, telekinesis, increased healing abilities, superhuman strength, flight, and energy emission (in the form of blasts). Additionally, time-travel, though rarely a power with mutants, has often been central to many storylines among X-titles. While mutants epitomize evolution as the natural progression of humankind in most narratives, Marvel has gone further to explain that the Celestials, god-like beings who visited Earth in its infancy, actually altered human DNA, allowing for later manifestations of powers in both mutants and other super-powered people alike. This idea came to fruition in the series, *Earth X* (1999) and, while the series as a whole has not been accepted as part of Marvel's main continuum, this origin of mutant powers has not been completely rejected.

With more than 40 years of stories about mutants, several have emerged as the most powerful, influential or popular. Charles "Professor X" Xavier is not only one of the first mutants (and ultimately, the first Marvel mutant), he is the world's most powerful telepath. Despite occasional respites, he has led the X-Men as mentor, tactical, and field leader throughout most of their run. Although Scott "Cyclops" Summers has served as a leader of an X-team repeatedly since his creation, his influence and even power as a mutant is surpassed by his long-time lover and (currently) deceased wife, Jean Grey. Since joining with the Phoenix Force in *Uncanny X-Men* #100–1 (1979), she has continually challenged her colleagues, her enemies, and entire planets and solar systems. James "Wolverine" Howlett has had the staying power and popularity to rival all other X-Men with a continued success of ongoing and miniseries comic books, a movie, *X-Men Origins: Wolverine* (2009), and several video games as well. His tough demeanor, mutant healing factor and adamantium-grafted skeleton have made him a popular antihero over the years, though his potential and power as a mutant have not been particularly more significant than many other mutants. Cable exhibits a similar motif as Wolverine, with cyborg limbs, a dubious moral code, and superior fighting abilities, but has the added bonus of being the temporally displaced son of Cyclops and having several mutant powers, including telekinesis and telepathy. Franklin Richard, the child prodigy of Susan "Invisible Woman" Storm and Reed "Mr. Fantastic" Richards of the **Fantastic Four**, has been hinted at many times as the world's most powerful mutant and in certainly story arcs this has become true (*Onslaught; Earth X*).

Among villains, Erik Magnus "Magneto" Lehnsherr stands as the first and most-common mutant foe of the X-Men. He has organized mutant teams of his own and even established entire mutant colonies. While Magneto's role as nemesis has fluctuated over the years, Apocalypse is the villain that has continually been a threat to X-Men teams and mutants everywhere. Like Magneto, he seeks a mutant-dominated world, but unlike Magneto, he is nearly immortal and has been working towards the goal for thousands of years. Glimpses into the future reveal that his success would mean tremendous devastation for humans and mutants alike. Nathaniel "Mr. Sinister" Essex has teamed with both Magneto and Apocalypse over the years in trying to orchestrate the demise of the X-Men, as well as gaining more mutants for him to experiment with.

Dozens of series have been published over the years featuring mutants. Though most have been miniseries, a significant number of mutant-based ongoing series have survived over the years with various reincarnations or re-launchings. Most mutant series have focused on teams or groups rather than individuals, with *Wolverine* proving to be the only substantial and long-standing solo success. *The Uncanny X-men* has proved most successful with consistent publication since 1963. Launched in 1983, **New Mutants** had the staying power for 100 issues before transitioning into the title *X-Force*, which lasted over 120 issues. This series deals with a second generation of mutants who start as students at Xavier's School for Gifted Youngsters in *New Mutants* and eventually strike off on their own under the leadership of Cable in *X-Force*. *X-Force* and *New Mutants* were revived as series in 2008 and 2009, respectively. Another spin-off series, *X-Factor*, appeared in 1986 and lasted until its 150th issue in 1998. This series focused on the original X-Men (Angel, Beast, Cyclops, Iceman, and Jean Grey) as they worked for the government to improve human-mutant relations and protect mutantkind. The series was revamped again in February, 2006, as a detective agency for mutants under Jamie "Multiple Man" Madrox. *Excalibur* served as the UK-based version of X-Men from 1988 to 1998, headed by Captain Britain, with a mixture of original mutants and expatriates from X-Men. This series has also been re-launched several times since its original run. The most erratic mutant-based title currently running is *Exiles*, which deals with a cast of ever-changing mutants who jump through the multiverse saving parallel Earths and entire universes from collapse. Though non-mutants occasionally make the team, the crux of membership contains mutants and the title itself suggests it is an "X-title."

In later X-titles and comics, mutants serve as a metaphor for outsider groups in general, but their initial stories in *X-Men* do not evoke a particularly strong theme of outsider status, beyond the typical "super-powered humans" model which certainly was not new within comics in 1963. Their focus in those early issues is to learn to use their abilities and to counteract those mutants who attack and attempt to rule over humankind. In that first issue, Professor X explains of mutants, "Not all of them want to help mankind!! . . . some hate the human race, and wish to destroy it! Some feel that the mutants should be the real rulers of Earth! It is our job to protect mankind from . . . from the evil mutants." In those early issues, the X-Men are met with applause and admiration among humans. In *X-Men* #2, Angel is accosted by a group of teenage girls enamored with him, while Cyclops is thanked by a group of construction workers. Resentment and angst do not have a presence in the first few issues.

Magneto and the Brotherhood of Evil Mutants create much of the groundwork for alienation and antagonism between humans and mutants in issue #4, but the metaphor of mutant as representative outsider was still negligible. Human-mutant relations took a turn for the worse in *X-Men* #14 with the first appearance of the Sentinels, mutant-hunting robots created by Bolivar Trask. They would return in stronger new forms and larger numbers in the years to come. However, this issue revealed the strong antagonism and growing application of mutant as outsider narrative that mutant-related titles and stories have capitalized on ever since.

For much of the 1980s and 1990s, academics and fans have drawn parallels between mutants and various minority groups, especially in terms of ethnicity or sexual orientation. For example, some discussions have proposed Charles Xavier as the Martin Luther King Jr. of mutants with his utopian vision of peaceful human and mutant co-existence, with Magneto as the Malcolm X figure who believes mutants have to violently achieve their ends. In the *X-Men* movies in the 2000s, the language used to explain being a mutant corresponds to that of non-heterosexual identity, with scenes where teen mutants "came out" to their parents or parents tried forcibly to remove the mutant (homosexual) gene from their children.

The Sentinels became the first in a line of mutant hunters who capture or execute mutants for the protection of mankind, or at the behest of a villain. Over the years, they have gone through many transformations as different X-Men enemies (Bolivar Trask, Stephen Lang, Sebastian Shaw, Cassandra Nova, etc.)and have modified and re-launched against the X-Men or the mutant population in general. The repeated and haunting fear is the capture, enslavement, and eradication of mutants in a form akin to the Jews and other minorities in the Holocaust. In several story arcs, this fear is solidified when glimpses of the future reveal a world ruled by Sentinels, with mutants mostly dead or enslaved. This was best captured (and habitually returned to) in the storyline "Days of Future Past" in *Uncanny X-Men* #141–42 (1981). This genocide analogy was pushed further in *X-Men* #181 (1984) when the long-time adversary of mutant-kind, Senator Robert Kelly, began work on launching the Mutant Registration Act, a law requiring forced registration for all mutants and thereby marking them much like any exploited group in a society where genocide occurs. Although used sporadically in the comics throughout the 1980s and 1990s, it never developed much further on its own, but it did act as a prototype for the Superhuman Registration Act; a law that spawns the events in the major crossover series **Civil War** (2006).

Many other mutant-killers and hate groups have been created over the years to reinforce the theme of mutant as ultimate outsider and victim. In *Uncanny X-Men*

#210 (1986), the Marauders entered the scene as a group of hired mutant assassins killing the Morlocks and extracting the mutant DNA for their employer, Mr. Sinister, an archenemy of all X-teams. The Friends of Humanity serve as the stereotypical hate-group akin to anti-Semitic groups in the real world. Since their first appearance in *Uncanny X-Men* #299 (1993), they have continued to threaten, harm, and even kill mutants within the Marvel universe. Under guidance of the Reverend William Stryker, the Purifiers are a fundamentalist cult seeking to purify the human race of mutants by violent means. Though first appearing in *Marvel Graphic Novel #5: X-Men: God Loves, Man Kills* (1982), it has only been after the "House of M" saga that they have taken on a more prominent role in several X-titles.

Marvel has created many external and direct threats to mutants over the years, but in the 1990s, Marvel began experimenting with indirect mutant extermination. The first came in 1993 with the conclusion of the crossover series, *X-Cutioner's Song*. In the final scene, the Legacy Virus is unleashed in the world and shortly thereafter, Illyana "Magik" Rasputin becomes the first casualty. The Legacy Virus infected many mutants, both popular and unknown throughout the 1990s, until Marvel writers created a cure. The Legacy Virus served as an analogy for HIV/AIDS, playing on the fears of the general population about means of transmission and anxiety of groups typically associated with the disease. Within the Marvel universe, a cure was created for the Legacy Virus, but in order for it to take effect one mutant had to be infected and die; Peter "Colossus" Rasputin, brother of Magik, sacrificed himself to end the plague.

The second major attempt to limit or reduce the ever-expanding cast of mutants came in 2005 with impact of the "House of M" story arc. During the run of *New X-Men* in the early 2000s, mutants became less of a tiny, feared minority and more of a subculture that was becoming increasingly fashionable among younger people. Mutants lived openly, clustering in their own neighborhoods in cities such as New York. However, this took the X-Men away from their traditional focus, so "House of M" and "Decimation" were written to return to prior status quo. The story focused on the attempts of Pietro "Quicksilver" Maximoff to protect his catatonic sister, Wanda "Scarlet Witch" Maximoff, from Professor X and others who looked to kill the Scarlet Witch since her power of probability was causing significant rifts and catastrophes within the world. Before they can intervene, her powers reorder the universe into a world where homo-superiors reign over homo-sapiens. Led by Wolverine, a cohort of superheroes realizes the change and seeks out the leading and most powerful mutant family (Magneto's family) to correct the altered reality. In the ensuing battle and revelations, the Scarlet Witch returns the world back to the way it was with one exception; in what is referred to as the "Decimation," the world's population of mutants has been reduced to less than 200, with several major mutants being depowered, including Professor X, Magneto, Robert "Iceman" Drake, and Quicksilver. This arc allowed Marvel Comics to regain control and reconstruct X-titles continuity while also returning to some of the roots of alienated and feared outsider status.

Despite repeated hunts for and attempted elimination of mutants, there have been several places that mutants have congregated in large numbers over the years. Some of these places were refuges; other places served as exile. The most obvious has been the X-Mansion, the property of Professor Xavier in Westchester County, New York. In the post-House of M world, the X-Mansion becomes a sanctuary for mutants. Eventually, the mansion comes to be protected by the Sentinel Squad O*N*E, an elite group of Sentinels with human operators mandated to protect the surviving mutants. This dubious relationship is understandably questioned by many of the older mutants who have been subjected time and again to Sentinel attacks. The sewer tunnels of New York City serve as home to the Morlocks (*Uncanny X-Men* #169, 1983), a collection of mutants whose physical mutations prevent them from properly integrating into common society. Over the years, the Morlocks have faced repeated resistance, infiltration, and attacks from mutants and humans who seek to either control them or eradicate them. Though they are essentially disbanded after the effects of the Decimation, there is still some indication that they will regroup in the near future. For a brief time, Magneto establishes his Asteroid M, an asteroid in Earth's orbit converted into a space station that serves as a mutant paradise for mutants wishing to escape the persecution and violence of human life. However, Magneto's benevolence is limited to mutants whom he deems genetically redeemable. Mutant town, or District X, serves as essentially a ghetto for mutants for much of the 2000s before Decimation, after which less than a handful of the hundreds of residents still have any power. Though Muir Island has never quite been a refuge for the general mutant population, it has served as the base of operations for Excalibur as well as a major research facility for Moira MacTaggert, Professor X, and other people for the purpose of studying and containing mutants.

The fictional island country of Genosha has served many purposes for the mutant population over the years. Initially, the island was a fully functioning and advanced civilization built upon the backs of mutant slaves. Appearing in *Uncanny X-Men* #235 (1988), the island served to represent real world issues as an African country (Genosha is located north of Madagascar) with a government-ordained apartheid easily invoked images of South Africa during this time. The X-Men, along with X-Factor and the New Mutants, undermine the government and its leaders. In the aftermath, Genosha attempts a more egalitarian government but is often subjected to attacks from mutants seeking revenge for past wrongdoings. Eventually, Genosha is given over to Magneto as a nation for mutants. However, the refuge that Genosha represents comes to an end in *New X-Men* #115 (2001) when the villain Cassandra Nova kills the vast majority of Genoshan citizens. The island had been used several times since this event but has been considered a deserted and desolate place.

By the 2000s, the proliferation of X-Men properties in comics, televisions series, films, video games, and books provided many avenues for consumers to understand mutants as the ultimate "others" who are simultaneously ostracized and fetishized by popular culture, similar to contemporary renderings of queer and non-Western identities. The evident duality of a subculture being both potentially beneficial and detrimental to the world correlates strongly with the U.S. culture in a post-9/11 paradigm.

**Selected Bibliography:** Irwin, William, Rebecca Housel, and J. Jeremy Wisnewski, eds. *X-Men and Philosophy: Astonishing Insight and Uncanny Argument in the Mutant X-Verse*. Indianapolis: Wiley, 2009; Wein, Len, Keith R. A. DeCandido, and Karen Haber. *The Unauthorized X-Men: SF and Comic Writers on Mutants, Prejudice, and Adamantium*. Dallas: Benbella Books, 2006; Zakarin, Scott, Dir. *Stan Lee's Mutants, Monsters & Marvels*. DVD, Sony Pictures/Creative Light, 2002.

*Lance Eaton*

**MYSTERY MEN.** Bob Burden's *Mystery Men* was a cult satirical **superhero** team series that first appeared in 1987, in a two-part, backup story in *Flaming Carrot Comics* #16 and #17. Burden's best-known character was published by Aardvark-Vanaheim, Renegade Press, and then **Dark Horse Comics** from 1984 to 1993. Born in Buffalo, New York, in 1946, Burden has won the Ignatz Award, The Inkpot Award for Outstanding Achievement in Comic Arts, and the **Eisner Award** for Best Single Issue. Republished by **Image Comics** since 2005, current incarnations of the title are listed as *Bob Burden's Original Mysterymen. The Original Cult Comic Classic*. Burden's work is characterized by self-aware postmodern humor about comics and superheroes in a similar fashion to Steve Gerber's **Howard the Duck** (1973) or **John Byrne**'s run on *The Sensational She-Hulk* (1989), but his independent status allows for more outrageous parodies. "The Flaming Carrot" wears a large carrot-shaped mask with a perpetually burning flame at the top, a white shirt, red pants, and flippers. His origins as revealed in issue #7 of *Flaming Carrot Comics* were that of a man who had a nervous breakdown after reading 5,000 comics in a single sitting for a bet.

The Mystery Men are down-at-heel, second-string blue-collar superheroes in a "world of superheroes." In its comic book incarnation, the team has included Flaming Carrot Man, The Shoveler, Jackpot, Mr. Furious, Screwball, Captain Attack, Bondo Man, Jumpin' Jehosaphat, Red Rover, The Strangler, The Spleen, The Metro Marauder, Hummer, Disc Man, Jumo the Magnificent, The Whisperer, Mystic Hand, Star Shark, the Zeke. Members invented for the movie include the Bowler, the Blue Raja, the Sphinx, and Invisible Boy. The comic and film explore the idea of the underside, ground level experience of superheroics before the trope became more popular in comic book series such as Keith Giffen and J. M. DeMatteis's *Justice League International*. If this trope was still a cult novelty among comic readers it was even more of an unknown quantity for movie-going audiences, so it is ironic that the Mystery Men characters gained wider prominence via Kinka Usher's 1999 film *Mystery Men*.

With its tagline, "They're not your average superheroes," *Mystery Men* spoofed the idea of the superhero team, a concept that cinematically had yet to reach its current prominence with the likes of the **X-Men** trilogy. Set in Champion City, the film concerns The Shoveler/Stan Belarsy (William H. Macy), Mr. Furious/Roy or the

William H. Macy, Ben Stiller, Hank Azaria, Janeane Garofalo, Paul Rubens, and Kel Mitchell in the 1999 film *Mystery Men*, directed by Kinka Usher. Universal/Photofest

self-created alter ego "Phoenix Dark" (Ben Stiller), and The Blue Raja/Jeffrey (Hank Azaria) as superheroes with negligible, if any, powers that must save the day when the city's **Superman** archetype, Captain Amazing/alter ego Lance Hunt (Greg Kinnear) disappears. The film is generally well-liked and has maintained a cult status, but in keeping with many **adaptations** of comic books before the recent renaissance, *Mystery Men* almost disguises its comic book sources rather than celebrating them.

*Lorcan McGrane*

**MY TROUBLES WITH WOMEN.** Originally released in 1992 by Knockabout Comics, and reprinted in 2000 by venerable underground publisher Last Gasp, *My Troubles with Women* collects 10 autobiographical stories by **Robert Crumb** (three in collaboration with his wife Aline Kominsky-Crumb) that first appeared in the comic books **Zap** and *Hup* and the magazine *Weirdo* between 1980 and 1989. The stories represent Crumb's ongoing work almost two decades after he emerged as the most prominent and influential creator of **underground comics**, or "**comix**," in the late 1960s. Like a few other survivors of that movement, Crumb's original location in the counter-cultural underground mutated into the realm of **alternative**, or independent comics, a shift also marked by Crumb's own transition from audacious autobiographical stories exposing his sexual fantasies (and frustrations) to more gentle chronicles of his life as a husband and father. However, the collection only surveys a decade's worth of what has been a career-long exploration of the women Crumb depicts as both the muses and demons driving his consistently controversial art.

Indeed, the title of the collection, from a story published in two parts in 1980 and 1986, could easily extend to most of Crumb's life and career: the rather mild term "troubles" only hints at a genuinely troubling aspect of his work (and many other underground comics) as a whole. Despite the liberation of the imagination that underground comics asserted, encouraging artists like Crumb to challenge cultural repression and self-censorship by exposing their most personal fantasies, this cathartic artistic freedom often led to shockingly misogynist images and narratives. In Crumb's case, indulgence in the sexual liberation of the 1960s and 1970s was often expressed in his comics by fantasies of physical domination, with women's bodies twisted into positions that allow Crumb's cartoon surrogates to have their way with them, an understanding of "free love" that appeared in direct conflict with the simultaneous women's liberation movement, which Crumb frequently parodied. While the misogyny of many male comics artists seems tacit or unconscious, Crumb perhaps deserves some credit for confronting his obsessions with brutal honestly. (This collection judiciously omits most of Crumb's racialized sexual fantasies, often centered around self-consciously stereotypical characters like the naïve black woman Angelfood McSpade, who wears mock-native dress and speaks in comic Negro dialect.)

The stories in *My Troubles with Women* depict Crumb as both unapologetically nostalgic for past indulgences and transgressions and grateful (as the opening story, "I'm Grateful! I'm Grateful!" from 1989 insists) for his settled married life and recent fatherhood. Another story, "Memories Are Made of This" (1988) recalls an earlier, awkward seduction before Crumb (as often, in direct address to the reader) swears that he has learned his lesson. "Footsy" (1987) is a richly illustrated memory of the origins of Crumb's infamous fetish for women's legs and feet, also explored in the more elaborate history of Crumb's psyche in "My Troubles with Women, Part II" (1986), which suggests more fully than earlier material that Crumb's difficulties with normative masculine identity, dating back to adolescent humiliations, are deeply intertwined with his ongoing views of women.

Four stories in the collection—"Arline 'n' Bob and That Thing in the Back Bedroom" (1983), "Uncle Bob's Mid-Life Crisis" (1982), "Our Lovely Home" (1988) and "Dirty Laundry Comics" (1986)—were all originally published in *Weirdo*, and depict Crumb's current married life and devotion to his precocious daughter Sophie (eventually a cartoonist herself), indicating that Crumb's gratitude for domestic life and fatherhood are sincere even if sometimes viewed with characteristic irony. In the three of these stories produced in collaboration with Aline Kominsky-Crumb, her flat and inconsistent drawings of herself contrast effectively with Crumb's familiar self-portraits in his cross-hatched, rounded style, visually representing the personality differences that define their unusual partnership. However, Crumb chooses to conclude the volume with "If I Were a King" (1987), another richly illustrated story that revives Crumb's most troubling fantasies (also on view in other stories in the collection), including his physical domination of one of his pantheon of imposing "beast-women." The fantasy concludes with an all-too familiar image of Crumb on top of a pile of comatose women, stuffing his penis into one of their mouths. Although an epilogue brings Crumb out of his fantasy, to be chastised by a "Lil' Hitler Pig," who calls him a "poor twisted devil," the shock effect is hardly vanquished by this final admonishment. Crumb's women are consistently objectified, often as bodies to be literally contorted for Crumb's self-caricatures to climb onto and penetrate; their misuse (often presented as passive or willing) is hardly tempered by Crumb's consistent presentation of himself as thoroughly dominated and deranged by their powerful stature, and in his later work, such as this volume, the image of Crumb as a self-identified pervert seems designed to be purposely unsettling alongside his depictions of himself as a doting father and subservient husband. Here and elsewhere, Crumb can be both narcissistic and masochistic, indulging and berating himself in turn: his claims to have reformed his life do not, he reveals, control his fantasies, which have remained consistently disturbing, stubbornly maintaining his emotional immaturity despite the remarkable accomplishment of Crumb's images. Indeed, if Crumb's depictions of women (at least in his narrative work, rather than his more flattering portraits) seem to have never developed beyond adolescent fascination and revulsion, this collection offers examples of his mature style as an artist. Such contradictions are perhaps at the heart of Crumb's career, an odd balance of hard-won artistic legitimacy and a still disreputable status, both in some measure celebrated by his fans.

A number of subsequent publications have also focused on Crumb's representations of women and sexuality, though these are again persistent themes of a now long career: both the gentle *Gotta Have 'Em: Portraits of Women* (Greybull Press, 2003) and the unapologetic *Robert Crumb's Sex Obsessions* (Taschen, 2007) were packaged as fine art collector editions. *The Sweeter Side of R. Crumb* (MQ Publications, 2006) also seeks to temper the artist's reputation as a misanthropic sexist. In addition to their collaborative work, collected in *The Complete Dirty Laundry Comics* (Last Gasp, 1993) and *Crumb Family Comics* (Last Gasp, 1998), Aline Kominsky-Crumb's perspective on her famous husband is provided by sections of her *Need More Love: A Graphic Memoir* (MQ Publications, 2007).

*Corey K. Creekmur*

N

**NAT TURNER.** In the historical comic, *Nat Turner*, artist **Kyle Baker** portrays the well-known Virginia slave uprising of 1831 from the perspective of the enslaved black man and self-proclaimed Christian prophet, Nat Turner. Kyle Baker Publishing initially produced the comic as a four-part series in 2005, but it was later re-issued in two volumes through **Image Comics** and appeared as a single graphic novel in 2008, from Abrams. Illustrated in black and white, *Nat Turner* contains virtually no dialogue and relies instead on the brutality and sorrow of Baker's arresting images, as well as narration from attorney Thomas R. Gray's 1831 publication *The Confessions of Nat Turner* to re-imagine one of the largest, most violent slave insurrections in the antebellum South. Baker's comic adapts *Confessions of Nat Turner* by expanding upon its assessment of Turner's motives; yet *Nat Turner* ultimately departs from Gray's account by minimizing the diabolical traits that white observers attributed to the slave rebellion. Where Gray viewed the insurrection as devious and desperate, and articulated Turner's silence as monstrous resignation, Baker's portrait endows Turner with dignity and courage as he struggles to free his people through righteous violence.

To develop Turner's heroism, *Nat Turner* begins with an origin story that illustrates key details of his mother's life and capture in Africa. Within the large borderless panels and splash pages, Baker's heavily-inked sketches use the large, expressive eyes of her emaciated face as the lens through which the reader experiences the horror of the Middle Passage and the New World auction block. The second part of the comic recounts young Nat's childhood as he learns to negotiate the restrictions of slave life, secretly learns how to read, and begins to develop a self-affirming religious identity. Bloodshed dominates Baker's depiction of Turner's upbringing; around him enslaved blacks are beaten, separated from their families, and humiliated without provocation. When Turner's own wife and children are sold, he cries out to God for justice, interpreting signs such as a solar eclipse as a divinely-sanction call for vengeance.

The final two sections of *Nat Turner* illustrate the slave uprising of August 1831 that resulted in the death of over 50 white adults and children. Baker's visual narrative is unflinching in its depiction of carnage through crude images of bloody axes, headless bodies and limbs that echo the prior treatment of slaves. The illustrations also highlight the unraveling of the rebellion by depicting participants such as the slave Sam, whose violent impulsiveness acts as a foil against Turner's methodical preparation. The stately image of Turner, broad-chested with sword in hand, is further juxtaposed by the shortsighted behavior of the recruits who resort to drinking and stealing during the night. Nevertheless, Baker carefully maintains the humanity of Turner's imposing figure from his capture to the moment of his execution, as he quietly confronts the hanging rope and, with his chin lifted, ascends from murderer to martyr.

In addition to being favorably compared to historical comics such as **Art Spiegelman's** *Maus* and Ho Che Anderson's *King*, Baker's complex rendering of Nat Turner adds a new dimension to creative interpretations over the years by Harriet Beecher Stowe, William Henry Shelton, Robert Hayden, William Styron, and other writers and artists. *Nat Turner* has also received several industry awards including an **Eisner Award** for Best Reality-Based Work (2006) as well as Glyph Comics Awards for Story of the Year (2006) and Best Artist (2006, 2008).

*Qiana J. Whitted*

**NAZIS.** "Nazi" is a widely used abbreviation derived from the fascist National Socialist Party that ruled Germany under Adolf Hitler from 1933 to 1945, committing some of the most egregious atrocities in modern history. The Nazis have long been staple villains in comics, notably **superhero** comics. In the same year that the Nazis took power in Germany, the modern American comic book format was born. By the end of the 1930s American comics were full of anti-Nazi imagery, from humor comics to the newly established superhero genre. Such popular propaganda sprung up all across America, ridiculing the enemy from the pages and covers of comics and magazines, on billboards and over the airwaves via radio, and through the cinema screen, with newsreels, animated cartoons, and Hollywood films pitting themselves against the propaganda being produced by the Nazis. Much of this imagery demonized the enemy as monsters, or ridiculed them, making the enemy, be they Nazi or Japanese, appear inhuman, monstrous, or laughable.

Humor comics, including those based on Disney and Warner Bros. animated characters, followed the example of animated films, poking fun at the enemy. Superhero comics adopted this strategy too, but being more orientated to adventure they usually drew more from the war films Hollywood was producing, such as *Confessions of a Nazis Spy* (1939) or *Guadalcanal Diary* (1943), focusing on fantasies of espionage rings and brutal combat with the enemy. However, whereas Hollywood films were heavily censored by the government to ensure that the right kinds of messages were communicated, the comics industry was far less regulated and therefore provided some of the most extreme examples of caricature and rhetorical exaggeration found in propaganda and popular culture of the period. In superhero comics, Nazis became supervillains, and World War II, as represented in comics, became a thrilling adventure against the forces of evil and oppression.

Superhero comics helped to fight the isolationism of the American people in the run up to war. Even before the attack on Pearl Harbor and American intervention in late 1941, superheroes routinely fought against war profiteers, spies, and saboteurs. One of the reasons for this eagerness to attack the Nazis was that many comic artists, writers and publishers were Jewish and used their comics to highlight the dangers of the Nazi state. As early as December 1939, The Sub-Mariner was shown on the cover of *Marvel Mystery Comics* #4 attacking a U-boat. The cover of *Action Comics* #54 (1942) showed **Superman** tying a periscope in a knot, although *Pep Comics* #2 (February 1940) was more violent, showing The Shield shooting the crew. The German U-boat menace was a very topical theme, as the main threat to American interests in 1940 came from the U-boats prowling the Atlantic. U.S. President Roosevelt attempted to use this threat to encourage Americans to support intervention, and comics like this followed his lead. Soon comics indulged in extreme fantasies, showing armies of spies, sympathizers, and saboteurs undermining American industry and morale. The most famous example is *Captain America* from **Timely Comics** (which would later become **Marvel**). On the cover of first issue (March 1941) Captain America bursts into a Nazi bunker full of invasion plans and film footage detailing an ongoing sabotage campaign, thereby justifying Captain America's pre-emptive strike. Captain America is identified as "The Sentinel of our Shores" and does what most Americans longed to, punching Hitler firmly on the jaw. Interestingly, this occurred at a time when many superhero comics, notably those produced by National (later **DC Comics**) only made oblique references to the enemy—perhaps because they felt **Superman**'s powers would allow him easily to defeat the Nazis, thus diminishing the importance of real-world fighting men. Following the example of Charlie Chaplin's film *The Great Dictator* (1940), an imaginary enemy was often substituted for the real one, although it was always clear who the intended target was. This was emblematic of the restraint of National as opposed to the brash streetwise nature of Timely's comics. However, one of the most overt attacks on the Nazis came in the form of MLJ's *Daredevil Battles Hitler* (1941), which, despite being rather crude in terms of its artwork, story, and politics, certainly made its message clear—the Nazis were a menace that must be stamped out. At this time most of the major publishers were featuring stories, or at least covers, that dealt with the war in some way. There was no lack of inspiration from Hollywood films, advertisements, propaganda posters, and political cartoons, all of which employed similar rhetorical strategies and comparable imagery in representing the Nazis. However, while few Americans had anything but contempt for the Nazis, most Americans did not want to get involved in another European war.

When Japan attacked Pearl Harbor in December 1941 the mood of the nation changed overnight. America declared war on the Japanese, Nazi Germany and the United States declared war on each other, and popular culture, which had been acting as a form of unofficial propaganda for so long, was finally vindicated. Primed and ready to fire, mass culture became a weapon against the enemy. Roosevelt knew that while the American people were eager for revenge against the Japanese, the war would not be won if the Nazis prevailed in Europe. In propaganda and popular culture images of the Nazis, and to a lesser extent, the German people, became increasingly aggressive. Superheroes took particular delight in attacking hordes of Nazi troops, or attacking Hitler himself, encouraging Americans to see the Nazis as the epitome of evil. This was not difficult, and comics also offered Nazi supervillains, such as Captain Nazi (*Master Comics*), The Red Skull (*Captain America*). These villains were usually cruel, monstrous, and perverse. In comics, as in other forms of popular culture, Nazis were particularly interested in assaulting women and poisoning children, or else destroying American industry. German officers were sadists and German troops were mindless automatons or ogres. Indeed, much of the imagery, especially in Timely comics, was drawn from horror films. For some reason Nazi strongholds were invariably gothic castles, and they employed medieval torture methods on helpless victims. The level of hatred and ridicule directed at the Nazis was challenged only by the levels of hatred directed towards the Japanese. In comics, as in reality, the war against Japan took on the hateful aspects of a race war, and propaganda and popular culture were extremely racist and irresponsible in promoting hatred of the Japanese as a people. This did not happen in terms of the German people. The Nazi leaders were despised, officers and troops were dealt with violently, but by and large the German people were presented as victims of their own government. As Western Europeans, the Germans had a similar racial heritage to the majority of Americans, so there was little mileage in presenting the Germans as a corrupt race of people.

While most superhero comics were content to deliver propagandist messages that were quite blunt and obvious a small number offered something more considered. One example is **Will Eisner's *The Spirit*** story, "The Tale of the Dictator's Reform" (1941), which imagined Hitler coming to America and being impressed with its people. Vowing to end the war, he returns to Germany only to be murdered by his lieutenants and replaced with a double. The story went beyond images of Hitler as a monster and suggested that rather than Nazism being driven by one madman it was instead a corrupt system, and that fascism was the actual enemy that had to be defeated. Such stories were rare, with most comics preferring to simply utilize the war as a convenient backdrop for adventure stories, or else, to make a simplistic point about combating the evils of the Axis.

Nazis appeared in other genres besides superheroes, notably **war comics**. Some of these comics were aimed directly at troops fighting overseas, so were particularly scathing about the enemies' courage and equipment, often suggesting that the Nazis and the Japanese were poorly trained and badly supported. This was intended to boost morale, but when such stories were contradicted so clearly by experience they could have the opposite effect. Interestingly, reality conflicted with comics in other regards too, as the majority of stories involving Nazis concerned spy rings and espionage on American soil. In reality, Nazi sabotage of American industry was practically nonexistent, and the few spy rings that existed had little success and were rounded up quite efficiently by the FBI, so never really posed much of a threat. If one were to believe the comics however, there were hundreds of plots and an army of saboteurs.

When the war ended in 1945 superheroes continued to fight the Nazis for a time, as there was a backlog of stories to work through. However, in time the superhero genre faltered, in part because it was so heavily invested in propagandist attacks on the enemy that, without Nazis or Japanese to fight, the superhero was largely redundant. In time, though, Nazis would reappear, first in the **war comics** of the 1950s, then again in the 1960s, when a revival of Captain America by **Stan Lee** and **Jack Kirby** brought Captain America's wartime exploits back to life, along with his old antagonist the Red Skull, and new Nazi villains, such as Baron Zemo. When Captain America was revived as a character in the Marvel universe of the 1960s, having been frozen in a block of ice since the end of the war, his enemies came with him, refigured as supervillains. However, by this time there was a new generation of readers and Nazis villains, when they appeared, had much less impact. By this time Nazis had been diluted somewhat in the popular consciousness by endless Hollywood films and television shows like *Hogan's Heroes*, which made the Nazis seem like buffoons. In addition, sensitivity about the Holocaust made the use of Nazi characters a cause for concern. Thus, for a time, the Red Skull was reconfigured as a communist, rather than a Nazi.

In the 1970s there was resurgence in fan and collector interest in what became known as the **Golden Age** of comics, roughly speaking, the war years. This resulted in Roy Thomas's homage to the comics of the 1940s, *The Invaders* (1975). This comic featured the previously untold wartime exploits of Timely's Golden Age heroes, Captain America, The Sub-Mariner, and The Torch, along with some more obscure 1940s characters, and a handful of new ones. *The Invaders* ran for four years. In the course of this run they faced the Red Skull, Hitler, and Masterman, a Nazi version of Captain America, who was an amalgam of various Nazi villains, notably Captain Marvel's wartime nemesis, Captain Nazi. Interestingly, this was also a time when Neo-Nazi groups were increasingly on the rise, as were instances of Holocaust denial. The reappearance of Golden Age heroes to defeat the Nazis all over again had a strong appeal for some older readers, but in the main, *The Invaders* was for lovers of nostalgia. The taste of the average comics fan at that time was for more cynical comics.

Allusions to 1940s comics and World War II continued to appear throughout the 1980s, in comics such as **Dave Stevens's *The Rocketeer***, which drew heavily from 1930s and 1940s radio adventures and movie serials such as *King of the Rocketmen*. This was another appeal to nostalgia, and perhaps a little old fashioned for most readers, but it was clear that creators seemed to continually return to the war. There was some connection between the war and comics that could not be broken. In Britain, **Grant Morrison** and

Steve Yeowell's superhero series *Zenith*, which ran in the British weekly **science fiction** comic *2000 AD* from 1988 to 1993, took World War II as its starting point, and in a direct allusion to *The Invaders* Zenith faced a resurrected Nazi supersoldier called Masterman. Here Morrison played with the occult associations of the Nazi party, elaborating on conspiracy theories that linked prominent Nazis with the Thule Society and occult practices. Rumored links between Nazis and the occult would also figure prominently in **Mike Mignola's** *Hellboy*, which began appearing in 1993. Also in 1993, wartime superheroes once again came to the fore in the four-part miniseries *The Golden Age*, published by DC Comics, which examined the fate of DC's 1940s heroes in the years immediately following the end of the war. By the end of the series the first of a new breed of superhero for the atomic age, Dynaman, who represents the coming superhero of 1950s and 1960s comics, is revealed as the villain, a superhuman body housing the transplanted brain of Adolf Hitler. Once again, World War II was the event that defined the superhero genre's origins. This was also the case in 1996, when a collaboration between Marvel and DC, Amalgam Comics, produced Super-Soldier by **Dave Gibbons**, a hybrid version of Captain America and Superman. In the story, Super-Solder fights a Nazi war machine, "Ultra-Metallo," who is programmed to destroy the White House.

In the wake of the attacks on American on September 11, 2001, many comics returned to imagery from World War II, presenting the ambiguous war on terror in terms of the certainties associated with the earlier conflict. This was particularly evident in the new volumes of Captain America comics, which featured versions of famous World War II propaganda posters as covers. Marvel Comics returned to the war in the first issue of **Mark Millar's** *The Ultimates* (2002), a post-9/11 version of *The Avengers*, and **Image Comics** re-launched their modern version of Captain America, SuperPatriot, in 2004. As a patriotic superhero, the latter has a host of Nazi enemies, including a Nazi supervillain who seems to be an amalgam of The Red Skull, Captain Nazi, and Masterman. Indeed, SuperPatriot even encounters a giant robot ape which houses the brain of Hitler.

In spite of the rather clichéd and superficial treatment of World War II in most comics, there have been several thought-provoking and intelligent responses to the war, such as **Art Spiegelman's** *Maus* (1973–91), which tells the story of the Holocaust, and portrays the Nazis as cats, the Jews as mice. However, for the most part Nazis have been, and continue to be, stock villains who represent evil and oppression.

**Selected Bibliography:** Jones, Gerard. *Men of Tomorrow: Geeks, Gangsters and the Birth of the Comic Book*. New York: Basic Books, 2004; Jones, Gerard, and Jacobs, Will. *The Comic Book Heroes*. Rocklin, CA: Prima Publishing, 1997; Wright, Bradford. *Comic Book Nation*. Baltimore: Johns Hopkins University Press, 2003; Wright, Nicky. *The Classic Era of American Comics*. London: Prion Books Ltd, 2000.

*Chris Murray*

**NEW MUTANTS.** The New Mutants **superhero** team first appeared in *Marvel Graphic Novel* #4 (1982) written by **Chris Claremont**. They launched their own title with

*New Mutants* #1, with a cover date of March, 1983. Most notably, New Mutants was the first **X-Men** spin-off ongoing series. Its success generated later ongoing X-Men series including *X-Factor*, *X-Force*, and *Generation X*. The premise of the series centers on a group of mutants who are just coming into their abilities and learning to use or master their powers. In real time, it had been 20 years since the X-Men first appeared, and though within the **Marvel Comics** universe they had not grown by 20 years, it was abundantly clear that the members of the X-Men should now be adults. *New Mutants* gave the opportunity to explore the complex issues of adolescent identity complicated by mutant powers and bigotry. The series would also prove a testing ground for characters (heroes and villains) in determining if they were successful enough to make it into the *X-Men* main series or into other splinter series later on. *The New Mutants* also provided staunch competition for the revived *New **Teen Titans*** (1980) from **DC Comics**.

Much like the relaunch of X-Men with *Giant Size X-Men* #1, the New Mutants' roster took on a diverse representation of cultures, some of which had not been previously represented in Marvel Comics. The team included Cannonball (American), Karma (Vietnamese), Mirage (Cheyenne), Sunspot (Brazilian), and Wolfsbane (Scottish). Other early members would include Magma, Magik, Warlock and Cypher, while former X-Factor wards Boom Boom, Rictor, Rusty Collins and Skids would join later. Bird Brain and Gosamyr were also members for short periods, and Kitty Pryde was briefly demoted to the team from the X-Men. Though often successful in their missions and challenges, the overall life of the New Mutants has been chaotic and traumatic. Several team members have been lost through death (Cypher and Warlock), loss of powers (Magik), and desertion (Wolfsbane, Rictor, and Sunspot). Partway into the series, Xavier leaves both X-Men and New Mutants, giving direction over to Magneto, who has rehabilitated himself. Magneto returns to a more sinister character as he assumes a position within the Hellfire Club, thus reinforcing the theme of abandonment that runs so strongly within the series from its leaders to the individual characters. Whether orphaned, abandoned, or disowned, most of the New Mutants, the original and later members, are parentless and their time with the New Mutants does not always offer substitute parental support.

Their adventures bring them to far-off places, including the Norse mythological Asgard and even outer space; often they are fighting foes much more powerful than themselves including the Hellfire Club, Freedom Force, Legion, Mutant Liberation Front, Shadow King, and Silver Samurai. However, often these external threats prove no more compelling than the group dynamics of the New Mutants and the burgeoning identities of the different characters as they deal with their own inner adolescent turmoil while also contending with the tragedy their team experienced.

The most significant run of the series came in its last 15 issues, when Rob Liefeld took over as penciller and eventually writer (with Fabian Nicieza) for the last three issues of the series (#98–100). Though the series as a whole maintains a dark edge to it, the final run of the series transforms the *New Mutants* into a small militant organization led (forcibly) by Cable, who first appeared in *New Mutants* #87. Cable is later discovered to be Cyclops's son who has been sent to the future. With Cable at the helm, the New Mutants face off against the Mutant Liberation Front, whose leader, Stryfe, is physically identical to Cable. Cable continues to lead the New Mutants in the absence of any other X-Men willing or able to take over the responsibility. However, when the X-Men and Professor X eventually return, Cable is challenged for leadership of the young mutants, accused of treating them as soldiers, not children. In a final break that ends the series, Cable and his followers splinter off from the X-Men and Xavier's School to form X-Force, with the initial roster consisting of Boom-Boom, Cannonball, Domino, Feral, Shatterstar, and Warpath—with the rest of the New Mutants quitting entirely or defecting to other teams such as X-Factor and Excalibur.

Though the ongoing series ends with issue #100 in 1991, the concept behind New Mutants carries on almost continuously in various series through 2009, as in the transition into X-Force with much of the same team members. By 1994, *Generation X* was launched, the third ongoing series of adolescent mutants under *X-Men* titles. Though the first issue's title, "Third Genesis," declares it the successor to *Giant Size X-Men* #1 (the issue's subtitle was "Second Genesis"), it also fits appropriately as a successor to *New Mutants* as a third series and class of mutants starting their education at Xavier's School. The series ran parallel to *X-Force* until it was cancelled in 2001, with *X-Force* canceled a year later (though the original premise of *X-Force* was significantly altered for the last 14 issues). During this time, Marvel released a miniseries, *New Mutants: Truth or Death* (1997). Marvel also released a second *New Mutants* miniseries in 2003 that ran for 12 issues and transitioned into *New X-Men: Academy X* in 2004. The series deals with some of the original members of New Mutants and Generation X returning to Xavier's School to become teachers and mentors to another young group of mutants. This series (after dropping the subtitle with issue #19) ran until 2008. It was replaced by *Young X-Men* (2008–9) and finally by a new ongoing series, *New Mutants* in 2009. Though the plots, reasons, and actions of the adolescent mutant teams are different, they often reflect the social and cultural dynamics of youth culture in specific ways that the adult teams cannot capture. The mixture of teenage angst, being accepted by peers, real world events, and saving the world meshed together well enough to have continued appeal for readers.

*Lance Eaton*

**NICIEZA, FABIAN** (1961–). Fabian Nicieza is a prolific American comics writer who has also held production, editorial, and executive positions in the publishing industry. Nicieza was born in Argentina and came to the United States at an early age. Best known for his work on **Marvel**'s *The New Warriors*, *X-Force*, and **X-Men** in the 1990s, he has written hundreds of comics—mainly **superhero** stories for **Marvel** and **DC** Comics, but also for other genres and publishers. Recurring features of Nicieza's stories include an emphasis on complex, at times convoluted plots; an abundance of references to back story and popular culture at large; diverse characters; and an awareness of social issues.

Holding a bachelor's degree in communication, Nicieza entered publishing in 1983, in a production capacity at Berkley Books, a paperback publisher. In 1985, he applied for a position at Marvel's book department and was accepted, but soon joined the company's burgeoning advertising department instead before moving on to work as an editor. In addition to being on staff at Marvel, Nicieza began to write for the publisher. His first professional comics work appeared in *Psi-Force* #9 in 1987, followed by a steady stream of other stories.

Nicieza's breakthrough as a writer came in 1990, when he launched *The New Warriors* with artist Mark Bagley. The series proved a sleeper hit whose sales kept climbing. Later that year, Nicieza joined artist and co-writer Rob Liefeld on **New Mutants**, where he co-created the characters Deadpool, Domino and Shatterstar, among others. Liefeld and Nicieza relaunched the series as *X-Force* in 1991, and its debut issue became the best-selling American comic book since World War II. When Liefeld and fellow artist **Jim Lee**, who had broken the sales record of *X-Force* #1 with *X-Men* #1 after only two months, left Marvel to found **Image Comics** in 1992, Nicieza became the sole writer of both *X-Force* and *X-Men*. By 1993, he was one of the most prolific writers in the industry, his name sometimes appearing in more than 10 comics per month. During this period of wild commercial success, Nicieza wrote series like *Cable*, *Deadpool*, and *Nomad*, among others.

In 1995, Nicieza, no longer on staff, left both *X-Force* and *X-Men* due to disagreements with editorial. In 1996, while producing less and less work for Marvel, Nicieza co-wrote the **DC Comics** miniseries **Justice League**: *A Midsummer's Nightmare*. In the same year, he joined Acclaim Comics, publisher of series such as *Turok* and *X-O: Manowar*, as editor-in-chief, eventually adding the roles of publisher and president. Although the creators assembled by Nicieza included names like **Kurt Busiek**, **Mark Waid**, and **Garth Ennis**, his line of comics failed to gain traction in an increasingly difficult comics market. Nicieza resigned from Acclaim in 1999.

Between 1999 and 2008, Nicieza wrote numerous comics for Marvel, notably the series *Thunderbolts*, *Gambit*, and *Cable & Deadpool*, but also for other publishers, including *Buffy the Vampire Slayer* for **Dark Horse**, various **Superman** and **Batman** projects for DC and *The 99* for Kuwaiti company Teshkeel Comics. In 2008, Nicieza signed an exclusive contract with DC. He has since co-written the weekly 52-issue series *Trinity* with Busiek and is set to helm the monthly title *Azrael* starting in October 2009.

**Selected Bibliography:** Martin, Madalyn. "Acclaim Entertainment Names Fabian Nicieza President and Publisher of Acclaim Comics." (April 14, 1997). Acclaim Entertainment, http://www.thefreelibrary.com/Acclaim+Entertainment+Names+Fabian+Nicieza+President+and+Publisher+of . . . -a019309402; McLelland, Ryan. "Valiant Days, Valiant Nights: Interview with Fabian Nicieza." (September 8, 2003). Valiant Comics.com, http://www.valiantcomics.com/valiant/valiantdays/FabianNicieza-Interview.doc; Wilson, Keri. "Fabian's Thunder: Fabian Nicieza." *Sequential Tart* (November, 2001). http://www.sequentialtart.com/archive/nov01/nicieza.shtml.

*Marc-Oliver Frisch*

**NIKOPOL TRILOGY, THE.** *The Nikopol Trilogy* is a 170-page **science-fiction** comic by the Belgrade born Parisian artist Enki Bilal (1951–). It consists of three comics (created originally in French): *La Foire aux Immortels* (literally "The Carnival of Immortals" but published in English as *Gods in Chaos*) of 1980, *La Femme piège* (*The Woman Trap*) of 1986 and finally *Froid Équateur* (*Equator Cold*) of 1992. The French title *Trilogie Nikopol* dates from 1995 when the French publisher *Les Humanoïdes Associés* collected the three stories in one volume, which was not Bilal's intention because he wanted every part to be quite different. Consequently there are three more or less separate stories but with various links among them: for instance, some characters as Nikopol, his son Niko, and the rebelling Egyptian god Horus reappear. The action moves from Paris in the first part, to London and Berlin in the second part, and finally to Africa in the last story.

The first part, *La Foire aux Immortels*, originally serialized in the French comics monthly *Pilote*, was a major step in Bilal's development as an artist, because it was the first time he drew and wrote a long story by himself and it was the first completely done in what has been called direct coloring. From then on Bilal would continue to use this technique of fully-painted-artwork in his comics and illustration work—except for his most recent album *Animal'z* (2009). In fact, this style would make him widely respected. In general Bilal's color scheme has a rather monochromatic feeling, as it is built around greys, but on the other hand a few prominent colored patches (foremost in yellow or red) show up now and then. Together with this somber palette of grey tones his baroque, decadent fictional worlds would become his trademark, not only in his comics but also in his other artistic work (illustrations, paintings, set design, films). At the time of the first publication, Europe was still in a rather gloomy atmosphere: the **Cold War** had been heated up by the installations of new nuclear arms, while the oil crisis of the 1970s provoked an economic recession with old industries closing down, causing skyrocketing unemployment. The idea of a pessimistic future was not solely shared by punks but also by artists in larger circles of Western European culture. For instance European comics saw a remarkable boom of post-cataclysmic stories (e.g., Howard's & Ezquerra's *Judge Dredd*, Auclair's *Simon de la Fleuve*, Hermann's *Jeremiah*). In the first part of the *Nikopol Trilogy*, readers learn that two nuclear wars were fought between 1990 and 2023, and that a fascist regime had been installed in Paris. Except for the male elite that is allowed to live in the center, the 2023 Paris is a rather disastrous place, in spite of some technological progress (new flying devices) it is clearly a world in decay. Though it all looks extremely grim and dark, Bilal injects some humorous elements, such as the Egyptian gods playing the famous board game Monopoly, or the unrelentingly procreating greyish flying "angels." Sources of inspiration for Bilal are multiple: from Baudelaire's poetry (which is often quoted by Nikopol) to the Egyptian gods of Roger Zelazny's science fiction novel *Creatures of Light and Darkness* (1969).

The comic struck a chord among adult readers and was an immediate critical and commercial success in France. When the second part was published, six years after the first, Bilal was already an acclaimed and well-known artist; *La Femme piège* was celebrated at the Angoulême festival, a year later Bilal himself was awarded the Grand Prix at the 1987 Angoulême Festival, and the third part was picked as best book of the year by the important literary magazine *Lire*.

Perhaps due to his bicultural upbringing, Bilal is an excellent builder of strange but fascinating worlds. This trilogy lays the foundations for his later work; most of his films and his comics would refer in one way or another to the universe created in the *Nikopol Trilogy*, most explicitly in *Immortel (ad vitam)* (2004), which is a very free filmic version using some characters and scenes from the trilogy but placing them in the new setting of a futuristic New York.

The first part of the trilogy was for the first time published in English in **Heavy Metal** as *The Immortals' Fete* (1981), while the complete trilogy was published in a single volume by Humanoids Publishing in 1999. In addition to the *Nikopol Trilogy*, Bilal has created other science fiction comics, such as the *Monstre Tetralogy* (1998, 2003, 2006, 2007) and *Animal'z* (2009). As of 2009 he had also directed three feature-length science fiction films: *Bunker Palace Hotel* (1989), *Tykho Moon* (1996), *Immortel (ad vitam)* (2004).

**Selected Bibliography:** "Enki Bilal Interview." *The Comics Journal* 129 (May 1989).

*Pascal Lefèvre*

**"OMAHA" THE CAT DANCER.** The creation of Minneapolis-based artist and writer Reed Waller, *Omaha* first appeared in the APA (Amateur Press Association) anthology *Vootie*, whose stated mission was the promotion of **funny animal comics**, including Disney and Warner Brothers characters, as well as original characters. Contributors created and published original material, which was collated into anthologies and redistributed to contributing members.

Dan O'Neill's *Air Pirates Funnies* was a 1971 underground anthology comic. Its central story concerned the sex lives and drug use of Mickey Mouse and other Disney characters. Disney sued for copyright infringement, bringing national attention to the comic. In 1978, in part inspired by O'Neill's work, Waller created his character *Omaha* in *Vootie*. As extensions of the ideas in *Air Pirates Funnies*, Waller gave his story political overtones and plausible continuity. The characters had active emotion-based sex lives. Waller made the characters more human than animal, inspiring the term anthropomorphic, a term Waller disliked, preferring funny animal. After reading issues of *Vootie* featuring Waller's nascent *Omaha* strips, **Kitchen Sink Press** publisher, Denis Kitchen, approached Waller about the prospect of a book. A 36-page *Omaha* story debuted in *Bizarre Sex* #9 in 1981.

*Bizarre Sex* #9 sold very well, and *Omaha* #1 was published in 1982 by a small Minneapolis publisher. However, Waller had ceased working on *Omaha* during issue #1. A variety of suggestions led to him offer the writing responsibility to his then-spouse Kate Worley. After issue #2, the title moved back to Kitchen Sink. Working collaboratively, Waller and Worley produced 20 issues of *Omaha*, as well as short *Omaha* stories for several political and/or sexual anthologies, and other work.

In Worley's writing, characters confronted disability issues, mental health concerns, blue laws and sexuality. The latter two are especially significant because Waller and Worley were the first comic creators to come out as bisexual. The relationships of bisexual character Shelley Hine and gay character Rob Shaw rang truer as a result. Shelley was also disabled, bringing that issue to the forefront.

In 1987, Friendly Frank's Comic Store in Chicago was raided. Six comics were seized, including two issues of *Omaha*. The Comic Book Legal Defense Fund, an organization dedicated to protecting the rights of comic creators, publishers, and retailers, began as a result. *Omaha* was the subject of further obscenity charges in Toronto and New Zealand in 1990. All charges were eventually dismissed.

Waller was diagnosed with colon cancer in 1991. His outstanding medical bills resulted in two benefit comics, titled *Images of Omaha*, again published by Kitchen Sink. Some of the most respected people in comics contributed to the benefit books, demonstrating the aesthetic respect *Omaha* commanded. Following Waller's recovery and an acrimonious breakup with Worley in 1994, the same year *Omaha* moved to **Fantagraphics**, the title was discontinued indefinitely, after four issues with that publisher.

In 2002, the rift between Waller and Worley was sufficiently mended and the two resumed work on *Omaha*. Kate Worley died of lung cancer in 2004. Her widower, fellow writer James Vance, began working with Waller on concluding the storyline from Kate's notes and manuscripts. As of this writing, the series is being concluded episodically in NBM's *Sizzle* magazine, with a final collection pending on the work's completion. In addition to spurring the creation of the erotic funny animal subgenre of comics, *Omaha* was nominated for three **Eisner Awards** in 1989, two in 1991, and won a Squiddy Award for Best Ongoing Series in 1994.

*See also:* Underground and Adult Comics

**Selected Bibliography:** Kitchen, Denis. *The Complete Omaha, Vol. 7.* New York: NBM Publishing, 2008.

*Diana Green*

**100 BULLETS.** A monthly series from **DC**'s Vertigo imprint that ran for 100 issues between 1999 and 2009, written by **Brian Azzarello**, with art by Eduardo Risso, *100 Bullets* is based largely on a single premise: *What if you could get away with murder?* As the series begins, unsuspecting individuals from various walks of life are approached by a man identifying himself only as "Agent Graves." Graves reveals to these individuals that certain misfortunes, tragedies, or traumas in their lives have been willfully caused by specific parties. Graves then provides each of his targets with an attaché case that identifies the perpetrator(s) and provides "irrefutable evidence" that his claims are true. Most importantly, each case contains a gun and 100 rounds of untraceable ammunition to be used as the bearer sees fit. Crucially, Graves never explicitly instructs those receiving an attaché to kill; rather, he tantalizes them with information and opportunity: whatever they choose to do, their actions will be above the law. The discrepancy between the reprisal offered by Graves and the means he provides to ensure it is indicative of the series' ongoing examination of the excesses of violence and authority. These excesses are recorded in the series' title itself, and visually reiterated as each new attaché is put into play: if retribution can ostensibly be attained with one pull on the trigger, then providing 100 bullets is disturbingly disproportionate, a point that serves to enhance the ominous premise of consequence-free revenge.

Although Graves's bullets prove to be untraceable, some recipients of the attachés nevertheless find that the promise of carte blanche is not enough to compel them to kill; others find that Graves's form of payback does not provide the peace they were seeking, or they do not follow his instructions. For example, Graves's first contact, Isabelle Cordova, ends up taking more vengeance and killing additional felons, while Graves's second client, Lee Dolan, chooses not to take revenge. More significantly, a grander plot explaining Graves's motivations slowly begins to take shape, becoming exponentially intricate with each issue. Readers learn that the briefcases are used by Graves in some—but not all—instances to recruit potential members of the Minutemen, a group of seven lethal and nearly unstoppable assassins associated with a powerful collective known as the Trust. The Trust is led by the heads of 13 "families," with the Minutemen acting as both their enforcers and as a kind of internal security mechanism that ensures no one family in the Trust gains a disproportionate share of power or influence. Should one Trust family make a move to destabilize or weaken the position of another, the Minutemen are mandated to respond in kind. A conflict between Graves and the Trust is revealed in snippets, as is the clandestine influence that the Trust has exerted throughout its long history (the Trust's role in the assassination of JFK is implied in a number of issues). Through a steady trickle of veiled conversations and layered flashbacks, it comes to light that the earliest incarnation of the Trust crossed the Atlantic and deployed seven killers of the original Minutemen to slaughter the original colonists at Roanoke. This killing was an act of revenge by the Trust because the Trust had offered the kings of Europe complete autonomy over the new world in exchange for relinquishing control of the old world (Europe) to the Trust. England ignored the offer and was punished by having its colonists murdered. Forgoing interest in European matters, the Trust staked a bloody claim to what would become the United States of America, and their descendants have reaped the benefits ever since. Graves once headed the modern-day collection of Minutemen, but he disbanded them and put them into hiding after the Trust seemingly violated its agreement with them in asking for the Minutemen's involvement in another grand crime of comparable magnitude; some of these hidden Minutemen have their memories wiped clean and are placed in mundane lives until they are reactivated by a mysterious watchword—*Croatoa*—that hearkens back to Roanoke and America's origins. Certain attachés are given to "sleeping" Minutemen as Graves, now ostensibly devoted to destroying the Trust, manipulates various players among constantly shifting factions comprised of the families of the Trust, and the Minutemen past, present, and future.

The series is rife with unrelenting brutality. Acts of violence—sometimes calculated, sometimes shockingly random—pervade nearly every issue, ranging from the absolutely savage to the grimly humorous. Extraneous violence even takes place in the background of many panels in such threatening forms as muggings, ravenous dogs, and drunken posturing. Risso renders this vicious world and its inhabitants with expressive and often elegant linework. His economical style, combined with his deft handling of shadows and silhouettes, gives the series its distinctive atmosphere of perpetual danger and tension, an atmosphere that is everywhere etched in the wrinkles, scars, snarls, and sensuous curves of the main characters. Risso also displays a remarkable array of page-layouts and pacing techniques that propel visceral confrontations and intense conversations alike, setting everything against richly-detailed backdrops (enhanced by particularly effective coloring) extending from inner-city slums to decadent highrises.

The other distinguishing feature of *100 Bullets* is its language. Characters exchange cryptic, fragmented dialogue that refers to events the reading audience has never been privy to; interlocutors constantly finish each others' sentences with razor-sharp puns; rivals spar with veiled truths, pointed threats, and expletives galore. Language is, as in much of Azzarello's work, not just a means of communication, but an expression of power. Fittingly, the series involves a devilish investment in onomastics: character names include Cole Burns, Wylie Times, Will Slaughter—one hardly bats an eye when, at a well-advanced stage of the series, readers learn that Graves's first name is Philip. Causal naming practices even help to order the series' trade paperback collections: the initial collection is *First Shot, Last Call*, followed by *Split Second Chance*; the 10th volume is *Decayed*, and so on. Its interest in emblematic language and names suggests that *100 Bullets* is a kind of modern morality play, though such a comparison is both apt and misleading. The backbone of the series involves temptation and opportunity assaulting the morality of individuals who are jolted from a seemingly mundane existence and forced to reflect on how their lives have been shaped by great personal tragedy produced by forces beyond their control. While this underlying emphasis on sanctioned retribution and the possibility of redemption provides so much of the series' energy, *100 Bullets* is much more than an allegorical struggle between virtue and vice. That is, the series as a whole greatly complicates simple distinctions between right and wrong. In blurring—if not destroying—the line between good and bad, right and wrong, the series returns time and again to matters epitomized in Graves's Faustian bargain: humankind's thirst for power and control, the violence upon which this power inevitably depends, and the widespread and always irreversible ramifications of life's decisions. If its intimate noir sensibilities help sustain the story's intensity, it must also be said that the series has a truly all-American scope: seemingly all major American cities—from New York to Los Angeles, New Orleans to Seattle—become a part of the narrative's landscape, immediately recognizable through the combination of Risso's stylized detail and Azzarello's sharp ear for regional dialects, as well as slang and street talk. The series also employs both women and ethnic minorities in major roles, further extending its scope. *100 Bullets* is momentous not only for the duration of the collaboration between Azzarello and

Risso (a modern day rarity), but for the undeniable synergy that these two creators were able to sustain from start to finish.

*J. Gavin Paul*

**O'NEIL, DENNIS** (1939–). Working his way up from editorial assistant, Dennis "Denny" O'Neil would become an acclaimed and prolific writer of comic books and novels and one of the most influential editors of American comic books, overseeing, most notably, the entire line of **Batman** titles. Born and raised in St. Louis, O'Neil was working as a crime-beat reporter in Cape Girardeau, Missouri, in 1965, when Roy Thomas, who had just accepted a job with **Marvel Comics**, encouraged O'Neil to take the **Marvel** writer's test. Subsequently, O'Neil soon joined what he calls the "second generation" of Marvel writers, the first writers to follow in **Stan Lee**'s footsteps. During his initial tenure at Marvel, O'Neil worked on such diverse titles as *Millie the Model*, *Kid Colt*, and *Doctor Strange*.

In 1967, O'Neil began moonlighting for **Charlton Comics** under the editorship of Dick Giordano, writing under the pseudonym Sergius O'Shaughnessy, a name borrowed from a Norman Mailer novel. O'Neil worked on such Charlton titles as *The Prankster* and *Wander* until the company folded its **superhero** line in 1967. O'Neil followed Giordano to **DC**, where he initially worked on titles like *The Creeper* and *Bomba the Jungle Boy*. Soon, though, O'Neil began writing for *Justice League of America* as well as stories featuring some of the League's original members: **Wonder Woman**, **Green Lantern**, and **Batman**.

One of the recurrent trends of O'Neil's work as writer and editor has been the re-humanization of superheroes. Early on at DC, O'Neil developed a storyline that saw Wonder Woman surrender her powers. Later, he greatly weakened the essentially omnipotent **Superman**. In a different vein, he turned the wealthy and aloof **Green Arrow** into a poor political activist. A decade later, after returning for a time to write for Marvel, O'Neil sent **Iron Man**'s alter ego, Tony Stark, on a six-month alcoholic binge.

In 1970, O'Neil wrote his first solo Batman story, "The Secret of the Waiting Graves," which teamed him up for the first time with an important long-term collaborator, artist **Neal Adams**. Later that year, O'Neil and Adams began developing the highly acclaimed Green Lantern/Green Arrow series in which the socially aware Green Arrow introduces a naïve Green Lantern to some of the woes facing American society. Many consider the short-lived series a turning point in comic book maturity, moving the genre beyond the realm of adolescent fantasy.

In 1986, O'Neil became the group editor of all of DC's Batman series, which included, at the time, *Detective Comics*, *Batman Comics*, and a few other titles. By the time of his retirement in 2000, O'Neil was editing 12 monthly Batman titles as well as graphic novels, miniseries, and one-shots, along with writing for the Batman spin-off *Azrael*. During his tenure, he oversaw the most significant evolution of the Batman character, changes that O'Neil says "went back and took what was implicit" from the original character. O'Neil helped return Batman to the brooding detective **Bob Kane** and Bill Finger first envisioned. Subsequently, O'Neil supervised some of the most acclaimed Batman storylines, including **The Dark Knight Returns**, *A Death in the Family, Knightfall*, and *No Man's Land*.

**Selected Bibliography:** O'Neil, Denny. "Interview." (December 3, 2007). *Around Comics*, http://www.aroundcomics.com/; O'Neil, Denny. "Interview." (December 10, 7007). *Around Comics*, http://www.aroundcomics.com/.

*Jason S. Todd*

**OPTIC NERVE** is an ongoing comics series created by Adrian Tomine in 1991, while he was midway through high school in Sacramento, CA. Originally published as a mini-comic three pages long and with a paltry print run of 25 copies, the series is now one of Canadian publisher Drawn & Quarterly's best-known series. The first seven issues, consisting of a combination of semi-autobiographical stories alongside fictional stories, were all printed as mini-comics of ever-increasing length closer and closer to the industry-standard 32 pages. As mini-comics with very limited print runs, they quickly sold out, while Tomine became increasingly well-known. He began a comic strip for *Pulse!* for Tower Records the following year, which brought more attention to his mini-comics work.

In 1994, when he was just 20, Drawn and Quarterly picked up *Optic Nerve* and began major publication and distribution of the series. It became extremely popular; as a result, Tomine and his series garnered a great deal of attention, though not all of it was positive. For example, the letters pages of his issues often include at least one letter where Tomine's readers take him to task for a variety of things, including his visual similarity to other comics artists (most notably **Daniel Clowes**, whom Tomine acknowledges as one of his major influences). Others cite his sad characters as being too entrenched in pop culture, too affected, of being too "emo" or "hipster" in his portrayals of them. Much of the work was informed by those around him, with a decidedly autobiographical aspect to the dialogue and characters.

However, despite this fan feedback, *Optic Nerve* gained momentum and widespread critical acclaim with the nomination of the series for a "Best New Series" **Harvey Award** and Tomine's win of a Harvey Award for "Best New Talent" in 1995. In this same year, the first seven issues of the series, long out of print in the original mini-comic format, were collected in *32 Stories*. This title has proved so popular that Drawn & Quarterly re-issued the series as a new boxed set in April 2009 with redesigned packaging and promotion, recognizing nearly two decades of work.

In 1997, the first four issues of *Optic Nerve* produced for Drawn & Quarterly were reprinted as *Sleepwalk and Other Stories*, one of Drawn & Quarterly's best-selling collections. Tomine continued work (along with finishing a degree in English from the University of California at Berkeley) on the series, publishing the second *Optic Nerve* collection, the critically acclaimed *Summer Blonde*, in 2002. Reprinting issues #5 through #8 of the series, *Summer Blonde* particularly showcases Tomine's skill at capturing various characters through dialogue so true to life that it feels almost like you are eavesdropping on their conversations.

One of the stories from this collection, "Bomb Scare," was included in Dave Eggers's *The Best American Nonrequired Reading* published by Houghton Mifflin in that same year, and Tomine was still publishing *Optic Nerve* as of early 2009, despite a hiatus between 2001 and 2004. He has also developed a career in commercial illustration work, including the creation of CD covers for a variety of bands and magazine covers ranging from *The New Yorker* to *Rolling Stone* and *Time*. All of these include the crisp and distinctive line work associated with his comics images. His style, both in *Optic Nerve* and in his commercial work, is crisp and clean, with bold lines and savvy detail, such as a hipster girl sitting in the back of a New York tourist bus, with her parents arm's length away snapping photos of Radio City Music Hall while she reads a J. D. Salinger book.

Published in 2007, Tomine's collection *Shortcomings* is made up of a narrative arc spanning issues *Optic Nerve* #9 through #11, taking a total of about five years to reach publication in collected form. This is his first work that is a multi-issue storyline; generally his pieces have tended to be more like a series of short stories and vignettes rather than a longer related piece divided over issues and published sequentially. This collection is also one of the first times that Tomine talks about racial issues and stereotypes in some great detail. Earlier stories deal with quirky characters; in "Summer Job" from *Optic Nerve* #2, readers learn about Eric, who is working a summer job at a photo reproduction place; in another, the story revolves around a woman scouring the "I Saw You" section of her local paper thinking there are ads placed there for her. There are characters who place prank phone calls, invite people they have recently met to funerals, and are generally profoundly lonely and unusual individuals sharing odd moments of similarity. They have more in common than they think. They share a sensibility about the world, the people in it, and their own intersecting identities.

More than anything, though, *Optic Nerve* is a series about identity. Some of it is Tomine's own, as a Japanese American cartoonist writing about race but without making race the primary defining lens of the work he produces. Some of it is simply about being in the world: Ben Tanaka, the primary protagonist of *Shortcomings*, is abrasive and conflicted. As a Japanese American man, Tanaka jokes about stereotypes about Asian men but seems intent on not questioning the double standard that makes it acceptable for him to pursue a series of blonde women, but causes him to condemn his former girlfriend Miko when she begins dating a white man, even though Ben learns about this situation long after they have broken up and she has moved across the country to New York. Meanwhile, what precipitated their breakup wasn't so much that Ben simply took Miko for granted, but more her discovery of his porn stash—focusing on imaging of white women. **Race** is an issue throughout *Optic Nerve*, but Tomine explores it in a different way, by calling stereotypes into question or simply giving them voice, such as when Ben says to his lesbian Korean friend Alice, who's passing for straight at a family wedding, "Why don't we just tell them that I'm Korean while we're at it?" "All Asians might look the same to you," she jokes, "but my family would spot your Japanese ass a mile away."

*Anne Thalheimer*

**PALESTINE.** An award-winning work of comics journalism by artist and journalist **Joe Sacco**, *Palestine* was published serially in nine installments from 1993 to 1995. The installments were collected in one volume published in 2001 and introduced by the eminent activist-academic Edward Said. Based on interviews and observations conducted by Sacco during a two-month stay in the winter of 1991–92 in Palestinian territories occupied by Israel, the comic takes readers from the spontaneous eruption of the First Intifada (uprising) of Palestinians against Israeli military occupation in1987 to the intifada's waning days in 1992. Historical interludes also describe the mass expulsion of Palestinians from what is now Israel-proper by Zionist terrorist groups in 1948.

The narrative begins with Sacco having a discussion with two men in Cairo, one absorbed in a love affair, the other absorbed in regional politics. The opening introduces us to Sacco's method, in which his presence—more explicit than in his later works—is an integral part of the narrative. Nearly everything he portrays is based on his observations and interactions with others, which inform and are informed by his impressions, perceptions, and emotions. The scene also sets the approach to the subject matter of the rest of the narrative, which highlights the ways and extent to which the everyday concerns of Palestinians run up against political realities largely outside of their control.

Indeed, *Palestine* is the story of occupation, about the daily indignities suffered by an entire population living under the yoke of the brutal military rule of Israel. Sacco does not hide readers from the conflicts within Palestinian society, such as the class differentials in the Gaza Strip between businessmen with large houses and unemployed people living in refugee camps, where houses have sand for floors, or the domestic abuse faced by many women, or the sometimes violent confrontations between different Palestinian political factions. However, like the ubiquitous "Palestinian room" where copious tea is served and young men sit around sharing stories, the one set of experiences that cuts across all differences is that of Israeli occupation. Every Palestinian has some connection with death, injury, destruction of homes, displacement, imprisonment, economic deprivation and/or generalized humiliation that is a direct, unmediated result of the violence of Israeli occupation. The psychological ramifications of occupation are also emphasized, as when one Palestinian asks, "Every home here has someone who is imprisoned, who has died, who is wounded . . . *this* is the childhood?" There is simply no escape, and all of Palestine (especially the Gaza Strip) is a prison—hemmed in on all sides by Israeli military outposts and regulated completely by Israeli military bureaucracy. Even those Palestinians who do manage to leave the occupied territories have no guarantee that they will ever be allowed back.

The concept of separation is central to *Palestine* as narrative and Palestine as lived experience. At one point, Sacco refers to parallel universes as in **Marvel Comics**: on the one hand, a seemingly normal cityscape in Jerusalem, with people in love, traffic, tourism, and so on; on the other hand, hidden beneath the surface, a world of brutal torture. The former world is largely for Israelis, whereas the latter is reserved exclusively for Palestinians. Sacco also notes the separate standards of justice for Israeli settlers who illegally occupy Palestinian land, and Palestinians who defend themselves against the violence of the former—settlers are rarely caught for murder, and when tried receive mild sentences; Palestinians caught for murder, however, typically receive life imprisonment and their families face collective punishment. Reminiscent of apartheid South Africa, there are even separate roads for the Israeli settlers and the indigenous Palestinians. In the closing chapter, two Israeli women discussing politics with Sacco in Tel Aviv declare that they simply do not want their normal lives (which, Sacco notes, are very Western lives) interrupted by the occasional burst of Palestinian violence. "We don't think about this stuff all the time, and we get a bit tired of hearing about it!" The very next morning, Sacco bumps into a friend in the Palestinian city of Nablus. Their seemingly normal reunion is almost immediately interrupted by violence—stones, settlers, and soldiers in a scene that is by now all too familiar to Sacco and to the reader. The contrast is clear: Israelis live in a universe where they have the choice to become tired of discussing violence, because violence is abnormal; Palestinians live in a universe where there is no choice but to discuss violence because of the omnipresence of a brutal Israeli occupation; in a society where violence is never normalized but it is the norm, it is the absence of violence that is abnormal.

Sacco's emphasis on Palestinian views might appear to be contradictory to objective journalism that ostensibly represents both sides of a conflict. However, his work seeks to deconstruct both the notions that Palestinians are a homogenous group of people and that mainstream journalism is anywhere near balanced: "I've heard nothing but the Israeli side most all my life. . . ." To counter the imbalance in mainstream media and the actual imbalance of power that sees a group of Israeli soldiers with automatic rifles standing under an awning while making an unarmed Palestinian boy stand in the rain and answer their questions, Sacco embeds himself with the people of Palestine. Indeed, the absence of Palestinian leaders or official spokespersons in his story is also indicative of his attempts to present the everyday lived experiences of Palestinians.

Yet, more than a narrative that seeks to upset in some small way a very large imbalance, *Palestine* is also a call to action. When interviewees ask Sacco what good his words or the words of supposedly pro-Palestinian people in the West are, he has little to say in return. The question is directed not only at Sacco, but at the reader who has—like the voyeur-cum-vulture Sacco—consumed the grief, pain, and suffering of Palestinians. It is not enough, Sacco implies, and the Palestinians in the narrative make clear, to feel sympathy for the Palestinian cause; the point is to take concrete actions to influence Western governments—and in particular the American government without which the Israeli state could probably not survive—to approach the conflict in a way that recognizes the rights of Palestinians to land and to humanity. There can be no solution, Sacco notes, "until this central fact—Israeli occupation—is addressed as an issue of international law and basic human rights."

**Selected Bibliography:** Sacco, Joe. *Palestine*. Seattle: Fantagraphics Books, 2001.

*Noaman G. Ali*

**PEKAR, HARVEY** (1939–). Harvey Pekar is a prominent comic book writer and memoirist as well as a widely published jazz and book critic. Born and raised in Cleveland, Ohio, Pekar lives in neighboring Cleveland Heights with his third wife, Joyce Brabner, and their adopted daughter. He is best known for his autobiographical series **American Splendor** (1976–), which provided the basis for a 2003 award-winning film adaptation of the same name. He has also written a series of nonfiction graphic novels, including *Our Cancer Year* (1994, with Frank Stack and Joyce Brabner), *The Quitter* (2005, with Dean Haspiel), *Macedonia* (2006, with Heather Roberson and Ed Piskor), and *Students for a Democratic Society: A Graphic History* (2008, with Gary Dumm, Paul Buhle and others). Pekar also worked with Buhle to produce two volumes designed to give voice to working class and oppositional cultural perspectives: *Studs Terkel's Working: A Graphic Adaptation* (2009) and *The Beats* (2009). Maintaining his interest in music, Pekar wrote the libretto for *Leave Me Alone!*, a jazz opera that premiered at Oberlin College in 2009.

Pekar was inspired to publish *American Splendor* as a result of his friendship with underground comix legend **Robert Crumb**, who contributed artwork to the first and subsequent issues. The occasionally published comics anthology centers on Pekar's life and in particular his experiences working as a file clerk in a large VA hospital in Cleveland, from which he retired in 2001. While Pekar self-published *American Splendor* for many years, **DC Comics** assumed the role of publisher from 2006 to 2008 via its Vertigo imprint. The list of artists who have contributed to *American Splendor* over the years—including Alison Bechdel, **Chester Brown**, **Eddie Campbell**, Hunt Emerson, Bob

Harvey Pekar as the "real Harvey," in the 2003 film *American Splendor*, directed by Shari Springer Berman and Robert Pulcini. Fine Line Features/Photofest

Fingerman, Drew Friedman, Gilbert **Hernandez**, Josh Neufeld, Spain Rodriguez, **Joe Sacco**, and Jim Woodring—is a de facto *Who's Who* of **alternative comics**. The fact that Pekar was invited to become the first guest editor of Houghton Mifflin's *Best American Comics* series (2006–) speaks to his sterling reputation in the comics field. While many of his artistic collaborators have been established figures, Pekar has made a special effort to encourage up-and-coming cartoonists who have undoubtedly benefited from their association with one of the most famous personalities in independent comics.

Pekar first gained national prominence as a result of his multiple guest appearances on television's *Late Night with David Letterman* in the late 1980s and early 1990s. He was eventually banned from the show for his confrontational personal style and pointed on-air criticism of NBC's corporate owner General Electric. The success of the *American Splendor* film, which starred Paul Giamatti and Hope Davis, further added to his cultural cache. He has leveraged this reputation to help secure publishing deals with trade publishers such as Ballantine, Doubleday, and the New Press. His most recent publishing effort to date (2009) is an **adaptation** of Studs Terkel's *Working*, published by the New Press. Like Studs Terkel, Pekar has a remarkable eye for transforming the prosaic details of everyday life into the stuff of serious entertainment. He has a sturdy work ethic, and he has found a way to make creative use of his somewhat curmudgeonly persona. Along with his longtime friend Crumb, he played a major role in inspiring the alternative comics surge of the past two decades.

*Kent Worcester*

**LA PERDIDA.** Created by Jessica Abel, the comic book *La Perdida* (literally translated as "The Lost") was first published serially in five installments by **Fantagraphics** Books from 2001 to 2005. A collected version was reprinted by Pantheon Books in 2006. The rather small original format (6.75" × 8.5") of the comic labels it as an independent comic. *La Perdida* was awarded with a **Harvey Award** in 2002 as "Best New Series" and was translated into French, Spanish, and Italian.

The New York-based comic-artist Abel (born 1969) started to draw comics while taking courses at the University of Chicago, where her work was first published in the student anthology *Breakdown*. After graduation she tried unsuccessfully to enter the world of comics. After receiving a Xeric Grant for her independently published comic book *Artbabe*, Abel produced a professionally printed version which put her on the map of independent comics. From 1997 to 1999, Abel's second volume of *Artbabe* was published by Fantagraphics Books, which won her a Harvey Award and a Lulu Award as "Best New Talent" in 1997. Her work was featured in various publications such as the *Best American Comics* anthology. Recently she produced a secondary comic book on comic books with her husband and comic-artist Matt Madden called *Drawing Words, Writing Pictures*.

Although Abel sums up the content of *La Perdida* very briefly as "a story about finding yourself by getting lost," the comic book offers a much more complex tale. The story is set in Mexico City, where the female protagonist Carla, in search of her heritage, must recognize that reality does not match with her romanticized image of the Mexican capital. On this quest "to find herself," concepts of belonging and of authenticity are questioned. While the façade of the exotic Mexico slowly fades away, Carla is confronted with the everyday life of expatriates and local inhabitants of the city. Influenced by these encounters Carla seems to lose herself and has to struggle in order to regain her sense of identity.

The story begins with a short prologue that shows the protagonist reviewing the events of the last year in retrospective. The reader is given single panels as flashbacks that foreshadow the complete story to come. Guided by retrospective observations in the captions, Carla arrives in the capital and meets up with Harry, a friend of hers. His apartment offers a point of refuge but also a starting point of a journey. Its simplistic white walls present an almost clinical space in the midst of the crowded cityscape of Mexico City. Similar to the following issues of *La Perdida*, issue one ends with a cliffhanger when Carla rips away the wallpaper on Harry's white walls.

The following two issues contrast the indigenous Mexican culture with the world of the expatriates Carla wants to ignore. She moves in with her Mexican boyfriend Oscar and discusses questions of cultural belonging with their friend Memo. In heated debates Carla tries to defend her search for identity, which seems to Memo as the mere luxury of a spoiled American daughter. A different perspective is provided by Carla's brother Rodriguez, who grew up with their Mexican father. His easy-going mentality is exactly what Carla is looking for ("Yeah isn't it funny how visitors can give you a new perspective?"). During his short vacation, Rodriguez takes Carla to places she has not been before and gives her a skeleton doll as a departure present. This souvenir from the famous Mexican holiday, the Day of the Dead, acts as a precursor of the events to come.

Without noticing, Carla succeeds in turning invisible: no longer being an expatriate, she has adapted to Mexican everyday life and blends in perfectly. Yet she begins to wonder if this is the life she wants to lead. When friends of Memo and Oscar abduct Harry in order to get a ransom, Carla is stuck with her new identity and is held as a prisoner in her own house. With the help of some friends she is able to free herself from imprisonment to tell her tale.

In order to construct these cultural differences on the printed pages of *La Perdida*, Abel uses language as a tool to express this otherness. While all the captions are Carla's or the narrator's internal monologue, the dialogues constantly shifts between English and Spanish. While the first two issues of *La Perdida* present Spanish and English sentences next to each other, the English passages tend to fade away in later issues. Sentences such as "You should make attention" offer further insight into the problems of communication. From issue three onwards almost everything printed in English should resemble Spanish dialogue; only some English phrases are displayed in parenthesis. Abel also introduces the reader into Mexican vernacular by adding special terms of the Mexican slang, which are translated in footnotes.

While these narrative techniques are rather innovative, Abel's drawing style is certainly influenced by America's independent scene. Yet her work with brushes gives her a unique outlook that she uses for *La Perdida*. With simple strokes of her finer brushes, she conveys the characters' emotions, while thicker lines are used for the backgrounds. Another trademark of Abel is her lettering, which gives the language its unique appearance.

The process of becoming, of change, is also displayed on a visual level. Abel's evocative black-and-white drawings tend to alter slightly over the course of the five issues of *La Perdida:* for example, facial features change. This leaves graphic space for the characters to evolve, especially as the protagonist Carla blends in with Mexican culture more easily. Scenes of Mexican everyday life are depicted as darker and more crowded, and clearly stand in contrast to the blazing white of Harry's apartment.

*La Perdida* is an imaginative journey not only in terms of displaying a different culture but also in thinking of a way to depict these differences visually in a comic book. While introducing her life in Mexico City in a retrospective, Carla's adventures are always contrasted by the captions that already encompass its outcome. This mode of displaying a duality of cultures is mirrored visually by Abel's unique lettering and her brushwork. Various levels of communication additionally evoke a process of adapting into an unfamiliar society, and yet always feature the constant struggle not to lose one's self.

*Daniel Wüllner*

**PÉREZ, GEORGE** (1954–). George Pérez was born in the South Bronx, New York, to parents who emigrated from Puerto Rico. He was a lifelong fan of **superhero** comics and started drawing at an early age. He ended his formal education after high school and tried to break into comics by working on fanzines and showing his work at conventions. **Marvel** artist Rich Buckler saw Pérez's folio and hired him as an assistant in 1973. Perez's first professionally published story was a backup in *Astonishing Tales #25*. Pérez left Buckler for personal reasons, but was immediately hired by Marvel to draw the Man-Wolf series in Marvel's *Creatures on the Loose* and the Sons of the Tiger series in *Deadly Hands of Kung Fu*. While working on these series, Pérez was hired to replace Buckler on **Fantastic Four**, and also took on a regular assignment on **Avengers.** Pérez's work on these titles gave him a reputation as an artist who could draw team superhero comics and actually enjoyed doing so. Most artists hated such assignments because they involved drawing more characters for the same page rate.

Pérez worked at Marvel throughout the 1970s, but in 1980 he was hired to draw **DC**'s new series *New Teen Titans*. He took this job because he was also offered **Justice League of America**, but *NTT* soon became one of DC's top-selling titles. By now Pérez was a major superstar, and he was the natural choice to draw the **JLA/Avengers** crossover in 1983. Negotiations on this project collapsed, leading Pérez to leave Marvel for 10 years. In 1985 he drew **Crisis on Infinite Earths**, which gave him a reputation as an artist of "crossover" series (i.e. those featuring large numbers of characters from one or more superhero universes). His first major writing assignment was on the post-*Crisis* revival of **Wonder Woman.** Pérez spent much of the late 1980s and early 1990s working on smaller projects such as *Sachs & Violens* and **Incredible Hulk:** *Future Imperfect*, but he returned to monthly comics in 1998 for a three-year run on *Avengers*. Health problems, including diabetes, have made it difficult for Pérez to maintain a monthly schedule, and most of his recent work has been on high-profile limited series such as *JLA/Avengers* and *Final Crisis: Legion of Three Worlds*.

Pérez is the preeminent contemporary artist of crossover and superhero team titles, largely because of his superb compositional ability (which made him a sought-after cover artist) and his willingness to draw large numbers of characters. The cover of *JLA/Avengers #3* alone features at least 200 characters. Pérez's artwork is also famous for its tight rendering and richness of detail. As a storyteller, Pérez consciously strives not to repeat the same layout on consecutive pages, and tends to include an unusually high number of panels on each page. His habit of giving fans more for their money has diminished his speed and volume of work, but has helped make him one of the biggest stars of contemporary superhero comics.

**Selected Bibliography:** Heintjes, Tom, ed. *Focus on George Pérez*. Agoura, CA: Fantagraphics Books, 1985; Nolen-Weathington, Eric, ed. *Modern Masters Volume Two: George Pérez*. Raleigh, NC: TwoMorrows Publishing, 2003.

*Aaron Kashtan*

**PERSEPOLIS,** by the Iranian born Marjane Satrapi (1969–), is not only an autobiographical comic of her personal and family life from the age of 10 to 24, but also offers a view of Iran's historical transformation during that time. It begins around the time of the revolution against the regime of the Shah in 1979 and ends with Satrapi's escape to Western Europe in 1994. Being a descendant of the royal Persian family dethroned by the father of the last shah, her account is willingly subjective. Though the regime of the shah was autocratic and very repressive towards its opponents, life was much easier for Marjane's modern family (her mother for instance did not have to wear a veil). The author presents herself as a child with extremely high aspirations (in her imagination she was talking to God). This enduring sense of superiority may explain her sometimes very critical tone, even towards family members, though her main target remains the Islamic dictatorship with its backwards beliefs. Satrapi presents a nuanced picture of her native country: she shows, for instance, that not all Iranians were so happy about the new Islamist regime and illustrates how the Iranian people tried to find ways to cope with it (e.g. organizing illegal parties with alcohol and dancing). She could of course not have produced this comic in her native country, but living in Paris she found the ideal working environment in the **alternative comics** movement: the French artist David B. guided her and the alternative French printing house *L'Association* put out the first part in 2000. Jean-Christophe Menu (Bellefroid, 2005, 13) of *L'Association* was afraid that they were taking a huge risk publishing the first volume of *Persepolis* by a then completely unknown Iranian artist: "The phenomenal success of Persepolis [...] is hallucinant. We could not have expected that. We thought to take a big risk when we published the first volume of Persepolis at 3,000 copies. Four years later, we had already sold more than 200,000 copies of the four volumes." By 2004 all four volumes of *Persepolis* were published in French; they have now been translated into many languages with similar success. The sequence is easily the best-selling comic of **L'Association**'s catalogue. Not only are the sales statistics stunning for a new artist, but the comic has exercised an important influence on the field. Like ***Maus*** by **Art Spiegelman**, *Persepolis* has attracted many readers who normally would not read comics. Both artists made a comic about a crucial historical and the repercussions on their family situation. Both comics were published in a format smaller than usual, a format resembling a novel. Though both comics were first published in parts, their final and integral versions each comprise more than 200 pages. Like *Maus*, *Persepolis* came at an opportune moment: just before the most spectacular terrorist attacks of September 11, 2001. From that moment on the threat of Islamic fundamentalists seemed more serious, though it was not their first strike and several others would follow. Those shocking acts have considerably raised interest in Islamic fundamentalism in Europe and the United States, including the events that are central to *Persepolis*. Other factors may also help to explain the success of *Persepolis*, including the fact that this comic was made by a young woman who opposes religious dogmatism and is living as a modern woman in the West, without a veil.

That Satrapi is proud of her country does not hinder the appeal of her work; instead it strengthens her credibility. The fact that readers get the events from the perspective of a young girl works efficiently and excuses the rudimentary drawing style. *Persepolis* proves again that one doesn't need to have refined artwork to sell a comic as long the content is interesting enough. In 2007 the comic was adapted with critical and public success into an animated film by Satrapi and Vincent Paronnaud, who himself is a celebrated French comics artist (working under the pen-name of Winshluss). After *Persepolis*, *L'Association* published (in 2004) another comic by Satrapi, *Poulet aux prunes* (*Chicken With Plums*, 2006) about Nasser Ali Khan, a renowned Iranian musician related to the family of the author. Again she has joined forces with Paronnaud to adapt this comic to the big screen, but this time it will be a live-action film.

**Selected Bibliography:** "L'interview! Marjane Satrapi." (2002). BD Sélection, http://www.bdselection.com/php/?rub=page_dos&id_dossier=51; Bellefroid, Thierry. *Les éditeurs de bande dessinée*. Paris; Niffle, 2005.

*Pascal Lefèvre*

**PHANTOM LADY.** Phantom Lady originated in the first issue of *Police Comics* (from **Quality Comics**) in 1941. In what had already become a comic book tradition, Phantom Lady is a rich girl when she is not fighting crime. The first panel of Phantom Lady's first story reads: "The society columns record the activities of Sandra Knight, debutant daughter of Senator Henry Knight . . . no one suspects that the frivolous Sandra is also The Phantom Lady, whose battle against spies and public enemies constantly make headlines." Artist Arthur Peddy designed her in a yellow costume with green cape, and gave her a kind of reverse flashlight, her "black ray," which blinded people. She also came with the requisite boyfriend, state department investigator Don Borden, who, even though Sandra Knight and Phantom Lady looked exactly alike (she did not even wear a mask) never caught on. The original Phantom Lady, while decently drawn, was not particularly memorable, and was interchangeable with many of the other superheroines who were being included in **Golden Age** comic books at that time. Neither she nor they survived for very long, and the original Phantom Lady's last appearance in her original run was in *Police Comics* #23, 1943.

Phantom Lady's stories were produced for Quality by the **Eisner**-Iger Shop. In 1947, that shop was producing work for Fox Comics, which became the new publisher for Phantom Lady, who got her own book, which lasted until 1949. She also got a complete new look, with a blue costume and red cape. Her new artist, the stylish and flamboyant **Matt Baker**, restyled her hair, giving her bangs and a passing resemblance to then-popular pinup queen Bettie Page. Baker, one of the rare African American artists in comics during the 1940s, excelled in drawing women. During Baker's all-too brief life—he died prematurely from a congenital heart condition—he drew jungle queens, aviatrixes, girl detectives and superheroines; they were always beautiful and always strong. Some of his best were Fiction House's Tiger Girl and Sky Girl, and the sarong-clad South Sea Girl, Alani, queen of "The Vanishing Islands," which he drew for Seven Seas Comics—and Phantom Lady.

It has been argued by male writers that Baker's women were drawn to appeal to men, and while that is certainly probable, they also appealed strongly to a female audience. His dashing and glamorous women have a kind of 1940s noir movie-star appeal. He also had a flare for fashion and paid loving attention to details of clothing and hair styles, at a time when the average male comic artist was satisfied to clothe his heroines in a featureless red dress. It should be noted that Phantom Lady's costume of blue shorts and a matching halter top, much-heralded by male critics and fans as eye-poppingly sexy, contains more fabric than what the average woman wears today on the beach. There is not a navel to be seen.

Phantom Lady's most famous—or infamous—cover, no, 17. from 1948, was featured in **Fredric Wertham**'s famous condemnation of comic books, *Seduction of the Innocent*. The superheroine stands on a dock, tied to a post, but not very well tied, as she has already made headway in undoing her ropes. Looking directly at the readers, she flashes her black ray at them. Her halter top is cut lower than usual, and exposes a generous expanse of pointed breast. Wertham described the cover as producing "sexual stimulation by combining 'headlights' with the sadist's dream of tying up a woman." A perusal of Golden Age comic books will reveal far stronger and more objectionable bondage scenes, including those in which the woman's clothing is ripped and she is being whipped. An equal perusal of "bad girl" comics of the 1990s will reward the prurient reader with breasts twice the size of Phantom Lady's. Still, because of this inclusion in Wertham's book, although all issues of Phantom Lady are extremely valuable to collectors, the price on #17 is now astronomical.

Phantom Lady was at her most interesting when she interacted with other women, and this happened often in her stories. In "The Condemned Venus," from *Phantom Lady* #14, 1947, she actually gets herself arrested and put into prison so that she can free her friend Kitty Manders, who, believing her husband is a killer, has taken the rap for him and has been condemned to death for murder. Together, on the lam from the law, they kidnap the governor and find the real killers.

"A Shroud for the Bride," in the same issue, is a kind of dark Cinderella story. Porky Mead, an alcoholic millionaire, breaks three dates to attend a masquerade ball with a pretty waitress he has picked up. ("Porky an' me is gonna get married," says the waitress.) A shot rings out and his date falls to the ground, dead. Phantom Lady learns that the victim was wearing a costume meant for someone else—one of the three jealous women who had been stood up by Porky. Stealing the dead girl's shoe, she tries it on each of the woman, knowing the shoe will fit the murderer.

Phantom Lady was revived by **DC** in the 1970s (in the Freedom Fighters, along with other Quality characters) and still makes occasional appearances in her civilian identity as the grandmother of Manhunter Kate Spencer. Also, two successor Phantom Ladies, Dee Tyler and Stormy Knight, have since been published. Dee Tyler was written by Len Strazewski and drawn by Chuck Austen with an even skimpier costume than her predecessor. Stormy Knight was created by writer Justin Gray and artist Jimmy Palmiotti, based on notes from **Grant Morrison**. The character is remembered today by mostly male writers and fans as being outrageously over-the-top in blatant sexuality. A fresh look at the comic, especially compared to the more recent treatment of women in comics, will reveal strong representations of beautiful women, and more glamour than pornography.

*Trina Robbins*

**PLANETARY.** A 27-issue series published by the Wildstorm imprint of **DC Comics** and written by **Warren Ellis** with art by John Cassady, *Planetary* is both the name of the series and of the organization within the series that seeks to uncover the secret history of the **superhero** world in which it is set. The series began publication in 1999, but has been plagued with delays and taken multiple hiatuses over the 10 years between *Planetary* #1 and *Planetary* #27. Besides the series proper, three stand-alone, one-shot stories have also been published, *Planetary/The Authority: Ruling the World* (2000), *Planetary/JLA: Terra Occulta* (2002), and *Planetary/Batman: Night on Earth* (2003). While these are not essential to the main storyline, *Planetary/Batman: Night on Earth* did utilize the same creative team as that of the regular series and certainly reads as if it could be an issue of the series. *Planetary* has also been released in a series of collections: *Planetary: All over the World, and Other Stories* (Volume 1) collects *Planetary* #1–6, *Planetary: The Fourth Man* (Volume 2) collects *Planetary* #7–12, *Planetary: Leaving the 20th Century* (Volume 3) collects *Planetary* #13–18, *Planetary Vol. 4* collects *Planetary* #19–27, and *Planetary: Crossing Worlds* collects the stand-alone one-shot stories.

The Planetary Field Team, a three-person group of superhumans, is funded by the Planetary Foundation and consists of Elijah Snow, Jakita Wagner, and The Drummer. Snow possesses the ability to subtract heat from his immediate area, while Wagner enjoys super-strength, super-speed, and virtual invulnerability. The Drummer operates as something of an informational "black hole" in that all things, especially computers, give him information. For instance, even a cup of coffee indicates its temperature to him (*Planetary* #23). The members of the Planetary Field team have been described as "archaeologists of the impossible."

Planetary's agenda of aiding mankind and making a finer world with the knowledge it acquires puts it directly at odds with the four Voyagers, the secret masters of the world. The four comprise four superhumans, Randall Dowling, Jacob Greene, William Leather, and Kim Suskind, modeled after **Marvel Comics' Fantastic Four.** Here, Ellis indulges in a bit of commentary on the American comics market. The four dominating the world of Planetary beginning in 1961 is no coincidence; 1961 marks the year that Marvel began publishing the *Fantastic Four*. It is also the year that the superhero genre began its dominance, to the extent that virtually all other genres disappeared of the American comics market. "The things these scum have cost us since 1961 . . ." (*Planetary* #6) serves as a condemnation of superhero comics and the American comics market, as well as a lament of what was lost in their dominance of said market.

The overriding plot structure of the first 12 issues of the series concerns itself with the mystery surrounding the identity of the Fourth Man of Planetary. The resolution of this mystery changes the focus of Planetary's agenda from that of mystery archaeologists to that of combating the four and their interests. This puts not only the Planetary

Field Team, but the entire Planetary Foundation in direct conflict with the four who destroy an entire Brazilian Planetary office building in an attempt to kill Snow, Wagner, and the Drummer. Snow methodically removes two members of the four, Leather and Greene, before finally confronting Dowling and Suskind and retrieving all of their hoarded knowledge.

*Planetary* is unique with respect to its covers, which change in both format and style with every issue and lend themselves to the contents of each issue much more so than typical superhero comics. For instance, the cover of *Planetary* #2 alludes to Japanese monster movie posters, while *Planetary* #3 suggests the widescreen still of a Hong Kong action film. Other covers hint at **Neil Gaiman's Sandman** (*Planetary* #7), **Doc Savage** paperback reprints of the 1970s (*Planetary* #5), and 1950s monster cinema (*Planetary* #8).

In *Planetary*, Ellis digs at the roots of the superhero sub-genre, what he terms superhuman fiction, and spotlights many of the early 20th-century pulp antecedents for modern superheroes. He also utilizes thinly disguised versions of existing characters such as **Superman**, **Green Lantern**, **Wonder Woman**, the **Shadow**, **Tarzan**, Doc Savage, and the Lone Ranger in an attempt to show why these characters have endured. By stripping the characters back to their respective cores, Ellis illustrates why the "mad and beautiful ideas" that spawned these characters remain compelling decades later.

Ellis brings a modernist sensibility to *Planetary*. Snow, in particular, seems very much a representative modernist man cast adrift in a postmodern world, unable to initially place himself in that world. He suffers from the postmodern condition of a lack of historicity in that his memories (his past) have literally been taken from him, at least until he recovers both his memories and sense of purpose in *Planetary* #12. With or without his memories, though, his driving motivation remains to discover a history that has been lost or hidden, and to put the pieces of the puzzle of history back together. This is no more apparent than in the cover of *Planetary* #26, which depicts Snow staring at the reader, holding the last piece of the puzzle which comprises the cover. In discovering the secret history of the 20th century, he rediscovers not only his own history, but a unifying sense of purpose that will carry him far into the future. Snow is dedicated to keeping the world strange, as he believes it should be. He and the entire Planetary organization fight what the German sociologist Max Weber called rationalization, or the tendency of capitalism to strip the world of magic, reducing all aspects of life to a routine sameness.

**Selected Bibliography:** Ellis, Warren, and John Cassaday. *Planetary: All over the World, and Other Stories.* Vol. 1. La Jolla, CA: WildStorm Productions, 2000; Ellis, Warren, and John Cassaday. *Planetary: Leaving the 20th Century.* Vol. 3. La Jolla, CA: WildStorm Productions, 2004; Ellis, Warren, and John Cassaday. *Planetary: The Fourth Man.* Vol. 2. La Jolla, CA: WildStorm Productions, 2001; Ellis, Warren, and John Cassaday. *Planetary: Spacetime Archaeology.* Vol. 4. La Jolla, CA: WildStorm

Productions, 2010; Ellis, Warren, et al. *Planetary: Crossing Worlds*. La Jolla, CA: WildStorm Productions, 2004.

*Will Allred*

**PLASTIC MAN.** A **Quality Comics superhero**, Plastic Man first appeared in *Police Comics* #1 (August 1941), written and drawn by Jack Cole. In the first story, readers are introduced to Eel O'Brien, a career criminal and former orphan. On a routine break-in at a chemical company, O'Brien is shot by a night watchman and falls into a vat of acid. Abandoned by his gang, a disoriented O'Brien passes out near a mountain. He awakens to find himself in a monastery, where a kind monk hides him from questioning police. Following this act of charity, O'Brien vows to reform. This vow receives a boost when he discovers the effects of the acid—he can now bend, stretch, or mold his body into any shape. Altering his face to form a new identity, he begins wearing goggles and a suit of red, yellow, and black. In this guise, he adopts the name Plastic Man. As O'Brien, he now works undercover to capture criminals, beginning with his old gang.

After his first appearance, Plastic Man soon became one of Quality's most prominent characters. While his origin had appeared in the final pages of *Police* #1, Plastic Man took over as the lead feature of the monthly series with issue #5. At the same time, the page count on the strip increased from 6 to 13. This was followed by a self-titled series. The undated *Plastic Man* #1 was released in 1943. Issue #2 was dated August 1944, with a third following in spring 1946. From that point, the series followed a quarterly schedule until #12 (July 1948), when it became bi-monthly.

While other superheroes had a rigid format, Plastic Man could become anything. This allowed the strip to have a looser, wilder form of storytelling. The increasingly comedic bent was aided by the introduction of sidekick Woozy Winks, a portly bumbler who assisted the hero on his adventures in *Police Comics* #13.

Initially, Plastic Man fought few super-villains, as most of his foes were racketeers and gangsters. As Cole found his footing, both the drawings and the stories got broader and more exaggerated. He defied expectations of the superhero genre, with villains such as Sadly-Sadly Sanders, a man so pathetic people could not help but throw their money at him (*Plastic Man* #26), and The Green Terror, a gardener whose creations include a plant that breathes enough carbon dioxide to smother a man (*Police Comics* #58).

This experimentation extended past the stories to the look of the series. At a time when many crime-fighters were interchangeable square-jawed tough guys, Plastic Man's bright, cartoony appearance stood out. He fooled criminals into thinking that he was a lamp, or a table, or a rug, only to revert to human form and catch them red-handed. As Cole's visual style developed, the strip became increasingly packed with visual information. Panels often contained several sight gags which could be easily missed by the casual reader.

Despite the unique style of the strip, *Plastic Man* still relied heavily on superhero conventions for much of its humor. Consequently, the series fell out of favor along with other superhero titles in the early 1950s. *Police Comics* #102 (October 1950) was Plastic Man's last appearance, as it switched to a straight police procedural with the following issue. *Plastic Man* itself continued for another six years, even becoming monthly with #49 (November 1954).

For the last several years, however, both series had become Jack Cole creations in name only. Beginning in the late 1940s, a succession of ghost writers and artists had taken over. In 1956, after several years of lackluster sales, Quality Comics closed its doors. *Plastic Man* was published until the very end, with a total of 64 issues. He would soon find a home at a new company, as **DC Comics** acquired the company's stable of superheroes. It wasn't until 1966 that Plastic Man received a new solo series, however. Written by Arnold Drake and drawn by various penciler included **Gil Kane,** it ran for 10 issues, ending in 1968. In the years that followed, the character made guest appearances in various series. A second attempt at a solo series was made in 1976, written by Steve Skeates with art by **Ramona Fradon**. It too lasted for 10 issues, numbered 11 through 20. Despite these series, Plastic Man's most prominent appearances in his first 30 years as a DC property were not in comic books at all. *The Plastic Man Comedy/Adventure Show* aired on ABC Saturday mornings from 1979 through 1981.

Following his integration into the DC universe proper after *Crisis on Infinite Earths*, the character got a major push with a four-issue miniseries (1988–89). This series, written by Phil Foglio and drawn by Hilary Barta, added a dark edge as it revealed that the chemical infected the hero's brain to see everything in a cartoony way. He was no longer simply light-hearted. Instead, he was brain-damaged.

The latter part of the next decade saw Plastic Man back to his old self as he joined the **Justice League of America. Grant Morrison** and later writers mostly used the character as comic relief. Some darkness remained, however. During his run, writer Joe Kelly revealed that Plastic Man had a son from a brief relationship 10 years earlier. The boy, named Luke, later took the name Offspring and began operating as a superhero in his own right.

In 2004, DC debuted a new Plastic Man series written and drawn by **Kyle Baker.** Unlike previous revival attempts, it was more in the vein of the **Golden Age** series. Plastic Man was once again a lawman (now an FBI Agent) operating as a double agent in his O'Brien identity, aided by the long-unseen Woozy Winks and the sensible Agent Morgan. The focus was on wild antics, and the series featured exaggerated versions of many other DC characters. It won the 2004 **Eisner Award** for Best New Series. However, DC canceled it in 2006 after 20 issues. Since that time, Plastic Man has once again been relegated to guest-star status.

*Anthony Strand*

**PLAYBOY, THE.** This collection of comics by Canadian cartoonist **Chester Brown** reveals his adolescent misadventures in suburbia while discovering, obsessing over, and, eventually, accepting his relationship to pornography. Originally serialized in the *Vortex*

*Comics* editions of his series *Yummy Fur* (which began as a self-published mini-comic), this autobiographical tale demarcated a split between his earlier, slightly surreal work with characters like *Ed the Happy Clown*.

Published by Drawn & Quarterly as a 170-page collection in 1992, *The Playboy* begins in 1975 when Brown is 15, growing up in a suburb of Montreal called Châteauguay. The opening panel centers on an illustration of what will later be revealed as a *Playboy* centerfold model. The second panel takes place in the clouds as Brown's id, (represented by a shirtless caricature of the cartoonist with demon wings), is lounging in thin air. His id appropriately serves not only as the narrator of the story, but also as an instigator.

As Brown's devilish id continues its narration, we see the young protagonist attending a church service. Brown is occupied with fantasies concerning a nude model he had seen on the cover of *Playboy* magazine in the convenience store the day before. After church ends and he has lunch at home with his family, Brown rushes back to the store to purchase his very first issue of *Playboy*, trembling, sweaty hands and all.

Thus begins a vicious cycle. Brown's near-addiction to pornography starts a binge-and-purge habit as a young man pursues self-discovery. "Chester managed to avoid the temptation of buying last month's *Playboy* but this month . . . well here he comes with something hidden under his shirt."

Each *Playboy* magazine Brown purchases, he hides under a plank of wood in a field or forest. As time passes, Brown rarely finds his latest issues left untouched when he returns, which leads Brown to experience cathartic guilt and the aforementioned *Playboy* purging paranoia. Time passes as Brown graduates high school and attends college where he continues his pornographic habits. This time, however, the purging is in response to his first real relationship with a woman, so he does not have to lie when she inquires about his pornography consumption. They break up amicably after several years and Brown finds himself having to fantasize about nude *Playboy* models in his second romantic relationship with a woman: "With my next girlfriend I found that in order to maintain an erection I had to imagine that I was having sex with one of my favorite playmates."

Brown comes to the discovery that he prefers masturbation to the actual sex act. At the end of this comics collection Brown confesses he maintains a four-inch thick stack of his favorite "photos of naked women," ultimately coming to terms with his formerly "guilty" habit and sexuality.

What rings true as a timeless facet in Brown's work concerning *The Playboy* is the nakedness of the story, his ability to allow himself to be the character whose beliefs and behavior are out of step with his rules, as he tries desperately to figure it all out. Brown's autobiographical work, beginning with *The Playboy*, sparked a confessional comics renaissance not seen since the hedonistic grandfather of autobiographical comics, **Robert Crumb**, began to lay it all out on the table in the swinging 1960s.

*See also:* Underground and Adult Comics; Memoir/Slice-of-Life Themes

**Selected Bibliography:** Brown, Chester. *The Playboy.* Montréal: Drawn & Quarterly, 1992.

*Jared L. Olmsted*

**POLITICS AND POLITICIANS.** Whether they feature **superheroes**, spy smashers, or countercultural bomb-throwers, comic books have from their earliest days been inextricably bound up with politics. Like other forms of mass culture, comic books both reflect and participate in the public sphere, registering and helping to shape popular opinion about political questions such as civil rights, international relations, and the role of government in private life.

Comic books emerged in the 1930s, the era of the Great Depression and the New Deal, a period when many Americans began to question and revise their understandings of American values and to deepen their engagements with politics. When superheroes—powerful crusaders usually created by working-class writers and artists—emerged, their adventures were often motivated by a blend of populism and leftism. **Superman**'s earliest foes included crooked industrialists and politicians whose most nefarious quality was their indifference to the economic hardships of ordinary Americans. Indeed, one early story featured Superman speaking up on behalf of a young juvenile delinquent, blaming his troubles partly on his miserable social situation, and eventually demolishing the slum the young man called home to make way for government housing (**Action Comics** #8, 1930). When Superman's popular success led to a horde of imitators such as **Green Lantern** and Hourman, these new characters often also emulated his politics. Comics historian Bradford Wright notes that although comics creators rarely criticized national political figures directly, their focus on "the failings of local government and the dangers of provincial demagogues" highlighted the "need for outside intervention and tacitly stressed a common interest between public welfare and a strong federal government" (24).

As World War II intensified in Europe, comic books in the United States shifted their emphasis from the internal problems of the nation to the external threat of the Axis powers. Comics helped to mold national consensus about the possibility of U.S. participation in the war. Perhaps the best-known example in this regard is the cover of **Joe Simon** and **Jack Kirby's** *Captain America* #1, released early in 1941, an iconic image of the patriotic hero socking Adolf Hitler in the jaw. Although **Nazi** villains were not unusual in comics by 1941, it was also common for superheroes to battle against foreign agents who wanted to drag the United States into a fight that many Americans thought it should avoid. The publication of *Captain America* #1 brought that tension home to Simon and Kirby in a very direct way: while the comic was a major success, they also received hate mail and even death threats from isolationists and Nazi sympathizers (Wright 36). Captain America was not the first patriotic hero, nor would he be the last, as a multitude of characters—whether star-spangled or not—leapt into the war effort after the bombing of Pearl Harbor. As William Savage observes, "comic books became an integral part of the Allied propaganda machine, emphasizing the need for a maximum war effort by portraying the enemy as the inhuman offspring of a vast and pernicious evil" (10). Japanese soldiers in particular were often caricatured as monstrous, slavering beasts.

After the close of the war, superhero comic books slipped into escapism, social irrelevance, and general unpopularity. Not even the menace of communism provided a compelling motivation for superheroes in this era. A telling example is that of Joe Simon and Jack Kirby's *Fighting American* (1954–55), whose patriotic title character did not meet with the same success as his more famous predecessor. The Fighting American began as an earnest communist-smasher, but the chronicles of his exploits—which involved vanquishing foes such as "Poison Ivan" and "Super-Khakalovitch"—quickly turned to lighthearted **satire** of **Cold War** political attitudes. Neither approach was enough to keep the book afloat. Among the new genres that arose to take the place of superhero tales, none was more engaged with political issues of the post-war era than **crime** and **horror** comics, especially those published by **EC** Comics. EC titles spun often grisly tales of murder and betrayal, but their stories also often took the United States to task for failing to live up to the ideals for which it had so recently gone to war, and for succumbing to the paranoia of anticommunist politicians such as Joseph McCarthy. *Shock SuspenStories* (1952–55), primarily featuring tales written by **William Gaines** and **Al Feldstein**, was the primary venue for EC's most pointed social commentary. Stories such as "In Gratitude" (#11, 1953) and "The Whipping" (#14, 1954) took on the evils of racism and segregation, while "The Patriots!" tackled the issue of anticommunist hysteria. EC's **war comics**, *Frontline Combat* and *Two-Fisted Tales*, edited and usually written by **Harvey Kurtzman**, tended to emphasize the futility of war and to critique post-war American exceptionalism. Even the more fantastic genres were sometimes pressed into the service of EC's social satire: *Weird Fantasy* #18 (1952) features an African American astronaut's exploration of an alien world divided and diminished by segregation.

Although EC's frequent renderings of decapitations and other forms of dismemberment were among the more overt targets for anti–comic book crusaders like Dr. **Fredric Wertham** and Senator Estes Kefauver, the **Comics Code** that emerged from this time of crisis did as much to blunt EC's political commentary as it did to tame its representations of violence. Among the code's regulations were prohibitions against depicting politicians, government officials, and other authority figures in a negative light. Although Kurtzman took his penchant for satirical broadsides to the wildly popular *Mad* magazine, the loss of EC's dissenting voice meant that most comic books in the later 1950s and early 1960s continued to enforce a vision of a Cold War-era United States whose major problems stemmed not from internal strife, but from the forces of communism. Although the short-lived war comic *Blazing Combat* (1965–66), from **Warren Publications**, questioned the morality of the Vietnam War in a manner that recalled Kurtzman's work, other war comics such as Dell's *Jungle War*

*Stories* and **Charlton Comics'** *Fightin' Army* portrayed the conflict as a noble and necessary struggle against the forces of communism. The Cold War was an important backdrop for **Marvel's** revitalization of the superhero in the early 1960s: The accident in space that gives the **Fantastic Four** their powers is the result of their urgent mission to beat the Soviets to the Moon, and superheroes such as **Iron Man** and Captain America found themselves facing off against communist enemies far more threatening than those so easily trounced by the Fighting American. However, as Matthew J. Costello observes, by the end of the 1960s, the Cold War consensus was beginning to fray, and "the virtue of the government also [became] more ambiguous" (74). Both Marvel and **DC** found that they could not keep representations of real-world political unrest out of their comics, but their responses to it were always carefully calibrated. Frequently, superhero comics presented exaggerated versions of right-wing and left-wing responses to political issues, with the star of the book advocating a moderate middle ground. **Batman** and **Spider-Man** both found themselves confronting militant activist groups with whom they sympathized but whose methods they deplored (*Amazing Spider-Man* #68, 1969, *Batman* #230, 1971). As Bradford Wright observes, "in an American society facing deepening political divisions, Marvel's superheroes worked to preserve what remained of the vital center. DC's superheroes tended to take the same position" (235).

Although mainstream comics were constrained in their ability to respond to the political upheavals of the day, a new model of comics creation and distribution was emerging in the late 1960s, one that offered its artists enormous aesthetic and ideological freedom: **underground comics**, or "**comix**." Because they were primarily distributed through venues such as "head" shops and record stores instead of through news vendors, and were thus free of the restrictions of the Comics Code, the undergrounds had license to offer graphic depictions of sexuality, violence, and drug use. Comix creators gravitated toward pointed satire of American mass culture and politics as well. The underground comics as a group offered no single coherent political vision; many were only "political" in the broad sense that their celebration of the counterculture functioned as an implicit critique of mainstream American values. However, within the diverse and idiosyncratic group of underground creators were several artists who placed politics at the center of their work. These included Manuel "Spain" Rodriguez, whose Marxist hero "Trashman" waged revolutionary violence against a fascist United States government in a bleak, dystopian future. Skip Williamson regularly satirized leading political figures of the day in the pages of *Bijou Funnies* (1969–70); he also brought together a group of underground cartoonists to create *Conspiracy Capers* (1969), a comic dedicated to defending the Chicago Seven. Explicitly political anthology titles including *Slow Death Funnies* (1969) and *All-Atomic Comics* (1976) leveled criticisms at a variety of powerful and destructive forces in American life, including the nuclear power industry and corporate agribusiness. Female underground cartoonists such as **Trina Robbins** and Lee Mars published a wide array of titles that brought **feminism** to comics, including *It Ain't Me, Babe* (1970) and *Wimmen's Comix* (1972), which dealt with political issues of particular interest to women, including reproductive rights, workplace discrimination, and the sexism prevalent in American culture—even in the counterculture. Gay and lesbian-focused titles such as Roberta Gregory's *Dynamite Damsels* (1976) and the anthology *Gay Comix* (1980–91), created by Howard Cruse, provided a venue for post-Stonewall reconsiderations of the intersections of the personal and political.

Although underground comics contained the most detailed and sustained treatments of the counterculture in the 1960s and 1970s, some mainstream writers and artists sought to examine the ways in which the counterculture was re-shaping the political landscape in the United States. The most notable of these was Captain America creator Joe Simon, who was responsible for two unusual, original, and short-lived series at DC Comics that explored the phenomenon of active, sometimes radical, political engagement among young people: *Brother Power the Geek* (1968) and *Prez* (1973–74). Lasting a mere two issues, *Brother Power* starred a tailor's dummy who comes to life in a hippie community and sets out to understand the nature of his existence. Simon's ambivalence about the counterculture is plainly evident: Although the hippies are portrayed as friendly and accepting, they are also depicted as directionless. While Brother Power appreciates his new friends, he is motivated to make something of himself, first running for political office (where he intends to promote "Love, Peace . . . Flower Power" (#1) and then becoming plant foreman at a factory making missiles for space exploration—where he eventually employs his hippie friends on the assembly line. Developing and extending some of its predecessor's themes, *Prez* is an exploration of the relationship between youthful idealism and political pragmatism, and of the ways in which revolutionary or subversive political energies can be appropriated and redirected by those who would see the status quo preserved. Its title character, Prez Rickard, "First Teen President of the U.S.A.," is swept into the U.S. Senate and then the White House following the 1971 constitutional amendment extending suffrage to 18-year-olds. Winning the presidency with a "Truth-and-Love campaign which polarize[s] the generations" (issue #1) Prez initially seems to represent a radical break with political orthodoxy, as evidenced by his diverse and unusual cabinet: Prez enlists his own mother to serve as vice-president, and he recruits a (rather stereotypically characterized) Native American youth named Eagle Free to serve as director of the Federal Bureau of Investigations. Yet though he promises a new and peaceful approach to the problems of the United States, his eventual compromises on the use of military force turn his once enthusiastic constituency of young people against him. Although the series ended before Simon could explore this tension further, *Prez* still stands as a fascinating consideration of the United States' political landscape in a complex time.

Another offbeat comic from a mainstream publisher which frequently dealt with political issues was Marvel's **Howard the Duck** (1976–79, 1986), written by Steve Gerber. In 1976, the anthropomorphic title character decided to mount a third party campaign for the presidency of the United States, appealing to a public uninspired by either Jimmy Carter or Gerald Ford. After dumping a smooth-talking campaign adviser who has written all of his speeches before finding out what his candidate believes on the issues, Howard chooses to run as a "people's candidate" (#8) who rejects the extremes of "animalistic conservatism" and "jellyfish liberalism" (#7) and favors educating and empowering individual voters to understand and make decisions about matters of war and economics. His campaign mainly functions as a vehicle for Howard's scathing critique of the cheap materialism and consumerism of American life. As one shocked voter remarks, "My god, he's telling the truth! He'll be dead in a week!" (#8). Although Howard is driven from the race in short order by a phony sex scandal, his candidacy served as a way for writer Gerber to satirize American politics as shallow, superficial, and ultimately destructive to democracy.

Political questions began to move to the forefront in the superhero comics of the 1970s as well. Costumed adventurers were beginning to find a political voice, and in most cases they were critical of the status quo in the United States. Writer **Dennis O'Neil** brought an earnest political relevance to his run on DC's *Green Lantern/Green Arrow*; in O'Neil's hands, the title characters frequently engaged in adventures that brought them into conflict over liberal and conservative versions of the American dream. O'Neil's premiere issue (#76, 1970) featured liberal gadfly Green Arrow chiding his sometime partner, Green Lantern, for his simple-minded approach to law and order—an approach that neglects the larger social problems underlying crime, including political corruption and racism. As an African American man tells Green Lantern, "I been readin' about you . . . How you work for the blue skins . . . And how on a planet someplace you helped out the orange skins . . . and you done considerable for the purple skins! Only there's skins you never bothered with—! The black skins! I want to know . . . How come?!" The heroes set out to investigate what Green Arrow calls the "hideous moral cancer [that] is rotting our very souls," taking on issues such as industrial pollution, the powers of the mass media, and the plight of Native Americans.

In Steve Englehart and Sal Buscema's *Captain America*, the title character vanquishes a racist, red-baiting 1950s version of himself, a victory which seems to suggest a rejection of a jingoistic, nationalistic American past (#153–56, 1972). However, Cap's further adventures complicated that cautiously optimistic conclusion: the "Secret Empire" storyline that ran through issues 169–73 (1974) reflected Watergate-era disillusionment with the American government and a growing cynicism with the political process itself. In these issues, Captain America finds himself the subject of a vicious smear campaign by the Committee to Regain America's Principles. CRAP—a clear allusion to Richard Nixon's CREEP (Committee to Re-Elect the President)—runs advertisements seeking to convince the public that the Sentinel of Liberty is a dangerous vigilante working in opposition to America's principles. As Cap and his partner the Falcon discover, CRAP is merely a front group for a shadowy cabal known as the Secret Empire, who intend to take over the United States. In a dramatic final confrontation in the Oval Office of the White House, Number One reveals himself to Captain America as a high-ranking politician who hungers for power that would not be "constrained by legalities" (#175). The revelation shakes Cap's faith in the very concept of America and leads him to take on a new identity, that of Nomad, the Man without a Country, for a short time.

Although not all of Captain America's adventures in the political realm were so dark, they did often continue to reflect a dissatisfaction with the limitations of the status quo in American politics. In the waning days of Jimmy Carter's presidency, Captain America even mulled a run at the nation's highest office himself. *Captain America* #250 (1980), written by Roger Stern and Don Perlin, features a story in which the New Populist Party seeks to recruit the hero to run on their ticket and defy the deeply entrenched two-party system. As one enthusiastic NPP member tells him, "People wouldn't have to settle for the lesser of two evils—they'd actually have someone to vote *for!*" Cap eventually decides against running, believing that he is better suited to preserve the American dream than to engage with the daily compromises of political reality.

Few politically focused comics of the 1980s shared the mostly upbeat attitude of Stern's Captain America. British comics scribe **Alan Moore** extrapolated from Prime Minister Margaret Thatcher's extreme conservatism to create the bleak, dystopian future England of *V for Vendetta* (1982–88), while his run on *Swamp Thing* featured a character, Nukeface, who becomes poisonous to those around him when he unwittingly drinks improperly stored toxic waste; pages crowded with newspaper clippings about the dangers of toxic waste suggested the urgency of the problem (#35–36, 1985). In *The Dark Knight Returns* (1986), **Frank Miller** portrays **Superman** as the passive dupe of a corrupt United States government led by a glib Ronald Reagan. The 1980s also saw the rise of **alternative comics**; distributed through the burgeoning direct market but creator-driven and unaffiliated with the major publishers, alternative comics faced few impediments to engaging with political questions in a sophisticated manner. **Howard Chaykin's** *American Flagg!* (1983–89) satirized a United States in which government-controlled mass culture had robbed American citizens of their ability to uphold the responsibilities of participatory democracy. In the first volume of *Love and Rockets* (1982–96) many of Gilbert **Hernandez's** "Palomar" stories critiqued United States involvement in Latin America. **Dave Sim's** *Cerebus* (1977–2004) began as a pulp genre pastiche but eventually became a complicated and controversial treatment of the themes of corrupting power, the intersection of religion and politics, gender roles, and the relationship between politics and art. Another important creator from the world of alternative comics, Paul Chadwick, began in the 1990s to use his sensitive man-monster **Concrete** to explore political questions. The most notable result was *Concrete: Think Like a Mountain* (1996) a miniseries which dealt with the ethical implications of extremism in the environmental movement.

In recent years, treatments of political questions in comics have often been inspired by the attacks on the World Trade Center and the Pentagon on September 11, 2001 and the subsequent wars in Afghanistan and Iraq, as well as by domestic debates over civil rights. **Art Spiegelman's** *In the Shadow of No Towers* (2004) not only reflects upon the trauma of 9/11 but also criticizes the way in which the George W. Bush administration exploited the attacks for political gain. Superheroes, always potent metaphors for the uses and abuses of power, have often been pressed into the service of political narratives. Superman villain Lex Luthor briefly served as President of the United States, and Iron Man took a turn as Secretary of Defense. **Brian K. Vaughan**'s ongoing series *Ex Machina* (2004–) offers a more sophisticated take on superheroes in politics; it stars Mitchell Hundred, also known as the superhero the Great Machine, who finds himself serving as mayor of New York after he successfully defends one of the World Trade Center towers from Al-Qaeda. *Ex Machina* deftly complicates the distinction between the superhuman action of costumed adventurers and the all-too-human process of politics. Perhaps the highest profile mainstream comic book to tackle politics in recent years is Marvel's 2006 miniseries *Civil War*. Its central conflict, involving a law requiring superhumans to register with and become agents of the government after a disastrous accident, has been widely interpreted as an allegory for the ongoing debate over the role of civil rights in a time of war. Not every comic to deal with politics in recent years has been so grimly serious, however. In early 2009, comic book enthusiast Barack Obama made an appearance in the pages of *Amazing* **Spider-Man** #583, in a story in which Spider-Man thwarts his old foe the Chameleon's attempt to disrupt Obama's inauguration—and gets a fist bump from the President in return.

**Selected Bibliography:** Costello, Matthew J. *Secret Identity Crisis: Comic Books and the Unmasking of Cold War America*. New York: Continuum, 2009; Danky, James, and Denis Kitchen, eds. *Underground Classics: The Transformation of Comics into Comix*. New York: Abrams ComicArts, 2009; Estren, Mark James. *A History of Underground Comics*. San Francisco: Straight Arrow, 1974; Rosenkranz, Patrick. *Rebel Visions: The Underground Comix Revolution*. Seattle: Fantagraphics, 2008; Sabin, Roger. *Comics, Comix and Graphic Novels: A History of Comic Art*. New York: Phaidon, 1996; Savage, William, Jr. *Commies, Cowboys, and Jungle Queens: Comic Books and America, 1945– 1954*. Middletown, CT: Wesleyan, 1998; Wiater, Stanley, and Stephen R. Bissette. *Comic Book Rebels: Conversations with the Creators of the New Comics*. New York: Donald I. Fine, 1993; Wright, Bradford. *Comic Book Nation: The Transformation of Youth Culture in America*. Baltimore: Johns Hopkins, 2003.

*Brannon Costello*

**POST-APOCALYPTIC NARRATIVES.** Though "apocalypse" or "Armageddon" originally refers to the Christian concept of the end of the known world as a result of the war between the Anti-Christ and Jesus Christ, a post-apocalyptic narrative is not necessarily spiritually derived. While some stories invoke Christian motifs and theology, others do not. Typically, the term "post-apocalyptic" refers to a world that has suffered a single or multiple cataclysmic events. Therefore, post-apocalyptic narratives speculate about life after a civilization's destruction and how the survivors attempt to rebuild civilization. These narratives often reflect the fears and anxieties of the times that produce them; projecting the concerns and anxieties in question into an extreme all-destructive power or event. The civilization's destruction can be a result of internal or external threats. Common triggers can include any one or more of the following: environmental devastation or destruction, plague, alien invasion, war, nuclear destruction or radiation, and genetic contamination.

Post-apocalyptic narratives are often confused with dystopian narratives but are distinctly different. Post-apocalyptic stories focus on the rebuilding or dealing with the destruction of organized civilization, whereas dystopian narratives deal with problematic ongoing societies that are often highly structured. There is also occasion to lump post-apocalyptic narratives with invasion or conquest narratives which again, do not necessarily fit together thematically. Therefore, stories from the classic comic strips and pulp fiction of *Buck Rogers* (1929) and *Flash Gordon* (1934) are not classified as post-apocalyptic, because civilizations are still intact.

Several authors contributed to the development of the post-apocalyptic genre and therefore, influenced comics' own developments of genre conventions. Mary Shelley's *The Last Man* (1826) is marked as the first modern post-apocalyptic narrative, though it was never as popular as later stories. Richard Jefferies's *After London* (1885) was similarly popular at the time but did not necessarily have long-lasting influence. By contrast, H. G. Wells's *The Time Machine* (1895), *War of the Worlds* (1898) and many more of his writings were popular throughout the 20th century and influenced plotlines for comics, films, and sequel novels by other authors. However, the early 20th century had a good share of popular post-apocalyptic narratives including M. P. Shiel's *The Purple Cloud* (1901), William Hope Hodgson's *The Night Land* (1912), Jack London's *The Scarlet Plague* (1912), Karel Capek's play, *R.U.R.* (1921), and Edgar Rice Burroughs's *The Moon Men* series (1926).

One could argue that the earliest comic to deal with a post-apocalyptic event was the **Superman** narrative, given that it takes place in the aftermath of the destruction of the planet Krypton. Meanwhile, Superman, like many **superheroes** after him, continually fought the apocalyptic destruction of society. On occasion, superhero stories will venture into post-apocalyptic settings, but usually as an alternative-universe or time-traveling accidents such as the story "Superman Under the Red Sun!" in *Action Comics* #300, where Superman is sent to the future by his enemies. Some one-million years in the future, Superman finds a decayed world where humans are virtually nonexistent and Earth's sun had become red.

From the rise of comic books through the early 1950s, few comics featured post-apocalyptic stories. Featured in *Hit Comics* #1 (1940), the "Blaze Barton" feature was essentially the first post-apocalyptic narrative in comics, though its direction and themes only marginally resemble how the genre is understood today. Initially the story revolved around Blaze Barton, his boss Professor Solis and Solis's daughter Avis, who have created a fortified city to protect against the increasing heat as Earth tilts extremely close to the sun. When they emerge from the city, they find that much of humanity is dead and Earth's vegetation and animals have mutated. Early plots had them rebuilding Earth while also encountering new monstrous or humanoid creatures. However, by *Hit Comics* #5, Earth had prospered enough that Blaze was sent on to explore the galaxy. Blaze Barton continued in *Hit Comics* until issue #13 when the series abruptly stopped.

Many comics stories have dealt with the eminent destruction of Earth, but it is typically either saved at the last minute by the story's protagonist, or the end of the world serves as the punch line for the story. Often, these latter stories were there to prove a point or teach a cautionary lesson. The stories revealed how Earth fell into decay, but few went beyond that to establish any substantial "life after the end of the world" scenarios. For example, in *Weird Tales of the Future* #6 (1953), the story "Plaything" features a perfect utopian Earth with civilization prospering until unexplainable environmental devastation destroys society. To explain the destruction, the narrator pulls back to show Earth as a toy for a child-like god who has decided to play catch with it. These kinds of stories attempted to reinforce the unexplained forces of the universe and how susceptible humankind was to the whims of nature.

Other narratives were informed by a sense of the futility of all human undertakings. These particularly were influenced by the destruction and devastation of World War II. In "Return" from *Weird Science* #5 (1951), the story focuses on a shuttle of scientists that leaves Earth just prior to atomic war, and returns some 500,000 years later to see if life still exists. They encounter a world of oversized humans who had not technologically progressed beyond the world in which the travelers had left. When they inquire as to what happened, they discover that the world is ignorant of the long ago atomic war and trace their history back only 200,000 years. The story ends with the present-day scientists, aware of impending doom, deciding to take a shuttle into space; thereby creating a cycle of avoiding or ignoring the destruction. "Flight of the Future" from *Weird Tales of the Future* #2 (1952) also presents a desolate future. The story tells of a murderer who escapes to a future by volunteering for suspended animation. He reawakens 20,000 years in the future, when humanity has decayed into hulking imbeciles. The only human alive turns out to be the man he believed he had killed in the past. In the final scene, the two last intelligent humans kill one another, leaving the lumbering masses to further devolve.

While the **Comics Code** in 1954 did not specifically forbid post-apocalyptic narratives, Part A, Section 6 states that "In every instance good shall triumph over evil and the criminal punished for his misdeeds," and Part B, Section 2 states that "Inclusion of stories dealing with evil shall be used or shall be published only where the intent is to illustrate a moral issue and in no case shall evil be presented alluringly nor as to injure the sensibilities of the reader." Such restrictions severely limited the types of narratives told, since the destruction of civilization by most means implied evil triumphing over good. Publishers often avoided this potential conundrum by placing post-apocalyptic stories on other planets, thereby bypassing any debate about the moral representation of a destroyed Earth. The main exception to this came in the form of the **Classics Illustrated** adaptation of *The Time Machine* (1956), which followed the published adaptation of Wells's *The War of the Worlds* (1955).

However, the mid-20th century was awash in post-apocalyptic themes in books, radio, and film. Many started as novels only to be turned into films (and some even comics) later on. Films such as *War of the Worlds* (1953), *The Time Machine* (1960),

*The Last Man on Earth* (1964), *Planet of the Apes* (1968), and *The Omega Man* (1971) all started as novels but eventually made their way into comics.

The comics industry was still capable of creating its own original material in this genre as well. **DC Comics** began the story of the Atomic Knights starting in *Strange Adventures* #117 (1960). After civilization's demise in the Hydrogen War of 1986, the Atomic Knights, under Sergeant Gardner Grayle, fight against the Black Baron, the ruler of a small Midwest fiefdom. These characters were featured in 15 stories and then occasionally appeared in the *Hercules Unbound* series (1977). DC Comics also launched *Kamandi: The Last Boy on Earth* (1972), which centers on a youth who lives in a world where anthropomorphic animals dominate the world, often stalking him as prey. The story had grown out of the story, "The Last Enemy," in the anthology comic *Alarming Tales* #1 (1957). In 1964, Gold Key Comics launched *Mighty Samson*, a series following a hide-clad warrior wandering the northeast region of the United States after a nuclear war. The series ran intermittently and barely made it to issue #32 (1982). **Marvel Comics** also played with post-apocalyptic themes in the 1970s with its creation of the character Deathlok in *Astonishing Tales* #25 (1974). After a fatal wound, Luther Manning is resurrected into the cyborgnetic body, Deathlok, in a future where the United States has all but been destroyed by factions. Eventually, Manning returns to his original time, but for a while he attempts to right the wrongs of the disheveled future. In 1975, **Charlton Comics** ran *Doomsday +1*, a 12 issue series in which a nuclear war results in the near annihilation of mankind; the crew of a returning space shuttle finds themselves in a very different world than the one they left.

From the 1980s to the 2000s, the standard triggers for an apocalypse continued to be ecological or environmental disaster, war (nuclear or otherwise), plague, or, particularly in the 2000s, **zombies**. Ironically, this range represented the Biblical Four Horsemen of the Apocalypse: Pestilence, War, Famine, and Death. The other major theme to emerge at this time, almost never addressed or referenced previously in comics, was post-apocalyptic worlds based upon religious or spiritual beliefs. Series such as *Curse of the Spawn* (1996), *Just a Pilgrim* (2000), *Ascend* (2004), and *Therefore Repent* (2008) all rely heavily on specific Christian elements of the build up to and aftermath of the Apocalypse. This was in part fueled by the rise in popularity of Christian fiction, particularly apocalyptic fiction, including *The New York Times* best-selling series *Left Behind*, by Tim LaHaye and Jerry Jenkins. Other series have spoofed the religious-oriented apocalypse, including *Jesus Hates Zombies* (2007) from Alterna Comics. This collection of shorts features the second coming of Jesus, a bat-wielding, jeans-wearing wanderer of a nearly abandoned Earth dishing out death to zombie horders.

*Xenozoic Tales* (1987) best represents the ecological disaster narrative. Environmental devastation and a series of cataclysmic natural disasters force humanity to resorts to underground cities for nearly six centuries. Upon reemerging, they discover that the world has been reclaimed by dinosaurs and other life forms, leaving humanity to attempt to recreate civilization. The war motif can be found in *Ex-Mutants* (1986), a series that takes place in the future after war has destroyed civilization and mutated the population. Five genetically-corrected people (ex-mutants) are sent to help bring hope to humanity, though with little success. *Y: The Last Man* (2002) illustrates the plague theme in post-apocalyptic narratives. After the near-instant violent death of the male population, Yorick, the sole male survivor in a world of women, works with others to figure out what happened and how to keep the human race alive.

The series *Deadworld* first appeared in 1987 and has continued to be published sporadically through the 2000s. Here, a zombie apocalypse is triggered when a portal is opened that ushers in King Zombie and a horde of zombies that wreak havoc upon the world. The series has been praised more for its violence and gruesome drawings than its plotline. By contrast, **Robert Kirkman's *The Walking Dead*** series (2003–) focuses more on the humans in the wake of zombies destroying the known world and has continued to receive acclaim from the industry.

Both British comics and Japanese **manga** have also had prominent influence in shaping post-apocalyptic narratives for American comics. The British **science fiction** weekly comic series, *2000 AD* (1977) has featured numerous narratives dealing life after civilization's demise. Yet the most influential series to come out of *2000 AD* is inarguable "Judge Dredd," first appearing in *2000 AD* #2 and in every issue since. After the "Apocalypse War," the world has broken down into giant city-states barely maintained by the Judge system: law officials who act as judge, jury, and executioner to any violators. Though the comic series never gained serious ground in American culture, it was used as source material for a big-production Hollywood film of the same name in 1995. Judge Dredd in some ways evoked similar themes and landscapes to those explored by authors such as Philip K. Dick and William Gibson, where despite a world with increasing technology, world systems continue to break down in the face of corporate greed and manipulation, a decaying public sphere, and increased dependence on technology that reoriented life to the point of being foreign to its readers. To this end, *Tank Girl* drew more on contemporary visions of the punk and popular culture when it appeared in *Deadline* (1988). The series focuses primarily on a former bounty-hunter who is now hunted by others. As the title suggests, she commandeers and drives a tank through her adventures in the ruined landscapes of civilization. Finally, **Alan Moore's *V for Vendetta*** (1982–88), while perhaps best viewed as a dystopian narrative, depicts a dystopia that arises in the aftermath of a nuclear war.

Manga became increasingly popular in the United States in the early 1990s, also influencing the production of a number of manga-influenced American comics. Some of the earliest and still most popular manga focused on post-apocalyptic situations; a genre thoroughly explored by a culture that had witnessed first hand the catastrophic effects of nuclear power. In *Akira* (1982), a motorcycle gang in Neo-Tokyo is torn apart as one member, Tetsuo Shima, gains psychic abilities and another, Shōtarō Kaneda, attempts to stop him from abusing his power. Both are pulled into a larger range of events in a post-nuclear war world with some people developing new abilities while others are unwilling lab experiments. *Fist of the North Star* (1983) follows the exploits of Kenshiro, a martial arts fighter who roams a world destroyed by nuclear war, taking down warlords and villains who prey upon the innocent. In the United States, Epic Comics began publishing *Akira* in 1988, and Viz Communications started *Fist of the North Star* in 1989. However, one of the earliest English translations of Japanese manga also offered what could be considered a real-world account of a post-apocalyptic situation. Originally serialized in 1973, the series **Barefoot Gen** first appeared to U.S. audiences in 1976. The story tells the story of Gen, a survivor of the Hiroshima bombing and his attempts to rebuild life among the ruins of Hiroshima with most of his family dead. The series reflects many of the experiences that the author, Keiji Nakazawa experienced as a survivor of the event.

Both Marvel and DC Comics have played around with the idea of post-apocalyptic futures for their continuity-based characters. Despite the many "Crisis" series that DC has published over the years, their real attempt at depicting a world in the aftermath of civilization's destruction and its ultimate revival came in 1996 with **Mark Waid** and **Alex Ross**'s miniseries **Kingdom Come**. Here, after many of Earth's original superheroes have retired or died, a new generation of super-powered people proves less responsible than their predecessors, generating widespread chaos. Eventually, Superman is coaxed out of retirement and joins up with others in an attempt to reestablish order, but with so many fronts and factions, he, **Batman**, **Wonder Woman**, and others are barely able to hold off nuclear destruction.

By contrast, Marvel has tread rather deeply into post-apocalyptic stories over the years and done so in such a way as to keep it relevant to mainstream continuity. One of the earliest storylines to do this was "Days of Our Future Past" in *Uncanny X-Men* #141–42 (1981). Though this story is initially set in a dystopian future where mutants were killed or herded into internment camps, it gives birth to a variety of future post-apocalyptic narratives taking place over the following three decades in which numerous time travelers visit their past (the X-Men's present) to prevent the future disruption. There, events were often focused around the assassination of Professor Charles Xavier as well as Senator Robert Kelly. The assassination of Charles Xavier also triggers the major crossover storyline known as "Age of the Apocalypse" (1995). Through the use of time travel, Xavier is killed even before he creates the X-Men. The world is reformed through the machinations of the evil immortal mutant, Apocalypse, who privileges mutants while also letting the world decay and fracture.

Building off the success of *Kingdom Come*, Ross and Jim Krueger created the **Earth X** series, a 42 comic series in which Earth becomes a central battleground for god-like beings. In the wake of the battle, the heroes, villains, and humans of Earth further mutate and eventually even defeat death. Marvel's most recent post-apocalyptic series, *Marvel Zombies* (2005), explores the concept of superhero zombies ravaging the known universe (and eventually multiverse) in search of more living beings to eat.

For most of its history, the post-apocalyptic narrative has fallen primarily into the genre of **science fiction**, but increasingly, in the second half of the 20th century, **horror** has also featured its share of post-apocalyptic titles influenced by Richard Matheson's novel *I Am Legend* (1954), and George Romero's *Living Dead* film series (beginning in 1968), as well as Stephen King's novel *The Stand* (1978). **Western** motifs inflected through such films as *A Boy and His Dog* (1974) and *Mad Max* (1979), as well as novels including Stephen King's *Dark Tower* series (1982) and David Brin's *The Postman* (1985) grew influential in the post-apocalyptic comics by the beginning of 2000s. Thus, both **Garth Ennis**'s *Pilgrim* miniseries (2001) and King's adapted and newly created *Dark Tower* comic series (2007) evoked a Western style. In any case, with a foreboding sense of millennialism upon the lead-up to the second millennium c.e., followed by heightened tension between the West and Islamic worlds in the aftermath of the September 11 attacks, the decline of U.S. hegemony, and the forthcoming Mayan date for the end of the world in December of 2012, contemporary concerns and anxieties have fueled a burgeoning interest in post-apocalyptic narratives in comics and all forms of storytelling.

*Lance Eaton*

**PREACHER** (1995–2000) was created by writer **Garth Ennis** and artist Steve Dillon, and originally released serially by **DC Comics**' imprint Vertigo. The series was collected in a trade paperback series of nine volumes. Ennis's best-known work to date, *Preacher*'s violent, humorous, and often absurd depiction of American culture and mythology has gained a large cult following and garnered Ennis numerous industry awards.

*Preacher* tells the story of Jesse Custer, a disillusioned preacher forced into ordination by his evil maternal grandmother, Marie L'Angelle, and her henchmen, Jody and T. C. During a sermon in his tiny Annville, Texas, church, Jesse is possessed by Genesis, the forbidden offspring of an angel and a demon. Genesis imbues Jesse with the Word of God, which forces anyone hearing it to obey his commands. Following his congregation's immolation, Jesse sets out to hunt down God and force the deity to answer for his flawed governance of creation, meanwhile battling such foes as the Grail, a conspiratorial network controlling the governments of the world and protecting the bloodline of Jesus Christ.

Jesse's quest reunites him with his ex-girlfriend Tulip O'Hare, a college-dropout turned hit-woman, and Cassidy, a 100-year-old Irish **vampire**, whose hard-drinking, party-loving attitude immediately endears him to Jesse. After Jesse falls out of an airplane during their escape from the Grail, Tulip believes he is dead and completely breaks down, turning to alcohol and tranquilizers, which Cassidy is all too happy to provide. After six months of running from the Grail and reluctantly living and sleeping with Cassidy, Tulip comes to her senses and seeks refuge at her friend Amy's house, where she is discovered by and reunited with Jesse.

For most of the series, Cassidy is Jesse's best friend and drinking buddy. Although he dedicates himself to helping Jesse complete his quest, Cassidy falls in love with Tulip, and gradually reveals himself to be a monster, as he all but kidnaps and rapes Tulip while they both believe Jesse to be dead. He finds Tulip shortly after her reunion with Jesse, and he and Jesse arrange a final meeting to hash out their differences. Before the meeting, Cassidy makes a deal with God: Cassidy will incapacitate Jesse long enough for God to rid him of Genesis, which will allow God to escape Jesse. In return, both Jesse and Cassidy survive the ordeal, since Genesis can only be removed upon Jesse's death and since Cassidy intends to let the sunlight destroy him in front of Jesse. Cassidy and God reach this agreement unaware of the deal Jesse has made with the Saint of Killers to have God killed.

Jesse encounters a host of nemeses on his journey, beginning with his demented grandmother and her lethal enforcer, Jody, who killed Jesse's father. Shortly after their quest begins, Jesse and Tulip are captured by Jody and his sidekick T. C., and taken back to Angelville, the L'Angelle family's plantation. Jody kills Tulip in front of Jesse in an attempt to break his will, which nearly works until God brings her back to life and tells her to warn Jesse off of his quest. They eventually escape, killing Jody, T. C., and Marie L'Angelle in the process.

Jesse's main opponent is Herr Starr, who leads the Grail, bent on bringing about Armageddon and ruling the world from behind its puppet messiah, a hopelessly inbred degenerate spawned by years of interbreeding within Christ's bloodline. Starr refuses to serve a warped messiah, and focuses on Jesse Custer, with his Word of God, as the most likely replacement. At the series' climax, Starr kills Jesse and then dies in a gunfight with Tulip.

Jesse also has to deal with the Saint of Killers, set on Jesse's trail by the angels who let Genesis escape in the first place. A former Confederate soldier turned bounty hunter, he is killed while attempting revenge on the bandits responsible for the deaths of his wife and daughter. Condemned to Hell, he is unable to let go of his hate, and is offered the position of Saint of Killers by the Angel of Death, who has grown weary of his duties. Indestructible and furnished with a pair of Colt revolvers that can kill anything, the Saint destroys armies in his attempt to kill Jesse. Jesse finally convinces him that God is at fault for his family's death, and sets the Saint on the deity's trail instead.

After Starr finally manages to kill Jesse, Genesis is set free. No longer having to deal with Genesis, God returns to heaven to take up his throne, from which he will be invincible. He arrives to find the Saint of Killers waiting amid a host of dead archangels. The Saint then blows God away, finally earning his rest. In the meantime, through Cassidy's deal with God, Jesse is brought back to life without Genesis or the Word of God, and Cassidy, who dies from exposure to sunlight shortly after Jesse is shot, comes back to life as a human. The series ends with Jesse and Tulip's reunion, while Cassidy sets about returning to life as a man.

Despite the Nietzschean resonance of God's death, *Preacher* is mostly an examination of American mythology, specifically frontier and Western narratives. *Preacher* dramatizes Richard Slotkin's argument that the defining American myth is that of the Anglo-Saxon **race** revitalizing itself through savage warfare on the frontier. According to Slotkin, the persistence of this myth accounts for the periodic resurgence of **Westerns** in popular culture, while *Preacher* suggests the extent to which **religion** is central to this national-racial myth. Jesse Custer, whose name derives from the near-mythological Western figures of Jesse James and George Armstrong Custer, is the quintessential self-made man; he educated himself from the public library and lives by his wits and the skills he learned "back home" from Jody—riding, shooting, and mechanical skills. Although a man of the cloth, Jesse's idols are his father and John Wayne, who appears periodically as a manifestation of Jesse's conscience. However, characters such as Amy and Tulip provide a far stronger female presence than is typical of the traditional Western. The series ranges from the bayous of Mississippi to the Grand Canyon and the deserts of Arizona, from New York to San Francisco, and culminates at the Alamo. Though an Irish writer, Garth Ennis writes like a patriotic American, and he seems to forgive America's faults because of its deeply ingrained belief in the ability to start over—though it is also the case that many of the most sinister forces in the series are distinctively American.

*Preacher* also further explores the disdain for religion Ennis expressed in his earlier original efforts *Troubled Souls* (1989) and *For a Few Troubles More* (1990), exploring the fallout of the early 20th-century Protestant-Catholic conflict in Ireland. From the millennial Grail, to the evil Marie L'Angelle, to a God who deserts his creation, every religious organization or figure depicted in *Preacher* is self-serving and power-seeking, and the series ultimately calls for America to desert the religion it no longer needs.

*Preacher* won two **Eisner Awards**, in 1998 and 2001 respectively. It also won Ennis the Comics Buyer's Guide Award for "Favorite Writer" five years running, from 1997 through 2001, and was nominated for a host of Eagle Awards in 1999, winning for "Favourite Colour Comic Book."

**Selected Bibliography:** Ennis, Garth. *Preacher*. New York: DC Comics, 1995–2000; Slotkin, Richard. *Gunfighter Nation: The Myth of the Frontier in Twentieth-Century America*. Norman: University of Oklahoma Press, 1998.

*Grant Bain*

**PRIDE OF BAGHDAD** is a graphic novel released in September, 2006, by **DC**-Vertigo, written by **Brian K. Vaughan** (*Ex Machina, Runaways, Y: The Last Man*) with art by Niko Henrichon (*Barnum!*). The story revolves around a pride of four lions living in the Baghdad Zoo at the time of the 2003 U.S. invasion on Iraq. After the zoo is bombed, they escape into the war-torn streets of Baghdad. Throughout their travels, they encounter other animals both friendly and antagonistic who introduce them to the world outside the zoo; but before they escape the city, they are shot down by U.S. Armed Forces. The concept was inspired by actual news reports of lions escaping from the zoo and roaming Baghdad until killed by U.S. forces. Vaughan fictionalizes the lions' internal experience as a means to engage in conversation about the invasion of Baghdad and the Iraq War.

The escaped lions include three adults: Zill, the alpha male who slides back and forth from being reasonable to being violent; Safa, a wounded elderly lioness who still maintains matriarchal influence, despite her acceptance of being caged; and Noor, primary partner to Zill and romantic about life in wild. They are joined by Ali, Noor's cub, who has known nothing but captivity. At the onset of the story, Noor is attempting to forge a peace and overthrow the zoo's human regime to gain freedom for all of its animals, but her potential allies hold no faith in the lions and their carnivorous predisposition. While Ali begs for more stories about life in the wild, Safa reflects on the violence, subjugation, and even rape she experienced in the wild from Zill and his kin. After an explosion that destroys their cage and sets free the pride, all but Safa move forward with many of the other animals as they stampede away from the fire and destruction. Along the way, Ali is kidnapped by a fanatical group of apes who wish to physically mark Ali so that he is part of their group. The cub is rescued by Safa, and the pride regroups and exits the zoo. Their progression leads them to encounter an aged turtle who warns them of the havoc and destruction experienced by him and his family in the last war (the first Gulf War). After averting a collision with U.S. tanks, the lions find themselves wandering the streets of a desolate and dead Baghdad, filled with human corpses. They follow a pack of horses only to find themselves entering the Republican Palace where they encounter a beaten and dying lion, Rashid. The dying lion is not the only curious creature held in captivity in Saddam's palace. A bear, Fajer, attacks the pride and a fierce battle ensures. While they do win against the savage bear, Safa loses her other eye. At the end of the day, the pride comes together on a rooftop to watch the setting sun—a privilege denied them while in captivity. Just after sunset, the lions are shot down by U.S. soldiers, who claim the animals were charging toward them.

The story itself runs parallel to the actual invasion of Baghdad and U.S. political intentions of dismantling weapons of mass destruction and installing a democracy. In interviews, Vaughan admits to no overall theory for his commentary but rather challenging the doctrine of preemptive strikes and interrogating the concepts of freedom and liberty in a post-9/11 culture. These concerns inform the text at different moments. Often skeptical and realistic about life before imprisonment, Safa's statement, "Freedom can't be given, only earned" evokes the anxiety about the pride's newly found freedom as well as the U.S. goals and mission. Later, the pride will encounter an antelope that Noor had been attempting to convince to join in the zoo rebellion. Isolated, the antelope is easy prey; but Noor lets it go with the reminder, "Let them all know that the antelopes could have been free ages ago if they had just been brave enough to trust me." The underlining commentary suggests that the different political and religious groups in Iraq might have earned their own freedom without the U.S. invasion. Meanwhile, The pride of lions has not attained but has been (temporarily) handed freedom: a not-so-proud moment. However, they are thrown into a world they do not fully comprehend; and in the end they cannot truly attain their freedom, as it is robbed from them by those who had initially, albeit unintentionally, liberated them—the U.S. Armed Forces. The suggestion that the American invasion was anything but the liberating event it was claimed to be is inescapable.

Unlike other successful ventures of Vaughan, *Pride of Baghdad* was planned and executed as a graphic novel from the beginning. It was well-received upon its release, winning accolades and awards, including the Best Original Graphic Novel of 2006 by

IGN.com. Independent publishers had directly dealt with the Iraq War by 2006 and both **Marvel** and **DC** had evoked parallels with Iraq (through often unnamed Middle-Eastern countries or even Kahndaq, the Middle-Eastern kingdom of DC Comics' Black Adam). *Pride of Baghdad*, however, was the first wide-release comic to deal directly with the U.S. invasion of Iraq.

*Lance Eaton*

**PRIEST, CHRISTOPHER** (1961–). Christopher Priest (born James Christopher Owsley) has been active in comics for over three decades, carving out a reputation as a writer of compelling, sophisticated, and original adventure genre stories. Priest also holds the distinctions of being the first African American editor at **Marvel** Comics (1984) as well as at **DC Comics** (1990), and of being the first African American to pen stories for either of the two major publishers without a collaborating writer. He is sometimes referred to as Christopher J. Priest to distinguish him from the well-known British **science fiction** and **fantasy** author Christopher Priest.

Priest began his career as an intern (as James Owsley) in 1978 at Marvel Comics, where he formed a friendship with writer and editor Larry Hama, an important early mentor. Priest eventually became Hama's assistant editor and soon began to try his hand at writing as well. He contributed several short pieces to *Crazy*, Marvel's humor magazine, and published his first **superhero** work with 1983's *The Falcon* limited series. Promoted to editor in 1984, Priest was given the reins of Marvel's three regular **Spider-Man** titles, where he helped launch the careers of renowned creators such as, Peter David, **Kyle Baker,** and Joe Quesada. After an editorial shake-up at Marvel, Priest left for DC, where he contributed stories for *Action Comics* Weekly and wrote the *Unknown Soldier* miniseries (1988). In 1990, Priest became an editor at DC, where he was eventually placed in charge of the Impact Comics line, DC's attempt to reach a younger audience. Priest was also instrumental in the genesis of **Milestone Comics**, a creator-owned line distributed by DC that featured an ethnically and racially diverse creative team and cast of characters. After changing his name for personal reasons in the early 1990s, Priest eventually left his editorial post but remained active in comics as a writer.

Though Priest's work is wide-ranging and diverse, a survey reveals several distinctive characteristics, including the (frequently humorous) defamiliarization of genre conventions, the examination of the ethical and political ramifications of the superhero, and a nuanced and mature approach to non-white characters in a genre with a long history of racial stereotyping. These themes are evident in early works, such as his 1987 *Spider-Man vs. Wolverine* one-shot, a story that places the title characters in physical and ideological conflict over the morality of killing, and his run on *Power Man and Iron Fist* (#111–25, 1984–86), in which Priest offers a complex treatment of **Luke Cage** (Power Man), a character whose depiction was to that point still largely tied to his roots in the blaxploitation genre.

Priest's later career includes such notable work as his lighthearted adventure series with frequent collaborator M. D. Bright, *Quantum and Woody* (1997–98), as well as several increasingly ambitious treatments of **race**, **politics**, and the superhero genre. His short-lived series for DC, *Xero* (1997–98) tells the story of a blond-haired, blue-eyed super-assassin whose secret identity was an African American basketball player; as scholar Marc Singer has noted, the series raised important questions about the implicit whiteness of the superhero ideal. Priest is perhaps best known for his critically acclaimed five-year run on Marvel's **Black Panther** (1998–2003). Priest revitalized the largely neglected character by focusing on his role as king of an enormously powerful and technologically advanced African nation in an uneasy relationship with the United States and other so-called first world powers.

After the cancellation of *Black Panther*, Priest worked on two acclaimed but short-lived series, *The Crew* (2003), **Captain America**, *and the Falcon* (2004). Since their cancellation he has been largely inactive in comics, focusing his attentions instead on his work as a minister.

*Brannon Costello*

**PROMETHEA.** Created by writer **Alan Moore** and artist J. H. Williams III, *Promethea* is a monthly comic book series originally published between 1999 and 2005. The series was one of the initial four titles published under the America's Best Comics (ABC) imprint of **Jim Lee**'s Wildstorm Comics. Moore, the primary creative force behind the small line of comics, was given substantial creative freedom; however, he was displeased that **DC Comics** purchased Wildstorm shortly after arranging his distribution deal. Although that corporate decision did not affect the content of Moore's comics, he had made a prior pledge to never again work for the large publisher. Nevertheless, ABC remained under DC's umbrella during the entirety of *Promethea*'s 32-issue run. With the exception of a short flashback sequence in issue #4 illustrated by Charles Vess, Williams was responsible for all of the artwork; consequently, the comic was frequently off its intended monthly published schedule to accommodate Williams's intricate style and the intense demands Moore placed upon his artist. Like the other ABC books, *Promethea* re-imagines the **superhero** genre, principally by blending it with other genres and disparate influences. Yet, within Moore's body of work at ABC, *Promethea* is where his various obsessions—such as the occult and magic, a skewed perspective on the superhero genre, and the purposes of **fantasy** and art—coalesce most evidently and, as many critics argue, successfully.

The plot of *Promethea* is frustratingly difficult to summarize. Sophie Bangs, a college student living in New York City, is conducting research for a term paper on a fictional, female character known as Promethea, who has appeared, over the years, in various incarnations and in different media. Sophie learns that "Promethea," existing as an idea, is a link between the physical, "real" world, and the Immateria, the realm of fantasy and imagination. Like many artists before her, Sophie is able to channel Promethea's powers—which alters Sophie's physical appearance and demeanor—by producing creative works about Promethea.

The 32-issue series is roughly structured into three acts. Act I involves Sophie adjusting to life as Promethea and learning more about her powers, magic, and those whom

Promethea inhabited before; Act II sees Sophie on a mystical journey through the 10 *sephiroths*, or spheres, that comprise the conception of the universe as described by the mystical teachings within Judaism known as Kabbalah; and Act III has Promethea fulfilling her cataclysmic prophesy to "end the world." Moore makes the argument that humanity's notion of reality is inextricably entwined with human imagination, and that stories and fantasy define reality, as opposed to reflecting it. Although not a totally original postulation, *Promethea* is nonetheless noteworthy in the way it not only manifests its core theme, but also serves as a meta-text that actualizes it, using a story to comment upon the functions and significance of other stories. It is also notable for its particularly effective use of the combination of image and text to further its own storytelling.

Superficially, *Promethea* corresponds to the conventions and expectations of the superhero genre. Sophie, a relatively recognizable and relatable character, is bestowed with remarkable powers through somewhat mysterious sources. Although these new-found abilities beleaguer her personal life, she is nonetheless compelled to use them for the welfare of others. Sophie is not the first, or only, super-powered person in the world of *Promethea*, and she occasionally allies herself with New York's premiere "science heroes," The Five Swell Guys, whose powers and history go largely unexplained. Yet, unlike most other superhero comics, Moore does not strive to represent a recognizable reality. New York City in the year 1999, as depicted in the series, is similar to the New York of the "real world," yet has clearly been transformed by the presence of "super" people and advanced technological progress: flying cars and "living" gels are seen as commonplace by the general populace. Whereas most superhero comics present fantastic elements as intrusions into a world that otherwise reflects our own, *Promethea* offers a world where verisimilitude and fantasy are inextricably, blatantly entwined.

The interconnectedness of fiction with reality in Moore's vision of New York City points to *Promethea*'s central concern: the roles of art, story, and imagination in human understanding. According to *Promethea*, when a person dreams or engages in creative thought, they enter the ethereal realm known as "The Immateria." This land is comprised of possibilities and thoughts, which can travel back to the physical plane; however, the translation from notion to reality is not perfect—the idea of a chair is not the same as an actual chair. The means to which these translations occur are stories, or more precisely, metaphors. Moore configures the indivisible relationship between imagination and reality around the importance of metaphor, and uses the mystical representational models of the Kabbalah and Tarot as means of illustrating how symbolism and story create meaning and participate in constructing the human framework of existence.

The interrelationship of fantasy with reality is made explicit as Sophie prepares to depart on her mystical tour through the Kabbalah's map of existence, whose 32 paths correspond to *Promethea*'s number of issues. As she begins her journey, Sophie meets the personified Universe: a celestial woman entwined with a glowing serpent. When told that the woman represents imagination and the snake indicates earthly, growing things, Sophie asks if the snake's head is at the woman's feet to represent imagination "growing up out" of material life. The snake replies, "No. It'sss there becaussse I am her ssservant." In other words, physical existence does not result in or engender imagination; rather, the material world is subordinate to and dependent upon human creativity. Promethea—who is a living story, or a story come to life—embodies this philosophy.

In *Promethea*, Moore demonstrates how reality is constructed through all forms of metaphors and stories, ranging from pulp fiction to religious myths to language itself. By the end of the series, Promethea has fulfilled her destiny to end the world, although not the physical realm, but the "world as we know it" by initiating a global moment of transcendence. In this new world, the division between imagination and reality is weakened, and ideas coexist in harmony rather than conflict. For example, a newly-enlightened friend of Sophie's tells her, "So, like I have this Baptist business going on, but at the same time . . . well, I'm sort of worshipping this pagan hearth-goddess called Hestia," to which Sophie replies, "Yeah, well, that's okay. It's okay to worship everything." The egalitarian pantheism that Promethea initiates illustrates Moore's reverence for stories and ideas as powerful, yet adaptable, entities that cooperate to create our notion of reality, and rejects a concrete vision of reality reflected by a universal "Truth."

*Jackson Ayres*

**PUNISHER, THE.** **Marvel Comics**' popular ultra-violent character, the Punisher was created in 1974 by writer Gerry Conway, and artists **John Romita, Sr.** and Ross Andru as a recurring guest feature for various *Spider-Man* titles. The Punisher was a frequent antagonist of Spider-Man, yet was portrayed as a sympathetic figure, neither hero nor villain. The Punisher dresses in a characteristic black uniform with a stylized skull emblazoned across the chest. While the Punisher lacks super powers, he makes up for this by wielding a variety of guns and other weapons. The character would later appear as a feature character in his own titles, where he has been portrayed as a troubled anti-hero engaged in a "one-man war on crime."

Like many popular characters, the Punisher's motivations are based in personal tragedy. His alter ego, Frank Castle, was a Marine and Vietnam veteran. Castle returns home to New York City and a promising future with his wife and two young children. While the family is walking through Central Park to find a place to have a picnic, they accidentally come across a mafia execution. Castle is then a witness to his family's murder, an event that motivates him to extreme ends in his drive for vengeance. The Punisher is not merely satisfied in eliminating the particular gangsters responsible for his loss; he extends his revenge to anyone guilty of criminal activity. What made the Punisher an original and successful character was his individual moral stance and his ruthless willingness to kill his foes. As a result, there are few recurring villains through various *Punisher* stories, because so few of them survive their encounters with Frank Castle.

The first true phase of the Punisher's popularity as a character was in the 1970s and early 1980s, when the character was a recurring feature in various Marvel titles, including *The Amazing Spider-Man* and **Daredevil:** *The Man Without Fear*. The character's first

Thomas Jane as Frank Castle, a.k.a. the Punisher, in the 2004 live-action film by the same name. Photofest

appearance, in *Amazing Spider-Man* #129, features the Punisher hired by the villainous Jackal to assassinate Spider-Man (at the time a suspected criminal in Marvel continuity). The Punisher's attempt on Spider-Man's life is interrupted when the Jackal, concerned that Spider-Man is too much of a challenge for the Punisher, secretly attacks Spider-Man and causes him to fall off of the rooftop the two are fighting on. Although Spider-Man survives this fall, neither the Jackal nor the Punisher are aware of this, nor is the Punisher aware of the Jackal's interference. The Punisher is enraged at the Jackal for so casually accepting Spider-Man's accidental death; although the Punisher would have taken Spider-Man's life as a retributive act of justice, the Punisher considered Spider-Man's accidental death both a failure and injustice on his own part. The Punisher begins to question the Jackal's motives, and in a subsequent encounter with Spider-Man he learns the true nature of the Jackal's treachery. The Punisher never fully accepts that Spider-Man is truly innocent, but the two often find themselves working toward the same goals in subsequent issues. By 1975, the Punisher was a solo feature in *Marvel Preview* #2, one of Marvel's black-and-white magazine format titles, which featured the first telling of the Punisher's origin story. In *Amazing Spider-Man* #162 (1976), one of the Punisher's few recurring foes was introduced: Jigsaw, a former hitman for a crime family. His name refers to his face, which appears to have been stitched together from pieces, owing to his having been thrown out of a plate-glass window previously by the Punisher.

Punisher remained a guest character until 1986, when Marvel debuted a five-issue miniseries, *The Punisher: Circle of Blood*, written by Steve Grant and Jo Duffy, and drawn by Mike Zeck, Mike Vosburg, and John Beatty. The story features the return of Jigsaw and the escape of the Punisher from Rikers Island Penitentiary. The popularity of the title led to the creation of an ongoing *Punisher* series the following year, further feeding fans' interest in the character. The ongoing series also introduced the character Microchip, who assists in creating and maintaining the Punisher's arsenal of weapons and gadgetry. Spin-off titles were additionally created, including *Punisher: War Zone* and *Punisher: War Journal*; the character's story was turned into a motion picture starring Dolph Lundgren in 1989.

Despite the character's explosive popularity and franchise status, interest in the character waned by the mid-1990s, and by 1995 all of the ongoing titles featuring the Punisher were canceled. In the latter half of the 1990s, Marvel attempted to revive the character twice, with little success. In 2000, however, Marvel successfully re-launched *The Punisher*, first as a 12-issue miniseries (published under the title *Welcome Back, Frank*), then as a regular ongoing title that has remained in publication in various incarnations since that time. Writer **Garth Ennis** and artist Steve Dillon, the creative team behind the DC/Vertigo series ***Preacher***, were the creators responsible for the Punisher's successful relaunch, though a variety of other artists and writers would contribute to the *Punisher* titles. Ennis used the Punisher character as a vehicle for a variety of storytelling possibilities: his characteristic contempt for super powered characters led to stories in which, for example, Frank Castle shoots Wolverine in the face with a rifle and rolls over him with a steamroller. Other stories feature Frank fighting an eastern-European prostitution ring, assisting Nick Fury and the American government in covert operations in Russia, or battling Irish mobsters both in New York and Ireland. Ennis also wrote various *Punisher* side-projects, such as *Born*, drawn by Darick Robertson, depicting Castle's days as a Marine in Vietnam, *The Tyger*, drawn by **EC Comics** legend **John Severin**, and *The End*, drawn by Richard Corben, depicting Frank's future death. *The Punisher* lasted 37 issues as a Marvel Knights title before it was moved to the Marvel MAX adult-oriented imprint with a new #1 issue in 2004. Ennis's run on the Marvel MAX *Punisher* title lasted until issue #60, and was subsequently retitled *The Punisher: Frank Castle*. Marvel also created a new main-continuity *Punisher* title, and licensed two new *Punisher* films, one in 2004 starring Thomas Jane, and another in 2008 titled *Punisher: War Zone* starring Ray Stevenson. Far more than many recurring characters, Frank Castle has earned legendary status as a comics character.

*Robert O'Nale*

**QUALITY COMICS.** Founded by Everett M. "Busy" Arnold, Quality Comics was an American comic book publishing company from 1939 to 1956. Before Quality, Arnold helped Bill Cook and John Mahon publish their Centaur line of original comic books. Seeing them struggle, Arnold began publishing Centaur publications filled with reprinted comic strips like *Joe Palooka* and *Mickey Finn*, beginning with *Featured Funnies* #1 (1937). Later renamed *Featured Comics* (1939), the series became the first of Arnold's Quality Comics. It and Arnold's second book, *Smash Comics*, featured original material. Centaur properties that carried over into Quality Comics included American comic books' first masked hero, the Clock.

Noting the comic book market's success, *Register and Tribune Syndicate* sales manager Henry Martin feared that newspaper strips might lose readers to them, and arranged for Arnold to print a tabloid-sized comic book supplement for newspapers. *The Spirit* debuted in 1940 as one of the insert's three titles, all created and jointly owned by **Will Eisner**. Quality Comics became known for quality art, much of it purchased from the Eisner-Iger workshop. Eisner creations for Arnold's comic book line included Doll Man (*Feature Comics* #27, 1939), Uncle Sam (*National Comics* #1, 1940), **Black Condor** (*Crack Comics* #1, 1940), and the Blackhawks (*Military Comics* #1, 1941). Eisner typically introduced these creations and then turned each over to other artists and writers to carry on. Chuck Cuidera's scripts with **Reed Crandall** and Bob Powell's art would popularize the *Blackhawk* tales. Lou Fine illustrated Uncle Sam and Black Condor in *Crack Comics*, before becoming best known for illustrating *Hit Comics* covers and, despite using the house pseudonym E. Lectron, working on the Ray in *Smash Comics*. By 1942, when other comic book publishers relied heavily on in-house or freelance talent, Quality continued purchasing content from independent studios. At their peak, Quality's nine titles collectively sold over one million copies per month. As the popularity of superhero comics declined, Quality Comics' new ventures included producing **romance** comics and the adventures of treasury agent *T-Man*.

When Jerry Iger left Quality Comics, he took the **Phantom Lady** from Quality to Fox Features, where the character became sexier to the point of controversy. During the United States Senate Subcommittee on Juvenile Delinquency's 1954 hearings and the **Comics Code** Authority's resultant creation, Quality remained among the few publishers with content considered consistently suitable for children. Nevertheless, Arnold closed a financially troubled Quality Comics in 1956, selling many creative properties to **DC Comics**, and retired.

Over the decades, Quality characters appeared sporadically in DC Comics publications. Uncle Sam, the Human Bomb, and several others became the Freedom Fighters, a superhero team from the parallel universe of **Earth X** where World War II had never ended. One of the most durable Quality characters would prove to be **Plastic Man**, Jack Cole's "India Rubber Man" character that enjoyed several DC revivals and appeared in animated cartoons. All of DC's Quality characters became part of the same continuity as other DC Comics characters as of *Crisis on Infinite Earths* #11 (1986).

**Selected Bibliography:** Duin, Steve, and Mike Richardson. *Comics Between the Panels.* Milwaukie, OR: Dark Horse Comics, 1998; Harvey, Robert C. *The Art of the Comic Book.* Jackson: University Press of Mississippi, 1996; Herman, H. *Silver Age: The Second Generation of Comic Book Artists.* Neshannock, PA: Hermes Press, 2004; Kaplan, A. *From Krakow to Krypton: Jews and Comic Books.* Philadelphia: The Jewish Publication Society, 2008; Wright, Bradford W. *Comic Book Nation: The Transformation of Youth Culture in America.* Baltimore: Johns Hopkins University Press, 2001; Wright, Nicky. *The Classic Era of American Comics.* Chicago: Contemporary Books, 2000.

*Travis Langley*

**RACE AND ETHNICITY.** The history of comics has been complicated by authors' considerations of racial and ethnic identity at least since the many 19th-century depictions of African slaves in English and American abolitionist cartoons. However, caricatures of African physiognomy that portrayed blacks as ignorant savages quickly became more common in European humor magazines and early American comics created by artists like the German cartoonist Wilhelm Busch and the Americans Richard Outcault, Frederick Burr Opper, and Winsor McCay. These authors' black characters prepared the ground for hundreds of later African and African American stereotyped comics characters whose history bears remarkable similarities to the evolution of American minstrelsy. The swollen lips, enlarged eyes, simply drawn faces, and predisposition to slapstick that distinguish characters like Sambo Johnson, Mickey Mouse, and **Felix the Cat** were also customary features of the minstrel stage from the late 18th century on. Many 19th-century British newspapers employed minstrel references to depict the Irish as a race of savage, subhuman degenerates, while American political cartoons expressed anxiety about increasing immigrant populations through exaggerated portraits of Italian, Jewish, and Irish citizens. Though many more recent artists have sought to undermine these and other ethnic stereotypes through complex characterization and socially conscious storylines, several mainstream publications continue to include few or no non-white characters.

Comics have engaged with the intersection of modern racial and political issues since 1932, when **Jerry Siegel** and **Joe Shuster** created **Superman** for *Action Comics*. Like many other Jewish American artists of the early 20th century, especially those working in film and theater, Siegel and Shuster espoused popular social views in their creative work. Such affiliations with the public imaginary served as a tool of assimilation for many immigrants, helping to undermine widespread nativist views in favor of a patriotism in which, theoretically, all citizens could participate. Superman's strong-arm opposition to the growing threat of **Nazi** Germany aligned his creators with the voice of the contemporary American military. A few years later, fellow Jewish American comics artist **Will Eisner** began drawing *The Spirit*, a 12-year-long serialized comic that followed the title character's attempts to fight crime in the fictional Central City. Though the Spirit's black sidekick, Ebony White, initially possessed stereotypical traits, Eisner assigned him a more complex and prominent role after World War II, and also introduced additional black characters. Siegel's, Shuster's and Eisner's characters also stand in stark contrast to the comic parodies of Jewish life that were popular in contemporary Nazi magazines such as *Der Stürmer*. Both Superman and the Spirit suggest that Jewish American artistic production could help to overcome social prejudice against ethnic minorities while promoting the new role of the United States as an emerging superpower.

In subsequent years, comics artists transformed a popular **superhero** convention, physical mutation, into a metaphor for racial diversity and difference. The most prominent example of this device is **Stan Lee** and **Jack Kirby's** *X-Men* (1963), which follows a group of superheroes whose powers manifest as a result of genetic mutation. Several of the **mutants'** genetic traits are accompanied by changes in physical appearance that simulate unique racial identities as well. Beast, who possesses superhuman strength and intelligence, has blue fur, fangs, and claws; Nightcrawler, a German character with the ability to teleport, has blue fur, yellow eyes, and a forked tail; and Wolverine, whose enhanced ability to heal enabled the implantation of an indestructible metal skeleton and claws, has body hair and a physical stance resembling a wolf's. Although the majority of the characters are Caucasian, the series also includes Storm, an African American women whose ancestors are Kenyan; the Native American Apache; and Sunfire, from Japan. The X-Men often tangle with the Brotherhood of Evil Mutants, whose leader, Magneto, is a Jewish concentration-camp survivor. Both groups battle social prejudice; though the X-Men seek to end the crimes that the Brotherhood perpetrates, the organizations are united in a struggle to combat society's fear of the unknown.

In 1993, African American publishers **Milestone Comics** created *Blood Syndicate*, a group of mutated characters with similarly unusual powers. However, this group's genetic differences have an identifiable origin—a radioactive gas that police used to break up a gang war—and its members, racially diverse before their mutations occurred, focus more on personal problems than on social justice. The group includes, among others, Brick House, an African American woman whose DNA fused with a brick wall to create physical invulnerability; Fade, a gay Latino man who can travel through solid objects; Third Rail, a Korean American man who can absorb and use electricity; and Wise Son, a Black Muslim man who cannot be physically harmed. Their experiences in the inner neighborhoods of the fictional city of Dakota demonstrate the real consequences of violence as well as the lack of easy solutions; the group eventually disintegrates because of internal dissension, most of the problems it had faced still unsolved.

Another specifically racialized perspective on superheroic abilities and responsibilities appeared in the United States in the 1970s, when a series of comics capitalized on the popularity of blaxploitation film characters like Shaft, Foxy Brown, and Dolemite. The most popular comics character in this vein was **Marvel's Luke Cage,** who first appeared in *Luke Cage: Hero for Hire* (later re-titled *Power Man*) in 1972. Cage gains his super-powers while unjustly imprisoned, when he volunteers for an experiment that gives him Superman-like strength and impenetrable skin. Unlike most superheroes up to this point, Cage exploits his abilities for a profit and consciously promotes his macho image. Marvel took advantage of this success by featuring a character introduced in *Fantastic Four* #52 (1966), the **Black Panther**, in their *Jungle Action* series from 1973 until 1976, then in his own self-titled book with two subsequent revivals. In his more recent incarnations, the character has typically been in the hands of African American creators such as **Christopher Priest** and Reginald Hudlin. This character's success was due in part to the title's resonance with contemporary Black Power movements. Other blaxploitation characters included **DC's** Black Lightning, who fought inner-city crime and drug use and earned recognition for his refusal to join the **Justice League of America** as its sole black member; and Marvel's short-lived Black Goliath, who could increase his size at will.

At the same time that American superheroes were undergoing a series of physical and ideological transformations that reflected the country's social preoccupations, Asian artists were developing a genre that would become one of the most commercially successful branches of comics. **Manga** appeared as a substantive entry into the field just after World War II, covering a wide range of subjects that includes **romance**, mystery, **horror**, sports, **history**, and more conventional action-adventure stories. Though many Western readers associate manga primarily with Japan, it has long been a popular form in Taiwan, Korea, and China as well. Part of the reason for manga's cultural specificity exists in its heavy reliance upon textually represented sound, which can be linked to oral features of the Japanese language. Its characters' exaggerated facial features—which include enlarged eyes, tiny mouths, and larger-than-life emotional reactions—invoke cultural **satire** and stereotype, but also recall Japan's centuries-long oral storytelling tradition. Manga has become one of the best-selling genres in the United States, France, and Germany, among other countries. Perhaps its most important contribution to the histories of comics and of print publication more generally has been its readers' expanded awareness of global cultural identities. A high consumer demand for titles such as *Barefoot Gen*, *Sailor Moon*, and *Ghost in the Shell* has resulted in the proliferation of related popular-culture fields like anime films, while American comics like Aaron McGruder's *The Boondocks* and the popular online *Homestar Runner* incorporate visual traits drawn from anime and manga.

Some comics artists have reacted to the commercial popularization of their art form by creating series and graphic novels that engage with racial and ethnic identity through dialogue with literary precedents, social issues, and historical events. Such historical revisionism generally takes one of two forms: representations of real history that address details or perspectives left out of more conventional accounts, or superhero origin stories that offer alternatives to the genre's mainstream standbys. In these superhero chronicles, a non-white main character often undergoes a set of challenges that contrast with the experiences of Superman, **Batman**, **Spider-Man**, and other comics superstars, pointing to the ways in which ethnic origins help to shape social experience. In Milestone Comics' *Icon: A Hero's Welcome* (1996), a compilation of the first eight issues of *Icon*, for instance, the title character comes to Earth when his spaceship crashes in a field—an origin story that has prompted some critics to label him a "chocolate-dip Superman." However, Icon is an adult alien who takes on the form of an African American baby boy before emerging from his craft, simply because it is 1839 and he has landed in a field tended by black slaves. He continues to live as a black man into the present, making the most of his immortality, but profits from his skill at business rather than helping others with his alien powers. It is not until he meets Raquel Ervin, a 15-year-old African American girl who tries to rob his house with a group of friends, that he gains a social conscience. Raquel renames herself Rocket, becomes Icon's sidekick, and teaches him the value of using one's abilities for the greater good. The series is notable for its attention to such issues as teen pregnancy, drug use, racial prejudice, and economic inequality. Icon and Rocket also interact with the Blood Syndicate, which exists in the same universe.

*Icon* only indirectly addresses the potential shortcomings of the American dream that Superman and his fellow heroes represent. However, Marvel's *Truth: Red, White, and Black* (2004), created by Robert Morales and **Kyle Baker**, deliberately challenges the easy equation that many superhero comics draw between physical prowess and patriotism. The book's main character, Isaiah Bradley, is a soldier on whose unit the U.S. government secretly tests a "super soldier" serum while they are serving in World War II. As a result, Bradley gains immense strength but is imprisoned for 17 years after a mission goes wrong. What the government covers up during this time is that Bradley was the original **Captain America**—a black man. The truth is not revealed until Steve Rogers, the white Captain America who has received all the public acclaim, learns about Bradley's existence and tracks him down to his New York City apartment, where he is living with his wife and a wall full of photographs, unable to speak due to brain damage sustained during his imprisonment. The book's final panel shows the two Captain Americas standing with their arms around each other's shoulders, smiling broadly. Rogers's costume is crisp and fitted, while Bradley's is in tatters, draped loosely over his T-shirt. Morales and Baker based their story on a number of historical sources, including accounts of the Tuskegee syphilis experiments, and slotted its new perspective on Captain America into the Marvel universe chronology. Morales and Baker's work, along with similarly satirical titles such as McGruder and Baker's **Birth of a Nation** and John Ridley's *The American Way*, suggest that many artists exploit their genre's often overstated visual elements in order to critique persistent issues of race and class. The field's many other black superheroes—including DC's **Green Lantern**, Amazing Man, and Cyborg; Milestone's Static; and Marvel's Blade,

Falcon, and Shard—also participate in ongoing conversations about unequal social opportunities and skewed cultural representation.

Graphic novels that narrate real historical events often personalize the trauma accumulated through disaster and deprivation by incorporating a narrator who experiences the events first-hand, or by considering the cultural mythologies that provide a framework through which to interpret that history. Ethnic identity thus helps to shape a book's unique historical perspective. **Art Spiegelman's** *Maus* (1986, 1991) is the best-known example of the former approach, featuring the story of his parents' sufferings during the Holocaust alongside World War II historiography and autobiographical ruminations on his identity as a second-generation survivor. All of the book's characters are historically real people, and all of the events he describes in the 1940s and 1980s actually occurred; Spiegelman gestures toward fictionalization only in his decision to represent ethnic groups as different animals, rather than as humans with distinctive facial features. Kyle Baker's two-volume *Nat Turner* (2005, 2007) also narrates a story of historical trauma, Turner's leadership of one of the largest slave rebellions to occur in the United States. Turner was captured just over two months after he and a small group of allies killed more than 60 whites in Southampton Country, Virginia. Although there is no observer character to put the events into a more personal perspective, Baker's decision to include almost no text (other than quotations from *The Confessions of Nat Turner*), and his smudged black-and-white drawings encourage readers to supply the narrative thread themselves. Filmmaker and founder of Virgin Comics/Virgin Animation, Shekhar Kapur, also created *Devi*, a graphic novel chronicling the adventures of Tara Mehta, an Indian woman who becomes a heroine prevailing against the forces of darkness in the fictional city of Sitapur. By invoking the mythology associated with Devi, both the Sanskrit word for "goddess" and the female embodiment of the divine essence in Hinduism, Kapur succeeded in carving out a space for Indian history and culture in the world of graphic novels. His company's other titles, which include *Ramayan 3392 AD* and *The Sadhu*, suggest that Indian ethnic identity could become as dominant a presence in comics as it is in film and music.

Many treatments of racial and ethnic identity in comics have also grown out of autobiographical works that focus on a central character's hesitation between fidelity to his or her native culture and assimilation into mainstream cultural practices. The rather astonishing proliferation of independent graphic novels since the early 1990s can be attributed, at least in part, to renewed reader interest in the genre of autobiography as well as a growing sense of transnational or global identity. In several instances, the narrator seeks to regain a set of cultural traits that he or she perceives as lost, but along the way various experiences result in a rejection or transformation of that sense of self. The narrative often includes a series of moments in which the main character comes to terms with what he or she perceives as an outsider or immigrant status as well, prompted by an engagement with the social issues prominent in a particular historical moment. One key example can be seen in **Joe Sacco's** *Palestine* (1996), which narrates the author's encounters while living for two months in the West Bank and the Gaza Strip. The book centers primarily on the Palestinian inhabitants' experiences of deprivation and frustration with unequal social conditions. Sacco focuses more on his interviewees' words than on his own experiences, though he does participate in, and comment on, the events unfolding around him. His role is ostensibly journalistic, but he becomes close to some of the people that he interviews and eventually acknowledges the shortcomings of his own story: its lack of objectivity and the need to represent the Israelis' lives more fully. His attitude toward his subjects shifts in kind, as he rejects an earlier desire to win awards from his work in favor of trying just to absorb the atrocities visible everywhere. The visual depictions of Sacco also change over time, as he first appears both physically and emotionally detached from the scene, standing on a wall above Jerusalem, but is later shown walking through marketplaces and city streets, drinking tea with Palestinian men, and guiding others through the very geographies that were once alien to him.

Marjane Satrapi's *Persepolis* (1999–2003) provides another important illustration of the mass appeal that ethnic autobiographies hold for diverse populations of readers. This graphic novel spans a 14-year period in Satrapi's life, from her girlhood in Iran to a period spent at a French high school in Vienna to her return to Iran, when she reflects upon her country's chaotic history and the possibility that she could live a more productive life elsewhere. Satrapi is careful to narrate contemporary political events in Iran alongside her personal experiences in romance, education, and work, suggesting that her sometimes misguided or impetuous behavior was a result in part of repressive social conditions. Satrapi also co-wrote and co-directed the animated film adaptation of her novel, which won the 2007 Cannes Film Festival Jury Prize. This event highlights not only the permeation of independent graphic narratives into other media, a milestone that superhero comics achieved long ago, but also Western audiences' increasing acceptance of and identification with other cultural experiences.

Although *Persepolis* includes some comedic moments to illustrate the main character's personal difficulties, it does not rely upon humor as a central narrative device, as many recent ethnic autobiographies have done. Gene Luen Yang's **American Born Chinese** (2006) alternates among three geographically and chronologically diverse narratives: the rise to power, downfall, and intellectual reawakening of the mythological Monkey King; the Chinese American Jin Wang's experiences of assimilating into the American school system and dealing with the traumas of adolescence; and the slapstick adventures of Danny, a white American teenager who represents Jin's fantasy self, and his visiting cousin Chin-Kee, whose exaggeratedly stereotypical traits repeatedly humiliate him. As the three stories progress, it becomes clear that their similar themes are meant to convey a joint message. Jin must learn to accept his own ethnic background and cultural traditions, refusing to succumb to either embarrassment over his ethnic roots or scorn for other Asians, before he can be comfortable in his own skin. The book concludes with Jin's discovery that his longtime friend Wei-Chen Sun is really the son of the Monkey King, sent to live among humans as a test of virtue. When Wei-Chen begins to crave human vices, the Monkey King takes his place in Jin's life as Chin-Kee.

In the end, the book's many cultural clashes, framed as farce, illustrate Jin's complicated negotiation of ethnic identities.

Jessica Abel's **La Perdida** (2006) offers another important example of the historically conscious ethnic autobiography, in the tradition of other Latino graphic novels like Ilan Stavans's *Mr. Spic Goes to Washington* (2008) and the **Hernandez Brothers'** collected **Love and Rockets** stories. The main character, Carla, moves from the United States to Mexico City as a way of coming to terms with her mixed-race background and her Mexican father's early abandonment. Though she lives in Mexico for a full year, she spends much of her time partying and fighting with various boyfriends. Her tenure there ends when she discovers that a group of her male friends have kidnapped her wealthy American ex-boyfriend and are holding him for ransom. After police unravel the kidnapping plot, she is forced to return to the United States and is forbidden to return to Mexico. Her essence may remain "lost," as the title suggests, since she never visits her father or loses the sense that she is exploiting a culture to which she has only tenuous links, but she succeeds in recognizing her own shortcomings. Abel's careful depiction of Carla's transition into Spanish fluency and the book's glossary of key terms render this graphic novel a crucial indicator of comics' new investment in issues of transnational identity and culture.

As the field of comics continues to diversify, more authors are responding directly to the genre's classic titles, heroes, and styles, while others see comics as a forum in which to create new perspectives on traditional literature and mainstream versions of history. **Alan Moore**'s *Supreme* (2002, 2003), for instance, parodies the uniform white American patriotism of heroes like **Superman** through an endless parade of Supremes at every age and a blindingly white costume. Paul Chadwick's **Concrete** (ongoing) tackles such issues as environmental decay and terrorism through a once-human hero who suffers social isolation after his brain is preserved within an impenetrable concrete body. **Harvey Pekar** and Gary Dumm's *Students for a Democratic Society: A Graphic History* (2008) represents an increasing number of nonfiction histories, dealing particularly with moments of social change, that are being produced in graphic form. Several literature series, including *No Fear Shakespeare* and *Graphic Classics*, take advantage of the form's visual characteristics in order to stress lesser-studied elements of classic literature such as gender roles, class concerns, and racial and ethnic identities. These trends suggest that diversity and difference have emerged as dominant preoccupations of modern comics.

**Selected Bibliography:** Brown, Jeffrey A. *Black Superheroes, Milestone Comics, and Their Fans.* Jackson: University Press of Mississippi, 2001; Buhle, Paul., ed. *Jews and American Comics: An Illustrated History of an American Art Form.* New York: New Press, 2008; Fingeroth, Danny. *Disguised as Clark Kent: Jews, Comics, and the Creation of the Superhero.* New York: Continuum, 2007; Strömberg, Fredrik. *Black Images in the Comics: A Visual History.* Seattle: Fantagraphics Books, 2003.

*Jennifer D. Ryan*

**RALL, TED** (1963–). Ted Rall is an acclaimed editorial cartoonist and columnist. He is currently president of the Association of American Editorial Cartoonists, a group dedicated to the promotion of editorial cartooning and association between editorial cartoonists. Rall publishes three cartoons and one column weekly through Universal Press Syndicate.

Rall was inspired to try editorial cartooning after meeting artist Keith Haring on a subway platform in Manhattan in 1986. He posted cartoons in his neighborhood in New York until he succeeded in syndicating his work in a number of weekly newspapers. Eventually he became syndicated by now-defunct San Francisco Chronicle Features, and moved to Universal Press Syndicate in 1996. Rall's cartoons espouse his politically liberal perspective, and are distinct in a number of ways from established traditions of editorial cartooning. Unlike traditional editorial cartoons, Rall uses multiple panels in a strip format instead of a single panel, a style typically used by cartoonists in alternative weekly papers. Rall also avoids traditional caricature styles in his cartoons: in traditional caricature, an artist will emphasize and exaggerate the physical appearance of a known person in order to suggest something about that person's personality. Rall infrequently illustrates known figures; instead, he prefers to satirize the reactions and behaviors of anonymous, everyday people. Frequently Rall does caricature known figures, yet sometimes he does not: Rall's depiction of former President George W. Bush is as "Generalissimo el Busho," a haggard, angry figure in a fascist military uniform who bears no physical resemblance to Bush.

Rall has also applied his craft to extended graphic narratives. Rall created a graphic novel parody of George Orwell's *Nineteen Eighty-Four* as *2024: A Graphic Novel*, and documented his travels through Afghanistan as a correspondent for radio station KFI and *The Village Voice* in the book *To Afghanistan and Back*, both published by graphic novel publisher NBM. Rall also edits a series of collections of cartoons by new editorial cartoonists in the *Attitude* series, also published by NBM.

*Robert O'Nale*

**RAW.** The brainchild of New York underground cartoonist **Art Spiegelman** and his wife and co-editor Françoise Mouly, *RAW* was from the start a groundbreaking graphics magazine and the premier anthology of its day for experimental and international comics. From 1980 to 1991, the sporadically published *RAW* helped to develop innovative cartooning talent outside of mainstream comics and assembled a stylistically diverse body of work that explored the formal and narrative capabilities of comics as a medium. With lavish production values unprecedented in a comics publication, *RAW* also promoted the idea of comics as a serious art form. Moreover, through its forays into book publishing and especially its serialization of Spiegelman's landmark *Maus*, *RAW* influenced the developing concept of the graphic novel as an artistically and commercially viable form.

*RAW* emerged from Mouly's experiments in printing and her burgeoning interest in comics as well as from Spiegelman's editorial work with the underground magazine *Arcade* (1975–76) and his dissatisfaction with existing venues for publishing comics.

After a 1978 trip to Europe during which they met many future *RAW* contributors, Mouly and Spiegelman agreed at the beginning of 1980 to publish a magazine of comics, graphics, and illustrated writing. Though *RAW* would explore the intersection between comics and other visual and literary arts, its primary intent was, in Mouly's words, "to make it manifest how good comics could be." The first volume of *RAW* (issues #1–8) focused on showing a wide range of visual work that had not been published before. It drew some of its talent from veterans of underground comics, including Bill Griffith, Kim Deitch, Justin Green, and **Robert Crumb**, though *RAW* used their work sparingly and went beyond the familiar underground content of sex, drugs, and violence. Moreover, *RAW* nurtured a new generation of alternative cartoonists, many of whom were students, teachers, or alumni of New York's School of Visual Arts, where Spiegelman taught and which offered considerable financial support to the magazine. Regular contributors included the **post-apocalyptic** punk artist Gary Panter, the pointillist and caricaturist Drew Friedman, urban chronicler **Ben Katchor**, **horror** master Charles Burns, and Spiegelman himself. *RAW* also introduced American readers to prominent international cartoonists such as France's Jacques Tardi, the Netherlands' Joost Swarte, Argentina's José Muñoz and Carlos Sampayo, and Japan's Yoshiharu Tsuge. By providing a common venue for cutting-edge cartoonists, *RAW* created a virtual community of contemporary artists and became the center of an international comics avant-garde. Moreover, throughout its run, *RAW* reprinted a judicious selection of comics from the turn of the century through the 1940s, including work by Winsor McCay, George Herriman, Milt Gross, Boody Rogers, and **Basil Wolverton**.

The early *RAW* presented contributors' work to its best advantage through an innovative format and impressive production values. Establishing the format of the first eight issues, *RAW* #1 was oversized (10½" × 14¼") to showcase its artwork. As with subsequent issues, the first issue was prepared to exacting standards on quality paper; according to a 1985 *Village Voice* article, Mouly approved just 3,500 of about 5,000 copies of *RAW* #1. Despite its relatively large printings, which reportedly ran as many as 7,500 copies, the first volume became a hybrid of the mass-market and the handmade with such features as a full-color image glued by hand onto the cover (#1) and a hand-torn cover (#7). At a time when Tribeca's Printed Matter was first bringing widespread attention to publications made by artists, *RAW* magazine emerged as an art object in itself, with extras that included comics booklets, trading cards and bubble gum (#2), an audio flexi-disc (#4), and mail-in stickers (#5). The cover for #3 with a Panter illustration even won a 1981 *Print* magazine design certificate.

Through 1986, *RAW*'s generous size and attractive presentation encouraged experimentation over narratives and shorter over longer works; content followed format. Because most of *RAW*'s early pieces were one or two pages, lengthier entries tended to stand out. Some noteworthy examples from the first volume include Muñoz and Sampayo's neo-noir "Mister Wilcox, Mister Conrad" (#3), Francis Masse's topsy-turvy "A Race of Racers" (#4), and Crumb's biographical "Jelly Roll Morton's Voodoo Curse" (#7). However, by far the most important work to appear in *RAW* was

Spiegelman's own epic Holocaust memoir *Maus*, one chapter of which was included as a small-format supplement in each issue from #2 onward.

With the 1986 publication of the first volume of *Maus* by Pantheon Books, Spiegelman and Mouly began their partnership with commercial publishers. Since 1982, *RAW* had released a series of "*RAW* One-Shots," stand-alone forerunners of today's graphic novels, featuring individual magazine contributors such as Panter, Sue Coe, and Jerry Moriarty. Pantheon and later Penguin continued this series, but Spiegelman and Mouly lost some of their creative control as they had to conform to industry production standards. Pantheon's reprinting of material from the first three issues of *RAW* in *Read Yourself Raw* (1987) brought a retrospective note to the magazine, but *RAW* itself was revived by Penguin in 1989 after a three-year hiatus. Even with Spiegelman and Mouly at the helm, *RAW* was a very different magazine under Penguin. Most important, it became *Maus*-sized, reduced to a digest format, but it grew in length to 200 pages, allowing it to show more work by more artists and reorienting it towards extended narratives. Despite *RAW*'s expansion and its mainstream distribution, it ended its run in 1991 after three issues with Penguin and the publication of volume two of *Maus*. By that time, though, *RAW* had fulfilled its mission of bringing together like-minded creators to show what was possible in making and publishing comics and validated their work as part of commercial culture.

**Selected Bibliography:** Kartalopoulos, Bill. "A *RAW* History: Part One" and "A *RAW* History: Part Two." *Indy Magazine* (Winter 2005), http://www.indyworld.com/indy/; Sabin, Roger. *Comics, Comix & Graphic Novels: A History of Comic Art.* London: Phaidon, 1996; Spiegelman, Art, and Françoise Mouly, eds. *Read Yourself Raw.* New York: Pantheon Books, 1987; Witek, Joseph, ed. *Art Spiegelman: Conversations.* Jackson: University Press of Mississippi, 2007.

*Michael W. Hancock*

**RED SON.** *See Superman: Red Son*

**RELIGION IN COMICS.** Religion is frequently a topic of comics, whether it involves the traditional organized faiths or goes beyond those to encompass a broader view of religion. As represented in comics, religion frequently extends beyond recognized modern institutions into the realms of myth, the supernatural, allegory, and outright fiction. Though only overt in select cases, the interaction between comics and religion is quite multifaceted. Comics have served as the medium for religious narrative, religious commentary, religious expression, pro-religious material, anti-religious sentiment, or simply for spiritual subtext. Conversely, comics have been used as the tool of religious organizations, creators, seekers, or critics. Given the plasticity of their dealings, comics and religion need to be considered separately first in order to assess the larger picture.

Creators' religions have been a frequent topic of academic and journalistic attention. Much, for example, has been made of the fact that a surprisingly large number of the medium's foremost creators have been Jewish. These include the creators of **Superman**, **Jerry Siegel** and **Joe Shuster**; the creator of *The Spirit* and early proponent of the graphic novel, **Will Eisner**; the creator of **Batman**, **Bob Kane**; and the creators of numerous **Marvel Comics** titles, **Stan Lee** (born Stan Lieber) and **Jack Kirby** (born Jacob Kurtzberg). The climate in which these pre–World War II Jewish artists worked became the inspiration behind Michael Chabon's Pulitzer Prize–winning novel *The Adventures of Kavalier & Clay*. Since that era, a number of other notable Jewish creators have made their marks in the field, among them Stan Goldberg (*Archie*), **William Gaines** (*MAD*), **Art Spiegelman** (*RAW*), **Harvey Pekar** (*American Splendor*), Joe Kubert (*Sgt. Rock*), **Trina Robbins** (*Wimmen's Comix*), **Howard Chaykin** (*American Flagg!*), and Peter David (*The Incredible Hulk*).

Outside of the Judeo-Christian tradition, the U.S. comics industry has felt the influence of writers and artists from other faith groups. Companies such as the Egypt-based AK Comics and Dr. Naif Al-Mutawa's Teshkeel Comics have brought Islamic English-language works to the fore, as have stateside creators such as G. Willow Wilson (*Cairo*) and Toufic El Rassi (*Arab in America*). The eight-volume story of *Buddha* has been translated from its original Japanese by **Osamu Tezuka** into English by publisher Vertical. Further, Liquid Comics (originally Virgin Comics) features a stable of Hindu talents; an adapted, New Age version of the Vedanta also appears in the chaos magic practices of **Grant Morrison** (*Invisibles*, *Vimanarama*). Along similar lines, Neo-Pagan voices can be found in the work of **Alan Moore** (*Watchmen*) and Holly Golightly (*Sabrina*).

Devout Christian authors and their products also fill significant corners of the field. **Mike Allred**, most popularly known for his **superhero** work on *X-Statix*, has produced *The Golden Plates*, a comic-book account of the Book of Mormon. Christian comic books themselves have become a cottage industry, with Jack Chick and his proselytizing Chick Tracts having continued publication since the early 1970s. International Christian publishing company Zondervan has expanded into comic books with their line of Z Graphic Novels including *Hand of the Morningstar*, *Kingdoms: A Biblical Epic*, and their series of *Manga Bibles*. Zondervan's should not be confused with *The Manga Bible* by British artist Siku nor with the *Manga Bible* from Living Bible publisher Tyndale. Even mainstream creator **Mark Millar** has begun exploring his own Christianity, starting with the miniseries *Chosen*, the first in his planned *American Jesus* trilogy.

In addition to these, a number of biblical accounts have been transposed into the comic book medium by faithful and non-faithful alike. The small press Archaia has released several works among its other **fantasy** and genre titles dealing with re-readings of the Bible: *The Lone and Level Sands*, a telling of Exodus from the Egyptian royal family's point of view; *The Secret History*, the story of ageless immortals living through biblical times into modern history; and *Some New Kind of Slaughter*, a compilation of flood myths from all time periods, including that of Noah's era. (The publisher has also produced series based on the Greek pantheon, *Hybrid Bastards!*, and Mayan and Aztec apocalyptic lore, *The Long Count*.) Portions of the Hebrew Bible have been turned into graphic novels, such as *Samson: Judge of Israel* and *Testament* from Metron Press, *Daniel: Prophet of Dreams* from Cross Culture Entertainment, and J. T. Waldman's *Megillat Esther* from the Jewish Publication Society of America. In addition to those already listed, the Christian Bible has seen numerous treatments in the medium, including *The Comic Book Bible* from Barbour Publishing, *The Illustrated Bible: Complete New Testament* from Thomas Nelson, and *The Lion Graphic Bible: The Whole Story from Genesis to Revelation* from Lion UK. Finally, *Rex Mundi*, an alternate world Holy Grail quest as murder mystery, gives both a sympathetic portrayal of Judas and a different account of Jesus's fate.

A chief mainstream source of religiously-themed works is the Vertigo wing of **DC Comics**. As a mature readers (adult) line, the Vertigo imprint has served as a home for the spiritual, Gaea philosophies in *The Saga of **Swamp Thing*** and the mystic, paranormal underworld of ***Hellblazer:*** *John Constantine*. Notably, **Neil Gaiman's Sandman** series—a mixture of pantheism, Abrahamic monotheism, polytheism, and henotheism—conducted its remarkable 75-issue run under the Vertigo banner, in addition to various specials and related miniseries. It led to *The Dreaming*, an exploration of the eponymous Sandman's kingdom, and *Lucifer*, the exploits of the first fallen angel now liberated from reigning over Hell. Vertigo also produced **Kyle Baker's** graphic novel *King David*, a semi-comical staging of the Goliath-slayer's rise to power, and the entirety of **Garth Ennis** and Steve Dillon's ***Preacher***, the gruesome story of a divinely-powered, lapsed clergyman's search for God in order to hold the Creator accountable. Like *Sandman*, *Preacher* had a 75-issue run, though largely confined to Judeo-Christian material. More recently, Vertigo has generated the postmodern Bible update *Testament*, the sexually charged *American Virgin*, and the Eastern-focused *Crossing Midnight* series, yet all three were canceled short of their creators' full visions.

A majority of the comics foregoing scriptural adaptation to address religious concerns of impact has arisen from independent presses or the graphics branch of major prose publishers. Originally published by Baronet Books in 1976, Eisner's **A Contract with God** was not only shaped around the Jewish tenement communities of Eisner's childhood but its title story directly addressed the issue of faith in the face of unjust loss. Popularly credited as the first "graphic novel," *A Contract with God* has since been reissued by Titan, **Kitchen Sink Press**, DC Comics, and W. W. Norton. From 1977 through 1991, Spiegelman developed ***Maus: A Survivor's Tale***, the memoir of his father's ordeals as a World War II-era Jewish concentration camp survivor and their subsequent relationship. Serially published in his ***RAW*** magazine, *Maus* was first collected in 1986, earning the 1986 Pulitzer Prize Special Award among other accolades.

Pantheon Books brought Marjane Satrapi's award-winning French-language ***Persepolis*** memoir to an American readership beginning in 2000. The book and its follow-up editions detail the childhood, adolescence, and young adulthood of Marjane as a Muslim girl coming of age and being impelled to leave post-war Iran. Her youthful course towards becoming a self-appointed prophetess is quickly derailed by the incursion of fundamentalist rule and her wider encounters with a disappointing world. Satrapi's studio-mate, Joann Sfar, has also had his French series *The Rabbi's Cat* translated into English and brought to American audiences by Pantheon. *The Rabbi's Cat* tells the story of a local Algerian rabbi who, along with his pet cat, must cope with the threatening arrival of a council-appointed rabbi from France and foreign suitors for the rabbi's daughter. Outside incursion also frames the majority of **Joe Sacco's Palestine**, a **Fantagraphics** book-length collection of comics journalism reporting on modern Palestinians' turmoil and faith. While Sacco may be a Christian American presenting an international readership with a particular people's perspectives, Craig Thomson, creator of **Blankets**, depicted his own childhood in an evangelical Christian community for a wider comic book reading audience through the publisher Top Shelf Productions. Thomson's own sexual awakening first conflicts then negotiates with the agapic love of Christianity through his first girlfriend, Raina. The relationship ultimately falters as does Thomson's faith.

Many comics are critical of religion and suspicious of faith's pernicious effects. For instance, Thomson's work on *Blankets* would not have been possible without Justin Green's pioneering underground work, **Binky Brown Meets the Holy Virgin Mary**. In it, the title character, Green's autobiographical alter ego, faces his conflict with the church in the wake of his sexual and compulsive obsessions. Other underground innovators, such as **Jaxon** and Frank Stack, produced titles like *God Nose* and *The New Adventures of Jesus* that have been considered blasphemous in their casual and even crass depictions of Christian divinity. More recently, creators such as **Robert Kirkman** and Tony Moore have published the irreverent *Battle Pope* series featuring a foul-mouthed, hard-drinking, super-powered, philandering Pope John Paul II and his sidekick Jesus fighting demons in a post-Rapture landscape. James Munroe and Salgood Sam also leverage a post-Rapture landscape in their graphic novel *Therefore, Repent!*, turning the remaining human population into the fortunate ones, free of false belief. Even the 1998 Stan Lee/**Moebius** collaboration on the cosmic *Silver Surfer: Parable* has been seen as a staunch critique of religion and morality, returning the world-eating Galactus character to the role in which Lee and Kirby first imagined him for *Fantastic Four* #48: a God surrogate.

Such stand-ins for religious figures are not always necessary. A number of fictional comic-book characters, even those featured in mainstream superhero titles, exhibit—to varying degrees, largely determined by their current writers—dedication to specific real-world faiths. When popularized by **Frank Miller**, the vigilante **Daredevil** had his Catholicism emphasized throughout the "Born Again" storyline. His alter ego, Matt Murdoch, had his life dismantled by the Kingpin of Crime, only to find his long-lost mother had become a nun. Similarly, as a member of Marvel's **X-Men**, the demonic-looking Nightcrawler became engaged for a time in studying for the priesthood, despite his Roma upbringing. Much of that involvement, though, was written away by subsequent inheritors of the *X-Men* books. More consistent has been the dedication of the Marvel character Marc Spector to his Egyptian god Khonsu as the vigilante Moon

Knight. Raised Jewish, Spector pledged himself to this deity in exchange for saving his mortal life. Complicating this, however, is Spector's own tenuous sanity, putting such devotion in a suspect light. Conversely, only in recent years has the Fantastic Four's Ben "The Thing" Grimm acknowledged his Jewish identity, something he quashed as a youth on the mean streets of New York; and the late Boston Brand's posthumous dedication to Hinduism as Deadman is also questionable, given no evidence that he was a believer until after he died and was reconstituted as a ghost. Further, while the Savage Dragon is a self-professed atheist, he has apparently met the Devil and God personally.

The supernatural is often folded into religion as a dogma-less, flexible theology with overt visual/physical results. This likely occurs due to the perceived overlap between demonic magic and the Judeo-Christian-Islamic concept of Satan and fallen angels. In addition to Gaiman's Lucifer, most of the major superhero publishers have a multitude of Satan-like or Hell-linked characters (e.g., Mephisto, Neron, Blaze, Satannish, Hades, Satanus, Malebolgia, Hela, etc.), all of whom occupy a realm not unlike Hell; sometimes these kingdoms even overlap and the "Satans" go to battle against each other, such as in the series *Underworld Unleashed* or *Reign in Hell*. Angels themselves play a variety of roles in the superhero genre, from adversaries (e.g. The Saint of Killers in *Preacher*) to allies (Zauriel in *JLA*) to weapons (**The Punisher**, briefly). Most often, though, this manner of religion is characterized more as supernatural sorcery or witchcraft, empowering would-be heroes like **Ghost Rider**, Zatanna, Hellstrom, Jason Blood, Brother Voodoo, The Doctor of *The Authority*, and **Dark Horse Comics'** eponymous *Hellboy*. In fact, in the case of the latter Hellboy, his native infernal realm is conceived little in the way of Christian soteriology, but instead his Hell is a Cthonic, Lovecraftian portal to the supernatural. These other portrayals sometimes further reduce the supernatural/religious into a form of super-science: rational, tamable energies just beyond the ken of modern investigation. **Image Comics'** *The Atheist* was predicated on the idea that stoic logic can investigate and defeat infernal possession. Alternately, **Kurt Busiek's *Astro City*** particularly plays with comics' religious/supernatural overlap in the Confessor, a **vampire**/priest hero. Through this brand of over-encompassing inclusion, a Norse god such as **Thor** can fight alongside a magic practitioner such as the Scarlet Witch, a technological **Iron Man**, and a devout Catholic such as Dagger all against an emissary of a monotheistic divinity (e.g., The Living Tribunal).

The superhero genre has also fashioned a large number of fictional religions for its storytelling purposes. Whether these faiths are being created as analogies to real-world denominations, as politically-correct straw men, as serious reflections on the concept of organized religion, or as easy targets for vilifying is to be determined on a case-by-case basis. In many estimations, the Triune Understanding depicted in Busiek's *Avengers* series is a riff on the Church of Scientology. Though they were responsible for the empowerment of the Avengers' ally Triathlon, the Triune Understanding was also linked to a pernicious alien race, making their motives dubious. Decades earlier, Jim Starlin further developed a malevolent incarnation of his Christ-figure Adam Warlock—who had died and resurrected for Counter-Earth—into the leader of the Universal Church of Truth. This alternate version of Warlock, now dubbed the Magus, could be read as Starlin commenting on the errant nature of institutionalized or papal Christianity, while the heroic Warlock retained pure Christ-like nobility. In the 1990s, Starlin would return to this theme through another of Warlock's discarded aspects, the Goddess, who would lead an apocalyptic sect of followers in what can be read as another critique of turn-of-the-century religious millennial alarm. Along with the Triune Understanding and Universal Church of Truth, Marvel Comics has also made religion the main impetus for many alien races' aggressions, notably the shape-shifting Skrulls and their foiled plans to infiltrate Earth, as prophesied by their scripture.

DC Comics has developed its own fictional religions, as well. Most notable among them would be the creation by Jack Kirby—and later development by **Grant Morrison**—of the New Gods. Though they often behaved and interacted with other extraterrestrial species as merely a powerful pantheon of warring aliens, the New Gods have taken on much more cosmically divine features in Morrison's later interpretations. Similarly, the inhabitants of planets Rann (the adopted home of Adam Strange) and Thanagar (the original world of Hawkman) have each become imbued with religious fervor in their 21st-century portrayals, leading to the miniseries *The Rann-Thanagar War* and *The Rann-Thanagar Holy War*. Also, following the death of Conner "Superboy" Kent, aka Kon-El, a human group led by Wonder Girl form "The Cult of Conner," based on Kryptonian technology and the belief that he can be resurrected; they are, however, broken up by a band of heroes who had themselves been previously resurrected.

The issue of resurrection and rebirth following mortal death is a particularly recurring theme in superhero comics. In fact, one of the few religious rituals consistently depicted in comics is the funeral (as opposed to, say, baptism or confirmation). Frequently, it is made as a universal, non-denominational service, though a casket, a congregation or funeral party, prayer leader, and some form of prayer book remain fixtures. Despite this reliability and apparent sincerity, an extraordinary number of characters have proven actual biological death—not a "fake death" or death-like state—to be temporary: **Aquaman**, Captain Britain, Colossus, Dr. Doom, Elektra, Elasti-Girl, **The Flash**, **Green Arrow**, **Green Lantern**, Hawkeye, Hawkman, Hellcat, Lex Luthor, Marvel Girl, Metamorpho, The Punisher, The Red Skull, Robin, **Spawn**, Thor, Wonder Man, **Wonder Woman**, and so on. Supposedly, in the case of DC Comics, the hero Kid Eternity, Agent of Chaos, was holding the metaphysical door between life and death open, allowing such ease of return for dead souls. In the case of Marvel Comics, several of these resurrections have been explained away either as the result of magical instability on the part of the Scarlet Witch or as the result of Skull imposters.

Of the many intersections between this medium and religion, the one engagement that has yet to take place is the creation of a new theology from a comic. These works have been used to contemplate religion, criticize it, degrade it, reflect it, honor it, and even proselytize for it. Given the increased quantity of these connections and the rising validation of the medium among U.S. audiences, the possibility of faith arising from panels is no longer impossible.

**Selected Bibliography:** Baskind, Samantha, and Ranen Omer-Sherman, eds. *The Jewish Graphic Novel: Critical Approaches*. New Brunswick, NJ: Rutgers University Press, 2008; Fingeroth, Danny. *Disguised as Clark Kent: Jews, Comics, and the Creation of the Superhero*. New York: Continuum, 2007; Garrett, Greg. *Holy Superheroes!: Exploring the Sacred in Comics, Graphic Novels, and Film*. Louisville, KY: Westminster John Knox Press, 2008; Knowles, Christopher. *Our Gods Wear Spandex: The Secret History of Comic Book Heroes*. San Francisco: Weiser Books, 2007; Lewis, A. David and Christine Hoff Kraemer, eds. *Graven Images: Religion in Comic Books & Graphic Novels*. New York: Continuum, 2010; LoCicero, Donald. *Superheroes and Gods: A Comparative Study from Babylonia to Batman*. Jefferson, NC: McFarland, 2008; McLain, Karline. *India's Immortal Comic Books: Gods, Kings, and Other Heroes*. Bloomington: Indiana University Press, 2009; Oropeza, B. J. *The Gospel According to Superheroes: Religion and Pop Culture*. New York: Peter Lang, 2005; "The Religion of Comic Book Characters." Adherents.com. http://www.adherents.com/lit/comics/comic_book_religion.html.

*A. David Lewis*

**RETCON.** Short for retroactive continuity, "retcon" is used as a verb to denote the process of revising a fictional serial narrative, altering details that have previously been established in the narrative so that it can be continued in a new direction or so that potential contradictions in previous events can be reconciled. The process is especially common in comic books, which traditionally seek continuity in their narratives over time, but which often involve large and complex narrative constructs that tend to get out of hand. This is especially the case with large publishers such as **DC** and **Marvel**, which generally attempt to maintain consistency among most of their various titles. With so many titles involved, however, discrepancies inevitably arise. Multiple Earths, parallel dimensions, and alternate timelines become the homes of different versions of the same characters, introducing potential confusion for readers. Retconning allows writers to revise existing stories, fill in missing details, or substitute entirely new versions of events.

The term "retcon" can also be used as a noun to designate the specific comics (or other works) that are published in this process of revision. The process of retconning is used in comics when it is felt that a narrative has become too complex or unwieldy and needs to be simplified, or when it is felt that a character's history has gone in a direction that is difficult to build upon and carry forward. **John Byrne**'s revision of the origin of **Superman** in the 1986 miniseries *The Man of Steel* is a prominent example of retconning in comics, though the most important example is probably **DC's *Crisis on Infinite Earths*** (1985), a 12-part series that includes all the company's major characters and resolves a number of contradictions in their backstories.

*M. Keith Booker*

**RICHIE RICH.** First appearing in Harvey Comics' *Little Dot* #1 (1953) in a story drawn by Steven Muffatti, Richie Rich continued as the protagonist of a back-up series in that title and other Harvey anthology series until finally graduating to his own book in 1960. Within the decade, Richie Rich would become Harvey's most popular character under the creative eyes of artists Warren Kremer and Ernie Colón.

Some debate exists over the creation of Richie Rich. Harvey Comics co-owner Alfred Harvey has claimed credit for the character, but Warren Kremer, who was responsible for many designs of Harvey characters, has also claimed to be the creator. At the height of his popularity in the early 1970s, Richie Rich comics sold more than 1,000,000 copies per month. At the point of highest saturation, Harvey Comics produced 33 Richie Rich titles in a single month, and he has starred in over 50 titles total.

Dubbed "The Poor Little Rich Boy," Richie Rich's stories originally focused on how the boy's wealth and privilege kept him from enjoying most of the more carefree pleasures of childhood. His girlfriend, Gloria Glad, rejects Richie's exorbitant gifts in an effort to keep him humble. As the series increased in popularity, Richie's adventures became more fantastic and often focused on the advantages that his enormous wealth provided. These adventures frequently took place on the international stage (or, in some cases, interplanetary) and were strongly influenced by comic predecessors like *Tintin* and Little Orphan Annie. In his world, Richie is a celebrity who is recognized world-wide for his wealth and adventures.

Richie's father owns Rich Industries, a multinational corporation, located in the city of Richville, that produces a wide variety of products. These products, usually invented by Professor Keenbean, often serve as the impetus for Richie's adventures. Richie Rich has a large supporting cast, including Cadbury the butler, Irona the robot maid, Dollar the dog (a rare breed of "Dollarmatians" with dollar signs in place of spots), his girlfriend Gloria, his best friends Pee-Wee and Freckles Friendly, child comedian Jackie Jokers, Billy Bellhops, and others. Richie's most common nemesis is his cousin, Reggie Van Dough. Reggie is the antithesis of Richie—a spoiled, rich child who uses his wealth to play practical jokes on others. Reggie always gets his comeuppance, but such lessons never have a lasting effect on him.

Covers to Richie Rich comics usually depict the boy using money for purposes other than currency: he carpets his floor and decorates his walls with it, he plays in piles of bills, and dollar signs often appear in his presence. Covers also depict Richie treating other signs of wealth, like gold, jewels, and oil, as playthings.

Harvey Comics ceased publication in 1982, only to return for a brief period from 1986 to 1994. Richie Rich also starred in his own Saturday morning television cartoon series beginning in 1980, and he was the subject of two feature films, the first (1994) starring Macaulay Culkin as the poor little rich boy.

*Andrew J. Kunka*

**ROAD TO PERDITION.** This graphic novel by writer **Max Allan Collins** (*Dick Tracy*) and artist Richard Piers Rayner (***Hellblazer***, ***Swamp Thing***) was published in 1998 by **DC Comics** under its Paradox Press imprint. Sam Mendes directed the award-winning 2002 film adaptation of the same name, which was written for the screen by David Self. Collins's inspiration for the 300-page novel was Kazuo Koike and Goseki

Kojima's important **manga**, *Lone Wolf and Cub*, the epic story of a shogun's enforcer, wrongly accused and widowed, who is forced to travel the road of vengeance with his toddler son in tow. *Road to Perdition* offers a distinctly American version of this father/son story.

Set in prohibition-era Rock Island, Illinois, the novel tells the tale of Michael O'Sullivan, devout family man, ex-soldier, and Irish crime boss John Looney's chief lieutenant. The story is seen from the point of view of O'Sullivan's son, Michael Jr., who narrates his childhood from a vantage point decades later in order to set the record straight, years after pulp writers and historians alike have established O'Sullivan's notoriety as the "Angel of Death." The story begins when young Michael stows away in his father's backseat and witnesses Connor Looney, the crime boss's slightly psychopathic son, turn a routine shakedown into a cold-blooded murder. Additionally, he witnesses his father's loyalty and efficient, unflappable skills with a Thompson submachine gun.

Because the Looneys suspect that Michael or O'Sullivan might betray Connor and the family's interests, the elder Looney orders a hit on his faithful servant, while Connor murders O'Sullivan's wife and younger son, leaving O'Sullivan and Michael on the lam, forced to defend themselves from Looney's long reach. Correctly fearful of O'Sullivan's vengeance and skills, Looney sends Connor into hiding under Al Capone's protection, and O'Sullivan launches an offensive against the revenue streams of both the Looney and Capone families, with the intent of making Connor's protection a

Tom Hanks as Michael O'Sullivan and Tyler Hoechlin as Michael Sullivan Jr. in the 2002 film *Road to Perdition*, directed by Sam Mendes. Dreamworks/Photofest

losing financial proposition. O'Sullivan and son thus begin their crime spree against Midwestern banks and their dirty deposits from Capone's and Looney's gambling, bootlegging, and extortion revenue. Looney increases the bounty on O'Sullivan's head to a quarter million dollars, and O'Sullivan provides Eliot Ness with a paper trail to indict the elder Looney in exchange for permission to continue his efforts to find and kill Connor Looney. When O'Sullivan burns and robs the mob's riverboat gambling operation, Capone decides that Connor Looney is more trouble than he's worth and hands him over to O'Sullivan, who gives him what he deserves. Unfortunately, in the end, O'Sullivan also must pay for his sins, himself shot down by an assassin, who is in turn shot down by young Michael.

Collins based his well-researched story loosely on actual characters and events: Rock Island-area crime boss John Looney did have a betrayed lieutenant, and the riverboat *Quinlan* did burn. Rayner's impressively detailed black-and-white art depicts Ness, Capone, and Frank Nitti, Capone's right-hand man, with nearly photorealistic historical accuracy. However, it is O'Sullivan and Michael, the most fictional of the book's characters, who bring the story to life. Following the murder of his wife, O'Sullivan wants to drop off Michael at a relative's farm in Perdition, Kansas, but mobsters are watching the farmhouse. Neither can he entrust Michael to any law enforcement agency in the Midwest; he tells Michael that all are corrupted by mob money: "There are no police in Chicago . . . just killers in blue uniforms" (121–22). The only way that he can make sure that Michael is safe is to keep him near, and readers see both anguish and tenderness in his face when he leaves Michael in the car while he tends to the business of retribution. Father and son develop a powerful emotional bond over the course of their violent adventure, one that would not likely have occurred if their lives had not been disrupted by violence.

Unlike *Lone Wolf and Cub*'s toddler son, *Perdition*'s Michael is nearly 10, capable of helping his father achieve vengeance by driving the getaway car and sometimes handling a gun, old enough to develop a deep relationship with his stoic father. O'Sullivan's serious demeanor with Michael during their long car rides and hotel stays is frequently tempered with displays of simple, genuine approval of his son's behavior. When Michael follows his instructions to wait until he returns, he says, "Good lad." On the country road where he teaches Michael to drive, he offers supportive praise: "You're doing fine." Never does he show anger or violence toward Michael. Neither does he wish that Michael follow in his occupational footsteps: "Be whatever you want—as long as it's not like me" (239). Unable ever to return home, Michael and his father are sealed off from their former lives, and Rayner strategically emphasizes this psychological loss and emotional distance when he shows the characters looking out through the car's windows, which reflects the city or the countryside outside, one image superimposed upon the other, neither complete. In the novel's many action scenes, Rayner's depictions of violence are both chaotic and beautiful; O'Sullivan leaps, lunges, and springs with the utmost grace, and his bullets do not miss. The angles of depiction are unpredictable, and the choreography is elegant.

While *Road to Perdition* qualifies as both a graphic crime novel and graphic historical novel, Collins's expert development of the father/son relationship and Rayner's exquisite artwork elevate the novel beyond generic limitations and expectations.

*Anthony D. Baker*

**ROBBINS, TRINA** (1938–). Trina Robbins is the world's foremost comics "herstorian," having written several major books on women in comics. She is also an important cartoonist in her own right, and a pioneer in publishing female comics artists. Robbins made her debut working in **underground comics**, or "**comix**," in the early 1970s, and was one of the very first female comics artists to emerge in these formative years for comic art. Robbins's first comics were printed in the *East Village Other*. She later joined the staff of the feminist underground newspaper *It Ain't Me, Babe*, where she produced the first American all-woman comic book, also titled *It Ain't Me, Babe*, in 1970. She would go on to become increasingly involved in creating outlets for, and promoting, female comics artists—who at the time were few and often not invited to the all-male underground comix anthologies.

Robbins next major project was the anthology *Wimmen's Comix*, started in 1972 and run by a group of female artists. *Wimmen's Comix* turned out to be an important springboard for a whole new generation of female comics artists, including Mary Fleener, Melinda Gebbie, **Phoebe Gloeckner**, Roberta Gregory, Aline Komisky Crumb, Carol Lay, Diane Noomin, Lee Marrs, Sharon Rudahl, Dori Seda, Carol Tyler, and Penny Van Horn. The magazine folded in 1992.

Even though she has always worked to promote other female artists, Robbins has also had the time to work as an artist herself, in the 1970s producing underground comix magazines like *All Girl Thrills* and *Girl Fight*. In the 1980s she, among other things, worked as penciler on **Wonder Woman** for the major publisher **DC Comics**. In the 1990s and into the 21st century she has worked on the comic *GoGirl*, with artist Anne Timmons for **Image Comics**.

Always working with a feminist goal, Robbins soon realized that the literature about comics was not paying enough attention to female creators, characters, and readers. In the 1980s she therefore set out to produce the very first book about comics from a decidedly female perspective. The result was *Women and the Comics*, published in 1985 and co-written by Catherine Yronwode. Since then, Robbins has become the world's leading comics herstorian, producing a number of books about comics, writing articles, curating exhibitions, and giving lectures.

Robbins has also written several books on other themes, but always from a feminist perspective. Today she is, among other things, producing scripts for biographical comics like *Hedy Lamarr and a Secret Communication System* and *Florence Nightingale: Lady with the Lamp*. Robbins won a Special Achievement Award from the San Diego Comic Con in 1989 for her work on *Strip AIDS U.S.A.*, a benefit book she co-edited with **Bill Sienkiewicz** and Robert Triptow. She was also one of the founders of the non-profit organization *Friends of Lulu*, created in 1994 to promote readership of comic books by women and the participation of women in the comic book industry.

*See also:* Feminism

**Selected Bibliography:** Robbins, Trina. *A Century of Women Cartoonists.* Northampton, MA: Kitchen Sink Press, 1993; Robbins, Trina. *The Great Women Superheroes.* Northampton, MA: Kitchen Sink Press, 1997; Robbins, Trina. *From Girls to Grrrlz: A History of Women's Comics from Teens to Zines.* San Francisco: Chronicle Books, 1999; Robbins, Trina. *The Great Women Cartoonists.* New York: Watson-Guptill, 2001; Robbins, Trina. *The Brinkley Girls: The Best of Nell Brinkley's Cartoons from 1913–1940.* Seattle: Fantagraphics, 2009.

*Fredrik Strömberg*

**ROCKETEER, THE.** Created in 1982 for Pacific Comics by writer/artist **Dave Stevens**, the Rocketeer is the alter ego of stunt pilot Cliff Secord, who is able to fly with the aid of a high-tech rocket pack. The character's physical appearance was based on the creator. However, there were obvious influences from other sources. Inspired by cliffhanger movie serials of the 1940s, the narrative drew on numerous influences. **Doc Savage** served as the inspiration for the nameless inventor of the rocket pack. The look of pin-up queen Bette Page inspired the character of Secord's girlfriend Betty. Stevens's friend and aesthetic inspiration Doug Wildey, creator of *Jonny Quest*, was the basis for Secord's friend and mentor Peavey. Stevens completed two Rocketeer stories, the original eponymous story and *Cliff's New York Adventure*. Though not named, **The Shadow** and his cadre are the catalysts of the second story. In the second storyline, Lothar is modeled on actor Rondo Hatton, who also appears in the 1991 Disney film adaptation of the series. Also in the second storyline, the magician The Great Orsinio is based on Orson Welles. Eclipse Comics serialized and collected the first story, and Comico published the second as a miniseries, later collected by **Dark Horse**. After the first book was adapted to film by Disney Studios in 1991, a graphic novel **adaptation** of the film was published by Hollywood Comics, written by Peter David and illustrated by Russ Heath. David authored a prose novelization of the film as well.

The first narrative begins with Secord as a down-on-his-luck stunt flyer. After a stolen rocket pack is stashed in his plane, he is thrust into a series of adventures involving **Nazis**, government agents, and organized crime. The first storyline of two is set in 1938 California, and uses the vehicle of the air show as a framework for adventure. Originally running as a backup story in Mike Grell's *Starslayer*, the series took advantage of its backup feature format to set up cliffhanger endings. Within this framework, the Rocketeer flew onto crashing planes, fought his way out of experimental aircraft piloted by Nazis, and escaped a hospital bed to run in search of his lady love—the stuff of true adventure. The first storyline offered an open-ended conclusion. As it proved quite popular, a second story was begun.

A poster for the 1991 film *The Rocketeer*, directed by Joe Johnston. Buena Vista Pictures/Photofest

In the second story, Cliff finds his way to New York. In contrast to the relatively open spaces of 1938 California, the milieu of the late-1930s New York club scene presents Secord as a fish out of water. The first storyline was to some extent a pastiche of the **Doc Savage** stories. The second was a pastiche of The Shadow. Both grew from Stevens's fascination with the 1930s. This fascination is also evident in the attention to detail in the art. Ranging from the accuracy of the Bulldog Diner to effectively capturing the technical aspects of stunt flying planes of the era, the look, pacing, storyline, and dialogue all read as a period piece rather than pastiche. To a great extent, the period look and feel carried over to the film.

However, the original narrative was altered for the film. In addition to the overt substitution of Howard Hughes for Doc Savage, offered merely as a throwaway gag in the original story, a matinee idol, a **Nazi** dirigible and a mob boss were added. Most significantly, the story was self-contained, as there was no guarantee of a sequel. Fan opinion is widely divided on the film. There was also some disappointment that Stevens was not assigned the art chores for the film's one-sheet. Some hold the film to be one of the most successful adaptations of a comic, while others were bitterly disappointed.

However, no such division exists on the comic stories. Stevens's work was widely recognized for its detail, expression, composition, fluid storytelling, and anatomies. The latter proved Stevens's forté. His rendering of a voluptuous, yet realistic and friendly female form echoed the work of 1940s pin-up artists, especially Gil Elvgren and Vargas. Stevens briefly succeeded Vargas as a pinup artist at *Playboy*.

Some regard Betty as the most significant contribution made by *The Rocketeer* to the comics. This character's look and aesthetic were consistent with the "good girl art" tradition of **Matt Baker** in the 1940s, and **Al Williamson**'s and **Frank Frazetta**'s renderings of sensuous women in the 1950s. This art also drew substantially on, and was a catalyst in renewing mainstream interest in the career of bondage pinup girl Bette Page, whom Stevens befriended after publication of *The Rocketeer*. Stevens's work on the character Betty was also reminiscent of "nose art" from World War II aircrafts. Stevens's pinup art proved so popular that it detracted from his narrative work, proving more lucrative. This disparity was partially due to the time taken on each comic page, reflected in the visual detail. However, he never lost interest in *The Rocketeer*.

Stevens's hope and plan for *The Rocketeer* was to allow other creators to take a turn with the character in a series of individual stories. Aside from some pinup pages in the individual issues, this never materialized. Stevens's own work on the title was slow to appear for two reasons. First, Stevens earned a better living doing commercial art and storyboard work than he did doing comics. Second, Stevens had leukemia, which eventually caused his death in March 2008. He was quite private about his condition, so the specific onset and its effect on his artistic output are unknown, but he is reported to have had the condition for several years before his death, so it seems likely to have limited his artistic output on *The Rocketeer*. Stevens's *The Rocketeer* won the Russ Manning, Inkpot and Kirby Awards.

**Selected Bibliography:** Stevens, Dave. *The Rocketeer*. Sacramento, CA: Eclipse Books, 1985; Roach, David. *The Superhero Encyclopedia*. Canton, MI: Visible Ink Press, 2004.

*Diana Green*

**ROMANCE COMICS.** Romance comics became an important phenomenon in American popular culture soon after World War II. However, contrary to some of the myths about the post-World War II comic book scene, they did not explode onto the newsstands overnight. Romance comics did not really catch on until the second half of 1949, but when they did, they became an American cultural institution read by untold millions of girls and women for more than a quarter century. By the mid-1970s, however, romance comics virtually disappeared, only occasionally resurfacing in the form of **satire**, or from independent publishers or in other **underground** comics. The original corporate romance comics, published almost entirely from 1947 to 1977, are now collected with enthusiasm by a handful of comic book and pop cultural historians and art enthusiasts.

The romance genre, so common in a variety of print sources during the first three-quarters of the 20th century, remains a powerful source of print revenue in the form of paperback (and hardcover) romance novels. Many of these stories continue to provide the fantasies that comic books and pulp magazines once did, along with their higher-caliber brethren, the "slick" fiction-filled magazines that have also disappeared from American culture.

Romance novels first comprised only a tiny fraction of the burgeoning paperback book industry, from its modern origins with the first Pocket Books shortly before World War II to the beginning of the Harlequin Romance line in the mid-1960s, which began an explosion of romance paperbacks that continues today. Instead, more than 7,500 pulp magazines were devoted to romance from the 1920s through the 1950s. Only the **Western**—featuring nearly 10,000 issues of the approximately 40,000 total issues published from 1896 to 1960 in more than 1,000 pulp titles—was a more dominant genre (and a number of pulps combined the two genres). Concurrently, hundreds of romance stories appeared every year for more than six decades in the weekly or monthly "slicks," such as *The Saturday Evening Post*, *Coronet*, *McCall's*, *Liberty*, and *Redbook*, along with the multitude of newspaper Sunday supplements of the era, plus the movie magazines and the lower-brow "true confession" magazines, which were printed on slick paper but had more in common with the pulp market. Beginning with the first of the modern pulpwood paper publications for adults, generally recognized as Frank Munsey's *Argosy* in 1896, romance stories appeared in many of the general-interest pulps before the pulp market exploded during the 1920s.

Pulps, indeed, were huge influences on the people who published, created, and in many cases read the nearly 150 romance comic book titles that suddenly appeared in the second half of 1949 and the first half of 1950. Street and Smith's *Love Story Magazine*, the best-remembered of the romance pulps, ran 1,158 issues from 1921 to 1947 and was so popular it was among the few pulps published weekly during most of its existence. *All-Story Love Tales*, begun by the Munsey Company and much later sold to the prolific pulp purveyor Popular Publications, ran 582 issues from 1929 to 1955. *Ranch Romances*, published from 1924 and the last pulp standing when it disappeared in 1971, ran 860 issues from three publishers. Many other titles from several leading publishers enjoyed huge commercial success, including *Thrilling Love*, *Rangeland Romances*, *Sweetheart Stories*, *Cupid's Diary*, and *Love Book Magazine*.

Comic books, though, were late to come to the romance profit party. The early modern comic books, with origins in the mid-1930s, were primarily anthologies of newspaper strips (including a few with romantic elements) until **Superman** debuted in *Action Comics* #1 (June 1938). It took more than a year, but Superman and fellow costumed hero **Batman**, who began in *Detective Comics* #27 (May 1939), brought about dozens of highly successful costumed heroes who began fighting crime in 1939–41, before World War II took center stage. By the end of the war, hundreds of colorful, bizarre, and fanciful characters had been created. As the **Golden Age** of Comics waned in the 1946–50 period, the vast majority of these characters disappeared until a handful of the best were revived and/or modernized in the late 1950s and 1960s, creating the **Silver Age**. Replacing them on post-war newsstands were **crime** comics, **horror** comics, humor comics, **fantasy** comics, Western comics, and romance comics.

Before romance could gain a foothold, however, the teen humor genre came first, complete with dozens of adolescents longing, panting, and scheming for the attention of the opposite sex. Following the template of Andy Hardy in the movies and Henry Aldrich on the radio beginning during the Great Depression, **Archie** Andrews made an inauspicious debut in the MLJ company's **superhero** titles *Pep Comics* #22 (December 1941) and *Jackpot Comics* #4 (Winter 1941–42). Archie was not the first teen in comics—his own company created the earlier non-related Wilbur for

*Zip Comics* #18 (September 1941)—but Archie eventually became by far the most successful teen in the funny books. He and his coterie of Betty, Veronica, and Jughead, plus many other characters, have been entertaining readers young and older ever since.

The first comic book directly marketed to girls—and featuring a smattering of romance in the text features—was the highly successful *Calling All Girls* #1 (September 1941) from the publishers of *Parents' Magazine*. Like the Archie titles, this and several much less successful imitators was a bridge to romance comics. Squeaky clean *Parents' Magazine* kept *Calling All Girls* going for more than two decades in a variety of formats, although the comic strip elements were gone by 1946. The firm left the comic book business in 1949 and did not participate in the blooming of romance comics.

The iconic comic book creators and entrepreneurial business partners **Joe Simon** and **Jack Kirby** established the romance genre in comic books virtually single-handedly, beginning with the first romance comic book, *Young Romance* #1 (September–October 1947) for the small Crestwood Publications line, otherwise known as Feature and Prize. Earlier in the same year, working for the second-tier publisher Hillman Comics, Simon and Kirby dropped strong hints of romance in the teen-humor title *My Date*, which ran from #1 (July 1947) through #4 (January 1948). An obscure 1946 one-shot with a romantically themed cover, *Romantic Picture Novelettes*, was merely a compilation of *Mary Worth* newspaper strip reprints.

Beginning in 1940, the Simon and Kirby team wrote and drew **superhero** adventures few competitors could match. They created *Captain America* #1 (March 1941) for **Timely/Marvel** Comics and produced the first 10 issues before moving over to larger National Comics (now **DC** Comics), for which they made the Boy Commandos a huge hit during World War II. Kirby, one of the most prolific comic book artists of all time, ultimately became most influential for his Silver Age work at Marvel, most notably with his co-creation of the **Fantastic Four** in 1961; but for the first two decades of his career, Kirby's most significant contribution to comic books was the co-creation of the romance genre with the immediate commercial hit *Young Romance*.

"I wondered how they (female readers) would accept a comic book version of the popular *True Story Magazine*, with youthful, emotional yet wholesome stories supposedly told in the first person by love-smitten teen-agers," Simon writes in his memoir, first published in 1990 (122). "Visually," he continues, "the magazine love stories seemed a natural conversion for comic books" (125). He could not have hit a longer, more timely grand slam in the comic book industry, which was in desperate need to re-tool because of the rapidly waning interest in superhero themes. The first story in the first issue of *Young Romance*, "I Was a Pick-Up!" could not have been more different than what had been appearing in any other comics designed to appeal to female readers. Such flamboyant stories, in fact, helped lead to the formation in September 1954 of the self-censorship industry organization, the **Comics Code** Authority.

*Young Romance* and Simon and Kirby's sister title *Young Love*, which debuted in 1949 for tiny Crestwood Publications, thrived with exciting, often highly original covers and themes. Even when 80 percent of the dozens of romance titles that had entered the field by 1950 were killed or suspended that year during industry turmoil, *Young Romance* and *Young Love* emerged as best-sellers on a monthly basis. In his memoir, Simon recalled that *Young Romance* #1 was a "complete sellout" and noted million-plus copy sales quickly became routine for both titles. In 2004, when comics historian Jerry Weist polled 44 leading people in the industry for a book entitled *The 100 Greatest Comic Books*, *Young Romance* #1 was the only romance comic book included, ranking 28th. In a sense, *Young Romance* #1 became a surrogate for an entire genre that existed without continuing characters like Archie or Captain America, but through tales of love set in an endless variety of backgrounds and situations.

Just as *Action Comics* #1 presented Superman for nearly a year without any superheroic competition, *Young Romance* had the love field to itself for nearly a year until Martin Goodman's Marvel Comics (also known as Timely) came up with *My Romance* #1 (August 1948). Goodman's company was long noted for its success with knock-off themes—indeed, Timely's *Captain America* #1 followed the first patriotic hero, MLT's The Shield, to the newsstands 14 months later.

Next in line was the sleazy minor-league publisher Victor Fox, also never one to miss a trend, although destined to remain in comics for less than three more years. Fox converted the radio teen humor **adaptation** of *Meet Corliss Archer* #3 to *My Life* #4 (September 1948), which began two years of a flood of somewhat lurid, short-lived titles from Fox. Fawcett, a major publisher of superhero and Western comics for whom Captain Marvel and Hopalong Cassidy made millions of dollars, jumped in next when it converted the superhero title *Captain Midnight* #67 to *Sweethearts* #68 (October 1948). Unlike the other three pioneering romance publishers, Fawcett boldly began *Sweethearts* as a monthly, perhaps with the knowledge that it was a comic book version of *True Confessions*, the same publisher's hugely successful adult "slick" magazine. Indeed, Fawcett was the only comic book publisher to begin a monthly title of any of the 147 romance titles to appear on the stands in 1949 and 1950. Fawcett also began *Life Story* as a monthly in 1949.

Interestingly, Fawcett did not market *Sweethearts* to the readers of its other comic books. The other Fawcett titles carried neither house ads nor listings for *Sweethearts*—this from a publisher that heavily plugged and listed all of its titles in all of its other comic books. The original readers of the early romance comics in 1947–50—mostly girls from 12 to 20 years old who grew up knowing only the hardships of the Great Depression, followed by World War II—eagerly grabbed the romance comics for a glimpse of what now seemed like the possibility of happiness and prosperity. On the other hand, many of the parents of these adolescent females, reared well before comic books got going in the mid-1930s, were not even aware of what the colorful pamphlet-style comic books were, since they did not yet exist during their childhoods in the era before the Depression.

All told, *Young Romance*, *My Romance*, *My Life*, and *Sweethearts* combined had only 15 issues with 1948 dates, also including the first two in 1947 from *Young Romance*. Publishers failed to pick up the pulse-pounding pace much in the first half of 1949, when only 42 romance issues hit the stands with dates of January through June. St. John and Harvey, then both minor publishers, got into the field with the fifth and sixth romance titles respectively, *Teen-Age Romances* and *First Love*. The always-enterprising Simon and Kirby then produced *Young Love* #1 (February–March 1949) and quickly followed with the first Western-romance hybrid, the short-lived *Real West Romances*, with #1 (April–May 1949), thereby precipitating an ill-fated craze for Western-themed romance comics over the next year. (Despite their rapid demise, these comics represented an interesting attempt to merge traditionally male- and traditionally female-oriented genres.)

Thus, over a 21-month span through June 1949, there were a grand total of only 57 issues devoted to romance. An explosive expansion followed. With publishers rapidly becoming aware of sales figures, no fewer than 256 issues dated July through December 1949 had romance themes, covering 118 titles and 22 publishers, including no fewer than 64 issues dated December alone—more than in the first 21 months of the genre's existence. In all, more than one in five comic books published in the second half of 1949 was devoted to love. Marvel Comics produced 27 titles, totaling 47 issues in 1949; during the same 12 months, Fox's numbers were 18 titles and 52 issues, not counting a plethora of rebound/reprint 25-cent giant issues.

Ironically, the two companies that would eventually dominate the romance field, National (DC) and **Charlton**, took few early chances as romance publishing began. DC, which published more than 900 romance comics through 1977, was a minor part of the second-half rush in 1949, beginning the highly successful 180-issue run of *Girls' Love Stories* and starting the hybrid *Romance Trail*, which lasted only six issues. Charlton, a minor song-hits magazine publisher that was just beginning its line of comics, converted *Tim McCoy Western* #21 to the five-issue run of the obscure *Pictorial Love Stories*, beginning with #22. Charlton went on to publish more than 1,400 romance issues, dominating the numbers, if not the quality, of the 1960s and 1970s when the only serious competitor was DC. Charlton and DC together produced well over one-third of the nearly 6,000 romance issues published from 1947 to 1977.

*Heart Throbs* #1 (August 1949) began a successful seven-year fling with romance for **Quality Comics**, which had been one of the leading heroic publishers of the Golden Age, with many of the most imaginative costumed heroes, illustrators, and cover artists. In fact, Quality creations **Blackhawk**, **Plastic Man**, and Dollman even managed to hold onto their own titles in the face of the industry's costume hero purge of 1949–50. By the second half of 1949, however, Quality decided to focus on other genres, including starting 14 romance titles from August 1949 through January 1950. Quality came up with the most evocative titles in the industry, including *Heart Throbs*, *Love Letters*, *Flaming Love*, and *Campus Loves*, and often set stories in exotic locations, ranging from South Seas islands to Hollywood film sets.

Simon and Kirby's Crestwood titles had serious competition not only from Quality, but also from publisher Archer St. John's comic line, which was a solid second-tier producer of numerous genres for a decade beginning in 1947. Not long after St. John began producing comics, the stylish **Matt Baker**, one of the few African American artists in comics, shifted to St. John from action-oriented circulation standout Fiction House, which produced no romance comics except for a 12-issue run of *Cowgirl Romances* in 1950–52. Baker's shift was fortuitous, since it gave him the opportunity to illustrate with a lavish, bravura style many of the best-written of all romance comics, notwithstanding Simon and Kirby's frequent gems. Baker, with a slick, realistic style reminiscent of syndicated comic strip superstar Alex Raymond, produced nearly 12 dozen gorgeous covers and a multitude of equally beautiful romance stories for St. John, which produced 165 romance issues from 1949 to 1955 along with several rebound/reprint giants. (Three more non-Baker issues followed in a last-gasp 1957–58 effort before the firm expired a little over two years after the original publisher's death.)

The St. John romance issues, among the most popular with collectors and historians, featured numerous stories grounded in psychological reality by Dana Dutch, whose career had largely languished in obscurity until comics historian John Benson wrote two books devoted to St. John, Baker, and Dutch—*Romance Without Tears* (2003) and *Confessions, Romances, Secrets and Temptations* (2007). These remain the only scholarly studies of romance comics history dealing with a single company, other than compilations of reprints from the likes of DC and Marvel. Had the St. John firm been better capitalized, it would be better remembered for the excellence of its all too short-lived romance line. The longest-running title, *Teen-Age Romances*, lasted only 45 issues.

So powerful was the 1949 phenomenon of romance comics that National even tried to change the emphasis of several stories featuring one of the firm's few remaining superheroes, the iconic **Wonder Woman**. There was always a hint of romance in the Amazon princess's adventures, which began in December 1941, the same month Archie first appeared. Yet a handful of 1949–50 adventures and covers in *Sensation Comics* clearly stressed romance at the expense of the usual colorful action for which Wonder Woman was noted as, by far, the most successful costumed heroine of all time.

Eventually the romance craze was unsustainable. The number of love comics dated January through June 1950 was a phenomenal 332—compared to the 322 issues of all types of comics produced in all of 1939. Thus, in the fiscal year from July 1949 through June 1950, there were no fewer than 588 romance issues from all companies combined, or nearly five dozen per month on the average. This does not even count the romance themes prominent in the likes of Wonder Woman and Marvel's *Venus* title, which turned the Goddess of Love into a costumed heroine.

The Love Glut, as comics historian Michelle Nolan has dubbed this period of comic book history, soon became the quickest genre blood-letting in comics history, absent censorship. Romance comics dated in the second half of 1950 totaled but 164 issues, a collapse that included only 61 issues dated October through December 1950. The Love Glut led to serious financial complications at Marvel, Fox, and Quality, among other firms. Even mighty National canceled *Romance Trail* and suspended *Secret Hearts*, which reappeared in 1952, cutting the goliath firm's romance line from four titles to two. Marvel killed 25 of 30 romance titles that appeared early in 1950, most of which did not make it beyond a second or third issue. Likewise, Fox abandoned all 21 of its short-lived love titles; soon, the entire firm disappeared. Major league publisher Fawcett killed or suspended 13 of 17 titles in 1950, and first-tier comic producer Quality concurrently purged or suspended 22 of its 30 titles in all genres, including all 14 romance types.

In all, only 30 of 147 romance titles, including Simon and Kirby's ever-popular *Young Romance* and *Young Love*, survived the Love Glut of 1950 unscathed. Several other titles were resumed in 1951 and 1952, when romance rallied strongly on the comic book racks before enduring a steady but slow decline, in large part because of the influence of television. Never again, however, would there be the likes of the romance craze of 1949–50.

**EC** Comics, best known for the **horror** and **fantasy** titles that helped precipitate the Comics Code Authority, killed its three short-lived romance titles, but not before producing the parody of all parodies. "The Love Story to End All Love Stories" in *Modern Love* #8 (August–September 1950), the company's final romance issue, featured satirical murders and the suicide of publisher T. Tot, a victim of the glut. (There really was a Tony Tot Comics sub-publishing company at EC.) "Put out anything … even … horror!" shouts the distraught Mr. Tot. Just before the luckless comic book tycoon's demise, respected creators Jack Lyman and Joe Curry sadly announce they are financially ruined and leap from Mr. Tot's penthouse window (ironically, at this time Joe Simon and Jack Kirby were among the few successful romance creators and were not suffering from the glut). This manic story would not have been out of place when editor **Harvey Kurtzman** began *Mad* as an EC comic book in 1952, though by then the romance market had stabilized.

In 1951, this stability permitted numerous titles to return, allowing for a market of 403 romance issues across 28 companies, including nine firms with but a single love title. There was, however, no genuinely new ground to be covered in the world of four-color love, other than St. John's introduction of *Wartime Romances* #1 (July 1951) one year into the Korean War. Romance went on to a single-year high of 522 issues in 1952, or one of every six of the record of 3,164 comic book issues—give or take a few sometimes listed issues that may or may not exist. The first wave of the baby boomers, born 1946–50, helped offset the negative influence of early commercial television on comic book circulation in the 1950s. Even so—until the late 1980s explosion of independent publishers and fan artists, along with the flooding of the market by Marvel and DC—corporate comics began a long, slow decline in circulation and title numbers following the highs of 1952.

Romance comics gradually lost out with all the rest, incrementally declining in numbers almost every year. The Comics Code Authority, which began placing its stamp in the upper-right hand corner of comics dated variously February, March, and April of 1955, would no longer allow cleavage, lingerie, or titles like "I Was a Pick-Up!" Censorship, of course, resulted in the death of horror and most **crime** titles, but romance persisted. There were 347 romance issues in 1955, the first year of censorship, followed by 296 in 1956, although the ensuing demise of publishers like Quality, St. John, Ace, and Lev Gleason inevitably resulted in a significant decline in romance-themed issues. By 1959, there was a decade-low 160 issues, mostly from Charlton, DC, and Joe Simon's output for Crestwood/Prize, along with two titles each from Marvel, and the tiny American Comics Group. Marvel suffered a massive distribution-company related collapse midway through 1957 and only two romance types remained among the 16 bi-monthly titles the once and future comic king could produce in an agreement with DC's distributor.

The long-running likes of *Young Love* and *Young Romance* from Crestwood/Prize (and, beginning in 1963, from DC following their purchase), along with success stories like DC's *Girls' Love Stories*, *Girls' Romances*, *Secret Hearts* and *Falling in Love*, plus ACG's *My Romantic Adventures* and *Confessions of the Lovelorn*, were the exception rather than the rule in the mercurial comic book industry. Even before the mom-and-pop stores and other grocery, drugstore and newsstand distribution outlets began to encounter serious problems in the 1960s, far more comic titles quickly vanished than succeeded on crowded newsstands. Superman and Batman, not to mention Captain America and the later Fantastic Four and Amazing **Spider-Man**, were the exception, not the rule. A few **funny animals** types, such as Donald Duck, Uncle Scrooge, and Bugs Bunny, lasted for decades, but most failed sooner or later.

Romance comics were no exception to the erratic nature of comic book circulation. During their 1947–77 run, there were some 301 love titles. Only 103—about one-third—lasted as long as a dozen issues, and fully 113 titles ran four or fewer issues. Only 15 romance titles ran to at least 100 issues, so, in hindsight, the odds were greatly against love.

Ironically, other than Simon and Kirby's epic *Young Romance #1*, the Holy Grail for most romance comic collectors is the once thoroughly obscure *Daring Love #1* from the tiny publisher Stanmor, except for the many collectors who treasure above all else Baker's St. John ouevre and eagerly pursue the rare reprint giants for which he did extraordinary covers.

*Daring Love #1* (September-October 1953), with a now-famous "roll-in-the-hay" cover, is distinguished by the first published artwork of **Steve Ditko**, who went on to co-create Spider-Man with Marvel editor **Stan Lee**. Ditko did the first 38 issues of *The Amazing Spider-Man* before leaving in a creative dispute with Marvel, but those 38 are among the most treasured in the collecting hobby.

Some of the romance failures were distinguished, such as Simon and Kirby's four-issue run of *In Love* in 1954–55 as part of the duo's ill-fated self-published Mainline imprint. The first three issues featured what was still a rarity in romance comics—nearly book-length "novels." *In Love #1* featured "Bride of the Star," one of the few baseball stories in romance comics; #2 was a soap opera entitled "Marilyn's Men," and #3 was "Artist Loves Model," the story of the frustrations of the nicely-named comic book illustrator Inky Wells.

Another noteworthy attempt at lengthy hybrid stories was Fawcett's three-issue run of *Love Mystery*, which was a victim of the 1950 Love Glut. The title included six nicely done stories that melded intrigue with romance. There were also remarkable period pieces such as "There's No Romance in Rock and Roll" from *True Life Romance* #3 (August 1956), one of several unsuccessful 1950s romance titles from the tiny publisher Ajax. In this story, a girl is forced to choose between a boy who loves the new rock-style tunes and one who prefers classical music. Having made the right choice, at least according to the author, the girl says, "Gee, I can't believe that I ever enjoyed that horrible rock and roll stuff—it's just plain noise!" Her clean-cut fellow responds, "Right! It'll never take the place of a sweet love song . . . by the way, let's get some records to share." This amazing tale was unearthed and reprinted as a curiosity piece in the satirical reprint title *My Terrible Romance* in 1994 by independent New England Comics.

When The Comics Code Authority was formed, formal rules of engagement, so to speak, were laid down for the publishers. The only major publishers not to participate were squeaky-clean Dell, which did not produce crime, horror or romance comics, and Gilberton, which published **Classics Illustrated**. Sexual imagery of all types was forbidden, right down to visible cleavage; meanwhile, respect for sanctity of the home, for marriage, for parents and for good behavior was always to be encouraged. No longer would there be titles like "The Savage In Her!" (*Young Romance* #22, June 1950). Controversy and conflict were out; dewy-eyed romance and domesticity were in.

The tiny American Comics Group, which for the most part published whimsical and character-driven romance stories from 1949 to 1964, inexplicably veered toward the sensational for a few months in 1954, only to be driven back to the mainstream by the Comics Code. "Jailbird's Romance"—billed as "The Most Sensational Confession of Outlaw Love Ever Published"—appeared in *My Romantic Adventures* #49 (September 1954), followed by an insane asylum epic, "Love of a Lunatic," in #50. In sister title *Confessions of the Lovelorn*, "I Sold My Baby" was the feature of #52 (August 1954), followed by "Heart of a Drunkard" in #53, "The Wrong Side of the Tracks" in #54 and "I Take What I Want" in #55. The code, if nothing else, produced a shift to titles like "The Man in My Past" and "My Own Heart," along with far tamer covers.

Likewise, stories like "I Joined a Teen-Age Sex Club!" in Harvey's *First Love* #13 (July 1951) were strictly forbidden. Harvey used a lot of pre-code reprints during the final years of its romance line in 1955–58, so the likes of "Sinful Surrender" in *First Love* #27 (April 1953) became "Foolish Dream" in the post-Comics Code *First Love* #61 (February 1956). Conflict-ridden dialog was expunged or rewritten; cleavage was covered over. Even advertising of questionable products was revised or dropped. The pre-code romance stories from DC, Marvel, and Charlton, however, generally required few changes, since those publishers had long since begun producing relatively tame romance stories.

By 1959, when Charlton produced 15 romance titles—more than any publisher had tried since the Love Glut year 1950—the low-rent firm dominated the genre in bulk, if not quality, since DC still had a headlock on production values in its five titles (the line expanded to seven when DC purchased Crestwood's then-venerable *Young Romance* and *Young Love* in 1963). Charlton published 72 of the 160 romance issues produced in 1959, most of them generically bland. Charlton tried stirring up a little controversy with its *High School Confidential Diary* #1 (June 1960), which top-billed "Reckless Rebels Tearing at Life . . ." perhaps in response to the spate of films dealing with juvenile delinquency in the late 1950s and early 1960s. These stories, of course, promised a lot more than they could deliver under the strictures of the Comics Code.

In the historic DC reprint compilation *Heart Throbs*, published in 1979, only two years after the last original DC romance issue, editor Naomi Scott spotlighted romance comics for the first time among books aimed at collectors as well as the general public. Among her observations were these telling lines: "Interestingly enough, romance comics were written and drawn primarily by men. Even the advice columns, with bylines attributed to Jane Ford and Julia Roberts, were written by men. Over the years there were women artists and story editors, but until recently the comic industry was dominated by men. That may have had something to do with the romance comic point of view—and why we (as girls) were never quite sure they were right" (11).

Scott also made this accurate observation: "Romance comics were popular for almost 30 years because they showed a simpler life. Love, romance and marriage were ends in themselves; problems were limited to finding the right mate, the person who would share the rest of your life. They satisfied a kid's need to know what was ahead, to know that dreams could come true and that life was a simple matter once you found your man. They were done in the same spirit as the Doris Day and Debbie Reynolds girl-next-door films of the fifties. In the late fifties and early sixties, television was stealing a large share of the comic book market—action-adventure comics, as well as romance. But the changing morality of the sixties and seventies killed romance comics forever" (12).

Before romance comics died, however, DC tried to make them topical in ways they never had been from the venerable firm. Since beginning to produce love stories in 1949, DC had often recycled plots and lines, but had consistently produced new art to account for changes in fashion. However, the situation began to change when DC produced its first serial in the long-running *Girls' Love Stories*. This epic starred April O'Day, Hollywood Starlet, who debuted in #104 (July 1964) and ran through #115 (November 1965). During the mid- and late-1960s, several other serials appeared in DC's love titles. The company's first serial character was Bonnie Taylor, airline stewardess (as they then were known), who ran in *Young Romance* #126 (November 1963) through #139 (December 1965–January 1966). DC picked up *Young Romance* with #125 (September 1963) and acquired *Young Love* concurrently with #39 (a renumbering complication of the original series), which began a serial starring the registered nurse Mary Robin.

Another early indication of DC's attempt to make romance comics more "hip" was the appearance of images of The Beatles in *Girls' Romances* #109 (June 1965) and *Heart Throbs* #101 (May 1966), though not the Fab Four themselves. Following the "Summer of Love" in 1967, DCs romance artists gradually phased in different fashions and lingo. DC first put hippies on a cover in a two-part story in *Girls' Romances* #135 and #136

(September and October 1968) entitled "My Time to Love." The heroine tells the hippie fellow, "Oh, Kip . . . I do love you . . . but you know how my parents feel about you . . . and that crazie, hippie life you lead!"

Black faces began to appear in a few stories of the 1970s, and editor/writer Robert Kanigher penned a 13-page story of interracial romance, "Full Hands, Empty Heart," for *Young Romance* #194 (July–August 1973). Kanigher, an innovator on several fronts and an outstanding editor and writer for DCs first-rate **war comics** since the 1950s, showed courage with this effort. In this story of the romance of a black female nurse and white male doctor—a twist on most interracial stories of the time, in which the black person was usually male—the doctor dies while saving the nurse from a drug-addled patient. "If we don't learn to love each other, the world will always be a jungle," the nurse says, holding the dead doctor. She finishes the tale saying wistfully, "In some worlds there's no color, only people."

Joe Simon briefly returned to romance as a DC editor in the 1970s, creating stories like "Daughter of Women's Lib" in *Young Love* #106 (October–November 1973); but neither images of The Beatles nor updated fashions, or even stories dealing with interracial love, hippies and women's liberation, could save DCs romance comics from falling circulation. Likewise, Marvel's experiment in bringing the genre back with two titles on a bi-monthly basis as the 1970s dawned ended six years later with *Our Love Story* #38 (February 1976) and *My Love* #39 (March 1976). Meanwhile, other than a few reprint issues, Charlton's extensive romance line ended in 1976.

By that time, DC had already dispatched *Secret Hearts* with #153 and *Girls' Romances* with #160, both in 1971. *Girls' Love Stories* disappeared with #180 and *Falling in Love* with #143, both in 1973; and *Love Stories* died with #152 in 1973 (the new title continued from *Heart Throbs* after #146). Finally, the pioneering *Young Romance* ended with #208 in 1975—the record for a romance comic—and *Young Love* vanished with #126 in 1977, with a last gasp of six issues after the title seemed to have been killed with #120 in 1975 along with *Young Romance*. Romance comics had thus come full circle, and romance in popular culture was left for movies, television, and paperback books.

**Selected Bibliography:** Nolan, Michelle. *Love on the Racks: A History of American Romance Comics*. Jefferson, NC: McFarland, 2008; Scott, Naomi, ed. *Heart Throbs: The Best of DC Romance Comics*. New York: Simon and Schuster, 1979; Simon, Joe. *Joe Simon: The Comic Book Makers*. New York: Crestwood, 1990.

*Michelle Nolan*

**ROMITA, JOHN, JR.** (1956–). An artist noted for his professionalism, consistency, and speed, Romita Jr. has spent nearly the entirety of his career detailing the **Marvel** universe and its characters. Since the late 1970s, he has styled every major figure in Marvel Comics, enjoying extended runs on titles such as *The Amazing **Spider-Man**, **Iron Man**, The Uncanny **X-Men**, **Daredevil**, The Punisher, The Incredible Hulk, Thor,* and ***Wolverine***. Despite this extensive resume, much like his father, **John Romita Sr.**,

Romita Jr. is most synonymous with Spider-Man. Though he has long since moved out from his father's shadow, the influence of the elder Romita can be seen in the energetic layouts and dynamic poses of Romita Jr.'s pages. Romita Jr.'s linework is distinctive in its angularity and grittiness; his comics are also recognizable for their effective use of shadow and detailed backgrounds.

Romita Jr. possesses a remarkable range; he has proven himself adept at creating both the grand, often cosmic scale required for the adventures of characters like the X-Men and Thor, as well as realistic urban environments. His fondness for New York—the city of his birth—shines through in much of his work (and perhaps helps to explain some of his fondness for Spider-Man). Romita Jr.'s work on Spider-Man is enriched with many of the city's identifying characteristics: majestic skylines, crowded streets, water towers, intricate networks of fire escapes, endless rows of brownstone buildings. Even the filthy, dangerous corners of Hell's Kitchen that were so integral to his work on the monthly *Daredevil* series in the 1980s and the limited series exploring the hero's origin, *Daredevil: The Man Without Fear* (with writer **Frank Miller** in 1994), speak to his commitment to detail. Shortly after the September 11, 2001 attacks on New York City, Romita Jr. and writer **J. Michael Straczynski** devoted an issue of *Amazing Spider-Man* to memorializing the victims; in it, Spider-Man, along with numerous Marvel heroes and villains, surveys the horrors of Ground Zero and attempts to comprehend the damage done to his city.

Romita Jr. entered creator-owned comics with *The Gray Area*, a three-issue limited series involving a dead New York cop exploring supernatural realms, co-written by Glen Brunswick and published by **Image Comics** in 2004. More recently, Romita Jr. has collaborated with writer **Mark Millar** on *Kick-Ass*, a creator-owned venture from Marvel's Icon imprint. This series, which has subsequently begun development as a major motion picture, involves violence that is more graphic and disturbing than most of Romita Jr.'s previous work.

Of contemporary artists working in mainstream comic books, Romita Jr. is among the most prolific. His ability to produce issue after issue without the assistance of a fill-in artist is becoming increasingly rare. During one span from 1998 to 2000 he was doing full pencils on two monthly series—*Peter Parker: Spider-Man* and *Thor*. This kind of productivity is almost unheard of in modern monthly comics. He returned to *Amazing Spider-Man* in 2008, becoming one of a rotating team of creators contributing to the title's weekly publication schedule. In yet another testament to his capabilities, Romita Jr. is set to pencil a 60-page story in an upcoming anniversary issue, *Amazing Spider-Man* #600.

*J. Gavin Paul*

**ROMITA, JOHN, SR.** (1930– ). Born in Brooklyn, New York, John Romita graduated from the School of Industrial Art (now known as Art and Design) in 1947. Milton Caniff and Noel Sickels were his primary early influences and he was a great admirer of **Jack Kirby** and **Gil Kane**. His first work was penciling a 15-page **romance** story for *Famous Funnies* which was never used. In 1949 he was asked by a friend who worked for **Timely Comics** to ghost pencil pages for him. Ultimately, this would help Romita meet Timely's art director, **Stan Lee**. Romita's first credited work was for "The Bradshaw Boys" in *Western Outlaws* #1 (February 1951) for Atlas Comics. He drew a number of stories in different genres and participated in the short revival of **Captain America** in *Young Men* #24–28 (Dec. 1953–July 1954) and *Captain America* #76–78 (May–September 1954).

Moving over to **DC comics** in 1958, Romita was assigned to work solely on romance titles. Tired of penciling and just wanting to ink, he returned to **Marvel Comics** to work on an *Avengers* issue. However, Lee had him do pencils over Jack Kirby's *Daredevil*—a title he enjoyed working on. This would lead to a two-part story guest starring **Spider-Man** (16–17, May–June 1966). Impressed with Romita's handling of the character, Lee handed him *The Amazing Spider-Man* (*ASM*) after co-creator **Steve Ditko** quit. Thinking it was a temporary job, Romita copied Ditko's style but after six months, he realized that the book was now his. It is Romita's version of Spider-Man that is now best remembered.

Working with the Marvel Method, where Lee would provide an outline of the story to the artist, Romita plotted many of the *Spider-Man* stories; sometimes even as he drove along with his family. Even his son **John Romita Jr.** (now himself a top comics artists) helped provide ideas. The two Romitas collaborated on *Amazing Spider-Man* 500. Romita's favorite issues of the series were #108 and #109, as he was able to play with some of his Milton Caniff influences.

Romita was responsible for the infamous "Death of Gwen Stacy" issue and drew the artwork that introduced Mary Jane Watson to the world (*ASM* #42). Romita left the series in the early 1970s to become the art director at Marvel, where he helped shape its new characters. He also worked on special projects such as children's books and coloring books, as well as overseeing "Romita's Raiders"—an apprentice program for new Marvel artists. From 1977 to 1980, Romita provided the artwork for the syndicated *Spider-Man* newspaper strip.

Romita once commented that he was a storyteller first and an artist second. "Art is only a tool, just like the lettering on the paper. If you don't tell a story, the best art in the world is a waste." After retiring, he has returned to contribute artwork to special Spider-Man events, including the 2007 USPS Spider-Man stamp.

**Selected Bibliography:** Lee, Stan, Tom DeFalco, Roy Thomas, Roger Stern, John Romita Sr. *Marvel Visionaries: John Romita Sr.* New York: Marvel, 2005; Thomas, Roy, Jim Amish, and John Romita, Sr. *John Romita: And All That Jazz.* Raleigh, NC: TwoMorrows Publishing, 2007.

*Jeff McLaughlin*

**RONIN.** While rising to fame with his run on **Daredevil** for **Marvel Comics**, the six-issue-miniseries *Ronin* for **DC Comics**, written between 1983 and 1984, can be seen as a landmark in the work of **Frank Miller**. Not only did he help strengthen the acceptance for creators' rights with his first creator-owned comic, but he also evolved as a comic artist on a visual level. Each of the six issues spans over 48 pages, a rather uncommon format for American mainstream comic books at that time.

In *Ronin*, Miller tells the story of a samurai warrior who, after losing his master, Lord Ozaki, sets out on a journey to kill his master's murderer, the demon Agat. Although the story starts out in 12th-century Japan, the demon and the ronin are transported into the New York of a **post-apocalyptic** future, where their battle continues. Simultaneously Miller depicts a completely different storyline about moral and human evolution that is altered by biogenetics, presented in the form of the Aquarius complex, a cooperation that develops new technologies based on bioorganic material. Both stories intertwine and thus reflect on each other when the samurai takes over the body of one of Aquarius' test subjects, the amputated boy Billy.

The story of *Ronin* is constructed out of a collage of different classical genres. While the prologue of the comic is situated in feudal 12th-century Japan and clearly resembles visually and thematically Eastern comic books such as **Lone Wolf and Cub**, the story is interrupted by a sudden time-travel into the future where a new protagonist is constructed as a symbiosis of two characters that overlap each other. The shape-shifting demon further strengthens this doppelganger motif when he takes over the role of Aquarius' director, Mr. Taggart. Although the setting, a dystopian New York City, resembles that of a **science-fiction** movie, the hard-boiled dialogue and the stand-off-like confrontations between the characters refer back to the classical **Western** genre.

In contrast to other comics of the same time, *Ronin* offers a positive female figure for identification, Officer Casey McKenna. As one of the three founders of the Aquarius complex and leader of its security force, she reminds the male characters and the readers of her status as a woman and also invites them to reflect on their own ways of thinking: "Gentlemen, it's the 21st century. You've got to have open minds."

Miller not only confronts his readers with gender issues but also with the society they are living in. While he is sometimes criticized because of the right-wing political implications of some of his comics, in *Ronin* he displays nearly all facets of the political spectrum, from a right-wing conservative to a leftist libertarian world-view. Although *Ronin* includes a wide range of racial slurs (such as "nip" or "chink"), Miller certainly does not present these stereotypes as acceptable. He rather reconstructs an over-exaggerated vernacular language in order to question the readers' perception for such terms and their implied meanings. After a rather heated debate about racial heritage, an African American character replies to his interlocutor, clearly recognizable as a **Nazi**, very ironically: "There goes the neighborhood."

What is more striking in *Ronin* than Miller's interest in politics is his use of visual methods (with the help of his color-artist Lynn Varley) to construct a world that challenges readers' typical reading habits. His panel designs offer more than a display of the action taking place; Miller rather structures the readers' perception of timing and pace and gives him a sense of direction on the two-dimensional printed page. Only some pages of the comic book are displayed in a traditional panel structure. From the second page onwards, Miller shows the difference between vertical and horizontal panels, using filmic devices such as close-ups and makes extended use of splash pages. *Ronin* predates the strict visual codex of black, white, and one supplementary color Miller would use in **Sin City**, beginning seven years later.

Miller closely connects the visual design of the comic book with its content. For the biogenetics housed in the Aquarius Complex, Miller uses a drawing technique that simulates biological organisms: tiny circles and fine lines connecting them resemble heaps of cells or molecules that construct more complex forms. This graphic method is not only used on the micro-level of the inside of the Aquarius complex, which appears as a giant living organism sheltering the characters, but also outside the complex. On a splash page that appears slightly changed in every single issue of *Ronin*, Miller displays the control the Aquarius Complex and its biogenetical engineered metabolism has over humanity. It literally spreads like a virus over New York City.

Another visual uniqueness can be witnessed in Miller's graphic handling of battle scenes. His break with more traditional modes of comic narration includes vivid violence with a special focus on the timing of the action. At the beginning of issue #3, for example, Casey McKenna reviews a videotaped battle between the ronin and her soldiers. The panels are not structured from left to right, but from top to bottom, and are printed in black and white in order to resemble a filmstrip. The strips exceed the format of the page and continue on the next page in a different scene. These panels are sometimes disrupted by an image of Officer McKenna, whose commentary describes the otherwise silent pictures of the film. Miller puts this device to a two-fold use: on the one hand he sets the comic visually apart from the medium film by placing its disrupted images in the sequence of a film-strip; on the other hand he evokes the feeling and speed that only films can produce in the viewer's mind.

With *Ronin*, Frank Miller created a heterogeneous comic book that blends various visual techniques and uses different genres in order to construct a reality that questions the society readers are living in. While Miller's **Batman: The Dark Knight Returns** stands out because of its revolutionary reading of preceding *Batman* comics, *Ronin* introduces new standards for graphic storytelling and creates a perfect symbiosis of graphic narration and content.

*Daniel Wüllner*

**ROSS, ALEX** (1970–). Alex Ross is an American writer, penciller, inker, colorist, letter, editor, and cover artist. While artists like **Mike Allred**, **Frank Miller**, and **Alan Moore** were placing a postmodern spin on the canonical **DC** and **Marvel** characters during the 1980s and 1990s, Ross created a postmodern take on the **superhero** canon by creating photo-realistic art and extremely true-to-life stories of superheroes relating to the real world. As Ross explains on his Web site, "Fans appreciate that [I] had an obvious affection for the characters [I] paint, demonstrated by [my] attention to detail and the fact that [I] took the time to make these characters look so believable," (www.alexrossart. com). He is best known for creating a series of graphic novels that combine the realism of his art and storytelling: *Marvels* (1994), *Astro City* (1995), *Kingdom Come* (1996) and the "Earth" series *Earth X* (1999), *Universe X* (2000), and *Paradise X* (2002).

Ross was born in Portland, Oregon, and grew up in Lubbock, Texas. His mother believes that he was destined to be an artist because at the age of three he would take pieces of paper and try to quickly draw whatever was being advertised on television during a commercial break. While his mother applauded his artistic ability, his father, a minister, was his moral compass, something that proved important when writing stories for characters like **Superman**. He remembers the defining moment of his childhood as being his discovery of the existence of **Spider-Man** from watching *The Electric Company*. Ironically, Ross would go on to be one of the foremost storytellers of the Spider-Man mythology during the 1990s, even helping design the superhero's costume for the 2002 film.

Having impressed Marvel editor **Kurt Busiek** with the art he created at the American Academy of Art in Chicago, Ross was asked to collaborate with Busiek in 1993 on a story about the average person on the street and their relationship with the superbeings of their world. Busiek was so impressed by the final product, *Marvels*, that he and Ross started designing characters the following year, for a monthly series for **Image Comics** that would explore the use of narrative perspective similar to the way that they experimented with it in the creation of *Marvels*. In *Astro City*, they conceived and designed over 50 superheroes and villains and used an ever-evolving cast of characters to tell an extended story about a city filled with superheroes. Not only were many stories told from the perspective of villains or individuals without superpowers, many issues were told from the first-person perspective with the panels reflecting the framing of the narrator's eyes. After the initial concept stage, Ross only continued to design the covers of subsequent issues preferring to continue with his own work looking at the connection between reality and superheroes.

Ross's follow-up to *Marvels* was a limited series for DC, *Kingdom Come*, which explored the future of DC's stable of superheroes, as they fought the passing of time, and each other, for personal, professional, and moral reasons. In 1997, *Wizard* magazine asked Ross to imagine a dystopian future for the Marvel characters, similar to the material that Ross had created DC in *Kingdom Come*. This issue of *Wizard* sold incredibly well, leading to *Wizard* partnering with Marvel on an additional issue in 1999 that featured a section called the *Earth X Sketch Book*. The *Sketch Book* was expanded into three miniseries that tell the story of **Captain America**, as he takes the reincarnation of **Captain Marvel** (Mar-vell) on a journey to repopulate the Marvel canon.

**Selected Bibliography:** Alex Ross Web site, (www.alexrossart.com).

*Jason Gallagher*

**RUCKA, GREG** (1969–). A multi-talented writer whose work includes novels, screenplays, animated features, and comic books, Greg Rucka is well regarded for his ability to craft narratives that are sympathetic to the humanity of his sometimes far-from-human characters. Known throughout the industry for skills honed as a crime novelist, Rucka has consistently proven himself a reliable comics writer by stressing the importance of story in a medium prone to visual excess and thin plotlines. Starting what would later become a pattern with his very first work in comics, Rucka is also known for writing strong female characters in his creator-owned properties as well as in corporate-owned, mainstream **superhero** titles.

Something of a rare breed in the world of comics, Rucka has a high degree of formal education. Graduating first from Vassar College, he went on to earn a Master's degree from the University of Southern California. His work is marked by deep, well-researched symbolism and extensive use of allusion—a tradition of writing not uncommon among erudite fiction writers.

Prior to the debut of his first comic book *Whiteout* (1998), created in collaboration with artist Steve Lieber and published through Oni Press, Rucka had already penned the first three installments of his Atticus Kodak novel series to critical acclaim. *Whiteout* and its sequel *Whiteout: Melt* (2000), both following U.S. Marshall Carrie Stetko as she investigates crimes in Antarctic research stations, received similar praise and helped solidify Rucka's place as a professional comic book writer. Still with Oni, Rucka next turned to what would be his longest-running creation, *Queen & Country* (2001–7), a British spy series centered on MI6 agent Tara Chace.

Transitioning into more opportunities at mainstream publishing houses, Rucka found his skills most at home in *Detective Comics* (1999–2002) and *Batman* (1999–2000), though his reach included the extended family of Batman titles at **DC Comics**. Fans and critics alike took particular notice of Rucka's stories that explored Batman's crime-solving prowess—that is, Batman's ability to live up to the "detective" moniker. During this time Rucka also dedicated a significant amount of energy to building the mythos of previously ancillary female Batman characters, including **Catwoman**, Batgirl, Oracle, and Huntress.

At **Marvel Comics**, Rucka contributed his vision to numerous characters in the House of Ideas pantheon. Interspersed at various times throughout the 2000s, Rucka wrote stories featuring **Black Widow**, **Spider-Man**, Elektra, **Daredevil**, and Wolverine, among others.

Today, most of Rucka's ongoing work can be found at DC, where he has left his mark on nearly all major characters in the DC universe. Having previously spent time on *Detective Comics*, Rucka has gone on to write **Wonder Woman**, *Adventures of Superman*, and **Action Comics**. He has also played major contributing roles in crossover events such as *Infinite Crisis*, *52*, *Countdown*, and *Final Crisis*. Despite the breadth of Rucka's oeuvre, however, his most acclaimed work at DC—including *Gotham Central* and *Checkmate*—sticks closely to his crime- and spy-influenced roots.

*Joshua Plencner*

**RUNAWAYS.** The popular series *Runaways* tells the story of a group of youths who discover that their parents are part of a murderous super-villain cabal, and that they themselves possess superpowers. **Brian K. Vaughan** and Adrian Alphona created the series in 2003 and produced 24 issues of the title before **Joss Whedon** and Michael Ryan took over the title for six issues; writer Terry Moore and illustrators Hubert

Ramos and Takeshi Miyazawa then produced nine subsequent issues, with Kathryn Immonen and Sara Pichelli scheduled to follow them.

Forced to go on the run, the runaways of the title plot to take down their parents' syndicate and atone for the previous generation's crimes by using their own powers for good. Since they have a very loosely constructed idea of themselves as a team, there is no cohesive group identity and no group costumes (much to the disgust of Molly, the youngest character). In contrast to other **superhero** groupings, there is a higher ratio of female characters and the group is diverse in age, **ethnicity**, and sexual orientation.

*Runaways* combines innovative content (fantastic plots and heroics often take a backseat to human relationships and themes regarding the journey to adulthood) with the traditional style and continuity of the **Marvel** universe of superhero narratives. Featuring quick-moving storylines that nonetheless give the reader emotional food for thought, a plethora of popular culture references, and engaging, well-rounded characters, the series has attracted both young adult and adult audiences.

Each of the multiple artists and inkers who have worked on the series has brought different artistic styles with them, but all share common features that complement and further construct the *Runaways'* world: a large color palette, realistically proportioned bodies, and clothing reflecting current trends in young adult fashion. While the art has changed significantly over the years, the individual characters are still instantly recognizable with their original personalities intact. As the series develops under new creative teams, it seems to have lost touch with the generational conflict of previous story arcs. The membership of the group, however, does not remain static as some of the characters are killed and still others, also runaways, are invited to join them in their quests for justice. The core characters include de facto leader Nico Minoru, a Japanese American who began the series as a 16-year-old Goth and is a sorceress like her parents. The son of mad scientists, Chase Stein turns 18 early in the series and is the most rebellious and unpredictable of all the characters. He possesses the world's most powerful gauntlets and, since the death of his girlfriend and fellow member of the group Gert Yorkes, has had an empathetic connection with the dinosaur Old Lace. Karolina Dean is a 16-year-old alien whose natural form is visually fluid, often depicted with waves of rainbow-like light enveloping her humanoid structure. Her early struggles with her homosexuality were treated respectfully and gradually at the onset of the series but her confidence has grown, particularly as result of her relationship with her Skrull fiancée, Xavin. Molly Hayes, the youngest member at age 11, is a mutant with superhuman strength and invulnerability. She provides a foil for much of the angst of the older members of the group as well as providing insight for crisis situations.

The various series of this title have been collected in diverse formats. There are, to date, three volumes of oversized hardcover editions: Volume 1 collects the premier single issues #1–18; Volume 2, the newly numbered issues #1–12, and the 2006 Free Comic Book Day crossover issue with *X-Men*; and Volume 3 gathers the remaining issues that were produced by Vaughan and Alphona (#13–24). Ten digest-sized trade collections, mostly in soft cover, include the material collected above (but grouped in individual story arcs) as well as subsequently published material. *Pride and Joy* (#1–6) introduces the main characters and their relationships with their parents, providing the initial main generational conflict concept and thrust of the series. *Teenage Wasteland* (#7–12) continues the saga of the parents' search for the runaway children with the involvement of Marvel's original teen runaway crime fighters, Cloak and Dagger. *The Good Die Young* collects the final issues from the first volume, #13–18, relating the last battle with the evil parents and the identity of the team mole. Five individual digests compose the second volume of the series: *True Believers* (#1–6), in which a wide variety of evil characters in the Marvel universe swarm to Los Angeles to fill the vacuum left by the defeat of the Pride; *Escape to New York* (#7–12) continues the adventure with Cloak and Dagger and the New **Avengers**; *Parental Guidance* (#13–18) centers on Molly Hayes's exploits with a youthful street gang; *Live Fast* (#19–24) focuses on decisions that must be made for the entire group; and *Dead End Kids* (#25–30) by Whedon and Ryan takes the group back to New York as well as a century into the past. The next two digests feature writer Moore and artists Ramos and Miyazawa in their supernatural spin on the adventures: *Dead Wrong* (#1–6) and *Rock Zombies* (#7–10). A film version of the comic is forthcoming with scripting by Vaughan.

There have also been a number of tie-ins with other series, notably **Civil War: Young Avengers/Runaways** (also called *Civil War: Young Avengers & Runaways* in the collected edition), a miniseries tie-in to Marvel Comics' Civil War crossover event. The miniseries was written by Zeb Wells with art by Stefano Caselli. Young Avengers co-creator Allan Heinberg and Runaways co-creator Vaughan served as creative consultants to Wells. A second team-up between the characters from *Runaways* and *Young Avengers*, *Secret Invasion: Runaways/Young Avengers*, was written by Chris Yost with art by Miyazawa. *Mystic Arcana*, published in 2007 as a series of four one-shot titles contains an individual main story followed by a back-up story whose plot continues through all four books. The main story in each book focuses upon a different fictional character, each of whom in previous Marvel publications have had associations with magic. In *Mystic Arcana: Sister Grimm*, Nico Minoru discovers her family's heirloom, the Black Mirror.

*Runaways* has been recommended by various library organizations for teen readers. It has won the 2006 **Harvey Award** for Best Continuing or Limited Series and Shuster awards, "Voters Choice—Outstanding International Creator" (2006, 2007), and was nominated for the Georgia Peach Award for Teen Readers in 2007.

*Gail de Vos*

**RUSSELL, P. CRAIG** (1951–). Craig Russell is a prominent illustrator, writer, and adapter. While earning his BFA in painting at the University of Cincinnati, awarded in 1973, he began drawing professionally for **Marvel**. After apprenticing under Dan Adkins, Russell's first penciling job was *Morbius, the Living* **Vampire**. Russell's opinion of his first published work is unclear, as he does not include it in his Opus listings (Russell lists all his work by Opus number, much like a classical composer). During this time, Russell also taught at Kent State University for two years and received a fellowship for comic creation from the Ohio State Arts Council.

His early Marvel work garnered significant attention in the mid- to late 1970s, when he became especially well known for his signature *War of the Worlds* (**Killraven**) series in *Amazing Adventures*. His compositions are posed and statuesque, reminiscent of Caravaggio in dramatic intent. Russell's quiet, delicate line and fluid composition, comparable to contemporaries Barry Smith and Mike Kaluta, helped define the quasi-Renaissance style that marked much of **Marvel's** most visually-significant 1970s work.

Following this, his work adapting Michael Moorcock's *Elric* achieved substantial fan and critical attention. A **Dark Horse** reprint of the run incorporated an adaptation of the **Neil Gaiman** short story *One Life Furnished in Early Moorcock*, also published later as a stand-alone comic. Russell inked the first of **DC's Elseworlds** stories, the 1989 *Gotham by Gaslight*, a Victorian **Batman** story that was penciled by then relative newcomer **Mike Mignola**. Russell has successfully illustrated Batman before and since, but critics and fans consider this book a landmark.

Russell has distinguished himself in his creation of a body of comic book and graphic novel work based on operas, especially Mozart's *The Magic Flute* and Wagner's Ring cycle. He has also adapted Kipling's *Red Dog*, *Fairy Tales of Oscar Wilde*, and *I Pagliacci*. His *Salome* uses Art Noveau elements to advance the narrative.

Russell was among the first mainstream comic artists to come out as gay. While he has been supportive of the gay community and defines himself as "just your average gay Libertarian comic book artist" (*Famous Comic Book Creators*), little of his work has dealt overtly with his sexuality. Working with co-creator David Singleton, Russell created a wordless story that occupies half of *Gay Comics* #23.

The work Russell has done illustrating Gaiman's writing may be his best known recent output. His work on **Sandman** #50, a 32-page story titled *Ramadan*, won an **Eisner Award** as best story of 1994. Additionally, Russell adapted the *Sandman* character Death in the story *Death and Venice*, in the anthology *The Sandman: Endless Nights*. More recently, Russell has written and illustrated a graphic novel based on Gaiman's story *Murder Mysteries*, and completed a graphic novel version of Gaiman's *Coraline* in 2008. Russell is completing a comic book adaptation of Gaiman's *The Dream Hunters*, originally illustrated by Yoshitaka Amano.

Russell has won Eisner, Inkpot, **Harvey**, Shazam and Parents' Choice awards. He remains prolific in the field.

**Selected Bibliography:** *Famous Comic Book Creators Trading Cards* #109: *Craig Russell*, Eclipse Enterprises, 1982; Raphael, Jordan, and Tom Spurgeon. "Interview: P. Craig Russell." *The Comics Journal* 111 (May 1991); "Brief Biographies: P. Craig Russell," (2005). Biography.jrank.org, http://biography.jrank.org/pages/1756/Russell-P-hilip-Craig-1951.html.

*Diana Green*

**SABRE.** A 38-page trade paperback written by Don McGregor and illustrated by Paul Gulacy that was first published in 1978, *Sabre* became the first publication issued by Eclipse Enterprises, which would go on to become Eclipse Comics. It can also lay claim to being one of the first graphic novels, appearing in the same year as **Will Eisner's** ***A Contract with God***, which is widely (though not quite accurately) cited as the first graphic novel. *Sabre* is also historically important because the original paperback was sold exclusively through comic-book stores, proving the viability of that method of distribution for longer and more expensive comics. The initial *Sabre* paperback, once again in print in a 20th-anniversary edition published by **Image Comics** in 1998, was followed by a 14-issue comic-book series, the first two of which reprinted the original black-and-white graphic novel in color. All of the *Sabre* comics feature the same eponymous African American hero, given his name by his favorite weapon, though he also totes a fancy high-tech pistol.

Sabre and his beautiful-but-deadly (white) lover-sidekick, Melissa Siren, have no actual superpowers, but both are preternaturally tough, courageous, and skilled in combat. Sabre, in particular, has become a hero and has developed his own staunchly held code of beliefs, tempered in the fires of a difficult upbringing in a series of rehabilitation centers, none of which were able to quell his fierce individualism and resistance to oppressive authority. He continues in this vein in the comics, which take place in a **post-apocalyptic** America in which the social system has collapsed beneath the pressures of greed and conformism. As Sabre explains to Melissa in one key (postcoital) conversation, his rebellion against society began when he realized that most in the general population were being "narcotized" by their "sensory video systems," a sort of futuristic form of television. As he puts it, "the materialistic carrot held under their noses" has caused most people to give up their individuality, while "I.Q. scores and salaries became more important than a sense of honor, or a measure of dignity in dealing with yourself or others."

Melissa shares Sabre's romantic rejection of the coldly calculating world around her, though from a different point of view that arises from her status as the first "test tube fetus," a product of a project designed, in a mode somewhat reminiscent of Aldous Huxley's *Brave New World*, to do away with sexual reproduction altogether, freeing up humans for "more important things." Melissa, however, feels that something important has been lost in freeing conception from its "orgasm origins." That something, she concludes, is "magic," a quality that is entirely lacking in the thoroughly routinized world in which she grows up.

In the *Sabre* graphic novel, the total triumph of consumer capitalism has led to an almost total collapse of civil society, creating a post-apocalyptic atmosphere of chaos and despair in which a few unscrupulous individuals have seized power, creating a (rather dysfunctional) dystopian state, the power of which is resisted by only a few determined rebels. The routinization theme is emphasized in the way Sabre and Melissa must make their way across a bizarre Disneyland-like amusement park in order to try to free a group of rebels who have been taken captive by the dark powers who run the park. The implication is clear: any apparent magic in this world is a mere simulacrum of magic, contained and commodified, bottled for mass consumption in carefully controlled doses. This park is run by the Overseer, a mysterious and sinister figure, though much of the actual work is carried out by his henchman Blackstar Blood, a villain with a certain sense of honor; this honor ultimately leads him to come to the aid of Sabre and Melissa at a crucial moment, helping them to defeat the Overseer, though even more powerful enemies remain on the horizon.

*Sabre*'s romanticism now seems a bit quaint, while its portrayal of Melissa is a bit sexist: despite the fact that she is strong and courageous, she functions in the text largely as a sexual object who must be rescued from a sexual fate worse than death by the hyper-masculine Sabre. Sabre himself is a hero somewhat in the Blaxploitation vein, though his swashbuckling style is modeled more directly on Errol Flynn's Captain Blood. Indeed, Sabre's **race** is largely beside the point, serving mainly to help establish his status as an outsider to the society around him, a status he shares with more mainstream African American comic-book heroes such as **Luke Cage**.

**Selected Bibliography:** McGregor, Don. *Sabre*. Fullerton, CA: Image Comics, 1978.

*M. Keith Booker*

**SACCO, JOE** (1960–). Joe Sacco is best known for practicing comics journalism, often reporting on politically volatile conflict zones. Born in Malta and raised in Australia, California, and Oregon, Sacco studied journalism at the University of Oregon, where he later published an alternative magazine before working as a news writer for *The Comics Journal*. After editing the humor anthology *Centrifugal Bumble-puppy* (**Fantagraphics**, eight issues, 1987–88) he focused on his own work in *Yahoo* (six issues, Fantagraphics, 1988–92), shifting from humor strips to autobiographical and documentary material, including accounts of Sacco's travels with a rock band in Europe and stories exploring his fascination with war. Issue #4, "Airpower through Victory," is a fully annotated history of modern military air attacks, followed by a vivid account of his mother's experience of World War II on Malta. Issue #5, "How I Loved the War," points towards Sacco's work in the next decade, while issue #6 sympathetically illustrates Susan Catherine's story of her life as a stripper.

His turn toward both autobiography and accounts of war confirmed Sacco as the most prominent artist employing comics as journalism or *reportage*. *Palestine*, his first major work, chronicled Sacco's trip to Israel and the Occupied Territories in the winter of 1991–92: serialized in nine issues (1993–95), *Palestine* was issued in a two-volume edition in 1994 and 1996 (winning an American Book Award), and in a collected edition featuring an introduction by Edward W. Said, in 2002. A 15th-anniversary "Special Edition" with valuable supplementary material, was published (like all previous versions, by Fantagraphics) in 1997.

Influenced by New Journalism, Sacco's comics allow his point of view to color the stories he gathers, although he often presents himself unflatteringly. While relying on photographs as sources for his drawings, he often employs visual distortion and jarring panel designs, with images eluding conventional borders, or humans drawn as if viewed from above or below through a fish-eye lens: the overall effect of Sacco's work, balanced between representation and interpretation, is to acknowledge the subjectivity inherent in even the most responsible attempts at objective journalism.

Some of Sacco's shorter pieces were collected as *War Junkie* (Fantagraphics, 1997), followed by three powerful books on the Bosnian war, including *Safe Area Goražde: The War in Eastern Bosnia 1992–1995* (Fantagraphics, 2000), *The Fixer: A Story from Saravejo* (Drawn & Quarterly, 2003), and *War's End: Profiles from Bosnia 1995–96* (Drawn & Quarterly, 2005). *Notes from a Defeatist* (Fantagraphics, 2003) reprints autobiographical material; some of Sacco's early and recent work on music, including posters and album covers, is collected in *But I Like It* (Fantagraphics, 2006). More recently, his stories on the Iraq War have appeared in mainstream publications, including *The Guardian* and *Harper's*.

**Selected Bibliography:** Groth, Gary, "Joe Sacco, Frontline Journalist." *The Comics Journal Special Edition* (Winter 2002): 55–72; Marshall, Monica. *Joe Sacco*. Library of Graphic Novelists. New York: Rosen Publishing, 2005.

*Corey K. Creekmur*

**SALE, TIM** (1956–). Born in Ithaca, New York, Tim Sale is a prominent comics illustrator and occasional writer. He attended New York's School of Visual Arts (SVA), in addition to participating in a comics workshop led by John Buscema. Before completing his degree at SVA, Sale returned to Seattle (where he grew up), and worked a variety of odd jobs while partnering with his sister to start a small imprint called Grey Archer Press.

In 1985, Sale was hired to pencil, ink, and letter *Thieves' World*, published by Starblaze. Eventually, Sale met Matt Wagner (of **Grendel** fame), as well as Diana Schutz (then working for Comico), and Barbara Randall of **DC**, at the San Diego Comic-Con. Randall introduced Sale to writer **Jeph Loeb**. Sale and Loeb struck up a partnership and the long-standing collaboration has produced a large portion of Sale's body of work. Their initial collaboration was on the first eight issues of the second volume of *Challengers of the Unknown* (1991), for DC, originally created by **Jack Kirby**.

Sale and Loeb then worked together on three Halloween specials for DC's **Batman: Legends of the Dark Knight** series: *Choices* (1993), *Madness* (1994), and *Ghosts* (1995). The specials led to an influential 13-issue limited series beginning in 1996 called, *Batman: The Long Halloween*. The series takes place during Batman's second year wearing the cape and cowl as he tries to hunt down a serial killer nicknamed "Holiday." (The killer murders people once a month on holidays). The miniseries was such a success that Sale and Loeb became star creators and developed a sequel beginning in 1999 titled, *Batman: Dark Victory*.

Between *Batman: The Long Halloween* and *Batman: Dark Victory*, Sale and Loeb collaborated on a four-issue limited series called **Superman** *For All Seasons*. Similar to the holiday device used in the two aforementioned Batman miniseries, this story involved a theme set around seasons and dealt with aspects of Superman's origins.

Eventually, Sale and Loeb would try to replicate their success with DC's most popular **superheroes** for DC's main competitor, **Marvel**. They collaborated on such titles as, **Daredevil:** *Yellow*, **Spider-Man:** *Blue*, **Hulk:** *Gray*, and **Captain America:** *White*. In 2006, Sale collaborated with writer/illustrator Darwyn Cook on *Superman Confidential*. Like Sale's collaborations with Loeb, this series concentrated on the character's early years and revealed Superman's first exposure to his Achilles' heel, Kryptonite.

Sale's line work can be best described as expressionistic and subtle. It is not cartoony in the most obvious sense, yet does not subscribe to the realm of realism either. He is influenced by many of the great American comic book illustrators, including Kirby, **Jim Steranko**, and **Neal Adams**. However, he has spent his time studying European cartoonists too, including Juanjo Guarnido and Ruben Pellejero, which gives his fat/skinny line brushwork a refreshing edge in the world of mainstream American comic book artists.

Recently, Sale has been creating artwork for the U.S. television series, *Heroes*, of which his frequent partner Loeb is a writer and producer. In addition to illustrating work for the show that is attributed to characters in the story, he also serves as an artistic consultant and even provides illustrations for the comics that are released between the show's seasons.

*Jared L. Olmsted*

**SANDMAN, THE (GAIMAN).** A 75-issue **DC**/Vertigo comics series, *The Sandman* (1989–96) was written by **Neil Gaiman** and illustrated by a number of artists, including Charles Vess, **Craig Russell**, **Steve Leialoha**, and Jill Thompson, with covers by **Dave**

**McKean**. The series was initially conceived as a **horror** comic, existing on the more magical end of the DC Comics mainstream. Over time, this gave way to a more mythological and meta-textual story, as well as a decreased interaction with the main DC universe. While there is an overall story arc, described by Gaiman as "the king of dreams must learn to change or die," a number of side stories lend a mythic depth to the series. All in all, however, the plot may be less important than are the quirky characters, bizarre twists, and occasional chilling or surprising moments that punctuate the series.

The main plot arc of *The Sandman* focuses on the character of Dream, also called Morpheus, who is one of the seven "Endless." These are personifications of fundamental forces in the universe: Destiny, a representation of historical process, is the eldest; Death is next, followed by Dream; then comes Destruction; the twins Desire and Despair; and, finally, the youngest, Delirium, who eons ago was Delight. These forces are behind all that sentient life experiences in the universe. As the story begins, Dream, returning to his kingdom after a long journey, is captured, in 1916, by the magician Roderick Burgess, who was hoping instead to capture Death and so gain immortality. The imprisonment of Dream has a number of immediate consequences for the 20th century: some people fall into a deep sleep while others remain awake; the land of dreams dissolves; and several people try to fill the "vacuum" left by Dream. Eventually, in 1987, Dream escapes, recovering his power and restoring his kingdom. He faces many challenges at first. Some nightmares escaped from Dream and he must regain control of them; in the process of doing so, Dream angers Hyppolita Hall, and sets in motion the seeds of his own destruction. Shortly afterward, Lucifer abandons Hell, turning out the demons and giving the Key of Hell to Dream, who must decide who among several competing divinities and powers may rightfully receive it. Later, Dream, at Delirium's request, sets out to find their brother Destruction, who abandoned his duties in the late 17th century; to succeed, he must kill his son Orpheus. For this action, and because of the threat that Hyppolita Hall feels he represents, Dream must face the Furies, and eventually choose between the complete dissolution of dreams and his own passing; he chooses the latter, and a new Dream—Hall's son Daniel, a child gestated in dreams—arises to take his place.

Alongside this main story arc are a number of tangential stories, many of which weave in and out of the main arc. A retelling of the Orpheus myth sets the stage for Dream's death, for example, while the story "A Game of You" expands the universe of dreams while commenting on the lack of female voices in comics storytelling. Some tales, such as his pursuit of the ancient queen Nada, elaborate on Dream's personality. Other stories illustrate the importance of dreams: they are the only thing to sustain the life of "Emperor" Joshua Norton of San Francisco, while their careful cultivation can end the Roman Empire or prolong its life by a thousand years. Some of these stories involve Dream as a primary character, while others relegate him to the background. Taken together with the main plotline, the overall point of the series seems to be that dreams, as a metaphor for the imagination or hope, are fundamental to human existence. Alisa Kwitney commented on the tale's multiple layers including "themes of sibling rivalry and passion turned to revenge, themes on the dangerous nature of gifts, particularly the gift of creativity, as well as recurrent meditations on the power of women, the nature of vision, and the distinction between Dream and Death."

Outside of the original, 75-issue run of *Sandman*, there have been numerous spin-off works. Gaiman himself wrote *The Dream Hunters* (1999), an illustrated novel taking place in Japan. The three-issue miniseries *Death: The High Cost of Living* (1993) and *Death: The Time of Your Life* (1996) both feature Dream's older sister, while *Endless Nights* (2003) contains seven separate tales about each of the Endless, some of which were set after the main series' end. DC also launched a number of titles connected with the world of Sandman, including Mike Carey's *Lucifer* (2001–6), which followed the title character after his abandoning of Hell; *The Dreaming* (1996–2001), a monthly series by several artists and writers that focused on the supporting characters (mostly Cain and Abel) within Dream's realm; and *The Sandman Presents* (1999–2004), another multi-author series that followed the large number of supporting characters from the main series.

The effect of *The Sandman* on comics in general has been to promote a sense of literary development in comics. In the early 1990s, *The Sandman* was the center of DC's new "mature" imprint, Vertigo. The success of *The Sandman* led to a boom in new titles that not only addressed adult themes—including more graphic violence and open discussions of sex—but also seemed to raise the perceived quality of the stories. Indeed, along with the work of **Alan Moore**, *The Sandman* is credited with adding depth to a medium often condemned as juvenile and sub-literary.

Curiously for a series that began as a horror comic, *The Sandman* also comments on the theme of hope in literature. More than just a story about "the shaper of dreams," Gaiman's stories touch on the importance of dreaming and hope in everyday lives, from African tribesmen to desperate writers to the Emperor Joshua Norton. As Death notes in *The Wake*, the passing of "Dream" is really the passing of a "point of view." The implication is that dreams will no longer be directly shaped by some higher power, but will be more open and free. The release of dreams back to the dreamers plays into that theme of hope.

**Selected Bibliography:** Bender, Hy. *The Sandman Companion*. New York: DC Comics, 1999; Kwitney, Alisa. *The Sandman: King of Dreams*. San Francisco: Chronicle Books, 2003.

*Jacob Lewis*

**SANDMAN, THE (GOLDEN AGE).** DC's original Sandman was a transitional figure between pulp heroes and the emerging **Superman**-style heroes that would soon dominate comics. Wesley Dodds (sometimes Dodd) wore a suit under his cape and a fedora over the gas mask that protected him from the effects of his sleeping gas gun. Like many pulp heroes, he left a sign at the scene of his activities—a few grains of sand. He first appeared in the 1939 *New York World's Fair Comics*, but the story in

*Adventure Comics* #40 is believed to have been written first. As World War II started, the Sandman was reworked into a traditionally costumed **superhero** with a matching sidekick, but as created by artist/writer Bert Christman with probable assistance from writer Gardner Fox, he stuck to battling ordinary gangsters and thieves. After a few adventures, he was joined by Dian Belmont, who became his girlfriend. Unlike many comic book love interests (but like many from the pulps) she was no damsel in distress but rather the Sandman's confidante and partner.

Dodds' superhero makeover was done by artist Paul Norris and writer Mort Weisinger, but it was **Joe Simon** and **Jack Kirby**'s slightly tweaked version soon afterwards that is most famous. Simon and Kirby gave the Sandman and his new ward, Sandy the Golden Boy (later recast as the orphaned nephew of the now-absent Dian), a series of creative adventures involving sleep and dreams. They produced most of his stories through his last original appearance in *Adventure Comics* #102. Along the way Dodds had been a co-founder and member of the **Justice Society of America** through most of the war, and made a few appearances in *World's Finest Comics.*

The Sandman returned in the **Silver Age's Justice League**/Justice Society team-ups, wearing his original costume. However, he had only minor appearances in JSA revivals throughout the 1970s, 1980s, and 1990s. Simon and Kirby created a completely different Sandman in the 1970s who never became very popular, but the most important new Sandman was **Neil Gaiman**'s incarnation of the character as the embodiment of "Dream," beginning in 1989. Gaiman acknowledged the first DC Sandman in his first issue, and also tied him in with the later Simon/Kirby character. More importantly, Gaiman's success led to a revival of the Sandman's original incarnation in *Sandman Mystery Theater*, a critically and commercially successful series set in the late 1930's that ran for 70 issues. In addition to the expected crime fighting, this series further explored the relationship between Dodds and Belmont, and the former's ties to dreams. Silver Age and later stories revealed that Sandy had been accidentally transformed into a "silicoid monster," although his human appearance was later restored. Wesley Dodds and Dian Belmont had long lives together although they never married. After Dian's death, Wesley sacrificed himself protecting the newly reincarnated Dr. Fate, transferring his prophetic dreams to Sandy and leading to the revival of the Justice Society. As Sand, Sandy became the first chairman of the revived JSA. More recently he has adopted the name Sandman (no longer exclusively associated with Gaiman's character) and the original costume of his mentor, restoring the pulp-influenced Sandman to an active place in the DC universe.

*See also:* Sandman, The (Gaiman)

*Henry Andrews*

**SATIRE.** Satire is the use of humor, irony, exaggeration or ridicule to expose human vice and fallibility, particularly in a political or social context. Satire has intertwined with the comic art form since the inception of comics. The most prevalent example of satiric cartooning in the popular consciousness is the political cartoon, which had its gestation in the grotesques of Leonardo da Vinci and the work of pamphleteers advocating the positions of Martin Luther. In early American newspapers, Ben Franklin used symbolism in cartoons to show the unyielding attitudes of American Revolutionary forces. This evolved into caricatures of political figures in the Civil War, and grotesques inspired by photographic representation in the same era. The contemporary political cartoon is an evolution of these works.

Bill Mauldin's body of work during World War II is one effort that must be noted in this area. Popularly known as the "Willie and Joe" cartoons, these single-panel gags showed the war from the viewpoint of the foot soldier. These cartoons included profanity and scathing attacks on the pompousness of ranking officers, made all the more biting by the cartoons being run in an official Army publication, *Stars and Stripes*. Many of these cartoons were later anthologized with added text as the very popular book *Up Front*.

As the comic art form evolved, its satiric elements followed suit. Social commentary on class issues appears in *Hogan's Alley* and *Bringing Up Father*. Even McCay's *Little Nemo in Slumberland* can be inferred to have a satiric element in its "Shantytown" storyline. The Tijuana Bible is one of the most neglected forms of satire in the comics. Within the framework of these 8 to 16-page pornographic comic books lurked scathing commentary on actors, politicians, and comic characters. Sexual performance and inhibition proved viable vehicles for taking the mighty down to size. In one early Bible, Al Capone is shown as impotent, while another portrays Cary Grant as gay. Tijuana Bibles were produced in the United States from the early 1930s until the early 1960s and satirized everything from Charlie Chaplin to the burgeoning feminist movement.

The advent of the comic book as an independent industry and as a burgeoning art form did not lack satiric content and intent. Though driven by the **superhero** model, comic books included parodic elements in the art (such as the grotesques of **Batman** villains, echoing those in the *Dick Tracy* strip) and the writing. The latter is evident in small moments in early **Superman** stories, in which Clark Kent slips sardonic one-liners in at the expense of cheap hoods, a minor recurring event throughout the first 10 appearances of the character.

In 1941, Jack Cole created **Plastic Man**. Cole's work on this series, which ran until 1956, was the best of all worlds in terms of satire. The central character, portrayed as the only sane man in an insane world, has the most ludicrous appearance, and serves as a foil for his own observations. Similarly, the early 1960s ACG Comics character "Herbie" used the perceptions of its central character and supporting cast as a satiric trope. Herbie Popnecker, an obese grade-schooler who eats lollipops and sleeps too much, is known to all the world as a superhero of the highest order—all except Herbie's parents. Herbie's incredible strength, abilities to fly, travel through time and the supernatural realms, talk to animals, and hypnotize anyone, all serve as devices for topical humor. Herbie interacts with world leaders and major figures, including Muhammad Ali, John

Kennedy, and Fidel Castro. Their ineptitude in contrast to Herbie's capability, itself contrasted with Herbie's ludicrous appearance, gives the stories a satiric bite.

Another significant comic character using wit and satire as ongoing weapons, debuting in the same time frame, is **The Spirit.** This aspect of the character, created by **Will Eisner,** evolved over the course of his 17-year run in a comic book that was distributed as a Sunday newspaper supplement. The character's origin story, dated June 1940, is rather straightforward; but within two months of beginning his weekly adventures, *The Spirit* ventured into the realm of parody with "The Kidnapping of Daisy Kay," a story that parodied *Li'l Abner.*

The latter strip was itself a continuous vehicle for satire and made a significant impact in the United States in the 1940s, contributing phraseology and social conventions to the public consciousness. Its creator, Al Capp, routinely used his characters as vehicles to show scorn and ridicule for greedy corporations and arrogant politicians, often with specific real-life models. Capp appeared on the cover of *Time* magazine on November 6, 1950.

Walt Kelly's *Pogo* is another overt example of comics satire from the same era. From its comic-book origins to its transition to the daily and Sunday funnies, *Pogo* was, like *Li'l Abner,* a vehicle for political commentary within the framework of an ongoing comic strip. *Pogo* hit its satiric peak with *The Jack Acid Society,* a storyline that ridiculed the McCarthy hearings. Within this narrative, Pogo uttered the phrase "we have met the enemy and he is us." This resonated in the public mind, and was resurrected as part of Kelly's work dealing with the burgeoning environmental crisis of the early 1970s.

The line between parody and satire is perhaps finer in comics than in other art forms. Parody deals largely in stylistic imitation, while satire is concerned with themes. Obviously, when dealing in an art form that incorporates word and image, the overlap is inevitable. The best satirists in comics are also often necessarily dealing in parody. For example, *Supersnipe* must be mentioned in the context of satire. Appearing a mere three years after Superman, this character existed primarily in the imagination of another fictional character. Koopy McFad, a prepubescent boy who "owns the most comic books in America," dresses in red long johns and a domino mask and imagines he is a superhero. His misadventures, which run from 1942–49, involve slapstick crime busting coupled with flights of super-powered fantasy. This motif is revisited in the **Marvel** character Forbush-Man from the 1960s parody title *Not Brand Ecch,* and in Don Martin's creation *Captain Klutz.* A later **DC** character, 'Mazing Man, is a melding of the superhero-fantasy parody character and the more gentle populist tone of *The Spirit.*

Similarly, the 1960s superhero team *The Inferior Five* was a satiric vehicle for DC. Not only did the title afford the opportunity to satirize the concept of generational heroes (the five are less successful offspring of **Golden Age** heroes), as well as heroic teams, but the storylines served as vehicles to poke fun at Marvel heroes and television. One issue parodied Marvel's **Thor,** another the **X-Men,** still another **The Fantastic Four.** Satiric reference to *The Man From U.N.C.L.E.,* a popular spy show of the mid-1960s and a comic from Dell, also appeared.

In fact, parodies of superhero comics have provided a major vehicle for satire in comics—with varying attitudes toward the superheroes being parodied. For all their idiosyncrasies, at the heart of Supersnipe, Captain Klutz, Forbush-Man and 'Mazing Man lay an appreciation, a reverence and love for the superhero form and for the ideals that form represented at its best. Jim Valentino's *Normalman*, created in 1983, is the only normal person on a planet of superheroes. As such, *Normalman* is a satiric vehicle for the celebration of the ordinary as special, but one that still treats the superhero genre respectfully. Other superhero satires lacked the same reverence for their inspirations. In the latter categories are The Badger, Ambush Bug, or Lobo. All three were mentally ill caricatures of the notion of hero. The Badger and Lobo were psychopathic and excessively violent. Ambush Bug was also criminally insane, but became a hero, albeit an unpredictable one. In fairness, all three can be seen partially as responses to the grittiness of some of the 1970s and 1980s dark heroes, including **The Punisher**, The Butcher, **Alan Moore's *Watchmen***, and **Frank Miller's Batman** in *The Dark Knight Returns*, and, all of which recast the role of the superhero into one of aggression, amorality, and cynicism. Thus, the satire of this trend took its subject to ludicrous extremes.

Moore and Miller, in revamping the superhero narrative, also themselves parodied it and infused it with satirical elements. Moore's *Top 10: The Forty-Niners* serves as parody of numerous superhero conventions and characters, as does Rick Veitch's 1990 *Brat Pack*, a scathing commentary on the nature of the superhero and the pathos of the kid sidekick. Both works use the often cited gay subtext of the superhero/sidekick relationship as an element of parody. Miller's *Dark Knight* books contain numerous characters intended to offend or provoke, but who also serve as satiric devices on social trends and human weaknesses. The character of Bruno from *The Dark Knight Returns* and the anime-inspired vacuous newsgirls in *Dark Knight Strikes Back* serve as prime examples. *Dark Knight Strikes Back* is notorious in this regard, as almost every character, major or minor, is an example of self-parody. However, Miller achieves a measure of balance with the effective use of *Plastic Man* as a vehicle to siphon attention from the antics of the other characters.

Another example of the insane superhero is gentler in its approach: Ben Edlund's *The Tick*, debuting in 1988, portrays an immensely powerful, slightly disturbed (issue #1 opens with *The Tick* in an asylum), very aggressive, but still lovable hero. Another dim-witted heroic parodic superhero character, Don Simpson's Megaton Man, appeared the same year. Megaton Man's primary satire related to the structure of superhero narrative and the extended superhero family.

Another variation of this form of parodic satire appears in the context of **Dave Sim's *Cerebus the Aardvark***. Originally a parody of the Barry Smith/Roy Thomas **Conan the Barbarian** run, the series quickly became a vehicle for the creator's views on politics, religion, comics, popular culture, and women. Using his central character Cerebus the Aardvark as a foil, Sim expanded the scope of the narrative into parody of any social or cultural issue that vexed him. The primary results of this were twofold. First, his peers questioned his mental health, often in print. Second, **Marvel Comics** threatened suit over the character Wolverroach, which they contended bore too close a resemblance to Wolverine. Sim relented, but his satire remained biting.

Another superhero satire related to a lawsuit appeared 33 years earlier. DC sued Fawcett Comics over perceived similarities between Superman and **Captain Marvel**. The suit, filed in 1941, was ruled in favor of Fawcett in 1949, but a 1951 appeals court favored DC. This provided the framework for another satire-related legal matter. A satiric story, Superduperman, which ran in *Mad* #4 (1953) was an apparent satire of the lawsuit itself, as Superduperman defeats Captain Marbles. DC threatened to sue publisher **EC** over this parody prior to its publication. EC's **Harvey Kurtzman** and **William Gaines** consulted two attorneys, got different opinions, and decided to publish nonetheless. Five issues later, *Mad* ran a satire titled Batboy and Rubin. This story was riddled with warning signs like "to lampoon is human, to forgive divine" and "note: any similarity between this and any other lampoon is strictly a lampoon." As much as a parody of Batman and Robin, this story was a satire of the proposed legal action.

*Mad* itself is a study in parody. Originally conceived as a vehicle for mocking other comic book work, *Mad* quickly evolved into a far-reaching venue for commentary on film, literature, and television. Under Kurtzman's editorial hand, the work in *Mad* was infused with a manic energy and irreverence. There had certainly been humor comics before *Mad*, but most had been modeled in the **funny animal** or *Archie* mode. *Mad* painted with a broader brush, and opened the doors for direct satirical assault. *Mad* also revisited the grotesque, using the work of **Basil Wolverton** for the cover of issue #11, as well as an interior story called "the *Mad* Reader." The cover in question was, by Kurtzman's admission, a deliberate and rather obvious parody of *Life* magazine. As the title ran on, its focus expanded. Issue #22, the Art Issue, had a *faux* Picasso cover. The first three stories were done with altered photographs, a subversive variation on Italian *fumetti*. In the last issue of its 23-issue comic run, *Mad* took on the McCarthy hearings directly. The story, Gopo Gossum, was a take on *Pogo*, remarking overtly on the dangers and inevitability of infusing politics into the funnies.

The commercial success of *Mad* led other comic companies to begin publishing imitations. Meanwhile, *PANIC* was issued by EC itself in response to the imitations of *Mad*, billing itself as "the only authorized *Mad* imitation." Issue #1 was banned in Holyoke, Massachusetts over its depictions of male and female cross-dressing in a Mickey Spillane parody, and over its interpretation of Clement Clark Moore's *The Night Before Christmas*. In response to these stories, the New York police raided EC's offices and sought to arrest whomever was in charge. Lyle Stuart, publisher of *Exposé* magazine (funded by EC publisher William Gaines) volunteered to be arrested. In response to the arrest, radio commentator Walter Winchell (who had previously been attacked in articles published by Stuart) called for a ban on all "the magazines Stuart publishes. The last four issues of *PANIC*'s 12-issue run were approved by the Comics Code Authority, and carried its seal on their covers, though code approval for this book was not easily obtained. Art was retouched to eliminate visible cleavage, references to alcohol were removed, and the gag name "Roughandtough" was inexplicably altered to "gunmen." Paradoxically, as

PANIC wound down, *Mad* became the sole survivor of the EC line by bypassing the code entirely and shifting to a magazine format, which it maintains to this day.

In the tradition of *Mad*, *PANIC*, and the Bibles, satiric comics continued to appear sporadically, albeit watered down by code limitations. Archie Comics' *Madhouse* was one of the better of the bunch, but still more driven by a sense of forced "wackiness" than by any real satiric zeal. However, satire magazines endured. After a falling out with Gaines over the editorial focus of *Mad*, Kurtzman left and started the short-lived *Trump*, published by Hugh Hefner. The 1957 *Trump* ran only two issues, and employed former *Mad* Comics staffers Al Jaffee, **Wally Wood**, and Jack Davis, along with a young Mel Brooks and Max Shulman.

Following *Trump*, Kurtzman, though completely broke, started another humor magazine, *Humbug*. Once again recruiting *Mad* alumni, Kurtzman added writer Larry Seigel, whose literary parodies echoed the presumed sophistication of the *Playboy* motif. In its 11 issues, *Humbug* managed to meld lowbrow schoolboy laughs with sophisticated literary wit. However, *Humbug* and *Trump* both fell prey to a trap inherent in satire; the work was topical, to the point of losing its edge if taken out of its time and context.

Kurtzman's following endeavor had some of the same problems, but overcame them with blatant audaciousness that transcended topicality. *Help!* Magazine, running 26 issues, recruited top writers, including Ernie Kovacs, Jerry Lewis, Mort Sahl, Dave Garroway, Jonathan Winters, Tom Poston, Hugh Downs, and Jackie Gleason, at meager rates. With editorial assists from a young Gloria Steinem and Terry Gilliam, Kurtzman produced some brilliant satire in *Help!* However, he neglected the comic form greatly in this endeavor, using few artists (including comrades from the *Mad* stable) and heavily favoring *fumetti*. *Help! Magazine* was, however, a vehicle for aspiring artists, who were paid $5 per appearance. Several luminaries of the comic world started in *Help!*, including **Robert Crumb** and Gilbert Shelton, whose first Wonder Warthog strips appear there.

Shelton's work, a scathing strip about a giant, super-powered, motorcycle-riding warthog, was a bridge between Kurtzman's work and car, biker, and drag racing cartoon magazines. These magazines, *Hot Rod Cartoons*, *Drag Cartoons*, *Cycle Cartoons*, *CARToons*, and the short-lived *Big Daddy Roth* and *Wonder Warthog* magazines, were brash and defiant. While their energy cannot be denied, they were aimed at a very select audience and mindset. Yet, like the best satire, they made those in authority quite nervous. They represented a repudiation of sanctioned cultural norms in favor of an anarchic reverie, albeit a reverie limited to drag racing and motorcycles, and their attendant way of life.

Shelton's crowning satiric achievement, the 50-page *Wonder Warthog and the Nurds of November*, appeared in 1980. Many of the events in this story have come to pass in the eyes of some, but were seen as ludicrous at the time: the corruption of a presidential election, corporate rule of the United States, pre-emptive war, wholesale financial ruin, and large-scale social apathy.

In addition to Shelton's work, just about all work from the early **underground and adult comics** movement can be construed as a work of satire. The most significant works in this arena are **Jaxon**'s *God Nose*, Foolbert Sturgeon's (Frank Stack) *New Adventures of Jesus*, Dan O'Neill's *Odd Bodkins*, and Crumb's early work in *Zap! Comics*. Crumb's work summed up the mantra of the undergrounds: violate taboos. Underground comics (often referred to as "**comix**") blithely ignored the Comics Code, as did Kurtzman's post-*Mad* efforts, the hot rod magazines, the Tijuana Bibles (dying out at this point), and the principal imitators of *Mad*, *Cracked* and *Sick*. However, the undergrounds, like the bibles, also thumbed their noses at conventional business models by not going through conventional magazine distribution channels.

In addition to the violation of societal taboos (primarily **race**, **religion**, violence, alcohol use, drug use, sex and sexuality), undergrounds excelled at the most potent satire, that which ridicules its own audience. Ostensibly about revolutionary concepts associated with the 1960s protest movements and hippies, sexual activity and drug use, many comix also pointed out the foibles of the counterculture they claimed to embrace and represent. Crumb's Mr. Natural can easily be seen as an archetype of the guru figure, but never does anything but exploit his pupils, much like Vaughn Bode's Cheech Wizard. The Freak Brothers were usually a vehicle for commentary on the asininity, stupidity, and treachery of both the so-called "establishment" and the fledgling counterculture.

Dan O'Neill's *Mickey Mouse Meets the Air Pirates* was the subject of a lawsuit by Disney, who claimed its characters were used illegally and that the image of the characters was denigrated by their portrayal engaging in drug use and sex acts. The suit was exacerbated by the specific use of the names of the Disney characters in the stories. O'Neill's response was that the character of Mickey was so widely visible in the public eye as to be deemed fair use. Details remain obscure, but it appears that, after eight years and three court victories, forcing O'Neill to incur legal fees that crippled him financially, Disney dropped its contempt charges and waived the $190,000 in damages and over $2 million in legal fees, on the sole condition that the *Air Pirates*, also the collective name given O'Neill and his fellow cartoonists on the two books, never violate Disney's copyright again. O'Neill is rumored to have celebrated by smoking a joint in Disney's office.

The *National Lampoon*, a rabidly irreverent if sophomoric humor magazine that ran from 1970 to 1988, succeeded the underground. The Lampoon's Comics section was a haven for underground cartoonists. Additionally, the magazine employed mainstream comics artists for comic book satires that served a dual function as social and political commentary. A prime example, Barry Smith's art on Sean Kelly's *Norman the Barbarian*, a parody of the *Conan* comic Smith was drawing at the time, appeared in the May 1972 issue. The story used Norman Mailer as the Conan figure, and staged him fighting a hydra with the heads of Mailer's "enemies," including Dick Cavett.

Bobby London, also an Air Pirate, was an artist whose strip *Dirty Duck* appeared in both comix and the Lampoon, and is currently running in *Playboy*. *Dirty Duck*'s style was overtly influenced by E. C. Segar, as was most of London's work. As London's career evolved, he landed his dream job in 1982, writing and drawing *Popeye* for King Features Syndicate. In 1992 he was fired. No specific reason was given. Speculation abounded that the firing was a direct result of his final unprinted storyline, involving Olive Oyl's addiction to the Home Shopping Club. She accidentally orders a baby Bluto. Deciding she does not want the artificial and evil child, she and Popeye resolve to "get rid of it." A priest takes action to stop them. Ironically, the editor who fired London over the abortion satire storyline was Jay Kennedy, editor of the Underground and New Wave Comix Price Guide. The irony was not lost on London.

While few undergrounds endured past 1975, Crumb's work continued to appear in a variety of venues, and new creators built on the legacy of the undergrounds. Crumb started the *Weirdo* anthology magazine in 1981. In addition to serving as an outlet for his most outrageous work, the magazine was a vehicle of artistic exploration for veteran cartoonists like the underground's Kim Deitch and Ed "Big Daddy" Roth, as well as new talents including Dori Seda. Dori's blunt, harsh, and hilarious autobiographical strips served to satirize the role of the artist in society, and the foibles of her own life.

In 1986, along with *"Omaha" the Cat Dancer*, *Bizarre Sex*, and *The Bodyssey*, copies of *Weirdo* were seized from Friendly Frank's, a Lansing, Illinois comic book shop. The owner of the store was charged with dealing in obscene materials. Publisher Denis Kitchen organized a defense fund. The case was won on appeal, and Kitchen used the funds remaining from the defense to organize the Comic Book Legal Defense Fund.

The most challenging case the CBLDF accepted came in 1993, when Mike Diana was charged with obscenity by Florida District Attorney Stuart Baggish. The work in question, Diana's comic *Boiled Angel 8*, depicted a man decapitating a woman for sexual pleasure (a visual device used by Crumb 25 years earlier). While most of Diana's work deals with dismemberment, mutilation, and children in a sexual context, he contended that the work was satirical in nature. The CBLDF lost the case. Diana was sentenced to an elaborate batch of punishments, including but not limited to having no contact with minors and attending journalism ethics school at his own expense. However, Diana moved to New York and is serving out his community service working for the CBLDF.

Other notable examples of recent comics satire include Charles Burns's work, especially the Big Baby stories, which combine horrific elements and adolescent sexual tension in an odd and effective satire of 1950s horror films. Devil's Due Publishing is publishing a political/barbarian parody along the lines of the *Lampoon* Conan/Norman Mailer piece of 36 years prior. This time the focus is on President Obama. The title, *Barack the Barbarian: Quest for the Treasure of Stimuli*, includes villains George the Dim and Red Sarah. Finally, the recent series *Battle Pope*, written by **Robert Kirkman**, echoes the religious satire of the recurring Lampoon comic feature *Son-O-God*, drawn by **Neal Adams**.

**Selected Bibliography:** Backer, Dan. *A Brief History of Political Cartoons*. Charlottesville: University of Virginia, 2000; Benson, John. *Interview with Harvey Kurtzman*. West Plains, MO: Russ Cochran, 1986; Levin, Bob. *The Pirates and the Mouse: Disney's War Against the Counterculture*. Seattle: Fantagraphics Books, 2003. Markstein, Don. "Supersnipe. Don Markstein's Toonpedia," (2003). Toonopedia.com, http://www.toonopedia.com/suprsnip.htm; "*Tijuana Bible Basics, Part One*." Tijuanabible.org, http://www.tijuanabible.org/articles/tijuana-bibles-a-history-of-dirty-comics.html.

*Diana Green*

# SCIENCE FICTION.

Science fiction has been a popular and durable genre of comics, which have sometimes been able to convey a sense of awe and wonder lacking in other forms of popular science fiction. The history of science fiction (sf) in modern comics can be traced back to January 7, 1929, with the debut appearance of *Buck Rogers in the Year 2429 A.D.*, America's first science-fiction newspaper comic strip. Buck Rogers is a U.S. Air Force lieutenant who finds himself waking in the 25th century, some 500 years in his own future. This is due to fumes inhaled during a mine cave-in, which engendered the effect of suspended animation. He is joined by Wilma Deering and Dr. Huer, citizens of this future, with Buck becoming its champion by defeating invaders and enemies including the Mongols, the tiger-men of Mars, the pirates from outer space, and Buck's nemesis, Killer Kane, accompanied by Ardala Valmar, his female companion.

The title of the strip would later change to *Buck Rogers in the 25th Century*, and finally *Buck Rogers*. It was initially drawn by Richard 'Dick' Calkins and scripted by Philip Francis Nowlan, and was distributed by John Flint Dille of the National Newspaper Service syndicate. Nowlan adapted his prose story *Armageddon 2419 A.D.*, which had originally appeared in *Amazing Stories*, a noted pulp science-fiction magazine, in August 1928. In this initial prose incarnation the protagonist was called Anthony Rogers, with "Buck" being a nickname. Nowlan also wrote a prose sequel, *The Airlords of Han*, which appeared in the March 1929 edition of *Amazing Stories*.

Later artists for the strip were Murphy Anderson (1947–49), Leon Dworkins (1949–51), Anderson again (1958–59), and George Tuska (1959–67). Calkins took over scripting duties after Nowlan (1940–47), followed by Bob Barton (1947–51), Rick Yager (1951–58) and others, including Fritz Leiber, the noted sf author.

A Sunday strip began on March 30, 1930. It initially focused on two supporting characters, Bud Deering (Wilma's younger brother) and Princess Alura from Mars. Buck Rogers later assumed the role of protagonist for this Sunday strip until it ended in 1965. Art duties on the strip were undertaken by Russell Keaton (1930–33), Yager (1933–58), Anderson (1958–59), and Tuska (1959–65). Script duties were assumed by writers including Nowlan (1930–40) and Yager (1940–58).

The strip was revived under the title *Buck Rogers in the 25th Century* in 1979 by Gray Morrow and Jim Lawrence. Cary Bates took over scripting duties in 1981, with Jack Sparling taking over art duties in 1982. The strip lasted until 1983. A brief comic book incarnation was published by TSR during 1990–91, co-written by Flint Dille (grandson of John Flint Dille) and Steven Grant (from a graphic novel by Grant), and later Buzz Dixon. It lasted for 10 issues.

The next significant work of science fiction to appear in the comics was *Flash Gordon*, which first appeared on January 7, 1934, as a Sunday strip. It was conceived as a means of competing with the popular *Buck Rogers* strip. It was created by Alex Raymond for King Features Syndicate, with scripting duties taken up by Don Moore soon after, which he continued with until the late 1940s. Moore was succeeded by a number of writers, including Fred Dickenson. The strip gained a reputation exceeding that of *Buck Rogers*, due in no small part to the seminal artwork created by Raymond, whose reputation holds strong to this day.

The Sunday strip was followed by a daily strip that first appeared on May 27, 1940, illustrated by Austin Briggs, who was previously Raymond's assistant. Briggs later took over from Raymond on the Sunday strip, finishing his run July 1948, to be followed by Mac Raboy (1948–67), and then Dan Barry, assisted by artists including **Frank Frazetta** and **Al Williamson**. However, the daily strip finished in June 1944, but was a revived in November 1951 by Barry and Ric Estrada.

Flash Gordon, "a Yale graduate and world-renowned polo player," and Dale Arden, his female companion, are taken on a journey to the planet Mongo on Dr. Zarkov's spaceship, after their plane crashes near Zarkov's observatory. On Mongo, they battle against the emperor of the planet, Ming the Merciless. They are helped in their struggle by Barin, King of Arboria, and his wife Aura, who is also Ming's daughter.

The visual appeal of *Flash Gordon* lay in the exotic alien scenery of locations including the undersea kingdom and the ice kingdom, and the equally exotic supporting cast: Tygrons, Wolvrons, and the Cerberus-inspired "Tsak, the Two-Headed Guardian of the Tunnel of Terror." Other visually interesting supporting characters in the cast were hawk men, lion men, and monkey men. This strip also shows evidence of formal experimentation, gradually leaving behind standardized frames and speech balloons and embracing a less defined, more consciously artistic style, in addition to replacing balloons with narrative captioning.

A central motif in the strip has Flash and Dale representing a moral humanism acceptable to its audience, with Ming epitomizing an amoral, inhuman, anti-human stance, an uncomfortable echo of the ideas propagated by Adolf Hitler, who became the Head of State in Germany in 1934, as well as the perceived threat of the "yellow peril" or Asian immigration. Like much sf, *Flash Gordon* would provide a reflection of the times in which it was created.

Science fiction proved to be an influential comics genre not only in the United States but in Great Britain as well. *Dan Dare—Pilot of the Future*, appeared as the lead feature in the very first issue of *The Eagle*, a seminal British comic, published on April 14, 1950. This feature occupied both the front and back page of this anthology publication. The strip was created by artist Frank Hampson and produced by a team of artists under his supervision. They employed photographic references in the form of specially constructed models (for such things as spaceships) and real people to pose as characters. The sequence's science fiction credentials were enhanced by the fact that noted author Arthur C. Clarke acted as an advisor for the first story. Other writers following Hampson included Alan Stranks, David Motton, and Eric Eden. Other artists working on the strip were Harold Johns, Donald Harley, Bruce Cornwell, Desmond Walduck, Frank Bellamy, and Keith Watson.

*Dan Dare* was initially devised by a clergyman, the Rev. Marcus Morris, as a reaction to the perceived threat posed to British morality by the U.S. **horror comics** that were being imported into the U.K. Dare himself was initially conceived as a chaplain until it was decided to make him a pilot, and he became Daniel MacGregor Dare, Colonel O.U.N. Interplanetary Space Fleet. This probably happened as a result of the fact that the potential of the comic outgrew its initial conception, that of a small Christian publication, instead aiming to become a national children's periodical, and it succeeded in this with the help of publisher Hulton Press.

Dare's nemesis was the Mekon, a green skinned alien with a huge, bulbous head, offset by a small torso and limbs. The Mekon ruled the Treens, the inhabitants of Venus, and Dan was aided in his fight against the Mekon by a strong supporting cast: Albert Fitzwilliam Digby, Dan's batman; Professor Jocelyn Mabel Peabody, nutrition expert; Henry Brennan Hogan, a pilot better known as 'Hank'; Pierre August Lafayette, another pilot; and Sir Hubert Gascoine Guest, Controller of Space Fleet.

Dan Dare was reinvented in 1977 for the first issue of the anthology *2000 AD*, which featured artwork by Massimo Bellardinelli and, later, **Dave Gibbons**. *The Eagle* was re-launched in 1982 and featured a protagonist who was the great-great-great grandson of the original Dare, with scripts by Pat Mills and John Wagner, and art by Gerry Embleton, followed by Ian Kennedy. In 1990, **Grant Morrison** and Rian Hughes produced *Dare*, a version of the original characters and strip but in the form of a political satire. **Garth Ennis** and Gary Erskine have also recently produced a new version (2008) for Virgin comics.

During this time **EC Comics**, infamous for its horror comics, also produced a number of significant science fiction comics. Both *Weird Science* and *Weird Fantasy* ran from May 1950 to December 1953 as bi-monthly publications. **William Gaines** started these sf titles by effectively discontinuing *Saddle Romances* at #11 (allowing issue #12 to become retitled as *Weird Science*) and *Moon Girl* at #12 (so issue #13 could become *Weird Fantasy*)—these became a part of what is referred to as EC's new trend publications, along with their **crime,** horror, humor and **military/war** titles. In line with Gaines's practice of saving money, he changed the titles of some of his existing comics, but retained the numbering, allowing him to avoid second class postage charges. This was a shrewd technique that he had employed when he began EC's horror titles, but he was soon discovered by the post office and, as of the January 1951 issue, *Weird Science* changed to issue #5 proper, with *Weird Fantasy* following suit with #6 in March 1951.

Both titles were later amalgamated as *Weird Science-Fantasy* in March 1954 (with issue #23 on the cover), as a quarterly title, due to comparatively lower sales than the horror titles. This would later be renamed as *Incredible Science Fiction* (issue #30), published at a bi-monthly rate until #33, when EC ceased publication of sf material.

Gaines's titles became noted for their **adaptations** of noted sf author Ray Bradbury's short stories. Their first adaptation was unauthorized, and combined elements of two stories in one strip. Bradbury praised the adaptation in a note to Gaines, and also wryly requested a payment for the use of his material. This led to further, authorized adaptations from EC of Bradbury's work, by Gaines and head writer **Al Feldstein**.

Advertisements for the sf titles proclaimed that EC were "proudest of our science fiction titles," and many of the stories published in those comics were political in nature. This led to friction between EC and the newly formed **Comics Code** Authority, who constantly pressured EC to change content, and outlawed the use of specific words in comic titles, predominantly those used by EC itself.

Matters reached a breaking point when EC was instructed to change the protagonists skin color from black to white in "Judgment Day," which would have undermined the point and effectiveness of the story itself—an exploration of the issue of skin color. Gaines would ultimately run the story, unchanged and without code approval, in their last comic, *Incredible Science Fiction* #33. Disillusioned with the politics of comics, Gaines and EC would go on to produce magazines that were exempt from the code, notably the humor magazine *Mad*.

Much of the success of **DC Comics** is an indirect result of the influence of science fiction, and is rooted in their most famous character, **Superman**. Writer **Jerry Siegel** and artist **Joe Shuster**, creators of Superman, were ultimately responsible for the growth of DC and superhero comics in general. Siegel's love of science fiction led him to create early fanzines, such as *Cosmic Stories* (1929), and it was in an issue of a fanzine, *Science Fiction* #3 (1933), that an early, villainous, telepathic version of Superman first appeared. For the version of Superman that gained success in comics they took much inspiration from science fiction, notably Philip Wylie's novel *Gladiator* (1930), where the protagonist Hugo Danner is born with enhanced strength, speed, and bulletproof skin as a result of a serum injected into his mother by his father, while pregnant with Hugo.

Another link with sf was provided by editor Julius Schwartz, who began his work in the genre by publishing another early fanzine, entitled *Time Traveller*, became an agent for sf writers including, Stanley G. Weinbaum and Ray Bradbury, and finally became an editor at DC. He hired Alfred Bester, a notable sf writer, to provide scripts, and was instrumental in DC's success with its **Silver Age** comics, editing sf-influenced revisions of older characters including the **Flash**, **Green Lantern**, and the Atom.

In terms of sf proper, DC Comics drew inspiration from EC comics. August 1950 saw the publication of *Strange Adventures* issue #1, an anthology that featured recurring characters. These included Chris KL-99 (Earth's first space-born human and genius), Star Hawkins (a sf detective), the Atomic Knights (heroes from the future), and Captain Comet and Animal Man (superheroes). It totaled 244 issues and ran from 1950 to 1973, and became best known for introducing Deadman to the world

(#205–16), following a transition to more supernatural, fantastic themes with #202. DC Comics' Vertigo imprint would later revive the title as a four-issue anthology series in 1999.

In April of 1951 DC published the first issue of *Mystery in Space*, its second sf title. This title followed the pattern established by *Strange Adventures*, utilizing an anthology structure, in addition to using recurring characters such as Knight of the Galaxy (from the 30th century) and Adam Strange. It totaled 110 issues, running from 1951 to 1966, resuming publication with #111–17 in 1980 and 1981, and finishing with an eight-issue miniseries revival in 2006, featuring a revived Captain Comet (originally from *Strange Adventures*) by Jim Starlin and Shane Davis.

**Marvel Comics'** success is also rooted in elements of science fiction. October 1939 saw the publication of *Marvel Comics #1*, the first comic published by **Timely Comics** (later Atlas, then finally Marvel), notable not only for the first appearance of the Sub-Mariner by Bill Everett, but for an early science fiction-influenced super-hero character, the Human Torch. Unlike the later version of the character it inspired (Johnny Storm of the **Fantastic Four**), Carl Burgos's original was an android created by Phineas Horton, a scientist. However, Marvel's major contribution to science fiction in comics was the sf-inspired work of the 1960s.

Much of the company's self-proclaimed "Marvel **Age of Comics**" was developed from sf-inspired scenarios and pseudo-scientific causes, usually a result of the fears raised by atomic energy in this period. The Fantastic Four gained their powers through their spaceship's exposure to a cosmic ray storm; Bruce Banner attempts to save a man who has wandered onto the test site of a gamma ray bomb, but is victim of the explosion which causes periodic transformations into the monstrous **Hulk** (inspired by *Dr. Jekyll and Mr. Hyde*, a work of proto-sf by Robert Louis Stevenson, published in 1886); Peter Parker's exposure to an irradiated spider causes him to develop the proportional abilities of a spider as **Spider-Man**. Such early scenarios are now attributed to writer/editor **Stan Lee** and the relevant artist on a given title, such as **Jack Kirby** and **Steve Ditko**. However, the true nature of such collaborations is shrouded in decades-long speculation and rumor.

Lee and Kirby's work on the *Fantastic Four* title (issues #1–102), contains amazing displays of sf-inspired design work, landscapes, ideas and characters, and is arguably the most influential sf run in comics. The members of the team are not standard superheroes: team leader Reed Richards is the world's most intelligent scientist, and creator of scores of inventions which would not be out of place in other genres of sf, like the Fantasticar and the portal to the Negative Zone. Kirby's design work portrays space and the negative zone as visually exciting, awe-inspiring environments rooted in a grounded sense of sf reality (as opposed to whimsical fantasy), and are examples of sf at its most wonderful and inspiring. Characters such as Galactus, the devourer of worlds, and his herald the **Silver Surfer** are born of an increasingly complex combination of science and mysticism that reflects popular interests in the period of the 1960s.

Science fiction has also held an important place in Japanese comics, known as **manga**. The most famous series is *Tetsuwan Atomu* (*Astro Boy* in the English translations), an important example of science fiction manga which first appeared in 1952, running until 1968. It was created and produced by **Osamu Tezuka**, popularly referred to as the God of Manga; Tezuka holds a place in Japanese culture, manga, and anime comparable to that of Walt Disney in the West; indeed, Disney was a major inspiration to Tezuka. He originally trained in medicine, becoming a doctor, although he never practiced. Instead, he became a key innovator in both manga and anime, creating work in a variety of genres, including science fiction, with *Astro Boy* arguably becoming his most successful creation.

Astro Boy is a robot that was created by Doctor Tenma, the head of the ministry of science. Tenma built him as a replacement for his own dead son, but soon came to realize that this would not work, and sold the robot to the circus. Astro is rescued by Tenma's successor, Professor Ochanomizu, and uses his powers to fight evil and further the cause of good. The stories were translated into English by Frederik L. Schodt. Meanwhile, Tezuka's growing recognition in the West can be seen in the fact that he was asked to become art director for *2001: A Space Odyssey* by Stanley Kubrick, but financial commitments forced Tezuka to decline the offer. Translations of his work have increased in recent years.

Another key manga series to make its mark in the West is *Akira*, by Katsuhiro Otomo, which is best described as fitting the cyberpunk sub-genre of science fiction. Set in a **post-apocalyptic** New-Toyko in 2019, the story concerns super-powered children involved in a government research program. It was originally serialized in Japan in *Young Magazine* between 1982 and 1990, and first translated and reprinted by Marvel's Epic imprint. More recently, it has been published in six English language volumes by **Dark Horse**. Another popular science fiction manga series to debut in *Young Magazine* was *Ghost in the Shell* (1989), by Masamune Shirow. This series is a thriller set in the future in which Public Security Section 9 agents are trying to capture the Puppeteer, who can gain control of human's minds, yet the puppeteer is revealed to be something more than was originally expected. Shirow's work is noted for the inclusion of footnotes and commentaries, and the original series has spawned two sequels—*Ghost in the Shell 2: Man/Machine Interface*, and *Ghost in the Shell 1.5: Human Error Processor*.

A major science fiction comic, *2000 AD*, debuted in England on February 26, 1977 and is still being published at the time of this writing. It is a weekly British anthology comic which was first published by IPC magazines. Initially printed on cheap newsprint paper, the genesis of the anthology came about as the result of a backlash against a predecessor comic, *Action*, which had to be cancelled following an outcry against violent and anti-establishment tendencies evident in the comic. Kevin Gosnell, an IPC magazines sub-editor, noticing the slew of upcoming science-fiction films, decided that an sf comic would be a good business opportunity, and asked Pat Mills to develop one. Mills, a writer and editor of some note in British comics, and the editor of *Action*, came to the realization that similar anti-authoritarian themes could be explored more safely through the veneer of a science fiction metaphor, and began to conceptualize what became *2000 AD*. The comic has transformed from a newsprint paper to a glossy format, in addition to embracing current technologies; it is available for downloading through the Internet, and can be viewed through iPhone and iPod touch versions.

Editors have assumed the role of Tharg the Mighty, a green-skinned alien, who says that the strips are produced by a group of robots; they intentionally resemble the actual comic creators employed by *2000 AD*. While its initial point of interest was a revamped Dan Dare, the comic soon became best known for the character of Judge Dredd, a future law-enforcement officer who performed the role of judge, jury, and executioner in Mega City One, the future eastern United States. The character gained his own monthly U.K. title in 1990, the *Judge Dredd Megazine*, still published at the time of this writing. Other science fiction strips for which *2000 AD* has become known include: "Rogue Trooper," a GI (genetic infantryman) with blue skin and three partners, Gunnar, Bagman, and Helm, which have been downloaded onto biochips located on his rifle, backpack and helmet respectively; "Robo Hunter," a series about Sam Slade, a bounty hunter who hunts robots; and "The Ballad of Halo Jones," an atypical sf story that eschewed *2000 AD*'s characteristic violence by focusing on the life of a young woman in the 50th century. The anthology has also had a significant impact in providing U.K.-based comics creators with a training ground to hone their talents for the American and international markets, including **Alan Moore**, Dave Gibbons, Brian Bolland, Grant Morrison and others. The downside of this trend is that once American and international markets open up to creators, the majority tend not to return to the magazine, although this has also been beneficial in allowing new creative opportunities for rising stars in the field to gain a public platform for their work.

Another significant work of science fiction in U.S. comics was **American Flagg**, a dystopian science fiction series published by First Comics (cover date October 1983). The year is 2031 and Reuben Flagg is an actor who has been sent from Mars to take on the responsibility of enforcing government law in Chicago, accompanied by a talking cat called Raul. His visual appearance is very much a modern, 1980's twist on previous patriot-heroes, such as **Captain America** and The Shield, in that all take the American Flag as inspiration, but Flagg is not a typical hero of this type and the series is very much a science fiction work of social **satire**.

*American Flagg* was created by **Howard Chaykin**, its principal artist and writer. It has also been scripted by Alan Moore and J. M. DeMatteis, and it has been penciled by Mike Vosburg and inked by Richard Ory. Distinctive lettering by Ken Bruzenak added to the effectiveness of the comic in creating and reflecting the future society in which the series is set. The series is an early example of work that dealt with more **adult** concerns and themes in comics, a rarity in 1983, but an approach that would bloom more fully as the decade progressed. Along these lines, it is notable that **post-apocalyptic narratives** (such as *Y: The Last Man*, *Ex Machina*, *V for Vendetta*, and *Tank Girl*) have been among the most popular science fiction comics in recent years.

This shift toward more adult audiences is often located in two major works, **Frank Miller's *The Dark Knight Returns*** (1986) and Moore's *Watchmen* (1986–87). Both of these deal with science fiction tropes. In *Dark Knight*, Frank Miller creates an older version of Bruce Wayne, retired for 10 years at the start of the story, who feels compelled to resume the mantle of **Batman**. Set in the near future, Gotham City is a media-saturated, violent nightmare version of a decaying urban landscape, and Miller offers the reader an uncompromising version of an iconic character. In *Watchmen*, Alan Moore and artist Dave Gibbons set their story of superheroes within a distinctive alternative Earth of 1985, where Richard Nixon remains president and where atomic science has created the ultimate superhuman. Essentially a murder mystery, this structural tour de force shows the potential of the medium while also making use of science fiction concepts familiar in other source materials, such as **Charlton** superhero comics and an episode of the science fiction TV series *The Outer Limits*.

In 1996, DC Comics launched Helix, an imprint devoted to science fiction; it featured work by noted creators including Michael Moorcock, Chaykin, and Garth Ennis. The imprint was short-lived, lasting until 1998, and its only major success was *Transmetropolitan* by **Warren Ellis** and Darick Robertson, which switched to publication under DC's Vertigo imprint with issue #13. The series follows the experiences of Spider Jerusalem, a journalist of the future inspired by Hunter S. Thompson's style of gonzo journalism (as featured in the novel *Fear and Loathing in Las Vegas* and other works). Jerusalem is a drug-taking, chain-smoking, hard-drinking, foul-mouthed crusading journalist of the future, who operates in an unnamed city (although clues point to it being New York). The series, which uses its dystopian setting to comment satirically on a variety of issues, ran for 60 issues, and is collected in a series of 10 trade paperbacks. Ellis has produced other sf and sf-influenced titles as well, and remains one of the writers most productive in the field.

*Andrew Edwards*

**SEAGUY.** *Seaguy*, created by writer **Grant Morrison** and artist Cameron Stewart, is a three-volume series of comic books, with each volume containing three issues. It is published by **DC Comics**' Vertigo imprint. Two volumes have appeared at the time of this writing, *Seaguy* (2004) and *Seaguy: The Slaves of Mickey Eye* (2009), with the final volume entitled *Seaguy Eternal* being still being planned for the future. The series uses a colorful, whimsical sense of visual design, which is tempered by a darker mood as it progresses.

The delay of five years between volumes one and two seems to have been the result of poor sales for the first series. It has been alleged that publication of the second volume was finally agreed to by DC as a result of a deal struck with them by Morrison, in which he offered his services to join other writers on DC's weekly series 52 in exchange for being allowed to continue with *Seaguy*. Despite these problems the series has become a critical success, with some critics declaring volume two to be some of Morrison's best work.

Seaguy is a non-powered **superhero** who wears a scuba suit. He is accompanied by his sidekick Chubby Da Choona, a talking, floating, cigar-smoking fish who wears a sailor's hat. They both live in New Venice, a Florida-style location set in the near future (some 50 to 70 years into the future, according to Morrison), full of color and energy. Seaguy and Chubby spend their days watching TV, specifically Mickey Eye, a character who has a television show and seems to be a twisted, panoptic version of a Mickey Mouse type icon, and is a disturbing looking eyeball with two legs and one arm. They also visit Mickey Eye's theme park on a daily basis. Seaguy also plays chess with Death, who is depicted in this series as a skeletal gondolier. Other characters include Old Seadog, Seaguy's mentor, and Doc Hero, a former superhero who is now compelled to continuously ride a Mickey Eye tilt-a-whirl, having lost the power of flight.

At the start of the first volume, Seaguy is consumed with the desire to have adventures and to be noticed by She-Beard, a warrior woman with facial hair who desires a mate but requires him to beat her in combat. However, the age of superheroes is over and Seaguy is finding it impossible to even get noticed by her. His boring existence changes when he discovers that a popular new food called Xoo has achieved sentience, and he feels compelled to protect it from forces who are after it. He also hopes to be finally noticed by She-Beard as a result of this. In addition, Moon rocks are falling to Earth in the form of small meteorites, which is made even more strange due to the fact that they are covered in hieroglyphics, with one such rock having the American flag embedded in it (as planted by astronaut Buzz Aldrin). All of this occurs in a world where, at some point in the past, the superheroes have triumphed over evil and have retired, after beating a supervillain called the Anti-Dad.

Series two, *Seaguy: The Slaves of Mickey Eye*, built upon the cult reputation of its predecessor, and was critically acclaimed in the comics press. It opens with Seaguy, who has retained no knowledge of what happened to him in series one due to the psychological manipulation he was subjected to at the end of series one; this is reminiscent of what occurs to the protagonists in the novels *1984* and *A Clockwork Orange*, by George Orwell and Anthony Burgess respectively. The second series is darker in tone than the first, a more somber echo of the predominantly joyful tone of its predecessor. Chubby has been replaced by Lucky the parrot, and Seaguy has no initial memories of his friend, although Chubby seems to invade his consciousness throughout the series.

Mickey Eye now dominates the landscape and Seaguy struggles to cope with life. Seaguy escapes from an institution where he has been incarcerated due to the intervention of Tree Guy, Pea Guy and Three Guy, three super-powered heroes who have been inspired by Seaguy. He is then given a new identity, that of El Macho, a "bull-dresser" who has to dress bulls, not kill them like a matador. He also has to deal with the impending marriage of Seadog and She-Beard and the growing power of Mickey Eye during the course if this second series.

Morrison has called *Seaguy* his attempt at a ***Watchmen***-style series in conceptual terms, not in plot or characterization. He is laying down his core beliefs regarding the superhero concept, and he has noted that the third volume will bring these concerns to the fore. He has declared it to be a new type of superhero comic, one which consciously avoids current trends that have elevated a violent type of coolness to the fore in the medium, a trend that he dislikes intensely. He sees *Seaguy* as a move to a more new-wave, **Silver Age**-inspired aesthetic combined with a modern literary sensibility. This idea, and the work on *Seaguy* that has occurred as a result of it, is perhaps similar in tone and execution to some of the work created by **Alan Moore** in his America's Best Comics (ABC) line.

Morrison and Stewart have generated a sense of surreal, weird mysteriousness that has its roots in work like *The Prisoner* TV series from the 1960s, which Morrison has stated as being a specific influence on *Seaguy*. Morrison gives full vent to his surreal and bizarre interests in this series, and while much can feel illogical or disconnected at times, he ultimately begins to draw the seemingly disparate threads together as each issue of both series progresses. Morrison has stated that *Seaguy Eternal*, the proposed final series of the trilogy, will form the ending to his ultimate statement on comic superheroes, and at the time of this writing is set for publication in the near future.

*Andrew Edwards*

**SETH** (born Gregory Gallant, 1962–) is a Canadian artist and illustrator living in Ontario. Educated at the Ontario College of Art, Seth first gained attention for his comics work with his autobiographical series *Palooka-Ville*, first published in 1991 by Montreal's Drawn & Quarterly, and re-issued in a 10th anniversary edition in 2001. In earlier issues of the series, he recounts daily events, ranging from an episode from 1984 where he was beaten up on the subway, to simply hanging out and talking with other characters. Most frequently, these people are the other two members of the "Toronto Three"—Seth, **Chester Brown**, and **Joe Matt**, who became the collective public face of mid-1990s autobiographical comics. All three were published by Drawn & Quarterly, worked at that time on largely autobiographical comics, and appeared in one another's works.

Where early *Palooka-Ville* issues were autobiographical and narrative-driven, later issues are more concerned with the small details of careful, slow story telling and beautifully rendered panels. Seth's work is elegant and demands that the reader both pay attention to the characters' facial expressions and notice the backgrounds suffused with nostalgia. For example, *Palooka-Ville* became a way for Seth to start crafting longer stories, such as 2004's *Clyde Fans* in which two brothers' fan business is driven to ruin by the rise of air conditioning. Overall, Seth's comics work displays a fascination with lost history and the past, be that traveling salesmen in small-town Canada, mystery *New Yorker* cartoonists, or collecting various artifacts—Pez dispensers, View-Master reels, or comic books (such as in 2005's *Wimbledon Green*).

Between *Palooka-Ville* and *Clyde Fans* rests what is Seth's most critically acclaimed work. In 1997, he won Ignatz Awards for Outstanding Artist as well as Outstanding Graphic Novel or Collection for ***It's A Good Life, If You Don't Weaken*** (Drawn and Quarterly, 1996, *Palooka-Ville* issues #4–9). On first pass, this work seems to interweave autobiography and history in Seth's search for a *New Yorker* cartoonist named Jack "Kalo" Kalloway, meant perhaps to evoke thoughts of Charles M. Schultz—something that makes sense, given Seth's current work as designer for **Fantagraphics'** 25-volume edition of *Peanuts* (winning both an **Eisner** and a **Harvey Award** in 2005). In time, astute readers deduced that Kalo never existed, that Seth created the drawings himself, and that much of the main story was elaborate fiction presented as autobiography.

Like other commercial illustrators, such as Adrian Tomine, Seth has done the cover art for magazine and CDs, including a 2001 Aimee Mann album (*Lost in Space*). Seth is also the designer responsible for the April 2006 Penguin Classics revised *Portable Dorothy Parker*. Seth spent a half-year, starting in September 2006 serializing *George Sprott (1894–1975)* for *The New York Times Magazine*, with a revised edition to follow. Other publications include *Bannock, Beans, and Black Tea* (2004), in which he illustrates some of his father's stories, and one volume of his sketchbooks, titled *Vernacular Drawings* (2001). His most recent work includes solo and touring shows of his fictional city of Dominion, and its sister city of Beaver, models created as reference for the buildings in his work. Both have been exhibited in small-scale model form, though Dominion was reworked to include a life-size working movie theater.

*Anne Thalheimer*

**SEVEN SOLDIERS OF VICTORY.** A large-scale series written by **Grant Morrison**, the umbrella title *Seven Soldiers of Victory* encompasses eight interlocking comic book series, totaling thirty issues, published by **DC Comics** between April 2005 and December 2006. Morrison's project comprises the bookends *Seven Soldiers of Victory* #0 and #1, with art by J. H. Williams III, and seven intervening four-issue miniseries that spotlight the individual "soldiers." The seven miniseries are: *Shining Knight*, with art by Simone Bianchi; *The Manhattan Guardian*, with art by Cameron Stewart; *Zatanna*, with art by Ryan Sook; *Klarion*, with art by Frazer Irving; *Mister Miracle*, with art by Pasqual Ferry and Freddie E. Williams II; *Bulleteer*, with art by Yanick Paquette; and *Frankenstein*, with art by Doug Mahnke. The miniseries were designed to be released on progressive monthly schedules, so that each week a different title under the *Seven Soldiers* banner would be on sale. Although missed deadlines curtailed this intended schedule, the unusual format of the series and Morrison's structuring of the narrative still contribute to a compelling—if somewhat disorienting—reading experience. The basic premise of Morrison's *Seven Soldiers* is to re-imagine the **superhero** team concept, most conspicuously by featuring revised versions of obscure or minor characters from the DC stable unwittingly cooperating together in order to stop an impending menace.

As with much of Morrison's work for DC, *Seven Soldiers* draws heavily upon the writer's extensive knowledge of the company's publishing history and lore. The *Seven Soldiers of Victory* first appeared in *Leading Comics* #1 (Winter 1941–42), but the team's continuity within the DC universe is convoluted and obscure. The original team, also known as "Law's Legionnaires," was created by Mort Weisinger and Mort Meskin in an attempt to capitalize on the success of the superhero team format utilized in the popular **Justice Society of America**, and ran for the first 14 issues of *Leading Comics*. The team's members were drawn from anthology books, and included **Green Arrow** and his sidekick Speedy, the Crimson Avenger, the Shining Knight, the Vigilante, and the duo Star-Spangled Kid and Stripesy, as well as an unofficial "eighth member," the Crimson Avenger's sidekick, Wing. This version of the team was reintroduced in *Justice League of America* #100 (1972), in a story where the Justice League is contacted by their Earth-2 counterparts, the Justice Society. The society is seeking assistance from the Justice League in locating the lost members of the legendary Seven Soldiers, who were scattered across time and space—and seemingly erased from collective memory—as an unfortunate consequence of their final victory against the threat known as the Nebula Man.

After this revival in *Justice League of America*, the Seven Soldiers franchise would remain effectively dormant until DC's company-wide retroactive continuity revamp in the wake of **Crisis on Infinite Earths** (1986). In the initial reworking of the Seven Soldiers, Wing was promoted to full membership and the Vigilante's sidekick, Stuff, was made an active member in order to replace Green Arrow and Speedy, who no longer had **Golden Age** counterparts. Even this revised version would be subsequently changed in the late 1990s, with Wing's spot as a soldier now filled by the archer known as The Spider, who had previously appeared in the *Crack Comics* feature, "Alias the Spider," published by defunct **Quality Comics**. This current version of the *Seven Soldiers* parallels the scenario presented in *Justice League of America* #100: the forgotten team is dispersed and lost throughout time after a battle with the Nebula Man. The major differences are that newly added member, the Spider, is actually a villain who sabotaged the team's final mission, and that the Vigilante spends 20 years fighting crime in the Old West before being rescued by the Justice League and Justice Society. This version of the team and its continuity is used as the starting point for Morrison's *Seven Soldiers of Victory*.

The plot of Morrison's *Seven Soldiers* centers around an invasion from a fairy-like race of beings from the future called the Sheeda. The Sheeda attack Earth periodically throughout history, devastating the planet through a process called the Harrowing, which leaves Earth and humanity with just enough resources to survive and rebuild in order to be conquered again. Prophesy states that a band of "seven soldiers" will eventually stop the Sheeda, so the army targets teams of seven during their invasions. To counteract this strategy, the mysterious Seven Unknown Men of Slaughter Swamp subtly orchestrate events that prod the current, individual soldiers into battling the Sheeda without ever realizing that they are cooperating with the others. Throughout the separate miniseries, the characters occasionally cross paths in their struggles against the Sheeda, and their respective journeys converge in the second bookend issue that concludes the story, but they generally remain unaware of each other and the ways their efforts coincide. Ultimately, the Sheeda are defeated and Klarion usurps the leadership of the assassinated Sheeda Queen, returning with them to their future as king, thereby fulfilling the prophesy that a soldier will turn traitor. Another prophesy states that one soldier will die, which seemingly comes to pass when Shilo Norman, Mister Miracle, sacrifices himself to defeat the villain who unleashed the Sheeda on humanity, Darkside. The series' final image, however, is of Norman's hands bursting from his grave, indicating that the world's greatest escape artist found a way to cheat death.

Despite complaints of lateness in the publication of individual issues, *Seven Soldiers* was a commercial success, due in part to Morrison's popularity and the consistently high quality of art. The maxi-series was also critically well-received, winning the **Eisner Award** for Best Finite/Limited Series in 2006. Although not Morrison's strongest or most incisive work, *Seven Soldiers* is nevertheless a considerable accomplishment, especially as an experiment in the possibilities of comic book storytelling. For example, the mosaic structure and unusual publication format allow for a variety of reading experiences. Moreover, the patterned structure highlights Morrison's desire to move away from cinematic comics and the increasingly popular screenplay style of comics writing. *Seven Soldiers* expands the borders of the superhero genre by incorporating disparate influences, such as speculative architecture, Celtic mythology, "Goth" subcultures, DC continuity, the occult, and hip-hop, among others.

As with much of Morrison's work, some critics have charged that—at least occasionally—*Seven Soldiers* borders on incomprehensibility, yet much of the appeal of the series lies in its zaniness and frenetic energy. In fact, the inevitable confusion one encounters when reading *Seven Soldiers* is one of its charms, as it replicates the disorientation a new comics reader faces when confronted with decades of complicated continuity. Unlike many writers of mainstream superhero comics, whose inclinations are to sieve and streamline continuity in order to make it as accessible and continuous as possible, Morrison (as exemplified by *Seven Soldiers*) embraces convolution and outlandishness as sources of unique storytelling opportunities.

*Jackson Ayres*

## SEVERIN, JOHN

**SEVERIN, JOHN** (1922–). In a career that has spanned over 60 years, John Severin has demonstrated that he is one of the very best artists to ever work in **war**/military and **Western** comic books. He has always had a tremendous passion for his subject matter and has illustrated countless stories in an exquisite, fine lined, realistic style. Not only is Severin an accomplished penciller and inker, but he is a talented humorist and caricaturist as well.

Though he began drawing cartoons professionally at the age of 10, Severin was not a fan of comic books and had only purchased a single comic as a boy. After graduating from New York's High School of Music and Art, he began to work with **Harvey Kurtzman** and Will Elder. After learning how much Kurtzman got paid for such work, he entered the field and published his first comic book story in 1947. The job was for **Joe Simon** and **Jack Kirby** and the story was published in Crestwood's *American Eagle*. Severin penciled it and Will Elder inked it. The two would collaborate for many years and become one of the great teams in comic book history.

In 1950, Severin and Elder followed Kurtzman over to **EC Comics** to work on *Two-Fisted Tales* and *Frontline Combat*. Kurtzman felt that both artists complemented each other wonderfully and created some of the finest work ever done in the genre of war books. Eventually this partnership did break up. Severin stated it was on friendly terms and that both were just "set to go on our own." Severin continued to work at EC and was an important contributor to Kurtzman's *MAD Magazine*, his work appearing in 9 of the first 10 issues. Severin never worked on any of the EC **horror comics** simply because, he claimed, working on such subject matter made him sick. Severin was editing *Two-Fisted Tales* at the time of EC's collapse in the mid-1950s.

In 1956 Severin accepted a staff position with **Stan Lee** at Atlas, working primarily on Westerns. When Atlas became **Marvel** in the early 1960s, Severin worked on a variety of material including *The Hulk*, and a long run inking *Sgt. Fury and His Howling Commandos* for which he won the Alley Cat Award for Best War Title of 1967 and 1968. Also, Severin was the main artist for *Cracked* from the first issue in 1958 until very recently and he freelanced for **Warren Publications** (*Creepy* and *Blazing Combat*) and **DC** (*Sgt. Rock*).

In the 1970s he teamed up with his younger sister and longtime EC colorist, **Marie Severin**, to work on Marvel's Kull the Conqueror. In 2003, Severin worked on Marvel's highly publicized and controversial gay interpretation of Rawhide Kid. When asked what his favorite work had been, Severin replied that it had been "at EC, Warren, and *Cracked* because he had the most free expression with them." In 2003, John Severin was inducted into the **Will Eisner** Hall of Fame.

**Selected Bibliography:** Geissman, Grant. *Foul Play!; The Art and Artists of the Notorious 1950s E.C. Comics!* New York: Collins Design, 2005.

*John F. Weinzierl*

**SEVERIN, MARIE** (1929–). Marie Severin is an award-winning, pioneering woman cartoonist. In the 1960s she was the only woman drawing for mainstream comic books. In the 1970s, she was one of two women drawing for the mainstream, the other being **Ramona Fradon**. It is symbolic that **Stan Lee**, who liked to give rhyming or alliterative names to the **Marvel** creators (Sturdy **Steve Ditko**, Jolly **Jack Kirby**, Genial **Gene Colan**) refereed to Marie Severin as "Marie the She," for indeed, she was the only "she" drawing for Marvel at the time.

Severin attended Pratt Institute for exactly one day before deciding that what they were teaching was not what she was interested in learning. Subsequently she attended and graduated from the Cartoonists and Illustrators school in the early 1950s. In 1952, at the suggestion of her brother **John Severin**, who was one of the **EC** artists, Severin went to work for EC Comics. She started as a Girl Friday, but soon progressed to doing full-time production, coloring, and researching as **Harvey Kurtzman**'s assistant. The first book she worked on was "A Moon, A Girl . . . Romance," which had formerly been Moon Girl comics, but she worked on all the EC books, finally leaving when, as a result of the 1954 Kefauver hearings, EC canceled all their comic book titles and turned *Mad* Comics into a magazine.

Severin was hired by Atlas comics in 1956, doing touch-up, paste-up, lettering, and other production work until the comic book implosion of the late 1950s, when Atlas, like most of the comic book publishers in the last 1950s, severely reduced their staffs to keep from going under. In 1958 she went to work as a staff artist for the Federal Reserve Bank, where she produced, among other things, a 20 page comic book called "The Story of Checks." During this period, she was also freelancing, and drew a story for **DC's** *Challengers of the Unknown* #4, in 1958.

She returned to **Timely**, now called Marvel Comics, on a freelance basis in 1964 and joined the staff in 1965. She continued doing production work until 1966, when she drew her first comic book for Marvel, an issue of **Doctor Strange.** Among the many titles Severin has worked on for Marvel over the ensuing years are *Sub-Mariner, Crazy, The* **Hulk, Iron Man**, *FOOM* (the Marvel in-house magazine), The first issue of *The Cat* (inks) and the first issue of *Star Wars* (colors), and a special one-shot, "The Life of Pope John Paul," in 1982. She also worked on Marvel's Star line during the 1980s, drawing the *Muppet Babies* and eight issues of *Fraggle Rock*, and has said in interviews that her favorite work has been light, humorous stories like the ones she drew for the Star line.

Marie Severin received the Inkpot Award at the San Diego Comicon in 1988, and in 1997 she was inducted into the Women Cartoonists Hall of Fame by Friends of Lulu, an organization that promotes participation in comics by women. She was inducted into the **Will Eisner** Hall of Fame in 2001.

*Trina Robbins*

## SGT. FURY AND HIS HOWLING COMMANDOS.

Sgt. Fury and His Howling Commandos were a heroic group of seven highly capable misfits led by Sgt. Nick Fury, whose cigar chomping, take-no-prisoners attitude informed their commando raids during World War II throughout all of Europe, and on occasion Japan. In the early 1960s, **Marvel** wanted to work off the formula that brought **DC** success with their army comic book *Our Army at War*, specifically the character Sgt. Rock. In response, **Stan Lee, Jack Kirby**, and Dick Ayers combined their efforts and created Sgt. Fury and his Howling Commandos, who first appeared in their own self-titled comic in 1963. The group was composed of fairly standard formulaic types, including the second in command "Dum Dum" Dugan, who was a former circus performer (and requisite Irishman, complete with bowler); Dino Manelli, a handsome man/movie star who joined the war to do his duty; Izzy Cohen, the jaunty Brooklynite who could fix anything; "Junior" Juniper, the Ivy League college graduate who met an untimely end early on in the series; "Rebel" Ralston, a southern Jockey who was wiry and a sure shot; and Gabriel Jones, an African American who liked to play his bugle while going into battle. This last member of the team is of interest, as regular units of the American Army in World War II were segregated until near the end of the war. The timing of the comic book coincided with the height of the Civil Rights movement in the United States as well.

The commandos were often used for behind the lines missions, similar to the true-life exploits of British commandos during World War II. The unit would often end up managing to get out of some close call that put them against the Germans in France. Eventually the Germans countered with their own unit, The Blitzkrieg Squad, led by a Colonel Baron von Strucker. The Germans were continually defeated, after which the Howling Commandos would return to England to be re-assigned by Captain "Happy Sam" Sawyer.

Even the death of "Junior" Juniper did not hamper the team. He was replaced with a British soldier, Percival Pinkerton. While affecting typical British manners and providing comic relief, Pinkerton proved himself to be an outstanding soldier. As with many of the comic books that centered on war themes, the Howling Commandos were always in the thick of the fighting, or training for action.

The story lines, while discussing combat in World War II, also took on concepts of bigotry, competition within services, vaudeville (through Dum-Dum's continual comments on his mother-in-law), and even some romance. Fury at one point was involved with a British countess, whose brother was a **Nazi** sympathizer. It was on a rescue mission to bring back the brother (Lord Haha) that Junior Juniper was killed. As always, the war interfered with the sergeant's love life. The countess Pamela Hawley was killed later in the series, and this further doomed Fury to be alone.

In keeping with their general policy of allowing popular characters to cross over from one comic to another, Marvel often had characters from other comics temporarily join the Howling Commandos. For instance, Reed Richards (Mr. Fantastic of the **Fantastic Four**) was an OSS officer in the famous Lord Haha episode, while **Captain America** sometimes fought alongside the Howlers. Many of the characters introduced in the *Sgt. Fury* series went on to be featured in the continuation series, *Nick Fury: Agent of S.H.I.E.L.D.*, in which Fury headed up an agency of super spies.

While *Sgt. Fury and His Howling Commandos* served as a counter to DC's *Sgt. Rock*, the two did have their differences. The Howlers were constantly involved with combat as first squad of Able Company, First Attack Division. DC's **war comics** were more serious in tone, as opposed to the Sgt. Fury comics, which used humor, **romance**, and slapstick in telling their stories. That humor also included a number of inside jokes. For example, Dick Ayers (artist) and Stan Lee (writer) made cameo appearances in *Sgt. Fury* #22, and the creators of the comic often identified themselves by their former service branch.

Often Fury showed a disobedience that would only be set off by outstanding results as a soldier. However, the Howlers were anything but realistic professional commandos. They fought with their fists rather than with weapons, and often exposed themselves unnecessarily to enemy fire or possible harm. While the concepts of honor and redemption were clearly used in the comic book story lines, the action was far different than the cold reality of combat, where people die, suddenly and violently. The stories also often addressed current events, as in several issues that dealt with racism.

The series was immensely popular, and soon *Nick Fury: Agent of S.H.I.E.L.D.* was created. Both series ran simultaneously for several years. The characters Fury, Dum Dum and Gabe continued on in the S.H.I.E.L.D. series. Fury has been re-imagined again and again over the years, and remains a popular character. He figured into the *Civil War* series as a man who no longer ran S.H.I.E.L.D. and whose stance on the question of superhero registration was generally unclear. Fury was also brought back to his World War II roots with the miniseries *Fury: Peacemaker*, created by **Garth Ennis** and Darick Robertson. Here, Fury was a far more realistic soldier, as well as a far more ruthless one. The new series showed his character flaws, and yet gave him believability as a man who had a drive to do "the right thing." In the end, Fury still served as a long lasting and popular character within the Marvel Comics stable.

*Cord Scott*

**SHADOW, THE.** "Who knows what evil lurks in the hearts of men? The Shadow knows!" Those chilling words were uttered by the mysterious vigilante known as The Shadow, first on radio and later through a series of adventures in pulp magazines, comic strips, comic books, and motion pictures. The Shadow was an ominous avenger who helped popularize the concept of a crimefighter operating under a secret identity. He terrified his adversaries with both his maniacal laughter and willingness to use deadly force. It was not uncommon for him to act as judge, jury, and executioner as he gunned down criminals with his two blazing .45s.

The Shadow debuted as the narrator of radio's *Detective Story Hour* in 1930. The program was sponsored by Street and Smith Publications in order to promote their weekly *Detective Story Magazine*. The character, which was originally voiced by James LaCurto, was intended to only introduce dramatizations of the magazine's stories. However, listeners soon became fascinated by the mysterious storyteller with the sinister voice and demanded to learn more of his exploits. To capitalize on The Shadow's unanticipated popularity and to protect their copyright interests, Street and Smith created a new pulp magazine, *The Shadow, a Detective Magazine*. Journalist Walter Gibson, an amateur magician who had ghostwritten for Houdini, was commissioned to develop the character. Gibson's first novel-length story, *The Living Shadow*, was published in 1931. He wrote 282 of the 325 Shadow adventures that appeared in the magazine over the next 18 years. Gibson, who wrote under the pseudonym Maxwell Grant, is credited with establishing many of The Shadow's most recognizable trademarks, gimmicks, and supporting cast.

The Shadow was depicted as a thin man with a hawk-like nose and piercing black eyes. He wore a long, black, crimson-lined coat, a broad-brimmed slouch hat, and later sported a red scarf to conceal the lower portion of his face. In print, The Shadow employed numerous identities in his war on crime, such as businessman Henry Arnaud, elderly gentleman Isaac Twambley, and Fritz, an old janitor who worked at police

Alec Baldwin as Lamont Cranston, a.k.a. the Shadow, in the 1994 film *The Shadow*, directed by Russell Mulcahy. Universal/Photofest

headquarters. His most prominent alias was that of Lamont Cranston, a millionaire playboy. In 1937, *The Shadow Unmasks* revealed the hero's true identity to be Kent Allard, a famed World War I aviator and spy. Seeking new challenges after the war, he faked his death in a South American jungle and returned to the United States to fight crime. Later adventures created more ambiguity as they raised questions regarding the validity of this origin. On radio and other media, this complicated back-story was discarded as Lamont Cranston was The Shadow's true self. While the hero possessed no true superpowers, he was said to have acquired "the mysterious power to cloud men's minds, so that they could not see him" while he was traveling throughout Asia.

The Shadow was often assisted by a network of agents who joined in his crusade against crime. The most notable were his right-hand man Harry Vincent, cabdriver Moe "Shrevy" Shrevnitz, radio operator Burbank, gangster Cliff Marsland, and Margo Lane, a wealthy socialite and potential love interest. He also gained numerous enemies, such as international spies, mad scientists, gangland kingpins, and various supervillains. The Shadow's most frequently recurring foes included The Voodoo Master, The Cobra, and The Wasp; Shiwan Khan, The Shadow's archenemy, first appeared in 1939. This descendant of Genghis Khan repeatedly fought the hero in his attempts to conquer the world.

The Shadow's popularity in the pulp magazines led to a wave of merchandise that included coloring books, wrist watches, sheet music, disguise and fingerprint kits, and comics. In 1937, the character returned to radio, but not as merely a narrator. Orson Welles starred as Lamont Cranston and Agnes Moorehead portrayed Margo Lane in the adventure series. Welles's Shadow was less deadly than the version seen routinely in the pulps. Although Welles left the show after only a year, the program remained a radio favorite until its cancellation in 1954. In newspapers, *The Shadow* comic strip, which ran from 1939 until 1942, was written by Walter Gibson and illustrated by Vernon Greene. The Shadow has also been seen many times in motion pictures. His first film appearance came in 1937's *The Shadow Strikes*, starring Rod LaRocque. A sequel, *International Crime*, was released in 1938. Victor Jory played the hero in a 1940 serial. Kane Richmond then took over the role in the low-budget *The Shadow Returns* in 1946. It was followed by two forgettable sequels. In 1994, Alec Baldwin took on the role of The Shadow/Lamont Cranston in *The Shadow*. This film combined both the pulp novel and radio versions of the character. In 2006, Hollywood director Sam Raimi expressed interest in producing a new film that would introduce The Shadow to another generation of fans.

The Shadow has routinely appeared in comic books over the decades. From 1940 to 1949, 101 issues of *Shadow Comics* were published. Beginning in 1964, **Archie** Comics published an eight issue series titled *The Shadow*. This is the most bizarre interpretation of the pulp hero, in which The Shadow is seen as a muscular blonde man wearing green and blue **superhero** costume. A more faithful and critically praised version of the character came in a12-issue series produced by **DC Comics** from 1973 to 1975. Written by **Dennis O'Neil** and drawn by Mike Kaluta, this series was highly influenced by Gibson's novels. The Caped Crusader even encounters The Shadow during this period in *Batman* #253 and #259. DC revived The Shadow again in the 1980s, but placed him in modern-day New York, a move that proved unsuccessful. **Marvel Comics** then published *Hitler's Astrologer* (1988), a Shadow graphic novel. From 1989 to 1992 DC published *The Shadow Strikes*. This series was set in the 1930s and is notable for featuring The Shadow's first team-up with **Doc Savage**, another pulp hero. **Dark Horse Comics** next took on The Shadow in two miniseries, *In the Coils of the Leviathan* (1993) and *Hell's Heat Wave* (1995). Dark Horse also published *The Shadow and Doc Savage* (1995), a miniseries that pitted the heroes against **Nazi** kidnappers. The Shadow is one of the most notable pulp heroes. His menacing vigilantism inspired later comic book heroes and taught generations of fans that "the weed of crime bears bitter fruit."

*Charles Coletta*

**SHOOTING WAR.** A web-comic and graphic novel written by Anthony Lappé and illustrated by Dan Goldman, *Shooting War* is a **satire** of contemporary journalism, war, and politics. The book is unique in that it integrates contemporary people and places with dramatic artistic styling and actual location photography. *Shooting War* is a modern fable about the power of media and celebrity, and what happens when one's ethics contradict one's career.

The central character of *Shooting War* is Jimmy Burns, a 20-something independent video blogger from Brooklyn who is determined to uncover corporate greed with his live independent vod-casts. While he is uploading a program to his Web site in a

Starbucks coffee shop, the shop explodes. The explosion, a result of a terrorist attack, has Burns in the right place at the right time, capturing it on video. Global News, a world-wide media conglomerate, gets the feed from his site and broadcasts it, making Burns an instant celebrity hounded by other media.

After the typical rounds of interviews with print and television personalities, Burns agrees to work for Global News, the epitome of the media entities critiqued by his anticapitalistic blogs. However, working from the inside to expose the gritty underbelly of life appeals to Jimmy, so he accepts. He is hooked on the adrenaline rush that comes with war reporting.

In pursuit of the ultimate war story, Jimmy Burns and a military crew head to Baghdad but get shot down and captured by the terrorist group, The Sword of Mohammed. Convincing the group to let him live by broadcasting their message live, Burns becomes the media outlet for the group. With this new role, Burns is released and finds himself back in his hotel awaiting contact with a new producer but is given an ultimatum—broadcast the group's messages or face the consequences.

As *Shooting War* continues, the plot has Burns encountering a variety of attacks, all controlled by the Sword of Mohammed. Torn between doing what is right and reporting the news, he realizes that he has become the media pawn for the group. This troubles Burns, but also intrigues him as a journalist. Another prominent journalist, Dan Rather (now reporting for the Dallas Mavericks), works with Burns to help him realize that reporting is more than just uncovering the facts, but being able to do the right thing for the good of society. Rather, in a tense battle scene, ends up saving Jimmy in a heroic turn of events that could have ended both of their lives. At the end of the book, Burns stands on his own and becomes an independent journalist in order to report breaking stories throughout the world.

The book satirizes media exploitation, truth, politics, and corruption of power. It also shows the power of public journalism and its responsibility to both society and the citizens who watch it. As Marshall McLuhan famously said, "the medium is the message." In this case, the message in *Shooting War* is one of caution because things are not always as they appear to be.

**Selected Bibliography:** For more information on *Shooting War*, go to, www.shooting war.com.

*Alec R. Hosterman*

**SHUSTER, JOE** (1914–92). Joe Shuster is the co-creator (with **Jerry Siegel**) of **Superman.** Shuster was born in Toronto, Canada, and moved to Cleveland, Ohio. Growing up, Shuster was a fan of the *Wash Tubbs* comic strip and the pulp illustrations of Frank Paul. Shuster would draw on his mother's breadboard on old wallpaper, packages, and anything else he could find. At Alexander Hamilton Junior High School, Joe drew comics for the school newspaper, *The Federalist*. At Glenville High School, Shuster was involved with set design for the drama club and won a cartoon contest about Thanksgiving.

He also won a citywide poster contest for a football game. Shuster agreed to illustrate and design a five-issue fanzine named *Science Fiction* written by Siegel. Unable to get a scholarship to the prestigious Cleveland School of Art (he received Honorable Mention), Shuster continued to draw from magazines and took night classes at the Huntington School of Art. Driven by Siegel's relentless drive to publish, Shuster was soon drawing many Siegel cartoon scripts including "Bruce Verne, G-man of the Future" and "Snoopy and Smiley," among others. Yet it was Shuster's ability to draw strongman heroes and gorgeous damsels that helped the duo get published starting in 1935 with several serials in **More Fun Comics**, *New Comics*, **Adventure Comics**, and **Detective Comics.** In these comics, Shuster used film techniques to provide emotional close-ups and stunning full-page action sequences, often elevated by Shuster's creative use of Craftint paper. At the same time, they worked on another character: Superman. Shuster designed the famous costume using elements of physical fitness culture, of which he was a strong follower. Superman was finally bought for $130 (including the rights) and the character debuted in **Action Comics** #1 (1938). Shuster (who was born with poor eyesight) opened his own Cleveland studio—with young artists such as Wayne Boring, Leo Nowak, and John Sikela—to help with the workload. Early stories were also lettered by Shuster's brother,

Frank. After World War II, Siegel and Shuster began proceedings to sue their employer, National Allied Publications (the primary direct forerunner of **DC Comics**) for the rights to Superman and were consequently fired.

Shuster teamed up with Siegel again on the comic *Funnyman* (1947), taught, and contributed pencils and covers to **horror** and racing comics. In the late 1950s and in need of money, he did anonymous work on the *Nights of Horror* magazines, which depicted his famous archetypal characters in outlandish fetish fantasies. Shuster tried to launch an art show and created a cartoon called "Kosmo," but neither worked out. He moved to California and was married briefly to Judy Calpini in 1975, the same year that he and Siegel were granted a pension by DC and were returned to the byline of *Superman*.

Artist Joe Shuster, who co-created Superman (ca. 1980s). DC Comics/Photofest

**Selected Bibliography:** Benton, Mike. *Masters of Imagination: The Comic Book Artists Hall of Fame.* New York: National, 1994; Jones, Gerard. *Men of Tomorrow.* New York: Basic, 2004; Yoe, Craig. *Secret Identity: The Fetish Art of Superman's Co-Creator Joe Shuster.* New York: Abrams ComicArts, 2009.

*Brad J. Ricca*

**SIEGEL, JERRY** (1914–96). Jerry Siegel was born in Cleveland, Ohio, to Lithuanian Jewish immigrants and is the famous co-creator (with **Joe Shuster**) of **Superman**. When his father died of a heart attack during a hold-up in 1932, Siegel turned to reading and writing as a means of escape and expression. In high school, he wrote prodigiously for the school newspaper, *The Glenville Torch.* Siegel also self-published five issues of an early fanzine called *Science Fiction* which included the story "The Reign of the Superman," a pulp homage illustrated by Shuster about a bald scientist who creates an evil mental marvel. Inspired by early comic books such as *Detective Dan*, Siegel and Shuster sent pitches for comics to early publishers (Consolidated Publishing) and local newspapers (*The Cleveland Shopping News*) but to no avail. They finally sold a series of short comics to **More Fun Comics**, *New Comics, and Adventure Comics* starting in 1935 with "Henri Duval," which was followed by "Spy," "Radio Squad," "Doctor Occult," and "Slam Bradley" which Siegel wrote for **Detective Comics** from 1937 to 1941. Siegel's narratives are heavily pulp in tone but also humorous as well, drawing from a variety of print, radio, and film sources. In the mid-1930s, Siegel and Shuster also worked up a new character called Superman who was a combination strongman and civic hero. The character went through a variety of incarnations, artists, and formats. Finally rescued from the slush pile, National Allied Publications (a forerunner of **DC Comics**) bought Superman's initial 13-page manuscript (and all subsequent rights) for $10 a page. Superman debuted in 1938's **Action Comics** #1. A new comic, *Superman* (1939), and a syndicated newspaper strip quickly followed, both written by Siegel.

Writer Jerry Siegel, who co-created Superman (ca. 1980s). DC Comics/Photofest

Siegel was drafted in 1943 and, upon his return from World

War II, instigated a complicated set of lawsuits in 1946 to regain control over Superman and the new character Superboy. Siegel and Shuster settled with their employer, National Allied Publications, the primary direct forerunner of DC, over Superboy, but were also summarily fired. Their last comics collaboration, "Funnyman" (1947) did not catch on. Siegel returned to write a host of un-credited Superman stories for DC during the late 1950s and 1960s. He also did limited work for **Marvel Comics**. Siegel worked in children's television, was the comic director for Ziff-Davis, and created (with Paul Reinman) The Mighty Crusaders for **Archie** Comics. He also worked on the Disney Duck comics, mostly for the Italian comic, *Mondadori Editore*. In 1975, after a long national campaign by fellow comics creators to coincide with the first Superman movie, Siegel and Shuster were given a pension settlement that also returned their names to the masthead of every incarnation of Superman.

Siegel was married twice: first, to Bella Lifshitz, with whom he had a son, Michael. He later married Joanne Carter, the original model for Lois Lane, and had a daughter, Laura.

**Selected Bibliography:** Daniels, Les. *The Complete History of Superman*. San Francisco: Chronicle, 1998; Jones, Gerard. *Men of Tomorrow*. New York: Basic, 2004.

*Brad J. Ricca*

**SIENKIEWICZ, BILL** (1958–). Born Boleslav Felix Robert Sienkiewicz in Blakely, Pennsylvania, and growing up in New Jersey, Bill Sienkiewicz is an innovative graphic novel artist and writer. Descended from the Nobel Prize-winning Polish novelist Henryk Sienkiewicz (*Quo Vadis*), he started drawing when he was about four or five and has stated that he was influenced by **Curt Swan** and **Jack Kirby**. As an adult, Sienkiewicz worked at construction sites in order to afford attending the Newark School of Fine and Industrial Arts in Newark, New Jersey.

Sienkiewicz started his comic book career doing the art for **Marvel**'s "Moon Knight," which was the back-up story in the *Hulk Magazine*, starting with issue #13 in 1978. Moon Knight received its own series in November 1980, and Sienkiewicz did the majority of the inside art and covers for the 30-issue run. From 1984 to 1986, Sienkiewicz established himself as a masterful cover artist when he was the primary artist on Marvel's *New Mutants* written by **Chris Claremont**. Sienkiewicz's impressionistic covers stood out among other **superhero** titles of the time, which classically depicted an action from inside the book. Instead, he simplified his figures to their iconic traits—the heroes were shadowy figures with identifiable characteristics. On many of his covers and in his interior pages, lines, often white, radiated from the center, conveying frenetic action as well as psychological turmoil, a trademark of his style throughout his career.

In January 1986, he teamed up with writer **Frank Miller** to produce *Marvel Graphic Novel* issue #24 titled ***Daredevil: Love and War***. Miller, after having produced the seminal ***Dark Knight Returns***, was a great fit for Sienkiewicz's experimental art; they produced the eight-issue *Elektra: Assassin* (August 1986–June 1987), which pushed the boundaries of superhero comics even further with its **adult** themes and political commentary. For his work on these issues, Sienkiewicz won international acclaim, receiving the 1986 Yellow Kid Award (Italy) and the 1987 **Jack Kirby** Award, presented by *Amazing Heroes* magazine. He also worked on the graphic novel, *Shadowplay: The Secret Team*, published in *Brought to Light*, with writer **Alan Moore** (Eclipse Comics 1988), about the history of the CIA. Sienkiewicz teamed up with Moore again in 1991 with the ambitious, but unfinished, series, *Big Numbers*; he produced art for only the first two issues before dropping out of the project.

From January 1988 to April 1989, Sienkiewicz became a writer and artist for his four-issue series, *Stray Toasters* (Epic Comics), which featured a detective hunting down a serial killer. Freed from the restrictions of the superhero genre, Sienkiewicz produced innovative text work and images that depicted the insanity of the killer and the world of his disturbed characters in his nonlinear narrative. Alternating splash pages with 9 and 12-panel pages, Sienkiewicz used a variety of media—from pen and ink drawings to mixed-media collages, to lush oil paintings—in order to evoke the inner chaos of his characters.

Since then, Sienkiewicz has worked on a variety of titles for **DC** and Marvel, notably winning the 2004 **Eisner Award** for his contribution to *Sandman: Endless Nights*, written by **Neil Gaiman** (DC-Vertigo 2003). Sienkiewicz's chapter, covering the character Delirium, is a cornucopia of techniques, from washes, to pen drawings, overlays, photographic images, and the combination serves the storyline admirably, blending the chaos of Delirium's mind with a pictorial delight in excess. Other notable illustration projects include the 1995 *Voodoo Child: The Illustrated Legend of Jimi Hendrix* (**Kitchen Sink Press**) and, in 1998, the children's book, *Santa, My Life and Times* (Avon Books). He also took his talent to other media, producing CD covers, movie promotional art, and trading cards. Further, Sienkiewicz has been an active character designer for television, earning two Emmy Award nominations in 1995 and 1996 for his work on *Where in the World is Carmen Sandiego?*

**Selected Bibliography:** Lerer, Mark. "The Marvel Age Interview: Bill Sienkiewicz." *Marvel Age* 28 ( July 1985): 20–22.

*Wendy Goldberg*

*SILVER AGE. See Ages of Comics*

**SILVER SURFER, THE.** The Silver Surfer is a **Marvel Comics** character created by **Stan Lee** and **Jack Kirby**. He falls under the category of a "cosmic" **superhero**. The character has powers on a vast scale and has been criticized as difficult to write for a monthly title. Generally, the character serves the genre convention of the "other" (or an outsider) used to provide an introspective perspective on a litany of human ills and social injustices.

Doug Jones as the Silver Surfer, in the 2007 film *Fantastic Four: Rise of the Silver Surfer*, directed by Tim Story. Actor Laurence Fishburne provided the voice of the Silver Surfer. 20th Century Fox/WETA/Photofest

The Silver Surfer first appears in a three-issue sequence of **Fantastic Four** (known today as the "The Galactus Trilogy") beginning with issue #48 in March 1966. Here the Silver Surfer comes to Earth, heralding the coming of Galactus, the devourer of worlds. While interacting with several characters, notably Alicia Masters, the Silver Surfer begins to feel conflicted between protecting what he deems as a worthy planet and his duties to Galactus. His outlook on the goodness and unlimited potential of humanity reflects similar humanistic progressive themes in much **science fiction** writing of the time, most notably in Gene Roddenberry's original *Star Trek*.

The Silver Surfer's defiance of Galactus echoes Lucifer's rebellion and subsequent exile from Heaven. Although Earth is spared, as a punishment for his transgression the Silver Surfer is exiled from the cosmos (i.e., Heaven). This exile is explored in the first series, running from August 1968 to #18 in September 1970. In this series, the Silver Surfer undergoes trials and temptations while continuing to reflect on the nobility of humanity despite the day-to-day bigotry and ignorance he sees. To further his Odysseus-like journey, the Surfer is feared and rejected by the majority of humans with whom he comes into contact, making his self-sacrifice and exile all the more bittersweet. This series is among Stan Lee's most introspective work and reflects many of the cultural and critical challenges of the social and political issues raised in the late 1960s.

The Silver Surfer wanders the Earth during his exile in the first series, longing to return to his home planet of Zenn-La and his mate, Shalla Bal. Here, again echoing *The Odyssey*, as the Surfer takes on the literary and mythological conventions of exile, trials, and temptation. The Surfer stands in for the incorruptible soul, constantly tested and tempted by a gallery of villains such as Dr. Doom, Loki, and the demon Mephisto. While Doom desires the Power Cosmic from the Surfer, Loki and Mephisto are attracted to the challenge of breaking the Surfer's will. As with many comics characters, the themes of willpower and moral clarity run deep in the narrative of *Silver Surfer*. Indeed, it is Mephisto who desperately wants to corrupt the "courage [. . .] purity [and] lack of malice" exhibited by the Surfer. Here again Mephisto stands in as a tangible representation of the baser instincts of human behavior opposed to the ideals of moral clarity.

Stan Lee's *Silver Surfer* series also includes the origin story of the Silver Surfer. Norrin Radd is an impatient scientist/astronomer from the planet Zenn-La, which has achieved such a degree of scientific advancement that all of the wants of its inhabitants are fulfilled. Such a culture frustrates young Radd as "the spirit of high adventure [and] the thrill of exploration" are lost on the contented people of Zenn-La. Anti-utopian currents run throughout the origin story, as Radd's individualism continually comes into conflict with the communal orientation of his advanced, seemingly utopian society. As was often the case in the Marvel comics written by Stan Lee, the aliens and monsters reflect aspects of human behavior, drawing obvious parallels to the social movements of the late 1960s. After the cancellation of the original series, the Silver Surfer made various appearances in other Marvel titles including *Fantastic Four* and *Defenders*. One-shots in 1978 and 1982 were followed by a continuing series in July 1987 that ran until issue #146 in November 1998, featuring the end of the Silver Surfer's Earth-bound exile. This series is oriented toward science fiction adventure, with less time given to social commentary and introspection. Various subsequent one-shot and special issues would feature the Surfer as a springboard for social commentary.

Placing the Surfer in the role of a messianic figure reaches its high point in *Silver Surfer: Parable*, a two-part sequence written by Lee with art by **Moebius**, published in 1988 and 1989. In this story, addressing wide ranging themes such as religious fanaticism; in one scene the Surfer is depicted in a crucified stance, with Lee's script quoting "They know not what they do." The depiction of the Silver Surfer in *Parable* thus takes the character away from its origins as a Lucifer deifying the destroyer God Galactus. Instead, his allegorical portrayal shifts to that of a Christlike, self-sacrificing figure defending a populace that hates him; at the same time he searches for "an oasis of sanity in this desert of [human] madness" that can reclaim his faith in humanity. Although leaving little room for ambiguity, *Parable* is among the most significant of Lee's later works commenting on the overall cultural materialism, social apathy, and religious narrow-mindedness of 1980s America.

*D. R. Hammontree*

**SIM, DAVE** (1956–). A longtime resident of Kitchener, Ontario, Dave Sim is one of the most successful self-publishers of comic books thus far. The creative work Sim is most known for is **Cerebus the Aardvark**, a sprawling and often challenging series published on a regular basis from 1977 until 2004. Prior to *Cerebus*, Sim contributed to and published fanzines, as well as creative work, including stories for a variety of independent publishers, and even a comic strip. *Cerebus* evolved from Sim's fanzine work, beginning as a sort of parody of various popular and, for the time, cutting-edge productions from **Marvel Comics**, particularly *Conan the Barbarian.* Sim, along with his then-wife, Deni Loubert, established his own publishing imprint, Aardvark-Vanaheim, as a vehicle for *Cerebus.*

Sim attracted interest in *Cerebus* for its high quality, his resistance to financial support from any outside publishers, and his vow to complete 300 regularly-issued numbers of the series. He was a tireless advocate of creator ownership, particularly through the vehicle of self-publishing, which he felt allowed the individual creator the best opportunities for financial success as well as artistic integrity. To that end, Sim published the *Cerebus Guide to Self-Publishing*, a collection of columns and written observations about creating and distributing comics independently. Together with his creative partner, Gerhard (who was responsible for the backgrounds), Sim also founded the Day Prize, named for his friend and mentor Gene Day, which was awarded yearly for outstanding achievements in self-publishing at the Small Press and Alternative Comics Expo (S.P.A.C.E.), held yearly in Columbus, Ohio. The prize gave critical recognition to independent creators from 2001 until 2007. In 2008, Sim withdrew from participation in the prize, which has been renamed the S.P.A.C.E. Prize.

For a time, Sim assisted other creators to achieve publication. With Deni Loubert as publisher, Aardvark-Vanaheim published several other titles for a time, including *Flaming Carrot Comics* by Bob Burden, *normalman* by Jim Valentino, and *Ms. Tree* by **Max Allan Collins** and Terry Beatty. Upon their divorce, Loubert would publish most of their old titles through her own company, Renegade Press, leaving *Cerebus* as the sole title published by Aardvark-Vanaheim. Subsequent titles (written and illustrated by Sim) published by Aardvark-Vanaheim include *Judenhass*, a prestige-format title about the Holocaust, and *Glamourpuss*, an unusual series that at times discusses Sim's opinions about the history of cartooning (in particular, early issues featured Sim's recreations of later illustrations by *Flash Gordon* creator Alex Raymond), and at other times lampoons fashion culture. While Sim's creative output has slowed somewhat since the end of *Cerebus*, he remains an important creative force in comics.

*Robert O'Nale*

**SIMON, JOE** (1913–). Raised in Rochester, New York, Joe Simon is one of the central figures in comic book history. After graduating high school and later working as art director for the *Syracuse Journal American*, Simon moved to New York City where he retouched publicity photos for Paramount Pictures and did illustrations for various magazines. In 1939 he did his first comics work assignment for Funnies, Inc. and then created his first comic book hero. He also did freelance stories and art for Centaur, Novelty, and Fox Publications. Working on *Blue Bolt* Simon met **Jack Kirby** and the two would soon become one of the most successful and influential teams in the comics business.

After leaving Fox, Simon found himself at publisher Martin's **Timely** (the future **Marvel**). As the company's first editor, Simon had a young **Stan Lee** as his office assistant. At Timely, Simon and Kirby created the one of the most famous comic book superheroes, **Captain America** in late 1940. Steve Rogers was an ordinary GI who was part of a secret Army experiment to create stronger soldiers, thus becoming Captain America. Along with his sidekick Bucky, Cap would fight the **Nazis** even before the United States had entered into World War II. Although their highly patriotic issues sold out, Simon and Kirby disagreed with Goodman over royalties. Yet, instead of challenging him, they sought out Jack Liebowitz at National Comics who would be only too happy to offer them a better deal. On hearing of this, Goodman fired the team.

At National, they took over the **Sandman** character and had hit after hit including the *Boy Commandos, Newsboy Legion*, and *Manhunter.* Simon created *The Fly* for **Archie** Comics and *Stuntman, Boy Explorers,* and *Boys' Ranch* for Harvey Publications—this last title being his favorite collaboration with Kirby. In 1953, the Simon and Kirby team would also create what would be another one of their favorites, the **Western** comic, *Bullseye.* For Prize Publications they created an early **horror comic** *Black Magic* and are also credited with creating the entire **romance** genre of comics with *Young Romance Comics* in 1947.

As the industry fell into a sharp decline in the mid 1950's, Simon focused more on commercial art, but also helped oversee many of the kid-friendly comics put out by Harvey Comics. In 1960, the business-savvy Simon created *Sick Magazine*, which competed favorably against *Mad.* The Simon and Kirby partnership ended in 1955, but they would come together over the years to work on updating old characters or creating new ones. Their last collaboration was in 1974 when Simon wrote the first issue of a new *Sandman* for **DC.**

Sixty-six years after his co-creation of Captain America, Simon commented: "We were movie directors, script men, penciler, colorers, inkers . . . we had dirty hands." Simon did it all and in doing so his creative force directly shaped the American comic book industry almost from its inception.

**Selected Bibliography:** Simon, Joe, and Jim Simon. *The Comic Book Makers.* Lakewood, NJ: Vanguard, 2003.

*Jeff McLaughlin*

**SIMONE, GAIL** (1974?–). In 1999, Gail Simone, a hairdresser and comics fan in her native Oregon, compiled a list of women characters in comics who had been raped, crippled, depowered, magically impregnated (without consent and therefore a form of rape), turned evil, given a life-threatening disease, or murdered. Because of extended continuity—made necessary by the longevity of medium—these characters were often subject to a combination of these atrocities. This trend, Simone observed, became known as "Women in Refrigerators"—after the particularly gruesome demise of the **Green Lantern**'s girlfriend, Alexandra DeWitt—who was murdered and stuffed in a refrigerator. The list was sent to several comics creators, along with a letter, asking for their thoughts. Simone went on to write a weekly column called "You'll All Be Sorry" for the Web site Comic Book Resources (1999–2003). She later began scripting *Simpsons* comics for Bongo.

**Marvel Comics'** Joe Quesada suggested Simone pitch for the title *Deadpool* which was later revamped as *Agent X*. Simone left Marvel over creative differences and began work at **DC Comics** where she wrote for various titles, including **Action Comics,** and a *Rose and Thorn* limited series (2004). Simone also wrote *Killer Princesses* for Oni Press with co-creator and artist Lea Hernandez.

In 2003, Simone took over DC's *Birds of Prey* title (formerly written by **Chuck Dixon**) with issue #56 and added Helena Bertinelli/Huntress to the line-up of Barbara Gordon/Oracle and Dinah Lance/Black Canary. Under her direction, *Birds of Prey* became one of DC's steadiest selling and most critically acclaimed books. Simone's success as a comic book writer, as well as her enjoyment of it, led her to give up hair-dressing to focus on writing full-time. In 2006, she was the writer for a limited series of *The Secret Six*, a DC **superhero** team that originated in the **Silver Age**. In 2007, she took over writing duties on ***Wonder Woman*** with Issue #14. Additionally, Simone's commitment to creating diverse casts of characters led her to win a Glyph Comics Award for Best Female Character in Thomasina Lindo—one of the lead characters in *Welcome to Tranquility*—a creator-owned comic published by WildStorm. Simone has also worked on a reboot of *Gen* for WildStorm and *All-New Atom* for DC. She has also done work in scripting for television and films based on comics. She wrote an episode of *Justice League Unlimited* and early drafts of the *Wonder Woman* animated direct-to-DVD feature film that was released in 2009.

**Selected Bibliography:** Garrity, Shaenon. "The Gail Simone Interview." *The Comics Journal* 286 (November 2007): 68–69; Stuller, Jennifer K. *Ink-stained Amazons and Cinematic Warriors: Superwomen in Modern Mythology*. New York: I. B. Tauris, 2010.

*Jennifer K. Stuller*

# SIMONSON, WALTER (WALT) (1946–).

Born in Knoxville, Tennessee, comic book writer and artist Walter Simonson graduated from Rhode Island School of Design in 1972. His thesis project *Star Slammers* would serve as his first portfolio and would later form the basis for a graphic novel and a miniseries. His widely recognizable signature in the shape of a brontosaurus reflects his early interest in paleontology. Although he started in the industry illustrating **war comics** for **DC Comics** and other companies, Simonson's big break actually came from writer Archie Goodwin, who invited him to draw *Manhunter* in 1973, which ran in the back of **Detective Comics.** Simonson's four-year stay with DC also included reviving the Metal Men.

At **Marvel Comics,** Simonson did a number of comic book movie **adaptations** including *Battlestar Galactica*, and *Star Wars*, and worked on *X-Factor* with his wife, writer Louise Simonson. He is best known for taking over *The Mighty **Thor*** in 1983 and creating story arcs that raised the level of the book to that of its earlier **Stan Lee/**

**Jack Kirby** days. Although Simonson injected a fine mixture of **science fiction** and mythology, fans typically remember two events during his approximately four years on the series. First, turning Thor into a frog for three issues (an homage to Simonson's favorite comic book writer and artist as a boy: **Carl Barks**) and second, the introduction of Beta Ray Bill, an alien who became only the second individual (at the time) deemed worthy enough to pick up Thor's hammer Mjolnir.

In late 1989, Simonson became writer and artist on *The Fantastic Four*. His year-and-a-half tenure included the memorable nonlinear presentation of a fight between Dr. Doom and Reed Richards that required the reader to read the issue twice. Simonson enjoyed working in the shared-universe concept where the various characters moved between different books, thereby creating complex back stories; thus he wrote and/or drew many characters for both Marvel and DC Comics including the **Avengers**, **The Hulk**, **Superman**, **Batman**, **Wonder Woman**, and Dr. Fate. This shared-universe concept was also part of publisher Malibu's Bravura line of creator-owned comics, which Simonson joined briefly before the company was bought out by Marvel.

As a fan of Jack Kirby's Fourth World mythos, Simonson was excited to bring back the character Orion for DC for a run that lasted 25 issues. Simonson also illustrated Michael Moorcock's miniseries *Elric: The Making of a Sorcerer*. Simonson had no preference for drawing covers or interiors as he found they offered different artistic challenges. When once asked which was more important in comics, writing or drawing, he responded that the question was like asking "Which is more important, breathing air or drinking water?"

Simonson's illustration influences include **Moebius**, Jim Holdaway, Frank Bellamy, Sergio Toppi and various **Silver Age** Marvel artists. His writing influences include J.R.R. Tolkien, numerous **science-fiction** writers, his friend Archie Goodwin, and wife Louise Simonson. A legendary talent, Simonson nevertheless remains an open-minded artist—willing and wanting to learn from anyone and anything.

*Jeff McLaughlin*

**SIN CITY.** The title refers to a variety of story arcs occurring in the same environment written and drawn by **Frank Miller**, who is renowned for his take on **Batman** in *The Dark Knight Returns*. The first *Sin City* story was published in *Dark Horse Comics Presents Fifth Anniversary Special* (1991) and then continued in the anthology *Dark Horse Presents* #51-62 (1991–92). These stories were later collected in graphic novel form and expanded along the years with more single issues and book collections coming along. There is no main protagonist in *Sin City*, but several characters appear regularly throughout the narrative threads (or "yarns" as they are referred to) as they weave in and out among each other. The individual yarns usually follow a central character but the stories are thoroughly intertwined and can be puzzled into a grand *Sin City* narrative chronology. Sin City is the nickname of the fictional Basin City—the setting in or around which the stories take place. The different parts of town act as the framing structure for the stories as they move from the rich neighborhood of Sacred Oaks to the worn-down projects, and city landmarks help anchor the fast-paced plot lines in areas like the surreal Tar Pits of the closed down amusement park and the fenced evil of The Farm. Old Town is a city within the city populated by prostitutes; as long as a fragile truce is kept, the mob and police leave the women of Old Town to carry out their own justice. Basin City has a very high frequency of violence and crime and is controlled by corrupt politicians, the mob, and various crime lords using hitmen as go-betweens. The police force is part SWAT team members and part regular cops, most of whom are in the pocket of one or the other powerful criminals. Miller uses an immediately recognizable style where great emphasis is put on the effects of light and shadow, using black and white to outline bodies, light up faces and keep things hidden in the dark. Contrasts between black and white shape the characters as black patches of ink are criss-crossed by falling white rain, and silhouettes in white or black take up big parts of the page design—their bodies striped by the light coming through numerous Venetian blinds. Grey tones are not an option in the visual execution of *Sin City*, but on rare occasion Miller uses a primary color for effect: a red dress, blue eyes or the yellow body of a vile villain known as the Yellow Bastard. The only exception to this black/white scenario is a passage in the volume *Hell and Back* where the drug- overdosed mind of the protagonist is reflected in a water-colored section featuring a wide variety of monsters and intertextual references to other comics. With the exception of *Family Values*, all the *Sin City* volumes were first published as single issues.

The Hard Goodbye (original title: Sin City) first collected in 1992, features Marv—a chivalrous but primitive muscle-man. After having spent a night with the beautiful Goldie just to wake and find her murdered in a way clearly intended to frame him for the crime, Marv swears revenge and starts killing his way through the people involved in her death.

Original comic panel of Nancy and Hartigan from Frank Miller's graphic novel *Sin City*. Dimension Films/Photofest

In *A Dame to Kill for* (1994) the photographer Dwight gets framed by his devious ex-girlfriend Ava Lord. Enlisting the help of Marv and the women of Old Town he is able to make Ava pay for her deeds and get his revenge. *The Big Fat Kill* (1996) finds Dwight in yet another precarious situation when he has to help cover up the murder of a crooked cop named Jack who was killed by the girls of Old Town. Both the mob and the police would love to take over Old Town and Jack's murder could be their chance. The final showdown refers to the battle of Thermopylae—a story Miller would later go on to elaborate in the graphic novel **300**. The main antagonist in *That Yellow Bastard* (1997) embodies all meanings of the word yellow. He preys on little girls and is maimed by the policeman Hartigan in an effort to save 11-year old Nancy Callahan from rape and murder. Eight years later he wants to get his hands on Nancy and Hartigan has to fight him again.

Once more Dwight is the main character in *Family Values* (1997), where he has been sent on a mission by the girls of Old Town. With him is deadly ninjette assassin Miho and their target mob family is made to understand that family can expand beyond blood relations. A collection of small stories with the characters from *Sin City* is put together in *Booze, Broads, and Bullets* (1998). Saving a girl from committing suicide takes ex-Navy Seal Wallace to *Hell and Back (A Sin City Love Story)*(2000) as he has to fight powerful moneyman Wallenquist to free the mysterious woman.

Benicio Del Toro as Jack Rafferty, in the 2005 film *Sin City*, directed by Frank Miller and Robert Rodriguez. Dimension Films/Photofest

*Sin City* is a revision of the classic noir **crime comics** bordering on pastiche but definitely an homage to a kind of comics the **Comics Code** helped obliterate. The setting is dark, the violence is graphic, and the heroes are men of action most often in pursuit of dangerous dames or damsels in distress. This central plot is underlined by the many close-ups of determined male faces and the repetition of silent, full-page images of scantily clad women. Sympathy is on the side of the lone avenger or the few and supposedly powerless against the many and powerful. No matter how hard the rain falls, how hopeless the situation seems or how black the night is, in *Sin City* there is always a way out for those who choose to fight.

*Sin City* was made into a movie in 2005 directed by Robert Rodriguez and co-directed by Miller himself. In the making are *Sin City 2* and *Sin City 3*, scheduled for release 2010 and 2011.

*Rikke Platz Cortsen*

**SPAWN.** Created by **Todd McFarlane**, Spawn made his first appearance in May, 1992, in the first issue of the comic book that bears his name. Spawn was one of the original creations from **Image Comics**, of which McFarlane was one of the co-founders. The central figure in *Spawn* is Albert "Al" Francis Simmons, a Detroit-born African American CIA agent whose boss, Jason Wynn, orders him assassinated. Simmons is sent to Hell because of his status as a mercenary. In Hell, Simmons, motivated by a desire to see his wife Wanda once more, unwisely strikes a deal with Malebolgia, a powerful lord, and returns to Earth as a Hellspawn, an officer in Hell's army.

His memory in tatters and his body misshapen beyond recognition, Spawn re-enters the world in a state of stupefaction. Once on Earth, he soon discovers that five years have passed since his death, and that his wife Wanda Blake has since married his friend Terry Fitzgerald, their union yielding a daughter named Cyan. Spawn was represented as a rather conventional crime-fighting anti-hero in the initial issues. His most significant encounters are with Anti-Spawn, or the Redeemer, who is later revealed to be Jason Wynn, and Angela, who was, like Cogliostro, created by **Neil Gaiman** in issue #9 of *Spawn*. Both the Redeemer and Angela were heavenly agents meant to counter Spawn, although Angela eventually comes to assist Spawn several times.

Following Spawn's encounter with the Redeemer, his suit, a crucial source of his power, undergoes a significant change (the first of many), becoming more powerful in the process. The suit is symbiotic and connected to his body and its nervous system; it is nourished by necroplasm, the hellish substance out of which Spawn was created. Spawn's necroplasmic power is limited, and its complete exhaustion would lead to eternal suffering in Hell.

Spawn, given his origins, functions within a good-evil dichotomy, represented in the early issues by, respectively, an old man named Cagliostro and the clown-like Violator, Malebolgia's earthly agent. That initial dichotomy is complicated by the introduction of an alternative realm to Hell and Heaven through the Heap. The Heap is a monstrous figure that formed when a man named Eddie Beckett inadvertently came into contact with necroplasm, leading to a merging of his body with the surrounding garbage. Spawn's battles with the Heap result in the latter swallowing the former, transporting Spawn to Greenworld, a kind of natural Purgatory independent of Hell and Heaven.

Spawn employs the powers accorded to him by the forces of that realm to defeat Urizen, a god released by Malebolgia in a failed attempt to assume control of all of Hell. Spawn, accompanied by Angela, enters Hell and destroys the weakened Malebolgia. He is then offered Malebolgia's place by Mammon, and after initially refusing it, decides to accept it in order to transform Hell into a paradisiacal realm. His plans are, however, thwarted by Cagliostro, who betrays Spawn, assumes control of Hell for

Michael Jai White as Spawn, in the 1997 film by the same name, directed by Mark A. Z. Dippé. Photofest/New Line Cinema

himself, and reveals himself as the Biblical Cain. Cagliostro returns Spawn to Earth seemingly transformed back to his original form as Al Simmons.

Simmons does not remain in that state for long, however, and is able to transform himself into Spawn again with the help of a witch named Nyx. He assumes a position strikingly similar to his original one, with Mammon replacing Malebolgia as the chief adversary. Spawn later finds himself at the center of Armageddon, where he rises to become as powerful as God and Satan (re-imagined as warring children of a more powerful figure named the Mother). Spawn destroys the armies of Hell and Heaven as well as all of humanity, and subsequently creates a new Earth with the sanction of the Mother. He asks the Mother to return him to Earth as Al Simmons thereafter.

Subsequent episodes in the Spawn narrative take a decidedly domestic turn, with Spawn's family relations and Mammon's long-time involvement in his life since early childhood taking precedence. The convoluted family history essentially centers on Mammon's intentions to create the ultimate Hellspawn, originally meant to be Al Simmons but afterwards his child Morana, whom Wanda miscarried after she was beaten by Simmons just prior to his death. Mammon's plans are foiled by the clairvoyant Cyan, who in cooperation with Nyx destroys Morana.

From the very beginning, the sense of uncertainty regarding Spawn's identity and past forms a central theme in the comic. In issue #2 of *Spawn*, for example, Spawn attempts to use his powers to assume a human shape, only to find that he has assumed the body of a blonde, white man. The issue of Simmons/Spawn's **race** is of striking interest given the dearth of main characters in comics that are African American. The matter has been addressed directly in the comic several times, nowhere as visibly as in *Spawn* #30, where Spawn, returning to the world after a sojourn in Heaven, finds himself in the U.S. South confronting the KKK while trying to protect an African

American family. He is shot in the head by the Klan members and then hanged, though he lives to exact revenge on them.

**Religion** forms another significant and consistent element in the comic, with Judeo-Christian mythology forming the basis for the comic's worldview. The resurrected Spawn, for example, has clear if somewhat antithetical predecessors in Lazarus and Christ. As well, the apocalyptic elements in the comic owe a great deal to *The Book of Revelation*, while the geography of Hell was clearly inspired by Dante's *Inferno*.

Spawn remained popular for much of the 1990s, and even starred in a feature film in 1997. Although his popularity has waned considerably since then, Spawn still remains a notable figure in comics. There have been several spin-offs, among them *Curse of the Spawn, Angela, Sam & Twitch*, a special featuring Spawn alongside **Batman**, and a **manga** titled *Shadows of Spawn*. The character's main narrative, however, is still found in the *Spawn* comic book, whose issues trace the myriad transformations that the character has undergone and continues to undergo.

*Denis Yarow*

**SPEEDING BULLETS.** A 52-page graphic novel written by J. M. DeMatteis and illustrated by Eduardo Barreto that was published in 1993 by **DC Comics** as part of its prestige *Elseworlds* line, *Speeding Bullets* won the Comic Buyer's Guide Fan Award for "Favorite Original Graphic Novel or Album of 1993." The premise of the story is based upon an amalgamation of the **Superman** and **Batman** myths: What would happen if the Kryptonian rocket ship that carried baby Kal-El to Earth had been discovered not by Jonathan and Martha Kent of Smallville, Kansas, but rather by Dr. and Mrs. Thomas Wayne of Gotham City?

Superman and Batman have had a long history of joining forces ever since the pair first discovered each other's secret identities and teamed-up in *Superman* #76 (May–June 1952). Beginning in 1954 with *World's Finest Comics* #71, the heroes regularly worked together in that title until its cancellation in 1986. The **Man of Steel** and the Caped Crusader were also seen together in a number of "Imaginary Stories" published by DC Comics over the years. As with the *Elseworlds* tales, the "Imaginary Stories" were not restricted by DC Comics canon. There are several notable Imaginary Stories from both the **Silver Age** and Bronze Age of comics history that combined Superman and Batman's supporting casts, villains, settings, and plotlines. *World's Finest* #136 (September 1963) contained a story titled "The Batman Nobody Remembered" which showcased a parallel universe where Superman is secretly Bruce Wayne and Batman never existed. *World's Finest* #167 (June 1967) presented "The New Superman-Batman Team!" in which baby Kal-El grows up powerless after his exposure to a gold Kryptonite meteor. Instead, Lex Luthor uses science to gain superpowers so he can become Superman. Batman is later revealed to be Clark's wealthy uncle Kendall, who is unaware of his Kryptonian heritage. A third interesting story is titled "Superman and Batman—Brothers!" and it appeared in *World's Finest* #172 (December 1967). In that tale, Bruce Wayne is adopted by the Kents after his parents are murdered. The kindly farm couple takes the sullen boy into their home so that their son Clark can have a brother. Together the boys fight crime in Smallville. By the end of this imaginary adventure, Batman joins the Legion of Super-Heroes in the 30th century, while Superman continues his never-ending battle against evil in the 20th century. In *Superman* #353 (November 1980) DC Comics began a short-lived backup series featuring the exploits of "Bruce (Superman) Wayne." In this alternative reality, baby Kal-El is discovered by James Gordon, who gives him to the Waynes. Bruce Wayne grows up to become Superman and later marries Barbara Gordon (Batwoman). One of the most unique amalgamations of the characters debuted in *World's Finest* #142 (June 1964); the composite Superman was a grotesque shapeshifting villain with green skin who formed a costume that was half Superman's and half Batman's. This rogue returned several times but was always soon defeated by the heroes.

*Speeding Bullets* continues the tradition of recreating the Superman legend by infusing it with elements from Batman's history. The graphic novel begins with the destruction of Krypton and the arrival of Kal-El's rocket on Earth. Instead of the Kents arriving at the crash site in their old pickup truck, the alien child is discovered by the Waynes who are being chauffeured by their butler Alfred. They name the boy Bruce and raise him to be cultured, respectful, and intelligent. As in DC Comics' established history, tragedy strikes years later as the Wayne family emerges from a theater when they encounter a hoodlum named Joe Chill. The thief brutally murders the elder Waynes during a robbery attempt. As young Bruce Wayne tearfully stares at his parents' killer, heat beams suddenly blast from his eyes and incinerate the murderer. The trauma of that night's events causes him to forget his unearthly abilities until years later when Alfred is threatened by a burglar. Bruce saves his faithful butler and begins to fully remember the facts surrounding his parents deaths. He soon discovers Thomas Wayne's journals relating how they found their son in the rocket ship. Again, as in the long-established DC canon, Bruce Wayne becomes the crimefighter Batman, although this Dark Knight is super-strong and can fly.

Other elements of the Superman and Batman histories are incorporated into *Speeding Bullets* as Bruce Wayne purchases the *Gotham Gazette* newspaper and hires editor Perry White and journalist Lois Lane. To protect his secret identity from Lois he pretends to be a shy, stuttering, klutz. Like the story's hero, the villain is a combination of Superman and Batman adversaries. Lex Luthor is presented as a ruthless billionaire, as had been established by **John Byrne**'s continuity revamp of the character during the 1980s. However, this Luthor harbors a dark secret. An earlier accident in a chemical plant had transformed him into the Joker. He also employs a lethal umbrella in the manner of the Penguin, another traditional Batman nemesis. Batman defeats the Joker in a violent encounter. Eventually, Lois convinces Batman that he could be an even greater hero if he abandoned Batman's darkness and instead became a symbol of hope. The story concludes with Bruce Wayne adopting a new costumed identity—Superman.

*Speeding Bullets* was one of several *Elseworlds* graphic novels that either combined the Superman and Batman legends in unique ways or placed the Man of Steel in new settings, such as medieval England, Soviet Russia, or Hollywood in the 1920s. *Elseworlds* stories provided interesting new perspectives on popular heroes and *Speeding Bullets* showcases the elements that have allowed both Superman and Batman to become enduring comic book icons.

*Charles Coletta*

**SPIDER-MAN.** Created in 1962 by illustrator/plotter **Steve Ditko** and writer **Stan Lee** with input from **Jack Kirby**, Spider-Man is arguably the most popular comic book **superhero** and certainly the most popular character of **Marvel Comics**. First appearing in the final issue of the **science fiction** and **fantasy** anthology comic book series, *Amazing Fantasy* #15, Spider-Man has appeared in several eponymous (and non-eponymous) comic book titles over 45 years, most centrally in *The Amazing Spider-Man*—first published in March 1963 and in continuous publication since. In addition to the issues produced by the initial creators, a particularly successful run of this title began in 1988, when artist **Todd McFarlane** joined writer David Michelinie beginning with issue #298. McFarlane also helped create the wildly popular villain Venom, an alien symbiote that can take over the bodies of humans, including, at one point, Spider-Man himself. In 2000, Marvel introduced *Ultimate Spider-Man*, written by **Brian Michael Bendis** and illustrated by Mark Bagley, to reboot the Spider-Man story for a newer audience. Spider-Man has appeared in several other media, such as animated and live-action television programs, toys, electronic games and live-action blockbuster films. Indeed, the films, *Spider-Man* (2002), *Spider-Man 2* (2004), *Spider-Man 3* (2007), and *Spider-Man 4* (due in 2011), directed by Sam Raimi and starring Tobey Maguire and Kirsten Dunst, constitute one of the most commercially successful franchises in movie history.

Peter Parker is an orphan being raised by his loving Uncle Ben and Aunt May. Upon being bitten by an irradiated spider at a science demonstration, the unpopular high school student finds himself acquiring spider-like powers: the proportionate strength, speed, and agility of a spider, the ability to stick to nearly any surface, and an uncanny "spider-sense" that senses impending danger. The bright science student invents a "web fluid" that mimics the strength and stickiness of spider webbing, as well as wrist-mounted web-shooters. Designing the now-iconic blue and red costume with superimposed web patterns, and a mask with large white eyepieces, Peter is ready to face the world as Spider-Man. Rather than using his powers for the greater good, Spider-Man at first appears on television variety shows to earn money. After one such appearance at a studio, Spider-Man fails to stop an escaping burglar, who kills Peter's beloved Uncle Ben later that day. Realizing that his self-interested inaction resulted in the death of his uncle, Peter realizes that "with great power there must also come— great responsibility!"

Spider-Man's debut story repeated many of the themes common in *Amazing Fantasy* and other comic books of the early 1960s, most notably the moralizing twist-ending and the anxiety over nuclear technology. Whereas in other stories the person who made the mistake would be held accountable for it, in this story the martyrdom of Uncle Ben establishes the moral. Moreover, the changes brought about by the irradiated spider and Peter's realization of responsibility can also be seen to stand in for puberty and the ways in which a teenager transitions to adulthood. Indeed, the interaction between Spider-Man using his powers responsibly and Peter Parker attempting to adapt to his often rapidly changing personal circumstances—and the ways in which one aspect of his life influences or interferes with the other—has come to characterize the essence of Spider-Man comics. For instance, a blood transfusion from Peter to Aunt May results in her becoming ill from radiation. The serum necessary for the cure is hijacked by the nefarious Doctor Octopus, and it is up to Spider-Man to find it. In one of the most iconic sequences of Ditko's art, a trapped Spider-Man frees himself from under tremendously heavy wreckage to reach the serum and save his aunt—all of this just before Peter is set to begin college.

As if the death of Uncle Ben was not enough, Spider-Man is often involved in the deaths of many others close to Peter Parker, and many of Spider-Man's most trenchant villains are linked to his private identity. Retired police captain George Stacy is killed when he saves the life of a child standing under falling debris from Spider-Man's battle against Doctor Octopus. Stacy's daughter, Gwen, Peter's girlfriend, is later killed during Spider-Man's battle with the Green Goblin. Meanwhile, the Goblin is actually Norman Osborn, the father of Peter's best friend, Harry. Although Norman Osborn had already been a manipulative tycoon, a chemical accident turns him into a super-powered villain and contributes to his mental degeneration. Osborn never tires of torturing Peter/Spider-Man, for instance kidnapping his and wife Mary Jane Watson's baby, presumably murdering her.

The Amazing Spider-Man issue #19, published in December 1964. Marvel Comics Group/Photofest

Being situated in contemporary contexts, Spider-Man comics have always dealt with social issues. Spider-Man comics in the 1960s and 1970s depict college protests and city politics, in which Peter is loath to get involved. A story arc in 1971 features Harry Osborn's addiction to drugs, whereas a 1982 single-issue questions the prevalence of guns in America. In 1974, Spider-Man teams up with **The Punisher** to fight the Tarantula, an operative of a repressive government in Latin America. While beating on the villain, Spidey delivers a speech in which he effectively aligns himself with revolutionaries fighting tyranny. The most sustained examination of Spider-Man's role in social realities comes during writer **J. Michael Straczynski**'s tenure in the 2000s. Separated from his wife, Peter returns to his high school to realize that the neighborhood has changed for the worse. He becomes a teacher and attempts to counsel students who might otherwise get into trouble. Spider-Man recognizes that he has never paid attention to the problems of street youth and the homeless, and a reformed thug questions why he only deals with things after they go wrong rather than trying to prevent them from going wrong.

Peter Parker's private life also becomes more complex as Aunt May learns of his secret identity and he restarts his relationship with Mary Jane, while joining the New **Avengers**. In the ***Civil War*** storyline (2006), Spider-Man unmasks to the world as Peter Parker in support of superhero registration, which he later realizes is a mistake. As a result, May is shot by a sniper sent by a villain and, in a coma, is on the verge of dying. Peter and Mary Jane make a deal with the devil (Mephisto) to keep May alive. The resultant resetting of the Spider-Man storyline means that Peter and Mary Jane had never married in the first place and Harry Osborn, long dead, somehow comes back to life, while Spider-Man's unmasking has been erased from collective memory. Peter is once again a bachelor, with a doting aunt, far removed from introspection about his role in society—other than knocking heads together in a superficial fulfillment of the dictum that great power entails great responsibility.

*Noaman G. Ali*

**SPIEGELMAN, ART** (1948–). An artist and writer whose work has done much to bring critical respect to comics and graphic novels, Spiegelman was born in Stockholm, Sweden. He emigrated with his parents, Vladek and Anya (Zylberberg) Spiegelman, to Norristown, Pennsylvania before settling in the Rego Park neighborhood of Queens, New York. Geographical transience and the importance of place in establishing one's identity have remained consistent themes in his work, particularly ***Maus: A Survivor's Tale*** (1986, 1991) and *In the Shadow of No Towers* (2004). He began drawing comics at an early age, publishing his first drawing at age 13 before becoming a student at Manhattan's High School of Art and Design. While doing freelance work for a small newspaper in Queens, he met Woody Gelman, art director of the Topps Chewing Gum Company, who would become a life-long mentor and friend. After graduation from the School of Art and Design, he attended Harpur College (now SUNY-Binghamton), where he worked as a cartoonist for the college newspaper and edited a humor magazine. In the summer of 1966, he became a creative consultant for Topps and began publishing his own **underground comics** work in such venues as the *East Village Other*.

Art Spiegelman with wife and collaborator Françoise Mouly (2000). Photofest

Tensions between independent artistry and the demands of commercial fame characterized Spiegelman's professional life, even as he drew upon such precedents as **Harvey Kurtzman**'s *MAD* magazine and **Robert Crumb**. A hospitalization for mental illness and his mother's suicide ended Spiegelman's time at Harpur in 1968. After a few years spent cartooning for men's magazines, he moved to San Francisco, where he published in *Gothic Blimp Works*, *Funny Animals*, and *Young Lust*, and co-edited *Short Order Comix* and *Whole Grains*. In 1975, he moved back to New York City, where he began co-editing *Arcade* magazine, married Françoise Mouly, and published a collection of his experimental comics in *Breakdowns* (1977; republished 2008). He and Mouly began the groundbreaking magazine *RAW*, which assembled a variety of graphic projects. At the same time, however, Spiegelman continued to work for Topps and began teaching at New York's School of Visual Arts. *RAW* serialized *Maus*, an exploration of his parents' Holocaust experiences and his own life as a second-generation survivor, for several issues before its two volumes, *My Father Bleeds History* and *And Here My Troubles Began*, were published. He ended his career with Topps in 1989, as the second volume of *Maus* was underway.

The publication of *Maus* marked both Spiegelman's emergence as a critically recognized artist and a widespread acceptance of graphic novels as serious literature. Particularly after receiving a special Pulitzer Prize in 1992 for the two volumes, he found himself at the center of a maelstrom of media attention and scholarly analysis. The book's success helped him to promote comics' visibility, a long-term goal, and garnered him significant acclaim. His black-on-black portrait of the missing Twin Towers for the *New Yorker*'s 9/11 cover was included in the American Society of Magazine Editors' 2005 list of "Top 40 Magazine Covers;" the image also appeared on the cover of *In the Shadow of No Towers*, his autobiographical study of both the devastation of New York City and its history in comics. His public commentaries on world events continue to generate controversy and esteem.

**Selected Bibliography:** Spiegelman, Art. *Breakdowns: Portrait of the Artist as a Young %@&\*!* New York: Pantheon Books, 2008; Witek, Joseph, ed. *Art Spiegelman: Conversations.* Jackson: University Press of Mississippi, 2007.

*Jennifer D. Ryan*

**SPIRIT, THE.** A comic book feature regularly produced by **Will Eisner** and his studio between 1940 and 1952, *The Spirit* was the lead feature in a comic book supplement licensed to newspapers by the Des Moines *Register and Tribune* syndicate. During its best periods, before and for several years after the artist's military service in World War II, Eisner was primarily responsible for the feature, writing and drawing, and closely collaborating with assistants to create the book. The eponymous hero of the series is a detective hero, Denny Colt, who is declared dead after a gas attack by criminal mastermind the Cobra. Colt is buried at Wildwood Cemetery, which subsequently becomes the Spirit's headquarters.

*The Spirit* section, usually titled The Comic Book Supplement, was created for newspaper editors worried about the competition from the new medium of the comic book, particularly after the success of **Superman**. Eisner never liked **superheroes**; when he got the chance to do his own comic book, he gave the Spirit a mask and gloves, but no secret identity (Denny Colt was dead) and, feeling that he had an adult, literate audience, not the children and lower literacy readers of comic books, he created mature and emotionally resonant stories. (The Spirit section included backup features, most notably those featuring the female detective Lady Luck, created by Eisner and drawn by Klaus Nordling, which were rather ordinary action and comedy stories.) Continuing characters included Police Commissioner Dolan, who brought the Spirit in on various cases; Dolan's daughter Ellen, romantically involved with the Spirit; and the detective's sidekick, an African American boy named Ebony White. After World War II, Eisner realized that this stereotyped character was offensive and, after several attempts to alter the character, including various professional roles, he was dropped from the series.

*The Spirit*, issue #1, published in 1974. Warren Publishing/ Photofest

The Spirit included lovingly depicted femmes fatales, notably P'Gelle, a dark-haired international adventuress; Dr. Silken Floss, a medical doctor and humanitarian; and Sand Saref, a blonde criminal mastermind. Villains included the Cobra, and the Octopus, a vicious gang lord who combined with former **Nazis** in violent criminal enterprises in Europe and America. The Spirit was set in Central City, which was clearly a version of New York, with subways, skyscrapers, and identifiable neighborhoods including the Lower East Side. Eisner told urban stories in the Spirit, exploring the world of machine politics and ward heelers, corrupt contractors building schools, and petty criminals captured through police work. The Spirit had no superpowers, and often took the kind of beatings more characteristic of a Philip Marlowe novel than the comics.

Eisner also incorporated **fantasy** and the supernatural in *The Spirit*, from Mr. Carrion and his love, the buzzard Julia; to eerie ghost ships; and even a refugee from Salem, Witch Hazel, featured in Halloween stories. Eisner felt that the circulation of the supplement in newspapers meant he had to do seasonal stories, including a series of Christmas Spirit stories that combined comedy with seasonal sentiment. In addition to villains and beauties, Eisner's recurring characters included the spoiled rich girl, Darling, whose stories were both humorous and reflected on the transience of wealth; Sgt. Grey, a competent, articulate, and professional African American police detective; the silent, baseball-capped P. S. Smith, who embodied anarchy and disruption; and several attempts at replacements for Ebony, including Binky and Bunky.

The stories Eisner created before he was drafted in 1941 were enjoyable and engaging, but when he returned from military service in 1944, he began to experiment with narrative and artistic effects in ways that are generally credited with expanding the aesthetic horizons of the comic art medium. Deeply shadowed narratives, which Eisner called "two bottles of ink" stories, jarring viewpoints and striking angles resonated with the effects of movies like Orson Welles's *Citizen Kane* (1941). Among Eisner's narrative experiments were the story "Ten Minutes" (September 11, 1949), multilayered storytelling that elapsed in the time it took to read it, and, most famous of all, "The Story Gerhard Shnobble" (September 5, 1948), the ironic story of a man who could fly, and dies aloft and unnoticed in the crossfire as the Spirit apprehends some small-time crooks. Eisner also experimented with longer continuities, including a six-part story in which the Spirit goes blind and has his sight restored by Dr. Floss. Eisner's women characters were beautiful, some based on movie stars, such as Skinny Bones, drawn from Lauren Bacall. However, unlike most popular culture beauties, all were professionally accomplished. P'Gell was a business woman and professional, including serving as headmistress of a girl's school. Ellen Dolan was an outspoken and strong female character, as often saving the Spirit or herself as being rescued. She successfully ran for mayor of Central City, over the opposition of the Spirit, in a series of linked stories that can only be described as proto-feminist. Eisner had a variety of talented and accomplished assistants on the Spirit. The polished superhero artist Lou Fine and the fantasy writer who would later become a noted regionalist, Manley Wade Wellman, produced *The Spirit* during Eisner's World War II service, but unfortunately produced mostly unremarkable stories. Political cartoonist, playwright, and children's book author Jules Feiffer began his career in Eisner's studio, producing memorable stories including one featuring his own strip character, Clifford. As *The Spirit* wound down, the excellent **science fiction** comics artist **Wally Wood** created a series in which the Spirit traveled to the Moon. By the last years of the feature, Eisner was really no longer involved. He had turned his attention to **educational comics**, particularly the magazine he had created for the U.S. Army, based on his World War II work, *P\*S, the Preventive Maintenance Monthly*. The economics of the section became more difficult, particularly as the price of newsprint rose, and Eisner ended the series in 1952. The growing attack on comic books in the media probably also helped motivate Eisner's decision. Interest in the Spirit was revived when Feiffer published his book, *The Great Comic Book Heroes*, in 1965, giving a prominent place to Eisner's creation alongside Superman, **Batman**, and **Captain Marvel**. Ironically, nostalgic interest in super-heroes helped restore Eisner's anti-superhero to prominence. In addition to reprints by **Kitchen Sink Press** of the original comics, the character was resurrected in new stories published by Kitchen Sink in the mid-1990s, by such writers as **Alan Moore** and **Neil Gaiman**. In 2007, **DC** picked up the character, first in **Jeph Loeb**'s one-shot *Batman/The Spirit*, then in his own ongoing self-titled series. A 2008 film adaptation, directed by comics writer and artist **Frank Miller**, was not well received.

*Christopher Couch*

**STAGGER LEE.** Writer Derek McCulloch and artist Shepherd Hendrix explore the folk legend surrounding the infamous African American "bad man" known as Stagger Lee in this critically-acclaimed graphic novel published by **Image Comics** in 2006. The comic demystifies the details behind "Stag" Lee Shelton's deadly quarrel with Billy Lyons in a St. Louis saloon on Christmas Eve in 1895 against a turbulent backdrop of racial segregation and political corruption. Hendrix's artistic style evokes a distant past fixed in sepia-tone panels, the old-fashioned typeface of **Western comics**, and deep, shadowy images of violence and racial terror. The graphic novel's primary concern, however, is the evolution of Stagger Lee's image through a century of song from every American era and musical genre. Richly supported by historical and cultural research, *Stagger Lee* intertwines the realities of **race**, nation, and manhood with the portrait of a villain in a Stetson hat who was born out of the blues.

In moments of subversive levity, Stagger Lee speaks to the reader from the gallows, laughs about the way singers and songwriters have portrayed him, and acknowledges the irony of his rebirth as a hippie folk hero, a 1970s pimp, or a gangster thug. Lee Shelton, however, rarely smiles and is often drawn with sober and reflective expression. In more poignant scenes, he offers advice and hard-won wisdom to his own lawyers. This dialogic strategy poses a kind of cultural and ethical challenge to readers as they confront not only the tragedy of Billy Lyons's death, but also other calamities in the context of black folk life from the late 19th and early 20th century. In addition, *Stagger Lee*'s multiple plots fictionalize Shelton's attorney's tragic struggle with morphine addiction, a blues musician who was among the first to tell Stagger Lee's story through song, a woman who struggles to break out of a life of prostitution, and even a glimpse into the title character's childhood.

It is not the aim of McCulloch and Hendrix to exonerate Shelton, but rather to offer a fuller, more complex frame of reference from which to evaluate his actions. The man immortalized as Stagger Lee committed cold-blooded murder, but the graphic novel makes clear that he is also caught up in a network of racial politics that make it difficult to demonize him. Three of the most memorable symbols of the legend—the hat, the gun, and the ghost—are used to epitomize Shelton's existential struggle in the graphic novel. A secondary story line, for instance, depicts the title character as a child in Texas on a fishing trip with a respected elder named Zell Baxley. When Baxley uses an outhouse that is off-limits to blacks, young Lee Shelton watches in horror as the older man is forced by two white officers to pick up his own feces and place it his hat. The scene not only insinuates a motive for Shelton's well-known outrage over his own Stetson, but also provides a deeper view into daily humiliations of racism for black men. In a later scene, Shelton's attorney recounts a West African folktale to his law clerk as a way of generating a more empathetic view of their client. He invites the Yoruba deity, Obatala, into his office as a reminder of how often and how flagrantly due process has been denied to the descendants of Africans in America. In seeking justice for a "bad man" like Lee Shelton then, the story also affirms the rights of humanity in a broader sense. The fact that the title character is ultimately sentenced to 25 years in prison instead of being dragged out of the jail by a lynch mob is, ironically enough, considered a step in the right direction.

It is for this reason, perhaps, that McCulloch and Hendrix push their story beyond the criminal court to the blues guitars and piano juke joints across the country. They leave the reader with a tortured and helpless Lee Shelton who has been systematically erased in his last years, unwritten as the blues songs proliferate and a fictional stranger named Stagger Lee (and Stack o' Lee, Stackalee, or Stagolee) takes his place. Lost, too, in the larger-than-life image of Lee slugging it out with the Devil in Hell is the fact that Shelton actually died of tuberculosis in prison in 1912. The reader is left to determine the extent to which the 12 bars of a Stagger Lee blues song also serve as the psychosocial manifestation of a prison from which Shelton will never escape.

In addition to earning nominations for the **Eisner Award** and Eagle Comics Award, *Stagger Lee* won four Glyph Comics Awards for Best Writer, Story of the Year, Best Male Character, and Best Cover (2007).

*Qiana J. Whitted*

**STAR SPANGLED COMICS** was the second to last of **DC**'s eight main **Golden Age** anthologies to debut. It is notable for its patriotic theme and for shifting focus several times, going through adventure and occult periods before changing its title to Star Spangled War Stories. Coming roughly half a year after the appearance of **Timely**'s successful **Captain America** comics, *Star Spangled* can be seen as an attempt to cash in on the patriotic hero market. Like Timely's new flagship, the first six issues featured its **Jerry Siegel**-created title character both on the cover and in multiple stories. Despite this heavy promotion, plus appearances in *World's Finest Comics* and with the original **Seven Soldiers of Victory**, the Star Spangled Kid and his adult sidekick Stripesy did not take off. They remained in the anthology for most of its run, but issue #7 saw numerous changes. The military-themed characters Captain X and Armstrong of the Army were dropped, while the **superhero** Tarantula remained for just another year. Taking over the cover was the Newsboy Legion, a **Joe Simon** and **Jack Kirby** kid gang who had a superhero-ish protector called the Guardian. Superheroes Robotman (another Siegel creation) and TNT, along with comedy feature Penniless Palmer, rounded out the new lineup. TNT was dropped soon after patriotic superheroine Liberty Belle replaced Tarantula, but after that *Star Spangled's* contents remained stable through late 1946.

In 1947 **Batman**'s sidekick Robin graduated to a solo spot in *Star Spangled* and took the cover as well. Frontier hero Tomahawk, a white Revolutionary War hero friendly with "Indians," was added shortly after, with the nautical adventure strip Captain Compass beginning a year later. Tomahawk replaced Robin on the cover in 1949 and began appearing in *World's Finest Comics*. He then became the only *Star Spangled* feature to gain his own series which lasted until 1972. The Star Spangled Kid was edged out of his own strip by his then-new Otto Binder-created sidekick, Merry, The Girl of 1000 Gimmicks, but her solo feature was short-lived. After a few fillers, *Manhunters Around the World* solidified the adventure-oriented lineup, with Robin the only remaining superhero, although Robotman found a home in **Detective Comics.** The Manhunters feature would itself be edged out by the Ghost Breaker, Dr. Thirteen, who became the series' last cover feature. This occult strip was an attempt to capitalize on the trend towards **horror** stories, but with much tamer fare than many of DC's competitors. The experiment was short-lived, and after July of 1952's issue #130, the title switched to *Star Spangled War Stories* and reset its numbering soon after, becoming the last of DC's Golden Age anthologies to be canceled or retitled due to shifting post-war tastes. All of Star Spangled's early superheroes, as well as Dr. Thirteen, would appear again in the 1970's and 1980's, with Liberty Belle becoming chairwoman of the All-Star Squadron (featuring Robotman, Tarantula and later TNT's sidekick Dan). The Star-Spangled Kid joined the **Justice Society** and formed Infinity, Inc., before his death. Additionally, Jack Kirby brought back the Newsboy Legion and the Guardian in his Fourth World saga. Before all of that, Robotman had even inspired a new hero with the same concept in the **Silver Age** Doom Patrol. So while Star Spangled never produced a hero as high-profile as some other anthologies, its characters and their children and successors continue to influence the DC universe.

*Henry Andrews*

## STERANKO, JAMES (JIM) (1938–). Challenging the **Comics Code** Authority with cinema-style action sequences and sexy, skin-tight outfits on females in his seminal

series *Nick Fury, Agent of S.H.I.E.L.D.,* Pennsylvania-born visionary artist Jim Steranko has worked in many media outlets. He was the concept artist for such films as Francis Ford Coppola's *Dracula* (1992) and Steven Spielberg's *Raiders of the Lost Ark* (1981), for which he designed Indiana Jones's iconic look. His performances as a magician and escape artist provided a living model for **Jack Kirby**'s Mr. Miracle and Michael Chabon's The Escapist (from the Pulitzer Prize–winning novel *The Amazing Adventures of Kavalier & Clay*). While in his teens, Steranko was also one of the top card-magic specialists in America.

Just out of high school, Steranko worked as a sign painter and printer, and eventually became Art Director for a major ad agency. In 1965, he broke into comics, creating Spyman, Magicmaster, and the Gladiator for editor **Joe Simon** at Harvey Comics. Migrating to **Marvel Comics**, Steranko tightened and inked Kirby's layouts for **Strange Tales** 151, and soon took over penciling, writing, and coloring duties for *S.H.I.E.L.D.* During his brief run on the **X-Men**, he redesigned the title logo; some consider his work on **Captain America** #113 the peak of artistic quality. The Steranko thriller "At the Stroke of Midnight," in the first issue of *Tower of Shadows*, won a 1969 Alley Award for Best Feature Story. The same year, he started his own publishing company, Supergraphics, generating the entertainment magazine *Mediascene* (later retitled *Prevue*) and the acclaimed two-volume *History of Comics*. Moving on again, Steranko went on to paint hundreds of book covers, including 30 *The Shadow* pulp reprints for Pyramid Books.

No other artist has had such a revolutionary effect on comics with such a relatively limited body of work. Steranko had the popularity of a rock star during the late 1960s and early 1970s. His combination of extreme cinematic flare with pop-art styling supports the argument that comic books provide readers with an inexpensive way to hold a work of art in their hands every month. Steranko has had his works exhibited around the world, from the Winnipeg Art Gallery to the Louvre in Paris. He was inducted into the Comic Book Hall of Fame in 2006.

**Selected Bibliography:** Steranko, James. *History of Comics.* 2 vols. New York: Crown Publishing, 1972.

*Jeff McLaughlin*

**STEVENS, DAVE** (1955–2008). Dave Stevens was an award-winning illustrator, and is most prominently remembered as the creator of **The Rocketeer**, his association with legendary pin-up model Bettie Page, and his participation in fan culture, particularly the early years of San Diego Comic-Con (now Comic-Con International).

Stevens was born in Lynwood, California, and although he was raised in Portland, Oregon, spent much of his life from high school onward in San Diego, California. Among Stevens's earliest work as an artist was working as an assistant to the illustrator Russ Manning on the newspaper comic strips for *Tarzan* and *Star Wars*. His work in comics fanzines would lead to an association with **Jack Kirby**, who was a fellow San

Diego resident late in his life. Stevens was also employed as a storyboard illustrator for Steven Spielberg's film *Raiders of the Lost Ark* and the video for Michael Jackson's song *Thriller*, directed by John Landis.

Stevens's high-profile work on *The Rocketeer* began in 1982, initially as a backup story, then as a solo title that was compiled into graphic novel collections from Eclipse Comics and **Dark Horse Comics**. *The Rocketeer* gained notoriety primarily for its adaptation into a 1991 film by Joe Johnson, released by Disney. Stevens also borrowed the likeness of Bettie Page for his title character Cliff Secord's girlfriend Betty. Stevens's use of Page's image is frequently cited as a reason for Bettie Page's resurgence in popularity as a sex symbol. Fans of *The Rocketeer* became interested in Page's work, and likewise new fans of Bettie Page discovered Stevens's work through *The Rocketeer*. Stevens became personally associated with Page, and often assisted her with personal business matters, including the licensing of her likeness.

Stevens is associated with a group of artists who revered the older techniques of comic book and strip illustration. Among Stevens's influences are **Frank Frazetta**, Hal Foster, and **Will Eisner**. Much of Stevens's work is set in the 1930s, and Stevens's art nostalgically evokes the aesthetics of the time, including references to the Art Deco style. After working on *The Rocketeer*, both in comic book and film form, Stevens focused more exclusively on illustration work, such as cover art, supported by an enthusiastic fan base.

Later in his life, Stevens fought against leukemia, which in 2008 ultimately took his life. Stevens is fondly remembered by his fellow artists as well as his fans, who keep his artistic legacy alive.

*Robert O'Nale*

**STRACZYNSKI, J. MICHAEL** (1954–). Born in New Jersey, Joseph Michael Straczynski, popularly known as JMS, is a writer and producer perhaps best known as creator, writer and executive producer of the **science fiction** television series *Babylon 5*. In addition to several television programs, Straczynski has written plays, short stories, novels, news articles and films, such as the Clint Eastwood–directed *Changeling* (2008). Straczynski has also written several comic books, beginning in the 1980s, and more prolifically in the late 1990s and 2000s.

In the 1990s, Straczynski wrote comic books based on *Babylon 5* for **DC Comics**, and in 1999, he created and wrote *Rising Stars* (1999–2005), a story about a group of super-powered individuals born in the aftermath of a cosmic event in an American town, for Top Cow/**Image Comics**. *Rising Stars* was soon published under Straczynski's own imprint, Joe's Comics, along with *Midnight Nation* (2000–2), a story about lost and forgotten souls caught in the battle between (presumably) God and the Devil. In the 2000s, Straczynski wrote several **Marvel Comics** titles, most notably *The Amazing Spider-Man* (2001–7), *Supreme Power* (2003–5), a reboot of Squadron Supreme, Marvel's pastiche of the **Justice League of America**, and *Thor* (2007–9). In 2008, Straczynski also resumed writing for DC Comics.

Straczynski's writings often explore broad social, political, and philosophical issues, but through the choices that individuals make due to or despite their social circumstances and backgrounds, and through the responsibility of people of conscience (and power) to help others make the correct choices. In *Rising Stars*, the group of **superheroes** created from a cosmic event realize after tremendous infighting and loss that they have the power and responsibility to change the world for the better. Indeed, the fundamental contradiction of a superhero like Spider-Man is, as a reformed thug says to him, "You stop things as they go wrong, but you don't do anything to keep them from going wrong in the first place." In other words, with great power comes truly great responsibility. However, while the powerful can bring about tremendous change and offer glimpses perfection, the true change has to come from the vast masses working collectively to make a better world. The lives of more normal people put in extraordinary circumstances are what Straczynski focuses on in *Midnight Nation*. A police officer near death finds himself in the realm of those lost and forgotten by society—the homeless, the friendless—and must make a decision between keeping his own soul and becoming a minion of the Devil, or giving his soul to an angel and thus becoming forever transient. While he is guided throughout his difficult journey by the angel, the final choice is his to make. Similarly, in *The Book of Lost Souls* (2005–6, Icon Comics), a character who commits suicide must help the lost and forgotten make correct choices about breaking out of the ruts they find themselves in. Straczynski's overall message is that the social systems we inhabit are not fair, and all people can use help in making choices, but choices are ultimately only an individual's to make.

*Noaman G. Ali*

**STRANGE TALES.** To read the history of this **Marvel** comic book anthology is to read the history of comics from **crime** and **horror** comics of the 1950s to the **Silver Age superhero**, **Cold War espionage** stories, and psychedelic images of the 1960s. Included in the series is the work of many noted comic book artists and writers, as well as the prototypes and first appearances of lasting characters in the Marvel universe. Like other Marvel anthologies, *Tales of Suspense* (which would become the Silver Age **Captain America** series) and *Tales to Astonish* (which would become *The Incredible Hulk*), this series launched individual characters in their own books: *Nick Fury, Agent of S.H.I.E.L.D.* and **Doctor Strange.**

*Strange Tales* was started by Atlas comics (later Marvel comics) in June 1951 and continued with some disruptions until issue #188 on November 1976. The first 34 issues were pre–**Comics Code** and were modeled after the very successful **EC** books, which featured tales of horror and crime. The magazine was subtitled "Strange Tales of Startling Suspense!" Because of growing sentiment against comic books, partly inspired by **Fredric Wertham**'s book, *The Seduction of the Innocent*, the U.S. Senate Investigation on Juvenile Delinquency in 1954 used a *Strange Tales* story, "With Knife in Hand!" issue #28 (May 1954) by Jack Katz, as an example of the depravity they were fighting against. The lead character, a surgeon, is asked to save a mobster's girlfriend, who has been shot. However, he discovers that the woman is his cheating wife whose greed had encouraged him to work for the criminals in the first place. The doctor then commits suicide by stabbing a scalpel into his stomach, leaving his unfaithful spouse to expire on the operating table. As a result of the senate investigation, starting with issue #35, *Strange Tales* prominently displayed the Comics Code seal; the series also had a new subtitle: "Strange Tales of Suspense!"

Starting with issue #67, *Strange Tales* turned to a **science fiction** theme, depicting monsters such as those favored in drive-in movies—the "creature features." Some examples included Grottu, "King of the Insects" (issue #73), Taboo, "The Thing from the Swamp" (issues #75 and #77) and the first appearance of Fin Fang Foom (issue #89)—the last of which became a recurring villain in the **Iron Man** comics. From here until near the end of its run, the series featured scripts by **Stan Lee** and art by **Steve Ditko** and **Jack Kirby** among many other luminaries.

Alongside these monster comics, Lee, Ditko, and Kirby introduced prototypes of characters that would later become **Ant-Man**, Iron Man, and the Human Torch, to name a few. Issue #84 (May 1961) featured a villain with Magneto-like powers two years before Magneto would make his first appearance in **X-Men** #1 (1963). Likewise, Aunt May and Uncle Ben from **Spider-Man** appeared in issue #97 (June 1962), two months before **Amazing Fantasy** #15 (August 1962). These Silver Age characters would come to dominate the pages of *Strange Tales* along with appearances by **The Fantastic Four**, among others.

In July 1963, with issue #110, Ditko introduced Doctor Strange who would become the character most associated with this anthology, along with Nick Fury (formerly of **Sgt. Fury and His Howling Commandos**) in issue #135 (August 1965) by Kirby. From issues #145–#68, *Strange Tales* alternated between Nick Fury and Doctor Strange. Starting with issue #150, the names of these characters shared the masthead, while the title, "Strange Tales," was reduced in size. After issue #168 (May 1968), both Nick Fury and Doctor Strange were featured in their own books.

After May, 1968, *Strange Tales* was put on hold until September 1973 when it was revived at issue #169 with the first appearance of Brother Voodoo, whose run lasted only until issue #173 (April 1974). In issues #178–#81, Jim Starlin revitalized the character of Warlock, whose self-titled book had been canceled, with a new origin in the "Magus Saga." In the 1980s, Marvel briefly revived the *Strange Tales* series with 19 issues from April 1987 to October 1988, featuring Doctor Strange and Cloak and Dagger stories. There was a one-shot Volume 3 in November 1994; a two-issue series that was never completed in 1998; and *Strange Tales: Dark Corners* in May 1998, a one-shot anthology, featuring a variety of writers and artists.

*Wendy Goldberg*

**STRANGERS IN PARADISE** (SiP) is a 90-issue series written and drawn by Terry Moore. It ran from 1993 to 2007 and has been compiled in 6 pocket books and 19 trade paperbacks. The comic book was first self-published by Moore with Antarctic

Press; for eight issues of the third volume, SiP moved to Homage, an **Image Comics** imprint. The remaining issues were self-published by Moore and his wife, Robyn, by their own imprint, Abstract Studio. The birth and success of *Strangers in Paradise* are connected to the self-publishing movement represented by works such as **Bone** and **Cerebus.** In 1996, the series received the **Eisner Award** for Best Serialized Story for *I Dream of You*; in 1997, SiP received the National Cartoonists Society Reuben Award for Best Comic Book, and in 2001 the Gay and Lesbian Alliance Against Defamation (GLAAD) named the series Best Comic Book.

SiP follows a love story among the three protagonists of the series: Katina Choovanoski (aka Katchoo), Francine Peters, and David Qin (aka Yousaka Takahashi). Katchoo is a character with sharp edges. She was sexually abused by her stepfather and ran away from home; once on the streets, she joined a criminal organization and became an agent, an escort, and the lover of the organization's leader, Darcy Parker. In contrast, Francine's personality was defined by a conservative and religious family that expected her to have a conventional life. She is a sweet and contained woman who loves Katchoo but has difficulties defining the nature of her feelings. David is a sensitive and artistic boy who is deeply in love with Katchoo. His past is almost as complicated as Katchoo's; he is Darcy Parker's brother and was part of the criminal organization run by his family. He becomes a Christian and adopts the name David Qin after killing a 15-year-old boy. The role of David in this triangle is complex, since he brings both stability and challenges to the relationship between Francine and Katchoo. The supporting characters are more than mere extras for this love triangle. They develop very distinctive personalities and roles during the development of the series.

This comic book blends together elements of different genres: **romance**, comedy, intrigue, and drama. The romance and intrigue components help to define three distinctive moments in the series. The first one corresponds with the first volume, a three-issue miniseries. Here, Moore introduces and defines the main characters and their relationships. Although these issues present a balanced and self-contained story, Moore provides some clues about the possible future of the series' plot. The tone of the story is light and comical, especially in comparison with the emotional weight of the rest of the series.

The second volume runs for 14 issues and represents a shift in tone and storyline. David and Katchoo's pasts introduce a certain darkness and heaviness into the plot. The past is represented by the character of Darcy Parker, David's sister and leader of a global crime organization. Katchoo has stolen a considerable amount of money from Darcy before disappearing, and Darcy is looking for revenge. In the process, David's blood relationship with Darcy is revealed, and Francine becomes aware of Katchoo's complicated past. This volume also introduces some pivotal supporting characters who help move the story and the protagonists forward. Two examples are Casey and Emma. Casey brings a happy tone and directness to the comic book; on the other hand, Emma, who dies of AIDS, is a character from Katchoo's past who adds softness and fragility to Katchoo's usual toughness.

The third and final volume of the series is the longest of the three, running from issues 17 to 90. Moore intertwines the romantic and noir plots to keep the reader wondering about the future of the love triangle and the influence of the crime syndicate in the characters' lives. For different reasons, David and Katchoo become the main players in the future of the criminal organization; at the same time, Francine falls in love with a doctor and gets married. She seems destined to have the life her mother always dreamed of for her; however, Francine's miscarriage and David's terminal tumor bring the trio together again. Ultimately, David's death pushes Francine and Katchoo to be together. During this lengthy third volume, Moore pauses the main story line to tell three other stories: the beginning of Katchoo and Francine's friendship in high school; David's youth and the context of the crime he committed; and the story of Molly Lane, a crime narrative that combines elements of terror, suspense, and some romance.

*Strangers in Paradise* is often described as a comic book to recommend to female readers and non-comic-book readers. The reasons for this are that SiP features strong and genuine female characters and develops a story line focused on the characters' lives and feelings. The presence of two main female protagonists has also drawn comparisons to the *Locas* subnarrative of **Love and Rockets.** The artwork is presented in black and white with the exception of the five issues published by Homage. Currently, the only pages available in color in the paperback editions are the ones drawn by **Jim Lee** for the beginning of volume three. The length of SiP allows the reader to appreciate the development of Moore's art. From the first issues, the reader sees his past efforts to become a newspaper strip cartoonist. This past reveals itself in the many comical pages where Charles Schulz or Bill Watterson seem to have taken over Moore's pencil. His drawing style is realistic, clean, and highly effective at connecting the reader and the story. The construction of the page is not fixed, varying from a fairly regular six-panel grid to other pages where Moore explores different designs to evoke moods and express intense feelings. A distinctive characteristic of SiP is Moore's artistic use of long portions of text, poetry, songs, and music notations to convey complex emotions and create a complete experience.

**Selected Bibliography:** Moore, Terry. *Strangers in Paradise: Treasury Edition.* New York: Perennials Currents, 2004; Moore, Terry. "Terry Moore Interview." *The Comics Journal* (June 2006): 60–99.

*Lucia Cedeira Serantes*

**STUCK RUBBER BABY.** First published under **DC's** short-lived Paradox imprint, *Stuck Rubber Baby* (1995) presents the story of Toland Polk, a southern white male coming of age in the 1950s and 1960s. Written and illustrated by the **underground** cartoonist Howard Cruse (1944– ), the book offers a multilayered account of **race**, class, and homosexuality in the era of Eisenhower, Kennedy, and Johnson. *Stuck Rubber Baby* was nominated for the American Library Association's Gay and Lesbian Book Award as well as the Lambda Literary Award, and was named Best Graphic Novel by the

U.K. Comic Art Awards. The book received the *Prix de la critique* in France, and the *Luche* award in Germany, and has been translated into several European languages. While *Stuck Rubber Baby* appeared a few years before the graphic novel went mainstream as a form, it remains a noteworthy example of ambitious, historically focused comics storytelling.

Howard Cruse reportedly spent four years creating this stand-alone, 210-page work of graphic historical fiction. Set in the Deep South of the United States during the Civil Rights movement, it combines an intimate portrayal of one man's struggle to come to terms with his place in the world, with a larger perspective on the sociocultural fallout of mid-century protest. While the lens remains resolutely focused on the main character, the story encompasses a full gamut of **Cold War** personality types, from hot-headed folk singers and enraged Klansmen to anxious administrators and fearful parents. As such, *Stuck Rubber Baby* offers a rare example of a comic book that could plausibly be assigned in undergraduate courses on memoir, historical fiction, the 1960s, and 20th-century social movements. While many of the story's plot elements are fictional, the narrative draws heavily on Cruse's experiences growing up on the outskirts of Birmingham, Alabama, as the son of a Baptist preacher and homemaker. The author somehow manages to convey the impact of large-scale cultural upheaval within the delicate framework of a *roman à clef*. Unlike many would-be contenders to the title, *Stuck Rubber Baby* actually is a graphic novel.

Cruse's earliest published cartoons appeared in *The Baptist Student* when he was still in high school. He studied drama at Birmingham-Southern College in the late 1960s and moved to New York City in 1977. By the mid-1970s he had already made a name for himself in cartooning and activist circles for his exuberant graphic stories featuring carefree hippie characters. He found particular success with the characters Barefootz and Wendel, both of whom were amiable young men finding their way in the big city. Headrack, a character in these comics, is arguably the first openly gay character in comics. The underground comics publisher Denis Kitchen helped bring Cruse's artwork to the national stage by featuring his work in such titles as *Snarf, Dope Comix, Commies from Mars*, and *Comix Book* from **Kitchen Sink Press**. In addition, Kitchen published three stand-alone issues of *Barefootz Funnies* in the early 1970s and invited Cruse to edit the groundbreaking anthology series *Gay Comix* at the end of the decade. Some of Cruse's work from this period is still in print, thanks to Olmstead Press and **Fantagraphics**. His most recent project, an illustrated children's book called *The Swimmer with Rope in His Teeth*, produced in collaboration with Jeanne E. Shaffer, was issued by Prometheus Books in 2004. While Cruse has generated dozens of comic book stories over the years, *Stuck Rubber Baby* is by far the most complex project that he has undertaken to date.

When readers first meet Toland Polk he is grieving for his late parents, who were killed by a drunk driver, and puzzling over some advice he received from his late father. Toland comes from a modest background, works in a gas station, and would easily blend into the crowd except for the fact that he tends to ask a lot of questions. He is uneasy about the separation of the races under Jim Crow, and anxious about his own sexual orientation. His inner conflicts mirror those reshaping the wider society, and the likelihood that Toland Polk will eventually shed his political innocence and racial prejudices, and embrace his same-sex desires, is pretty much a given. Yet the hero's journey toward enlightenment is both engrossing and believable. Toland is an every-man type who happens to be gay; over the course of the narrative he inadvertently gets swept up in a tsunami of counter-cultural protest. He is neither a rabble-rousing militant nor a hide-bound traditionalist, and his transformation from small town naïf to open gay artist unfolds gradually. A little gullible perhaps, but at the same time an honest soul, Toland Polk is an appealing stand-in even for readers who were not yet born in the 1960s.

Historical graphic fiction is sometimes rendered in stark, declaratory lines that seem to convey a certain seriousness of purpose. Much of the pleasure of *Stuck Rubber Baby* can be found in Cruse's sensuous linework, which favors sloping curves and fragile shadows over sharp rectangles and brightly lit pages. *Stuck Rubber Baby* is fun to look at quite apart from the appeal of the story. As a work of visual imagination and recreation, it is obviously the product of a lot of thought and hard work. Densely illustrated and crammed with visual information, Cruse's pages are sometimes almost pointillist in their commitment to molecular detail. Like **Robert Crumb**, Cruse here makes extensive use of cross-hatching (a stylistic departure from his trademark stippling technique), takes advantage of the expressive possibilities of black-and-white, and composes whole pages rather than sequences of panels. Unlike Crumb, however, Cruse does not make fun of his characters or his readers. Cruse is not a cynic, or even a skeptic. Rather, he is one of the most hopeful and life-affirming cartoonists to have emerged out of the underground comics movement.

*Kent Worcester*

**SUMMER OF LOVE, THE.** A comics series republished under this title by Drawn & Quarterly in 2002, *The Summer of Love* was originally created by Debbie Drechsler for her five-issue (1996–99) Drawn & Quarterly series *Nowhere*. The feminist undergrounds of the 1970s and 1980s, especially *Wimmen's Comix*, inspired Drechsler, as did Peanuts and *MAD Magazine*. Her largest influences in stylistic terms are **Lynda Barry** and Richard Sala, though her visual style does not overtly resemble either. The correlation to Barry's work is most evident in subject matter. Both creators deal with adolescent pain and young girls' coming to terms with difficult situations with little or no help.

Drechsler's background in commercial art is evident in the visual look of the book. *The Summer of Love* is printed in two ink colors, a forest green and an earth brown. No black is used, even in the lettering. James Vance used a similar duo-tone effect in the **Kitchen Sink Press** series *Owlhoots* (1991). This color scheme gives the art a sort of coloring book effect. It also mutes the darks, using color to reinforce the sense of nuance and uncertainty experienced by the characters. Though the use of art tools (straightedge, triangle, templates, etc.) in the preliminary stages is evident, all aspects of the final printed art appear to be hand rendered. This is significant in that Drechsler began using a precision tool, the computer, with her subsequent commercial artwork.

The appearance of handwork also reinforces the childlike (though not childish) nature of the art, reinforcing the intimacy of the narrative. As is the case in Barry's work, the story is concerned with the emotional state of its protagonist, and told in omniscient first person and past tense. The narrative parts company with Barry's work in its addressing of teenage concerns, where Barry's characters were slightly younger for the majority of her primary work, *Ernie Pook's Comeek*. Drechsler has cited Barry as her primary influence in comics (*Comics Journal* 249). The tone of *The Summer of Love* is also reminiscent of the 1995 film *Welcome to the Dollhouse*, in that both works are unrelenting in their depiction of the traumas of female adolescence.

The title of *The Summer of Love* has two significant references. It refers to a teenage girl's first exposure to the myriad forms of physical love and sexuality. It also refers to its setting in the year 1967. In *The Summer of Love*, ninth-grader Lily is confronted with moving, the need for isolation, her own sexual awakenings, and her sister Pearl's experimentation with lesbianism. This confrontation is presented externally more than internally. While readers are privy to Lily's thoughts, the story is driven more by actions than reactions. Several introspective moments, such as the final two panels of Book Three, are wordless. The reader is left to infer Lily's thoughts in these situations rather than being told those thoughts outright. This increases the level of involvement with Lily, requiring the reader to sort through the character's feelings in the complex situation along with the character.

Era-specific icons permeate the narrative. The boys in the neighborhood have a garage band that plays ersatz psychedelic rock. The eponymous Jefferson Airplane album is new, and a topic of conversation. The girls wear granny dresses, miniskirts, beehive hairdos, and cutoffs. The boys sport short hair, but there are hints of the length changing. These trappings have an air of authenticity, consistent with Drechsler's age. She was 14 in 1967, so it is clear that she is versed through personal experience in the motif of the era, though she has never claimed *The Summer of Love* as autobiography or **memoir**; but her age does speak directly to the authenticity of her depiction of the period.

However, this is not a simple period piece. The period trappings are just that, and no more: the real focus is on Lily's personal experience, not her historical context. While this work can be distinguished from Drechsler's previous graphic novel *Daddy's Girl* by its calmer demeanor and subject matter (*Daddy's Girl* was a story of incest), it maintains the sense of urgency of its predecessor, despite the comparatively tame subject matter. The placidity of the subject matter is deceptive. The reader is taken with Lily on her missteps through the treacherous path of ninth grade and its betrayals, nuanced, and contradictory relationships.

Lily's experiences are not ominous or threatening in the sense of suspense or terror. However, the level of empathy created by this approach is consistent with a neglected aspect of events in the comic book marketplace of the time. Self-published zines burgeoned in the early 1990s. Many of these were by young women, and were published as a facet of the Riot Grrl movement. That movement was pervaded by the dominant themes echoed in *The Summer of Love*: alienation, frustration, betrayal, and cynicism, couched in the trappings of a specific time. Though much more complex than this list of themes might suggest, both the movement and Drechsler's work echo those themes.

Drechsler has subsequently removed herself from the intensity of the work but not from its honesty. In a 2002 interview, Drechsler remarked on both *The Summer of Love* and *Daddy's Girl*, stating, "I find it very hard to reread those stories and that makes me wonder how hard it is for other people to read (and see) and if that was the best way of presenting the material. I guess my sense of propriety drifts around, depending on where I am at any given moment. When I wrote those stories, I was much angrier at life than I am now, and much unhappier, so maybe I had less to lose? Or maybe it felt more necessary to slam people in the face with that stuff. I don't know for sure. (aka Simon)." Drechsler has done very little comics work since *The Summer of Love*, concentrating on her commercial art career.

*See also:* Feminism; Memoir/Slice-of-Life Themes; Underground and Adult Comics

**Selected Bibliography:** A.K.A. Simon. "Reality: the Debbie Drechsler Interview." (2002). Comics Bulletin, http://www.comicsbulletin.com/nuclear/98705880048391. htm; "Debbie Dreschler Interview." *The Comics Journal* (249) (December 2002), http://archives.tcj.com/249/i_drechsler.html; Drechsler, Debbie. *The Summer of Love*. Montreal: D & Q Press, 2002.

*Diana Green*

**SUPERHEROES.** The superhero is the protagonist of the superhero genre, which began with the appearance of **Jerry Siegel** and **Joe Shuster's Superman** in *Action Comics* #1 (cover date June 1938). By 1942 the term *superhero* was in use to describe comic book stories of heroic figures who wore colorful costumes and possessed superpowers. Parodies of the genre, which indicate an acceptance of the genre by both producers and consumers, emerged as early as 1940, with the Red Tornado by Sheldon Mayer, followed by Supersnipe and **Plastic Man** the next year.

The genre's immediate sources come from three adventure-narrative figures: the **science-fiction** superman, beginning with *Frankenstein* (1818); the dual-identity avenger-vigilante, beginning with *Nick of the Woods* (1835); and the pulp ubermensch, beginning with *Tarzan* (1912). The science-fiction superman is typically a tragic figure endowed with superior abilities by science who poses the threat of either tyranny over or evolutionary replacement of the human race. Influential science-fiction superman novels include H. G. Well's *Invisible Man* (1897) and *The War of the Worlds* (1898), and *The Food of the Gods* (1904); J. D. Beresford's *The Hampdenshire Wonder* (1911); and Olaf Stapledon's *Odd John* (1936). Edgar Rice Burroughs created one of the few heroic models of the science fiction superman with John Carter (1912). The most influential of these figures were Hugo Danner, hero of Philip Wylie's *Gladiator*

(1930), and **Doc Savage** (1933). Both Danner and Savage influenced the creation of Superman.

In America, the avenger-vigilante figure is rooted in Robert Montgomery Byrd's *Nick of the Woods*, a classic Indian-hater. The avenger-vigilante urbanized with dime-novel detectives like Nick Carter (1886). Influential dual-identity characters include the British penny-dreadful figure Spring-Heeled Jack (1837) and Baroness Orczy's Scarlet Pimpernel (1903). Frank Packard's Jimmie Dale, the Gray Seal, transferred the dual-identity character to a gritty urban setting and placed him in opposition to both the authorities and the underworld. The two most influential dual-identity avenger-vigilante figures for the superhero genre were Johnston McCulley's Zorro (1919) via Douglas Fairbanks's portrayal in *The Mark of Zorro* (1920), and the pulp vigilante **The Shadow** (1930), written primarily by Walter Gibson, both of which served as direct inspirations for the creation of **Batman**.

The pulp ubermensch refers to the practice of referring to heroes of pulp fiction adventure stories as supermen. The figure is rooted in the adaptation of Friedrich Nietzsche's Übermensch by Jack London in works like *The Sea Wolf* (1904) and *The Iron Heel* (1908), and Edgar Rice Burroughs's use of London's work as an inspiration in the character of Tarzan, who is referred to as a superman in *Tarzan of the Apes* (1912). Tarzan imitators Polaris of the Snows by Charles B. Stilson and Kioga of the Wilderness by William L. Chester are similar supermen raised outside of civilization. Although a villain, Dr. Fu Manchu (1912) fits the pulp-ubermensch mold, as does Blackie DuQuesne, the villain of E. E. "Doc" Smith's Skylark series (1928), as well as its hero Richard Seaton. The term *superman* is used in the *Armageddon 2419* (1928) novelettes by Philip Francis Nowlan to refer to Anthony Rogers, inspiration for the Buck Rogers comic strip and its adaptations, and all Americans living under the rule of the Han invaders. The two most influential of these figures for the superhero are The Shadow and Doc Savage, who are presented as superior to other people physically, mentally, morally, and socially, but serve as defenders of the middle class in opposition to the revolutionary ideological meaning imputed to the Übermensch by Nietzsche.

The superhero genre also has roots in comics strips, primarily through the depiction of strongmen like Popeye (1929) and Alley Oop (1933), who helped to establish comics as a medium in which fantastic feats of incredible strength could be depicted, and enabled the ability of comics to depict the fantastic with equal levels of surface realism as the mimetic. Costumed precursors of the superhero in comics include the short-lived Phantom Magician in Mel Graff's strip *The Adventures of Patsy* (1935) and Dr. Occult (1935), an occult detective by Superman creators Siegel and Shuster, which served as a kind of trial run for elements of their later hero Superman, including a red cape in **More Fun Comics.** The Phantom, a costumed and masked mystery man and adventurer, debuted in his own comic strip in 1936 and laid important groundwork for the superhero because in his adventures can be found nearly all the elements of the superhero genre. Other important influences on the superhero genre include the Jewish **folklore** figure, the golem, and physical culture strongmen like Eugene Sandow and Bernarr Macfadden.

One can identify the three primary conventions of the superhero genre. The most identifiable element of the genre is that the protagonist has superpowers—extraordinary abilities, advanced technology, or highly developed physical and/or mental skills (including mystical abilities). Second, the superhero has a selfless, pro-social mission, which means that his fight against evil must fit in with the existing, professed mores of society and must not be intended to benefit or further himself. Finally, the protagonist has a specific superhero identity, which is embodied in a codename and iconic costume, which typically express the superhero's biography, inner character, powers, or origin— the transformation from ordinary person to superhero. Often superheroes have dual identities, the ordinary one of which is usually a closely guarded secret.

The identity element comprises the codename and the costume, with the secret identity being a customary counterpart to the codename. The identity convention most clearly marks the superhero as different from his predecessors. Superheroic identities externalize either their alter ego's inner character or biography. Superman is a super man who represents the best humanity can hope to achieve; his codename expresses his inner character. The Batman identity was inspired by Bruce Wayne's encounter with a bat while he was seeking a disguise that would strike terror into the hearts of criminals; his codename embodies his biography. The superhero costume iconically represents the superhero identity—Batman wears a bat costume, **Spider-Man** a spider costume, and **Captain America** an American flag costume. The superhero's chevron—the shield or emblem typically worn on the chest—specifically emphasizes the character's code-name and is itself a simplified statement of that identity; Batman's bat, **Green Lantern**'s lantern, and **Captain Marvel**'s lightning bolt each indicates the source of the character's mission, powers, or identity.

These three elements—mission, powers, and identity—establish the core of the genre. Yet specific superheroes can exist who do not fully demonstrate these three elements, and heroes from other genres may exist who display all three elements to some degree but should not be regarded as superheroes. The similarities between specific instances of a genre are semantic, abstract, and thematic, and come from the constellation of conventions that are typically present in a genre offering. If a character basically fits the mission-powers-identity definition, even with significant qualifications, and cannot be easily placed into another genre because of the preponderance of superhero-genre conventions, the character is a superhero.

The **Hulk** can be said to be a superhero without a mission. During the Hulk's periods of low intelligence, his adventures do not arise from his attempts to fight crime or to improve the world. Instead he wanders the planet primarily seeking solitude while being drawn, or stumbling, into the plans of supervillains. He acts effectively as a superhero but does not have the mission or motivation to do so. He clearly has super-powers, and his superhero identity is composed of his codename—the Hulk—and his body, which effectively acts as a costume, especially given the Hulk's iconic green and purple color scheme. His tales, though, are suffused with secondary conventions of the superhero genre: supervillains—the Leader, the Abomination; superhero physics—the transformative power of gamma rays; the limited authorities—General Thunderbolt Ross; a pal—Rick Jones; superteams—the **Avengers** and the Defenders; and so forth. These conventions keep the Hulk within the superhero genre.

Batman was originally designed as a superhero without superpowers. His mission of vengeance against criminals is clear, and his identity—represented by his codename and iconic costume—marks him as a superhero. While he has no distinctly "super" powers, his physical strength and mental abilities allow him to fight crime alongside his more powerful brethren. Batman operates in a world brimming with conventions of the superhero genre: supervillains—the Joker, the Penguin; the helpful authority figure—Police Commissioner Gordon; the sidekick—Robin; superteams—the **Justice League** and the Outsiders; and so forth.

Arnold "Arn" Munro, Roy Thomas's Superman figure in the World War II era *Young All Stars*, has no superhero identity—no costume and no codename. He typically appears in street clothing, most often white pants and a black t-shirt, only once wearing (then quickly abandoning) a costume in the *Young All-Stars* series. While he has the nickname, "Iron," based on the pronunciation of his first name, he does not use this name as an alternative identity. He has a clear mission—protecting America from **Nazi** supervillains during World War II and serving the government as an agent. He possesses superstrength and invulnerability. He fights costumed, superpowered supervillains alongside other superheroes as part of the superteams the Young All-Stars and the Freedom Fighters, and has a solid place in the **DC** universe as the husband of the **Phantom Lady.**

These three examples demonstrate how a character who lacks one of the primary conventions of the superhero genre can still be considered a superhero because of the use of a number of other supporting conventions. Characters from other genres who do good and have enhanced abilities like Buffy the Vampire Slayer (**horror**), The Shadow (pulp vigilante), Beowulf (epic), or Luke Skywalker (**science fiction**) might best be considered heroes who are super, or super heroes, rather than the protagonists of the superhero genre. Generic distinction is a useful concept for understanding and defining the boundaries of the superhero genre. It makes the superhero genre's origins, evolution, and social function easier to grasp, delineate, and trace.

The superhero genre proper began with the appearance of Superman in the first issue *Action Comics*, which already contains the major conventions of the superhero genre. This story fully employs the primary conventions of mission, powers, and identity. The very first page presents the origin, the costume, the dual identity, and the urban setting. Other conventions, such as the secret identity, the superhero code, the supporting cast, the love interest, the limited authorities, and the super/mundane split emerge in the story itself.

In the next year, a flood of superheroes appeared, firmly establishing the genre. Between *Action Comics* #1 and ***Detective Comics*** #27 (cover date May 1939) only the Crimson Avenger, the Arrow, and the **Sandman** appeared to be following the superhero model, and they were more indebted to their pulp and radio predecessors.

Batman and Wonder Man, both direct responses to Superman, appeared in May of 1939, as did the Sub-Mariner. In the first three years, from 1938 to 1941, the primary superhero archetypes were created. Superman and Batman provide the two primary superhero paradigms: the superpowered superhero and the non-super superhero. **Wonder Woman** provides the next central paradigm, the superheroine, as well as the mythical or mythology-based hero. **The Flash** is the preeminent example of the single-powered hero. Parody comes with the Red Tornado. Captain America is the patriotic superhero par excellence. Batman's partner Robin stands as the first sidekick and can also be considered the first kid superhero. The **Golden Age** Sub-Mariner's status as the first anti-hero superhero places him within the troubled-hero category, thereby rounding out the superhero archetypes.

Fans use the concept of **ages of comics** to periodize the history of superhero comics. While not a scholarly term, the concept of ages has become so embedded in the discussion and analysis of the superhero genre that it is germane to any discussion of the genre. In addition, the established ages roughly parallel the evolution of genre put forward by film scholars Christian Metz and Thomas Schatz. The names and dates for the ages have achieved a rough consensus in the fan and scholarly communities.

The Golden Age began with the appearance of Superman in *Action Comics* #1. During the Golden Age, the superhero genre narratively animated and ritualistically resolved social conflicts of the period in ways that expressed the prevailing social ideology of the times. During this period the various conventions of superhero stories were isolated from the adventure literature out of which the superhero emerged and formalized so as to make the superhero genre distinct from other related genres. At this stage the narratives worked to transmit and reinforce the genre's social message—particularly New Deal-style social reform and the patriotism of World War II—as directly as possible. The conventions were not seen as problematic or needing to be questioned. The stories tended to be straightforward confrontations between good and evil in which the superhero, society, and the audience were all presumed to be on the same side and working for the same goals.

The primary marker of the **Silver Age** is the revival of superheroes, who had largely fallen out of favor with the public in the early 1950s. There is a firm consensus that the Silver Age began with the debut of the new Flash in *Showcase* #4 (cover date October 1956). Although some superheroes—such as **Marvel**'s Captain America, the Human Torch, and the Sub-Mariner—were revived prior to the Flash, these revivals failed, unlike the revivals of these three characters a decade later. The success of the Flash revival led to similar revivals of **Green Lantern**, the Atom, Hawkman, and the **Justice Society** (as the **Justice League**). The success of the Justice League led directly to the creation of the **Fantastic Four**, which prompted the other major innovations of the Silver Age: continuity and melodrama.

In the Silver Age, creators elaborated on all the conventions developed in the Golden Age. The secret identity was broadened to include characters who maintain both their superidentities and their alter egos in a public way (Fantastic Four, the Hulk).

Superheroes dated and married (Spider-Man and his various girlfriends, the Flash and Iris Allen, and Mr. Fantastic and the Invisible Girl). **Stan Lee's** "hero-with-a-problem" melodrama added depth to the characterization of the alter egos. Continuity expanded with DC's multiple Earths, the Marvel universe, crossovers, and extended storylines. The supervillain was complicated by turning some noble ones into superheroes (Sub-Mariner, Hawkeye, Quicksilver, Scarlet Witch). While the tales still featured contests between good and evil, these concepts are complicated slightly with virtuous villains and reluctant, selfish, or bickering heroes.

The Silver Age began with a whole-hearted acceptance of the status quo and constructed authority and ended with superheroes doubting the status quo and resisting authority. The melodrama that marked the beginning of the age at Marvel evolved into a confrontation of social issues, such as drug use and campus unrest in series like Spider-Man and the **Teen Titans**. The **Dennis O'Neil** and **Neal Adams** stories of Green Lantern and **Green Arrow** traveling the country and discovering social problems like over population, racism, pollution, and corporate greed exemplify these shifts (*Green Lantern* #76–89, April 1970–April/May 1972).

While there is no clear break between the end of the Silver Age and the start of the Bronze Age, several changes in superhero comics between 1968 and 1973 are generally recognized as marking a shift in the tone and nexus of concerns of the genre, with 1970 being the most commonly designated year for the changeover of ages. Some extra-textual events of 1970 that mark the end of the Silver Age include **Jack Kirby's** shift from Marvel to DC; the purge of veteran writers at DC that was nearly complete in that year; the fading of MLJ and **Charlton** as superhero publishers; the publication of *The Comic Book Price Guide* by Robert Overstreet, which provided a nearly complete index of comics published since 1933 and standards for grading and pricing comics, making public knowledge that had been the private preserve of specialists and institutionalizing the monetary value of old comic books; and the publication of *All in Color for a Dime*, edited by Don Thompson and Dick Lupoff, and **Jim Steranko's** *The Steranko History of Comics*, both of which looked back with nostalgic fondness on the Golden Age of superheroes.

Within the comics themselves the deaths of Gwen Stacey and the Green Goblin (*Amazing Spider-Man* #122–123, July–August 1973); Captain America's disillusionment at discovering the President of the United States to be the head of the Secret Empire, a fictionalized depiction of Watergate, and his subsequent adoption of the Nomad identity (#175–76, July–August 1974); the end of the Teen Titans' experiment in social activism, and the series return to formula (*Teen Titans* #31–32, January–April 1971). These issues can be seen as the end of relevance for these characters.

The Bronze Age featured few innovations in the superhero genre, with the primary movement being to refine the advances of the Silver Age. Few new characters were created at either Marvel or DC during the 1970s—Nova and Firestorm seem to be new versions of Peter Parker, but neither was groundbreaking, as the troubled teen superhero soap-operatic saga had already been around for over a decade. Peter Parker himself shifted from being a nerdy loser high school student to a handsome, successful, Pulitzer Prize–winning college graduate and professional photo-journalist. African Americans as both superheroes and supporting characters became more common. The Defenders, proclaimed as a "non-team," began in 1971, a twist on the pro-social vision of Julius Schwarz's Silver Age Justice League. Superman's powers were reduced with the creation of the Qward sand-Superman, and Kryptonite was denuded and transformed into K-iron. Other refinements included the cosmic stories (Kirby's Fourth World, Starlin's Warlock), and the growth of team books (the *X-Men*, the *Avengers*, the *JLA*, and the *Legion of Super-Heroes* all expanded).

The Iron Age, which began about 1980, featured a turning inward of the genre, driven by two industry trends. First, the creative staffs of the companies changed from primarily professional writers and artists who viewed their work as merely one way to make a living, to fans who specifically wanted to work in the comics industry, a trend begun in the 1960s. Second, as the traditional system of newsstand distribution and sales waned in the late 1970s, comic book publishers increasingly turned to direct distribution and comic-book specialty shops because of the higher profit margin the new system offered. The primary customers of these stores were self-identified comic-book (especially superhero) fans, and these fans became the target market for the publishers. With the producers and consumers largely coming from the same small segment of the population and sharing the same cultural and literary interests, the superhero genre turned in on itself away from the larger social concerns that had driven the genre in the Golden Age and the interest in relevance in the late Silver Age.

A primary thrust of the Iron Age was the reinvigoration of old, tired concepts. Self-conscious revivals sprouted everywhere: the Fantastic Four and Superman by **John Byrne**; *Daredevil* and Batman by **Frank Miller**; *Thor* by **Walter Simonson**; **Captain Marvel** in *Miracleman* and the **Charlton** heroes in *Watchmen*, both by **Alan Moore**; the new Teen Titans by **Marv Wolfman** and **George Pérez**. Perhaps the greatest example of reinvigoration in the Iron Age is the *Crisis on Infinite Earths*, which combined DC's multiple Earths into a single planet with a single unified history and necessitated a rewriting of the history of the DC multiverse.

In the Iron Age, the superhero's selflessness became problematic. Heroes either moved "up" into governance or "down" out of superhero status. In *Watchmen*, Miller's *Batman: The Dark Knight Returns*, *Miracleman*, and *Squadron Supreme*, superheroes who had formerly protected society from the machinations of outside evil move into formal participation in the governance of society. On the "down" side, **Iron Man** sank into alcoholism (issues #160–82). The Justice League disbanded (issues #258–61); and in *The Sensational She-Hulk* under John Byrne, She-Hulk drifted completely away from serious superhero status into flippant postmodernism.

The Iron Age of superhero comics was marked by the deaths of numerous superheroes, perhaps most notably Marvel's Captain Marvel, whose reconfiguration in the 1970s seems a hallmark of the impetus of the Bronze Age. Batman and Rorschach, the ostensible heroes of the two central texts of the Iron Age—*The Dark Knight Returns* and *Watchmen*, both die at the end of their series, Batman figuratively and Rorschach literally. Superman himself, who had been completely revamped in 1986, was killed in 1992. These deaths can be seen as emblematic of the exhaustion of the genre. Perhaps most emblematic of the death of the superhero is the Iron Age's self-proclaimed greatest success, **Spawn**, the corpse as superhero.

There is no consensus on the name of the current age of superhero comics or when it started. It is sometimes referred to as the Renaissance Age, but the Modern Age is the most common term, clearly serving as a placeholder until a consensus emerges. It has no firm start date because individual creators responded to the darkness of the Iron Age at different times and in different ways. An early non-comics indication of this shift was television's *Batman: The Animated Series*, begun in 1992, and the subsequent other Batman, Superman, and Justice League cartoons helmed by Paul Dini and Bruce Timm. In comics, **Kurt Busiek**'s and **Alex Ross's** *Marvels* (1994), Busiek's *Astro City* series (1995), James Robinson's *The Golden Age* (1993) and *Star Man* (1994–2001), and Ross's **Kingdom Come** (1996) all worked to rebuild the conventions of the genre that had broken down or become burdensome during the Iron Age. At Marvel, the Renaissance Age fully came in with Joe Quesada's assumption of the editor-in-chief position in 2000. Marvel came later to the Renaissance Age because during the Iron Age it was much more taken up with manipulating the speculator market through multiple, embossed, or enhanced covers, and empty formulaic stories with cluttered artwork. One sign of the shift into the Renaissance Age at Marvel is the influx of artists and writers from outside the superhero mainstream, such as **Peter Bagge** (*The Megalomaniacal Spider-Man*), **Brian Azzarello** and Richard Corben (*Banner and Cage*), and James Sturm (*Unstable Molecules*).

The other primary convention of the Modern Age is the event comic. An event comic is a series that tells a major story in a superhero universe, crosses over from its primary series into the majority of a company's titles, and pulls in the majority of its characters. Event comics go back to the annual summer crossovers of the Justice League with the Justice Society and other superteams (1963–85). Marvel's *Secret Wars* (1984–85) initiated the tradition of the company-wide crossover, which DC also used in the *Crisis on Infinite Earths* (1985). Several other events followed in the 1980s and 1990s, but gradually they became much more orchestrated campaigns, with each year's event series leading to the next year's series. At DC this integration of connected annual events has been strongest since **Identity Crisis** (2004), which led directly into the series of crisis events: *Countdown to Infinite Crisis* (2005), *Infinite Crisis* (2005–6), *52* (2006–7), *Countdown to Final Crisis* (2007–8) and *Final Crisis* (2008). At Marvel, the integration of event comics became most evident with **Civil War** (2006–7) and the subsequent event series *Secret Invasion* (2008) and *Dark Reign* (2008–9), though *Civil War* was itself tied to the previous event series *Secret War* (2004–5), *Avengers Disassembled* (2004–5), *House of M* (2005), and *Decimation* (2005). The main difference between Modern Age event comics and those of the past is the way the effects of the events series linger in the storytelling at both companies. Previously with series such as *Final Night* (1996) or *Infinity Gauntlet* (1991), the event would absorb the respective universe but pass and leave few long-term traces. The current series of event comics lead into each other and continue to have effects within the continuities of both companies' universes.

**Selected Bibliography:** Brown, Jeffrey A. *Black Superheroes, Milestone Comics, and Their Fans.* Jackson: University Press of Mississippi, 2001; Coogan, Peter. *Superhero: The Secret Origin of a Genre.* Austin: Monkey Brain Books, 2006; Kaveney, Roz. *Superheroes! Capes and Crusaders in Comics and Films.* New York: I. B. Tauris, 2008; Klock, Geoff. *How to Read Superhero Comics and Why.* New York: Continuum, 2002; Schatz, Thomas. *Hollywood Genres.* Philadelphia: Temple University Press, 1981; Stuller, Jennifer K. *Ink-stained Amazons and Cinematic Warriors: Superwomen in Modern Mythology.* New York: I. B. Tauris, 2010; Wright, Bradford. *Comic Book Nation.* Baltimore: Johns Hopkins Press, 2001.

*Peter Coogan*

**SUPERMAN.** Superman is the name of a fictional comic book character created in 1934 by writer **Jerry Siegel** and artist **Joe Shuster**, first published by the company that would become **DC Comics** in *Action Comics* #1, 1938. Superman was the first published superhero; sporting blue tights, a red cape, and an "S" emblematically placed on his chest, Superman routinely fights for truth, justice, and the American way as the longest running continuously published character in history.

Canonically, Superman is an alien visitor from the planet Krypton, rocketed to Earth while an infant by his father Jor-El as a precaution against the destruction of his native planet. Raised into adulthood by a kindly couple, the Kents, Superman champions the citizens of the fictional city of Metropolis, fighting crime in his dual identity as Superman and mild-mannered reporter Clark Kent by displaying an impressive array of powers inherited from his alien physiology including flight, super strength, invulnerability, super hearing, and both heat and x-ray vision. Over 70 years of publication, however, the remaining details of his origin have been significantly altered. His origin was first told in a one-page piece of exposition in *Action Comics* #1, which was expanded to fill two pages for the publication of *Superman* #1 in 1939. It took up nine pages in the 1948 "Origin of Superman" in *Superman* #53, 13 pages for *Superman* #146 "The Story of Superman's Life" in 1961, 15 in 1973 for *The Amazing World of Superman*'s "The Origin of Superman!," 143 pages in the 1986 miniseries **The Man of Steel**, and over 280 for the 2005 maxi-series **Superman: Birthright.** The character of Superman has thus constantly been in flux since his debut and has existed in subtly different forms throughout his publication. He has also been the source of several spin-off characters and comics, as in the detailing of his boyhood adventures as Superboy or in the creation of his female counterpart, Supergirl.

Superman's powers were actually far fewer and far less impressive in the first few years of his publication; for example, he did not gain the ability to fly until 1943.

*Superman*, issue #1, published Summer, 1939. DC Comics/ Photofest

The initial stories featuring Superman reflected this decreased power-level, pitting Superman against mostly mobsters and thugs as he fought against unsafe mining conditions, racketeering, and spousal abuse. During this period Superman displayed a tougher, grittier persona as Siegel and Shuster had modeled him after the hard-hitting pulp heroes popular to comics at the time.

The more charming, light-hearted version of Superman would not develop until Mort Weisinger's run as editor in the 1950s and 1960s. Hiring Otto Binder, the writer responsible for the wild popularity of the more comical and child-friendly series featuring **Captain Marvel**, *Whiz Comics*, Weisinger set about capturing the audience of the aforementioned publication by running highly imaginative—if not sometimes weirdly strange— stories with a heavier focus on **science fiction**. DC had recently won a lawsuit against Fawcett Publications, publisher of *Whiz Comics*, causing them to cease publication of **Captain Marvel** in 1953 due to his similarity to Superman, and with the institution of the **Comics Code** Authority in 1954 severely limiting the content printable in comics, light-hearted seemed the way to go. It is in this era that Superman's mythos was expanded to include the bottle city of Kandor, the Fortress of Solitude, Supergirl, and Krypto the Superdog.

During his tenure as editor of the Superman comics from 1971 to 1985, Julius Schwartz had already significantly modernized the character. The 1986 **retcon** of Superman by **John Byrne** in his miniseries, *The Man of Steel*, then started another new era for Superman comics by bringing a new focus to the interpersonal relationships in Superman's life In *The Man of Steel*, Byrne integrated Superman's Clark Kent persona into his fundamental identity since, in Byrne's origin story, his powers did not manifest until puberty, meaning that Clark Kent was no longer merely a guise for Superman to interact with the world. Because of this change, Byrne also kept Martha and Jonathan Kent alive into Superman's adulthood to help give him moral direction, whereas they had earlier died when he was still young. Clark started a relationship with Lois since he was no longer the one-dimensional weakling from previous portrayals, and in 1996 Lois Lane and Clark Kent married after nearly 60 years of courtship.

Lois Lane, introduced in *Action Comics* #1; Perry White, introduced in *Superman* #7 (1940); and Jimmy Olsen, introduced in Superman #13 (1941) comprise the core supporting cast in most Superman stories, and Lex Luthor, Superman's most recognizable arch-nemesis has been a thorn in Superman's side since *Action Comics* #23 (1940). The newspaper for which Superman works as Clark Kent, however, was first called *The Daily Star* in *Action Comics* #1 and only changed to *The Daily Planet* in *Superman* #4 (1940). Likewise the names of Superman's adoptive parents underwent frequent changes from John and Mary, to Silas and Mary, to finally settle on Jonathan and Martha in the early 1950s.

Predecessors to Superman can be found in the early **science fiction** stories and pulp comics Siegel and Shuster worked on before successfully pitching the Man of Steel to M.C. Gaines in 1937. The name "Superman" was first attributed to the villain of a short story Siegel published in 1933 titled "Reign of the Superman" about an out of work derelict who gains enormous mental powers after being subjected to a science experiment and uses his newfound abilities to conquer the world. Superman's appearance and attitude were prefaced by Siegel and Shuster's character "Slam Bradley" who first appeared in **Detective Comics** #1 (1937) as a hard-boiled pulp detective, but ultimately Siegel cites the myths of such heroes as Samson and Hercules as a major source for their own strong man with powers beyond those of a mere mortal, giving The Man of Tomorrow roots that stretch far back into our cultural past.

Five major motion pictures have been made about Superman, starting with Richard Donner's 1979 *Superman: The Movie* and ending with Bryan Singer's 2006 *Superman Returns*. The franchise enjoyed a movie serial in 1948 and 1950, a radio program running from 1940 to 1951, several cartoon shows, a Broadway musical in 1966, and four live-action television shows: *The Adventures of Superman* (1952–58), *Superboy* (1988–92), *Lois and Clark: The New Adventures of Superman* (1993–97), and *Smallville* (2001–). Beyond these representations have been thousands of product endorsements, toys, games, and merchandise saturating almost every aspect of American culture. Superman is one of the most widely recognized icons in the world, inspiring the entire superhero genre. The character's mark can be felt on our very language when someone refers to something that disturbs or frightens them as their "kryptonite." With any form he has taken, from parody to homage, Superman has become an indelible part of the cultural landscape into the 21st century.

**Selected Bibliography:** Daniels, Les. *Superman: The Complete History*. San Francisco: Chronicle Books, 1998; Daniels, Les. *DC Comics: Sixty Years of the World's Favorite Comic Book Heroes*. Boston: Bulfinch, 1995; Fleisher, Michael L. *The Original Encyclopedia of Comic Book Heroes*. Vol. 3. New York: DC Comics, 2007; Yeffeth,

Glenn, ed. *The Man from Krypton: A Closer Look at Superman*. Dallas: Benbella, 2005.

*Jackson Jennings*

**SUPERMAN: BIRTHRIGHT.** *Superman: Birthright* was a 12-issue limited series published by **DC Comics** from 2003 to 2004, written by **Mark Waid** and penciled by Leinil Francis Yu, which updated Superman's origin story, giving it a more modern context.

The series begins traditionally on Krypton where Jor-El, Superman's father, sends his son to Earth to escape the cataclysmic explosion that obliterates his birth planet, before immediately switching scenes to an African village where a 25-year-old Clark Kent, now a reporter, is investigating a story about a young a political leader fighting for representation for his tribe in their nation's parliament. The story of Clark's life on Earth only unfolds gradually through dialogue and flashbacks, as the issues explore the connection between heroism, identity, and belonging. It is not until issue #4 that Superman appears in full costume, his dual identity undertaken in order to both achieve his full potential as a superhuman being and belong to society in a way that he never felt he could, having been perceived solely as a savior. The main plot of the story, revealed in issue #7, involves Lex Luthor planning to discredit the **Man of Steel** as an alien spy by staging a Kryptonian invasion using advanced holographic technology and a small army of thugs dressed as Superman's long dead kinsmen. Waid sets up Luthor as a foil to Superman in this and the subsequent issue, showing flashbacks of their childhood friendship in their hometown of Smallville, and revealing that Lex, due to his staggering intellect, also felt like an outcast, who, unlike Superman, decided to reject society and instead work merely for individual gain. The climax of the story reaffirms Superman's heroic status to the public after he and Lois expose the invasion, smashing Luthor's machinery and foiling his forces.

*Superman: Birthright* is not the first comic detailing Superman's origin, nor is it even the first comic to **retcon** his origin: **John Byrne**'s 1986 miniseries *The Man of Steel* is *Birthright*'s predecessor in that respect. Waid's retcon diverges greatly from Byrne's, however, and is the longest Superman origin story ever produced as a Superman comic. The most notable change is in the character of Superman, who is now deeply concerned with his place in society. Instead of gradually gaining his powers throughout puberty, Waid shows Superman as having grown up with them, forcing much of his life to be spent hiding his true nature from the rest of the world. Consequently, Clark Kent returns to the timid bumbler familiar from the **Silver Age** of comics. Jonathan and Martha Kent appear to be younger than their previous incarnation and have a more active role in helping Superman both come to grips with his origin, and guard his secret. Lex Luthor is also modified, growing up alongside Clark and returning to his roots as more of a mad scientist than Byrne's previous conception of Lex Luthor as the industrialist fat-cat. Leinil Yu's designs also restore Krypton to its more colorful pre-Byrne aesthetic (albeit, with its projection screens and sleeker corners, a more technologically modern one), featuring the classic Superman "S" as Superman's family crest.

Waid's approach to the story is also different than most of his predecessors; there is a lot more time devoted to showing Superman as a young adult and what he was like before adopting his costume. The story also focuses on Metropolis's reaction to Superman, making his acceptance by the public centrally important to the narrative, though traditionally a non-issue in his origin. Lex Luthor's and Superman's relationship is more personal, too, giving their inevitable clashes a more emotional context. While the core aspects of Superman's origin remain—he came from technologically advanced Krypton, was raised by a kindly couple on a farm, keeps all the amazing powers expected from Superman, and fights for truth and justice in Metropolis—the story itself spends much of its time embellishing the inner struggles of its cast, and projecting those inner struggles onto the conflicts associated with superhero comics.

This new emphasis on internal motivations, however, is not new to the Superman mythos as a whole. The genesis of Waid's creation can be found in the television adaptation of Superman's adolescence, *Smallville*. *Smallville*, beginning in 2001, introduced a new style of pathos into the Superman mythos by focusing heavily on the interpersonal relationships around Superman. Like many of the other hits on the WB (the network which originally aired *Smallville*), such as *Buffy the Vampire Slayer*, *Dawson's Creek*, or even *The Gilmore Girls*, the show's creators designed their new Superman show around the drama created between its characters. The Kents' younger appearance, Lex Luthor's residence in Smallville, and even Clark Kent's longing to be accepted by the people around him were all popularized by the show, which has been the longest running Superman television series in history. Waid himself even acknowledges the similarity in the afterword to the graphic novelization of *Superman: Birthright*: "The entirety of *Superman: Birthright* is built around the same thing *Smallville* is built around, the same thing that ALL teenage lives are built around, the one bonding element we can count on our audience to find in common with this alien being who can fly: the search for identity" (301).

While *Superman: Birthright* heavily influenced the design of Kryptonians for works such as **Brian Azzerello**'s and **Jim Lee**'s *Superman: For Tomorrow* (*Superman* #204–15) and Michael Turner, Joe Kelly, and Talent Caldwell's *Superman: Godfall* (*Action Comics* #812–13, *Adventures of Superman* #625–66, and *Superman* #202–3), it did not remain the predominant version of Superman's origin for long. After DC's maxi-series *Infinite Crisis* changed the company's continuity, and with the collaboration of Richard Donner on *Superman: Last Son* (*Action Comics* #844–46, 851 and *Action Comics Annual* #11), the design for Krypton changed more to resemble Bryan Singer's 2006 movie, *Superman Returns*, which itself relied heavily on Richard Donner's *Superman: The Movie* in 1979, making *Superman: Birthright* no longer canonical.

**Selected Bibliography:** Waid, Mark. "Reimagining the Man of Tomorrow." *Superman: Birthright*. New York: DC, 2004, 292–302.

*Jackson Jennings*

**SUPERMAN: RED SON** (2003) is a three-issue *Elseworlds* miniseries written by **Mark Millar** and penciled by Dave Johnson and Kilian Plunkett. The story, narrated by

**Superman** himself, imagines the outcome of Superman's capsule landing in the Ukraine (rather than Kansas) in the 1930s. The first part of the story begins in America in the mid-1950s, as President Eisenhower announces the existence of the Superman. Reaction to his existence gives way to paranoia, and Eisenhower calls on Lex Luthor to devise ways to stop Superman. Several attempts are tried: Luthor attempts to crash a Sputnik into Metropolis, then uses DNA Superman left on the satellite to create a clone (Bizarro). Both are defeated handily by Superman. At home, Superman clashes with Stalin's illegitimate son Pyoter Roslov (Pete Ross), although the two seem to put differences aside in the wake of Stalin's death. Initially hesitant to elevate himself above his fellow communists, Superman eventually agrees to lead the Soviet Union by becoming its president.

In the second part of the story, the action fast-forwards to 1978, and shows Superman's attempts to build a global utopia, in which he is aided by **Wonder Woman**. The Soviet Union controls most of the world, and while most of the world is grateful for Superman's protection, he still faces challenges from both without and within. Luthor continues to send CIA-funded, superpowered agents, including most of Superman's traditional adversaries, to Russia with little success. Superman also faces dissent from a Russian version of **Batman**, who is funded by Roslov's KGB. Superman eventually defeats the combined efforts of these villains, and completes his totalitarian state. By the end, only the United States, reduced to 38 member states, remains outside his control.

The story's conclusion picks up in the year 2001. Superman's paradise is orderly, regulated, and finally free of dissent; all enemies, even Brainiac, have their proper place in the Soviet Union. Lex Luthor becomes president of the 35 remaining United States, and within a year has restored its prosperity to pre-Superman levels. Having achieved this, Luthor sets out to defeat Superman using a modified **Green Lantern** Corps, a contingent of Amazons led by a now-embittered Wonder Woman, and Luthor's own superior intelligence. Luthor is quickly captured by Brainiac, who convinces Superman that he must launch an attack on the United States in order to complete his utopia. Luthor ultimately defeats Superman with a letter comparing him to Brainiac: "Why don't you just put the whole *world* in a *bottle*, Superman?" Brainiac reveals that he has been using Superman all along; Luthor disables Brainiac only to cause his ship to self-destruct, and Superman, in a "last" act of heroism, tows the ship out of the solar system. Luthor picks up the pieces and establishes a truly utopian state, guided by "Luthorism," that expands the limits of human potential. In the last pages, readers discover that the future Earth is actually Superman's original home, and before its destruction by the red sun, Jor-L sends his son into the past to "fix" humanity.

While it does not speak clearly to any contemporary issues, other than the continued existence of totalitarianism in human society, *Red Son* does address a number of themes. The origin of Superman's values is one of these themes. Despite his growing up in the Ukraine, Superman continues to care for the welfare of humanity, implying that his defense of truth and justice is not a product of his American origins, but is an inherent part of his identity. While this fact is common to many of the *Elseworlds* tales featuring Superman, it is even more interesting given the truth about Superman's terrestrial origins. Human or Kryptonian, being Superman seems to require caring about one's neighbors.

Another theme woven through *Red Son* is that of competing utopian models. These include the idealized Communist model under which Superman grew up, and in which he persists in believing; Stalinism and its less brutal expression under Superman; American idealism; and the progressive and less totalitarian model provided by "Luthorism." Indeed, *Red Son* is one of the few Superman stories to depict Lex Luthor's victory as a good thing for humanity, as the centuries after Superman's defeat are ones of peace, prosperity, social growth, and universal good health and education. While these also seem to be features of Superman's 20th-century communist state, the advantage of Luthor's utopia is that it is a synthesis of Soviet and American philosophy, in which Luthor "combined his own ideas with notes from the archives, creating a brand-new style of government unlike anything we'd ever seen." Luthor thus creates a government that is beyond both capitalism and communism, freeing humanity "to become the most advanced species in the *known universe.*"

Working along with these utopian issues, *Red Son* focuses on the notion that a few central actors can change the course of world events. Despite his occasional claims to believe in equality, Superman's effect on world historical forces is clear and direct; his presence shapes, and in some cases distorts, world events. The same is true for Lex Luthor, who reshapes the world despite Superman's realization that "leaving them [humanity] alone means they can make their own mistakes again." Yet Millar hints that the presence of both characters is the key to humanity's success, as Superman notes: "Perhaps [Luthor] existed to keep me in *check*, or, as someone once hypothesized, perhaps it was the other way *around.*" Without the presence of the other, either Luthor or Superman would have affected the world negatively; together, they bring a better future about.

*Jacob Lewis*

**SWAMP THING.** One of the most popular and enduring **horror comics** characters of the past half century, Swamp Thing was launched in an eight-page story by Len Wein in 1971. Les Daniels wrote that "a gigantic mass of moss unexpectedly emerged as one of **DC's** most beloved heroes, and one of the few comic book characters recognized by people who don't read comics" (160). Swamp Thing's saga has always produced human, adult, disturbing, horror/**fantasy** stories with ecological and folkloric themes.

Sensing in 1971 that superhero dominance was ebbing, Wein and Artist Berni Wrightson were part of a 1970s rebirth of the popular horror comics that dominated the early 1950s. The original story cast Swamp Thing as Doctor Alex Olsen, and the characters all wore ruffled shirts and longish hair suggesting a faintly Romantic era with a Mary Shelley-Frankenstein atmosphere. The plot involved a Damien Ridge, Olsen's assistant who loves Olsen's wife, Linda, and plots to kill her husband. Olsen is bathed in a bio-restorative formula when Ridge detonates the lab; the doctor is subsequently transformed into the Swamp Thing. The paranoid Ridge begins to think Linda

Adrienne Barbeau as Alice Cable and Dick Durock as Swamp Thing, in the 1982 film *Swamp Thing*, directed by Wes Craven. MGM/Photofest

suspects him, and he plots to kill her. Swamp Thing bursts into the room, killing the murderer. Sadly, he finds himself unable to communicate with his wife, because his vocal cords have atrophied. He returns to the swamp realizing his human life is gone.

The character was given his own series in November, 1972. Wein and Wrightson revamped the origin tale, changing the scientist's name to Alec Holland, and introducing an **espionage** subplot. A criminal cartel, the Conclave, seek Holland's bio-restorative formula, leading to a fiery explosion in which Holland is saved only by the formula. His wife Linda is killed. In the second issue, Swamp Thing meets the mad Dr. Anton Arcane and his Un-men. Arcane offers to restore Holland to his human body in exchange for Swamp Thing's near immortal body. Using an incantation in front of a mysterious *soul jar* Holland is restored; realizing that Arcane is insane, he smashes the jar, and reverts back to Swamp Thing. Wrightson's art—placing Swamp Thing in murky castles, dismal swamps, and dark foreboding alleys—is a triumph. In issue #3, Wein performs a nice spin on the Frankenstein myth by introducing Arcane's brother, The Patchwork Man, Gregori Arcane, father to Abigail Arcane. In the story, a blown-up Gregori is pieced back together by Anton. As he says, "there wasn't much left of you, you realize—I had to improvise my repairs from the material at hand."

*Swamp Thing*, despite a great creative team, only lasted for 24 issues. Following a film in 1982, by horror auteur Wes Craven (an early fan of the comic book) the character re-emerged in a new comics series in the 1980s. Initially the new edition was only modestly popular. On the verge of cancellation it was revitalized by British comic auteur **Alan Moore**, who re-imagined Swamp Thing not as an undead muck monster, but as a vegetative elemental. Under Moore's guidance, Swamp Thing's chronology and mythology were completely rewritten. Now the Sunderland Corporation seeks the secrets of Alec Holland's research, assassinating Swamp Thing in a barrage of bullets (issue #20). The creepy Dr. Jason Woodrue is hired by Sunderland to autopsy the dead Swamp Thing in issue #21's pivotal story, "The Anatomy Lesson." He discovers that the creature is simply plants and roots, all vegetation with only vestigial forms of human organs. Swamp Thing is really a plant that *thinks* it is human, a consciousness of Earth known as *the Parliament of Trees* or simply, *the Green*. Abigail Arcane is re-introduced and quickly becomes the Swamp thing's lover and muse. At first, she is married to Mathew Cable, an FBI man investigating the murder of Holland and his wife. He thinks the Swamp Thing is the killer. For a time, Cable is possessed by the spirit of Anton Arcane and briefly has an incestuous affair with niece Abby. This story line created a serious challenge to the **Comics Code**, which prohibited stories of sexual perversion, including incest. DC stood behind Moore's work, running the tale without the Comics Code Seal and with a mature content advisory with future issues. The result was profitable sales and an ability to produce more **adult** fantasy, something that comics had lost following the fearful censorship episode of the 1950s.

Moore takes Swamp Thing on ever more exotic and fantastic crusades. Cable goes into a coma and Swamp Thing must rescue Abby, who has descended into Hell. There, Abby and Swamp Thing encounter many of DC's supernatural characters, laying the groundwork for DC's Vertigo line in the 1990s. By issue #34, the pair recognize their mutual love and after taking a hallucinogenic tuber (the Swamp Thing's seed?) they are able to consummate their affair. Swamp Thing became a pop culture phenomenon, appearing in a film sequel (1989), a cartoon series (1990) (with new lyrics to "Wild Thing": "swamp thing, you are amazing,") and also a popular USA Network television series (1990–92).

In the *American Gothic* story line, Moore's Swamp Thing meets modern incarnations of various horror characters including **vampires** and **zombies**. Moore also includes an affectionate tribute to Walt Kelly's *Pogo* gang of characters. Notably, Swamp Thing often crosses paths with **Batman**. The Dark Knight, with his own troubled childhood, seems a natural soul mate for the mournful Swamp Thing.

In later adventures, Swamp Thing meets the Parliament of Trees, becoming an Earth elemental, a demi-diety; he impregnates Abby by possessing the body of fellow supernatural hero, John Constantine of the *Hellblazer* comics. At one point (in a story by **Grant Morrison**), Swamp Thing is briefly split into two characters, a mindless Swamp Thing and a human, Alex Holland; he also battles the influence of post-Hurricane Katrina land developers in the Bayou.

*Stuart Lenig*

**SWAN, CURT** (1920–96). Curt Swan, born Douglas Curtis Swan, was the son of a railroad worker and a hospital employee. After being drafted into the U.S. Army in 1940, Swan was staff artist for *Stars & Stripes* newspaper. After his discharge, Swan met Eddie Herron, a former **DC Comics** writer. At Herron's suggestion, Swan applied at DC. Swan's first assignments were *Boy Commandos* and *Newsboy Legion* stories, assigned in 1945 and published in 1946.

Following these assignments, Swan largely abandoned inking, preferring penciling. This increased his output to three pages per day. Following the advice of Steve Brody, Swan began using illustrative shortcuts, such as minimal backgrounds for selected panels. Demonstrating an affinity for space opera, he was assigned a new strip in **Action Comics**, *Tommy Tomorrow*, in 1948. His success on this strip led to his work on *Superboy*, beginning in 1949. The sense of Americana that Swan bought to the title came in part from his upbringing in rural Minnesota and resonated with many of the feature's readers. In 1953, he began working on his signature character, **Superman**.

His portrayal of Superman was defined by attention to detail, imagination and realistic anatomy. Swan was one of a cadre of artists who redefined the character in the 1950s and 1960s, along with Al Plastino, Wayne Boring, **Jim Mooney**, and Murphy Anderson. Swan also penciled the cover of the issue of **Adventure Comics** that introduced *Supergirl*.

Also drawing the *Superman* newspaper strip from 1958 to 1961, Swan's style became the signature look for the character. Andy Warhol's *Superman* screenprint is based on an iconic Swan drawing of Superman in flight. Swan's *Superman* remains the default image of the character to this day.

Swan drew literally thousands of pages for DC over his 50-year career, spanning most of DC's line. His work on **World's Finest Comics** helped define that title in the 1960s. Aside from Superman, he was best known for his work on the *Legion of Super-Heroes*. Though the series' writers include **Jerry Seigel** and Otto Binder, many hold that the title was at its creative zenith when Swan was drawing Jim Shooter's scripts.

Swan worked for DC almost exclusively. He did a smattering of work for independent publishers in the 1990s, and worked for **Marvel** only once. He retired from Superman in 1986, but returned to the character and other DC projects for financial reasons. Though not his last work on the character, Swan's 1986 illustration of **Alan Moore's** two-part story **Whatever Happened to the Man of Tomorrow?** is regarded as canon for both defining and closing the **Silver Age** of comics. Here Swan's elegant pencils raised the emotional level of Superman's struggle with chaos to Wagnerian heights. One of Swan's last DC jobs was an issue of **Swamp Thing**, which he described as "rather strange, but these days, what isn't?"

Swan won the 1984 Inkpot Award and was inducted into the **Will Eisner** Hall of Fame in 1997. His unfulfilled desire was to be taken seriously as a professional illustrator. It is appropriate and a bit ironic that he is often called "the Norman Rockwell of comics."

**Selected Bibliography:** Zeno, Eddie, et al. *Curt Swan: A Life in Comics*. Lakewood, NJ: Vanguard Press, 2002.

*Diana Green*

**TALES FROM THE CRYPT.** *Tales from the Crypt* was **EC Comics'** flagship **horror comics** anthology title; it has become culturally synonymous with gory, twist-in-the-tale horror and has been adapted into a number of media. *Tales from the Crypt* was launched with the April/May 1950 issue (the same year as other notable bi-monthly EC Comics titles *The Haunt of Fear*, and *The Vault of Horror*); it ran for 46 issues until the February/March 1955 issue. All three titles were reluctantly axed by EC's publisher **William Gaines** in the face increasingly stringent restrictions by the **Comics Code** after a campaign against horror and **crime comics** in the late 1940s and early 1950s.

Although **Fredric Wertham's** notorious expose of comic violence and its effects on young readers, *Seduction of the Innocent* (1954), constantly cites **crime** and horror comics, the book's *raison d'être* is not comics scholarship or genre studies. Wertham classifies **Western comics** as crime comics because they involve criminal schemes, like cattle rustling, and takes the descriptions of comics from his subjects, often young people in care, at face value without looking at the comic book sources in context. Thus, **Blue Beetle** "turns into" **Superman**, according to one child. *Tales from the Crypt* is cited by name only once in the text by one of the interviewees, from a small group of 11 children (9 boys and 2 girls between 9 and 13 years old) and none of the scurrilous illustrations chosen for Wertham's centerpiece are from *Tales from the Crypt*. The famous baseball game played with entrails is from *Haunt of Fear* 19, and a stark cover of a hanged man above the unconvincing description "Cover of a children's comic book" is from EC's *Crime Suspense Stories* issue #20. What Wertham overlooked was the rising age of comic readership, and the mostly adult audience of EC comics in the World War II and the postwar period, where horror and crime comics gained a new adult readership. In the Congressional subcommittee held in April and June 1954, Gaines said (in the 1988 documentary film *Comic Book Confidential*) of his comics output and its most famous detractor:

> Some may not like them. That is a matter of personal taste. It would be just as difficult to explain the harmless thrill of a horror story to a Dr. Wertham as it would be to explain the sublimity of love to a frigid old maid. . . . What are we afraid of? Are we afraid of our own children? Do we forget that they are citizens, too, and entitled to select what to read or do? We think our children are so evil, simple minded, that it takes a story of murder to set them to murder, a story of robbery to set them to robbery?

It would be unfortunate, however, if the moral panic of the 1950s would overshadow how visually and stylistically progressive *Tales from the Crypt* was. Described by artist and writer **Al Feldstein** (EC Comics 1948–53, *Mad* Magazine 1956–84) as "new icing on old cakes," the comic was inspired by such popular culture staples of the 1950s as horror and **science fiction** B-movies, and such writers Edgar Allan Poe, H. P. Lovecraft, and Ray Bradbury, some of whose stories were adapted directly by the comic. Gaines and Feldstein had a shared love of such stories, and Gaines would come up with one-line plots or "springboards" that Feldstein and others would flesh out into twist-in-the-tale stories with often gruesome moral retribution for adulterers and murders. American literature from Ambrose Bierce to O. Henry to Damon Runyon has long had a love of quirky short stories with twist endings. In Ron Mann's 1988 documentary, *Comic Book Confidential*, Feldstein comments that what he and Gaines did was much like what television series such as *The Twilight Zone* and *Alfred Hitchcock Presents* did subsequently. The graphic design and dynamic cover art of *Tales from the Crypt* have also become iconic. The cover to issue #28 featured a cutaway of a character being buried alive while the

A three-dimensional issue of *Tales from the Crypt of Terror* (1953). Photofest

gravedigger walked away on the surface, and the startling cover of issue #41 shows a knife-thrower's assistant pinned to a wooden wheel while an ax is depicted inexorably approaching her horrified face yet never making contact in a dynamic and unsettling piece of comic art.

The visceral and straightforward storytelling of EC Comics as a whole, and *Tales from the Crypt* in particular, inspired the subsequent generation of horror writers and directors including Stephen King, George A. Romero, and John Carpenter, where supernatural horror tropes often happen against a mundane or modern rather than gothic background. Bands such as the American punk rock group The Cramps, used the distinct cover font for their band logo and got Feldstein to provide cover art for album *Songs The Lord Taught Us* (1980). *Tales from the Crypt* has been adapted into various films, television series and cartoons. Veteran director Freddie Francis's film *Tales from the Crypt* (1972), from Amicus Productions cast Ralph Richardson as the Crypt Keeper and such actors as Joan Collins and Peter Cushing. However, only the stories "Reflection of Death" (issue #23) and "Blind Alleys" (issue #46, February-March, 1955) by Feldstein and Gaines are actually from *Tales from the Crypt*, while the remaining three are from *The Vault of Terror* or the *Haunt of Fear*. HBO's television series *Tales from the Crypt* (1989–96) featured an animatronic Crypt Keeper, voiced by John Kassir, who introduced each episode with stories taken from EC's *Tales from the Crypt*, *Haunt of Fear*, *Vault of Fear*, *Crime SuspenStories*, and *Shock SuspenStories*. The popularity of the series, which (due to the subscription cable nature of the cable station) could show more gore and sexual situations, led to two more theatrically released films: *Tales from the Crypt Presents: Demon Knight* (1995) and *Tales from the Crypt Presents: Bordello of Blood* (1996). A third film, *Ritual*, was released straight to DVD in non-U.S. markets in 2001 and was not released in America until May 2, 2005, with specially filmed Crypt-Keeper segments with Kassir returning to the role. In the surprising trend of cartoons aimed at younger viewers based on such adult movies as *The Toxic Avenger* (1984) and *Robocop* (1987), the cartoon *Tales from the Cryptkeeper* lasted for two series from 1993 to 1994, returning as new *Tales from the Cryptkeeper* in 1997. Gemstone Publishing, producers of *The Official Overstreet Comic Book Price Guide* currently holds the rights to reprint *Tales from the Crypt*.

*Lorcan McGrane*

**TARZAN.** Tarzan, the Lord of the Jungle, was created by Edgar Rice Burroughs (1875–1950) and first appeared in *All-Story Magazine* in 1912. Burroughs created his feral hero only after having failed at numerous professions. He began his career as a pulp fiction writer in 1911 and his first serialized adventure, *Under the Moons of Mars*, was published the following year in *All-Story Magazine*. That tale introduced John Carter, a Civil War veteran who is transported to Mars. Burroughs achieved even greater success in 1912 with the publication of *Tarzan of the Apes*, a serialized adventure that also debuted in *All-Story Magazine*. Tarzan soon became one of the most enduring heroes of 20th-century popular culture as his exploits were seen in a variety of mass media, including novels, pulp magazines, comic strips, comic books, radio, film, and television.

In any medium, Tarzan's adventures are filled with untamed beasts, savage natives, lost cities, beautiful damsels, and thrilling action.

Burroughs's creation of the jungle hero was influenced by his reading the works of authors like Rudyard Kipling and H. Rider Haggard. Tarzan's origin, which was first published as a novel in 1914's *Tarzan of the Apes: A Romance of the Jungle*, has become one of the most famous tales in all of popular literature. Tarzan was born John Clayton, the future Lord Greystoke, in a hut after his aristocratic British parents had been marooned by their mutinous crew as they sailed along the African coast. Within a year the infant is orphaned as his mother dies and his father is killed by an attacking band of great apes. Miraculously, the baby is adopted by a female ape named Kala who is grief-stricken at the death of her own offspring. The boy is raised by the simians and called "Tarzan," which means "white skin" in the ape language. Burroughs described Tarzan as growing into a tall, handsome, and extremely athletic man with grey eyes and black hair. He is fully integrated into the ape society as he speaks their language and lives in the trees. Eventually, he discovers the hut where he was born and teaches himself to read with his family's books. He also takes to wearing a leopard skin loincloth. After years in the jungle, he encounters an American woman named Jane Porter who is lost in the wild along with her father. Tarzan becomes her protector and ultimately chooses

Bruce Bennett as Tarzan in the 1935 serial, *The New Adventures of Tarzan*. Burroughs-Tarzan Enterprises Inc. /Photofest

to follow her back to civilization where he can reclaim his noble birthright. Burroughs immediately followed this story with two more novels, *The Return of Tarzan* (1915) and *The Beasts of Tarzan* (1915); ultimately there would be dozens of Tarzan novels, many of which were serialized in the pulp magazines.

Unlike many of the film and television interpretations of the ape-man, Burroughs's hero was an articulate gentleman who is stronger and more courageous than other men because he has not been softened by the comforts of civilization. The famed line of movie dialogue "Me Tarzan, you Jane" never appeared in a Burroughs story. Tarzan was always presented as intelligent, loyal, and ethical; he rarely displayed any character flaws. His jungle upbringing gave him superior strength and unparalleled athletic ability. The stories are filled with many descriptions of his great speed, agility, reflexes, balance, as well as his swimming, leaping, and climbing skills. Burroughs also showed Tarzan as having enhanced senses of hearing and smell. Furthermore, he is capable of communicating with nearly every animal species in the jungle.

Tarzan came to comics in January 1929 when *Tarzan of the Apes* was adapted into a newspaper strip illustrated by Hal Foster. A Sunday page came in 1931. Foster's artwork revolutionized the comics page with his masterful use of cinematic techniques like angle shots and depth of field. His African scenery was stunning and Tarzan himself appeared to practically leap from the newspaper page. Foster left the strip in 1937 and went on to create *Prince Valiant*. Artist **Burne Hogarth** subsequently took over the feature for several years. Many other artists and writers worked on the comic strip during the next several decades. One of the most notable is Russ Manning, who took over the strip in 1968 after having drawn Tarzan's comic book adventures for years. Celebrated comic book writer and artist Mike Grell handled the Tarzan strip for several years in the 1980s. Tarzan still appears in a few newspapers, but the strip merely reprints older material.

Tarzan has had an extensive comic book career. The hero has appeared in comics published by a variety of publishers, such as Western Publishing, **Charlton Comics**, **DC Comics**, **Marvel Comics**, and **Dark Horse Comics**. Most of the Burroughs novels have been adapted over the years. Tarzan was featured in text stories in Dell's *Crackerjack Comics* from 1939 to 1942. In 1947, Tarzan was seen in two issues of Dell's *Four Color Comics*. A regular Tarzan series was launched the following year. Artist Jesse Marsh remained on the book for the next 18 years, while Gaylord DuBois wrote the stories for 25 years. DC Comics took over Tarzan in 1972. Legendary artist Joe Kubert drew many of the best stories during this period. He also wrote and edited the *Tarzan of the Apes* book for several years. From 1964 to 1972 Gold Key Comics published *Korak: Son of Tarzan*. DC Comics continued the series until 1976 where it ran under the title *Tarzan Family*. In 1977, the ape-man moved to Marvel Comics and starred in *Tarzan, Lord of the Jungle*. Dark Horse Comics published several Tarzan books beginning in 1996. Dark Horse and DC Comics joined forces to have the jungle hero team-up with two of the most popular superheroes. ***Batman*/*Tarzan: Claws of the Cat-Woman*** (1999) is set in the 1930s, while ***Superman*/*Tarzan: Sons of the Jungle*** (2002) is set in an alternate reality where Lord Greystoke grows up in England, while the infant Superman is raised by the apes. In 1996, *Tarzan vs. Predator at the Earth's Core* has the hero battle the aliens from the popular film franchise.

In 1967, Burne Hogarth captured the essence of Tarzan when he wrote of the jungle hero: "He is energy, grace, and virtue. He symbolizes the inevitable life source, the earth, the speed, the rain, the harvest, achievement, the triumph over adversity and death" (Richardson and Duin 433).

**Selected Bibliography:** Richardson, Mike, and Steve Duin. *Comics, Between the Panels*. Milwaukie, OR: Dark Horse Comics, 1998.

*Charles Coletta*

**TEEN TITANS.** A team of teenage **superheroes**, the Teen Titans elevated adolescent characters from their traditional role as sidekicks to become the protagonists of their own adventures. Teenage sidekicks were a popular element in comic books of the 1940s beginning with the debut of Robin as **Batman**'s apprentice in *Detective Comics* #38 (1940). Writers often employed these characters to provide their protagonists with allies with whom they could confide and advance plotlines. The teens further gave the young comics-reading audience characters with whom they could identify. The inclusion of Robin into the Batman franchise caused sales to nearly double. Robin's popularity was so strong in the **Golden Age** of comics that most superheroes of the era were nearly obligated to form a partnership with a hero-in-training. In 1964, **DC Comics** introduced the Teen Titans, a superhero team which placed the kid sidekicks at the forefront of the action.

During the **Silver Age** of comics, DC Comics introduced *Justice League of America*, a powerhouse title that combined the company's top superheroes. Its success spurred editor George Kashdan to approach writer Bob Haney with the notion of creating a "junior Justice League." The team, which included Robin, Aqualad, and Kid Flash, made its debut in *The Brave and the Bold* #54 (1964) as the teens joined forces to battle the villainous Mr. Twister. The heroes returned for another adventure and were formally called the "Teen Titans" for the first time in *The Brave and the Bold* #60 (1965). They were joined by Wonder Girl, whose earlier comics appearances had presented her merely in stories depicting the exploits of **Wonder Woman** as a youth. The quartet's popularity led to an appearance in *Showcase* #59 before they were ultimately rewarded with their own title, *Teen Titans* #1, in 1966. By issue #4 Speedy, sidekick to the **Green Arrow**, joined the roster. Numerous other teen superheroes, such as Beast Boy, Aquagirl, feuding brothers Hawk and Dove, psychic go-go dancer Lilith, and Mal Duncan—the first black Titan—made guest visits to the title.

The most notable feature of the 1960s Teen Titans stories is the unbearable dialogue with which the middle-aged writers strained to be "hip" for a younger readership growing up in the counterculture era. The writers did mildly explore current events as stories dealt with issues surrounding racial tensions in the inner cities and Vietnam War protesters. The Titans also faced a notoriously weak rogue's gallery that included villains like The Mad Mod, Captain Rumble, and Ding-Dong Daddy Dowd. While the writing may have been somewhat pedestrian, the artwork provided by Nick Cardy was lush. By issue #16 (1968), a new and more serious approach to the stories was implemented. One of the most important tales of this period involved a revised origin for Wonder Girl. *Teen Titans* #25 (1969) revealed her to be Donna Troy, an orphan rescued by Wonder Woman and given the power of the Amazons while being raised on Paradise Island. The Teen Titans' initial run was cancelled with issue #43 in 1973. However, the team was revived in 1976 with several new heroes, including Bat-Girl, Golden Eagle, Bumblebee, and Harlequin who claimed to be the daughter of various supervillains. Eventually, the team fractured as some of the heroes left to form a new group called "Titans West." This incarnation of the team was short-lived as it was canceled following issue #53 (1978).

In the early 1980s, when DC Comics decided to re-launch the Teen Titans once again, few within the industry believed the title would be successful. However, these concerns were quashed as this new version of the team, which debuted in *DC Comics Presents* #26 (1980), proved to be an immediate hit. *The New Teen Titans*, written by **Marv Wolfman** and drawn by **George Pérez**, climbed to the top of the sales charts in six months and remained DC's most popular title for most of the decade. Wolfman had worked on the title in the late 1960s before spending most of the 1970s at **Marvel Comics**, where he eventually rose to the position of editor-in-chief. Upon returning to DC he reinvigorated the Titans with many of the stylistic techniques that had made Marvel's titles popular with modern readers. In many respects, the new Teen Titans were DC's answer to Marvel's **X-Men** franchise as both series presented a diverse cast of young heroes combating villains and their own growing pains and doubts. Wolfman employed a large cast that included both established and new, intriguing characters. Robin, Kid Flash, and Wonder Girl from the old team were joined by Raven (a half-demon empath), Starfire (an alien warrior princess), Cyborg, and Beast Boy, now renamed Changeling. Wolfman's stories were action-packed but readers seemed to especially appreciate the quieter moments in the Titans' lives when they took off the masks. He presented the heroes as having an emotional depth previously absent from DC Comics' other creations. His goal was to show respect for the characters and not depict them as stereotypical teens. Pérez's contribution to the title was invaluable. He possessed a keen ability to draw books with large casts and was equally adept at depicting epic battles and subtle facial expressions. Pérez eventually joined Wolfman as the series' co-editor. After Wolfman and Pérez left the series for other projects, the Teen Titans lost much of their luster. Numerous writers and artists have attempted to re-launch the series since in 1980s heyday with varying success. The cast has also changed with each new creative team.

The Teen Titans' appearances have not been limited only to the comics pages. The team featuring Speedy, Kid Flash Wonder Girl, and Aqualad made their first animated appearance in segments within *The **Superman/Aquaman** Hour of Adventure* (1967). The character Cyborg joined the *Super Friends* Saturday morning cartoon show in the

1980s. In 2003, a Teen Titans animated series premiered that was aimed largely at a younger audience with its anime style. Older fans appreciated that many of the storylines were based upon plots from the Wolfman–Pérez comics era. The series was cancelled after five seasons. The Teen Titans remain one of DC's most prominent superhero groups as their adventures continue to resonate with fans.

*Charles Coletta*

**TERMINAL CITY.** *Terminal City* is a nine-issue miniseries published in 1996 by the Vertigo imprint of **DC Comics**. A sequel, the five-issue *Terminal City: Aerial Graffiti*, was published in 1997. Both titles were written by **Dean Motter** and penciled by Michael Lark.

The primary focus of both series is the rehabilitation of protagonist Cosmo Quinn, once a famous daredevil performing as "The Human Fly," but in the present time of the story a common window-washer in the architecturally sumptuous Terminal City, a city of deco glamour that has also fallen on hard times. Quinn hires enterprising young B. B. as an apprentice window-washer and general sidekick when she learns that the promise of construction work that lured her to town will never be fulfilled. *Terminal City* commences with the appearance of an amnesiac man with a briefcase bolted to his wrist. Speculation over the identity of the man, and the contents of the briefcase, pulls together much of the rest of the cast, including policeman Captain Sahib and underworld figure Big Lil. The amnesiac disappears shortly after the briefcase is somehow removed from his wrist, and the briefcase itself is barely mentioned again until the epilogue at the end of the series when it is found in the trash and taken away by a maniacal figure, never to be seen again.

The amnesiac and his briefcase provide Motter and Lark with a pretense to introduce Cosmo Quinn's disgraced or absent friends from 1984, the year of the Brave New World's Fair. Among those making return appearances is big game hunter Monty Vickers, who arranges for the comeback of another of the 1984 group, boxer Kid Gloves. Gloves boxes "Evolution" in a series of matches against the Piltdown Man, a Great Ape, and what Vickers claims is the missing link, a simian from Tibet. Later in the first series, Gloves boxes "Science" in the form of a robot. Though he defeats the robot, Gloves dies in the attempt. Another leftover from 1984, Eno Orez, the Man of 1,000 faces, succeeds in killing the current mayor of Terminal City after several failed attempts, though Orez's motivations for undertaking the assassination remain unclear.

*Terminal City: Aerial Graffiti* also features a man falling from the sky, but in this instance the man's identity is known from the start: he is Jose Hoffman, a bit player in a criminal scheme that involves the opening of the Transatlantic Tunnel connecting Paris and Terminal City. *Aerial Graffiti* also introduces readers to more figures from the 1984 Brave New World's Fair. This time, readers meet skywriter Raymond Alexander, who writes obscene messages in the air over Terminal City that embarrasses the acting mayor in front of business interests who might invest in the city's revival. Also present from the 1984 group is former fire eater and current arsonist Torch Johnson who, like Orez in the earlier series, works for underworld interests. Concerns over urban redevelopment motivate most of the actors in *Aerial Graffiti*, a wry contemporary comment on the state of urban cores in the mid-1990s when these stories were published. Despite all plotlines seeming to converge at the Transatlantic race from Paris to Terminal City featuring a magnetic train, a Zeppelin, and an experimental gravity-defying airship, the race itself is not part of this series. In an epilogue, Quinn promises that the race is "another story," one that remains untold since the second Terminal City story was the last to be published at this writing.

The two *Terminal City* stories read as much like one continuous serial as two separate stories. Motter's narration in both incorporates archival newsreel footage and contemporary television reports to develop characters' backgrounds and introduce plot elements, and alternating issues feature voice-overs from two characters: Cosmo Quinn from his memoir, "On the Wall," and mystery woman Monique Rome, the Lady in Red, who fights crime in an unofficial capacity and whose voice-over (in the form of a journal) presents the city as a jungle environment with shifting zones of safety and danger. The architectural designs are as interesting as readers might expect from a Dean Motter series, and Lark's crowd scenes are filled with visual jokes, like the recognizable figures from **science fiction** films in the background of a scene at a used robot lot.

Instead of the dystopian paranoia that characterizes much of Motter's other work, the *Terminal City* stories feature a low-key nostalgia and some silly humor. There is something comfortable and quietly impressive about the deco designs of the city, which shares design elements with *Mister X*'s Radiant City but which is much less oppressive. Despite protagonist Quinn's proclamation that "We were really competing against the NEW AGE itself. We were fighting against our own obsolescence," that fight is over before the first issue. Over the course of the two series, Quinn will move past fear and regret over his own past to integrate his past Human Fly experiences into his present, where he still works as a window washer but also has regular if unspectacular engagements as a daredevil. Meanwhile, the series is populated with characters whose wacky names refuse attempts at treating them seriously. These include low-level thug brothers Micasa and Sucasa, Quinn's ex-girlfriend Charity Ball and her sisters Faith and Hope, and Mayors Orwell and Huxley. Past Motter collaborators Ken Steacy and Paul Rivoche have buildings named after them, and sky-writer Raymond Alexander is clearly an homage to *Buck Rogers* creator Alex Raymond. There is an element of vaudeville, a dancing-as-fast-as-we-can spirit of joy that leavens the series.

Lark's pencils are impressive, especially in the second series, where the colors and fine pencil lines begin to show the polish and snap that characterize his later work in *Gotham Central* and **Daredevil.** Here readers can see the development of his distinctive down-to-earth style as he captures clearly human poses of characters, like Human Fly Cosmo Quinn, engaged in almost superhuman behaviors.

**Selected Bibliography:** Motter, Dean and Michael Lark. *Terminal City*. New York: DC Comics. 1996; Motter, Dean and Michael Lark. *Terminal City: Aerial Graffiti*. New York: DC Comics. 1997.

*Matthew Dube*

**TEZUKA, OSAMU** (1928–89). Widely known as the "Father of **Manga**," or even the "God of Manga," Osamu Tezuka was a medical doctor, an illustrator, and a filmmaker; more importantly, this prolific artist was the greatest comics author that Japan has ever known. At a very young age, Tezuka acquired a love for stories from his mother, while his father allowed him the rare privilege of going to the movies regularly. It was Walt Disney and the Fleischer brothers who inspired little Tezuka to draw his first manga by copying Mickey Mouse and Popeye during his primary years, where his talent was recognized and encouraged by a Samaritan schoolmaster. At the outbreak of World War II, Tezuka continued to produce manga for his entourage in junior high in spite of a general manga-bashing mentality. After the war, Tezuka registered in the school of medicine and set his mind to earn his degree but his heart was already turning towards manga creation.

Drawing continuously for more than 50 years (about 150,000 plates in 700 works), creating manga was Tezuka's way of shielding himself against various persecutions throughout life. For his primary school classmates ridiculed his small size, the wartime militaries loathed manga, the Tokyo publishers made fun of the provincial young artist from Osaka, and the general readership of the 1950s considered manga pernicious, just as comic books were coming under fire in the United States as a bad influence on young people.

A self-taught artist, Tezuka broke away from the common farcical stories four to five pages long of the pre-war period, and molded the modern manga landscape with "story manga," which feature a strong and fluid narrative. He also invented the "star system," which recasts the same recognizable key characters in different manga, thus giving readers a sense of familiarity. His work influenced the generation of the postwar years immensely, not only because his *Jungle Taitei* (1950–54) defined *shonen manga*, and his *Princess Knight* (1954–68) gave birth to *shôjo manga*, but also because of his avant-garde use of dynamic techniques. Color plates, use of boldface in dialogues, and onomatopoeia spreading beyond the edge of the frame were frowned upon at first but well accepted a decade later. His humorous and deceptively simple drawings lent weight to the themes that he wanted to convey and explore—ecology and human dignity, guilt and redemption, evil and moral decay—all adroitly blended in a variety of genres: **science fiction**, social fiction, medical thriller, biography, **history**, and the sublime.

Although his very first manga was a science fiction story (*The Ghost Man*), the best-known one was *New Treasure Island* (1947), which pioneered cinematic movements ranging from panoramic shots to close-ups. Other popular works for young readers include *Lost World* (1948), *Astro Boy* (1951–68), and *Black Jack* (1973–84). Starting in the mid-1960s, Tezuka entered his mature period with high-caliber, multi-volume works such as *Ode to Kirihito* (1970–71), *Ayako* (1972–73), **Buddha** (1974–84), *MW* (1976–78), *Adolf* (1983–85). However, several series were regretfully left unfinished at his death, including *Phoenix* (1956–), *Dororo* (1967–), and *Ludwig B.* (1987–).

*Nhu-Hoa Nguyen*

**THOR.** Based on the Norse mythological character of the same name and originally adapted into comics by the **Marvel Comics** creative team of **Stan Lee**, Larry Lieber, and **Jack Kirby**, Thor made his debut in the pages of *Journey into Mystery* #83 in 1962. The son of Odin, ruler of Asgard (realm of the Gods) and Gaea, protector of Midgard (realm of Earth), Thor was banished to Earth and forced to inhabit the mortal body of Donald Blake, a physically impaired medical doctor, without any memory of his true identity. After discovering his past on a vacation to Norway, Blake is able to transform into Thor, and back again, at will with the help of Mjolnir, Thor's mystical war hammer given to him by his father. As the God of Thunder, Thor has the power to create and control weather phenomena, including rain, wind, and lighting. After centuries of practice he is also highly skilled in hand-to-hand combat and, with the help of Mjolnir, can fly as well as open inter-dimensional portals, among other abilities. Since his introduction, Thor has continuously proven to be one of the most powerful characters in the Marvel universe, drawing on the magical Odinforce in battles against mortal, superhuman, mythological, and cosmic villains. Thor is also a founding member of The **Avengers** and regularly appears in major Marvel universe crossover events.

Writers and artists have been able to utilize the richly complex stories within Norse mythology to propel Marvel's version of the character. The primary conflicts within the *Thor* narrative explore the tension between Thor's allegiance to Asgard and his innate desire to protect Earth from harm. Often compounding this strain is Thor's step-brother Loki, a shapeshifting master of dark magic who desires to rule Asgard as his own. Other Asgardian characters, such as Balder, Thor's lifelong friend; Heimdall, guardian sentry of Asgard; Tyr, Asgardian God of War; and Sif, Thor's sometimes love interest, offer the narrative ample amounts of depth and breadth in storytelling options. Perhaps desirous of even more storytelling freedom, Lee and Kirby made several additions to Asgardian lore throughout their tenure on the book; notably absent in the original mythology, The Warriors Three—consisting of Fandral, Hogun, and Volstagg—were introduced in *Journey into Mystery* #119 in 1965 and have since played a popular supporting role within broader story arcs.

Like Thor's family, friends, and allies, many of his enemies are drawn from mythology as well. Fire demon Surtur, frost giant Ymir, and the Midgard Serpent all make appearances as the most powerful enemies of Asgard, with new Lee and Kirby creations the Mangog (*Thor* [Vol. 1] #154) and the Enchanters Three (*Thor* [Vol. 1] #143) also testing Thor's might. Besides these mythological creatures, however, Thor has developed several other foes on Earth, including Radioactive Man (*Journey into Mystery* #93) and the Wrecking Crew (*Thor* [Vol. 1] #304). Thor's most dire threats have come from villains empowered by the trickster Loki. These include the Absorbing Man (*Journey*

Thor. Marvel Comics/Photofest

*into Mystery* #114), the Destroyer (*Journey into Mystery* #118), and the Wrecker (*Thor* #148).

Despite his immense power, Thor has, at several different times, taken leaves of absence from his superheroic duties, opening the door for other characters to wield Mjolnir and channel the Thunder God's strength. Because only worthy souls can even lift Thor's hammer from the ground, however, the list of substitutes was very short until the 1980s, when Beta Ray Bill (*Thor* [Vol. 1] #337), Tyr (*Thor* [Vol. 1] #355), **Captain America** (*Thor* [Vol. 1] #390), and Eric Masterson (*Thor* [Vol. 1] #433) all took control of Mjolnir for short periods of time. Beta Ray Bill, an alien warrior originally created by writer-artist **Walt Simonson** in 1983, proved so worthy that Odin eventually gave Bill his own mystical war hammer named Stormbreaker, a weapon equal in power to Mjolnir.

Jack Kirby's vision of Thor was tangibly different than his work on other Marvel strips. The grandiosity of Asgard was a challenge to Kirby; unlike outer space environments, he had to craft not only power and immensity but an environment of elegance and profundity. Kirby's eclectic take on medieval Norse God garb was a colorful patchwork of latex and leather, with characters so multi-colored their costumes seemed more Asian than Germanic. He found the perfect complement in the work of inker Vince Colletta, whose clean, light line lifted Kirby's work from gruff superhero pounding to beautiful, atmospheric poetry. Where the **Hulk** smashed, Thor grasped in an elegant set of moves that were lovingly conveyed.

In addition to the long formative run by writer Lee and artist Kirby, *Thor* has had the privilege of being crafted by some of the comic book industry's most venerable creators. Writers Gerry Conway, Len Wein, Tom DeFalco, Dan Jurgens, and Michael Avon Oeming—among others—have all made contributions to the title, with artists John Buscema, **Neal Adams**, Keith Pollard, and Ron Frenz having given visual shape to the Thunder God throughout his publication history. One of the most notable runs in the series, however, was Simonson's critically acclaimed tenure on the book as writer and artist from *Thor* (Vol. 1) #337–67. He stayed on the title as a writer—and sometimes artist—until issue #382.

Though Simonson's groundbreaking run on *Thor* is considered to be the definitive take on the character after the Lee/Kirby run, several other story arcs have made lasting impressions on fans. "The Eternals Saga," an epic tale spanning 28 issues (*Thor Annual* #7 and *Thor* [Vol. 1] #284–300) follows Thor as he learns about the Eternals and Deviants, genetically engineered superhuman races, and their cosmic creators the Celestials. "The Dark Gods" takes place after the major Marvel crossover event "Heroes Reborn" and chronicles Thor's search for his fellow Asgardians, who have mysteriously gone missing (*Thor* [Vol. 2] #1–13). The "Ragnarok" story arc sees the mythological end of Asgard come to bear, with Thor and his allies locked in a fateful battle they know they will lose (*Thor* [Vol. 2] #80–85).

Marking Thor's return to the Marvel universe, the most recent run in the series (*Thor* Vol. 3) has been written by **J. Michael Straczynski** with pencils from Olivier Coipel. It brings with it a dramatic re-imagining of the Thor mythos, as Thor must rebuild Asgard after the decimation caused by Ragnarok. With Odin gone, the return of Donald Blake, Asgard transported to rural Oklahoma, and Loki taking a female form, the current run is staking ground as a significant extension and modification of *Thor's* narrative history.

*Joshua Plencner*

**300.** **Frank Miller's** retelling of the Spartan battle of Thermopylae in 480 B.C., *300* was first published in 1998 as a limited edition comic book series from **Dark Horse Comics**, and later released as a trade paperback. Here, Miller, as artist and writer, and Lynn Varley, as colorist, undertake a major challenge of recounting the past: the ability to interweave historical fact with a narrative that is compelling enough for readers to accept the tale as reality.

In the opening salvo of *300*, "Chapter One: Honor," readers are introduced to the Spartana: resilient, harsh, skilled, and loyal combatants. Spartan warriors are the ultimate warriors. As a band of Spartans settle in for the night, they tell tales of battles long past and the heroic adventures of their king, Leonidas, and then drift off to sleep. As they rest, King Leonidas reminisces about the events of the past year, beginning with the sudden arrival of a messenger from King Xerxes of Persia. The messenger sought out the King of Sparta, asking him to capitulate to the Persian Empire. The answer, predictably, is not good for the messenger and his fate is sealed in the depths of a bottomless pit.

"Chapter Two: Duty" finds Leonidas thinking back upon his visit to the Ephors, the priests to the "Old Gods." From these seers he seeks wisdom and guidance. Upon his return, Leonidas consults the Spartan council and is warned against going to war with Persia. In the end, he defies the council and travels to the Hot Gates (Thermopylae) only to see the Persian fleet's boats wrecked upon the seaside rocks. Leonidas's army is jubilant but he is not, thinking to himself, "The fools. The dear young fools. They actually think we have a chance." In this statement is more than a precursor; it is commentary on the experience of a trained soldier who sees the reality of the real battle still to come. King Leonidas is more than just a leader; in this statement he becomes a seer of sorts, seeing the only true path of what will happen.

Any epic tale needs a diversion. Shakespeare's *Hamlet* had Rosencrantz and Guildenstern. Miller's *300* has Ephialtes, a deformed Spartan whose only desire is to become a Spartan soldier. Interspersed among "Chapter Three: Glory," Miller gives readers a glimpse at Ephialtes's own quest to become a warrior. His resolve, travels, and kills are tame next to the graphic portrayal of Xerxes's scourge of Spartan scouts.

Ephialtes finally arrives at Leonidas's camp and begs him to join the battle, only to be turned down because he is unable to raise his shield high enough to engage in phalanx, a military move that allows Spartans to form a single rectangular unit in order to fight and protect one another with weaponry. Denied, Ephialtes flings himself over the nearby cliff to his death; however, readers learn (later in the chapter) that he survived his fall. Feeling betrayed by the Gods, he forsakes the Spartan life and seeks out Xerxes.

"Chapter Four: Combat" covers the first day of the final battle. Through graphically detailed imagery, readers see the warrior Spartans holding off the Persian army. During a break in the battle, Leonidas goes to meet his enemy. In this meeting, Xerxes offers Leonidas the chance to surrender in exchange for wealth and power. Sarcasm abounds as Leonidas refuses, saying, "But this kneeling business—I'm afraid killing all those slaves of yours has left me with a nasty cramp in my leg. I think I'll walk it off," which he does, leaving Xerxes camp.

A panel from Frank Miller's graphic novel *300*, next to the corresponding scene from the 2007 film by the same name, directed by Zack Snyder. Warner Bros./Photofest

"Chapter Five: Victory" begins on day two of the great battle. The forces engage one another and the death toll rises, all the while the Spartans are holding their own against the Persians. That night, Leonidas realizes this is the end and prepares his army for the finale. Also, Ephilates finds Xerxes and declares loyalty to him.

At the end, surrounded by Persian soldiers, Xerxes offers Leonidas one last chance to capitulate. Hesitant, he falls to his knees but then suddenly lunges his spear at Xerxes, a call to arms for his troops to attack. The Persian king is wounded, but not killed. However, all of the other Spartans are killed on the spot. The last scene in the book is set a year later and Captain Dilios recounts the story of brave Leonidas going into battle, much the same as was done in Chapter One.

The unique shape of the hardback book is wider than it is tall, forcing the reader to engage the artwork in a different way than traditional comics or graphic novels. This double-page spread format also allows Miller and Varley to detail profile shots or illustrate the sweeping battles from varying perspectives, all the while giving the reader an experience akin to that of watching an epic movie on the silver screen. The detailed drawings creep across some spreads, bleeding into various panels. It is, by many standards, a momentous undertaking, not just for the historical nature of the story but also in constructing a believable story around what little is really known.

In 1999, *300* won **Eisner Awards** for "Best Limited Series," "Best Writer/Artist," and "Best Colorist," and also won **Harvey Awards** for "Best Continuing or Limited Series" and "Best Colorist." In 2007, Warner Brothers released *300* to moviegoers worldwide. The film version was applauded for its visually stunning CGI graphics; however it was also criticized for being historically inaccurate and insensitive in its "Orientalist" depiction of Persians.

Between fact and fiction lays the real story of Thermopylae; but that is not the point with Miller and Varley's *300*. Rather, their rendition engages readers on a different, more emotional level not seen in previous works. In this way it brings history alive for readers to experience, right alongside Leonidas and the Spartan army.

*Alec R. Hosterman*

**TIMELY COMICS.** *See* **Marvel Comics**

**TINTIN.** The young investigative reporter Tintin, celebrated for his bravery, quick thinking and positive moral outlook, is perhaps the most recognizable European comic-book hero and was **Hergé**'s most successful creation.

On January 10, 1929 in the pages of *Le Petit Vingtième*, the children's supplement of the Belgian Catholic newspaper *Le Vingtième Siècle*, Tintin began his first adventure accompanied by his white fox terrier Snowy. Over the next five decades, the pair was joined by a large cast of supporting characters, including the bungling detectives Thomson and Thompson, the opera singer Bianca Castafiore, Tintin's fellow adventurer Captain Haddock, and the hard of hearing scientist Professor Calculus—in addition to ruthless villains such as Dr. Müller and Rastapopoulos.

The modern Tintin canon comprises 24 books, from the black-and-white *Tintin in the Land of the Soviets* (1930) to the posthumously issued drafts for *Tintin and Alph-Art* (1978–82). A complex publication history means, however, that this tally of 24 books should be very nearly doubled, as the majority of the stories exist in at least two distinct authorial versions. There were also a number of false starts and abandoned projects for which rough sketches have been preserved. All of the *Tintin* narratives were initially published as serials and later converted into book form (in black-and-white until 1942, and then in color). Graphic conventions and narrative content were significantly influenced by the prerequisites of the serial form.

First, drawings had to be easy to reproduce in print. Hence the contained dynamism of Hergé's "clear line" pen strokes and the simple yet highly effective system of graphic notation—speed lines, sweat droplets, stars, spirals, arabesques—used to depict movement and emotional reactions.

*The Adventures of Tintin: Cigars of the Pharaoh* showing Tintin with his dog, Snowy. Little, Brown & Company/Photofest

Second, each installment had to capture the attention of the reader with a mixture of suspense and entertainment. Hero and reader were driven forward in the face of hostile forces by a certain "will to know," giving heed to both short-range enigmas (revealed from week to week) and the promise of a long-range uncovering of secret information (deferred until the very end). At the same time, compelling depictions of foreign lands provided a note of exoticism while unsettling themes were everywhere held in balance with knockabout routines reminiscent of the *commedia dell'arte*.

As the stories gained in artistic complexity during the 1940s and the 1950s, Hergé increasingly drew inspiration from a personal archive of magazine articles, newspaper cuttings, and a variety of reference books. Borrowings can also be identified from a wide range of classical literature, popular novels, theater, silent cinema and travel writing (some via suggestions from Hergé's friends and collaborators).

Critics occasionally take Hergé to task for his treatment of **race**, gender, and politics, but the books are overwhelmingly positive and little seems to undermine their continued relevance. Indeed, there is something almost universal about Tintin. He is frequently described as a hero without qualities, his ageless neutrality facilitating reader identification, regardless of gender or nationality. While there is certainly some validity to this argument, his more distinctive attributes should not be overlooked.

Above all, Tintin is the personification of a dynamic principle—neatly symbolized by his raised forelock—and expressed through a capacity for purposeful action. Any task, quest, or duty he undertakes is carried through to completion and readers are compelled, at least in imagination, to raise themselves to his level of skill. This goes some way toward explaining the broad and lasting appeal of the series, which has been translated into over 60 languages, and which traces out a fascinating developmental arc.

The early books, from *Tintin in the Land of the Soviets* to *King Ottokar's Sceptre* (1939), serve almost as a play-space within which readers vicariously experience the hero's passage through trials and dangers. Younger readers are thus provided with an opportunity to achieve mastery over common fears and anxieties while safely living out an impulse for adventure.

The intermediate books, from *The Crab with the Golden Claws* (1941) to *Tintin in Tibet* (1960), remain concerned with problem-solving and journeys of discovery—including a mission to the Moon—but are more intricately composed and place a new emphasis on the emerging group of secondary characters. Captain Haddock in particular, raising laughter with his immoderate love of whisky and a unique repertory of extravagant curses, takes on a very prominent role.

The later books, from *The Castafiore Emerald* (1963) to *Tintin and the Picaros* (1976), present a more ironic postmodern *Tintin*, less liked and frequently misunderstood, yet deserving of equal attention. They engage in sophisticated games with the constituent elements of the *Tintin* universe, almost in the manner of experimental fiction, yet at all times within a medium designed to reach a mass audience. The final unfinished adventure, *Tintin and Alph-Art*, would have combined Hergé's two artistic passions: the contemporary art scene and the comic strip world of his fictional hero.

Although Tintin's appearance and behavior undergo changes over the years, he remains at all times a seeker after truth. Hergé, in much the same fashion, continuously aimed at artistic perfection. The original inked sheets bear witness to his refinement and attention to detail, while extensive prepublication materials allow us to reconstruct his working procedures. Large-format preparatory pencil drawings for the last seven books, for example, provide much evidence of the developing work, from the elaboration of alternatives and the working out of compositional problems to last-minute changes of mind (and it is often particularly interesting to discover what Hergé chose not to do).

Notwithstanding the impressive body of secondary literature devoted to *Tintin*, many documents have yet to be studied in detail, most notably Hergé's working papers and a voluminous correspondence (including letters exchanged between Hergé and his publisher). Around 90 percent of Hergé's original artwork is held by the "Studios Hergé." A wide-ranging selection is on display at the Musée Hergé in Belgium, opened in 2009.

**Selected Bibliography:** Farr, Michael. *Tintin: The Complete Companion*. London: John Murray, 2001; Goddin, Philippe. *Hergé: Chronologie d'une œuvre*. 6 vols. Brussels: Moulinsart, 2000–9.

*Raphaël Taylor*

**TOMB OF DRACULA.** The most successful product of **Marvel's horror** revival of the early 1970s, *Tomb of Dracula* was a landmark in the evolution of long-form comic book narratives and is also remembered for introducing the character Blade. From its inception, the **Comics Code** prohibited **vampire** stories, but the controversy over the publication of *Amazing Spider-Man* #96–98 (1971) without the code seal led to a liberalization of the code, one of the results of which was to permit the portrayal of vampires. Marvel was quick to get into this newly available genre: a vampire villain, Morbius, was introduced in *Amazing Spider-Man* #101 (1971), and in 1972 Marvel added an ongoing series, *Tomb of Dracula*, starring literature's most famous vampire. The art assignment for the series was offered to Bill Everett, but **Gene Colan**, a lifelong Dracula fan, convinced **Stan Lee** to give him the job. The series got off to an inauspicious start: by issue #7 it was on its fourth writer, **Marv Wolfman**, and seemed doomed to cancellation. Wolfman thus felt he had a certain degree of creative freedom and chose to write the series in a personal and experimental vein. Unexpectedly, the series became a high seller and lasted 70 issues, ending only when Colan quit due to alleged creative interference by new editor-in-chief Jim Shooter. Following *Tomb of Dracula*'s cancellation, it was briefly restarted as a black-and-white magazine, and Wolfman and Colan revived *Tomb of Dracula* in 1991 as a four-issue miniseries.

Wolfman's only knowledge of Dracula came from Bram Stoker's novel; he was not a fan of horror movies, and his *Tomb of Dracula* bears little resemblance to conventional works in that genre. It is closer to a **superhero** comic in that it focuses on a cast of heroes with unique abilities who struggle against a supervillain. The villain, of course, is Dracula, and the principal heroes include Frank Drake, a descendant of Dracula; Rachel van Helsing, a descendant of Dracula's nemesis Abraham van Helsing; Quincy Harker, the elderly son of another of Dracula's foes, Jonathan Harker; and Blade, one of Marvel's most prominent African American characters, a vigilante whose mother was killed by the vampire Deacon Frost while giving birth to him. However, whereas most superhero comics of the time featured episodic narratives whose premises rarely changed, *Tomb of Dracula* had an overarching and evolving storyline that had been planned out years in advance. The series begins by chronicling the struggle between Dracula and the heroes, but eventually Dracula is killed by the mad scientist Doctor Sun, who seeks to turn the entire human race into vampires, and the heroes are forced to revive Dracula and ally with him against Sun. In the second half of the series, Dracula becomes the head of a Satanic cult, claiming to be the devil, but he gains a new enemy: his newborn son, Janus, who magically ages and is revealed as an agent of Heaven. (Unusually for a Marvel comic, ToD dealt explicitly with **religion** and did so in a notably sensitive way.) Furthermore, its characters underwent significant change over the course of the series—it lacked the "illusion of growth" typical of contemporary Marvel comics. Dracula (based visually on Jack Palance) is a disgusting monster; his lack of thought balloons discourages the reader from identifying with him, whereas Wolfman makes each of Dracula's victims more sympathetic by giving them names and brief biographies. Yet Dracula also has his noble side. As early as issue #22 he saves a woman from her undead abusive husband; his love for Janus and his wife Domini is genuine, and his struggle with Janus convinces him of the superiority of good to evil, to the point where, in #69, he uses a crucifix to defend children from other vampires. Yet Dracula ultimately proves to be beyond redemption, and the monthly series ends with his death. By contrast, the heroes are changed for the worse by their encounters with Dracula. Whereas the heroes in Stoker's novel have mostly altruistic motivations, the chronically depressed Frank fights Dracula only because he has nothing else to do, while Rachel, Quincy, and Blade are motivated by their desire for revenge on the vampires who killed their loved ones. Eventually Quincy sacrifices his life to kill Dracula. Frank and Rachel are thus left with no purpose in life, and their romance proves unsustainable. The series illustrates Nietzsche's aphorism that whoever fights monsters risks becoming a monster. Because *Tomb of Dracula*'s only title character is the villain, the roster of the heroes is subject to change without notice. Other recurring heroes include Quincy's daughter Edith, the mute Indian Taj Nital, the Dracula groupie Aurora Rabinowitz, the vampiric detective Hannibal King, and the hack writer Harold H. Harold, who provides much-needed comic relief.

Wolfman and Colan collaborated on every issue of the series from #7 onward, and Tom Palmer inked every issue starting with #12. Such longevity for a creative team was almost unheard of at the time and perhaps explains why the series is often praised for its consistency. Colan's painterly pencil work is effectively complemented by Palmer's tight inking.

The characters in *Tomb of Dracula* appeared in many later Marvel titles, including **X-Men** *Annual* #6, in which Rachel is turned into a vampire and killed by Wolverine, and the 1992–94 series *Nightstalkers*, which stars Frank, Blade, and King. A 1980 animated movie based on the series was released in Japan but has never received widespread distribution in the United States. A major motion picture based on Blade, starring Wesley Snipes, was released in 1998, becoming a box office success and spawning two sequels (2002, 2004). The film version of Blade bears only a superficial resemblance to the character from the comics, and the film version of Deacon Frost has nothing in common with the comics version but his name. Wolfman sued Marvel in 1998 for ownership of Blade and Frost, but the court found in favor of Marvel, ruling that Marvel's uses of the character were different enough from the original characters that Wolfman could not claim ownership. This decision was viewed by many as a setback for creators' rights.

**Selected Bibliography:** Cooke, Jon B. "Marv Wolfman Interview: Wolfman by Day." *Comic Book Artist* 1(13) (May 2001): 30–47.

*Aaron Kashtan*

**TOM STRONG.** Published between 1999 and 2006, *Tom Strong* is a monthly comic book series created by writer **Alan Moore** and artist Chris Sprouse. The series was one of the initial four monthly titles from the America's Best Comics (ABC) imprint of Wildstorm Comics. Alan Moore—the writer and co-creator of all of the initial ABC comics—was the principal creative force behind the small line of comics. Shortly after Moore, who was given substantial creative freedom, made the deal with **Jim Lee**'s company Wildstorm to publish his books, the publisher was purchased by **DC Comics**, inadvertently making Moore renege on a pledge never to work again with DC. Moore and Sprouse were responsible for most of *Tom Strong's* 36 issues, but several artists and a few writers—including **Ed Brubaker** and **Brian K. Vaughn**—also contributed stories. The series also inspired a 12-issue spin-off, the anthology series *Tom Strong's Terrific Tales*. In 2003, ABC published *The Many Worlds of Tesla Strong*, starring Tom's daughter, Tesla. That year also saw the six-issue miniseries, *Terra Obscura*, which fleshed out the story of a parallel Earth introduced in *Tom Strong*; a second *Terra Obscura* miniseries came the following year. Like the rest of Moore's work with ABC, *Tom Strong* is a genre-bending adventure series that, in this case, merges elements of **superhero** comics with those of comic books' predecessors, pulp fiction, and the adventure novel.

Tom Strong's origin is explained in the first issue, in a story entitled, "How Tom Strong Got Started." His parents are American scientists who, in 1899, locate a supposedly mythical island known as Attabar Teru in the West Indies. Upon arrival, Sinclair Strong assembles "Pneuman," a robotic manservant with prototypical artificial intelligence. Susan is soon impregnated and the couple meets Attabar Teru's other inhabitants, the native Ozu tribe, when some members assist with the delivery of Tom Strong, born in the first year of the 20th century. The Ozu share their customs with the Strongs, including the chewing of the indigenous "goloka root," which promotes vitality and substantially retards the aging process.

The Ozu also allow the Strongs to freely conduct their experiment, which, according to Sinclair Strong, is "to produce a child raised by pure reason, away from society's influence." Young Tom is kept within a pressurized chamber, and administered "progressive schooling" and a vegetarian diet. The experiment is cut short in 1908 when an earthquake devastates the Strongs' laboratory (housed within a dormant volcano), and Tom is orphaned at the age of eight. Removed from his chamber for the first time, Tom Strong spends his formative years under the guidance of the Ozu chief. In 1921, as a brawny and highly scientific young man, Tom decides to finally visit "the world beyond the rainbow mists," with Pneuman as his only companion. Tom travels to his parents' hometown, the fictional American metropolis Millennium City, where he instantly becomes a celebrity as a savior from the city's colorful criminals. Of these flamboyant "science villains," the most notable—and persistent—is the evil Paul Saveen, an enemy cast in both the "mad scientist" and "gentleman crook" molds. Tom eventually returns to Attabar Teru in order to marry the Ozu tribe's princess, Dhalua, making them one of the relatively few interracial couples in mainstream comics, and they produce a daughter, Tesla.

Tom's adventures in Millennium City continue over the course of the century. The family frequently returns to Attabar Teru, but lives primarily in "The Stronghold," a massive skyscraper in Millennium City that functions as residence, laboratory, and fortress; as philanthropists and heroes, the Strongs become the city's biggest celebrities. The regenerative effects of the goloka root keep the Strong family youthful and vital, even on the verge of Tom's centennial birthday. In addition to the Strong family and Pneuman, the regular cast of *Tom Strong* also includes the "educated ape," King Solomon, an intelligent, articulate gorilla with the manners and accent of an Edwardian England gentleman; Tesla's boyfriend Val, the exiled prince of a subterranean society; as well as Timmy Turbo and a handful of pre-pubescent members of Tom's fan club, the Strongmen of America. Frequent flashback scenes, and references to past adventures that go largely unexplained, give the impression of a fully realized world with a rich history.

Moore has said that the premise behind *Tom Strong* was to imagine contemporary comic books if the popularity of **Superman** had not instigated the superhero genre; therefore, *Tom Strong's* cultural ancestors are pulp fiction and popular adventure novels from the early 20th century. However, although Tom Strong's "scientist-adventurer" persona suggests **Doc Savage** and his origin seems undoubtedly influenced by **Tarzan**, *Tom Strong* is still steeped in the tropes and history of superhero comics. In many ways, the foundational model for *Tom Strong* is the pulp adventure, upon which Moore then grafts superhero elements. The superhero genre provides inspiration for stories that involve Strong's analogue Tom Strange, versions of the Strong family from parallel dimensions, and alternate timelines. Additionally, Moore uses frequent flashbacks to evoke not only the character's long life, but also *Tom Strong's* nonexistent publication history, and the types of adventures Tom has at various points in his 100-year biography roughly correspond to the trends in superhero comics at that particular historical moment. In fact, many *Tom Strong* covers are parodies of those of famous superhero comics throughout the decades. Yet, Moore also manipulates superhero conventions. For example, although the Strongs have physical encounters with their enemies, the ultimate resolutions are generally peaceful and brought about by compromise.

Strong characterization and clever storytelling makes *Tom Strong* notable, but the potency of the series is in its playful demonstration of the power of fiction. While still maintaining consistent—as well as relatively mature and sophisticated—characterization, Moore uses *Tom Strong* as a vehicle for a wide range of stories, including lighthearted adventures, tense action-thrillers, melodrama, quirky **science fiction**, and **satire**. Many fans who expected a straightforward adventure series bristled at the drastic fluctuations of tone, but, in doing so, Moore highlights fiction's flexibility and adaptability, qualities that are particularly potent in comics. Without disrupting the basic integrity of either, Tom Strong the character, and *Tom Strong* the series, can exist and operate in a nearly infinite variety of ways—depending on context, subject matter, authorial intention, and reader's response—and Moore seems determined to demonstrate that Tom Strong can succeed, in different ways and for varying purposes, in every milieu and genre. Representative of all fiction, *Tom Strong* (and Tom Strong) is a vehicle for the expression of ideas: stable enough to maintain coherence, yet malleable enough to serve any number of possible artistic purposes and styles.

*Jackson Ayres*

**TOTH, ALEX** (1928–2006). Alexander "Alex" Toth was an American writer, penciller, inker, colorist, letterer, and cover artist. Although remembered more for his time as a character and art designer for the Hanna-Barbera Animation Studios (designing characters like Space Ghost, Birdman, and Jonny Quest), Toth was an acclaimed comic book artist who is also remembered for his introduction of adult design while drawing the comic book based on Disney's *Zorro* television series, and for redesigning **DC**'s stable of **superhero** characters for the extremely popular *Super Friends* television series. While not a household name, Toth was, in the words of *Comics Journal* editor Gary Groth, "among the greatest comic book artists ever . . . an artist's artist, just because of his mastery of the form. And though not particularly popular among general comic book readers, every cartoonist who cared deeply about [. . .] craft learned something by looking at [Toth's] work" (Hevesi 2006).

Toth was born in Manhattan to a father who worked as a printer. He graduated from the High School of Industrial Arts and was taken under the wing of Milton Caniff, the creator of the comic strip *Terry and the Pirates*. Because of his apprenticeship with Caniff, Sheldon Mayer, an editor at DC Comics, hired Toth in 1947 to work on **Green Lantern**, **The Flash**, The Atom, and *Dr. Mid-Nite*. Over the next two decades, he developed a sparse style, employing sharp contrasts through working for DC and as the "ghost" illustrator of Warren Tufts's *Casey Ruggles*, a realistic strip set during the California Gold Rush of 1849. Not being allowed to create and design his own characters, Toth left DC and moved to California in 1952 to start a career with Standard Comics.

Toth was drafted into the military in 1954 and served in Tokyo, where he wrote and drew a weekly adventure strip, *Jon Fury*, for a military base paper. After returning to the United States in 1956, he got a job with Dell Comics and was selected to work on the comic book series based on the Walt Disney Company's television series, *Zorro*.

In 1960, Toth left Dell to work as an art director in animation because he was beginning to see the comic book industry as too interested in producing violent products. 1961 was his breakout year in television animation, as he was offered a job with the Hanna-Barbera Company. At Hanna-Barbera, he was able to create his own line of superheroes, as well as re-design the **Fantastic Four** for their first television series in 1967.

During the 1970s, Toth returned to DC Comics with the short-lived series *Hot Wheels*. He created the character Jesse Bravo, a daredevil pilot, for the comic book *Bravo for Adventure*. In 1973, Toth became art director on Hanna-Barbera's *Super Friends*, an effort to bring the DC characters to the children of the 1970s,

Toth died on May 27, 2006, at his home in Burbank, California at the age of 77. According to his son, Eric, he died of heart failure while at his drawing board.

**Selected Bibliography:** Hevesi, Dennis. "Alex Toth, 77, Comic Book Artist, and 'Space Ghost' Animator, Dies." *The New York Times* (June 6, 2006), http://www.nytimes.com/2006/06/06/arts/design/06toth.html?scp=1&sq=Alex%20Toth&st=cse; http://www.comicbookdb.com/creator.php?ID=151;http://http://www.twomor rows.com/comicbookartist/articles/11toth.html.

*Jason Gallagher*

**TRANSMETROPOLITAN.** A 60-issue series published initially by the Helix imprint and later by the Vertigo imprint of **DC Comics** and written by **Warren Ellis** with art by Darick Robertson, *Transmetropolitan* is the story of gonzo journalist Spider Jerusalem in an unnamed postmodern city of the future. The series began publication in 1997 and ended with the publication of *Transmetropolitan* #60 in 2002. Besides the series proper, two stand-alone, one-shot stories have also been published: *Transmetropolitan: I Hate It Here* (2000) and *Transmetropolitan: Filth of the City* (2001). These contain excerpted columns by Spider Jerusalem as illustrated by a number of comics artists. Also, two short stories were published in the anthologies *Vertigo: Winter's Edge II* ("Edgy Winter") and *Vertigo: Winter's Edge III* ("Next Winters"). *Transmetropolitan* has also been released in a series of collections as well.

*Transmetropolitan* chronicles the return of Jerusalem to a future megalopolis simply known as the City. His return from the mountain retreat that has been his home for the preceding five years only occurs under the threat of lawsuit from his former publisher. The first year of the series follows Spider as he irritates the local government and reacquaints himself with the City in the company of his "filthy assistants," Channon Yarrow and Yelana Rossini. The second year sees Spider, whose original fame and fortune were due to his coverage of the previous presidential election, forced to cover politics as another presidential election campaign grinds on. His rare and genuine affection for Dr. Vita Severn, Political Director for Senator Gary Callahan, leads to a backhanded endorsement from Spider of Callahan, whom he refers to as the Smiler. Spider later exposes Callahan's running mate, though, as having been grown in a "bastard farm" within the last two years by an extreme fascist wing of Callahan's party. While Callahan's ratings plummet, the approval rating of Severn remain extremely high, and as she is about to address the press to answer Spider's charges, she is assassinated on the orders of Callahan. The sympathy vote for Callahan wins him not only his party's nomination, but ultimately the presidency. Over the course of the next few years, Spider, with the help of his "filthy assistants," finally amasses enough evidence to expose Callahan as a murderer and bring down his presidency.

*Transmetropolitan* contains many postmodern elements. Commodification, loss of historical sense, waning of affect, and fragmentation are all readily illustrated by the City. Ellis quickly establishes the City as a postmodern consumer heaven/hell where anything and everything is for sale. Denizens of the city can buy virtually anything, including Ebola Cola, bowel disruptors, dolphin steaks, trained attack cancers that grow on faces, packets of fresh baby seal eyes, powdered children, both temporary and permanent body modification, and air Jesus sports shoes that enable the wearer to walk on water, to name only a small sample. Everything is a commodity, and everything is for sale. Spider also notes that City dwellers seem to live more in the present "because it's difficult to refer back to the past." This loss of historicity is another symptom of the postmodern condition. Humanity has also become a relative term, with some deciding to become half alien, others becoming cyborgs, and some even becoming "foglets," which are billions of tiny machines that float in the air. Yet Ellis keeps them all recognizably human in their behavior. Oddly enough, though, even with all this technological progress, the City is still saturated with religion, although in a highly fragmented way: it has "one new religion invested every hour" (*Transmetropolitan* #6).

Ellis utilizes *Transmetropolitan* as a vehicle to satirize media, politics, **religion**, marketing, and consumer capitalism, among many other subjects. The dark humor injected into the series, however, only serves to balance the stories of very real suffering that happen every day in the City. Spider may be a loathsome person, but he does believe in the truth, and it is this unwavering belief that drives him to confront President Callahan.

*Will Allred*

**UNDERGROUND AND ADULT COMICS.** Commonly referred to as "**comix**," underground comics are a form of outsider comics art characterized by one or more of the following: counter-culture ideology, irreverence, and depictions of drug use, graphic sex, and other subject matters usually taboo in comic books. Because they are usually self-published or published by a small press, these comics manifest an artistic freedom and personal vision seldom found in mainstream comic books.

Across the United States, creative and unconventional young people who had grown up reading the genre fantasies mass produced by the East Coast comic book industry began to make their own comics with an aesthetic derived from sources as diverse as **Harvey Kurtzman's EC Comics**, Rick Griffin's surfer magazine cartoons, Robert Williams's dragster illustrations, and even the t-shirt designs of Big Daddy Roth. The content and even the style of the artwork were a conscious rebellion against **Comics Code** Authority restrictions, editorial policies, and genre formulas of traditional comic books. They did not compete with traditional comic books on the newsstands, but developed a distribution system of alternative bookstores, record stores, and head shops. These convention-defying, politically charged, and independently produced comic books eventually became widely known as *underground comix*.

The underground comix movement is strongly associated with San Francisco, but it has roots in Texas, Cleveland, Wisconsin, New York, and possibly Tijuana. There is no proof that any of the crude little sex comics that began appearing in the 1930s and became know as Eight-Pagers or Tijuana Bibles were actually produced in Tijuana. The creators of these wallet-sized sex romps had to be much more underground than the comix artists of the 1960s and 70s, because the eight-pagers were illegal due to both obscenity violations and copyright infringement. The Tijuana Bibles depicted, in graphic detail, celebrities, political figures, or fictional characters using obscene language and enjoying a wide variety of sex acts, most of which were illegal at the time. By far the favorite subjects were characters from the newspaper comic strips. By the 1950s, the eight-pagers were rare artifacts and most of the underground comix creators were probably only vaguely aware of them as anti-authoritarian ancestors. More direct influences were the early *Mad* and even the outrageously gruesome and occasionally politically subversive **horror** and **science fiction** comics of the 1950s, done by creators who were more likely to have been exposed to the Tijuana Bibles.

Some of those influential creators might have also been exposed to the so-called kinky comics that developed in the subculture of sexual fetishism. One of the pioneers of these comics was John Alexander Scott Coutts, who changed his name to John Willie when he moved to New York in the mid-1940s and began publishing the bondage and fetish magazine *Bizarre*. Willie's bondage comic "Sweet Gwendoline" was serialized in *Bizarre* during the late 1940s, reprinted by Irving Klaw in the 1950s, and collected in a graphic novel in 1958. Fetish entrepreneur Irving Klaw also serialized the bondage comics of Gene Bilbrew (Eneg), Eric Stanton, and others in his *Movie Star News* magazine during the 1950s and published some of their collected stories in book form through his Nutrix imprint. These kinky comics were not widely available and more people knew them by reputation than ever saw one. However, they did establish a tradition of drawing taboo sexual practices that a number of underground cartoonists gleefully continued.

The tap root of the undergrounds goes back to **William Gaines**'s infamous EC line that included *Vault of Horror*, *Crime SuspenStories*, and *Mad*. For approximately five years the EC writers and artists crafted tightly plotted, but lurid, short stories that delighted their adolescent fans (including virtually all of the future underground cartoonists) and shocked polite society. The gore, violence, sensuality, and occasional political commentary of these works strained against and often violated the boundaries of what was considered good taste until EC became the primary target of the of the wrath of censors in the form of the Comics Code Authority (CCA). When most of Gaines's titles were denied code approval and distributors refused to carry them, EC stayed afloat on the back of one title—*Mad*, which shifted to a magazine format and thus moved outside the purview of the code.

Most of the pioneer underground cartoonists cite the Kurtzman-edited *Mad* magazine as a major influence on their consciousness and their style. Kurtzman left EC in 1956 due to a dispute with Gaines over control of *Mad*. After two failed attempts to start his own humor magazine (*Trump* and *Humbug*, both in 1957), Kurtzman had a remarkable five-year run editing and doing much of the writing for *Help!*, a magazine with even more aggressive and risqué humor than he had employed in *Mad*. Kurtzman not only foreshadowed the content of the soon to emerge underground comix, but he provided encouragement and a taste of publication to future comix superstars **Robert Crumb**, Jay Lynch, Gilbert Shelton, and Skip Williamson in the amateur section of *Help!*.

It is difficult to identify when and where the first underground comic book was "published," but a strong case can be made for Austin, Texas, as the birthplace of underground comix. In the fall of 1962, Gilbert Shelton took over as editor of *Texas Ranger* humor magazine at the University of Texas in Austin. The adventures of Shelton's superhero parody, Wonder Wart-Hog, appeared in all but one of the issues Shelton edited and became the first underground comix "hit." Just weeks before his *Texas Ranger* debut, the "hog of steel" was presented to a national audience in the pages of *Help!*, and via a profile in *Mademoiselle* magazine. Shelton, Jack Jackson, and Tony Bell began publishing *The Austin Iconoclastic Newsletter* (known simply as *THE*) in 1964. Six of the seven issues contained a one-page Frank Stack comic, "The Adventures of J" (the name Jesus was spelled out in the seventh installment). Shelton collected about a dozen of the Jesus strips in a photocopied 14-page comic book that he distributed to friends in Austin. The fifth issue of *THE* advertised *God Nose Adult Comix* by Jack Jackson, but signed **Jaxon**. Jackson's friends in the state capital print shop ran off 1,000 copies of the 42-page *God Nose* comic book. In 1968, the underground newspaper *The Austin Rag* published the first of Shelton's comics about The Fabulous Furry Freak Brothers, who would eventually become the best known and most widely marketed characters from the underground comix.

Underground newspapers such as the *East Village Other* and the *Berkeley Barb* began appearing in the mid-1960s. Robert Crumb turned to the underground newspapers as a promising venue for his LSD-inspired creations of 1967 (including Mr. Natural, Eggs Ackley, and Angelfood McSpade). The Philadelphia-based underground newspaper *Yarrowstalks* published a couple of Crumb's strips in its first two issues during the summer of 1967. It was underground newspaper publisher Don Donahue who paid for printing 5,000 copies of Crumb's **Zap** *Comix* #1. Donahue sold the majority of the print run to Third World Distribution from where the books went to head shops and record stores across the nation.

With issue #2, *Zap* became an anthology and provided an outlet for the talents of Manuel "Spain" Rodriguez, Victor Moscoso, Rick Griffin, and **S. Clay Wilson.** *Zap* inspired Jay Lynch and Skip Williamson to convert their humor magazine, *The Chicago Mirror*, to *Bijou Funnies*, a comix anthology that published some of the early work of **Art Spiegelman.**

A very stoned Ron Turner encountered a copy of *Zap* and was inspired to create a benefit comic book, *Slow Death Funnies*, for an ecology center in Berkeley. The ecology center did not care for the comic, but with the help of Gary Arlington, proprietor of the San Francisco Comic Book Company, Turner sold enough copies that he began running Last Gasp Eco-Funnies out of his garage. **Trina Robbins** convinced Turner to publish *It Ain't Me, Babe*, the first all-women produced comic book. Robbins helped form the wimmen's comix collective, which, beginning in 1972, produced seven issues of *Wimmen's Comix* for Last Gasp. Another significant title from Last Gasp was Justin Green's **Binky Brown Meets the Virgin Mary**, the inspiration for many of the autobiographical **alternative** comics of the following decades. Turner also began to distribute other publishers' books, such as the 1971 *Air Pirate Funnies* with a parody of Disney characters that embroiled Dan O'Neill and his fellow Air Pirates in a decade-long legal battle.

As a comix scene developed in the wake of *Zap*, it was only natural that it gravitated toward the counter-culture center, San Francisco. In the summer of 1968, Shelton packed up his old Plymouth, headed west and joined Jackson, Dave Moriaty, Fred Todd, Janis Joplin, and other transplanted Texas who were becoming known around San Francisco as the "Texas Mafia." When the Texas Mafia bought a used printing press in hopes of printing rock posters for fellow University of Texas dropout Chet Helms's Family Dog Production, it was the beginning of Rip Off Press, which quickly became a major publisher of underground comix, publishing such titles as *Hydrogen Bomb Funnies* and *Freak Brothers*.

Before Rip Off Press, The Print Mint was the dominant publisher of underground comix. Their large print runs and practice of paying royalties to the artists for every edition made it possible for some cartoonists to make a living from their comix. However, as more cartoonists questioned the aesthetic judgment and accounting practices of The Print Mint, other publishers entered the underground scene. When Wisconsin-based cartoonist Denis Kitchen became disgruntled with The Print Mint he started **Kitchen Sink** Enterprises in conjunction with Krupp Comic Works in 1970.

At the peak of the underground phenomenon in 1973, there were over 300 comix titles in print; a Comix Convention was held in Berkeley, and it was not unusual for a book to sell 40,000 copies, and the most popular titles achieved six-figure circulation. Yet, by the mid-1970s, the death rattle of underground comix was unmistakable. With the end of the conflict in Vietnam, youth subculture was no longer galvanized by the anti-war movement, and by the mid-1970s many former flower children had started families, taken jobs, and were paying mortgages. They were less receptive to the counter-culture messages of the underground comix. The informal distribution system was also under siege. The 1973 Supreme Court ruling in Miller vs. California reaffirmed that obscenity was not protected by the First Amendment and made it more dangerous to sell the more explicit underground material. As more states attempted to make it against the law to sell drug paraphernalia, many of the head shops that sold underground comix were forced out of business.

Even the creators themselves were changing. The informal cartoonists' cooperatives of the late 1960s had become publishing companies, and the subculture had become an industry, with less distance from and less revulsion for mainstream comics. Hoping to tap into the underground market, **Marvel** publisher **Stan Lee** convinced Denis Kitchen to edit the 1974 *Comix Book* for Marvel. *Comix Book* featured work from top underground talents, but because the stories were too tame for the underground audience and too bizarre for the mainstream fans, Marvel only published three issues before Kitchen Sink took over publication for the final two issues.

Both the revolutionary and risqué aspects of underground comix were continued, at least to some degree, by former underground cartoonists taking subgenres of the underground comix to new audiences, by comics in a magazine format that allowed more freedom, and by a new distribution model that circumvented the Comics Code and encouraged independent publishers. Most recently, the Internet has become an important vehicle for the on-line distribution of these successors to the underground comix.

Tijuana Bibles sometimes featured gay or lesbian orgies, but the GLBT comic book genre began with underground comix such as *Come Out Comix* (1972), *Dynamite Damsels* (1976), and *Gay Heart Throbs* (1976). In 1980 Howard Cruse edited the *Gay Comix* anthology for Kitchen Sink. The anthology not only featured the work of pioneering underground cartoonists such as Mary Wings, Roberta Gregory, and Trina Robbins, but also provided an outlet for the work of up-and-coming cartoonists such as Donna Barr and Sam Kieth. Cruse only edited the first four issues, but the anthology continued for 25 issues and helped insure that transgressive comic book work survived beyond the demise of the underground. For example, in 1991 Roberta Gregory introduced Midge or Bitchy Bitch in *Naughty Bits* and Diane DiMassa began combining outrageous violence and dry wit in *The Hothead Paison*.

Comic books by lesbian, gay, bisexual, and transgender creators have matured in content and have found an audience far beyond the GLBT community. Some of the most critically acclaimed graphic novels have been produced by GLBT cartoonists. Howard Cruse spent years crafting the semi-autobiographical graphic novel **Stuck Rubber Baby** that was eventually published by **DC**'s Paradox Press imprint in 1995. Alison Bechdel's **Fun Home** was a finalist for the 2006 National Book Critics Circle Award and *The Guardian* included *Fun Home* in its list of 1,000 novels everyone must read.

There were a handful of underground comix, for instance the earliest offerings of Turner's Last Gasp Eco-Funnies, that were intended to educate about and advocate for social issues. Some of these works were no doubt an inspiration to Leonard Rifas when he put together *All Atomic Comics* in 1976. Rifas established EduComics and also pursued other projects, such as *Corporate Crime Comics* and *Tobacco Comics* that went beyond the visceral anti-establishment attitude of underground comix to make reasoned attacks on hegemonic institutions. In 1980, Seth Toboman and Peter Kuper channeled the ideological spirit of the underground comix when they created the activist anthology *World War 3 Illustrated*.

Except as an object of parody, undergrounds generally eschewed genre fiction, but even as the underground comix movement was getting underway there were comics in magazine format that combined mainstream genres with the more prurient aspects of the undergrounds. The **horror**, **science fiction**, and **fantasy** magazines published by **Warren Publications**, Skywald, and others contained little of the social commentary of the underground comix, but because magazines were not subject to the restrictions of the Comics Code Authority, they provided plenty of nudity and gore. Warren's first magazine comics anthology, *Creepy*, appeared in 1964, followed two years later by *Eerie*; the erotic *Vampirella* debuted in 1969. At the end of 1970, Skywald entered the magazine comic book market with *Nightmare*. Also in the 1970s, Marvel launched an array of fantasy and horror comics, such as *Savage Tales* and *Tales of the Zombie*, containing material that could not have received code approval.

In 1977 *National Lampoon Presents French Comics (the Kind Men Like)* introduced **European comics** erotica to an American audience. It also tested the waters for their launch of **Heavy Metal**, an American version of the French magazine *Métal Hurlant*, later that year. Inspired by the best of the American underground comix, *Metal Hurlant*, which debuted in 1974, offered wildly imaginative science fiction and fantasy in comics form. Early issues of *Heavy Metal* relied heavily on reprints of material from the European magazine, but soon had home-grown content, including the lushly rendered sex and violence of Richard Corben.

Comic book writer and entrepreneur George Caragonne, along with Mark McClellan, sold *Penthouse* publisher Bob Guccione on the idea of *Penthouse Comix*. The title was launched in 1994 and ran for 33 issues. Guccione's subsequent adult comix titles, *Men's Adventure Comix*, *Omni Comix*, and *Penthouse Max*, only lasted a matter of months. Penthouse paid top rates and attracted talent such as Richard Corben, Gray Morrow, Adam Hughes, and Arthur Suydam.

The advent of the direct market distribution of comic books in the 1970s allowed independents, alternatives, and even a few of the residual undergrounds to be sold side-by-side with mainstream comics in comic book specialty stores. Comic books distributed through the direct market did not have to carry the Comics Code seal that was required on newsstand comics, and the comics specialty shops attracted an adult clientele. These conditions encouraged the emergence of independent publishers who provided edgier content. One of the earliest and most significant of these independent publications was Mike Friedrich's *Star\*Reach* anthology that debuted in 1974. It was considered a ground level comic, a blending of the mainstream and the underground. *Star\*Reach* allowed mainstream creators such as **Walt Simonson**, Jim Starlin and **Howard Chaykin** to produce work that mainstream publishers would have found unacceptable, but the result was generally no more radical that what was appearing in Marvel's black and white magazines—genre adventures with a few topless women.

However, Chaykin, perhaps stimulated by this taste of freedom, went on to create comics more reminiscent of the underground comix. He shocked mainstream audiences with his suggestive **American Flagg!** comic, but his 1988 erotic noir miniseries *Black Kiss*, with its dark comedy and explicit sex, became one of the most controversial comic books of the decade. The 1980s and 1990s were decades in which sex comics proliferated. In 1984, Larry Welz began *Cherry Poptart* (later simply *Cherry*), a sex-filled and **satire** laced series drawn in the style of **Archie** comics. The title was first published by Last Gasp, later by Tundra and Kitchen Sink, and eventually self-published by Welz. Former exotic dancer Sylvie Rancourt and artist Jacques Boivin teamed to create *Melody: The True Story of a Nude Dancer*, which was published by Kitchen Sink beginning in 1988. When **Fantagraphics** was in financial trouble in 1990, Groth funded his literary comics with an Eros line of comics that offered every aspect of erotica, from virtually plotless sex romps, to hardcore bondage and discipline, to parody. Also in the early 1990s, rocker Glenn

Danzig's Verotik line of comics offered characters ranging from demonesses to zombie hookers in a heady mix of horror and sex.

The first publisher specializing in graphic novels, the New York based NBM, began publishing European albums in English in 1976. The Eurotica imprint brought the erotic work of Milo Manara, Georges Pichard, and other Europeans to American audiences. The Amerotica imprint has had limited offerings, but did publish Michael Manning's S&M hit *The Spider Garden*. NBM also issued trade paperback collections of works such as Reed Waller and Kate Worley's **"Omaha," the Cat Dancer**, a soap opera with anthropomorphic characters engaged in abundant and graphically depicted sex. Omaha first appeared in a strip in the 1978 anthology *Vootie*, became a series issued sporadically by a variety of publishers, and the finale of the story was serialized in NBM's erotic anthology *Sizzle* beginning in 2006.

Japanese comics (**manga**) with a sexual aspect had been around for decades, but comic books referred to as *ecchi*, for the milder form, and *hentai*, for the more perverse works, became something of a phenomenon in Japan during the 1970s. For some time only the most dedicated manga fans outside Japan knew about these comics, but as scans became available online erotic manga gained a following worldwide. The Internet has allowed for a proliferation of readily available sex comics. Content ranges from those sites like Dirty Comics that offer single character titles, such as *Chicas*, created by a single cartoonist, to online "publishers" like Adult Comics that offer half a dozen different titles by a variety of creators to Comixxx Archive with hundreds of comics, some original and some scanned from print comics. On the darker side there are the extreme S&M comics offered on sites like DOComics, which began as a marketing tool for the printed fetish comics of Gary Roberts, Tempelton, and others, but like many online comics sites, has begun selling only electronic PDF versions of the comics.

Even mainstream creators began to push the boundaries and find varying degrees of freedom from the constraints of the Comics Code. Following the popularity of Marvel's **Conan the Barbarian**, which debuted in 1970, fantasy comics emerged as a popular genre. Fantasy comics always contained an erotic element that ranged from chain mail bikinis in traditional format publications, to full frontal nudity, in magazine format. Marvel's *Red Sonja* was mildly titillating, but artist Frank Thorne left the Red Sonja book to create his own warrior woman, Ghita, who was prone to lose her chainmail bikini and fight topless or nude. During the 1980s he did a *Li'l Abner* parody, *Moonshine McJuggs*, for *Playboy* and created a couple of hardcore erotic series, *The Iron Devil* and *The Devil's Angel*.

Mature content in the mainstream has been most evident at DC Comics. When DC began the Vertigo imprint the titles were crafted not merely for adult readers, but for sophisticated readers. Sex and violence were plentiful in some of the titles, but it never seemed gratuitous. The protagonists in **Preacher** have hearty sexual appetites and the villains engage in a wide range of sexual deviance. *The Extremist* presents an adventure set in a highly fictionalized version of San Francisco's fetish scene. However, it was the moral dilemmas, fascinating characters, and clever storytelling that attracted readers to these and other Vertigo titles. The books under the Marvel Max imprint and the occasional adult title from **Image Comics**, such as the tongue-in-cheek adventures of a super-powered prostitute in *The Pro*, often seemed sophomoric compared to the Vertigo books. As DC and Marvel tested the boundaries of what was allowable during the 1970s and 1980s, the code was repeatedly relaxed. Eventually, it became irrelevant. Marvel opted out in 2001, and DC only submits selected titles intended for young readers.

Kitchen Sink, Last Gasp and Rip Off Press survived beyond the 1970s by diversifying their offerings, including reprinting classic comics material and publishing the emerging alternative comics. The underground comix tradition has been most directly sustained by the alternative comics that began to appear in the mid-1970s as underground comix were fading away. Alternative comics are self-published or small-press works that resist the clichés of mainstream genre fiction in order to present a personal vision, but (unlike underground comix) they are aimed at the general culture rather than a particular subculture.

In 1976, **Harvey Pekar**, a file clerk in Cleveland veterans hospital, decided to chronicle his daily frustrations and occasional triumphs in an ironically titled comic book, *American Splendor*. Pekar used old jazz records to entice acquaintance Robert Crumb to draw his script. *American Splendor* is one of the earliest examples of the type of comic book that has come to be referred to as alternative comic.

*Arcade* magazine was created by editors Art Spiegelman and Bill Griffith to compete in a mainstream magazine market, but the magazine never got distribution beyond the dwindling underground outlets. *Arcade*'s cancellation in 1976, after only seven issues, is sometimes pointed to as the end of the underground movement. Yet *Arcade* can also be viewed as a transition from an underground vibe to an alternative aesthetic that was more evident in the experimental *RAW*. Spiegelman and future wife Françoise Mouly published the first issue of this comics anthology in 1981. In *RAW* #2 Spiegelman began serializing *Maus* as a mini-comic insert. The 11 issues of *RAW* contained work by both underground stalwarts and emerging alternative cartoonists, such as Gary Panter and Charles Burns. About the time *RAW* was being conceived Robert Crumb created the anthology *Weirdo* to fill the void left by the collapse of the underground comix industry and the cancellation of *Arcade*. Crumb featured work by a number of his underground contemporaries, but he also sought out undiscovered talent. When Crumb passed the editorship of *Weirdo* to **Peter Bagge** the book took on more of a punk sensibility and became an important venue for the work of new wave cartoonists.

*Arcade*, *RAW*, and *Wierdo* were rooted in the underground comix, but they created an alternative to both the underground and the mainstream. Former superhero fan Gary Groth was converted to this new aesthetic; he not only championed alternative comics as publisher and editor of *The Comics Journal*, but in 1982 his company, Fantagraphics, began publishing innovative comics aimed at an adult audience. The first offering was **Love and Rockets**, in which the **Hernandez Brothers** told character-driven tales with a Latino perspective that was unique in American comics. With an attitude that was often considered elitist, self-aggrandizing and antagonistic toward the mainstream, Fantagraphics made enemies, but they also did more than most publishers to force the comic book medium to mature in the 1980s.

In 1989, Chris Oliveros began the Canadian Drawn and Quarterly to publish an anthology of art and literary comics in the experimental tradition of *RAW*. Soon the company expanded to publish ongoing comic book series and graphic novels by such notable creators as Adrian Tomine, **Chester Brown**, and Julie Doucet. Drawn and Quarterly publishes works that might have occasional sex scenes, but are adult by virtue of the intelligence with which they examine the human condition.

Top Shelf Productions, which began in 1997, has published work by **Eddie Campbell**, Craig Thompson, Nate Powell and other critically acclaimed cartoonists. Founders Chris Staros and Brett Warnock feel part of their mission as a publisher is to change the perception of comic books by getting works of merit into the market-place. *Lost Girls*, **Alan Moore** and Melinda Gebbie's work of erotica featuring the children's literature icons Dorothy, Wendy and Alice began in Stephen R. Bissette's *Taboo* anthology in 1991 and was eventually collected in three volumes by Top Shelf Productions. The work brings together the traditions and evolving ambitions of comic books as an outsider art form. Featuring popular culture characters reminiscent of the Tijuana Bibles, it blends explicit sex with social commentary reminiscent of the undergrounds, and aspires to make pornography, the term Moore prefers for the work, an aesthetic and intellectual experience that can be enriching rather than soulless or merely escapist.

Underground creators and publishers had a fierce commitment to freedom of expression that could produce offensive work, but also stimulated creativity and experimentation. As the creators matured there developed an impressive variety of work in the underground comix. This work inspired the next generation of cartoonists to create alternative comic books and graphic novels that, due to their sophistication of theme and form, are beginning to find acceptance in mainstream culture.

*See also:* Satire

*Randy Duncan*

**VAMPIRES AND ZOMBIES.** While vampires and zombies have been common stock for films and books for much of the 20th century, their presence in comic books has not been consistent due to censorship practices in the mid-1950s. In the early comic industry of the 1920s and 1930s, comics steered clear of tales involving vampires, zombies and most **horror** motifs. Horror comics arose in the 1940s and with them also came an abundance of stories presenting vampires and zombies.

Vampires and zombies have been used in many ways throughout history to represent fears and anxieties about death; particularly the disruption of a peaceful transition into some sort of afterlife. However, these undead creatures are also used to reveal human fear of fates worse than death. Common elements include returning from the dead, biting or bodily fluid exchange as a means of infecting, and significant violence to permanently kill the creature (stake through the hearts for vampires and blunt trauma to the head or decapitation for zombies). Vampires are known to have a range of supernatural powers including flight, body transformation, telepathy, and super-strength; while zombies rarely have any powers, they typically have a maniacal appetite for human flesh. Both are typically depicted as gaunt and pale figures with vampires weakened or killed by sunlight but often appearing relatively normal with the exception of protruding fangs.

Zombies are often reanimated in a posthumous state, rotting flesh, disheveled appearance and all. Most early zombies narratives (though few contemporary ones) are connected with typically non-Western spiritual beliefs, particularly from African and Caribbean cultures in the form of Voodoo. Zombies can also be singularly reanimated corpses seeking revenge for personal injustices or cursed begotten creatures. However in the last few decades, zombies have largely represented a plague of human mindlessness triggered by any number of reasons including disease, spiritual invocation, alien infestation, or scientific experimentation.

Vampires often come from non-Western sources (for instance Dracula comes from the periphery of Europe and the Ottoman Empire), but their mythology is deeply rooted in Christian theology; vampires are generally vulnerable to crosses, holy water, and other Christian relics. While the vampire also invokes anxieties about safe transition into the afterlife, their more conscious nature and more calculated approach to survival means their narratives are predatory by nature. The vampire is seductive, scheming, and often subtle in its actions, while the zombies tend to be mindless, ceaseless, and simplistic. Because of its consciousness and overall alluring nature, vampires also carry more over erotic (heterosexual and homosexual) undertones. Over the years, vampires more than zombies have become sympathetic antagonists and even in some narratives actual protagonists.

Several external sources have influenced comic depictions of vampires and zombies in the 1940s and 1950s. Bram Stoker's classic book, *Dracula* (1897), its predecessor novella, *Carmilla* (1872) by Joseph Sheridan LeFanu, and several cinematic adaptations—including F. W. Murnau's *Nosferatu* (1923) and Tod Browning's *Dracula* (1931)—helped to shape the early manifestations of vampires in comics, while Mary Shelley's *Frankenstein*, many short stories of H. P. Lovecraft (in particular, "Herbert West: The Reanimator"), and films such as Victor Halperin's *White Zombie* (1932), Jean Yarbrough's *King of the Zombies* (1941), Jacques Tourneur's *I Walked With Zombies* (1943) created the backbone of the popular understanding of the zombie during this time. These sources helped shape the visual depiction, the mythological background, and the narrative range of vampire and zombie comics for much of their early history.

There is some fluidity in these definitions and portrayals of "vampire" and "zombie" since traits like genre conventions can fluctuate or be manipulated in order to keep stories fresh and interesting. Therefore, in some stories, vampirism might be identified as a blood-born virus; in others vampires might have an aversion to sunlight but have no need to return to the tomb during the day. Also, one's status as a zombie can sway back and forth depending on the depiction. Characters inspired by Shelley's *Frankenstein* are the best example. In narratives that stick closely to the original story, Frankenstein's monster is less often seen as a zombie since the creature is eloquent, quick-witted, and ultimately, left to his own devices in the Arctic at story's end, wanting nothing to do with humanity. However, Frankenstein stories inspired by the James Whale film, *Frankenstein* (1931), are more likely to be read as a zombie since the Boris Karloff version of the monster is lumbering, monosyllabic, and, constructed in large part from a freshly buried body, much more clearly than the original novel suggests. Mummies and ghouls, too, have a way of fitting or being excluded from the category of zombie depending on the circumstance of their creation, their means of destruction, and intentions as such beings. While vampire stories were easily identifiable, the same could not be said for zombie stories. Many horror stories of the 1940s and 1950s featured people who came back from the dead but for different reasons and with different capabilities. Many returned to avenge their death, others came because they were just overwhelmingly evil, and still more were beckoned from the grave or revived by the living. These were the major tropes for zombie stories in the late 1940s and 1950s.

Few stories containing horror were published in the 1930s and usually the horrific elements were mere extensions of the some other genre story. Typically, **Classics Illustrated's adaptation** of *The Strange Case of Dr. Jekyll and Mr. Hyde* in 1943 is identified as the first horror comic. *Eerie Comics* #1 (1947) is often credited as the first ongoing horror series, though there is some debate since Dick Briefer's *Frankenstein* series (1945) was inspired by horror but often the early issues were more humor than horror. Regardless, by the end of the 1940s, vampires and zombies were being featured prominently in many horror comics.

Often, early vampire stories were formulaic in that they followed in the tradition of both the film and book versions of *Dracula*. For instance, in a story published in *Adventures into the Unknown* #3 (1948), "The Vampire Prowls" features many things that invoke the film, *Dracula*, more so than the book. The story contains a well-dressed vampire akin to Béla Lugosi's film version of Dracula who lusts after a woman he meets at the theater though she is married to another. The doctor of the story wields an herb (juniper sprig) to repulse the vampire and later stakes the vampire through the heart in its coffin. This is more aligned with the film since in the book, there is no theater scene and it is the husband who helps slay Dracula.

Regardless, vampires and zombies continued as reliable characters in the increasingly gory and violent comics of the 1950s. The visual and moral debauchery exhibited in **crime** and horror comics led to the publication of *Seduction of the Innocent* by Dr. **Fredric Wertham** and to meetings of the U.S. Senate's sub-committee to Investigate Juvenile Delinquency with a focus on comics. October, 1954 saw the creation of the **Comics Code** of the Comics Magazine Association of America, Inc, in which comic stories involving vampires and zombies would be all but eliminated in comic books for about 17 years. Under General Standards Part B, the Comics Code stipulated several clauses that would significantly hinder these narratives, including the second clause which prohibited "all scenes of horror" and the third clause which banned "all lurid, unsavory, gruesome illustrations." But vampires and zombies were officially sent back to their coffins en masse with the fifth clause which clearly stated, "Scenes dealing with, or instruments associated with walking dead, torture, vampires and vampirism, ghouls, cannibalism and werewolfism are prohibited." For most publishers, this kept them from publishing such stories until 1971.

The revised Comics Code in 1971 amended and opened up some room by rewording the fifth clause as such: "Scenes dealing with, or instruments associated with walking dead, or torture, shall not be used. Vampires, ghouls and werewolves shall be permitted to be used when handled in the classic tradition such as Frankenstein, Dracula, and other high caliber literary works written by Edgar Allan Poe, Saki, Conan Doyle and other respected authors whose works are read in schools around the world." With horror reemerging as a popular film genre in the wake of creation of the Motion Picture

Movie Association of America's new rating system in 1968, comics also looked to cash in on the macabre. Films such as George R. Romero's *Night of the Living Dead* (1968) helped shape the minds and visual expectations for the next decade as they have continued to do to the present.

Therefore, while the Comics Code clearly indicated that stories with zombies were off limits and vampires would be limited; this did not prevent these tales from publication in horror comics during this time. By the late 1960s, publishers were bypassing the Comics Code altogether by publishing their "comics" as black and white magazines, thereby not needing the Comics Code's Seal of Approval. The tradition was started by **EC Comics** in the 1950s with their publication of *Mad* as a magazine but others followed this tradition including **Warren Publishing** with *Creepie* (1964), *Eerie* (1966), and Forrest J. Ackerman's *Vampirella* (1969). The initial run of *Vampirella* presented the title character as hostess and even character in a few stories in each issue. In comics, Vampirella is the first sympathetic recurring vampire to appear, and her pleasing, voluptuous appearance led to legions of fans.

Seeing the success of bypassing the code, **Marvel Comics** moved forward with its imprint, Curtis Magazines (also known as Marvel Monster Group), to publish some of its most famous monster stories including *Dracula Lives* (1973), *Tales of the Zombie* (1973),

and *Vampire Tales* (1973). *Tales of the Zombie* portrayed a revamped character from a short piece previously published in *Menace #5* (1953), Simon Garth. Brought back from death by voodoo magic, Garth is enlisted repeatedly to do harm and occasional good. He is the earliest sympathetic recurring zombie to appear in comics. Within the actual comic books, the word "zombie" was prohibited, so publishers used other replacements including Marvel Comics use of the term, "zuvembies."

Marvel Comics also responded to the relaxed code with the creation of the character Morbius. This "Living Vampire" first appeared in *Amazing **Spider-Man*** #101 in October, 1971, then continued in the horror anthology series, *Adventures into Fear* starting with #20 and finally, into the *Vampire Tales* comic

Bela Lugosi as Count Dracula in the 1931 film *Dracula*, directed by Tod Browning. Universal Pictures/Photofest magazine. This human with vampire powers was a foray into the new territory. Once the character was approved by the code and accepted by readers, Marvel Comics followed up with the series, *Tomb of Dracula* in 1972. The other famous human-vampire hybrid character, Blade, made his first appearance in *Tomb of Dracula* #10.

**DC Comics** too was publishing zombie and vampire stories in horror or speculative anthologies series such as *Ghosts* (1971), *Secrets of Haunted House* (1975), *Secrets of Sinister House* (1972), *The Unexpected* (1968), *Weird Mystery Tales* (1972), and *Weird War Tales* (1971). However during the 1970s, Marvel Comics dominated horror with ongoing series that featured recurring zombies (Simon Garth) or vampires (primarily Blade, Morbius, and Dracula), as well as many anthologies series, including *Crypts of Shadows* (1973), *Dead of Night* (1973), *Monsters Unleashed* (1973), *Giant-Size Chillers* (1974), *Haunt of Horror* (1974), *Supernatural Thrillers* (1972), *Tomb of Darkness* (1974), *Uncanny Tales* (1973), *Vault of Evil* (1973), and others.

**Marv Wolfman** both wrote and edited many of these series for Marvel Comics including extended stints on both *Tales of the Zombie* and *The Tomb of Dracula*. Both series portrayed and developed these monsters beyond their typical cinematic representation of unambiguously evil. For most of their history, comics featuring zombies and vampires took their lead from books and film, but with Wolfman and others, comics developed distinct trends within the overall vampire and zombie mythology.

Since the change in the Comics Code, vampires have been featured regularly within Marvel Comics' continuum. Blade and Morbius made it into mainstream continuum of Marvel Comics on a regular basis, while Dracula and vampires in general make occasional appearances. Dracula fought the Defenders in *The Defenders* #95 (1981), the **X-Men** in *Uncanny X-Men Annual* #6 (1982) and also encountered Apocalypse (*X-Men: Apocalypse vs. Dracula*, 2006), and Captain Britain (*Captain Britain and MI13*, 2009). In the 1990s, Marvel Comics launched the crossover series, *Rise of the Midnight Sons*, which featured many of the supernaturally-based superheroes including Morbius, Blade, and characters related to, or inspired by, Abraham van Helsing and Dracula. Plots focused on the occult, thus vampires and zombie characters were reoccurring villains.

DC Comics pitted both **Superman** and **Batman** at different times against Dracula and other vampires, though not always in their main continuum (*Batman & Dracula: Red Rain*, 1991; *Batman: Bloodstorm*, 1994; *Batman: Crimson Mist*, 1999; *Superman* #180, 2002; *Superman and Batman vs. Vampires and Werewolves*, 2008). There are occasional vampire and zombie villains, but DC Comics has few recurring vampires or zombies. Andrew Bennet was a "good vampire" attempting to fight against evil ones. He appeared as a regular character in *House of Mystery* starting with issue #290 for 30 issues and then appeared sporadically in different series throughout the 1990s and 2000s. DC Comics also created Solomon Grundy, a recurring zombie supervillain who first appeared in **All-American Comics** #61 (1944) and has repeatedly battled Batman, Superman, **Green Lantern**, Starman and others over the years.

In the 1980s and 1990s, there were several short-lived zombie series among the various independent publishers but one series, was repeatedly revived, *Deadworld* (1987). First published by Arrow Comics and created by Stuart Kerr and Ralph Griffith, the series was praised for its gore factor, compelling black and white art and complicated plot. When Arrow Comics folded, Caliber Comics gained control of the title and finished the initial series, released a series of one-shot issues and miniseries before relaunching the series again in 1993. While the first series lasted 26 issues, the second series lasted only 15. However, *Deadworld* received another reprieve in 2005 when it was relicensed and published as an ongoing series by **Image Comics**. The series revolved around a set of characters trying to survive in a **post-apocalyptic** setting where the world is dominated by both brain-dead and intelligent zombies, including King Zombie who seeks to open a portal to another dimension.

Vampires also grew in popularity in the 1980s and 1990s, owing much to Anne Rice's *Vampire Chronicles* books and an inundation of vampire films. Taking a lead from this trend, independent publishers also launched new series and revamped old ones. Gary Reed of Caliber Comics published a miniseries on Reinfeld, the servant of Dracula, and the *Vampirella* series, now under Harris Comics, was relaunched as well as featured in dozens of one-shot editions and cross-over series. Cassidy, an Irish vampire featured prominently as a side-kick to Jesse Custer, the main character in the **Eisner Award**-winning series, **Preacher** (1995).

An explosion of zombie stories occurred in the first decade of the 2000s. Comics featuring or centering on vampires had been continually increasing since the 1980s. However, zombie narratives became very popular, very quickly, at this time. Of over 100 titles in which zombies feature prominently in the comic series published in the last 50 years, over 70 were published in the 2000s. Many factors played a role, including the disintegration of the Comics Code and the cultural legitimacy comics were now receiving. The boost also stemmed from highly successful zombie films in the theaters including the release of *Resident Evil* (2002), *28 Days Later* (2002), and the remake of George R. Romero's *Dawn of the Dead* (2004), all of which hit record box-office receipts that had not been seen for zombie films since the original *Dawn of the Dead* (1978).

Added to this, comics were experiencing a general horror renaissance that balanced on several factors. IDW Publishing was hitting its stride publishing both original horror content including the vampire series, *30 Days of Night* (2002), as well as licensed titles based on television, movies, and video games such as *Angel* (2005), *Underworld* (2003), and *Silent Hill* (2004). Steve Niles and Ben Templesmith (*30 Days of Night*) quickly became very popular and were involved in numerous horror projects throughout the 2000s. Niles' miniseries *Remains* (2004) revolved around survivors of a zombie apocalypse in the middle of a show-down of fast-moving zombies (represented in movies such as *28 Days Later* and the 2004 *Dawn of the Dead*) and slow-shambling zombies (also known as the classic Romero zombie). This marked the first acknowledgement and use of this shift in zombie abilities.

This reciprocal relationship of genre film and television with comics is best exemplified by **Joss Whedon**'s *Buffy the Vampire* series. While a comic series ran concurrently with the television series, Whedon went on to craft a comic book continuation of the television series after its termination called *Buffy the Vampire Slayer Season Eight* (2007). This comic series was distinct from previous *Buffy* series, which did not advance the ongoing plot of the TV show. Niles performed a similar feat as writer of *28 Days Later: The Aftermath*, published in April, 2007, a month after the launch of the first issue of *Buffy the Vampire Slayer Season Eight*. This graphic novel filled the gap between the film *28 Days Later* and its sequel *28 Weeks Later* (2007).

*30 Days of Night* was the most influential vampire narrative in the comics of the 2000s. Meanwhile, Image Comic's **Walking Dead** (2003) was the most powerful and impressive zombie series to come out, surpassing *Deadworld* as the most popular ongoing zombie series. Written by **Robert Kirkman**, the story revolves around former police officer, Rick Grimes and his family as they try to live in a world where zombies have destroyed civilization.

In 2005, Marvel Comics launched its *Marvel Zombies* series, which was well received by fans and critics alike. The premise originated in *Ultimate **Fantastic Four*** in which Reed Richards taps into a parallel universe where a virus has turned all of Marvel's **superheroes** into zombies who feast on the entire world (and eventually universe). The zombies appeared in two short runs on *Ultimate Fantastic Four* and by year's end, Marvel Comics had hired Kirkman to write what would be the first of several Marvel Zombies series.

By the end of the decade, zombies continued to thrive with the vast majority of narratives still focused on the zombie as villain. Very few narratives were particularly sympathetic towards these undead, though there were a few exceptions, such as *Zombie Cop* (2009), in which one "good" fights against the other zombies. However, vampires had developed much more complex narratives in large part thanks to the Rice's *Vampire Chronicles*, Whedon's *Buffy the Vampire Slayer* and *Angel* series, Charlaine Harris's *Southern Vampire Mysteries*, and Stephanie Meyer's *Twilight* series. Certainly, narratives still focus on vampires as villains such as the *Blade* series and *30 Days of Night*, but the shift to vampires as complex, sometimes tragic figures rather than clear villain continues to influence comic narratives and sales.

**Selected Bibliography:** Kendall, David, ed. *The Mammoth Book of Zombie Comics*. Philadelphia: Running Press, 2008; Normanton, Peter. *The Mammoth Book of Best Horror Comics*. Philadelphia: Running Press, 2008; Reed, Gary. *Deadworld—Complete Comic Collection on CD-ROM*. CD-ROM. Macomb, MI: Eagle One Media, 2007.

*Lance Eaton*

**VAUGHAN, BRIAN K.** (1976–). Writer of award-winning graphic novels and creator-owned comic books, Vaughan was born in Cleveland, Ohio. While studying film at New York University, he participated in a **Marvel Comics** writers' workshop for new talent and was subsequently given small writing jobs. His first major work was **DC**-Vertigo's *Swamp Thing* but it was not well-received and resulted in the book's cancellation after 20 issues. In 2006, his graphic novel *Pride of Baghdad*, illustrated by Niko Henrichon, was inspired by the true story of four lions who escaped the Baghdad Zoo during Operation Iraqi Freedom. A parable about the ongoing Iraqi conflict, the work was acclaimed by mainstream critics and fans alike.

Vaughan has written single and multiple issues for various DC and Marvel titles, however, it is his work on his own creations (or co-creations) where his unique voice stands out. Such works include *Runaways* (for Marvel), *Y: The Last Man* (for Vertigo), and *Ex Machina* (for DC-Wildstorm). *Runaways* is an all-ages comic book where a group of children discover that their parents are super-villains. *Y* concerns a young man named Yorick Brown who quickly realizes he is the last man standing while the rest of his gender has been killed by some unknown plague. As he travels around the world he is befriended by those women who wish to protect him and find a cure, and threatened by those women who want him dead. Vaughan planned the entire 60-issue run from the start and rarely diverged from his original storyline. Co-creator Pia Guerra's interiors were essential to maintain the sense of continuity over the five years of the series. *Y* treats what could have been a bad B-movie storyline with intelligent (and often humorously, if naughtily phrased) observations regarding growing up, the nature of gender, and extremism.

While living in Brooklyn, Vaughan witnessed the collapse of the World Trade Center Towers and he has suggested that this experience has shaped much of what he has written. *Ex Machina*, another one of Vaughan's long but finite series, concerns a **superhero** who becomes Mayor of New York City after September 11, 2001. The work is a commentary on the failures of political leadership and ponders whether there can be real heroes. Much of his work has been optioned for films, and Vaughan himself has contributed to the popular television series *Lost* starting in 2007. Vaughan's work features his gift for clever yet natural dialogue, his ear for pop culture references, interesting twists on mainstream storylines, and his ability to create exciting cliff-hangers.

*Jeff McLaughlin*

**V FOR VENDETTA.** A dystopian tale of a near-future fascist Britain terrorized by a mysterious freedom fighter known only as V, this brooding story, written by **Alan Moore** and drawn by David Lloyd, initially appeared in the short-lived but hugely influential British comic *Warrior* (1982–85), created by Dez Skinn, a former editor at **Marvel UK**. Published by Quality Communications, *V for Vendetta* appeared alongside Moore's *Marvelman* (known as *Miracleman* in the United States), and was originally in black and white. *V for Vendetta* was incomplete at the time when *Warrior* ceased publication, but Moore's rising stardom in American comics, especially with his acclaimed *Watchmen*, ensured that *V for Vendetta* was reprinted by **DC Comics**, allowing Moore and Lloyd to complete the story. The American comic was colored by Lloyd and was collected as a book in the wake of the graphic novel boom of the mid-1980s.

Hugo Weaving as V in the 2005 film *V for Vendetta*, directed by James McTeigue. Warner Bros./ Photofest

*V for Vendetta* emerged from a number of sources. In his early 20s, Moore had submitted a proposal for a character called The Doll to DC Thomson, the Scottish publishers of long-running comics *The Beano* and *The Dandy*. The idea was rejected, and Moore later admitted that expecting DC Thomson to publish a story about a transsexual terrorist was perhaps unrealistic. When *Warrior* launched, editor Dez Skinn paired Moore with Lloyd and asked for a dark, mysterious strip, capturing the edgy tone that *Warrior* was striving for. Lloyd had previously worked on *Night Raven* for Marvel UK, a dark thriller set in the 1930s. Asked to do another 1930s mystery Lloyd resisted, wanting a chance to do something more contemporary. Moore turned back to his idea for *The Doll*, and things slowly came together. From initial character designs that were quite conventionally superheroic emerged the idea to blend a range of influences that would make this a uniquely British series. In his companion piece "Behind the Painted Smile," which appears in the graphic novel, Moore recounts a long and eclectic list of influences on *V for Vendetta* (270). It was apparently Lloyd who suggested that the central character be modeled on Guy Fawkes; Moore seized on the idea and V was born. Fawkes was Catholic soldier who was executed for his part in the Gunpowder Plot of November 5, 1605, when a small group planned to blow up the English Houses of Parliament in order to destroy Protestant rule. Every year, on November 5, the plot is remembered by British school children who burn Guy Fawkes effigies, singing "Remember, remember the fifth of November, The gunpowder treason and plot, I know of no reason why the gunpowder treason should ever be forgot." By turning the protagonist into a modern Guy Fawkes, Moore and Lloyd tapped into something that was emblazoned in the memories of British readers from childhood, turning a bogey-man into a hero of sorts. Lloyd also contributed greatly to the style of the story with his idea that it should dispense with sound-effects or thought-balloons, making the pacing and atmosphere much more somber and restrained. Moore's innovations included an episode presented as a song, complete with musical notes.

*V for Vendetta* was a platform for Moore's political views, showing a society on the verge of collapse and divided by the inequalities that were associated with the government of conservative Prime Minister Margaret Thatcher. Moore's vision of this world was very much influenced by George Orwell's *Nineteen Eighty-Four* (1948), but also drew on post-war British comics. The main character, V, is an anarchist, reflecting Moore's politics. He is never clearly identified, although it is clear that he has been a victim of the fascist government's repressive policies towards dissidents, minorities, and homosexuals. Escaping from a concentration camp where cruel experiments have been performed, V disguises himself in a Guy Fawkes costume, clearly identifying himself as a terrorist, rebel, and martyr. The story opens with V rescuing a young woman, Evey Hammond, from the police, who intend to assault her following her arrest for prostitution. V takes Evey to a rooftop and blows up the Houses of Parliament. She is taken to his hideout, the Shadow Gallery, and becomes his accomplice in his war against those who have tortured him. A police detective, Eric Finch, investigates V, but has little luck in discovering his identity, as V is systematically murdering everyone who might identify him. Eventually Evey becomes disenchanted with V's methods and after an argument he abandons her. Some time later he kidnaps her, subjects her to an ordeal modeled on his own torture, and shows her how she can free herself from fear, and from oppression. V continues his war on the government, as Finch slowly closes in. Upon finding V's hideout Finch shoots and mortally wounds V. As V dies he passes on his legacy to Evey, who adopts his costume, sending his body in an underground train full of explosives to destroy Downing Street. Evey announces that with the government gone people must now choose what comes next. In the aftermath of this revolution Finch stumbles out into the now chaotic streets, leaving London behind. With the once repressive mechanisms of state control now destroyed, the future is left unclear.

As indicated by the list of influences given above it is clear that *V for Vendetta* can be read in many ways, as a response to many different sources. One interesting point to note in the context of British comics of the time is that it can be read as a critique of the politics celebrated by some readers of Judge Dredd, a popular character created by Pat Mills, John Wagner, and Carlos Ezquerra in *2000 AD*. Dredd was originally a fascist, and the stories were a **satire** on his inflexibility and the cruelty of the world he inhabits. Some readers actually approved of Dredd's politics, missing the point entirely. Moore's response is an anarchist hero, clearly set against the horrors of a fascist society. There is little room to empathies with the fascist characters here.

In 2005, a film adaptation was released, directed by James McTeigue, produced by Joel Silver and the Wachowski brothers (who wrote the screenplay), and starring Hugo

Weaving as V, Natalie Portman as Evey, Stephen Rea as Finch, and John Hurt as Adam Sutler, the leader of the fascist government. In keeping with his view that such adaptations are not representative of his original work, Moore demanded that his name be removed from the credits. The film was controversial from the outset. Its release was reportedly delayed by the London bombings of July 7 and June 21, 2005, although this was denied by the filmmakers, though it is clear that there was some unease about a story that celebrated a terrorist radicalizing a young woman and justifying mass revolts against the police and government. This was also at the time of ongoing protests against the war in Iraq. However, some (including Moore) felt that the film missed the point of Moore's politics entirely; it does, in some ways, seem to comment more on the contemporary Bush administration in the United States while keeping the British setting.

**Selected Bibliography:** Moore, Alan. *V for Vendetta*. New York: DC Comics, 1990.

*Chris Murray*

**WAID, MARK** (1962–). Born in Hueytown, Alabama, Waid's first connection to the comic book industry was freelance reporting for comics trade publications *Comics Buyer's Guide* and *Amazing Heroes*. This led to a brief stint as editor of *Amazing Heroes* in 1986. In 1985 and 1986, Waid began the transition from writing about comic books to writing comics books themselves, with two backup stories about his favorite character, **Superman**, in **DC's** *Action Comics*. In 1987, DC hired Waid to edit *Legion of Super-Heroes*, *Secret Origins*, *Doom Patrol* and a number of one-shot titles. He also worked closely with writer Brain Augustyn and artist **Mike Mignola** to create the first of DC's *Elseworlds* tales, *Batman: Gotham by Gaslight*.

In 1989, Waid left the editorial position to pursue a freelance writing career. He wrote two titles, *The Comet* (co-written with artist Tom Lyle for half the run) and *Legend of the Shield* (co-written with Grant Miehm), in DC's Impact imprint. Waid's rise to prominence began in 1992 with *Flash*, a revamp of the title in which former Kid Flash, Wally West, assumed the mantle of the Flash. Waid felt an emotional connection with the Wally West character and his eight-year run on *Flash* resonated with fans. Along with Mike Wieringo, Waid gave the fans a new character, Impulse, in the pages of *Flash* and then wrote most of the first 27 issues of the *Impulse* comic. His status as fan favorite writer was cemented in 1996 when he worked with **Alex Ross** on the *Kingdom Come* limited series, an entertaining polemic about the true heroism of DC's icons contrasted with the type of troubled and violent heroes prevalent in **Image** and **Marvel** books. Waid was voted Best Writer by *Comics Buyer's Guide* readers in 1997.

Waid used his new fame to pursue opportunities outside DC. At **Marvel** he had two brief, but well received, runs on **Captain America**, and, a few years later, redefined the **Fantastic Four** as a family of adventurers ("imaginauts") during a nearly three-year stint. In 2000, a number of high profile creators, including Waid, developed the Gorilla Comics imprint for creator-owned titles that were published through Image Comics. Only a handful of issues ever saw print, and Waid and Barry Kitson completed their *Empire* project through DC a few years later. In 2001, Waid began a one year exclusive contract at CrossGen Comics. He contributed to a number of titles, but his most fondly remembered CrossGen work was on the first 10 issues of the Sherlock Holmes pastiche *Ruse*.

In 2005, Waid signed an exclusive contract with DC, and immediately began playing a major role in redefining the DC universe. His 2003, 12-part limited series **Superman: Birthright** presented an up-dated telling of Clark Kent's decision to become Superman, and was, for a time, the official Superman origin story. Beginning in 2005, he wrote the first 30 issues of a rebooted and re-imagined *Legion of Super-Heroes*, renamed *Supergirl and the Legion of Super-Heroes* halfway through his run. Waid was one of four prominent writers given an editorial role in guiding the events of the DC universe in the wake of *Infinite Crisis*. From mid-2006 to mid-2007, the four also co-wrote the weekly limited series *52*.

In the summer of 2007 Waid assumed the position of editor-in-chief at Boom! Studios. In addition to guiding the company's development and mentoring young writers, Waid continues to write, not only titles such as *Irredeemable*, *The Unknown*, and *The Incredibles* for Boom! Studios, but also *Amazing* **Spider-Man** for Marvel.

*Randy Duncan*

**WALKING DEAD, THE.** Debuting in October, 2003, this ongoing series revolves around a cast of ever-changing characters living in a world infested by **zombies**, where only pockets of humanity still exist. Written by **Robert Kirkman** (*Invincible*, *The Astounding Wolf-man*), the series came at a time when the zombie-themed films were gaining momentum with films like *Resident Evil* (2002) and *28 Days Later* (2003) participating in a renewed interest in zombie narratives. However, unlike these films and the later remake of George R. Romero's *Dawn of the Dead* (2004), *Walking Dead* contained the cinematic slow-shambling rotting corpses made famous by Romero in his zombie films since the original *Night of the Living Dead* in 1968. Additionally, like many other zombie narratives that focus solely on the outbreak phase of the zombie attacks, *Walking Dead* bypasses the outbreak altogether and follows a group of survivors as they change, adapt, and accept a new world order. The power of the story lies in the richly developed characters and plot complications that occur over dozens of issues.

The story revolves around the main character, Rick Grimes, and his family. At the onset of the story, Rick is a policeman who has awakened in an abandoned hospital where he had been recovering from a gunshot. He manages to find his wife Lori and son Carl with a group of survivors, including his former partner, Shane. Strain occurs between Shane and Rick as Rick assumes leadership and directs the group to make an effort to get to Atlanta, Georgia. This escalates until the two are pitched to fight, only to have Carl kill Shane to protect his father. From this point forward, Rick leads the hodgepodge group of people who vary considerably in size, shape, intelligence, orientation, philosophy, and so on, which fuels tension, problems, and feuds within the group; this internal threat often seems as serious as the external threat of the zombies.

As leader, Rick finds himself arming Carl and other children, teaching them to shoot to kill, and providing a new moral code that is nothing like any he himself has experienced or readers of the comic series are likely to experience. Rick's arc as a leader is a challenging one, filled with hard decisions that have irrevocable consequences that sometimes include losing loved ones or people that he has fought alongside and gained a deep respect for.

After a period of wandering, attempting to find the last vestiges of civilization, Rick and his group settle down in an abandoned but intact prison, believing that it will provide protection from the zombies. In the backdrop of this, they have lost and gained people; characters have formed conventional and unconventional relationships; and some, including Lori, are having children. Settling into the prison entails regulating living quarters and delegating day-to-day responsibilities such as farming. Much as in Romero's *Dawn of the Dead* (1978), zombies become only one of the legitimate threats to the group. During this period of stability, the group encounters another camp of survivors in a nearby town named Woodbury; but, unlike the egalitarian nature of Rick's group, this second group is ruled by a tyrannical governor, a sadistic and deviant being. Rick and two others are captured by the Woodbury camp that plan to use them as entertainment in their gladiator arena where humans face off against zombies. In the ensuing altercation, the Governor chops off Rick's right hand, but, Rick escapes and returns back to the prison camp.

The camp prepares for the inevitable battle with the other group, and characters clash over whether to stay and fight it out or to run and get free of the Woodbury camp. The crux of the battle occurs over issues #43–48 in which the prison defenses are irreparably destroyed and those who survive the battle with the Woodbury camp flee in different directions. Lori, their new baby, and Rick's close friend Tyrese lie among the dead. Now more than ever, Rick's ability to lead is held suspect—more by himself than anyone else. In the aftermath, Rick becomes quite ill from the wounds sustained by the battle, and Carl is left to take care of his ailing father alone while also dealing with the zombies. Though Rick physically recovers, it becomes clear that his sanity is barely intact and that he cannot allow himself to lead the group any further.

The series became instantly popular and continues to gain much accolades for Kirkman's masterful storytelling, often pushing the story in irreversible directions and not hesitating to set an entirely new and unexpected course as was best exemplified in the gruesome deaths of Rick's wife and newborn daughter. The compelling and diverse characters with their own agendas often take precedence over the zombie-fighting, which (according to Kirkman) is the point. In several interviews, he has emphasized that the zombies are the back story and that the main story involves the attempts of the characters truly to rethink some very fundamental and philosophical beliefs.

Statements such as "We are the walking dead," in issue #24, provide moments of pause within the narrative for characters and readers alike to think about the gravity of a real-life apocalyptic world.

The successful launch and reception of *The Walking Dead* gave rise to several more zombie series including the reprised *Deadworld* in 2005 by **Image Comics**. Additionally, **Marvel Comics** hired Kirkman to write a miniseries about the end of the Marvel Universe through its own zombie apocalypse, which won many accolades and spawned several sequels and spin-offs.

The first six issues of *The Walking Dead* were drawn by Tony Moore, who would continue on as cover artist for the first 24 issues. Moore received an **Eisner Award** nomination in 2005 for Best Cover Artist, while the series itself was nominated for an Eisner Award for Best New Series in 2004. Charlie Adlard has served as story artist and eventually cover artist up through 2009. The entire series is drawn in grayscale black and white, nostalgically evoking Romero's original black-and-white *Night of the Living Dead* (1968), while also helping to create an eerie atmosphere that is appropriate to the subject matter of the series.

*See also:* Vampires and Zombies

*Lance Eaton*

**WAR COMICS.** Comics have long been deeply implicated in presenting military themes, and in times of war, providing commentary, either in support of the state, or in opposition to it. This association between war and comics should come as no surprise, given the close historical association of comics with politics and propaganda. After all, comics excel at presenting caricatures and at celebrating mythological heroes and exaggerated villains, which makes them an ideal medium for propaganda.

The first example of an editorial cartoon in an American newspaper was Benjamin Franklin's 1754 illustration of a snake with a severed head, representative of the various colonies, with the slogan "Join, or Die." This appeal to form a union that would eventually become the United States was intended as a call to arms, and is therefore the first American propaganda cartoon. Editorial cartoons with clearly political purposes later appeared in cartoon magazines like *Puck* and have remained an important form ever since. Meanwhile, comic strips in newspapers, know as the Funnies, began to appear. Primarily designed to entertain, these strips often featured adventure strips alongside humor, and these adventure strips frequently featured military and war themes. In the 1930s, newspaper strips transformed into comic books. The adventure strips once again proved extremely popular, and **superheroes** dominated the market from the late 1930s onwards, with a peak in their popularity during World War II. With the onset of the war the superhero comics, and indeed, all genres, dealt with military and war themes explicitly. Since then comics have responded in one way or another to all the major world conflicts, often simplifying these complex political circumstances to straightforward battles between good and evil. From their origins to the present day, comics have been used for political purposes, and have been particularly useful in presenting images of war that are at once emotive and entertaining. This is their power, but it can also be quite dangerous if used to manipulate and misinform, as all kinds of propaganda invariably are at some point.

War comics first emerged as a distinct genre in 1940, with the publication of *War Comics* by Dell, a company known primarily for **funny animal** comics. However, the comic was not an initial success, probably because America was not yet at war in 1940, and the official stance of the United States was still neutral and non-interventionist. Such overt militarism may have been too much for readers, despite the fact that around the same time superhero comics were preparing Americans for war with interventionist messages. It would seem that readers needed the gloss of fantasy that the superheroes provided. Regardless, by 1943 the genre of war comics started to disentangle itself from superheroes, with titles that seemed to be directly targeted at the armed forces, such as *The United States Marines* and *Camp Comics*, which featured pin-up girls and was aimed at troops buying comics at the PX on military bases (Goulart 2000, 159–71). The obvious change in circumstances was that American was now at war, and with the conscription of millions of American men there was a large market for such stories. Many of the covers of these comics looked exactly like propaganda posters, and communicated similar messages, sometimes about practical issues related to health, such as how to avoid sexually transmitted diseases.

An important factor when considering war comics is that some were created by writers with direct experience of war or military life, which, combined with the fact that they were written and drawn with troops in mind, meant that they were often very accurate in how they presented military hardware. This was especially important for cover artists, who were often chosen because they could render realistic aircraft, tanks, and the like. In contrast, such realism was rarely an aspect of the writing, with many of the stories being jingoistic, extremely patriotic, sexist, and occasionally racist, especially against the Japanese. Of course, a good proportion of the readership was civilian, and quite young, so these aspects were sometimes restrained, though war comics of the time could be quite lurid as well. Extremes of violence happened out of frame, or were rendered in euphemistic terms, when the violence was directed against American troops, although enemy troops were dealt with in much harsher terms, with some of these comics being quite lurid in their depiction of the killing of the enemy. The appeal to morale was the recurring excuse for such excess. Whereas the artwork could be quite striking and inventive, the stories were usually quite predictable, with outnumbered and outgunned good guys versus the enemy, who were presented as cruel, dishonorable, and monstrous. The enemy would resort to "dirty tricks" like ambushing the Americans, and after scenes of disbelief, horror, then anger, the American troops would get their revenge. It was a story seen over and over again in Hollywood films, such as *Guadalcanal Diary* (1943), and replicated in endless comics. It was also a microcosm of the popular perception of the American experience of the war.

The character types were similarly predictable, a range of characters drawn from different backgrounds to represent the melting pot of America, although African American characters were rarely present. There were also recognizable types, such as the rookie, the experienced sergeant, the crazy lieutenant, or indeed, the cowardly officer, but the backbone of the squad was almost always a heroic everyman character who could be roused to near superhuman acts of violence to defend his buddies and kill the enemy. The counterpoint to all this was the battle-weary "Willie and Joe," Bill Mauldin's famous creations who preferred a dry manhole and clean socks to acts of heroism. These characters, much beloved of the troops, represented the reality of military life much more than anything offered by comics or films of the time.

As World War II drew to a close in 1945 the popularity of war comics waned, but in the early 1950s the Korean War (1950–53) provided war comics with a new audience. The result was a spate of publications such as *War Comics*, *Battlefield*, *Battle Front*, *Battle Action*, *Marines in Battle*, *Fightin' Marines*, and *G.I. Joe*, most of which presented the war as a grand adventure and portrayed soldiers as heroic supermen. This was very much the tried and tested strategy from the earlier conflict, but this time things did not ring true. The Korean war was a bitter battle of attrition, and the news from the front was rarely worth celebrating. National (later to become **DC Comics**) published *Our Army at War*, *Our Fighting Forces*, and *Star-Spangled War Stories*, which were of better quality than most war comics of the time (Wright), however, the most innovative war comics were those produced by **EC** Comics, who published intelligent antiwar comics such as such as *Two-Fisted Tales* and *Frontline Combat*, written and drawn by **Harvey Kurtzman**. The subversive stance of these publications (and their success) would contribute to EC's downfall, as they were effectively put out of business as a comics publisher following the introduction of the **Comics Code** in 1955.

In the 1960s, war comics declined in popularity, most likely due to the fact that superheroes were on the rise once more, and because the Vietnam conflict was a much more ambiguous and morally complicated war, and one that sparked protests and riots in the United States and worldwide. It was, like the Korean war, not a war where victories were particularly numerous. There was little to celebrate, and comics retreated into **fantasy** instead. Notable exceptions were National's *Our Army at War* (1959), which introduced Sgt. Rock, and **Marvel's *Sgt Fury and His Howling Commandos*** (1963), which combined war stories with the dynamic excess of superhero comics. DC had notable success with *Enemy Ace* (1965), which told the story of a German fighter pilot, loosely modeled on the Red Baron, who fought in World War I and II. DC's *The Unknown Soldier* first appeared in 1966, then sporadically through the 1970s to the present. The character is a World War II soldier whose brother is killed at Pearl Harbor. With his face destroyed by an explosion he vows to make a difference in the war to avenge his brother, becoming a covert operative with no identity. From 1965 to 1966, **Warren Publishing** published *Blazing Combat*, a war comic in a similar format to their successful horror comic *Creepy*. Written and edited by Archie Goodwin, *Blazing Combat* featured art by some of the best artists of the day; it promoted realism over hyperbolic adventures and attempted to recapture both the antiwar stance and the quality of Kurtzman's work for EC. The result was a series of excellent stories, so with a grim inevitability the title was short-lived, largely due to the controversy surrounding the story "Landscape," which appeared in the second issue. This story, told from the point of view of an old Vietnamese peasant, makes the American intervention in Vietnam seem particularly unheroic. Mainstream popular opinion was still divided on the war at this point, and there was not yet the widespread condemnation of the war that would emerge by the end of the 1960s and the early 1970s. The military objected to the story and military bases refused to stock the offending issue, as did a campaign against the title by the American Legion, ultimately contributing in its cancellation.

In 1974, as the Vietnam war was ending, the most violent and cynical character in **Marvel Comics** at the time made his appearance, **The Punisher**. A former U.S. Marine turned vigilante, the Punisher became hugely popular. Unlike most superheroes, the Punisher used extensive weaponry and tended to kill his enemies. He eventually gained his own series in 1986, the same year that Marvel published *The 'Nam* by Doug Murray, who was himself a Vietnam veteran. Based on real events, and told in "real time," with each issue advancing the characters lives by one month, *The 'Nam* aimed to capture the view of the war from a rookie's point of view in the same way as Oliver Stone's film *Platoon* (also 1986). The success of *The 'Nam*, though modest, was greater than expected, prompting Marvel to release *Semper Fi': Tales of the Marine Corps* in 1988. *The 'Nam* lasted until the early 1990s and the final issues co-starred the Punisher in order to boost sales. Throughout this time, Marvel was also publishing G.I. Joe comics based on the popular toy, which was quite different in tone from any of its other war related comics.

In 2001, British writer **Garth Ennis** started his revival of war comics with *War Stories*, his homage to, or attack on, British war comics such as *Commando*, published by DC Thomson since 1961. These were brutal and violent stories that punctured the rather restrained nature of many war comics, especially *Commando* comics, showing in graphic detail the carnage and bloodshed that war comics often elide. Ennis also wrote an Enemy Ace miniseries, *War in Heaven*, in 2001.

Several examples of military and war themes in comics move the action to a **science fiction** setting, creating a sub-genre of "future war" stories. Examples include *Rogue Trooper*, from the British weekly *2000 AD*, and the 1988 adaptation of Joe Haldeman's novel *The Forever War* (1974) by Mark van Oppen (also known as Marvano).

Since the events of September 11, 2001, military themes have become increasingly prevalent in comics, with advertisements for the Marine Corps in many mainstream comics, and the comics themselves acting as a kind of propaganda mechanism for the War on Terror. **Mark Millar**'s *The Ultimates*, which began in 2002, is very much *The Avengers* for the post-9/11 world, which is to say, The Ultimates are a much more violent, ruthless paramilitary organization than The Avengers have ever been. However, following the unpopular and costly occupation of Iraq, the military themes evident in some comics turned to an anti-war sentiment, or are at least moved beyond the propaganda imagery that appeared immediately in the wake of 9/11. One **Captain America** miniseries, *The Chosen* (2007) was written by David Morrell, author of *First Blood* (1972) and creator of Rambo. It is set in Afghanistan and follows a U.S. Marine who seems to be hallucinating that he can see Captain America at times of stress.

In recent years there have been an increasing number of comics that have tackled the subject of war and have taken an anti-war stance from the perspective of non-American characters, notably *Maus* (1972–91) by **Art Spiegelman**, *Barefoot Gen* (1973–85) by Keiji Nakazawa, and *Palestine* (1993) by **Joe Sacco**. These comics have told the story of traumatic events in war from a civilian point of view, something that war comics too often ignore.

**Selected Bibliography:** Goulart, Ron. *Comic Book Culture.* Portland: Collector's Press, 2000; Jones, Gerard, and Jacobs, Will. *The Comic Book Heroes.* Rocklin, CA: Prima Publishing, 1997; Wright, Bradford. *Comic Book Nation.* Baltimore: Johns Hopkins University Press, 2003; Wright, Nicky. *The Classic Era of American Comics.* London: Prion Books, 2000.

*Chris Murray*

**WARE, CHRIS** (1967–). Among the most celebrated contemporary American comics artists, Chris Ware has been crucial to the widespread recognition of comics as works of literary and artistic merit. Ware's cutting-edge work derives from his immersion in the early history of American comics (and commercial graphic design), resulting in some of the most elaborately crafted and formally complex comics in the history of the medium. Ware is best known for his ongoing series of intricately designed publications *The Acme Novelty Library* (1994–present, with #1–15 published by **Fantagraphics** before Ware began self-publishing subsequent issues) and his award-winning, semi-autobiographical graphic novel *Jimmy Corrigan, the Smartest Kid on Earth* (Pantheon, 2000). He has also worked as an illustrator, designer, and editor, helping to shape the appreciation of both historical and contemporary comics as an art form.

Ware was born in Omaha, Nebraska, and began publishing comics in the student newspaper while he was enrolled at the University of Texas, including the mock **science fiction** strip *Floyd Farland: Citizen of the Future*, published in 1988 by the **Marvel** offshoot Eclipse as a prestige format comic. (The notoriously self-critical Ware is dismissive of the strip and has not allowed it, or much other early work, to be reprinted since.) In the same period, he also drew a number of increasingly complex strips (often wordless, or foregrounding language as a visual element) featuring the characters Quimby the Mouse and Sparky the Cat (in fact only a cat head). These early strips (collected in *Quimby the Mouse* from Fantagraphics in 2003) announce many of Ware's later, ongoing concerns, employing nostalgic influences (the **funny animals** that populate early comic strips and animated cartoons) in the service of grim irony and highly inventive formal play. The direction of his future work was also signaled when Ware was invited to contribute to the final issues of the prestigious anthology *RAW*, edited by **Art Spiegelman** and Françoise Mouly: Ware's ingenious strips combined autobiographical anecdotes with the clichéd devices of **superhero** comics, functioning as a meta-commentary on the grammar of the comics form.

After Ware moved to Chicago to briefly attend the School of the Art Institute of Chicago, he began contributing strips to local arts newspapers *New City* and *The Chicago Reader*, slowly building the story of Jimmy Corrigan, which would also unfold (with many alterations along the way) in his *Acme Novelty Library*. In both *Jimmy Corrigan* and subsequent work Ware often draws upon iconographic forms such as architectural blueprints, flowcharts, and medical illustrations in addition to earlier comics. His page layouts veer from single-page panels to pages of incredible density, with transitions exploiting a vast range of temporal and spatial possibilities: few other comics push so often towards the limits of the form, especially to tell stories devoted to exploring tender and painful human emotions.

Ware's published sketchbooks, *The Acme Novelty Date Book Volume One, 1986–1995* (Drawn & Quarterly, 2003) and *The Acme Novelty Date Book Volume Two, 1995–2002* (Drawn & Quarterly, 2007) reveal a much looser style than the extreme precision of his published work. Ware has also edited a volume of *McSweeney's* (#13, 2004) devoted to comics and featuring a typically elaborate Ware-designed dust jacket, and *The Best American Comics 2007* (Houghton Mifflin). He has also played a key role in reprints of the classic comic strips *Krazy Kat* by George Herrimann and *Gasoline Alley* by Frank King, both of which have strongly influenced his own work. Ware has received frequent recognition for his comics, including multiple **Eisner** and **Harvey Awards**, and his work has been featured in several museum exhibitions. He has also created toys and sculptures as offshoots of his comics work, and published *The Rag-Time Ephemeralist*, devoted to the early American musical style that Ware claims informs his understanding of the structure of comics and the emotions both forms generate in their audiences.

**Selected Bibliography:** Kannenberg, Jr., Gene. "The Comics of Chris Ware." In *The Language of Comics: Word and Image*, ed. Robin Varnum and Christina T. Gibbons. Jackson: University Press of Mississippi, 2001, 174–97; Raeburn, Daniel. *Chris Ware.* New Haven: Yale University Press, 2004.

*Corey K. Creekmur*

**WARREN PUBLISHING.** Founded by James Warren in 1969, Warren Publishing published **horror**, dark **fantasy**, and **science fiction** comics with an adult twist that bypassed the **Comics Code** by virtue of the magazine format until 1983. Their most well-known publications were *Creepy, Eerie, Vampirella,* and *Famous Monsters of Filmland*. *Creepy, Eerie,* and *Vampirella* were all characterized by lush painted covers, an inner front cover with a color drawing of the flagship character often by Bernie Wrightson in *Creepy* and *Eerie,* and Jose Gonzales in *Vampirella* (112 issues from September 1969 to March 1983) introducing usually six stories. Warren's *Eerie* was not connected with the January, 1947 one-shot horror comic of the same name published by Avon Publications, which ran for 17 issues from May/June 1951. Similar to EC comics hosts The Crypt Keeper or the Vault Keeper, "Uncle Creepy," a wizened old man, and "Cousin Eerie," a rotund grotesque figure in pilgrim style attire, warned of the gruesomeness of each tale in the Warren publications. Titles like *Creepy* occasionally had issues on a different theme, thus science fiction stories such as *Purge* (which prefigures Judge Dredd with a similar tale of a fascist cop on a motorbike enforcing over-strict rules, in this case owning copies of Warren titles) and *Executor One* (a robotic executioner with the consciousness of a man) feature in issue #73 of *Creepy*, where six science fiction stories are presented as fairytales told by an old man to deformed children in a **post-apocalyptic** city. *Edgar Allan Poe's Creepy Stories* issue #69, February 1975, and issue #70, March 1975, featured comic strip adaptations of such Poe stories as "The Pit and Pendulum," "The House of Usher," and "The Oval Portrait." There were also articles on how comics were created with a section called "Everything You Always Wanted to Know . . . about the Comics!" This feature added to an active fan culture, and the letter pages of most Warren publications had critical and incisive letters on story and quality. This sense of fandom and community was one of the hallmarks of *Famous Monsters of Filmland*. Along with the hosted titles that included in-joke puns and humor, the readers pages of the magazine featured photos of readers and fostered a community spirit of early fandom. Vampirella was created by Forrest J. Ackerman and first appeared as a horror story host in *Vampirella* issue #1, September 1969, but was recreated as an ongoing character in her own right in storylines that combined horror and science fiction. Vampirella was an updated vampire story, which although superficially supernatural and gothic, has a science fiction basis. Vampirella is an alien from the planet Draculon, where the inhabitants lived on blood that flowed in the planet's rivers. After an Earth spaceship crashes on the planet, Vampirella is sent to investigate and ends up piloting the ship back to Earth. Her red, one-piece leather thong and black boots have almost iconic status in certain circles. When Warren became bankrupt in 1983, Vampirella was a notable character that was sold in auction to Harris Comics, which has made intermittent attempts to resurrect the character. Hollywood exploitation veteran Jim Wynorski helmed a direct-to-DVD film version of *Vampirella* (1996) starring Puerto Rican Talisa Soto in the title role, and The Who's Roger Daltrey as villain Vlad. In comparison to the much-discussed gore of EC horror comics tales, Warren's output was characterized more by its atmospheric black and white art and more adult, sexual themes, which was influenced by the influx of Spanish artists.

*Lorcan McGrane*

**WATCHMEN.** One of the defining comics of the 1980s, and one of the benchmarks against which intelligent and literate storytelling in comics have been judged ever since. Written by **Alan Moore**, drawn by **Dave Gibbons**, with color by John Higgins, *Watchmen* is an insightful homage to the **superhero** genre, as well as a deconstruction of its clichés, forms, and influences. Originally published as a 12-issue series beginning in

September 1986, *Watchmen* was collected as a book in 1987, finding enormous success alongside other **adult comics** of the 1980s, **Frank Miller's *The Dark Knight Returns*** and **Art Spiegelman's *Maus***, the collected versions of which contributed to the rise of the graphic novel format. The origin of *Watchmen* was **DC Comics'** purchase of the rights for characters previously published by the defunct **Charlton Comics**. Moore, a British writer who had been head-hunted by DC and was enjoying success with his re-vamp of the ailing *Swamp Thing* title, wrote a treatment outlining how he would perform the same alchemy with the Charlton characters. However, as the proposal was a radical departure from the established characters, Moore was given the go-ahead to create new characters based on the Charlton heroes. The result was a degree of creative freedom that Moore and Gibbons thrived under. The story was ambitious, with a complex narrative structure and a disciplined adherence to a nine-panel grid format, only broken occasionally for dramatic effect. Moore's scripts were unusually dense for a comic script, full of extraneous detail and description, as is his habit, but he was not prescriptive about the artwork, allowing Gibbons more-or-less free reign. The format of

the comics was equally bold, with distinctive covers, and no letters page, instead Moore used the extra pages to present supplementary material such as text stories that related to the main narrative, as well as song lyrics and quotations from famous thinkers. Moore also consciously decided not to use an external narrative voice in captions, or to use thought-balloons, forcing himself and Gibbons to tell the story primarily through dialogue and images, leaving characters' motivations and thoughts ambiguous, something that was also done in Moore's *V for Vendetta*. The result was a comic that seemed, in terms of both story and artwork, to be much more sophisticated than most superhero comics of the time, and indeed, somewhat more akin to American **underground** comics such as *RAW*, where stylish layouts and narrative innovation were reshaping conceptions of what the medium was capable of.

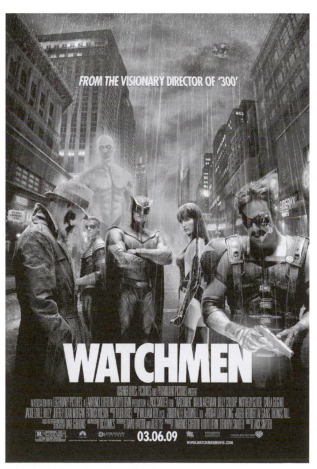

A poster for the 2009 film *Watchmen*, directed by Zack Snyder. Warner Bros./Photofest

In terms of the story, Moore broke with the conventions of the superhero story from the outset, displacing the action/adventure genre for a murder mystery structure, slowly unveiling clues to the identity of the villain, if such a thing could be said to exist in the morally complex and compromised world that Moore presents. Beginning with the murder of Edward Blake, a masked vigilante and government operative also known as The Comedian, the story follows the unhinged vigilante Rorschach (aka Walter Kovacs) as he investigates his hunch that there is a "mask killer" targeting superheroes. This investigation brings him into contact with his retired former team-mates, Dan Dreiberg (Nite Owl), Laurie Juspeczyk (Silk Spectre), Jon Osterman (Dr. Manhattan), and Adrian Veidt (Ozymandias). Through flashback and supplementary material it is revealed that in this alternate world costumed heroes (without genuine super powers) known as The Minutemen appeared during World War II but disbanded following the war. A genuine super-being is created in an accident in a nuclear research facility in the 1950s, later taking the name Dr. Manhattan. In the 1960s an attempt to resurrect The Minutemen falters and soon after superheroes are outlawed. Dr. Manhattan becomes a tool of U.S. government policy, and is used as a weapon in Vietnam, leading to a U.S. victory and to the re-election of President Richard Nixon for multiple terms running into the 1980s, while other superheroes either retire or become vigilantes or outcasts. As Rorschach's investigation begins to cast light on a larger conspiracy, tensions between the Soviet Union and America escalate, moving towards an apocalyptic showdown between the superpowers. Will the superheroes avert disaster, and who is behind a mysterious plan to save the world from itself?

The extensive flashback structure and the interpolation of a pirate comic as a commentary on the story adds to the complexity of the narrative, which gains power through its literary treatment of time and memory, its recurrent symbolism and the ingenuity with which Moore weaves together all the disparate elements with exacting precision, which is matched by Gibbons's artwork. All of these elements invoke the image of the universe, and the fictional universe created by Moore, as a mechanism, a watch being disassembled and reassembled by a watch-maker. Themes of determinism, fate and free will move from the cosmic scale down to the sub-atomic, through the intermediate stage of everyday human affairs. Dr. Manhattan adopts a relativist view, seeing no difference between past, present, and future, or between life and death. While Moore and Gibbons can at times seem preoccupied by the formal experimentation of the text, at its heart the story is a morality tale disguised as a superhero story, disguised as a murder mystery. Ultimately the story reveals that the smallest moments matter, and that events reverberate through time and memory with devastating consequences.

The story is also interesting as a meta-textual commentary on the superhero genre itself. The alternative history mapped out by Moore corresponds very closely to the history of American comics, from wartime popularity to a post-war lull where other genres, especially **horror**, **crime** and **science fiction** prospered, to the resurgence in the popularity of superheroes in the 1960s, and the darker comics of the 1970s and 1980s, typified by **Neal Adams**'s version of **Batman** and **Marvel Comics' The Punisher**.

Moore's treatment of superheroes is a **satire** of the genre, as it undermines the clichés and generic codes, allowing Moore to explore a question that he had already addressed in his British comics *Captain Britain*, and especially *Marvelman* (known as *Miracleman* in the U.S.): what if superheroes existed in the real world? However, *Watchmen* moves far beyond this conceit, becoming something rarely glimpsed in superhero comics, a meditation not only on the genre, its political implications and fetishistic nature, but also the psychology of the characters, and the nature of the comics medium itself, the structure, vocabulary, and grammar of which is fully exploited by Moore and Gibbons.

Hailed as a masterpiece by many critics at the time of its release, a *Watchmen* film seemed inevitable. Terry Gilliam was one name attached to the project in the early years, but after years in development and several scripts, the film version seemed like it would never emerge. However, in 2009, after complex litigation, Warner Bros. eventually released a film based on *Watchmen* directed by Zack Snyder, which, despite mixed reviews from critics, was something of a commercial success and attempted to remain true to its source. However, Moore had long claimed that Watchmen was deliberately intended to be unfilmable, designed to showcase resources that were unique to the medium of comics. After having been frustrated by adaptations of his work in the past, and having previously resolved never to work for DC Comics following the dispute over merchandising royalties from the original comic series, Moore insisted that his name be removed from the credits for the film. Despite such controversy, Watchmen remains a byword for well-crafted and intelligent story-telling in comics, as well as a striking deconstruction of the superhero genre.

*Chris Murray*

**WEIRDO.** A black and white comics anthology, *Weirdo* was published in magazine format by **underground comics** stalwart Last Gasp for 28 issues (1981–93). Edited by **Robert Crumb** for 10 issues, followed by **Peter Bagge** (issues #11–17, and #25) and Aline Kominsky-Crumb (issues #18–24, and #26–28), the legendary Crumb's presence always loomed over the magazine, and his regular contributions, including striking color covers, remained the primary draw despite the impressive range of contributors over the full run. *Weirdo* followed *Arcade* (7 issues, 1975–76), edited by **Art Spiegelman** and Bill Griffith, as a venue carrying still active underground artists towards a more independent or alternative status while also introducing the work of rising artists, including Bagge. Since their runs were almost simultaneous, *Weirdo*'s emphatically lowbrow aesthetic implicitly set it against the artistically ambitious and slickly produced *RAW* (1980–91), edited by Spiegelman and Françoise Mouly. As with most anthologies, the quality of *Weirdo* was erratic, but it provided a regular space of resistance against mainstream **superhero** comics when there were few such alternatives available to its unconventional artists. In retrospect, *Weirdo* filled the gap between the waning underground in which Crumb had been the dominant figure, and the growing but more diffuse world of **adult comics** and **alternative comics** that would soon be transformed by many of its younger contributors.

*Weirdo* began as Crumb's attempt to emulate comics magazines that had influenced him, especially the early *Mad* and **Harvey Kurtzman**'s *Help!* (1960–65): many of *Weirdo*'s covers, packing small figures into elaborate borders, were in homage to Crumb's models. Designed more like a magazine than a typical comic book, *Weirdo* included advice columns (by Terry Zwigoff and **Harvey Pekar**), notably cranky letters pages, and ads promoting like-minded publications, including the first wave of hand-made mini-comics. Under Crumb's editorship, a series of *fumetti*, or photo-funnies, were also featured: depicting the large women that obsessed him acting out silly scenarios (often with Crumb participating); they were a regular source of complaints from readers. (Somewhat peevishly, Crumb has since refused to reprint them in collections of his work.) In addition to Crumb, who contributed significantly to every issue, key underground figures such as Spain Rodriguez, **S. Clay Wilson**, Robert Williams, Bill Griffith, Justin Green, Robert Armstrong, Frank Stack, and Kim Dietch were frequently represented, although not always with their most memorable work. *Weirdo* may have been more beneficial for the space it offered to younger artists who had missed the earlier underground as a publishing option; in addition to Bagge, the magazine included early work by eventually notable artists Kaz, **Daniel Clowes**, Drew Friedman, Raymond Pettibon, David Collier, **Joe Sacco**, Doug Allen, and Gilbert **Hernandez**.

Even before Kominsky-Crumb established a tongue in cheek policy promoting (as the cover of #18 stated) "the grueling, gritty world of young women cartoonists," *Weirdo* had also welcomed female artists, in marked contrast to all-male precursors like **Zap.** Along with Kominsky-Crumb's regular strips, *Weirdo* eventually showcased **Phoebe Gloeckner**, Terri Boyce, Diane Noomin, Mary Fleener, Carol Tyler, Carol Lay, Julie Doucet, and Debbie Dreschler. Early on, the editors had discovered Dori Seda, who remained a regular (and rapidly improving) contributor until her death in 1988, with #22 presented as a "Dori Memorial Issue." *Weirdo* also reprinted historical material that suggested a lineage for its creators: the first issue has a Brueghel engraving as a center-spread, and later issues gather Gene Deitch's 1940s jazz cartoons, obscure strips from 1950s African American magazines, and Ed "Big Daddy" Roth's hot-rod cartoons. Finally, *Weirdo* also included technically crude work by outsider artists such as Bruce N. Duncan, Norman F. Pettingill, prison cartoonist Macedonio Garcia, and Crumb's own troubled brother Max. Issue #12 included work by (and a memorial to) the notoriously unstable underground legend Rory Hayes, who died in 1983.

Crumb's contributions to *Weirdo* included many important autobiographical strips, including "I Remember the Sixties" (#4), "Uncle Bob's Mid-Life Crisis" (#7), "Footsy" (#20), "Memories Are Made of This" (#22), and "I'm Grateful! I'm Grateful!" (#25). He also provided parodies, including a rather strained series of strips centered on the ultra-fashionable Mode O'Day (ultimately an easy target), and a wicked imitation of the independent erotic comic ***"Omaha," the Cat Dancer*** (#24). Yet the magazine was also Crumb's chosen venue for a number of remarkable historical comics, including an illustrated section of James Boswell's 18th-century *London Journal* (#3), case studies from Krafft-Ebing's 19th-century *Psychopathia Sexualis* (#13), and a biography of the

**science fiction** writer Philip K. Dick (#17), each produced in what had become Crumb's increasingly distinctive "late" style, marked by intensified cross-hatching and realistic detail. Crumb also illustrated popular songs and fairytales (including in #11 a contemporary "Goldilocks and the Three Bears") in similar, jarringly realistic style. However, for the final issue Crumb provided one of his most shocking strips in an often shocking career, the two part "When the Niggers Take Over America!" and "When the Goddamn Jews Take Over America!" Apparently created following a return trip to America once he had moved to France, the willfully offensive strip blurs the thin line between outrageous **satire** and genuine racist paranoia. Most (but not all) of Crumb's *Weirdo* work has been collected and reprinted, but it is worth seeking out issues of the magazine to appreciate them in their original, often messy context, rubbing shoulders with the more elusive comics and creators collected by the magazine.

While *Weirdo* appears less unified in its origins and function than either the underground comics or humor magazines it derives from, it is no less a product of its own time, staging a milder but still persistent protest against the return to conservatism marked by the Reagan administration in the United States, which it almost exactly paralleled. Redeploying a schoolyard taunt for its title, *Weirdo* offered an rare space for strange and even disturbing comics when the mainstream, once home to a range of genres, had narrowed to a near-exclusive focus on superhero titles and just before independent comics and the rise of the graphic novel would expand to offer unconventional artists additional venues for their uncompromising work.

*Corey K. Creekmur*

**WERTHAM, FREDRIC** (1895–1981). Born in Nuremberg, Fredric Wertham received his MD from the University of Wurtzburg in 1921; he trained under Emile Kraepelin, the founder of contemporary psychiatry, in Munich, then left Germany in 1922 to join the Phipps Psychiatric Clinic at Johns Hopkins University. In Baltimore, Wertham established a friendship with journalist H. L. Mencken and worked with famed attorney Clarence Darrow, becoming one of the first psychiatrists willing to testify on behalf of indigent black defendants. During this time Wertham married Florence Hesketh, a distinguished artist and sculptor, published studies on the effects of mescaline, developed a mosaic test to evaluate a patient's mental state, wrote *The Brain as an Organ: Its Postmortem Study and Interpretation* (1934), and received the first psychiatric grant made by the National Research Council.

During the 1930s Wertham moved to New York City where his expertise as a forensic psychiatrist became well known. With the encouragement of prominent African American writers Ralph Ellison and Richard Wright, Wertham enlisted a multiracial, volunteer staff to establish in 1946 a clinic in Harlem dedicated to alleviating the "free-floating hostility" afflicting many in that community and to understanding the realities of black life in America. Named in memory of Karl Marx's son-in-law, Dr. Paul LeFargue, the LeFargue Clinic became one of the most noteworthy institutions to serve poor Americans and to promote the cause of civil rights. As a result of his work at the

Clinic, NAACP Legal Defense Fund lawyers Jack Greenberg and Thurgood Marshall asked Wertham to research the effects of segregation on children. This research later became part of the groundbreaking anti-segregation case *Brown v. Board of Education of Topeka* (1954). During this period, Wertham treated the sons of the executed spies Julius and Ethel Rosenberg, was appointed by Senator Estes Kefauver as sole psychiatric consultant for the Senate Subcommittee on Organized Crime (1950), and became lead witness for the Senate Subcommittee to Investigate Juvenile Delinquency (1953–56).

In addition to bringing psychotherapy to a neglected community, Wertham's work at the Lefargue Clinic provided the foundation for his ideas on the contribution **horror** and **crime comics** made for a climate of juvenile violence. In 1948, Wertham organized the first symposium on media violence at the New York Academy of Medicine. Wertham identified media-induced violence as a public health issue; his arguments about the harmful effects of media-induced violence and its connection to the rise of juvenile delinquency are summarized in his book *Seduction of the Innocent* (1954). Here, he argued that the brutal and sadistic activity in many comics promoted a climate of violence and a coarsening of society. He was also concerned with sexual images in comics, especially with what he saw as the promulgation of images of homosexuality. Wertham concluded that access to violent comics for children younger than 14 must be controlled. Although Wertham, as a progressive, vigorously denied that he was advocating censorship, his work stimulated the comic book industry to adopt a tactic of self-censorship via The Code of the Comics Magazine Association of America (1954), generally known as the **Comics Code**.

Wertham continued to probe not only how comic books, but also mass news publications, television, and the movies influenced behavior and distorted perceptions of teenagers and different ethnic groups. *The Circle of Guilt* (1956) analyzes the paradigm of fear, racism, and prejudice in New York and exposes both the failure and hypocrisy of the legal system in complicity with the social service establishment.

In 1966, Wertham published *A Sign for Cain: An Exploration of Human Violence*, a sociological history of violence in Western culture. This book focuses on the effects of mass media exposure on the virulence of political tyrannies in the 20th century, on the emergence of the legal and medical legitimization of violence, and on the willing acceptance of the value of violence.

His interest in youth and how communication shapes culture led Wertham to publish his last book, *The World of Fanzines: A Special Form of Communication* (1973). He sees fanzines not as a product of our society but a reaction to it. The culture of fanzines expresses a genuine voice wanting to be heard, defying the overpowering roar of the mass media.

**Selected Bibliography:** Beaty, Bart. *Fredric Wertham and the Critique of Mass Culture.* Jackson: University Press of Mississippi, 2005; Gilbert, James. *A Cycle of Outrage: American's Reaction to Juvenile Delinquency.* New York: Oxford University Press, 1995; Lent, John, ed. *Pulp Demons: International Dimensions of the Postwar Anti-Comics Campaign.*

Madison: Fairleigh Dickinson University Press, 1999; Nyberg, Amy. *Seal of Approval: History of the Comics Code.* Jackson: University Press of Mississippi, 1998; Reibman, James E., ed. *A Fredric Wertham Reader.* Laurel, NY: Main Roads Books, forthcoming; Reibman, James E. *My Brother's Keeper: The Life of Fredric Wertham.* forthcoming; Wertham, Fredric. *Seduction of the Innocent.* Laurel, NY: Main Roads Books, 2004.

*James E. Reibman*

**WESTERNS (COMICS).** Comics and the American West have always shared a strong affinity, as Maurice Horn observes: "Just as the Western pioneers were conscious of opening a new geographical frontier, the pioneers of the comics were quick to realize that they were exploring a new artistic frontier" (10). Another medium can be added to this relation: film. The history of Western comic books is strongly connected with Western movies. Hundreds of heroes from television and movie Westerns have been adapted into comic book series and vice versa. The medium of film learned a lot from the hyperbolic atmosphere of comics and comic strips, especially derived syntactic techniques from film editing. The iconography of the American West is already situated in the pictures of Frederic Remington (1861–1909) and Charles Russell (1864–1926), which constitute a model for the whole visual and graphic tradition. The adventures of Western comics derive from two different traditions. The fantastic one, addressed to juvenile readers, found its roots in the dime novels of the 19th century (and in the 20th century in Western pulp magazines, e.g. by Zane Grey), in Wild West shows like those of Buffalo Bill and in the "horse operas" of silent films. The second tradition, the realistic illustration of the West, was targeted at adult readers; newspapers, diaries, photographs, and chronicles are the sources of its pictures.

Three major elements define the genre: setting (what became the Western United States, extending also to Alaska, Canada, Mexico, Argentina, and even Australia), period (the later half of the 19th century), and the characters who lived in this time and place. Furthermore, the depiction of violence plays a central role in the genre. The history of the genre enlarged this close definition and added new themes and interpretations to the traditional stories. These concepts will be illustrated using examples from some of the most significant Western comic books.

## Setting

The most recognizable feature of any Western is its setting, an idealized "Garden of the West" with a wide geographical palette. Film director John Ford established the unmistakable Monument Valley (Utah) as the Western landscape par excellence. Depending on the knowledge or skills of the authors and artists, the deserts, plains, rivers, and mountains of the West are elaborated in a more or less authentic way. The vegetation, like the ever-present cactus, is not only used for decorative reasons, but can even become an allegorical motif as in the comic strip *Krazy Kat*. Landscape can also reflect the feelings of the figures or the atmosphere of the situation. The conflict between man and nature often develops into real battles against blizzards, dust storms, and the merciless sun. The latter is often used as an instrument for torture, examples of which can be seen in *Blueberry*. Comics of the American West portray the development of the land in every form of human settlement; from primitive huts to already flourishing towns with their obligatory main streets, saloons, and railroad stations. Military forts and Indian villages are hot spots for conflicts.

## Period

The genre is structured by archetypes of American mythology developed through history. Indeed, while typically pretending to historical accuracy, the Western (in comics and otherwise) has often contributed to the growth of legend and myth. Western comic book authors frequently base their plots on historical events, especially those of the 19th century, when the American West still presented the challenge of a frontier to be tamed. Western comics have drawn extensively upon events associated with the conquest of the West, including the American Indian Wars, the American Civil War (1861–65), the construction of the railroads or the settlement of the western frontier with its most visible symbol, the wagon train. Key events include the activity of Pony Express (which in fact only lasted for 18 months), the running of stagecoach lines, or the Gold Rush of 1849. The search for gold is a leitmotif of Western comic book series. Many writers use avarice as one of the primal human motivations for violent conflicts. The figure of the gold seeker joins the Native American and the adventurous Westerner as key images in these comics.

The legendary bloody encounter at the O.K. Corral (October 26, 1881) in Tombstone Territory between Wyatt Earp with his marshals and a group of cowboys established the gunfight and the showdown as a favorite focal point for Western comics such as *Hopalong Cassidy*, *Tom Mix*, or *Tex Willer*. Meanwhile, such events helped to make the gunfighter a central figure in the Western genre in any medium, including comics.

One of the few long-lasting Western comics set in the atypical period of the 18th century was *Tomahawk* (published 1950–73), created by Joe Samachson and Edmund Good, with **Frank Frazetta** as one of the artists. Here, Tomahawk and his group of rangers fight behind the British lines for General George Washington in the American Revolutionary War (1775–1783).

## Characters

Both historical figures and fictional characters have contributed to the image of the Western hero. Western legends are based on true accounts of historical figures such as Kit Carson, Billy the Kid, the Apache Geronimo or—the most often mythologized Western figure—Buffalo Bill Cody. Like most of the comic book heroes from other genres, the Western hero, apart from a few exceptions such as Blueberry, does not age, making him available for continuing adventures over long periods of time. Generally speaking, there are five types of Western heroes: the cowboy, the lone rider/reformed outlaw, the lawman, the (ex-)military man and the Indian.

The archetype of the Western hero is the cowboy, still virtually a national symbol in the present-day United States. Classic examples of the idealized hero who represents the social values of the "good guy" include heroes like Tom Mix and Roy Rogers (stars of American film and television Westerns) and Jim Boum (from the French comics by Marijac). The cowboy's obligatory sidekick is his horse, mostly a stallion, which adds traits like loyalty, compassion and stamina to the powers of the hero.

Fred Harman's (1902–82) red-haired *Bronc Peeler* (created in 1933, known as *Red Ryder* from 1938 on) was an unconventional comic-strip cowboy character. Sometimes guided by his sense of justice, sometimes simply by more pragmatic motives, he always remains impenitent. Over time, he undergoes a metamorphosis from traditional cowboy to car-driving and plane-flying undercover agent. With his companions, Coyote Pete and Little Beaver, a little Navaho Indian boy, Red Ryder soon moved beyond the original comic strip to appear in a vast number of comic books from 1940 to 1957. Originally based on reprinted newspaper strips, these books soon moved into original territory, using the same cast of characters, but adjusting their adventures to juvenile readers. The pencils on the first original comic book material belonged to **Jack Kirby**, with *Lightnin' and the Lone Rider* in 1937. The details of costumes (e.g. Red's Stetson) and accessories (e.g. the Mexican saddle) and the setting (southwestern Colorado) are depicted with an almost archaeological authenticity. Characterized by its attention to detail, a touch of pathos and its wry humor, the series is a Western of the old school, despite its later setting, which allows for the presence of cars and airplanes.

The archetypal cattle driver is also represented in **European comics**. Marijac's (Jacques Dumas, 1908–94) *Jim Boum* (1934–50) fights cattle rustlers, train robbers, outlaw gangs and also natural forces like blizzards and wavy rivers. He later transforms into an enemy of the Nazis in Africa and of the Japanese in the Pacific, until he eventually even becomes a space-cowboy.

The vast number of "Kid" characters in Western comics are often masked like **superhero**es and capable of fighting with super-human stunts and methods. These more entertaining and juvenile cowboy figures include such characters as Kid Colt, hero of a series that started as *Kid Colt, Hero of the West* in 1948 scripted inter alia by **Stan Lee** and drawn by masters such as **Jack Kirby**, **Reed Crandall**, Joe Maneely, and others, who where engaged at the same time with **Marvel Comics'** *Two-Gun Kid*. The huge number of *Kid*-titles in Western comic books was enlarged in 1954 by three other young-looking justice-fighters: *The Ringo Kid* (mainly by Joe Maneely and Joe Sinnott), *The Outlaw Kid* (with Doug Wildey's photographic art style) and *The Western Kid*—all of them dropped in 1957 and reprinted in 1970. The foundation of the **Comics Code** Authority also came about in 1954, which sought, among other things to diminish the violence in comic books. Ironically, the rise of the code had little effect on the Western, which was relatively immune to the strictures of the code because its violence was so traditional and ritualized. Thus, Stan Lee's Rawhide Kid, a ruthless gunslinger using gun and bullwhip with brutal effectiveness, was born in 1955 (with art by Kirby), the year after the establishment of the Comics Code.

The "Kid-characters" diminished the idealized image of the ethically conscious cowboy. One alternative is the figure of the "lone rider," who knows no moral code other than his own. In particular, Zane Grey's *Tex Thorne* (1936) gave an example of the unconventional hero who is driven by an inner conviction or by personal motivations. The ambiguity of this anti-heroic and pessimistic figure did not suit the habits of the American comics readership, but was enthusiastically absorbed by authors from abroad such as the Belgian Jijé (Joseph Gillain, 1914–80) with his *Jerry Spring* (1954–90). Unlike the lone rider, the so-called "reformed outlaw" only seems to be an anti-hero; his failures and incomprehensible reactions (overstepping his authority, brutally killing, abusing women) are forced by external circumstances. A model for such a reformed outlaw is Jean Valjean, the protagonist in Victor Hugo's *Les Misérables*.

Partly deriving from the *Zorro* novels and films, partly because of the more popular concept of the superhero, the masked hero also fights in Western comic books. Fran Striker introduced the character of the costumed Western hero with *The Lone Ranger* (in comic book form mainly published by Dell from 1948–62). The ranger and his white horse Silver were born in 1933 in a radio broadcast from station WXYZ of Detroit, and were then adapted for a comic strip, first drawn by Ed Kressy, who was replaced early on by and Charles Flanders, in 1938. With its stagecoach robberies, bank holdups, cattle rustlings, heroic rescues of defrauded widows, victimized orphans (mostly young girls) and illegal land take-overs, the series builds a classical Western repertoire of narrative patterns and can be considered the most representative of all American Western comic strips, with regard to the strong presence and variety of Western myths. Because of Flanders's limited drawing skills, the reprints for a comic book series beginning in 1947 lasted only for 37 issues; the franchise then passed on to Paul Newman (no relation to the actor) and Tom Gill, who created new material for Dell until 1962 (followed by reprints and original material by Gold Key 1964–77). In Newman's plots, the Lone Ranger became a kind of master sleuth and unofficial guardian of the peace on the frontier; Gill's drawings gave spirit, especially to horse riding and shooting scenes, two of the main iconographic actions of the Western genre. Though perhaps now best known as the protagonist of a television series (1949–57), the masked rider's career in the comics continues up to present day (Dynamite Entertainment, 2006– ), scripted by Brett Matthews and drawn by Sergio Cariello in a new, very cinematic manner with soft, brownish colors (by Dean White). The figure of the Lone Ranger includes the aspects of the lone rider and of the lawman, another typical figure in Western comics. Meanwhile, his Indian sidekick Tonto has become an icon in his own right, though in many ways a problematic one.

The Lone Ranger is a lawman, a member of the Texas Rangers. In Western towns, the lawman is embodied in the marshal or sheriff, archetypes that clearly emerged from Western history and folklore. The lawman's aura of righteousness and invincibility derives from such spectacular historical gunfights as the one at the O.K. Corral and was enshrined by film figures such as Gary Cooper in *High Noon* (1952). The paradoxical fact of the small number of sheriff or marshal titles in comic book series can be explained by the open-ended structure of the comics. Lawmen in long-lasting series like Tex often bend their official duties into wild adventures without strong rules.

Dell's *Maverick* (1959–62) shows another lawman-type who fights more with his cleverness than with his gun. Dan Spiegle's camera-like compositions present Bret and Bart Maverick, two brothers of the post-Civil War days. The tendency toward detective fiction and soft-hearted heroes who impress more with their brains than with their physical strength was continued in 1968 with *Bat Lash* by Sergio Aragones and Nick Cardy.

Westerns with the Civil War as historical background either portray the military man as a patriotic figure or criticize him. The heroic portrayal of the soldiers of the U.S. Cavalry was one of the favorite motifs for American Western comics. With army deserter *Sgt. Kirk* (1953–59), Italian creator Hugo Pratt (1927–95) gave a very European and critical view on the theme. The American perspective changed with Michael Fleischer's *Jonah Hex*, which first appeared in 1972 and has appeared sporadically ever since. An ex-officer of the Confederacy, his face partly blown away by gunfire, Hex stands out in the crowd of good-looking John Wayne copies. His ambiguous stance between good and evil is symbolized in a Jekyll-and-Hyde-theme; but unlike the **Batman** character Two-Face, Hex never loses his heroic power. The artists of *Jonah Hex* all came from abroad: the Filipinos Tony de Zuñiga and Noly Panaligan, and the Latin Americans George Moliterni, and José Luis García-López. In January 2006, writer Jimmy Palmiotti, together with new artists, revived Hex for DC by making the character more mystical and adding elements of **horror** to the series.

In Western comics, Native Americans have mostly been treated as the antagonists of the Cavalry or to symbolize the wildness of the frontier. However, individual Indians, acting as sidekicks of the white heroes, quickly became a basic feature of the genre. Tonto (with the Lone Ranger) and Little Beaver (with Red Ryder) show bravery and pure heroism, joining a legacy of Indian companions that dates back to the novels of James Fenimore Cooper.

As a reaction to the trauma of the Vietnam War and the oppositional political movements of the 1960s, one can observe a change in Westerns from pure action and violence to a new examination of the problems of the displacement of Native Americans, which began to reflect also present situation of ethnic minority groups. The Swiss francophone cartoonist Derib (Claude de Ribeaupierre, 1944– ) marked with his *Buddy Longway* (1974–87; 2002–6) a movement toward "political correctness," telling a sentimental family saga of the interracial relationship between the white trapper and his Sioux Indian wife, Chinook. Buddy's vulnerable character and the deep psychological conflicts between different cultures are set in an allegorical rough wilderness, which Derib created with the highest feeling for atmosphere.

Together with Swiss francophone scriptwriter Job (André Jobin, 1927–) Derib created another "ethnophile" Western series, aimed with its cartoonish style at a younger audience: *Yakari* (1973–2008 and still running). Here, the small Sioux Indian protagonist and his predominately animal friends (he is able to speak animal languages), live adventures without any "White Men," as the stories take place long before the European colonization. In addition, the concluded series *Les Peaux-Rouges* (1974–82) by Dutch artist Hans Kresse, focused on the world of the American tribes and tried to show their culture in an objective manner, free of mystifications and epic narration, and set apart from modern culture.

Because of its central emphasis on good guy/bad guy oppositions, the Western comic requires a strong antagonist to the Western hero. The antagonist, as the incarnation of evil, serves to enhance the image and powers of the hero. Among other things, the villain gives the hero a reason to fight, thus initiating the plot; meanwhile, violent and even criminal acts by the hero are often legitimated by the necessity of defeating the evil villain.

While the Indians were long depicted as evil, crazed savages, the most vilified ethnic group in the Western comics of the 1930s may be Mexicans, characterized by their Spanish surnames and stereotypical Latin American mannerisms (mustached, in tight pants and wide sombreros). Only a few Western comics, such as *The Cisco Kid* or *Jerry Spring*, used a Mexican as the hero's sidekick, but then the Cisco Kid is himself a Mexican *caballero*.

Women characters were also often important to the genre, especially as a motivating factor for masculine action. Such characters generally served either as the reason for vengeance and the hero's helping hand, or the object of desire, as represented by the Indian princess, the saloon girl, or the schoolmarm. Historical figures like Calamity Jane even got their own comic books. Annie Oakley became a popular female hero in comics, while a vogue for **romance** Westerns in the late 1940s and early 1950s offered opportunity to feature women as key characters.

## The History of the Western Comic Book

The Western genre of comics is as old as the medium itself. The first Western comic book stories were reprints of newspaper strips. As early as in 1889 the French series *La Famille Fenouillard* by Georges Colomb confronted their characters with Native Americans and cowboys. A growth-spurt in the development of the genre started in the 1930s with Harry O'Neill's *Broncho Bill* (1930–52); the "adventurous decade" increased the interest of the part of syndicates for Western stories.

The 1940s signified the peak of the Western newspaper strip, as World War II helped to develop **superhero** and **war comics**, but the overall success of the Western film (epitomized by the movies of John Ford) prompted comics artists to change to the genre. Among them, **Burne Hogarth**, known for his work with *Tarzan*, shifted to the Western with the Tarzan-like Drago (1945–46), a bare-breasted hero who rides virtuously through Hogarth's landscapes and fights postwar **Nazis** in Argentina. The years 1948–52 are often considered the **Golden Age** of the Western, when American Western comics reached the pinnacle of their popularity.

American Western comics maintained a reasonable success through the 1950s, but many Western titles were discontinued in the 1960s and 1970s, as the popularity of the genre declined. The same period, however, saw a rise of the Western in Europe, where American Westerns remained popular even as European-produced Westerns rose to the fore, especially in France and Italy. Indeed, the Western strip flourished in all parts of the world (mainly Spain, Argentina and Japan) while it was slowly dying in the United States. Maurice Horn partly accounts for this fact with the European and Latin American view of "the Western as a modern allegory of the eternal struggle between good and evil" (174). The lone cowboy symbolizes the rightful heir to the knight of medieval epics of chivalry. Built by Western movies and Western comics, the mythology of the American West shares many of the classical elements of Homer's *Iliad* or *Odyssey*.

Jijé's previously mentioned *Jerry Spring* can be considered the founding text of the Franco-Belgian Western comic tradition. Pressure from the publisher (Dupuis) forced Jijé to employ assistants for his successful series from 1960 on, among them **Jean "Moebius" Giraud**. In 1963, Moebius created the famous Western series *Lieutenant Blueberry* with Jean-Michel Charlier. His style would imitate Jijé's at least until 1965. Very impressed by his first sojourn in Mexico (1955), Moebius's fascination with the Mexican landscape spilled over into his panels, and his "hallucinatory, desert-like landscapes" became one of his trademarks. "American Western comics remained overshadowed by the movies, but Gir[aud] used devices peculiar to comics to produce effects that are impossible on screen" (Screech 2005, 100). Nevertheless, Giraud was influenced by both American and Italian cinema, as *Blueberry* adapted the styles of Sergio Leone's Italian Spaghetti Westerns and of the American director Sam Packinpah. On the other hand, Hermann (Hermann Huppen) and Greg's (Michel Régnier) *Comanche* (1969–80) shows more conventional styles and influences. Set on a ranch, it tells the story of a young and pretty heroine, Comanche, and her taciturn but strong foreman Red Dust.

Spaghetti Westerns still influence the European Western comic, as well as the very few new American series of recent years such as *Loveless* (2005–8) by **Brian Azzarello**. With *Bouncer* (2001–8), Chilean writer Alejandro Jodorowsky (1929–) and French artist François Boucq (1955–) presented the Wild West after the American Civil War. The grotesque poetical style of Jodorowsky and the surreal super-naturalistic drawings of Boucq unmasked all the myths of the West. In a near glorification of violence, the borders of good and evil are erased in *Bouncer* and the reader is confronted with bare brutality and mystic, bloody action.

## Subgenres

In addition to comics that can directly be identified as examples of the Western genre, a number of comics have participated in a more marginal way. Numerous comics, for example, have combined aspects of the Western with those of other genres, such as **science fiction** or **horror**. For example, DC and **Marvel** especially pushed the "Weird Western" as a subgenre, as Kid Colt and the Rawhide Kid fight against monsters, aliens, and other characters from horror comics. Meanwhile, the mix of genres was joined by a mix of media; several Western television series were adapted to comics, which became a form of merchandising for the TV series.

The most important subgenre of the Western is the parody of the Western proper, which dates back at least to Ferd Johnson's *Texas Slim* (started in the Chicago *Tribune* in 1925). Outside the United States, a satirical view of the American West was brought forth by Italian Benito Jacovitti in *Cocco Bill* (1957–98) with his chamomile-drinking cowboy and his cigarette-smoking horse. The most popular and successful parodic Western comic book is the French series *Lucky Luke*. In 1946, the cartoonist Morris (Maurice de Bevère, 1923–2001) created this affectionate parody of the Western mythos and was joined in 1955 by scriptwriter René Goscinny (1926–77), creator of *Astérix*. Lucky Luke and his talking white horse Jolly Jumper confront the whole world of the "real West," always with a passion for authenticity: Lucky Luke tries to put the parodied version of the Dalton brothers behind bars, he teaches Calamity Jane how to be a real lady, and runs across Billy the Kid, Jesse James, and a bounty hunter that looks strikingly like Lee van Cleef, an actor in many Spaghetti-Westerns. To this day (with the help of many ghost-writers and artists) Lucky Luke always rides away into the sunset in the last panel of every album, humming his famous: "I'm a poor lonesome cowboy and a long way from home . . ."

**Selected Bibliography:** Bonelli, Sergio. *Le Frontiere di carta. Piccola storia del western a fumetti*. Milan: Sergio Bonelli Editore, 1998; Briou, Jean-Michel, ed. *Le nouveau Western. De Jijé à Blanc-Dumont*. Brussels: 1981; Brown, Dee. *The Westerners*. New York: Holt, Rinehart and Winston, 1974; Frasca, Giampiero. *C'era una volta il Western. Immagini di una nazione*. Novara: De Agostini, 2007; Frayling, Christopher. *Spaghetti Westerns*. London: I. B. Tauris, 1981; Horn, Maurice. *Comics of the American West*. New York: Winchester Press, 1977; Screech, Matthew. *Masters of the Ninth Art. Bande dessinées and Franco-Belgian Identity*. Liverpool: University Press, 2005.

*Martha Zan*

**WHAT IF?** The *What If?* series explores the motif of the alternative history within the world of **Marvel** comics, as much as **DC Comics** had explored this motif in their "imaginary stories," out of continuity tales (often about **Superman**), that explored various possibilities in the character's life. This would later lead to their extensive *Elseworlds* line of stories, such as those that place **Batman** in the Victorian era or in a modern world in which the country is run by a theocracy, or putting Superman in the U.S. Civil War or in Camelot. Yet when it comes to alternative comics history on a regular basis, no one did it like Marvel and *What If?*

The original *What If?* series were 47 double-sized titles that ran, often bi-monthly, from 1977 to 1984. Series creator and writer Roy Thomas summed up the origins of the series:

> I was looking for a new series to write that would keep me out of the Marvel mainstream (so that, now that I was no longer editor-in-chief, I wouldn't have to

keep up with continuity of the main characters) . . . just as **Conan**, *The Invaders*, et al., were doing. Still, I liked the idea of writing an occasional story about the **Fantastic Four**, **Hulk**, Spidey, or whoever. And Stan was in the habit of saying that the way he thought up some of the story directions was to ask himself, "What if" this happened or that happened . . . how would it affect a hero's life going forward? So I proposed a comic called *What If* which would feature a different hero every month, starting with one of the strongest possibilities—what if **Spider-Man** had actually joined the F. F. as he had tried to do in *Amazing Spider-Man #1*?

A one-time *What If?* special appeared in 1988, and the following year a new monthly series began that lasted for 114 issues (plus an issue numbered -1) until 1998. The "host" of these stories is Uatu, The Watcher, an immortal alien who lives on the moon and whose race watches but does not interfere. He was able to look into alternative universes and tell of what happened in those worlds. Due to events in other comics the Watcher stopped appearing after issue #76 of the second series and with issue #87 the book's format changed, with the major difference not being spelled out on the cover (it simply became "*What If? Starring . . .*" The most notable of these was issue #105, which was set in the near future and introduced Spider-Girl, the daughter of Spider-Man. This character soon got her own book and this led to a number of titles (known as MC2) that were set in that time period. While none of the others lasted for more than a year, Spider-Girl lasted for 100 issues in one title, and 30 issues in another. Some stories from this era were also listed as part of the Marvel "Alterniverse," which includes a few other "alternate world" tales.

For the next seven years, Marvel's only visits to various alternative worlds was through the *X-Men* spin-off *Exiles*, but beginning in 2005, Marvel began to publish a series of "one-shot" *What If?* stories. Usually with five to six issues (all numbered #1) the comics that were published around the same period often had a common thread or theme. The first of these had various "hosts," including **Brian Michael Bendis** acting as the narrator in his own stories. The next batch of stories all took place on the same alternative world, with the "host" being a man from the Marvel world who was able to read about these historical figures (such as a Civil War-era **Captain America** or a feudal Japan version of **Daredevil**) on his computer. This group also had an additional comic, a humor title called *Wha . . . Huh?!* The next three groups of one-shots had no host, and often dealt with divergences on major storylines from recent years such as *Civil War* and *World War Hulk*. The fourth group is notable for a **Fantastic Four**-themed story that was to be drawn by Mike Wieringo, but was unfinished at the time of his death. Other artists helped to complete it, and the volume was sold as a special with proceeds going to the charity, The Hero Initiative. In addition, the fifth collection had a back-up story that ran throughout all five issues.

Many issues of the original series have been collected in a series of books called *What If? Classic* and random issues from the first two series have been collected in various books. The one-shots have been collected as *What If: Why Not?*, *What If: Mirror Mirror*,

*What If: Event Horizon*, *What If: Civil War*, and *What If: Secret Wars*. While most of the stories in the two ongoing titles were done-in-one types, there was the occasional multi-part story or sequel and some stories have been re-imagined in later volumes. Some issues contained more than one story and the first series also contained a few back-up stories that were in continuity, such as the history of The Eternals or a story set in the 1940s that adjusted the history of Captain America. As expected the more popular characters appeared in the most issues including Spider-Man (28), The Fantastic Four (26), and The **X-Men** (50—both as a team and solo members such as Wolverine).

Some points of divergence were revisited multiple times (sometimes even in the same issue). For example, in the regular continuity a burglar whom the newly created Spider-Man failed to stop ended up killing Peter Parker's Uncle Ben, leading Spider-Man to become a crimefighter. *What If?* explored such possibilities as what if he had stopped the burglar or what if his aunt had been killed instead. Alternatives to the Fantastic Four gaining powers by going into space ranged from them having different powers, to all of them having exactly the same power, to their not going at all. There was even a story (Vol. 1 #11) in which **Stan Lee**, **Jack Kirby**, and two others at Marvel became the Fantastic Four.

Some *What If?* stories involve a large number of characters while some only a handful or less. Yet even the latter could have an effect of the greater Marvel universe. For example, a Fantastic Four story in Vol. 1 #31, in which the Thing goes on a rampage, shows how his actions prevented the origins of Spider-Man, **Thor**, and The Hulk. Some issues have happy endings while others end in tragedy, sometimes with the death of the hero, sometimes with the entire world being destroyed. While there may not be another ongoing series in the near future, one way or the other, Marvel will continue to ask "What If?"

*David S. Serchay*

**WHATEVER HAPPENED TO THE MAN OF TOMORROW?** First published in two parts in *Superman* #423 and *Action Comics* #583 (both September 1986) "Whatever Happened to the Man of Tomorrow?" was, conceptually if not literally, the last **Superman** story. Written by **Alan Moore** (who, by legend, threatened **DC** editor Julius Schwartz to get the assignment), a "final" Superman story was made possible because of the planned re-launch of Superman by artist and writer **John Byrne** in the 1986 miniseries *The Man of Steel*, following the extensive streamlining of the entire DC "universe" in *Crisis on Infinite Earths* in 1985. The "new" Superman, along with most DC titles, would proceed as if many of the details of the character's past had never happened, so Moore's story would be the last to draw freely upon story elements about to be officially erased from DC continuity. However, the popularity and success of Moore's story in wrapping up 50 years of previous Superman stories had the curious effect of quietly undermining much of what came later, even suggesting that the legendary character might have been best left alone after this elegant conclusion.

Moore's story followed "For the Man Who Has Everything," his notable contribution (drawn by **Dave Gibbons**) to *Superman Annual* 11 (1985), which revealed Superman's "heart's desire" to live a normal life on his native planet Krypton, married with children. Moore's only other Superman story, "The Jungle Line," appeared in *DC Comics Presents* 85 (1985), and featured **Swamp Thing**, the character who elevated the British Moore to fame as a writer in the United States. (Otherwise, Moore has explored the Superman mythos extensively through surrogates, including Miracleman, Supreme, and **Tom Strong**, all stand-ins for the Man of Steel.) Although Moore would soon be most famous for his "deconstruction" of the superhero in *Watchmen* (1986–87), his Superman stories are affectionate tributes, even as they end an era in the character's fictional life. It is therefore especially appropriate that **Curt Swan** (with inking by **George Pérez** in *Superman* and Kurt Schaffenberger in *Action*), the character's definitive **Silver Age** artist, penciled this "swan song" for Superman. (The cover of *Action* #583, depicting Superman leaving the characters in the series behind on the roof of the Daily Planet building, also includes cameo drawings of Swan, as well as editors Julius Schwartz and DC President Jenette Kahn.) In Swan's seasoned hands this last story looks like a classic DC comic, in contrast to the more experimental visual styles then accompanying other revamps of **superheroes**; the easy collaboration of Moore and Swan thus avoids the generational conflict one might have expected in the meeting of a young Turk and old pro.

Set in the future year of 1997, former reporter Lois Lane (now Lois Elliot, married with a baby boy) is interviewed for a "Superman Memorial Edition" of the Daily Planet, her old employer: she recounts a series of traumatic events, beginning with the logically illogical "genocide, homicide, and finally suicide" performed by Bizarro, Superman's "perfect imperfect duplicate." This is soon followed by Superman's "unmasking," the long delayed revelation to the world that Superman's secret identity has been mild mannered reporter Clark Kent. As the story continues, piece after piece of the accumulated Superman mythology is brought to a conclusion with a finality that the ongoing, serial production of Superman stories had persistently withheld. The longstanding rivalry between Lois Lane and Lana Lang, the repetitive cycle that allowed Superman's villains to be endlessly captured and to escape or be released, and even the often vague status of Superman's pet dog Krypto are all resolved without the open-endedness readers had learned to expect from decades of previous comics. In the story's most delicate moment, the arrival of Supergirl from the future upsets Superman, who had recently mourned her dramatic death in *Crisis on Infinite Earths* and *Superman* #414: in Moore's story, at least, Superman respects DC's enforced continuity (misleading Supergirl as to her fate), even as Moore tugs at one of its many loopholes. Rather than just an aside for DC fans, the scene hinges on the free-wheeling devices of time-travel and multiple dimensions that DC now sought to control, turning the narrative puzzles raised by DC's recalibration of its stories into an ethical dilemma, one of the remarkable ways in which Moore breathes new life into established conventions.

In effect, the entire story is both a tribute to and work of mourning for the often silly but fun Superman legacy then being rejected for greater realism and seriousness.

So, before they are banished, Moore makes grand use of the "Superman family" that had included not only spin-off comics featuring "girlfriend" Lois Lane and "pal" Jimmy Olsen, but futuristic cohorts the Legion of Superheroes, the Legion of Super-pets, and super-villains such as Lex Luthor, Brainiac, and Mr. Mxyzptlk, all at long last killed in this tale, the last by Superman himself in violation of his personal code, which requires the end of his career. Revealed as the source of all the trouble in the story, Lois notes that Mr. Mxyzptlk, the cartoonish imp from the Fifth Dimension (introduced in *Superman* #30 in 1944) "looked different somehow. He didn't look funny anymore," one of the story's wry acknowledgments of the revisions under-way in superhero comics. The story thus blends elements of the trend towards grim "revisionism" that would be most dramatically marked by Moore's *Watchmen* and **Frank Miller's *The Dark Knight Returns*** (as well as Moore's **Batman** one-shot *The Killing Joke*) with a much more sentimental quality, which would characterize later DC stories, such as **Mark Waid** and **Alex Ross's *Kingdom Come*** (1996), which also envisions a future, happily married Superman. The clever line that concludes Moore's expository introduction to the story ("This is an Imaginary Story . . . aren't they all?") has often been cited as a gentle riposte to attempts to distinguish "real" events in the continuity of the DC universe from what it had explicitly identified as "Imaginary Stories" or (beginning in 1989) as *Elseworlds* tales. Like many of the fanciful Silver Age Superman stories it simultaneously emulates and puts to rest, Moore's story ends with a wink to the reader, letting us in on the secret of Super-man's disappearance and presumed death, and providing the seed for future stories even as a long run is being officially shut down. Eventually Moore's battles with DC would make his work on the central figures in DC's pantheon unthinkable, but his rare take on the company's central icon remains a highlight from a half-century of stories.

DC repackaged the two comic book issues as a single square-bound volume in 1996, and the story has since been reprinted in *DC Universe: The Stories of Alan Moore* (2006). *The Deluxe Edition* of the story (joined by Moore's two other Superman stories) appeared in 2009.

**Selected Bibliography:** Klock, Geoff. *How to Read Superhero Comics and Why.* New York: Continuum, 2003.

*Corey K. Creekmur*

**WHEDON, JOSS** (1964–). Joseph Hill Whedon was born in New York City to television writer Tom Whedon and high school teacher and writer, Lee Stearns. His parents divorced when he was nine years old and he subsequently divided time between them. His teenage years were spent at a private boys' school in England and he went on to study feminism and film at Wesleyan University. Whedon lists his film studies professor Jeanine Basinger, his mother, and his wife Kai Cole as the three most important and influential women in his life and his work.

Whedon began his career in Hollywood writing for the sitcom *Roseanne*—a job that made him a third generation television writer (his father wrote for *The Electric Company* and *The Golden Girls* and his grandfather, John Whedon, wrote for *The Donna Reed Show*). Whedon also co-wrote several movies including, *Toy Story* and *Alien Resurrection*, and worked as a script doctor on *Speed* and **X-Men**—the latter of which kept only two of his original lines.

Whedon has noted he was a fan of comic books growing up, and more specifically, of *girls* in comic books. Therefore he was disappointed with the lack of female characters in the medium, especially when it came to **superheroes**. He was particularly drawn to Kitty Pryde of the X-Men—a character he calls a figure of both affection and identification. Whedon's early frustration with this scarcity of interesting women characters in comics later carried over to film and television. It was one of several factors that inspired him to create a female superhero in Buffy Summers, who first appeared in the 1992 film *Buffy the Vampire Slayer* and then in the critically acclaimed television series of the same name from 1997 to 2003.

While he acknowledges that film and comics are different media, Whedon frequently utilizes storytelling techniques he learned from reading comic books in his film and television work. These include plotting devices and rhythm as well as superhero tropes. Additionally, the impact of **Chris Claremont**'s early run on the X-Men can be seen in Whedon's narrative focus on friendship and the created family in his television series *Buffy the Vampire Slayer*, *Angel*, and *Firefly*. Whedon's series challenge the conventions of commercial television work, partly because he draws so heavily upon alternative traditions, especially the comics, though the comics have come to influence numerous other television series as well, including *Alias*, *Battlestar Galactica*, and *Lost*—not to mention more obvious cases, such as *Heroes* and *Smallville*.

Whedon's interest in comics came full-circle when he began to write comics himself. First he contributed to comic books based on *Buffy the Vampire Slayer* that were published by **Dark Horse Comics** from 1998 to 2004. He also wrote a limited series about a future Slayer for **Dark Horse** called *Fray*. It was drawn by Karl Moline and appeared between the years 2001 and 2003. Whedon scripted issues #1 through #24 for **Marvel**'s *Astonishing X-Men* title with art by John Cassaday. He was involved in writing a **Wonder Woman** film script for Warner Bros. but the project dissolved over creative differences.

In 2007, five years after the series finale of *Buffy the Vampire Slayer*, Whedon began producing an Eighth Season of the series—but in an innovative twist he did so in comic books rather than on television. Published by Dark Horse, *Buffy the Vampire Slayer Season Eight* has expanded the Slayer mythology in a canonical fashion and has featured scripts by Whedon, as well as by guest writers such as **Jeph Loeb** and **Brian K. Vaughan**. The success of this transition from medium to medium led to a continuation of *Angel* in comic book form as well, published by IDW Publishing. Whedon also wrote an arc for **Marvel's Runaways** after Vaughan left the title.

**Selected Bibliography:** Kaveney, Roz. *Superheroes! Capes and Crusaders in Comics and Films.* New York: I. B. Tauris, 2008; Stuller, Jennifer K. *Ink-stained Amazons and Cinematic Warriors: Superwomen in Modern Mythology.* New York: I. B. Tauris, 2010; Whedon, Joss. "Introduction." In *Fray.* Oregon: Dark Horse Books, 2003.

*Jennifer K. Stuller*

**WILLIAMSON, AL** (1931–). Artist Al Williamson's clean and articulate drawing provided a touch of elegance to the sometimes crude and overwrought expressionist style delivered by the **EC** (Entertaining Comics) brand of grotesque **horror** in the 1950s. Williamson was the youngest of EC's stable of regular artists, and his work was inspired by the romantic draftsmanship of Alex Raymond (*Flash Gordon*) and Hal Foster (***Tarzan*** and *Prince Valiant*). Williamson, of Colombian descent, worked in the New York commercial art world, studied with anatomy and sequential art master, **Burne Hogarth**, and performed his first comic book art in *Heroic Comics* in 1948 at the age of 17. Later, he took over the *Flash Gordon* strip from Raymond. Collector Ray Cuthbert relates that Williamson wished to emulate Raymond's style precisely, so he used a lightbox to trace Raymond's delicate figurative work, even though his own hand was beautiful and clear.

Despite the typically crude and shocking appearance of ghouls, **vampires**, and other monsters in EC comics, Williamson's brand of horror was more restrained, dignified, and elevated. His work served the story and eschewed showboating. A former publisher at **Marvel**, Shirrel Rhoades, writes that, "it would take more than half a century for Hollywood's special effects to catch up with the dazzling visuals drawn by **Wallace Wood** and Al Williamson for the EC Comics' celebrated sci-fi titles" (50). After the extinction of EC, Williamson was employed by a host of companies in the 1950s including Harvey, Atlas, and AGC.

Williamson distinguished himself as the artist of *Flash Gordon* in the 1960s, working on the daily comic strip and creating memorable *Flash Gordon* comic books for King Features. Williamson's world featured floating cities, sleek spacecraft, grotesque monsters wedded to classical proportions and a strong sense of balance. Heroes, like Flash Gordon, were always supple, erect, and placid, representing an ideal of Greek and Renaissance humanism.

By the 1980s, **Marvel Comics** and George Lucas tapped Williamson to do the Marvel Comics **adaptation** of *The Empire Strikes Back* from the *Star Wars* film series. Williamson augmented the fairytale wonder of *Star Wars* with a grit and realism that provided gravity to the storyline and underscored its classicism.

Much of Williamson's prowess in recent years has been in exceeding expectations with ephemeral material. In the 1980s, he created a new ***New Mutants*** series with Brett Blevins, collaborated with Jim Shooter and **John Romita Jr.** on *Star Brand*, and inked a wide array of Marvel graphic novel covers including *Cloak and Dagger*, *The Inhumans*, and the *Squadron Supreme*. In his work on ***Spider-Man*** 2099, artists Rick Leonardi and Williamson provided a delicate sensibility that prevented the dark-age futuristic

Spider-Man (Miguel O'Hara) character from being an overstated heavy metal basher. In the 1990s, he created a new comic adaptation of Lucas's *Star Wars: The Phantom Menace* and collaborated with Romita Jr. on the *Spider-Man* series.

**Selected Bibliography:** Cuthbert, Ray. "The Search for Al Williamson's *Flash Gordon* Number 1" (2002), http://www.comicartville.com/flashgordon.htm; Rhoades, Shirrel. *A Complete History of American Comics.* New York: Peter Lang, 2008.

*Stuart Lenig*

**WILSON, S. CLAY** (1941–). Among the original contributors to *Zap* Comix, S. Clay Wilson is infamous for his violent and hyper-sexual drawings, often containing a recurring character, the Checkered Demon. An influential figure in the **underground comics** scene, he shattered conventionality with his densely detailed strips crammed with deviancy, carnage, and confusion.

Born in Lincoln, Nebraska, Wilson later attended the University of Nebraska and earned a bachelor of fine arts degree in 1964. Wilson has described his academic experience there as tumultuous. In spite of his distaste for the mandatory ROTC training at the University of Nebraska, Wilson was a sharp student of anthropology and art history, which underscored his horrific images with subtle moral tales and astute reflections of contemporary society and civilization.

After graduating from UNL, Wilson fled Lincoln for a short stay in New York. He then moved to Lawrence, Kansas, and began doing a series of full-page drawings for *Grist*, a literary magazine published and edited by John Fowler. On a trip to San Francisco to visit Charles Plymell, in 1968, Wilson met **Robert Crumb**, who was in the midst of printing the first issue of *Zap* Comix. Wilson showed Crumb his artwork, which Crumb described as "something like I'd never seen before, anywhere, the level of mayhem, violence, dismemberment, naked women, loose body parts, huge, obscene sex organs, a nightmare vision of hell-on-Earth never so graphically illustrated in the history of art!" Crumb expanded *Zap* to include Wilson, with his premiere of the Checkered Demon in *Zap* Comix #2.

In addition to his contribution to the *Zap* collective that also included Spain Rodriguez, Robert Williams, and Rick Griffin, Wilson published his own titles such as *Pork, Snatch,* and *Feltch*. He also played in a blues band called Yukon Pete and the Muff Divers. Wilson's art continued to contain lurid degeneracy, tempered with dark humor. Wilson's signature style is to pack every inch of space packed with action and crazy details. His artwork is said to have even offended **Harvey Kurtzman**, who was nonetheless drawn to it. Though certainly controversial, Wilson has avoided some of the criticisms directed towards many of his contemporaries for their portrayal of women, as many consider him to be an equal opportunity sadist.

Wilson has illustrated the books of William S. Burroughs, and created a volume of children's fairy tales, *Wilson's Grimm*. He continued to produce comics, watercolors, and book illustrations until he suffered a severe brain injury in 2008. After attending a publishing event in San Francisco, Wilson left the house of a friend and was later found unconscious, with injuries that included a fractured neck. After a week in intensive care, Wilson was put on an accelerated therapy program and has shown signs of improvement. A controversial figure, at times he reflected the excess found in his comics.

**Selected Bibliography:** Rosenkrantz, Patrick. *Rebel Visions, The Underground Comix Revolution 1963–1975.* Seattle: Fantagraphics Books, 2002; Wilson, S. Clay. *The Art of S. Clay Wilson.* Berkeley, CA: Ten Speed Press, 2006.

*Richard L. Graham*

**WITCHBLADE.** *Witchblade* is an ongoing monthly comic from independent U.S. publishers Top Cow Productions, an imprint of **Image Comics**, primarily featuring tough independent female New York Police Department homicide detective Sara Pezzini. Created by Mark Silvestri, David Wohl, Brian Haberlin, and Michael Turner, *Witchblade* concerns Penzini's discovery and use of the Witchblade, a supernatural ancient weapon that envelops the body and imbues the user with superhuman powers. The title has maintained popularity and is an interesting take on female **superheroes**. Pezzini first appeared in *Cyblade/Shi #1: The Battle For Independents* (1995), where she was mortally wounded during an undercover case, the Witchblade made its choice to include her in the long line of women that has shared its power and healed her wounds, allowing her to survive the resulting confrontation with villain Kenneth Irons. She then passes a Periculum test, after which the Witchblade bonds with her at a cellular level and slows the aging process. Similar to **Green Lantern,** "Witchblade" refers both to the power-giving device and colloquially to the character who possesses it any given time.

Yancy Butler and David Chokachi in the TNT television series *Witchblade*. TNT/Photofest

Although the comics fetishistically represent Pezzini in full Witchblade armor and little else, the moderately successful television series, *Witchblade*, which debuted on August 27, 2000 on TNT as a pilot film, directed by Ralph Hemeker and written by Silvestri and John David Zeik, and starring Yancy Butler in the title role, was less titillating in its representation of women. It ran for two series: from June 12, 2001 to August 26, 2002. In 2009, talks occurred about the possibility of a major motion picture, directed by Michael Rymer and produced by Platinum Studies, IDG Films, and Relatively Media. In the wake of the unsuccessful films *Elektra* (2005) and *Catwoman* (2005), and the problems in getting **Wonder Woman** to the screen, this may be difficult, however. As a television show, *Witchblade* could be seen as part of a robust female action hero genre on television with the likes of *Birds of Prey* (2002–3) and the more well-known *Buffy the Vampire Slayer* (1997–2003), and *Xena Warrior Princess* (1995–2001). The idea of handing down a mythical power from warrior woman to warrior women was as rather clumsily inserted into **DC Comics'** Catwoman franchise with the roundly panned *Catwoman* film. Witchblade has had many crossovers with both other Top Cow characters, and characters from **DC Comics**, **Marvel**, and **Dark Horse Comics** that strain any sense of continuity. These have included *Witchblade/Wolverine* (2004) and *Witchblade/The Magdalena/Vampirella* (2005). These constant crossovers are reminiscent of the crossovers of such film licensed properties as *Robocop*, *Terminator*, and *Aliens* in the Dark Horse comics of the 1980s and 1990s. In 2004, Japanese animation Studio GONZO started to produce an anime version of the character set in the far future, which ran for 24 episodes from April 2006 onwards. A **manga** incarnation *Witchblade: Taker*, created by Yasuko Kobayashi started a serial run in March 2006.

*Lorcan McGrane*

**WOLFMAN, MARV** (1946–). Marv Wolfman began working for **DC Comics** in 1968 as a freelance writer on their mystery titles and *Blackhawk*, soon contributing to **superhero** books like *Teen Titans*, *Supergirl*, and *Batman*. By the early 1970s, after a brief period as story editor at **Warren Publications**, he had moved over to **Marvel**, where he created Skull the Slayer, Nova, Bullseye, and the Black Cat, but he is probably best known for his monumental 70-issue run on *Tomb of Dracula* with **Gene Colan**, which included the first appearance of the **vampire** hunter, Blade. Wolfman also edited Marvel's black-and-white magazine line, before he was promoted to editor-in-chief, but he stepped down after less than a year to devote more time to writing, including extensive runs on *Fantastic Four*, *Daredevil*, and *The Amazing Spider-Man*. In 1980, toward the end of his run on *Dracula*, he had a falling out with then editor-in-chief Jim Shooter over Wolfman's editing duties on the title, and Wolfman then moved back to DC Comics as a writer/editor.

Upon his return to DC, Wolfman embarked on the most prolific and significant period in his career. Along with artist **George Pérez**, he created *The New Teen Titans*, which quickly became DC's bestselling title. *The New Teen Titans* combined original Titans Robin, Wonder Girl, Kid Flash, and Beast Boy (renamed as Changeling) with brand new characters: Raven, Cyborg, and Starfire. Wolfman and Pérez also transformed

Robin from Batman's sidekick to the independent hero, Nightwing. Wolfman also reunited with his *Tomb of Dracula* collaborator Gene Colan on another supernatural title, the short-lived *Night Force*. In 1985, Wolfman and Pérez created **Crisis on Infinite Earths**, a year-long crossover that combined DC's multiple universes into a single one with a single continuity. During the *Crisis*, several long-running characters died, including **The Flash** and Supergirl. Following the series, most DC heroes underwent a revamp; Wolfman joined writer/artist **John Byrne** in the revamp of **Superman**, and Wolfman in particular revised the villain Lex Luthor from an evil scientist to a ruthless corporate executive. While continuing to write *New Teen Titans* for more than 10 years, Wolfman also wrote *Batman*, where he introduced the character Tim Drake as the new Robin after the death of Robin II, Jason Todd.

Wolfman's writing on *New Teen Titans* combined soap-opera-style continuity and detailed characterization with superhero action, wherein some subplots would last for a year or more. For example, the storyline that involved new team member Terra betraying the Titans to the villain Deathstroke, the Terminator, ran for more than 18 issues. This kind of long-range plotting became a hallmark of Wolfman's style. In addition, after the success of *Crisis on Infinite Earths*, he became known for his ability to write large-scale "event" comics that involved many characters and plotlines.

With the end of his writing on *The New Teen Titans* in 1995, Wolfman's comic work decreased significantly while he pursued a career in television and animation. In 1998, he sued Marvel Comics over the ownership of the Blade and Deacon Frost characters, which had recently been featured in a successful film from New Line Cinema, but a judge issued a ruling in favor of Marvel in 2000. He returned to comics again in 2006, writing *Nightwing* and a revival of *Vigilante* (a version of which he created in *New Teen Titans*) for DC.

*Andrew J. Kunka*

**WOLVERTON, BASIL** (1909–78). Basil Wolverton is most widely known as an illustrator for the early issues of **EC Comics'** *MAD*, covers for **DC Comics'** **horror**-humor anthology title *PLOP!*, and his character for **Timely** (later **Marvel**) Comics, *Powerhouse Pepper*. Among Wolverton's most popular images were his bizarre, distorted caricatures of the human figure, although his total body of work included **science fiction**, horror, and humor.

Wolverton illustrated the *Powerhouse Pepper* series for Timely comics from 1942 to 1947, as a popular backup feature in various titles from Timely, including *Joker, Gay*, and *Tessie the Typist*. The character also briefly had his own title, spanning five issues in 1948. The series was acclaimed for its humorous similarities to E. C. Segar's Popeye the Sailor. *Powerhouse Pepper* was eventually compiled and reprinted in a single volume from **Fantagraphics** Books in 1997. Wolverton's numerous other humor, **science fiction** and horror stories appeared from a number of publishers from 1938 to 1954, spanning, as some have estimated, over 1,300 pages. Some of these stories have been reprinted in *Basil Wolverton in Space* (**Dark Horse Comics**, 1997), *Basil Wolverton's Gateway to*

*Horror* (**Dark Horse Comics**, 1988), and *The Basil Wolverton Reader*, volumes one and two (2003 and 2004, Pure Imagination Publishing).

After 1954, Wolverton began his association with EC Comics, primarily as an illustrator for *Mad*, and to a lesser degree their other humor title, *Panic*. Wolverton had previously developed an unusual style of cartooning he described as the "spaghetti and meatballs" style, so named for its distinctive tendency to distort the human form into drooping, veined, protuberant, and stringy shapes. Perhaps the best examples of this style are found in "MAD Reader" (*Mad* #11, 1954) and "Meet Miss Potgold" (*Mad* #17, 1954). These images created by Wolverton were beyond basic gross-out humor: Wolverton crafted imagery that was psychologically affecting and reflected an almost Freudian sexual symbolism. Wolverton revisited this style for the covers for *PLOP!*, which was reminiscent of early *MAD*, crafting covers for the series' first 19 issues in the early 1970s.

In his personal life, Wolverton was a conservative, religious, and private person. He crafted a series of cartoons describing the events of the Bible, largely covering the Old Testament. These stories were published for Herbert Armstrong's Radio Church of God, which would later be known as the Worldwide Church of God. These stories have since been compiled and published by Fantagraphics Books in 2008. Wolverton also illustrated scenes from the Christian Apocalypse in his 1959 title *1975 in Prophecy*. Unquestionably some of Wolverton's finest work, these illustrations are meticulously detailed and utilize Wolverton's sense of horror and the grotesque to emotionally impact the viewer.

Wolverton died in 1978, four years after a debilitating stroke. His son, Monte Wolverton, continues to maintain his father's legacy, through books and articles about his father's life and work. Thanks to such efforts, Wolverton's work is being rediscovered by new generations of artists and readers.

*Robert O'Nale*

**WONDER WOMAN.** Created by William Moulton Marston (a well-known psychologist and the inventor of the systolic blood pressure test, a forerunner of the polygraph) Wonder Woman debuted in *All Star Comics* #8 (December 1941). Writing under the pseudonym Charles Moulton, Marston died in 1947, but stories he had written continued to appear for two years after his death. The early Wonder Woman stories were drawn by Harry G. Peter in a distinctive, blocky style until his death in 1958. Since then, she has gone through numerous writers and artists (mostly male) and has become the most important female **superhero** in comics history. Long thought of as a sort of female counterpart to **Superman**, she has regularly appeared in a variety of **DC Comics** titles since her debut, giving her the longest continuous run of any superhero in comics other than Superman and **Batman**. She is also a particularly interesting and complex example of the superhero. Marston infused Wonder Woman with proto-feminist characteristics and themes such as independence, self-worth, and sisterhood. Over the years, and with the death of her creator, she was subjected to the whims of writers and the mores of various eras—many of which deprived the Amazon of her authority in favor of a more normative femininity. Her appearance on the cover of the first issue of *Ms.* magazine (1972) reinforced her status as a symbol of female empowerment and assured she would always be recognized as an icon of feminist ideals.

Because of the length of her run in DC's complex and changing universe, Wonder Woman has gone through a number of transformations in her look and other characteristics over the years. Her origin story has undergone changes as well, though the best-known version has her as an Amazon princess living on isolated Paradise Island when American intelligence agent Steve Trevor crashes his plane there. Helping to nurse Trevor back to health, she then wins a tournament designed to choose a champion to return with him to the United States to help fight the **Nazis**. She then remains in "Man's World," living as her alter ego Diana Prince while using her powers to fight against Nazis and other villains. Trevor, meanwhile, remains her love interest, but importantly remains in a secondary role relative to Wonder Woman herself, playing Lois Lane to her Superman.

Conceived by Marston as a role model for the "new woman," Wonder Woman was originally envisioned as a tall, beautiful Amazon with superhuman speed, strength, and agility. The possessor of special Amazonian hand-to-hand combat skills, she also bore a variety of weapons, including a golden Lasso of Truth with which she could force the obedience and truthfulness of anyone she encountered; she also owned an invisible airplane that she could control by telepathy. As her origins evolved to include important Hellenic roots, she acquired forearm bracelets (forged from the shield of Zeus) that could ward off bullets and other attacks, while also producing a powerful concussive force of their own when slammed together.

Lynda Carter, as Diana Prince, a.k.a. Wonder Woman, in the CBS television series by the same name, which ran from 1976–79 and brought the character to a new level of celebrity in American culture. ABC/Photofest

Early on, she joined the **Justice Society of America**, becoming its first female member, though (in a reflection of the expectations of the early 1940s and in contrast to Marston's vision) she served as the group's secretary. In 1960, she joined the **Justice League of America**. Her long and varied career has included appearances in her own long-running self-titled comic; indeed, along with Superman and Batman, she was one of only three superheroes to appear continuously in their own titles through the 1950s with the demise of superhero comics in that decade. She was, however, considerably toned down in response to charges by critics such as **Fredric Wertham** that comics were dangerous influences on children and that her stories, in particular, had a lesbian subtext. Critics of that time also complained of the unusual amount of bondage in comics featuring Wonder Woman, often involving her golden lasso, though bondage was in fact a common image in the comics of the day.

In the 1960s, Wonder Woman's Hellenic roots were emphasized in a revamping of the character. By 1969, however, in what can be interpreted as one of a number of attempts on the part of male writers to tame the Amazon Princess (sometimes by hyper-sexualizing her), she lost her super powers when she gave them up in order to remain on Earth after the other Amazons decided to move to another dimension. Now as Diana Prince, without a superhero identity, she became the owner of a mod boutique. Even without super powers, however, she trained under her Chinese mentor I Ching to become enough of an expert at martial arts and weapons to continue her fight against evil even as a mortal human. Wonder Woman was brought to new prominence in American culture with the success of the popular *Wonder Woman* television series that aired from 1975 to 1979, with Lynda Carter in the title role.

The popularity of this series (in which Wonder Woman has super powers) caused the character to return to her superhero roots. After the 1985 ***Crisis on Infinite Earths*** series she was re-launched by **George Pérez** and Greg Potter with a completely reworked origin story. Now an emissary to our world from the fictional island nation of Themyscira (formerly Paradise Island), her body is revealed to be composed of the mystical clay surrounding the island, given super abilities by a group of Olympian gods. Since then the character has made a number of important appearances and gone through a variety of transformations, playing a key role in the main DC continuity as well as in the *Elseworlds* miniseries ***Kingdom Come*** (1996), in which she becomes pregnant with Superman's daughter, or in Darwyn Cooke's ***The New Frontier*** (2004), in which she challenges Superman over U.S. involvement in Vietnam. The 1986 miniseries *Legend of Wonder Woman* is an affectionate tribute to her legacy by writer **Kurt Busiek** with art in homage to Peter by **Trina Robbins**; the 2002 graphic novel *The Hiketeia*, by **Greg Rucka** and J. G. Jones, stages a notable confrontation between Wonder Woman and Batman. In 2007, **Gail Simone** became the first woman to regularly write Wonder Woman stories. Meanwhile, Wonder Woman's origin story was clarified in a self-titled direct-to-DVD animated movie released in 2009.

Whatever her importance within the DC universe, Wonder Woman is probably most important as an icon of feminine strength and capability within the popular culture of the real world. She is an iconic figure often referred to in other works of popular culture and has exerted a central influence on the evolution of female heroes in the comics. Her influence extends to other media as well, and she is often cited as one of the inspirations behind the recent rise of action-oriented female heroes in television and film, such as the protagonists of the television series *Xena: Warrior Princess* (1995–2001) and *Buffy the Vampire Slayer* (1996–2003). Moreover, as an ongoing image of feminine courage and strength beginning in a time when there were few such images available in American popular culture, she has exercised an incalculable influence on generations of young women in need of such powerful and positive role models.

**Selected Bibliography:** Beatty, Scott. *Wonder Woman: The Ultimate Guide to the Amazon Princess.* New York: DK, 2003; Daniels, Les. *Wonder Woman: The Complete History.* San Francisco: Chronicle Books, 2004; Robbins, Trina. *The Great American Superheroines.* Palace Press International, 2010; Stuller, Jennifer. *Ink-Stained Amazons and Cinematic Warriors: Superwomen in Modern Mythology.* London: I. B. Tauris, 2010.

*M. Keith Booker*

**WOOD, WALLACE (WALLY)** (1927–81). Born in Minnesota, Wood was one of the greatest artists in the comics field. Best known for his artwork for **EC Comics** and *Mad* Magazine, Wood also illustrated book covers, **science fiction** digests, men's magazines, posters, record albums and even the roughs for the Topp's *Mars Attacks!* cards.

After Wood graduated from high school in 1944, he joined the Merchant Marines and then enlisted in the U.S. Army in 1946. He was hired by **Will Eisner** to do lettering on *The Spirit* and then became an assistant to George Wunder on the newspaper strip *Terry and the Pirates*. His first professional comic book job was as a letterer for Fox Publications in 1948. He then branched out drawing various **romance** titles in 1949.

"The Werewolf Legend," in *Vault Of Horror* #2, was Wood's first story for EC Comics. Wood penciled and inked approximately 150 EC stories in various genres, many now considered true classics. After the collapse of EC, the company's most popular title, *Mad*, was continued as a magazine for which Wood was a major contributor through 1964.

In 1958, Wood inked the pencils of **Jack Kirby** on the syndicated strip *Sky Masters of the Space Force* and also worked with Kirby on *Challengers of the Unknown*.

Wood did stories and artwork for **Warren Publishing's horror** magazines, as well as for **Charlton comics**, Fox, Harvey, Atlas, and others. Wood also established **Daredevil's** distinctive red costume for **Marvel Comics** during the **Silver Age**.

Wood's dedication to his field often resulted in expressions of resentment concerning what he saw as exploitation of the artists (e.g., low pay, no benefits). So, in 1965 Wood enjoyed the opportunity afforded by Tower Comics to create, write, and draw his own **superheroes**. The result was T.H.U.N.D.E.R. Agents (The Higher United Nations Defense Enforcements Reserves). He would hire many of his colleagues to assist him in this enterprise. While the work is now highly prized, it would only last for two years. In 1966, Wood launched the independent magazine *witzend* based on a concept by Dan Adkins. The magazine's philosophy was based upon Wood's view that artists should retain copyright to their own work. In a keynote address at the 1966

NYC comic convention, artist **Gil Kane** spoke of how *witzend* represented the future of comic book art.

During the early 1970s Wood worked sporadically for Marvel and **DC Comics**. In 1972 Wood began writing and drawing the sexy strips *Cannon* and *Sally Forth* for a servicemen's magazine. He also contributed x-rated stories and illustrations to pornographic magazines. When it seemed his future was past, in 1978 he produced the *Wizard King* with artwork as fine as any of his career.

Suffering from a number of debilitating ailments including the loss of vision in one eye due to numerous strokes, Wood took his own life in 1981 at the age of 53. The prodigious amount of his published work is staggering.

**Selected Bibliography:** Starger, Steve, and J. David Spurlock. *Wally's World: The Brilliant Life and Tragic Death of Wally Wood, the World's 2nd Best Comic Book Artist.* Lakewood, NJ: Vanguard Productions, 2006.

*Jeff McLaughlin*

**WORLD'S FINEST COMICS.** A series published by National/**DC Comics** from 1941 to #323 (January 1986) featuring **Superman** and **Batman** stories and team-ups. The title "World's Finest" was originally derived from *World's Fair* comics published by National/DC during the 1939–40 New York World's fair. The series itself (initially titled *World's Best Comics* with issue #1) began as *World's Finest* with #2 in the summer of 1941. Like many anthology series of the day, each 96-page magazine featured a variety of **superhero** stories. Superman and Batman appeared in separate adventures in its **Golden Age** run. The series also anthologized the adventures of numerous other characters, including **Sandman**, Johnny Thunder, Hop Harrigan, TNT, Crimson Avenger, Star Spangled Kid, **Aquaman**, and **Green Arrow**. In the Golden Age, the series almost exclusively featured characters who had first appeared in other anthologies.

The series survived the post-war downturn of the superhero genre by featuring Superman and Batman together rather than in separate adventures. These team-ups began in July–August 1954 with issue #71 and would continue to highlight the two most popular characters in the DC Comics line throughout the **Silver Age** (argued to begin with issue #84). These Superman/Batman adventures (also featuring Robin) would also see the team up of various villains, such as the first Lex Luthor and Joker paring in issue #88.

Even with the emphasis of the series as a Superman/Batman vehicle, *World's Finest* would, on occasion, get back to its roots as an anthology series at times featuring Green Arrow, Tommy Tomorrow (issues #102–24, 1959–60), and **Aquaman** (beginning with issue #125) along with the standard Superman/Batman adventures (usually written by Dick Sprang until issue #135).

Some Silver Age *World's Finest* stories would also cross over with Legion of Super-Heroes characters (at that point featured in *Adventure Comics*). The Composite Superman, an android villain with the powers of the Legion with a half-Superman, half-Batman appearance was introduced in issue #142, while the Adult Legion would make an appearance in issue #172. These Superman/Batman adventures would help define the characters for an innocent Silver Age audience.

The late 1960s and early 1970s saw attempts to reposition characters to be more aligned with the socio-cultural changes of the times. At the same time, however, the superhero genre was influenced by the pop culture camp style of the Adam West *Batman* television series. *World's Finest* reflects this conflict by on one hand spotlighting covers by **Neal Adams** (issues #199 and #200) and on the other hand, featuring a Metamorpho run from issues #217–20.

In the mid 1970s up until its cancellation in 1986 Batman/Superman team-ups would continue for the majority of the run. Like many other series during this time, 100-page specials and 80-page anthologies would be featured in *World's Finest* as it picked up the load from the "Canceled Comic Cavalcade" implosion of the late 1970s. Anthologized adventures in these 80-page editions featured Green Arrow, Hawkman, Shazam (the Marvel Family), Zatanna, Challengers of the Unknown, Black Lightning, Creeper, Vigilante, and Deadman.

By 1983, the series settled into the standard 24-page Superman/Batman adventures until its cancellation at the dawn of the post-***Crisis on Infinite Earths*** era.

*D. R. Hammontree*

**WORLD'S GREATEST SUPERHEROES, THE.** *The World's Greatest Superheroes* is a hardcover graphic novel published by **DC** in 2005 collecting a series of works created by **Alex Ross** and Paul Dini from 1998 to 2003 about various DC **superheroes**. Ross conceived of the project while working on ***Kingdom Come***, and the six oversized works that comprise *The World's Greatest Super-Heroes*—**Superman**: *Peace on Earth*, **Batman**: *War on Crime, Shazam!*: *Power of Hope*, **Wonder Woman**: *Spirit of Truth*, **JLA**: *Secret Origins*, and *JLA*: *Liberty and Justice*—all feature the Ross's characteristic paintings with dialogue and narrative supplied by Dini.

The first selection in the collection is *Superman: Peace on Earth*, originally published in 1998 and featuring a story about Superman combating world hunger. Superman decides throughout the course of the story that with his incredible powers and the resources of the United States, he could ensure that the entire population of Earth would be fed for one day. His mission, however, ends in failure as he encounters distrust from other countries who see him as a spokesperson for an American agenda, or who feel his benevolence is a threat to their power structure. Ultimately, Superman learns that his greatest power is to inspire the people around him to do good for their communities, and that the only viable solution to the world's problems is through education and cooperation.

The humanistic theme established in *Superman: Peace on Earth* is echoed throughout the other five works collected in *The World's Greatest Superheroes*, and more often than not the heroes in these stories fail in their overt missions, requiring them to change their approach to ultimately succeed. Thus, *Batman: War on Crime*, published in 1999, forces

Batman to confront poverty as he attempts to keep a juvenile whose parents were killed in a violent crime from succumbing to the cycle of violence that plagues the inner city. Batman's realization is that he bears a double responsibility to his community: not only is he obliged to help as the Batman, but his alter-ego, Bruce Wayne, must also actively strive to revitalize the urban landscape using the vast resources of his multinational company. This realization leads Batman to reject the industrialist Randall Winters as a business partner since Winters is more concerned with lining his pockets than with urban renewal.

*Shazam!: The Power of Hope*, published in 2000, involves **Captain Marvel**'s interactions with sick children at a local hospital. There he meets an adolescent who has been abused by his father. Unable to connect to the boy as Captain Marvel, and disquieted by this failure, he decides to return as Billy Batson, his alter-ego, since Billy himself is merely a child. Captain Marvel finds that he is able to approach the boy freely without the imposing trappings of an adult superhero and he befriends him. The experience teaches Captain Marvel that it is hope itself that is essential to the role of a superhero, and that the smallest gestures can sometimes make the biggest difference in the lives that he touches.

*Wonder Woman: Spirit of Truth*, published in 2001, addresses **Wonder Woman**'s role as an ambassador of peace to the nations of Earth. Near the beginning of the book she fails time and time again in her overtures of cooperation with foreign nations because of their perception of her as an outsider to both the countries' affairs and to life as a normal human. In a pivotal scene she discusses her frustrations with Superman, who encourages her to be less flamboyant in her approach so that she can gain a new perspective on the situation. She then dons a series of disguises in order to walk among people without drawing attention to herself, and in so doing gains a more intimate knowledge of the cultures with which she wishes to connect in order to better operate as a superhero.

The last two works are companion pieces, *JLA: Secret Origins*, published in 2002, acting as a preceding volume and preview to *JLA: Liberty and Justice*, published in 2003, by containing a series of two-page origin stories for its main characters. *JLA: Liberty and Justice* itself is about the **Justice League of America** combating an alien disease that paralyzes its victims. The overt threat to the public that emerges from the confusion as the Justice League attempts to isolate and cure the disease, however, is from the people themselves as widespread riots begin to break out from fear of the global pandemic. The Justice League pacifies the riots, but in doing so takes a hit to their reputation as news organizations and public leaders speak out against even their mild use of force on the general public. Rampant fear grips much of the populace and the alien plague is even blamed on the Justice League, the league itself having several members of extra-terrestrial origin. Told mostly from the perspective of the Martian **Manhunter**, the story comes to a conclusion when he speaks about the Justice League's intentions in front of the United Nations, asking for the people of the world to realize that the Justice League has always honored the trust the public has given them and that the members of the League ultimately wish to be perceived as part of the global population, not as outsiders to be feared.

The works comprising *The World's Greatest Superheroes* are meant to ground superheroes in the real world, diverging greatly from the epic battles seen in many superhero comics by giving the heroes real-world problems to face, such as hunger or street crime. Each work takes particular care to stress the humanity of its heroes, showing that each hero's greatest asset is the ability to connect to the people around them in meaningful ways. Consequently, the stories are narrated from the heroes' perspectives in their own voices. This technique is bolstered by Ross and Dini's decision to place the text uncharacteristically outside of speech and thought balloons in most of the works, relying on speech balloons only in *JLA: Liberty and Justice* to facilitate the interactions of a larger cast.

The genesis of the work owes itself somewhat to Ross's style of illustration; he wanted to bring the same realism that he portrays with his art to the story that he told. The oversized format of the stories hearkens back to the tabloid size one-shots that Ross remembered from his youth, and like these, Ross wanted *The World's Greatest Superheroes* to be appealing to a larger audience who might not find the heroes as familiar as long-time fans. This rationale also prompted the two-page origins that begin each story, as each one is a simplified version meant to allow easy-access to the characters by the largest audience possible.

While the publication, being placed outside of DC's regular continuity, did not heavily influence further comics, *Superman: Peace on Earth* did win the **Eisner Award** for best graphic album in 1999, also netting Ross an Eisner Award for best interior painter/ multimedia artist in that same year. The original drawings for *Superman: Peace on Earth, Batman: War on Crime, Shazam!: Power of Hope,* and *Wonder Woman: Spirit of Truth* were all auctioned off for charity, netting UNICEF $81,000 from *Peace on Earth,* The Reisenbach Charter School in Harlem $157,400 from *War on Crime,* The Make-A-Wish foundation $110,000 from *Power of Hope,* and the Twin Towers Fund $50,000 from *Spirit of Truth.*

*Jackson Jennings*

**X-MEN.** The X-Men superhero team was created by **Stan Lee** and **Jack Kirby**; they first appeared in September 1963 and have since become the basis for one of **Marvel's** most enduring projects, spawning countless spin-offs, video games, cartoons, action figures, and feature films. The *X-Men* comics would eventually include contributions from some of the leading writers and artists in the industry, including **John Byrne**, **Jim Lee**, **Grant Morrison**, and **Chris Claremont**. Though perhaps uninspired in its inception, *X-Men* grew into one of the most popular comics of its time; its characters and stories have touched on some of the most intense social and political questions of our time, cultivating a rich thematic history unusual in a mainstream series.

The X-Men phenomenon began with the creation of the original X-Men team of **mutants** by Professor Xavier, himself a powerful telepath, in the hopes that his team will be able to protect humanity from those mutants who would seek to use their powers for evil. In the first issue they face the man who would become their greatest foe: Magneto. A mutant who could create and control magnetic fields (and who was later revealed to be a survivor of the Jewish Holocaust), Magneto would go on to become the most important oppositional force the X-Men would face—not only because of his enormous power but also because, in insisting that humanity will never accept mutants and that they must struggle against humans in order to protect and preserve their own existence, he presents the most compelling ideological challenge to Xavier's dream of peaceful human/mutant coexistence.

Indeed, while arch-nemeses Xavier and Magneto are enemies, they are also old friends who often treat one another with mercy and mutual respect—in some cases they even work together against more traditionally evil characters like the time-traveling agent of social-Darwinist destruction, Apocalypse. Thus, in a sense, Xavier is Martin

Luther King to Magneto's Malcolm X; joined by the recognition that they are victims of human violence and exclusion, but divided by the manner in which they seek to respond. Further complicating the moral compass of the series are characters like the immensely popular Wolverine who, despite ultimately accepting Xavier's liberal humanism, takes very different and sometimes questionable paths to the same ends.

Xavier's original X-Men team went through a number of lineup changes and, in the process, spawned a variety of closely related titles. The primary team was documented in *Uncanny X-Men* and later in *X-Men*, while younger mutants who trained and fought with the X-Men joined teams like the government sponsored X-Factor, the British Excalibur, and the rebel group X-Force, each of which had their own titles for many years. Continuity was maintained across all of the X-books and major events were increasingly marked in the 1990s and 2000s by crossovers implicating mutants across the various titles.

Among the most important of these crossovers was the "X-Cutioner's Song" which was published across four months in 1992. In this story, a character named Stryfe returns from a dystopic future seeking vengeance against those whose failures led to his nightmarish existence. As part of his plan, he attempts to assassinate Professor Xavier by infecting him with a techno-organic virus. The professor survives, but so does the virus; in fact, Stryfe's Legacy Virus became an ever-present factor in the lives of mutants for long after; it was a terminal disease, thought at first to only strike mutants but later infecting non-mutants too.

The virus was, naturally, meant to parallel the rise of HIV and this was one of many instances where mutants seemed to explicitly represent victimized minorities in American society. In particular, the treatment of mutants often served as a venue for the exploration of attitudes towards homophobia and racism. Xavier is the consummate liberal, inspiring his students to follow and fight for his dream of peaceful coexistence in the face of intolerance, hatred and violence

*The Uncanny X-men*, issue #135, published July 1980. Marvel Comics Group/Photofest

from a public unable and unwilling to understand that mutants deserved the same rights as humans. Yet Xavier's liberalism contains an implicit contradiction: mutants can, in fact, by their nature pose significant threats to public safety. Unlike racialized minorities or homosexuals, the danger posed by mutants is not a social construction; it is real and palpable. Liberal reasoning can easily refute homophobic claims that gay people pose a danger to society; but charges that mutants are dangerous are wholly legitimate (if incomplete), given the extraordinary powers they possess, and are often borne out in the stories themselves through powerful characters like Onslaught. In that context, when anti-mutant crusaders like Senator Robert Kelly propose Draconian measures to register, control or cure all mutants, it is not altogether impossible to sympathize with their position, even if the execution of their plans sometimes makes readers recoil.

Indeed, despite attempts by writers to show the dark and dehumanizing nature of these measures, depicting scenes that can evoke the most horrifying images of the Jewish Holocaust, the Soviet police state or Apartheid in Israel, there remains the consistent problem that mutants' powers give them uniquely destructive powers that German Jews, Soviet dissidents, or Palestinians under occupation do not. As a result, the books might be seen to partly legitimate the very discrimination they seek to critique; after all, if registration or genetic re-configuration is a legitimate response to "the mutant problem," what is to say that sterilization is not a legitimate response to "the gay problem?"

Naturally, this is not the intention of the writers, but rather it is a logical flaw inherent in the use of potentially dangerous mutants to dramatize the liberal ideology to which the books try to adhere. It is notable, too, that while Xavier and his brood preach tolerance and respect, their writers are reluctant to embrace that same spirit; gendered behavior norms are regularly reinforced and there have been very few gay or lesbian characters in the X-books. Some characters, like Northstar, Destiny and Mystique, were given "gay characteristics" but Marvel Comics refused to allow any explicitly gay characters until Northstar, then a member of the **Alpha Flight** team, outed himself in 1992. In the mid-1990s, a homoerotic attraction began to develop between two members of X-Force, Rictor and Shatterstar, but before it could blossom into an explicit relationship, new writers took over the title and the storyline was abruptly dropped. The two characters have since shared an on-panel kiss in the *X-Factor* series. Indeed, by the early 21st century, gay and lesbian characters were more widely accepted by American culture as a whole, and Northstar officially became a temporary member of the X-Men in 2001 and a regular member in 2002. The dynamic of the X-books was significantly altered in 2005 in the "Decimation" crossover. During that event, a deranged and hysterical Scarlet Witch inadvertently caused the un-mutation, and in some cases the death, of all but 200 of the world's mutant population. This posed newer, tougher questions for the remaining mutants: are mutants a separate and now-endangered species that should seek to rebuild its genetic stock, or were they always simply the human products of genetic 'accidents' who should greet the end of these mutations as an invitation to re-enter the human society from which they came?

*Tyler Shipley*

**YOSSEL.** In this historical graphic novel, first published in 2003, writer and artist **Joe Kubert** combines an account of the Holocaust in Poland with a "**What if?**" story from his family's personal history. Kubert's family emigrated to the United States from Poland in 1928, and in *Yossel* he explores what might have happened if he and his family had been in Poland when the **Nazis** invaded in the early days of World War II in 1939.

The story centers on a Jewish family living in Poland as the war starts. The young son, Yossel (like Kubert) shows aptitude with pencil and paper, and draws everything he possibly can. As the war comes closer to his village, the drawings occasionally reflect the imagery around him, but more often serve as a form of escapism, as real comics were. When the family is relocated to the Ghetto of Warsaw, his skills come in handy to keep him alive, as he is often brought into the German military headquarters to draw pictures for the entertainment of the soldiers. Interestingly, Yossel even drew **Superman**, but with Nazi symbols and look rather than his traditional one. His talents served as a way to gain food, and later information.

An interesting sub-plot to the main story of Yossel's struggles involves a man who escapes the concentration camp at Auschwitz. He had been imprisoned and served as a *sondernkommando*, who were Jews chosen to do special jobs in the camp. As the man tells of the horrors he has seen, he notes how cruel the Germans are, and how God has seemingly abandoned the Jews. When the old man first appears before Yossel, he calls Yossel by name. In time, the reader finds out that the old man is in fact the rabbi for Yossel's family, and that the family has died in the showers of Auschwitz.

Yossel then takes on the role of a partisan. The leader Mordechai is only in his early 20s, but the necessity of staying alive has driven all remaining youths into hiding.

As the full story of the horrors visited on Jews becomes clear, so too does the need to fight back, and make the Germans pay for their acts. From this point on, Yossel uses his gift of art to spy on the Germans, and eventually plants a bomb in their headquarters.

The comic ties in well with many of the other Holocaust themed books in recent years, including **Art Spiegelman**'s *Maus* (1973–91), which set the standard for such works. As with *Maus*, *Yossel* relates the Holocaust via a personal family history, though this time an imagined one. Kubert notes in the preface that the story is based on correspondence with relatives in the area as well as on later recollections of those who survived. Other recent graphic novels about the Holocaust include Miriam Katin's *We Are on Our Own* (2006), Pascal Croci's *Auschwitz* (2004, first published in French in 2002), and **Will Eisner**'s *The Plot: The Secret Story of the Protocols of the Elders of Zion* (2005).

The black and white artwork of *Yossel* is significant as it relays a type of documentary-style storytelling, while reinforcing the notion that, in some cases, moral oppositions are not complex and ambiguous but can be as simple and stark as the opposition between black and white. One can see a similar black-and-white form of storytelling in works such as *Persepolis* (1999–2003), by Marjane Satrapi, and *Palestine* (2001), by **Joe Sacco**.

*Cord Scott*

**YOUTH CULTURE IN COMICS.** The connection between the comic book world and youth is strong and undeniable. Although children and teenagers are not the only component of the comic book audience, they constitute a majority that has represented the modern comic book audience par excellence. This link between comics and youth has two sides that are closely interrelated: the evolution of comic books as a form of youth entertainment and the many representations of youth in the comic medium.

Since youth has been the most important audience, comic book publishers and creators have often looked for stories that appeal to this age group, transforming comics into a channel to express and represent the interests and concerns of different generations of (especially American) youth. The rise of comics as a cultural phenomenon came at a moment of history when children and adolescents were increasingly becoming a distinctive target market for the entertainment industry. Comics were one of the only forms of entertainment that bypassed the control of parents and other cultural authorities. Accessibility was and has been a main issue in the past and present of comic books; two factors were decisive during the infancy of the medium: the low price that permitted the independent purchase by youth; and the easy access through newsstands.

The content of the comic books published at the birth of the industry is easily encapsulated in two titles: *Superman* (1938) and *Archie* (1941). Both titles are still in print and represent two leading genres at the time: the **superhero** narrative and the teen humor narrative. Superheroes dominated the industry from the late 1930s until the end of the World War II. By then, the market was saturated with superhero stories and started a slow decay; at the same time, works like *Archie* or Dell's **funny animals** titles had been showing steady sales and at this point started their dominance of the publishing market. Funny animal titles were aimed primarily at younger children, *Archie* and other similar titles, such as *Penny* (1943) and *Bobby Sox* (1944) were meant for adolescents. These titles helped to define the concept of adolescence in society.

Culturally, movie studios, radio stations and music producers were starting to recognize teenagers as a distinctive and economically interesting age group. In the world of comics, it was probably in 1919 when a teenager was first made the protagonist of a comic strip. Carl Ed created *Harold Teen*, a comic strip for the *Chicago Tribune*. Harold was, in many ways, very similar to Archie: he talked, dressed, and hung out in the same places that the average American teenager would do in the 1920s. However, it is interesting to note that in that period the concept of adolescence was still emerging, and that a comic like *Harold Teen* was probably helping to reinforce the differences in behavior and interests between children and teenagers.

During the 1940s and 1950s many titles with children, teens and young adults as main characters were published, including *Little Lulu* (1935), **Dennis the Menace** (1951), *Millie the Model* (1945), *Leave it to Binky* (1948), and **Richie Rich** (1953). However, none of them can be compared in success and lasting history to *Archie*, featuring America's favorite teenager. The comics about the redheaded and freckle-faced Archie Andrews helped to build and capitalized on the newborn teenage culture. Following the success of Mickey Rooney's movies and similar themed radio shows, John Goldwater at MLJ Publishing decided that the market was ready for something different from superheroes, something closer to the everyday life of the average reader. Archie's first appearance was as a backup story for *The Shield* in *Pep Comics* #22. Archie is an idealized and sanitized version of the American teenager of the 1940s. He lives in a peaceful suburban area, Riverdale, and his friends correspond with character types often found in any

Betty and Veronica from the Archie Comics. Photofest

high school narrative. Jughead is the faithful and funny friend who is more interested in food than girls, and girls are Archie's greatest problem. Betty is the typical sweetheart, romantic but also pragmatic, excellent in class and sports, and always ready to help Archie. On the other hand, Veronica is the spoiled girl, daughter of the richest man in Riverdale, Hiram Lodge. In contrast to Betty, Veronica is sophisticated, in many cases manipulative and less reliable than Betty. Finally, Archie could not succeed without a rival, and that is Reggie Mantle. Reggie is the jock who shares class upbringing with Veronica. His personality is egocentric and vain, which combines with his witty sense of humor to make him the perfect opposite for the easy-going Archie. The content is rather formulaic, following everyday life situations and incidents in the life of this group of characters, always avoiding the controversy that issues like sexuality or identity would bring. These teenagers speak properly, obey their parents, and do not smoke, drink or get into serious fights.

Bob Montana and Dan DeCarlo are responsible for giving Archie its characteristic drawing and narrative style. Montana joined the company in 1947 and was a major influence in the narrative style of the comic. De Carlo became part of the team in the late 1950s and he developed the clear and clean drawing style that is now a trademark of Archie's comics.

The popularity of *Archie* was such that most of the characters in the comic book got their own titles, while MLJ Publishing changed its name to Archie Comics in 1946. In the 1960s, Archie Comics created two other relatively successful teen titles: *Sabrina, the Teenage Witch* and *Josie and the Pussycats*. These three works expanded their success beyond the print world and were adapted to other media. Archie and Josie had their own television cartoon shows and later on the three comic books became live-action movies.

Archie's contemporary titles still portray an idealized and clean view of adolescence, although they keep themselves culturally relevant with the introduction of technology, popular culture references, and a cast that include more ethnically diverse characters. Clearly Archie's formula works since, along with **superhero** comics, it is the only surviving title from the **Golden Age**. Society's interest in Archie is proven by the press coverage that the recent engagement between Archie and Veronica has attracted. Archie is also one of the few comics that continues to be easily accessible in newsstands and supermarkets, the same as in the 1940s.

In addition, Archie's influence can still be seen in such contemporary works as *Zits* (1997–) whose protagonist, Jeremy Duncan, is essentially a modernized version of Archie Andrews. In this comic, Jerry Scott and Jim Borgman have created a realistic portrait of the contemporary teenager from a humorous and ironic perspective. It focuses in Jeremy's daily life: the everyday misunderstandings between him and his parents, his love for music, his unpredictable relationship with Sara, and his friendship with Hector and Pierce. The depiction of teenage life is full of popular culture commentary and use of technology (from headphones to cell phones) and, although Jeremy can be described as a more rebellious character than Archie, his stories are still rather harmless.

During the 1930s, 1940s, and 1950s comic books were ever-present in the lives of many children and teenagers; this circumstance attracted the attention of many adults: parents, teachers, librarians, and other culture gatekeepers. Comic books became a new instance of the struggle between popular and highbrow art, especially when serving the cultural needs and tastes of youngsters. Like pulp magazines before them, comic books were accused of being mere entertainment, having no educational purpose, lowering the literacy skills of youth, and even damaging their eyes with bright colours and low quality printing. Before the infamous attack of **Fredric Wertham** in his book *The Seduction of the Innocent* (1954) and the trials that led to the establishment of the **Comics Code**, Sterling North declared comic books a "national disgrace" and listed the many format and content weaknesses of the medium. However, in order to strengthen his argument, North also recognized the ubiquity of the medium in society, noting that virtually every child read these "color 'comic' magazines." Wertham increased the virulence of the attack on comics, highlighting two ideas: comic books were a product of a decadent capitalistic industry lacking any cultural value and they also affected the innocent minds of children and teenagers, transforming them into criminals.

Although every comic book was considered a menace, the ones published by **EC** were judged as especially dangerous. **William Gaines** inherited this publishing company from his father and decided to shift the content from funny animal stories to titles like *Weird Science* or *The Vault of Horror*. EC represented a counter-cultural effort during the conservative 1950s, the attraction of youth for these company's titles is more than understandable. In a historical moment characterized by a conservative and conformist society, EC published comic books that had children and teenagers as protagonists and challenged every idealized institution: parenthood, marriage, education, legal authorities, and so forth. EC paid a high price for their rebellious line of publication, since it almost disappeared after the Senate trials and the rise of the **Comics Code**.

The magazine *Mad* was one of their only regular publications after these events. Originally *Mad* was published as a comic book, but soon it changed its format to magazine to move outside the purview of the code. Created almost solely by **Harvey Kurtzman** in 1952, its satiric take on popular culture would make it a cultural icon for teenagers and young adults in the 1960s and 1970s. As well, many underground writers who succeeded in the late 1960s and 1970s, among them **Robert Crumb** and **Art Spiegelman**, have acknowledged the influence of *Mad* in the birth and development of **underground comics**.

After the establishment of the Comics Code, the only publisher that strengthened its position was Dell due to its publishing line focused on innocuous and children-oriented titles. The code eliminated the possibility of publishing edgy, violent, challenging, and counter-establishment stories, and it also helped to reinforce two ideas about comics in the mainstream society: comic books were something just for children and, from that moment on, nothing more than cheap and clean entertainment. However, something changed in the content of comic books in the 1960s. Parallel to the development of underground comics, superhero comics also found the need to response to cultural and social changes. The youth of the time was a complex and confused one but the storylines inherited from the 1950s did not reflect any of those feelings. **Stan Lee** realized that **Marvel** could capitalize on the feelings of modern youth and recover the teenage audience for the comic book medium. Working with **Steve Ditko** and **Jack Kirby**, Lee developed a new kind of superhero in such figures as the **Fantastic Four** (1961), **The Hulk** (1962), **Spider-Man** (1962), and the **X-Men** (1963). The nature of these superheroes set them apart from the ones published by the rival company **DC**, though DC itself soon countered with the **Teen Titans**, a youthful superhero team who began to appear in 1964. The superheroes created by Marvel showed a complexity never seen before in the superhero realm: they struggled with their secret identities and their superpowers; their relationship with authorities and the public was ambivalent, with moments of admiration but also persecution. Spider-Man and The Human Torch were young adults whose behavior and issues did not differ much from the typical teenager, from love matters to money problems. Many members of the X-Men were teenagers as well. The Thing and The Hulk were superheroes alienated from society because of their superpowers. As well, most of The Hulk's stories were often focused on his struggles with the Army and other forces of authority that tried to capture him because of the perceived threat posed by his power.

Nonetheless, Lee was seeking a connection with the teenage reader beyond storylines. He devised several strategies to establish and strengthen a connection between readers and creators, such as bulletins and the Bullpen that accompanied every comic book and helped to create a vibrant fan culture and sense of community among fans. Some examples of fan behavior can be found as early as the 1930s in connection with science fiction literature. During the 1950s, EC readers managed to organize themselves. However, the first instances of modern fandom are located in the early 1960s mainly caused by two circumstances: the phenomenon of Marvel Mania and the inclusion of readers' addresses in the letter pages of the comics published by DC. Fanzines and comic book conventions soon became part of the comic book culture and readers and creators had the opportunity to establish a dialogue. Since then, fandom culture has become highly relevant for the world of comics in many ways: it supports the publishers' efforts to keep their titles relevant to teen readers; it has sustained the careers of many readers that dream of becoming comic book creators; and finally, fandom has become an important and recognizable part of youth culture.

At the same time that Marvel was tapping into the interests of the teenage audience, the development of underground comics (**comix**) was attracting an older audience of college readers with edgy, sexually charged, and anti-authoritarian storylines and characters. Around the figure of **Robert Crumb** and other authors, the comics medium initiated an alternative route away from mainstream publishers, the Comics Code, and **superhero** storylines. Comix became part of a youth subculture concentrated around head shops and the hippie movement. As soon as this culture weakened, comix started a slow decay. However, their relative success proved the possibility of creating something alternative to mainstream comics. Comix publishers were defenders of freedom of expression and pushers of creative boundaries. This movement nurtured and opened doors to **alternative** and independent artists that flourished in the 1980s and 1990s. It also allowed authors to experiment with drawing and narrative styles as well as storylines. An example of the influence of this movement in the storylines of following decades is the work *Binky Brown Meets the Holy Virgin Mary* by Justin Green (1972). Through this work, Green explores with great honesty how he suffered from an incipient obsessive-compulsive disorder during his childhood and teenage years in an environment dominated by Catholicism. This comic is one of the first examples of autobiographical work or **memoir** in the comics medium. Interestingly, it focuses the narrative on the author's youth, something that has become common in contemporary works, such as Craig Thompson's *Blankets* (2003), **Phoebe Gloeckner's** *A Child's Life* (2000), and **Chester Brown's** *The Playboy* (1992). The biographical content of these titles demands very distinctive styles, voices, and storylines, each of them representing three different ways of looking back on one's past.

In short, *Blankets* looks at the conflict between the religious family and environment Thompson grew up in and his first romantic and sexual relationship. The semi-autobiographical *A Child's Life* shows a different story about childhood and adolescence; it focuses on the life of Minnie, an abused teenager who early in her life had extreme experiences with sex and drugs. Even the rather humorous *The Playboy* discusses sexuality and the obsession with pornography in terms that were probably inconceivable without the edgy and experimental years of underground comics.

The example of underground comics and the changes in distribution brought by the direct market supported the birth of independent publishers and the self-publishing phenomenon. Two authors who emerged under these circumstances are John Porcellino and Ariel Schrag. Both cartoonists bring a distinctive perspective to the analysis of adolescence in the comics medium. Porcellino is a well-known author mainly through his minicomic *King-Cat*. His piece *Perfect Example* (2000) collects several stories about Porcellino's adolescence previously published in this minicomic. In these stories, Porcellino presents himself as a quiet teenager who is dealing with an incipient case of depression. With a style that can be described as simple but not simplistic, Porcellino transmits his emotional state and how it affected his social life and first romantic relationships. The slow and controlled pace of Porcellino's work markedly contrasts with Ariel Schrag's lively and noisy style. She first self-published her stories to later release them under the label of Slave Labor Graphics. One of the main peculiarities of Schrag's work is that it is not an adult reflection on her past teenager years; her comics are contemporary to the experiences, therefore, the reader gets a more visceral and raw account of Schrag's life: her growing doubts about her sexuality; her experimentations with drugs and alcohol; her parents' divorce; and especially her ever shifting obsessions with different bands. Schrag's autobiographical work brings a richness of detail and energy seldom found in other titles. She managed to keep a similar tone in the volume she edited entitled *Stuck in the Middle*, in which authors such **Joe Matt**, **Daniel Clowes**, and Gabrielle Bell dig into their own memories about what it was like to survive middle school.

These titles mentioned are extremely difficult to categorize under any other label than that the general one of memoirs. The drawing styles, the character's voices and the main themes of the stories are a product of a personal process of introspection and sharing that makes each unique, but extremely enriching for any reader, adolescent or adult.

The view brought by the autobiographical works is complemented by other comics that succeed at describing not just the experiences but also the cultural and social moment. *Archie* and titles like it were for a long time the only example of a realistic, although idealized, voice about what it meant to be a teenager in America. The works published during the 1960s and 1970s opened the door for a less juvenile and more introspective take on youth culture and experiences. An excellent example is *Locas*, a sub-narrative of *Love & Rockets* (1982), a **Hernandez Brothers'** creation. This comic follows the lives of Maggie Chascarrillo and Hopey Glass, two young adult Latinas in Los Angeles during the 1980s. Part of the novelty in this title was the realistic description of the punk culture in the city at that moment, as Jaime Hernandez managed to successfully portray the expectations, dreams, and the reality of an entire generation. Another peculiarity of this title is that the characters have aged over time and nowadays readers can follow the life of Maggie as an adult.

In a completely different style and tone, Daniel Clowes follows the life of another pair of girls, Enid and Beck, as part of the grunge generation. ***Ghost World*** (1997) is populated by typical teenage sentiments like angst, boredom, irony and cynicism; everything works perfectly to construct this search for one's place in society. The same way that Hernandez used Los Angeles as the setting for Maggie and Hopey, Clowes creates an unnamed city populated by fast-food restaurants and shopping malls that resembles any North American city. Both settings work extremely well to represent the society and culture that surrounds the main characters and how they navigate it or react against it. Also linked to the Generation X is the character of Buddy Bradley. A creation of **Peter Bagge**, Buddy is the personification of the grunge young adult in the 1990s who dreams of abandoning the family home to live in the grunge Mecca: Seattle. Bagge's characteristic drawing style is perfect to describe Buddy's chaotic and improvised life where peculiar roommates, angry girlfriends, and meaningless jobs are common ingredients. Compared with the introspective and rather serious tone of some of the works aforementioned works, this comic book presents a humorous, sharp and ironic view of the youth culture and the society of the time.

Ross Campbell and Charles Burns use **horror** to examine different aspects of a teenage life. Through the metaphor of a "teen plague" that physically affects to teenagers that have had sex, Burns's ***Black Hole*** (1995) explores issues of sex, emotional relationships, and what it means to be "normal" in a rather aseptic society. On the other hand, Campbell's *The Abandoned* (2006) and the series *Wet Moon* (2004) are populated by characters that are already far from being the typical teenager. They are outcasts, mainly Goths and Punks, who are basically trying to navigate life in the South of United States. In *The Abandoned*, Campbell makes everybody over 23 a **zombie** that feeds on these 23 and under, who remain human. Both comic books take on typical teenage issues, such as relationships with friends and family, love and sexuality, identity and maturing, but the peculiarities of most protagonists and the setting make these works a stimulating and different view of adolescent culture.

Another relevant characteristic of Campbell's work is the influence of **manga**. The popularity of manga with contemporary youth audience has not only increased exponentially the number of translations from original titles and series but has also influenced enormously the drawing and narrative style of new authors. A perfect example of this phenomenon is the work of Bryan Lee O'Malley in *Scott Pilgrim*, beginning in 2004. The story follows the adventures of the title character, a 23-year-old Canadian slacker who does not have a job, shares an apartment with a gay friend, and plays in a rock band. The main plot focuses on the love story between Scott and Ramona, and her seven evil ex-boyfriends whom Scott must defeat to be able to date Ramona. This comic book combines humor, some **fantasy**, and many manga-influenced fights to explore the difficulties one confronts when is in love. Beyond some of the fantastic elements of the story, *Scott Pilgrim* portrays youth culture in a realistic manner, seamlessly including the use of cell phones, video games, as well as references to skateboarding culture, and other trivial elements like eating and dressing habits that are relevant in contemporary youth.

The other major change that manga has brought to North American comics is the acknowledgment of the female audience in the comics world. A predominantly male industry, both on the creative and reading ends, the explosion of manga titles has helped to make more visible and strengthen an already existing female audience. A consequence of this has been the attempt of one of the major publishers, **DC**, to capitalize on the teen female market with the development of the imprint Minx. This imprint was created to develop stories that spoke directly to a teen female audience. Although of short duration, from 2007 to 2008, Minx published 12 titles that had in common their teen and young adult female protagonists, an everyday life focus and a positive critic reception. The reasons for the imprint's cancellation are still unclear and it has received a rather unusual attention from the mainstream press, reflecting the opinions of readers, creators, and critics. Some consider that the female audience in comic books is not as large and strong as expected; others criticized the lack of time given to the project in order to establish a name and audience.

In the world of superheroes, the need to connect with a new generation of teen readers has also forced some changes. After years of their respective superhero universes, the two main comic book publishers realized that most of their titles had become almost unmanageable to follow for non-expert readers. Marvel, for instance, decided to revisit the birth and first steps of some of their best-known superheroes. The Ultimate Marvel series focuses on updating the style and narrative of these stories, especially for a younger audience, eliminating some of the many intricacies that make the storylines too obscure for new readers. One of the most successful works is *Ultimate Spider-Man*, from the hands of **Brian Michael Bendis** and Mark Bagle. *Runaways* is another title that has clearly attracted the attention of preteen and teenagers. Created by **Brian K. Vaughan** and published in two imprints targeting younger readers, Tsunami and Marvel Next, this title represents a different take on the superhero theme. The Runaways are a group of teenagers who discover that their parents are evil villains. Trying to stop them, the teens realize that they have powers of their own and become a rather dysfunctional and atypical superheroes group. One of the most salient characteristics of this title is the constant presence of teen culture. These teenagers are not superheroes that happen to be teens, but teens that happen to have superpowers, therefore their interests, feelings, concerns, language and relationships are kept in a realistic realm.

The connection between comic books and youth is complicated but it remains strong. Even though recent developments, such as the graphic novel phenomenon, have increased the importance of the adult and non-fan audience, comic books still tend to both reflect and influence youth culture.

**Selected Bibliography:** Brown, Jeffrey A. "The Readers." *Black Superheroes, Milestone Comics, and their Fans.* Jackson: University Press of Mississippi, 2001, 93–132; Lavin, Michael R. "A Librarian's Guide to Archie Comics." *Serials Review* 25(1) (1999): 75–82; Pustz, Matthew. *Comic Book Culture: Fanboys and True Believers.* Jackson: University Press of Mississippi, 1999; Wright, Bradford W. *Comic Book Nation: The Transformation of Youth Culture in America.* Baltimore: Johns Hopkins University Press, 2001.

*Lucia Cedeira Serantes*

**Y: THE LAST MAN.** This series begins with one horrifying moment in which every single male mammal, human, and animal, on the face of Earth dies—except for one man and one monkey. One survivor is a would-be escape artist in his early 20s named Yorick Brown and the other is a Capuchin helper monkey named Ampersand that Yorick is training. This is the premise of *Y: The Last Man*, the award-winning series published by **DC Comics** as part of their Vertigo line from 2002 to 2007 (last issue cover date January 2008). **Brian K. Vaughan** and Pia Guerra created the series, all of which was written by Vaughan and most of which was penciled by Guerra and inked by Jose Marzan Jr., Goran Sudzuka, and Paul Chadwick contributed additional artwork, with J. G. Jones and Massimo Carnevale providing the covers. The series was written for **adult** readers and contains mature language and both male and female nudity. The 60 issues have been collected into 10 collections as well as a series of oversized hardcover editions. The collections are subtitled: *Unmanned* (#1–5), *Cycles* (#6–10), *One Small Step* (#11–17), *Safeword* (#18–23), *Ring of Truth* (#24–31), *Girl on Girl* (#32–36), *Paper Dolls* (#37–42), *Kimono Dragons* (#43–48), *Motherland* (#49–54), and *Whys and Wherefores* (#55–60). The hardcovers are simply numbered by volume and contain at least 10 issues each.

While a number of characters appear regularly in the series, there are three primary characters—Yorick, Agent 355, and Dr. Allison Mann. At the time of the "gendercide," Yorick is in his early 20s and about to propose on the phone to his girlfriend Beth, who is in Australia. When he realizes he was the only human male still alive he takes to concealing himself with a cloak, hood and gas mask and using a slight falsetto when talking to the women that he encounters (explaining fear of whatever caused the males to die as a reason to keep wearing the mask). Ampersand often perches on his shoulder. Yorick makes his way to Washington D.C. in search of his mother, a member of Congress who is working with the new president (the highest surviving woman in the order of succession) and who, with the president, ends up sending Yorick out to discover the truth regarding what had happened. Yorick accepts the mission, but all he really wants is to find Beth. Over the next five years, his mission and his quest will take him across the country and the world.

Assigned to protect Yorick is Agent 355, a member of the Culper Ring, a mysterious organization that dates back to the Revolutionary War. At the time of the "gendercide," she was removing a supposedly cursed artifact from Jordan, crossing the border just as it happened. Her skills help Yorick to survive on many occasions over the years and their relationship grows, moving to close friendship and then close to something more. Their first task is to go to Boston to the lab of geneticist Dr. Allison Mann (born Ayuko Matsumori), who at the time of the "gendercide" was (unsuccessfully) giving birth to a cloned baby. Yorick and 355 find her, but after her lab is destroyed the trio is forced to head to the West Coast in search of her back-up notes, which provide the key to keeping the human species alive. It is her work that often dictates where the group must go. There are a number of additional supporting characters who have both positive and negative effects on the three main characters.

The effects of the "gendercide" upon the world are shown in various ways throughout the series. At first there is the destruction caused by multitudes of car and plane crashes, the reorganization of government (including a group of widows who want their husband's old positions to restore the Democrat-Republican balance), and changes in society, such as how a former supermodel now must make a living disposing of dead bodies. Among the antagonists in the series are the "Daughters of the Amazon," an ultra-radical feminist group seeking to destroy the remnants of the "patriarchy" that "Mother Earth" saw fit to dispose of. Yorick's sister, Hero, becomes a member of the group and, for a time, is a threat to her brother's life. At one point, a traveling group of performers offering a show to a small town find that many of the women there would like the troupe to create new versions of their favorite soap operas.

Other allies and threats to the trio come from the new role of women in the world's militaries. Due to the number of women in its armed forces, Israel's place in the Middle East is stronger and since it allows women to serve on submarines, it is now Australia that rules the waves. Religion in this new world is touched upon with a group of women from the Vatican that are following rumors of a new born male whom they wish to make into the new Pope.

While there are those who wish to capture Yorick for political reasons (such as an Israeli soldier who wants him as a way to strengthen her country or at least weaken others) or personal gain (a journalist who wants a great story). What is generally not seen in the series is the stereotypical "last man" scenario in which all women just want to have sex with him. While on his travels, Yorick wants to stay faithful to Beth, and the one encounter he does have causes feelings of guilt. The series also discusses the sex lives of the surviving women, including those in same-sex relationships (though some were lesbians beforehand), prostitutes who specialize in dressing and acting like men, and those who use mechanical means (including a "robotic" substitute used in Japan).

The series gives some possible reasons for the sudden death of all males on earth, ranging from the scientific to the supernatural, but no definitive answer is provided. In fact, many questions remain unanswered, but Vaughan has insisted that the series is complete and will not be revisited.

*David S. Serchay*

**Z**

**ZAP** was the best-known and most influential **underground comic** book, featuring taboo-breaking work by the movement's key figures. Upon its initial appearance in San Francisco in 1968 with a cover price of 25 cents, and the "fair warning" that it was "for adult intellectuals only," *Zap Comix* (the spelling itself virtually a declaration of independence) linked comic books directly to the counterculture, otherwise being expressed through popular music, fashion, drugs, and lifestyle. Soon thereafter underground comics (now routinely known as "**comix**") would be sold in "head shops," since regular distribution was unavailable to them.

The first issue of *Zap* was printed by Beat writer and publisher Charles Plymell and Don Donahue of Apex Novelties. Apex would publish six more issues (including #0, 1967–74); The Print Mint published issues #7–9 (1974–78), and Last Gasp published issues #10–15 (1982–2004). The first two issues (#1 followed by #0, recreated from photocopies of the stolen art for the issue intended to appear first) were entirely the work of **Robert Crumb**, who quickly became the most famous and influential underground cartoonist despite his own ambivalence toward the hippie movement; thereafter the comic functioned as an anthology of disconnected pieces featuring what soon became a stable group consisting of **S. Clay Wilson**, Robert Williams, "Spain" Rodriguez, Gilbert Shelton, Rick Griffin, and Victor Moscoso, the latter two often working in entirely nonnarrative modes associated with psychedelic drugs and rock concert posters. Much later, for the last two issues, Paul Mavrides came aboard.

The initial all-Crumb issues announced many of the themes that would dominate Crumb's career, and featured one of his most important characters, the irreverent bearded sage Mr. Natural (introduced in *Yarrowstalks* in 1967), along with his hapless disciple Flakey Foont. The strip "Whiteman" indicated Crumb's skill at social **satire**, although

Title panel of "Whiteman," issue #1 of Zap Comix. Sony Pictures Classics/Photofest

its reliance on "comic Negroes," as well as a genuinely shocking fake ad for canned "nigger hearts" in the first issue also indicated Crumb's willingness to employ outrageous racial stereotypes, derived from earlier cartoons and animated films, leading to decades of debate over their subversive or irredeemably racist meanings. If Mr. Natural was a brilliant condensation of the era's fascination with (and perhaps hoodwinking by) alternative lifestyles and modes of consciousness, the naïve, dialect-speaking African Amazon Angelfood McSpade (her name alone a provocation) has seemed to some critics less a wicked commentary on the period's volatile racial and gender politics than Crumb's indulgence in racist and sexist fantasy.

With issue #2, the semi-abstract work of Griffin and Moscoso (often daring to distort classic Disney characters) was added, along with the outrageously violent, sex-drenched drawings of Wilson, whose uninhibited Checkered Demon was one of the underground's many embodiments of an entirely unrepressed id. Whereas Crumb's unsettling impact in part derived from his presenting taboo content in the nostalgic style of earlier cartoons, and while Griffin and Moscoso's drawings were built out of curving lines and mandala-like symmetries, Wilson's incredibly dense panels, ignoring the illusion of depth that might provide breathing space for his pirate and biker characters, fully embraced the grotesque as an aesthetic style. Issue #3 added Gilbert Shelton, whose Wonder Wart-Hog (a parody of **superheroes**) adventures seemed more willing to entertain readers than others. The issue also included the first "jam," a non-narrative strip that included contributions from all of the issue's artists, a group effort that soon became an underground tradition. The issue was also a cleverly designed "Special 69 Issue," which could be read from either front or back, with a Moscoso mirror-image spinning the reader around at the comic's center. Issue #4 added Robert Williams, whose talent for precise design distinguished his work from Wilson's, despite their shared affinity for densely packed panels and odd creatures (such as Williams' Coochy Cooty). The "outlaw" status of underground comics was also fully affirmed by the appearance of

*Zap* #4, which contained Crumb's "Joe Blow," a simultaneously cute and explicit depiction of an incestuous all-American family: the issue was the focus of a number of obscenity trials in various communities, and was for a time prohibited in New York.

By issue #6 Spain Rodriguez joined the group, which remained stable for the next seven issues. The roster only changed with issue #13, which was dedicated to Griffin, who had died after a motorcycle accident. Paul Mavrides joined for issue #14 (1998), which in part chronicled divisions within the group in response to Crumb's desire to put the comic to an end. (With wicked wit, Crumb is killed in a visual homage to his own killing of his most lucrative character, **Fritz the Cat**.) Issue #15 appeared after a gap of five years, and though not identified as a final bow, seemed to be a quiet but redundant return to business as usual, with Mavrides still on board with the core group of Crumb, Shelton, Wilson, Williams, Moscoso, and Rodriguez.

Always constructed as an anthology (even when Crumb was the sole contributor), *Zap* also maintained a degree of continuity due to recurrent characters (noted above, as well as Spain's macho Trashman, and even some of Moscoso's semi-abstract figures) as well as the consistent style and obsessive themes of its artists. For all of its initial innovations and boldness, there was little experimentation once the formula for the comic was established, with a few notable exceptions: Crumb, who had moved increasingly toward autobiographical stories (a genre no other *Zap* artist embraced) offered a serious biography of the blues singer Charlie Patton in #11, rendered in a richly detailed, semi-realist mode unlike his earlier contributions. In the same issue Spain provides a strip with detailed renderings of airplanes that suggest he might have had a career drawing **war comics** for the mainstream, and in #18 even Shelton contributes a story on a Paris cemetery with unusually realistic drawings. Otherwise, the radical cartoonists tended to stick with what was ironically familiar as the series continued.

Despite its own tendency toward repetition and familiarity, *Zap* would remain the model for other underground and independent anthology comics, such as *Bijou Funnies* (8 issues, 1968–73), *Snarf* (15 issues, 1972–90), and the digest-sized *Snatch* (3 issues, 1968–69), as well as the later magazines *Arcade* (7 issues, 1975–76) edited by Bill Griffith and **Art Spiegelman**, and Crumb's own **Weirdo** (28 issues, 1981–1993). The entirely male, frequently misogynist, and generally heterosexual (if not polymorphously perverse) perspective of *Zap* also presumably motivated the creation of the feminist and gay underground anthologies *Wimmen's Comix* (17 issues, 1972–92) and *Gay Comix* (25 issues, 1983–98).

**Selected Bibliography:** Estren, Mark James. *A History of Underground Comics*. 3rd Edition. Berkeley, CA: Ronin Books, 1993; Rosenkrantz, Patrick. *Rebel Visions: The Underground Comix Revolution 1963–1975*. Seattle: Fantagraphics, 2002.

*Corey K. Creekmur*

**ZOMBIES.** *See **Vampires and Zombies***

# Selected General Resources

Atlas Tales. Accessed September 20, 2009. http://www.atlastales.com/.

Benton, Mike. *Masters of Imagination: The Comic Book Artists Hall of Fame*. New York: National, 1994.

Booker, M. Keith. *"May Contain Graphic Material": Comic Books, Graphic Novels, and Film*. Westport, CT: Praeger, 2007.

Brooker, Will. *Batman Unmasked: Analyzing a Cultural Icon*. New York: Continuum, 2005.

BPIB Art Samples Database. Accessed September 20, 2009. http://www.bpib.com/.

Brown, Jeffrey A. *Black Superheroes, Milestone Comics, and Their Fans*. Jackson: University Press of Mississippi, 2001.

Buhle, Paul., ed. *Jews and American Comics: An Illustrated History of an American Art Form*. New York: New Press, 2008.

The Comic Book Database. Accessed September 20, 2009. http://www.comicbookdb.com.

Comic Book Reference Bibliographic Datafile. Accessed September 20, 2009. http://www.crbd.eu/.

Comic Book Resources Link Database. Accessed September 20, 2009. http://comicbookresources.com/resources/links.

Comic-Con International: San Diego. Accessed September 20, 2009. http://www.comic-con.org/cci/.

*The Comics Journal*. Seattle: Fantagraphics Books.

The Comics Reporter. Accessed September 20, 2009. http://www.comicsreporter.com/.

Comics Research Bibliography. Accessed September 20, 2009. http://www.rpi.edu/~bulloj/comxbib.html.

Comics Scholarship Annotated Bibliographies. Accessed September 20, 2009. http://www.comicsresearch.org/.

Comix Scholars Listserve. Accessed September 20, 2009. http://www.english.ufl.edu/comics/scholars/.

Coogan, Peter. *Superhero: The Secret Origin of a Genre*. Austin, TX: Monkey Brain Books, 2006.

Costello, Matthew J. *Secret Identity Crisis: Comic Books and the Unmasking of Cold War America*. New York: Continuum, 2009.

Daniels, Les. *Marvel: Five Fabulous Decades of the World's Greatest Comics*. New York: Harry N. Abrams, 1991.

Daniels, Les. *Batman: The Complete History*. San Francisco: Chronicle, 1999.

Daniels, Les. *The Complete History of Superman*. San Francisco: Chronicle, 1998.

Daniels, Les. *DC Comics: A Celebration of the World's Favorite Comic Book Super Heroes*. New York: Billboard Books, 2003.

Danky, James, and Denis Kitchen, eds. *Underground Classics: The Transformation of Comics into Comix*. New York: Abrams ComicArts, 2009.

Dark Horse Comics Homepage. Accessed September 20, 2009. http://darkhorse.com/.

DC Comics Homepage. Accessed September 20, 2009. http://dccomics.com/dccomics/.

Duin, Steve, and Mike Richardson. *Comics Between the Panels*. Milwaukie, OR: Dark Horse Comics, 1998.

Duncan, Randy, and Matthew J. Smith. *The Power of Comics: History, Form, and Culture*. New York: Continuum, 2009.

Eisner, Will. *Comics and Sequential Art*. Tamarac, FL: Poorhouse Press, 1985.

Estren, Mark James. *A History of Underground Comics*. San Francisco: Straight Arrow, 1974.

Fingeroth, Danny. *Disguised as Clark Kent: Jews, Comics, and the Creation of the Superhero*. New York: Continuum, 2007.

Fingeroth, Danny. *The Rough Guide to Graphic Novels*. London: Rough Guides, 2008.

Fleisher, Michael L. *The Original Encyclopedia of Comic Book Heroes*. New York: DC Comics, 2007.

Garrett, Greg. *Holy Superheroes!: Exploring the Sacred in Comics, Graphic Novels, and Film*. Louisville, KY: Westminster John Knox Press, 2008.

Geissman, Grant. *Foul Play!: The Art and Artists of the Notorious 1950s E.C. Comics!* New York: Collins Design, 2005.

Golden Age Comics Downloading Site. Accessed September 20, 2009. http://www.goldenagecomics.co.uk.

Gordon, Ian, Mark Jancovich, and Matthew P. McAllister, eds. *Film and Comic Books*. Jackson: University Press of Mississippi, 2007.

Goulart, Ron. *Comic Book Culture*. Portland: Collector's Press, 2000.

The Grand Comic-Book Database. Accessed September 3, 2009. http://www.comics.org/.

Gravett, Paul. *Graphic Novels, Stories to Change Your Life*. New York: Collins Design, 2005.

Groensteen, Thierry. *The System of Comics*. Jackson: University Press of Mississippi, 2007.

Harvey, Robert C. *The Art of the Comic Book*. Jackson: University Press of Mississippi, 1996.

Hatfield, Charles. *Alternative Comics: An Emerging Literature*. Jackson: University Press of Mississippi, 2005.

Heer, Jeet, and Kent Worcester, eds. *Arguing Comics: Literary Masters on a Popular Medium*. Jackson: University Press of Mississippi, 2004.

Heer, Jeet, and Kent Worcester, eds. *A Comics Studies Reader*. Jackson: University Press of Mississippi, 2009.

Herman, H. *Silver Age: The Second Generation of Comic Book Artists*. Neshannock, PA: Hermes Press, 2004.

Horn, Maurice. *Comics of the American West*. New York: Winchester Press, 1977.

Horn, Maurice, ed. *The World Encyclopedia of Comics*. New York: Chelsea House, 1976.

Howe, Sean, ed. *Give our Regards to the Atomsmashers*. New York: Pantheon, 2004.

Image Comics Homepage. Accessed September 20, 2009. http://imagecomics.com/.

Inducks Disney Comics Database Portal. Accessed September 20, 2009. http://inducks.org/.

Institute for Comics Studies. Accessed September 20, 2009. http://www.instituteforcomicsstudies.org/.

*International Journal of Comics Art*. Published three times yearly through Temple University, Philadelphia, PA.

Jones, Gerard. *Men of Tomorrow: Geeks, Gangsters and the Birth of the Comic Book*. New York: Basic Books, 2004.

Jones, Gerard, and Will Jacobs. *The Comic Book Heroes*. Rocklin, CA: Prima Publishing, 1997.

Jones, William B., Jr. *Classics Illustrated: A Cultural History*. Jefferson, NC: McFarland, 2001.

Kannenberg, Gene. Jr. *500 Essential Graphic Novels*. New York: Collins Design, 2008.

Kaplan, A. *From Krakow to Krypton: Jews and Comic Books*. Philadelphia: The Jewish Publication Society, 2008.

Kaveney, Roz. *Superheroes! Capes and Crusaders in Comics and Films*. London: I. B. Tauris, 2008.

Klock, Geoff. *How to Read Superhero Comics and Why*. New York: Continuum, 2002.

Knowles, Christopher. *Our Gods Wear Spandex: The Secret History of Comic Book Heroes*. San Francisco: Weiser Books, 2007.

Lewis, A. David, and Christine Hoff Kraemer, eds. *Graven Images: Religion in Comic Books & Graphic Novels*. New York: Continuum, 2010.

Markstein, Donald D. *Don Markstein's Toonopedia*. Accessed September 3, 2009. http://www.toonopedia.com/.

Martin, Douglas. "Gil Kane, Comic-Book Artist, Is Dead at 73." *New York Times*, February 3, 2000. http://www.nytimes.com/2000/02/03/arts/gil-kane-comic-book-artist-is-dead-at-73.html?pagewanted=1.

Marvel Comics Homepage. Accessed September 20, 2009. http://marvel.com/.

Marvel Masterworks Resource Page. Accessed September 20, 2009. http://marvelmasterworks.com/.

McCloud, Scott. *Understanding Comics: The Invisible Art*. New York: HarperPerennial, 2003.

McLaughlin, Jeff. *Comics As Philosophy*. Jackson: University Press of Mississippi, 2005.

Mike's Amazing World of DC Comics. Accessed September 20, 2009. http://www.dcindexes.com/.

New York Comic Con. Accessed September 20, 2009. http://www.newyorkcomiccon.com/.

Nolan, Michelle. *Love on the Racks: A History of American Romance Comics*. Jefferson, NC: McFarland, 2008.

Nyberg, Amy. *Seal of Approval: History of the Comics Code*. Jackson: University Press of Mississippi, 1998.

Pearson, Roberta E., and William Uricchio, eds. *The Many Lives of the Batman: Critical Approaches to a Superhero and His Media*. New York: Routledge, 1991.

Platinum Age Comics Group. Accessed September 20, 2009. http://groups.yahoo.com/group/PlatinumAgeComics/.

Pustz, Matthew. *Comic Book Culture: Fanboys and True Believers*. Jackson: University Press of Mississippi, 1999.

Richardson, Mike, and Steve Duin. *Comics, Between the Panels*. Milwaukie, OR: Dark Horse Comics, 1998.

Roach, David. *The Superhero Encyclopedia*. Canton, MI: Visible Ink Press, 2004.

Robbins, Trina. *A Century of Women Cartoonists*. Northampton, MA: Kitchen Sink, 1993.

Robbins, Trina. *The Great Women Superheroes*. Northampton, MA: Kitchen Sink, 1997.

Robbins, Trina. *From Girls to Grrrlz: A History of Women's Comics from Teens to Zines*. San Francisco: Chronicle Books, 1999.

Robbins, Trina. *The Great Women Cartoonists*. New York: Watson-Guptill, 2001.

Rosenkranz, Patrick. *Rebel Visions: The Underground Comix Revolution*. Seattle: Fantagraphics, 2008.

Sabin, Roger. *Comics, Comix and Graphic Novels: A History of Comic Art*. New York: Phaidon, 1996.

Savage, William, Jr. *Commies, Cowboys, and Jungle Queens: Comic Books and America, 1945–1954*. Middletown, CT: Wesleyan, 1998.

Scott, Naomi, ed. *Heart Throbs: The Best of DC Romance Comics*. New York: Simon and Schuster, 1979.

Simon, Joe. *Joe Simon: The Comic Book Makers*. New York: Crestwood, 1990.

Steranko, James. *History of Comics*. 2 vols. New York: Crown Publishing, 1972.

Strömberg, Fredrik. *Black Images in the Comics: A Visual History*. Seattle: Fantagraphics Books, 2003.

Stuller, Jennifer K. *Ink-stained Amazons and Cinematic Warriors: Superwomen in Modern Mythology*. New York: I. B. Tauris, 2010.

Varnum, Robin, and Christina T. Gibbons, eds. *The Language of Comics: Word and Image*. Jackson: University Press of Mississippi, 2001.

Versaci, Rocco. *This Book Contains Graphic Language*. New York: Continuum, 2007.

White, David Manning, and Robert H. Abel. *The Funnies: An American Idiom*. New York: Free Press, 1963.

Who's Who in the DC Universe. Accessed September 20, 2009. http://www.super manartists.comics.org/.

Wiater, Stanley, and Stephen R. Bissette. *Comic Book Rebels: Conversations with the Creators of the New Comics*. New York: Donald I. Fine, 1993.

Wolk, Douglas. *Reading Comics: How Graphic Novels Work and What They Mean*. Cambridge: Da Capo Press, 2007.

Wright, Bradford. *Comic Book Nation*. Baltimore: Johns Hopkins University Press, 2003.

Wright, Nicky. *The Classic Era of American Comics*. London: Prion Books, 2000.

Yeffeth, Glenn, ed. *The Man from Krypton: A Closer Look at Superman*. Dallas: Benbella, 2005.

# About the Editor
# and the Contributors

## Editor

**M. Keith Booker** is the James E. and Ellen Wadley Professor of English at the University of Arkansas, Fayetteville, where he is director of the program in Comparative Literature and Cultural Studies.

## Contributors

**Noaman G. Ali** is a PhD student in the department of Political Science at the University of Toronto. He completed his MA in Social and Political Thought at York University, Canada.

**Will Allred** currently writes comics, is a PhD candidate in English at the University of Arkansas, and has been a member of the Grand Comic-Book Database Project since 1996, and a member of its Board of Directors since 2000.

**Henry Andrews** is a software engineer and member of the Board of the Grand Comic-Book Database.

**Jackson Ayres** is a PhD candidate in English Literature at the University of Arkansas. His research interests include 20th-century British and American literature, the political novel, film studies, comics, literary theory, and popular culture. His dissertation examines the contemporary role and status of the public intellectual.

**Grant Bain** is currently pursuing his doctorate in modern American literature, and working on a dissertation on the Southern Gothic at the University of Arkansas. He completed his master's degree there in 2006 and plans to complete his PhD in 2010. His research interests include critical theory, modern literature, and popular culture.

**Anthony D. Baker** is the director of composition at Tennessee Technological University, where he teaches undergraduate and graduate courses in writing, rhetoric, research methods, and literature, including a course about graphic novels. His recent publications include chapters in *Approaches to Teaching the Graphic Novel* and *Autism and Representation*.

**Patrick Scott Belk** is a PhD candidate at the University of Tulsa and book review editor and Web site manager of the *James Joyce Quarterly*. His dissertation project, tentatively titled "Imperial Rags," focuses on adventure narratives and mass-media technologies in the early decades of the 20th century.

**Tim Bryant** is a PhD candidate in the English Department of the University at Buffalo, where he studies American literature, cultural studies, and religious history. He teaches Alan Moore's *Watchmen* in his composition and humanities course, and has an essay about the experience forthcoming in a collection from Fountainhead Press.

**Brian Camp** received his MA in Film Studies from Memphis State University in 1991.

**Stanford W. Carpenter** is a cultural anthropologist and assistant professor in the Department of Visual & Critical Studies at the School of the Art Institute of Chicago. Carpenter conducts ethnographic research among cultural producers with an emphasis on artists, editors, and writers to address the construction and depiction of community and identity in everyday life. He uses his ethnographic research both for scholarly manuscripts and arts-based projects.

**James Bucky Carter** is an assistant professor of English Education at the University of Texas at El Paso. He edited and contributed chapters to *Building Literacy Connections with Graphic Novels: Page by Page, Panel by Panel* (NCTE 2007). In 2009, he won the inaugural Fordham GSE Excellence for Education in Graphica Award.

**Lucia Cedeira Serantes** is working towards her PhD in Library and Information Science at the University of Western Ontario, London, Ontario. Her general area of work focuses on the intersection of young adults, reading and libraries, with special attention to comic book readers. Previously she worked as young adult librarian and researcher for the International Center for Children's and Young Adults' Books (Salamanca, Spain).

**Charles Coletta** earned both his BA and MA in Literature from John Carroll University, Cleveland, Ohio and his doctorate in American Culture Studies from Bowling Green State University, Bowling Green, Ohio. He has taught in the Department of Popular Culture at BGSU since 2000. In 2006, he assisted Eva Marie Saint in preparing for her role as "Ma Kent" in *Superman Returns*.

**Peter Coogan** is the director of the Institute for Comics Studies and the co-founder and co-chair of the Comics Arts Conference. He teaches at Webster University and Washington University, both in St. Louis. He is the author of *Superhero: The Secret Origin* of a Genre (2006).

**Rikke Platz Cortsen** is a PhD student at the University of Copenhagen. She holds an extended MA in Comparative Literature, graduating with a thesis about the construction of time and space in comics written by Alan Moore. She teaches classes in literature and comics, and writes for Danish comics magazine *STRIP!*.

**Brannon Costello** is associate professor of English at Louisiana State University, where he specializes in American literature, Southern studies, and comics. He is the author of *Plantation Airs: Racial Paternalism and the Transformations of Class in Southern Fiction, 1945–1971* (2007) and numerous articles and essays.

**Christopher Couch** teaches comparative literature at the University of Massachusetts, Amherst. He is the author of numerous books and articles on Latin American art and on graphic novels and comic art, including *The Will Eisner Companion: The Pioneering Spirit of the Father of the Graphic Novel* (with Stephen Weiner), and *Will Eisner: A Retrospective* (with Peter Myer).

**Corey K. Creekmur** is an associate professor of English and Film Studies at the University of Iowa, where he also directs the Institute for Cinema and Culture. His publications include studies of American and Indian cinema, popular music, and comics.

**Craig Crowder** is a PhD student at the University of Kentucky's Department of English and a life-long reader of comics. His research interests include 19th-century British literature and cultural studies.

**Ed Cunard** graduated with an MA in Literature from Indiana University of Pennsylvania in 2009.

**Gail de Vos** is a professional storyteller and an adjunct associate professor for the School of Library and Information Studies at the University of Alberta, Edmonton, Alberta. She is the author of eight books on storytelling, folklore, and popular culture, and has taught her online course, "Comic books and graphic novels in school and public libraries," for over six years.

**Matthew Dube** teaches in the English department at William Woods University in Fulton, Missouri. He has presented critical responses at national conferences sponsored by the College English Association and the Popular Culture/American Culture Association.

**Randy Duncan** has a PhD in Communications from Louisiana State University and has taught at Henderson State University since 1987. He is co-author of *The Power of Comics: History, Form and Culture* (Continuum 2009) and the co-founder of the Comics Arts Conference. He serves on the Editorial Board of the *International Journal of Comic Art*.

**Lance Eaton** teaches at several colleges in Massachusetts including the University of Massachusetts and Emerson College. As a freelance writer, he has written for *Publishers Weekly*, *Library Journal*, *Foreword Magazine*, and *Audiofile Magazine*. His areas of study include gender and sexuality, comics, audiobooks, and adaptation.

**Andrew Edwards** is a writer, comics critic, independent scholar, and assistant director for Great Britain for the Institute for Comics Studies. He holds a BA Honors in English and History, an MA in English, and postgraduate qualifications in both teaching and librarianship.

**Marc-Oliver Frisch** is a student of North American Literature and Culture at Saarland University, Saarbrücken, Germany. His writing on comics appears regularly at *Publishers Weekly/The Beat* (http://pwbeat.publishersweekly.com/blog/), in the German comics magazine *Comicgate* (http://www.comicgate.de/), and at his weblog Comiks Debris (http://comiksdebris.blogspot.com/).

**Jason Gallagher** is a graduate student in the Media Studies program at the S. I. Newhouse School of Public Communication at Syracuse University. He received his MA in English in 2009 from the University of Nebraska-Omaha, where he studied textual analysis and Native American and Chicano/a studies.

**Wendy Goldberg** has presented papers at national conferences and published essays on comics, anime, and manga for the last 14 years. Her most recent article is titled

"The Manga Phenomenon in America" in *Manga: An Anthology of Global and Cultural Perspectives* (ed. Toni Johnson-Woods, Continuum, 2009). She has been an English instructor at the United States Coast Guard Academy and is currently serving as submission editor for *Mechademia: An Annual Forum for Anime, Manga and the Fan Arts* (ed. Frenchy Lunning, University of Minnesota Press).

**Richard L. Graham** is a media services librarian and assistant professor at the University of Nebraska-Lincoln. He reads and writes about comics, television, and popular culture while maintaining and developing a media collection—from microfilm to PS3 games.

**Diana Green** has a BFA in Comic Book Illustration from the Minneapolis College of Art and Design and an MA in Liberal Studies, Hamline University, St. Paul, Minnesota. She teaches studio and liberal studies classes, including comic history and graphic novel, along with presenting at the Comic Scholars Conference (2006–). She continues to publish on comics history and theory.

**Alex Hall** is a doctoral student at Kent State University in Kent, Ohio. His master's thesis looked at dystopian cultural production of the early 21st century, and the suitability of the dystopian narrative framework for exhibiting the utopian imagination. He is an active member of the Society for Utopian Studies.

**D. R. Hammontree** began his love of comics with *World's Finest* #282. He holds a PhD in English Studies (with an emphasis on Cultural Rhetoric) from Illinois State University and is a professor of Writing at Jackson Community College, Jackson, Michigan. He has written on issues of writing pedagogy, civic literacy, and comics.

**Michael W. Hancock** teaches English and graphic novels at the Illinois Mathematics and Science Academy in Aurora, Illinois.

**Alec R. Hosterman** is a doctoral candidate in Technical Communication and Rhetoric at Texas Tech University. He is writing his dissertation on hyperreality and the graphic narrative. He is also a Senior Lecturer in the communication arts area at Indiana University, South Bend. He teaches courses in visual communication, rhetoric, comics, and new media.

**Jackson Jennings** completed his BA in English and Philosophy and Religion at Truman State University in Kirksville, Missouri. He is now working on his PhD in English at the University of Arkansas, where he also received his MA.

**Aaron Kashtan** is a doctoral student in the Department of English at the University of Florida, specializing in Media Studies and Comics and Visual Rhetoric. He is the moderator of the comix-scholars listserv and was a co-organizer of the 2009 University of Florida Conference on Comics and Graphic Novels.

**Andrew J. Kunka** is an associate professor of English at the University of South Carolina, Sumter. He co-edited, with Michele Troy, the collection *May Sinclair: Moving towards the Modern*, from Ashgate Press (2006), and his essay on Siegfried Sassoon's elegies appears in the collection *Modernism and Mourning* (2007), edited by Patricia Rae.

**Travis Langley** is a professor of psychology who teaches courses on psychopathology, personality, crime, and comics at Henderson State University, Arkadelphia, Arkansas. He helps organize the Comics Arts Conference and academic tracks for Wizard World and other fan conventions. He runs the ERIICA Project (Empirical Research on the Interpretation & Influence of the Comic Arts).

**Pascal Lefèvre** teaches on comics and visual media in various Belgian university colleges of art and is affiliated researcher at the University of Leuven. He has published widely on visual culture in various languages and he is a member of various international editorial boards and consultative committees of academic journals.

**Stuart Lenig** is a professor of communication and media studies at Columbia State Community College, Columbia, Tennessee. He is currently working on projects about glam rock, graphic novels, and steampunk culture. He produces cultural affairs programming, directs the film/performance program, and promotes the digital media initiative.

**A. David Lewis** is a Boston educator who has lectured nationally on comics studies. He founded the Religion & Graphica Collection at Boston University and co-edited the book *Graven Images: Religion in Comic Books & Graphic Novels*. His graphic novels include *The Lone and Level Sands* and *Some New Kind of Slaughter* with mpMann.

**Jacob Lewis** is a doctoral candidate in the English Department at the University of Arkansas. He is currently finishing a dissertation that charts the utopian function in several medieval dream-visions. His scholarly interests include medieval dream visions, Marxism, and utopianism.

**Lorcan McGrane** has studied at the University of Ulster, Dublin Institute of Technology, and the University of East Anglia in the areas of film and television studies. He has taught at UEA, Norwich University College of the Arts, and Lowestoft College, and is currently writing *Superheroic Bodies: The Corporealities of Contemporary Film Superheroes*.

**Jeff McLaughlin** is an Associate Professor of Philosophy at Thompson Rivers University, Kamloops British Columbia. He is author/editor of *Comics as Philosophy* (2005), *Stan Lee: Conversations* (2007), and *An Introduction to Philosophy: In Black and White and Colour* (2010).

**Chris Murray** lectures on English and Film Studies at the University of Dundee, Scotland, where he is the head of English. His main research interest is comics. He is a central member of the Scottish Word and Image Group (SWIG), which organizes annual conferences on aspects of word and image study. His book on superheroes and propaganda is being published by Hampton Press. He organizes an annual conference on comics as part of the Dundee Literary Festival and is editor of the new journal *Studies in Comics*, forthcoming from Intellect.

**Nhu-Hoa Nguyen** holds a PhD in Semiology (Université du Québec à Montréal) and teaches Visual Semiotics, Comics Critical Analysis, and History of Comic Art in the comics undergraduate program at the Université du Québec en Outaouais, in Québec. Her fields of research include rhetorical figures, comics studies and Peircean studies.

**Michelle Nolan** is a journalist and widely recognized authority on romance comics. She is the author of *Love on the Racks: A History of American Romance Comics* (2008).

**Mark O'English** is the university archivist at Washington State University in Pullman, Washington, where he works with their underground comics collections. He has worked for Marvel Publishing as a researcher/writer on numerous reference publications, including their lines of encyclopedias and official handbooks.

**Jared L. Olmsted** is a budding comics historian currently residing in Brooklyn, New York. He is a former Picturebox Inc. volunteer as well as the founder and curator of *Marginalia*, a mini-comix festival housed in downtown LA's infamous multi-use space, The Smell.

**Robert O'Nale** lives in Arkadelphia, Arkansas and graduated from Henderson State University's Master of Liberal Arts program in 2008. He is revising his master's thesis for publication, which focuses on Gestalt psychology and comic books. He has presented on comic books and visual theory at the Comic Arts Conference at Wondercon in San Francisco and Comic-Con International in San Diego.

**J. Gavin Paul** is a postdoctoral research fellow and instructor in the Department of English at Simon Fraser University, Burnaby, British Columbia.

**Joshua Plencner** is a doctoral student in the Department of Political Science at the University of Oregon, where his broad research interests include American political culture and institutional development. A current ongoing project connects theories of race and ethnicity, political assimilation, and early superhero comics.

**James E. Reibman** taught literature and media studies at Lafayette College, Easton, Pennsylvania. A specialist on law and literature, he has published on legal writings of the Scottish Enlightenment and on Samuel Johnson and his circle. His most recent lectures and writings concern the graphic novel, popular culture, 20th-century American intellectual history, the Roman world, and violence in the media. Reibman is the biographer of Fredric Wertham and is the editor of the forthcoming *A Fredric Wertham Reader*.

**Michael G. Rhode** is an independent comics scholar who is editor of the book, *Harvey Pekar: Conversations* and a contributing editor to the *International Journal of Comic Art*.

**Brad J. Ricca**, PhD teaches English at Case Western Reserve University, Cleveland, Ohio. He has been published in *The Emily Dickinson Journal, Leviathan, Culture and Cosmos*, and elsewhere. His comics work includes presentations at the Comics Art Conference and the Popular Culture Association. He wrote a documentary film on Superman titled *Last Son*.

**Leonard Rifas** is the proprietor of EduComics, a part-time educational comic book company. He teaches courses in Sequential Art at Seattle Central Community College. He has an MA and a PhD from the University of Washington's School of Communications. He welcomes correspondence pertaining to comics scholarship at rifas@earthlink.net.

**Trina Robbins** is an independent scholar, writer, historian, and feminist. An important cartoonist, Robbins has also written histories of women cartoonists and of superheroines, and is responsible for the rediscovery of pioneer women cartoonists such as Nell Brinkley and Lily Renee. Her collection of original art by 20th-century women cartoonists has been exhibited in Germany, Portugal, Austria, Spain, and Japan, as well as New York and San Francisco.

**Mark C. Rogers** is professor of communication at Walsh University, North Canton, Ohio. He has previously written about the media industries for the *International Journal of Comic Art* and several books about television.

**Julia Round** (MA, PhD) lectures in the Media School at Bournemouth University, UK, and edits the academic journal *Studies in Comics*. She has published and presented work internationally on cross-media adaptations, the graphic novel redefinition, the application of literary criticism and terminology to comics, and the presence of gothic and fantastic motifs and themes in this medium. Further details at www.juliaround.com.

**Jennifer D. Ryan** is an assistant professor of English at Buffalo State College, Buffalo, New York, where she teaches courses in American poetry, the 20th-century American novel, and African American literature. Her article on *Icon: A Hero's Welcome* appeared in the "Graphic Narrative" issue of *Modern Fiction Studies*; her book, *Post-Jazz Poetics: A Social History*, is forthcoming in 2010 from Palgrave Macmillan.

**Kyle Ryan** is an art historian and conservator.

**Cord Scott** is currently a doctoral candidate in American History at Loyola University, Chicago. He has written for several encyclopedias and academic journals, most recently an article in *Captain America and the Struggle of the Superhero*. His dissertation is on war-themed comics and American society.

**David S. Serchay** is a youth services librarian for the Broward County (Florida) Library System where his duties include selecting graphic novels for the system. He is the author of *The Librarian's Guide to Graphic Novels* series of books from Neal-Schuman, and has lectured and written elsewhere on the subject.

**Tyler Shipley** is a PhD candidate in the Department of Political Science at York University in Toronto. His research areas include political economy, popular culture, and Marxist theory. He has published work on the current financial crisis and contemporary imperialism, labor under neoliberalism, and the implications of the three month strike of 2008–9 at York University.

**Matthew J. Smith** is the co-author of *The Power of Comics: History, Form, and Culture* (www.powerofcomics.com) and an associate professor at Wittenberg University, Springfield, Ohio, where he teaches courses in media studies. He holds a doctorate in Communication from Ohio University, and has served as the president of the Ohio Communication Association.

**Anthony Strand** is currently a graduate student at the University of Missouri working on his master's degree in Library Science.

**Fredrik Strömberg** is the editor of *Bild & Bubbla*, Scandinavia's largest magazine about comics; the president of the Swedish Comics Association; and head of the Comic Art School of Sweden. Among the books he has written are *Swedish Comics History*, *Black Images in the Comics*, and *The Comics Go to Hell*.

**Jennifer K. Stuller** is a professional writer, critic, scholar, pop culture "herstorian," and public speaker. She is the author of *Ink-Stained Amazons and Cinematic Warriors: Superwomen in Modern Mythology* (I. B. Tauris 2010) and has written for *Geek Monthly* and *Bitch* magazines. Stuller is a Charter Associate of the Whedon Studies Association and she can be reached through her Web site: http://www.ink-staine damazon.com/.

**Raphaël Taylor** is an independent scholar and holds a PhD from King's College London. He is completing a book on Hergé's "Adventures of Tintin" considered as works of art, and is also preparing a study of André Franquin's *bandes dessinées*. His other area of scholarship is Mozart studies, and projects include a monograph on comedy, games, and the carnivalesque in Mozart's life and works.

**Anne Thalheimer** finished her PhD ("Terrorists, Bitches, and Dykes: Gender, Violence, and Heteroideology in Late 20th C. Lesbian Comix") at the University of Delaware in 2002 and is currently a chief reader for the evaluation systems group of Pearson.

**Jason S. Todd**, PhD is the writing center director and an assistant professor of English at Xavier University of Louisiana, New Orleans.

**John F. Weinzierl** is an associate professor of Modern European History at Lyon College, Batesville, Arkansas. His areas of specialization are 19th-century Europe, the Middle East, and the evolution of war. Research interests include Napoleonic Europe and popular culture during World War II.

**Qiana J. Whitted** is associate professor of English and African American Studies at the University of South Carolina. Her publications include the book, *A God of Justice?: The Problem of Evil in 20th Century Black Literature*, as well as articles and reviews in *African American Review*, *Callaloo*, and *Southern Literary Journal*. She is also co-editor of a forthcoming collection on comics and the U.S. South.

**Kent Worcester** is an associate professor of Political Science at Marymount Manhattan College, New York. He is the author or editor of six books, including *C.L.R. James: A Political Biography* (1996), *Arguing Comics: Literary Masters on a Popular Medium* (2004) and *A Comics Studies Reader* (2009), co-edited with Jeet Heer. He is a member of the Board of Advisors of the Museum of Comic and Cartoon Art (MoCCA) and a regular contributor to *The Comics Journal*.

**Daniel Wüllner** is currently writing his doctoral thesis about the novels of William Gaddis at the Ludwig-Maximilians-University of Munich (*Ludwig-Maximilians-Universität München*). For the past five years, he has been working for the German online-magazine *Comicgate* (www.comicgate.de), and has published articles on comics in online newspapers. His academic achievements as a comic scholar can be followed at http://neuesausdemelfenbeinturm.blogspot.com/.

**Christine Yao** recently completed her MA in English Literature at Dalhousie University, Halifax, Nova Scotia, preceded by an Honors BA at the University of Toronto.

**Denis Yarow** recently completed his MA in English at the University of Toronto, from which he also received his Honors BA in English and Literary Studies.

**Martha Zan** studied history of art in Cologne, Germany and Florence, Italy; she received her MA at the University of Cologne in 2009 with her thesis "Jean Giraud´s Blueberry and the Spaghetti-Western. The Relation Between the Language of Comic Book and Movie." During her studies she held journalist jobs for the local newspaper and radio station; she was initiator and author of an audio guide project for children.

**Eugenia Zuroski Jenkins** is assistant professor of English and Cultural Studies at McMaster University, Hamilton, Ontario, and associate editor of *Eighteenth-Century Fiction*. She specializes in Orientalism, material culture, and taste and aesthetics in literature and culture of the long 18th century.

# Index